Contemporary Issues in the Law of Treaties

CONTEMPORARY ISSUES IN THE LAW OF TREATIES

by

MALGOSIA FITZMAURICE

and

OLUFEMI ELIAS

eleven
international publishing

Published, sold and distributed by Eleven International Publishing
P.O. Box 358
3500 AJ Utrecht, the Netherlands
Tel.: +31 30 231 0545
Fax: +31 30 225 8045
info@elevenpub.com
www.elevenpub.com

Cover: The Interior of the Palace des Glaces during the signing of the Peace Terms.
Versailles, France. June 1919. (Photo credit: U.S. National Archives)

Printed on acid-free paper.

ISBN 90-77596-06-2

© 2005 Eleven International Publishing

Printed in The Netherlands

Table of Contents

Preface

The central role played by treaties in the international legal system cannot be overestimated. It is often remarked that treaties are the principal means of international law-making, whose characteristics offer several self-evident advantages over customary international law in the regulation of both traditional and more recent areas of international law. in particular, a number of fields of contemporary international concern, such as environmental protection, international trade and human rights, are regulated to a very large extent by treaties. Even the functioning of treaties themselves is regulated to a significant extent by a treaty, the Vienna Convention on the Law of Treaties ("VCLT").

Testimony to the continued importance of treaties, if it is needed, is provided by the continued development and renewed controversy in respect of many of the rules contained in the VCLT. The relevance of the rules governing the law of treaties for other central fields of international law – for example, the relationship between the law of treaties and specific rules contained in specific treaties on the one hand, and the rules of state responsibility on the other – continue to be the subject of frequent doctrinal discussion.[1] in addition, some rapidly developing newer areas of public international law, which are regulated for the most part by treaties, have renewed the importance of some older problems;[2] for example, the question of conflicts between treaties regulating the same subject-matter.[3] One other important issue is the relevance of the emergence of new actors and factors, other than states, in the international legal order in general, and in the law of treaties in particular.[4]

---

[1] See, e.g., Chapter 3.
[2] See, e.g., Chapters 4, 6 and 8.
[3] See, e.g., Chapter 9.
[4] See, e.g., Chapter 2.

Furthermore, the fact that states use a variety of legal means and methods to regulate their relationships and mutual undertakings has given rise to a number of developments that call into question the true meaning of the term "treaty". This is an important question given that the law of treaties would apply if a given arrangement qualifies as a "treaty", and would not apply if the arrangement is not.[5] This issue is one that has been discussed in a number of recent cases before international tribunals, including the international Court of Justice (ICJ). The recent jurisprudence of the ICJ has also contributed to the development and clarification of on a number of aspects of the law of treaties.[6]

This book is a collection of discrete essays dealing with the issues of contemporary significance in the law of treaties. Accordingly, it neither purports nor aspires to provide a general overview of all aspects of the law of treaties, and it is by no means intended to be a comprehensive textbook. It is hoped that the discussion of the subjects selected in this book will shed some light on a number of areas of the contemporary law of treaties, and consequently on some important features of the international legal system at the beginning of the twenty-first century, and that the discussion will highlight the living character of the law of treaties and of public international law.

We would like to acknowledge the contributions of Ms Anneliese Quast and Dr Maria Vogiatzi, who co-authored Chapters 5 and 8 respectively. We are also grateful to Dr Rosalie Balkin, Director of the External and Legal Department of the IMO, for her comments on the participation of IGOs and NGOs in the treaty-making process in the IMO, discussed in Chapter 2. The authors would also like to express their gratitude to Ms Fiona Mucklow for her scrupulous editing of the manuscript, and also to Ms Selma Hoedt of Eleven International Publishing for her continuous support and for obtaining permission to use some previously published material.[7]

Malgosia Fitzmaurice
Olufemi Elias
London, 2005

---

[5] See, e.g., Chapters 1, 5, 7 and 11.

[6] See, e.g., Chapters 1, 5, 10 and 11.

[7] The authors are grateful to the following journals/publishers for permissions to use some previously published material: Australian Yearbook of international Law; the Australian National University; British Yearbook of international Law; Oxford University Press; Leiden Journal of international Law; Cambridge University Press; Nordic Journal of international Law; Brill Academic Publishers; Singapore Yearbook of international Law; Wolf Law Publishers.

Abbreviations

AFDI	Annuaire française du droit international
AJIL	American Journal of international Law
ARIEL	Austrian Review of international and European Law
AYIL	Australian Yearbook of international Law
BYIL	British Yearbook of international Law
Colo. J. int'l Envtl.L&Pol'y	Colorado Journal of international Environmental Law and Policy
Colum.J. Transnat'l L	Columbia Journal of Transnational Law
Cornell ILJ	Cornell international Law Journal
EJIL	European Journal of international Law
EPL	Environmental Policy and Law
FYIL	Finnish Yearbook of international Law
GYIL	German Yearbook of international Law
Hague YIL	Hague Yearbook of international Law
ICJ	International Court of Justice
ICJ Reports	Reports of Judgments, Advisory Opinions and Orders of the international Court of Justice
ICLQ	International and Comparative Law Quarterly
ILC	International Law Commission
ILM	International Legal Materials
ILR	International Law Reports
LJIL	Leiden Journal of international Law
NAFTA	North American Free Trade Agreement
NILR	Netherlands international Law Review
NJIL	Nordic Journal of international Law
NYIL	Netherlands Yearbook of international Law
OJ	official Journal of the European Communities

ÖZÖRV	Österreichische Zeitschrift für öffentliches Recht und Völkerrecht Austrian Journal of Public & International Law
PCIJ	Permanent Court of international Justice
RIAA	United Nations Reports of international Arbitral Awards
RCADI	Recueil des cours de l'Académie de Droit International
RGDIP	Revue générale du droit international public
SOLAS	Convention on the Safety of Life at Sea
UNCLOS	United Nations Convention on the Law of the Sea 1982
VCLT	Vienna Convention on the Law of Treaties (1969)
VCLT 1986	Vienna Convention on the Law of Treaties Between States and international Organizations Or Between International Organizations (1986)
VJIL	Virginia Journal of international Law
WTO	World Trade Organization
YIEL	Yearbook of international Environmental Law
YILC	Yearbook of the international Law Commission
ZaöRV	Zeitschrift für Ausländisches Öffentliches Recht und Völkerrecht

CHAPTER ONE

The Identification and Character of Treaties and Treaty Obligations Between States[*]

1. Introduction

1.1 The Problem

The "VCLT" contains an apparently simple definition of a treaty. Article 2, paragraph 1 (a) of the VCLT defines a treaty as "an international agreement concluded between States in written form and governed by international law, whether embodied in a single instrument or in two or more related instruments and whatever its particular designation". Nonetheless, the question of what constitutes a treaty, and the nature of treaty obligations, remain difficult problems in the law of treaties. According to Judge Jessup, "[t]he notion that there is a clear and ordinary meaning of the word "treaty" is a mirage".[1] The problem has been the subject of much writing,[2] and has been considered by the ICJ in a number of cases. It has been remarked that although "the definition of an international treaty seems at first sight to be a purely academic question, judicial experience shows that the determination

---

[*] This chapter is an updated and revised version of M. Fitzmaurice, "The Identification and Character of Treaties and treay Obligations Between States in International Law", published in 73 *BYIL* 2002 and reprinted with kind permission of Oxford University Press.
[1] Separate Opinion, Judge Jessup in South West Africa (Ethiopia v. South Africa; Liberia v. South Africa), Preliminary Objections, Judgment of 21 December 1962, 1962 ICJ Rep. 402. Similarly, G.J.H. van Hoof, *Rethinking the Sources of International Law* (1983), at 117.
[2] See, for example, the valuable and thought-provoking study by J. Klabbers, *The Concept of Treaty in International Law* (1996).

of whether a certain instrument constitutes a treaty has important practical consequences".[3]

One reason for the difficulty is the development of various new forms of interstate relations and of new branches of international law, such as international environmental law. These have seen the emergence of multifaceted forms of co-operation which have, in turn, produced new forms of international instruments, such as the so-called "soft-law" instruments, or instruments (often called "agreements") which are not intended to be legally binding at all but which have a certain political or moral force. This diversified co-operation between States has resulted in changes in the form of treaties, including the exponential growth of treaties in "simplified form".[4]

This chapter focuses on treaties concluded between States, and asks whether the formal definition of a treaty in the VCLT is adequate, given the wide variety of instruments used in modern international relations. It considers both "core" instances of the concept of a treaty, and also certain developments in the field of international relations, which test the borders of that concept. As a background to these issues, it is necessary to look also at the formal aspects of the concept, which are embodied in the positive rules derived from the definition of treaty in the VCLT.[5] In short, it is necessary to analyze, both in terms of form and substance, those consensual relationships between States that create rights and obligations.

On the other hand, acts that generate obligations but are unilateral in nature, or acts that are of a hybrid character (such as optional clauses in the ICJ's system of compulsory jurisdiction), will not be dealt with; nor will the problem of treaties concluded by international organizations. Although the provisions of the 1986 Vienna Convention on the Law of Treaties between States and International Organizations or Between International Organizations exhibit many similarities to those of the VCLT, there are certain legal issues that are specific to treaty-making by international organizations (such as the issue of juridical transparency of organizations) and that merit separate study.[6] The advent of international organizations has resulted in a diversified practice which does not fall fully within the ambit of international law relating to treaty-making between States.

---

[3] J. de Arechaga, "International Law in the Past Third Century", 159 *Recueil des Cours* (1978-I), at 35.

[4] See, e.g., J.E.S. Fawcett, "The Legal Character of International Agreements", 30 *BYIL* (1953), at 381-400.

[5] See D.P. Myers, "The Names and Scope of Treaties", 51 *AYIL* (1957), at 574-605.

[6] See, e.g., the excellent study of C. Brölmann, "The Vienna Convention on the Law of Treaties: The History of Draft Article 36 BIS", in J. Klabbers and R. Lefeber (eds.), *Essays on the Law of Treaties, A Collection of Essays in Honour of Bert Vierdag* (1998), at 121-143.

We first consider (in Section 2 below) the definition contained in the VCLT, and in particular its provisions concerning formal aspects of a treaty and its inadequacies in relation to substantive aspects. In Section 3, we consider a number of more recent developments in international law and international relations that illuminate the limits of the concept of the treaty.

The jurisprudence of the ICJ in this context is to be viewed with a certain degree of caution. In many cases, the main issue arising before the Court is whether the "agreement" in question suffices to establish its jurisdiction, and it can be difficult to distinguish between the Court's observations concerning the character of treaties in general, and those regarding the definition of agreement of the parties for the purposes of jurisdiction. The *Aegean Sea*[7] and the *Qatar/Bahrain* cases[8] are good examples. As will be seen below, the ICJ itself has adopted a pragmatic approach to this matter.[9]

1.2 Binding Agreements in Legal Systems – General Remarks

In principle, treaty obligations comprise those international obligations that arise directly by operation of the general principle of law embodied in the well-known maxim *pacta sunt servanda*. This principle – that agreements are to be upheld, or supported by the law – is undoubtedly one of the "general principles of law recognized by civilized nations" referred to in Article 38(1) of the Statute of the ICJ, existing in all major legal systems in broadly similar form. As a result, similar problems are encountered as to what constitutes a legally binding agreement. No legal system upholds *all* agreements. A detailed comparative study of the various methods used by legal systems to distinguish between those agreements which are upheld by

---

[7] Aegean Sea Continental Shelf case (Greece *v.* Turkey), Jurisdiction, 1978 ICJ Rep. 4, at 41-44, paras. 101-108.

[8] Maritime Delimitation and Territorial Questions between Qatar and Bahrain (Qatar v. Bahrain), Jurisdiction and Admissibility, 1994 ICJ Rep. 112, at 120-122, paras. 21-30; see J. Klabbers, "Qatar v. Bahrain: the Concept of a 'Treaty' in International Law", 33 *Archiv des Völkerrechts* (1995), at 361-376; S. Rosenne, "The Qatar/Bahrain case, What is a Treaty? A Framework Agreement and the Seising of the Court", 8 *LJIL* (1995), at 161-182; see also Case Concerning Maritime Delimitation and Territorial Question Between Qatar and Bahrain (Qatar v. Bahrain), Jurisdiction and Admissibility, 1995 ICJ Rep. 4; C. Chinkin, "A Mirage in the Sand? Distinguishing Binding and Non-Binding Relations Between States", 10 *LJIL* (1997), at 223-249; E. Vierdag, "The International Court of Justice and the Law of Treaties", in V. Lowe and M. Fitzmaurice (eds.), *Fifty Years of the International Court of Justice* (1996), 145, at 153.

[9] For example, in the Aegean Sea case, the Court, having satisfied itself as to the lack of jurisdiction, stated that "...the Court is not concerned, nor is it competent, to pronounce upon any other implications which that Communiqué may have in the context of the present dispute". See *supra* note 7, 1978 ICJ Rep. 4, at 44, para. 108.

the law, and those which are not, is beyond the scope of this chapter. However, it may prove useful to consider certain particular features of international law in this respect.

1.2.1 The concept of international legal obligation

Treaties are one of the sources which give rise to international legal obligations. In its commentary to the Articles on Responsibility of States for Internationally Wrongful Acts of 2001, the International Law Commission explained that:

> [i]nternational obligations may be established by a customary rule of international law, by a treaty or by general principles applicable within the international legal order. States may assume international obligations by a unilateral act. An international obligation may arise from provisions stipulated in a treaty (a decision of an international organ of an international organisation competent on the matter, a judgment given between two States by the International Court of Justice or another tribunal, etc.) ... Moreover these various grounds of obligation interact with each other ... Treaties, especially multilateral treaties, can contribute to the formation of general international law; customary law may assist in the interpretation of treaties; an obligation contained in a treaty may be applicable to a State by reason of its unilateral act, and so on.[10]

---

[10] The Report of the International Law Commission, on its fifty-third Session; 23 April – 1 June and 2 July – August (2001), Chapter IV, 'State Responsibility', at 126, General Assembly, Official Records, Fifty-fifth Session, Supplement No.10 (UN Doc. A/56/10), see <http://www.un.org/law/ilc/report.htm>. The Commission gives several examples of such various sources of international obligations. France undertook by a unilateral act not to engage in further atmospheric nuclear testing, see Nuclear Tests cases (Australia *v.* France and New Zealand *v.* France), Judgments of 20 December 1974, 1974 ICJ Rep. 253, at 267-272, paras. 42-60 and 457, 472-477, paras. 45-63, respectively. See also Request for an Examination of the Situation in Accordance with Paragraph 63 of the Court's Judgment of 20 December 1974 in the Nuclear Tests *(*New Zealand *v.* France*)* Order of 22 September 1995, 1995 ICJ Rep. 288, 305, paras. 60-61. See also Rainbow Warrior (New Zealand *v.* France), 1990 UNRIAA, Vol. XX, 217, 251. The Tribunal said that: "[a]ny violation by a State of any obligation, of whatever origin, gives rise to State responsibility and consequently, to the duty of reparation"; Case Concerning Gabčikovo-Nagymaros Project (Hungary and Slovakia), 1997 ICJ Rep. 7, at 38, para. 47: it is "well established that, when a State has committed an internationally wrongful act, its international responsibility is likely to be involved whatever the nature of the obligation it has failed to respect". See also J. Crawford, *The International Law Commission's Articles on State Responsibility – Introduction, Text and Commentaries* (2002), on content, forms and degrees of international responsibility, see at 6-8. On the interaction between treaties and international customary law, see M. Mendelson and R. Müllerson, *Statement on Principles Applicable to the Formation of General Customary International Law*, Final Report of the Committee on Formation of Customary Law (General) International Law, International Law Association, Sixty-Ninth (London) Conference (2000),

This lack of differentiation as regards the legal origin of an international obligation is evident in cases of breach of that obligation. As Article 12 of the ILC's Articles states: "There is a breach of an international obligation by a State when an act of that State is not in conformity with what is required of it by that obligation, regardless of its origin or character".[11] Treaties, as a source of international obligations and of responsibility arising from a breach of such obligations, are not distinct from other sources of international law. In absence of any specific provision to the contrary, breaches of treaty entail the general consequences that derive from the law of State responsibility.

1.2.2 Absence in international law of tools for analysis of the substantive nature of agreements

Municipal legal systems make use of a number of different analytical tools that assist in determining the substantive distinctions between those agreements that are upheld by the law and those that are not. For instance, there is the nominative system in the law of contract, in which only particular "named" types of contract, each of them defined, are upheld. This system was fundamental in Roman law and remains a significant characteristic of the law of contracts in French law. Again, both civil and common law systems have greatly developed the analysis of the substantive aspects of the formation of legally binding agreements through the concept of offer and acceptance (as well as the concept of consideration in common law). Furthermore, both have also developed the concept of necessity for certainty in the subject matter of contracts (in French law, for instance, in the form of the requirement of an *objet;* and in common law in the concept of contracts, or clauses in contracts, being void for uncertainty).

International law, by comparison, makes very little use of such analytical tools, in effect basing the substantive distinction between international agreements that are binding and those that are not almost entirely on the "intention" of the parties, no doubt, in part, as a legacy of its voluntarist origins. As will be seen below, this intention is treated from an objective point of view based on the apparent or external facts of the case, rather than on the subjective state of mind of the parties (or their representatives). In deciding this issue on the facts, international law does in fact take into

---

at 753-765; R. Higgins, *Problems and Process: International Law and How We Use It* (1994), at 32-38.

[11] Responsibility of States for Internationally Wrongful Acts, adopted by the International Law Commission, on 9 August 2001, see Official Records of the United Nations General Assembly, Fifty-sixth Session, Supplement No. 10, and corrigendum (UN Doc.A/56/10 and Corr. I). See also: Resolution of the General Assembly, UN Doc. A/RES/56/83, Fifty-sixth session, item 162.

account, albeit indirectly, some of the factors referred to above, such as certainty of the subject matter. Nevertheless, the international law test of intention is more elusive and gives rise to greater problems of proof than do more specific tests in other legal systems.

1.2.3 Particular characteristics of the international legal system

Notwithstanding similarities between the law of treaties in international law and that of contracts in municipal law systems, it is important to bear in mind some fundamental differences between legal systems operating on the international and on the national planes that are relevant to the distinction between binding and non-binding international agreements. The first is the relative importance in international relations of structured, relatively formal, and often continuous relations between States, which take many forms ranging from relations between government departments, through diplomatic relations, to meetings of heads of State, some of which are not intended in themselves to have, and do not have, specific legal consequences. This factor in international relations, which has led to the increased use and importance of non-binding informal instruments, has no real equivalent at the national level. This point is considered further in Section III below.

A second factor operating at the international level is the use made, in the absence of any international legislative body, of agreements to achieve objectives, which at the national level, would generally be achieved through legislation. This has given rise, among other things, to the growing importance of international instruments that are negotiated and drafted in ways virtually indistinguishable from binding treaty instruments, but which are not intended to be, and are not, legally binding. They may eventually become binding, either through their influence on the formation of customary international law or through their eventual incorporation into a binding treaty; and they are often intended to do so. These are often, and perhaps confusingly, called "soft-law" instruments, and are discussed further in section 3 below.

A third difference, of a more practical nature, is the sheer difficulty and expense of negotiating and concluding international agreements, especially at the multilateral level. This is an additional element in States' preferences for informal agreements and the use of "soft-law" instruments.

1.3 The VCLT and the Concept of Treaties

It is impossible to consider any aspect of the law of treaties without reference to the VCLT, which, broadly speaking, codified international law on the subject of the conclusion, interpretation and termination of treaties. In relation to the subject of the present chapter, however, it must be said that the VCLT is only of limited assistance. The definition of a treaty as "an international agreement concluded between States in written form and governed by international law, whether embodied in a single instrument or in two or more related instruments and whatever its particular designation" does, indeed, lay down a number of positive formal rules as to what constitutes a treaty. However, the VCLT is essentially silent with respect to the substantive issue as to which "agreements", which meet the positive formal requirements as set out in the VCLT, are to be upheld by international law and which are not. It simply refers to an "international agreement", but gives no further indication of what is meant by that expression.

2. The Definition of Treaty in the Vienna Convention

2.1 "Legal Obligation"

In his first Report on the Law of Treaties, Brierly merely mentioned the problem of the establishment of a relationship under international law.[12] Lauterpacht, while not proposing a comprehensive definition of a treaty, sought to include as elements thereof the creation of legal obligations, and the entering by the parties into undertakings of a legal character.[13] This legal obligation was the element that singled out a treaty from a political instrument. This line of reasoning was shared by Fitzmaurice, who presented several drafts, all of which referred to the creation of "legal obligations" or the establishment of a "relationship" governed by international law.[14] In his first draft, however, he added the requirement of the intention to create international obligations and the intention to establish a relationship under international law. Once established, treaties would automatically be governed by international law. Article I(2) of the Expository Draft Code, presented in 1959 to the General Assembly, contained only the phrase "governed by international law",[15] as opposed to other instruments which are governed by domestic law, even if they regulate matters of an international character.

---

[12] J. L. Brierly, First Report on the Law of Treaties (Art. I(a)), below note 24, at 226.

[13] H. Lauterpacht, First Report on the Law of Treaties, see below note 24, at 90; see also Sir G. Fitzmaurice, *The Law and Procedure of the International Court of Justice* (1986), Vol. 11, at 822-823.

[14] G. Fitzmaurice, First Report on the Law of Treaties (Art. 2(I)), below note 24, at 117.

[15] YILC (1959), Vol. II, Report of the ILC to the General Assembly on the work of its eleventh session, UN Doc. A/4169, at 95-97. The ILC admitted that there was a vast group of treaties that, although concluded between States (e.g., commercial transactions), were governed by private, national law.

As has been mentioned, one of the main problems relating to the concept of a treaty in the context of the VCLT is the inadequacy, in certain respects, of its definition as it relates to the substantive aspects of a treaty. In particular, essential questions remain as to what constitutes an international agreement governed by international law, as well as what the test is for deciding whether such an agreement has come into existence in a particular case. Early drafts presented to the ILC went some way towards providing answers to this problem. Thus, the relevant words in the definition of "treaty" contained in Article 2 of Fitzmaurice's draft were: "... a treaty is an international agreement ... intended to create rights and obligations, or to establish relationships, governed by international law". Leaving aside the rather fine distinction contained in this definition between an agreement intended to create rights and obligations and one intended merely to establish a relationship, it does contain the essential element implied by the term "international agreement governed by international law". This term is meant to imply that in order to constitute a treaty, an agreement must be legally binding in international law and create legally binding rights and obligations: it is not enough that it falls within the ambit of international law or that international law is applicable to it. In other words, for an agreement to constitute a treaty, not only must international law (as opposed to any other legal system) be applicable to it, but international law must also designate the agreement as one that is legally binding on the parties (as opposed to an agreement which is merely morally binding or merely political in nature). Even on this basis, there remains a further crucial element in establishing a comprehensive definition of the concept of a treaty, namely, the distinction between legally binding agreements and other agreements or arrangements between States.

2.2 "Treaty"

The ILC explained that the expression "treaty" is a generic term and that "an extraordinarily varied nomenclature has developed which serves to confuse the question of classifying international agreements", adding that "there is no exclusive or systematic use of nomenclature for particular types of transaction".[16] This has not, however, deterred a number of authors from attempting to relate particular designations of international agreements to their contents. For example, Myers[17] asserts, on the basis of Article 102 of

---

[16] The Official Records of the United Nations Conference on the Law of Treaties (1968), UN Doc. A/Conf/39/11/Add.2, at 8; YILC (1966), Vol. II, Report of the ILC to the General Assembly on the second part of its seventeenth and its eighteenth session, UN Doc.A/6390/Rev.I, at 188.

[17] Myers, *supra* note 5, at 578.

the United Nations ("UN") Charter, which appears to uphold a distinction between "treaty" and "international agreement",[18] "that one category emanates from the highest authority in the State and the other from subordinate executive authority". This distinction has not been maintained in practice, case law, nor in the literature.

Only very general conclusions may be drawn from the name of a treaty or its subject matter. Treaties bear a wide range of names, such as "covenant"; "agreed minutes"; "charter"; *notes verbales*; "memorandum of understanding"; "convention" and "agreement".[19] In most cases the names such as "charter" or "covenant" are applied to the more solemn type of instruments. The term "treaty", when applied to agreements that concern technical or other matters, constitutes a less solemn designation. Nonetheless, nomenclature cannot be relied on in order to characterize the substance of an international agreement.[20] The ICJ stated in 1962 that: "[t]erminology is not the determinant factor as to the character of an international agreement or undertaking", and this is borne out by numerous examples.[21]

---

[18] Art. 102, 1. "[e]very treaty and every international agreement entered into by any Member of the United Nations after the present Charter comes into force shall as soon as possible be registered with the Secretariat and published by it. 2. No party to any such treaty or international agreement which has not been registered in accordance with the provisions of paragraph 1 of this Article may invoke that treaty or agreement before any organ of the United Nations".

[19] YILC (1962), Vol. I, 638th meeting, at 529: The Vienna Convention has adopted the term 'treaty' as a generic term rather than the term 'agreement'. It has to be noted, however, that other terms are also used interchangeably, without an explanation as to the choice. The ILC has said: "[t]hus, in addition to "treaty", "convention" and "protocol" one not infrequently finds titles such as "declaration", "charter", "covenant", "pact", "act", "statute", "agreement", "concordat", whilst names like "declaration", "agreement" and "modus vivendi" may well be found given both to formal and less formal types of agreements. As to the latter, their nomenclature is almost illimitable, even if some names such as "agreement", "exchange on notes", "exchange of letters", "memorandum of agreement", or "agreed minute" may be more common than others. It is true that some types of instruments are used more frequently for some purposes rather than others; it is also true that some titles are more frequently attached to some types of transaction rather than to others. But there is no exclusive or systematic use of nomenclature for particular types of transaction".

[20] See, for example, an informal designation of a treaty establishing bilateral relationships between the United States and the former German Democratic Republic, which was called the 'Agreed Minutes', see 98 ILR (1994), 1-13. See also the 'Memorandum of Understanding on Port State Control' which establishes a very sophisticated system, 21 *ILM* (1982), at 1.

[21] South West Africa cases, *supra* note 1, at 331.

2.3 "In Written Form"

The VCLT refers to treaties as international agreements concluded in written form. This does not, however, mean that international agreements concluded entirely orally do not have any binding force in international law.[22] It merely means that the provisions of the VCLT, *as treaty provisions,* only apply to agreements in written form. This limitation of the VCLT was dictated by the exigencies of practicality and clarity.[23] The principles set out in the VCLT that are relevant to purely oral agreements may nonetheless apply to them as provisions of customary international law. Furthermore because, as has been noted, the VCLT provides no assistance as to what actually constitutes an "international agreement", this fundamental question remains one of customary law, with respect to which there seems to be no distinction between written and oral agreements. On the other hand it has to be admitted

---

[22] Art. 3, concerning "International agreements not within the scope of the present Convention", provides as follows: "[t]he fact that the present Convention does not apply to international agreements concluded between States and other subjects of international law or between such other subjects of international law, or to international agreements not in written form, shall not affect: (a) the legal force of such agreements; (b) the application to them of any of the rules set forth in the present Convention to which they would be subject under international law independently of the Convention; (c) the application of the Convention to the relations of States as between themselves under international agreements to which other subjects of international law are also parties".

[23] See note 15.

[24] J.L. Brierly, First Report on the Law of Treaties (Art. 1(a)), YILC (1950), Vol. II, UN Doc. A/CN.4.23, at 222 and 227; idem, Second Report on the Law of Treaties, YILC (1951), Vol. II, UN Doc.A/CN.4,/43, at 70; idem, Third Report on the Law of Treaties, YILC (1952), Vol. II, UN Doc. A/CN.4/54, at 50; Fitzmaurice on the other hand asked the question: "[w]ould an oral agreement recorded (a) with the knowledge and by the intention of the parties, (b) secretly by one of them only, on disc or tape recorder, amount to an agreement in writing?": G. Fitzmaurice, First Report on the Law of Treaties, YILC (1956), Vol. II, UN Doc.A/CN.4/101, at 104, at 107, note 4; idem, Second Report on the Law of Treaties,YILC (1957), Vol. II, UN Doc.A/CN.4/107, at 16; idem, Third Report on the Law of Treaties, YILC (1958), Vol. II, UN Doc.A/CN.4/115, at 20; idem, Fourth Report on the Law of Treaties, YILC (1959), Vol. II, UN Doc. A/CN.4/120, at 37; idem, Fifth Report on the Law of Treaties, YILC (1960), Vol. II, UN Doc.A/CN.4/130, at 69; H. Lauterpacht, First Report on the Law of Treaties, YILC (1953), Vol. II, UN Doc. A/CN.4/63, at 90; idem, Second Report on the Law of Treaties, YILC (1954), Vol. II, UN Doc.A/CN.4/87, at 123; C. H. M. Waldock, First Report on the Law of Treaties, YILC (1962), Vol. II, UN Doc.A/CN.4/144 and Add.1, at 27; idem, Second Report on the Law of Treaties, YILC (1963), Vol. II, UN Doc.A/CN.4/156 and Adds.1-3, at 36; idem, Third Report on the Law of Treaties, YILC (1964), Vol. II, UN Doc.A,/CN.4/167 and Adds. 1-3, at 5; idem, Fourth Report on the Law of Treaties, YILC (1965), Vol II., UN Doc.A/CN.4/177 and Adds. 1-2; idem, Fifth Report on the Law of Treaties, YILC (1966), Vol. II, UN Doc.A/CN.4/183, and Adds. 1-4, at 1; idem, Sixth Report on the Law of Treaties, YILC (1966), Vol. II, UN Doc.A/CN.4/186 and Adds. 1-7, at 51.

that there are no convincing modern examples of an oral agreement amounting to a treaty.

2.4 The Particular Form of a Treaty

The VCLT does not specify any particular written form for an international agreement to constitute a treaty. Certain problems were addressed by the ILC's Rapporteurs on the Law of Treaties. For instance, the first Rapporteur, J. L. Brierly, explained that the requirement for treaties to be "recorded in writing" was fulfilled by "typewriting and printing and, indeed, any other permanent method of recording".[24] Similarly, the number of documents in which an agreement is contained has no influence on its legal character.

The main problem that divided the ILC was the legal character of so called exchanges of notes and letters, which are intended to acquire legal force upon mutual exchange. Brierly was of the view that instruments of this kind should be covered;[25] and despite doubts raised in the ILC, later drafts did include exchanges of notes and letters within the definition of a treaty. For example, the 1962 ILC Draft Articles referred to treaties concluded in simplified form, which, the Commission explained, included exchanges of notes, exchanges of letters, agreed minutes, memoranda of agreement, joint declarations and "any other document concluded by any similar procedure".[26] In the end, due to inherent difficulties connected with defining treaties in simplified form, the ILC abandoned the inclusion of an express general *chapeau* describing their form.[27]

The ICJ and its predecessor the PCIJ have had to decide on several occasions whether certain instruments were treaties or not. In the *Aegean Sea* case,[28] the question was whether the Joint Brussels Communiqué issued by Greece and Turkey amounted to an agreement in international law embodying the intention of both parties to the dispute to submit the case to the ICJ. It did not bear any signatures, nor was it initialled. According to the Turkish government, it did not constitute an agreement under international law and accordingly had not been ratified, "at least at the part of Turkey".[29]

---

[25] Brierly, First Report on the Law of Treaties (Art. 1(b)), *supra* note 24, at 229.

[26] Waldock, First Report on the Law of Treaties (Art. 1(b)), *supra* note 24, at 33. It must be noted that the inclusion of this group of treaties influenced the drafting of the Article on presentation of full powers, which provided that the production of full powers will be dispensed with for treaties in simplified form, unless they are requested by other negotiating States (Art. 4, para. 1(b) of the Draft).

[27] See note 18.

[28] See note 7. See L. Gross, "The Dispute Between Greece and Turkey Concerning the Continental Shelf in the Aegean", 71 *AJIL* (1977), 31-59.

[29] Aegean Sea case, *supra* note 7, at 39, para. 95.

The Greek government maintained that the Joint Communiqué did constitute an agreement. According to the Greek government, "…it is necessary, and it is sufficient, for the communiqué to include-in addition to customary forms, protestations of friendship, recital of major principles and declarations of intent-provisions of a treaty nature".[30] During the oral proceedings before the ICJ, Greece submitted that the Joint Communiqué was "a modern ritual which has acquired full status in international practice". The Court declined jurisdiction in this case, but it did observe that treaties may appear in their "infinite variety";[31] and that, in order to conclude whether an instrument is a treaty or not, the nature of the act or transaction must be determined by its actual terms and by the particular circumstances in which it was drawn up.[32]

In the 1994 *Qatar/Bahrain* case,[33] the ICJ had to decide on the legal character of two instruments upon which Bahrain filed a case against Qatar: first, a double Exchange of Letters concluded in December 1987 between Qatar and Saudi Arabia, on the one hand, and between Bahrain and Saudi Arabia, on the other hand; and second, a set of minutes signed by the Foreign Ministers of Qatar and Bahrain in December 1990, on the occasion of the meeting of the Co-operation Council of Arab States of the Gulf. Again the question arose whether the instruments in question constituted a treaty, in this case a "special agreement", to give the Court jurisdiction. This case also illustrates the importance of the interpretation of treaties in determining whether an instrument constitutes a treaty.

An important element of the dispute was the agreement of both parties that the 1987 Exchange of Letters was an international agreement with binding force in their mutual relations. According to Bahrain, however, the 1990 Minutes were only a simple record of negotiations, and, therefore, did not constitute an international agreement and, thus, could not serve as the basis for the Court's jurisdiction.[34]

The Court observed that international agreements might assume a number of forms and have many denominations. It adopted the same approach as it had in the *Aegean Sea* case, finding it necessary to analyze the actual terms

---

[30] *Id.*

[31] Temple of Preah Vihear (Cambodia *v.* Thailand), Preliminary Objections, Judgment of 26 May 1961, 1961 ICJ Rep. 17, at 31; South-West Africa cases, *supra* note 1.

[32] Aegean Sea case, *supra* note 7, para. 96: "… it does not settle the question simply to refer to the form – a communiqué – in which that act or transaction is embodied. On the contrary, in determining what was indeed the nature of the act or transaction embodied in the Brussels Communiqué, the Court must have regard above all to its actual terms and to particular circumstances in which it was drawn up". See also the Case Concerning the Land and Maritime Boundary between Cameroon and Nigeria, (Cameroon *v.* Nigeria: Equatorial Guinea Intervening) Judgment of 10 October 2002, discussed in chapter 11 below.

[33] See note 8.

[34] *Id.*, 21-22.

and particular circumstances in which the alleged agreement was drawn up.[35] Taking all the facts of the case into consideration, the Court decided that the double Exchange of Letters and the 1990 Minutes were international agreements creating rights and obligations for the parties. The Court decided that by the terms of those agreements the parties had undertaken to submit to the Court the whole dispute between them, as provided for by the text proposed by Bahrain to Qatar on 26 October 1990 and accepted by Qatar in December 1990, and referred to in the 1990 Minutes as the "Bahrain formula".

In paragraph 25 of its judgment, the Court laid down the elements of an international undertaking that constitutes a treaty.[36] It said:

> ... Accordingly, and contrary to the contentions of Bahrain, the Minutes are not a simple record of a meeting, similar to those drawn up within the Tripartite Committee; they do not merely give an account of discussions and summarize points of agreement and disagreement. They enumerate the commitments to which Parties have consented. They thus create rights and obligations in international law for the Parties. They constitute an international agreement.

As has been observed, the word "thus" in that paragraph is of great importance, because it is the link between "commitments to which the Parties have consented", on the one hand, and the creation of "rights and obligations in international law" on the other.[37] The Court's ruling may be interpreted as indicating that the consent to commitments is of fundamental importance for the creation of a treaty under international law.

The *Eastern Greenland* case[38] shows clearly the limitations of the VCLT definition in the face of multifaceted sources of international legal obligations - in that case, obligations created by unilateral acts. The act in question was the Ihlen Declaration. On 14 July 1919 the Danish Minister accredited in Norway said, in a conversation with Mr Ihlen, the Norwegian Minister of Foreign Affairs, that Denmark would not object to any claim to Spitzbergen which Norway might submit at the Peace Conference, if Norway would not oppose the Danish claim at the same conference to the whole of Greenland. In another conversation on 22 July 1919, Mr Ihlen stated that: "... the plans of the Royal [Danish] Government respecting

---

[35] *Id.*, para. 24. One of the arguments presented by Bahrain was that the Minutes related to the territory of the State and that, therefore, they could only be considered binding according to the Constitution of Bahrain, i.e. after their positive enactment as law (para. 26 of the judgment). The Court rejected this argument. See also Cameroon *v.* Nigeria case (*supra* note 32), where Nigeria further relied on Art. 46 para. 2 of the VCLT, discussed in Chapter 11 below.

[36] Klabbers, *supra* note 2, at 366-367.

[37] *Id.*

[38] Legal Status of Eastern Greenland (Denmark *v.* Norway), 1933 PCIJ, Series A/B, no. 53.

Danish sovereignty over the whole of Greenland ... would meet with no difficulties on the part of Norway". These were words recorded by Mr Ihlen in the form of minutes, and submitted to his Government. One of the questions before the Court was the legal character of the Ihlen Declaration: was it simply a unilateral declaration, or a hybrid instrument combining the features of an agreement with those of a unilateral declaration?

The Court's judgment did not fully address any of these questions. It focused rather on the binding nature of an international obligation, regardless of its source. The Court said:

> [t]he Court considers it beyond all dispute that a reply of this nature given by the Minister for Foreign Affairs on behalf of his Government in response to a request by the diplomatic representative of a foreign Power, in regard to a question falling within his province, is binding upon the country to which the Minister belongs.[39]

The Court, having taken into consideration all circumstances, concluded that it was "unable to regard the Ihlen declaration of July 22nd 1919 otherwise than as unconditional and definitive", since "[i]t was so understood by the Norwegian Minister for Foreign Affairs when he told the Danish Minister at Christiania on November 7th 1919, that 'it was a pleasure to Norway to recognise Danish sovereignty over Greenland'". It was also in the same sense that the Danish Minister at Christiania had understood the Ihlen Declaration, when he informed the Danish Minister for Foreign Affairs on July 22nd 1999, that Mr Ihlen had told him "that the plans of the Royal Government in regard to the sovereignty of Denmark over the whole Greenland would not encounter any difficulties on the part of Norway".[40] Finally, the Court found that it followed that "as a result of the undertaking involved in the Ihlen Declaration of July 22nd 1919, Norway is under an obligation to refrain from contesting Danish sovereignty over Greenland as a whole, and *a fortiori* to refrain from occupying a part of Greenland".[41]

Perhaps the most interesting aspect of the analysis was the Court's indication that interdependence of mutual obligations might not necessarily create a bilateral engagement. The Court stated that:

> [i]t is clear from the relevant Danish documents which preceded the Danish Minister's démarche at Christiania on July 14th 1919, that the Danish attitude in the Spitzbergen question and the Norwegian attitude in the Greenland question were regarded in Denmark as interdependent, and this interdependence appears to be reflected also in Mr Ihlen's minute of the interview. Even if this interdependence – which, in view of the affirmative reply of the Norwegian Government, in whose name the Minister for Foreign Affairs was speaking, would have created a bilateral engagement – is not held

---

[39] *Id.*, 71.
[40] *Id.*, 72-73.
[41] *Id.*, 73.

to have been established, it can hardly be denied that what Denmark was asking of Norway ('not to make any difficulties in the settlement of the [Greenland] question') was equivalent to what she was indicating her readiness to concede in the Spitzbergen question (to refrain from opposing 'the wishes of Norway in regard to the settlement of this question'). What Denmark desired to obtain from Norway was that the latter should do nothing to obstruct the Danish plans in regard to Greenland. The declaration which the Minister for Foreign Affairs gave on July 22nd 1919, on behalf of the Norwegian Government, was definitely affirmative: 'I told the Danish Minster to-day that the Norwegian Government would not make any difficulty in the settlement of this question'.[42]

The Court appears to have based its decision as to the binding nature of the declaration in part on the formal legal ground of the inherent power of Ministers of Foreign Affairs to bind States by virtue of their statements (as now codified in Article 7 of the VCLT).[43] The Court emphasized that the position of the Minister for Foreign Affairs who had made a statement binding his government was sufficient to create an obligation for such a State, even without its having been an "interdependent" commitment. The Court held that it resulted in "an undertaking" on the part of the Norwegian government, its content being to refrain from making difficulties for Denmark in asserting its sovereignty over the whole of Greenland (but

---

[42] *Id.*, 70-71.

[43] Of special interest is Art. 7, para. 2: "[i]n virtue of their functions and without having to produce full powers, the following are considered as representing their State:

(a) Heads of States, heads of Governments and Ministers of Foreign Affairs, for the purpose of performing all acts relating to conclusion of a treaty;

(b) heads of diplomatic missions, for the purpose of adopting the text of a treaty between the accrediting State and the State to which they are accredited,

(c) representatives accredited by States to an international conference or to an organ of an international organisation or one of its organs, for the purpose of adopting the text of a treaty in that conference, organisation or organ".

See on this the Cameroon *v.* Nigeria case (*supra* note 32): Nigeria invoked Art. 7, para. 2, of the VCLT and argued that Cameroon, according to an objective test based upon the provisions of the VCLT, either knew or should have known that the Head of State of Nigeria did not have the power to make legally binding commitments without referring back to the Government of Nigeria, i.e. then the Supreme Military Council. Art. 7, para. 2, of the VCLT according to Nigeria, refers only to the way in which a person's function as a State's representative is established, and does not deal with the extent of that person's powers when exercising that representative function. Cameroon also submitted that according to Art. 7, para. 2, of the VCLT as a matter of international law a Head of State is always considered as representing a State for the purpose of expressing the consent to be bound by a treaty (para. 260 of the judgment). The Court did not accept the argument that Art. 7, para. 2, of the VCLT is solely concerned with the way that a person's function as a State's representative is established, but does not deal with the extent of that person's authority when exercising the representative functions (para. 265 of the judgment).

without constituting a direct acknowledgement of Danish sovereignty) and to refrain from occupying any part of Greenland. The Court, thus, characterized the Ihlen Declaration as a unilateral statement of a purely verbal nature. However, this was perhaps an oversimplification, dictated no doubt by the exigencies of the case. It is difficult not to acknowledge some force in the position of the Danish government, which claimed that in this case there existed, if not a treaty, then at least two interdependent engagements in the form of two unilateral acts.[44] The understanding of the Danish government was that the statements made by the Danish representative and the Norwegian Minister for Foreign Affairs were "interdependent". Thus, establishing a so-called *do ut des* reciprocal contractual recognition of Norwegian interests in Spitzbergen by Denmark and recognition of Danish interests in Greenland by Norway. Although not satisfactory if viewed in terms of a definition, it may be said that the Ihlen Declaration was in law a hybrid instrument where unilateral and bilateral obligations were inextricably interlocked.

2.5 "Concluded Between States"

2.5.1 The issue of international organizations

At the time of drafting, the controversial issues included the question of what subjects of international law the VCLT should cover, and the notion of a "State". As to the first of these issues, it was debated from the outset whether to extend the scope of the Convention to include international organizations. In Brierly's First Report, followed by the Reports of Lauterpacht,

---

[44] Judge Anzilotti said as follows: "[t]he dispute is one between Denmark and Norway regarding the sovereignty over a territory in Eastern Greenland. Denmark's position formed the subject of a request addressed by the Danish Government to the Norwegian Government in July 1919, and of a declaration on the part of the latter Government accepted by the Danish Government. Accordingly, in my view, the first thing to be done was to decide whether this constituted a valid agreement between two governments; if so, the rule to be applied for the solution of the dispute should first and foremost have been sought in this agreement." Later he continued: "The outcome of all this is therefore an agreement, concluded between the Danish Minister at Christiania, on behalf of the Danish Government, and the Norwegian Minister for Foreign Affairs, on behalf of the Norwegian Government, by means of purely verbal declarations. The validity of this agreement has been questioned, having regard, in the first place, to its verbal form, and to the competence of the Minister of Foreign Affairs. As regards the form, it should be noted, to begin with, that as both Parties are agreed as to the existence and tenor of these declarations, the question of proof does not arise. Moreover, there does not seem to be any rule of international law requiring that agreements of this kind must necessarily be in writing, in order to be valid." Judge Anzilotti, Dissenting Opinion, *supra* note 38, at 76 and 91.

Fitzmaurice and Waldock,[45] as well as at the Vienna Diplomatic Conference,[46] it was proposed that the VCLT should extend to include international organizations. In 1950, the Commission was in favour of extending the scope of the Convention to international organizations.[47]

However, in 1962, the Commission confirmed its decision to defer examination of treaties entered into by international organizations until it had made a further progress with its draft on treaties concluded by States.[48] In 1965 the ILC finally decided to limit the scope of the Draft Articles to treaties concluded between States and inserted a new Article expressly so providing.[49] In 1966 the Commission expressly reaffirmed its position that "the principles set out in the draft articles are to a large extent relevant also in the case of treaties concluded between States and other subjects of international law and between two or more such other subjects of international law". Following this statement, the Commission inserted a new provision, which became VCLT Article 3(a), the purpose of which was to safeguard the legal force of such agreements.[50]

As is stated in VCLT Article 1, the VCLT relates only to treaties concluded between States.[51] However, the formulation of VCLT Article 3(c), stating that the fact that the VCLT does not apply to agreements concluded between States and other subjects of international law shall not affect the application of the VCLT to the relations of States as between themselves under international agreements to which other subjects of international law are also parties, read in conjunction with Article 73 of the 1986 Vienna Convention on the Law of Treaties between States and International Organizations or between International Organizations ("[a]s between States parties to the [VCLT], the relations of those States under a treaty between

---

[45] See note 24. J. L. Brierly, First Report on the Law of Treaties (Art. 1(a)), at 228; H. Lauterpacht, First Report on the Law of Treaties (Art. 1), at 94; G. Fitzmaurice, First Report on the Law of Treaties (Art. 1(3)), at 117; C. H. M. Waldock, First Report on the Law of Treaties (Art. 1(a)), at 32.

[46] See the proposals of the United States and Vietnam, The Vienna Diplomatic Conference, UN Doc.A/Conf.39/11/Add.2, at 110.

[47] YILC (1950), Vol. II, Report of the ILC to the General Assembly on the work of its second session, UN Doc.A/1316, para. 162, at 381: "A majority of the Commission were also in favour of including in its study agreements to which international organisations are parties ...".

[48] YILC (1962), Vol. II, Report of the ILC to the General Assembly on the work of its fourteenth session, UN Doc.A/5209, para. 21 of the Introduction, at 161.

[49] YILC (1965), Vol. II, Report of the ILC to the General Assembly on the work of the first part of its seventeenth session, UN Doc.A/6009, at 159.

[50] YILC (1966), Vol. II, Report of the ILC to the General Assembly on the work of the second part of its seventeenth session, UN Doc.A/6309/Rev.I, at 190.

[51] Art. 1, "Scope of the Present Convention": "[t]he present Convention applies to treaties between States".

two or more States and one or more international organizations shall be governed by [the VCLT]"), indicates that the 1969 VCLT applies also to some extent to relationships between States and international organizations.[52]

The scope of this applicability was, however, never clearly specified. Therefore, it has been said that

> ... the Vienna Convention, applying specifically to treaties between States, is limited to agreements governed by international law between subjects of international law. But how the codified law applies to subjects of international law which are not States (other than, now, international intergovernmental organisations), or even how those other subjects are to be identified, are issues left completely open.[53]

The 1986 Vienna Convention evolved from the Vienna Diplomatic Conference where a resolution was adopted to request the International Law Commission to analyze the problem of treaties between States and international organizations or between two or more organizations. [54]

2.5.2 Agreements between States and non-state entities and individuals or corporations – the Anglo-Iranian Oil Co case

Agreements between States and individuals or corporations are not generally considered as belonging to the category of international agreements. The *locus classicus* on this issue is the *Anglo-Iranian Oil* case.[55]

---

[52] Art. 3(c) of the VCLT, on "International Agreements not within the scope of the present Convention" provides that "[t]he fact that the present Convention does not apply to international agreements concluded between Stares and other subjects of international law or between such other subjects of international law, or to international agreements not in written form, shall not affect: ... (c) the application of the Convention to the relations of States as between themselves under international agreements to which other subjects of international law are also parties". Art. 73 of the 1986 Convention on "Relationship to the Vienna Convention on the law of treaties" provides that "[a]s between States parties to the Vienna Convention on the Law of Treaties of 1969, the relations of those States under a treaty between two or more States and one or more international organizations shall be governed by that Convention". See, e.g., G. Gaja, "A New Vienna Convention on Treaties and International Organisations or between International Organisations: A Critical Commentary", 58 *BYIL* (1987), at 253-269; see also E. W. Vierdag, "Some Reflections on the Relationship between the 1969 and the 1986 Vienna Convention on the Law of Treaties", 25 *Archiv des Völkerrechts* (1987), 82-91, at 89.

[53] S Rosenne, *Developments in the Law of Treaties 1945-1986* (1989), at 22.

[54] "Resolution Relating to Article 1 of the Vienna Convention on the Law of Treaties", in the Official Records of the United Nations Conference on the Law of Treaties (1968), Final Act of the United Nations Conference on the Law of Treaties, UN Doc.A/CONF.39.26+corr., at 285.

[55] Anglo-Iranian Oil Company (United Kingdom *v.* Iran), Preliminary Objections, Judgment of 22 July 1952, 1952 ICJ Rep. 20, at 93.

The Iranian government granted a concession in 1933 to the Anglo-Iranian Oil Company for a period of sixty years. Article 22 of the concession agreement provided that all the differences relating to the concession were to be submitted to arbitration. The procedure to be followed was that of the PCIJ, and it was stated that the award was based on the juridical principles contained in Article 38 of the Statute of the Court. By Article 21 it was agreed that performance of the agreement would be based on principles of mutual good will and good faith, as well as on reasonable interpretation of the agreement. The Government of Iran also agreed that the Concession shall not be annulled and the terms shall not be altered either by general or special legislation in the future, or by administrative measures or any other acts whatever of the executive authorities.

On 15 and 20 March 1951, the Iranian Majlis and Senate passed a law nationalizing the oil industry in Iran. The British government, exercising its right of diplomatic protection, submitted an Application to the Court on the basis of Optional Clause Declarations made by itself and Iran. The case raised difficult issues in relation to jurisdiction. The Iranian Optional Clause Declaration referred to disputes arising in regard to situations or facts relating directly or indirectly to the application of treaties or conventions accepted by Persia and subsequent to the ratification of this Declaration. The question, thus, was whether the concession in question belonged to the category of such treaties or conventions. The argument submitted by the British government was based upon the involvement of the League of Nations in the cancellation of an earlier concession in 1932 by the Iranian government. The matter was submitted to the League of Nations. In 1933, the League of Nations Rapporteur submitted his Report on the matter to the League Council, together with the text of a new concession which replaced the earlier concession, and declared that "the dispute between His Majesty's Government in the United Kingdom and the Imperial Government of Persia is now finally settled". Since the representatives of both countries were satisfied with the outcome, the matter was removed from the agenda of the Council. Importantly, the government of the United Kingdom argued before the Court that, as a result of these proceedings, the government of Iran undertook certain treaty obligations in relation to the United Kingdom. The government of the United Kingdom claimed that because of these obligations, the agreement signed by the Iranian government and the Anglo-Persian Oil Company "has a double character, the character of being at once a concessionary contract between the Iranian Government and the Company and a treaty between the two Governments".[56]

The Court rejected the United Kingdom's argument based on the "double character" of the agreement:

---

[56] *Id.*, at 112.

> The Court cannot accept the view that that the contract signed by the Iranian Government and the Anglo-Persian Oil Company has a double character. It is nothing more than a concessionary contract between a Government and a foreign corporation. The United Kingdom is not a party to the contract; there is no privity of the contract between the Government of Iran and the Government of the United Kingdom. Under the contract the Iranian Government cannot claim from the United Kingdom Government any rights which it may claim from the company, nor can it be called upon to perform towards the United Kingdom Government any obligations which it is bound to perform towards the Company. The document bearing the signatures of the representatives of the Iranian Government and the Company has a single purpose: the purpose of regulating the relations between that Government and the Company in regard to the concession. It does not regulate in any way the relations between the two Governments.[57]

The Court further stated that the legal nature of the contract was not altered by the submission of the dispute to the Council and that submission did not convert its terms into the terms of a treaty by which the Iranian government is bound *vis-à-vis* the United Kingdom government.[58]

On this analysis, there is a range of treaties of quasi-international character which do not fall within the ambit of the VCLT. Mention may be made in this context of agreements concluded between Israel and the Palestinian Liberation Organization, including the Agreement on Preparatory Powers and Responsibilities of 29 August 1994;[59] the Palestinian-Israeli Interim Agreement on the West Bank and Gaza, the "Oslo II Agreement" of 28 September 1995;[60] and the Agreement on the Gaza Strip and the Jericho Area, the so-called "Cairo Agreement", of 4 May 1994.[61]

2.6 "Governed by International Law"

The term "governed by international law" forms part of the definition of a treaty contained in Article 1, paragraph 1(a), of the VCLT. This term has two aspects. First, it is aimed at excluding from the definition those agreements, even if international – and, indeed, even if made between States – which are governed by some other legal system in the sense that the applicable law is not international law. Second, the term "governed by international law" implies not just that international law is the law applicable to the agreement in question, but also that, under international law, that agreement is binding. Furthermore, this implication also contains within in it

---

[57] *Id.*

[58] *Id.*, 113.

[59] 34 *ILM* 455 (1994).

[60] 35 *ILM* 55 (1995).

[61] 34 *ILM* 622 (1994).

the concept of "intention" which was, as we shall see below, included in the definition of treaty in earlier drafts of the VCLT. This will be considered further in section 3 below.

Of course, merely specifying in an agreement that international law is to be the applicable law is not sufficient to turn the agreement into a treaty subject to the VCLT. This is of some importance in view of the phenomenon of "internationalization" of investment contracts, under which it has become increasingly common for capital-exporting countries to require that the proper law governing investment agreements should be international law – a technique that aims to prevent adverse exercises of sovereignty by the host country.[62]

The element "governed by international law" was one of the more problematic issues of the definition of the treaty in international law and Special Rapporteurs used various formulations to reflect this element.[63] The Commission finally came to the conclusion that the element of intent is sufficiently referred to by the phrase "governed by international law".

2.7 Registration

A final formal aspect may be mentioned, though it is not a formal rule constituting part of the definition of a treaty in the VCLT. It is sometimes suggested that the international registration of an agreement is an indication

---

[62] See P. Muchlinski, *Multinational Enterprises and Law* (1999), Ch. 14; F.A. Mann, "The Law Governing State Contracts", 21 *BYIL* (1944), at 11; F.A. Mann, "The Proper Law of Contracts Concluded by International Persons", 35 *BYIL* (1959), at 34; Sir R. Jennings, "State Contracts in International Law", 37 *BYIL* (1961), at 156; D.W. Bowett, "State Contracts with Aliens: Contemporary Developments on Compensation for Termination or Breach", 59 *BYIL* (1988), at 49; C. Greenwood, "State Contracts in International Law", 53 *BYIL* (1982), at 27-81.

[63] J.L. Brierly, First Report on the Law of Treaties (Art. 1(a)): "a relation under international law", note 24, 226; Lauterpacht, First Report on the Law of Treaties (Art. 1): treaties as "intended to create legal rights and obligations", note 24; G. Fitzmaurice, First Report on the Law of Treaties (Art. 2(1)): "a treaty is an international agreement ... intended to create legal rights and obligations, to establish relationships, governed by international law", *supra* note 24. Later, the ILC dropped the element of intention and simply stated in draft Art. 2, that treaties must be governed by international law: 1 *YILC* (1962), 638th meeting, at 52. At the Vienna Diplomatic Conference, Waldock stated that "[t]he phrase "international law" serves to distinguish between international agreements regulated by public international law and those which, although concluded between States, are regulated by national law of one of the parties (or by some other national law system chosen by the parties.)", Official Records of the United Nations Conference on the Law of Treaties (1968), UN Doc.A/Conf.39/11/Add.2, para. 6, at 9.

of its being an international treaty.[64] The duty to register was very strongly formulated in the Covenant of the League of Nations (Article 18), which read as follows: "[e]very treaty or international engagement entered into hereafter by any member of the League shall be forthwith registered with the Secretariat and shall as soon as possible be published by it. No such treaty or international engagement shall be binding until so registered". Of course, the duty to register only applied to League members. However, Article 18 of the Covenant did not have a significant impact on the practice of States and the PCIJ admitted cases that involved unregistered agreements.[65]

The United Nations (UN) system of registration was formulated in Article 102 of the UN Charter: "[e]very treaty and every international agreement entered into by any Member of the United Nations after the present Charter comes into force shall as soon as possible be registered with the Secretariat and published by it", and further: "[n]o party to any such treaty or international agreement which has not been registered in accordance with the provisions of paragraph 1 of this Article may invoke that treaty or agreement before any organ of the United Nations".[66] Article 102 of the Charter is less strongly worded than Article 18 of the Covenant. Non-publication does not defeat the binding force of any international treaty; it only indicates that it will not be possible to invoke it before any organ of the United Nations, including the ICJ. In relation to Article 102, the General Assembly has adopted a regulation, which requires, in paragraph 2, the registration of "[e]very treaty or international agreement, whatever its form or descriptive name..." with the exception, according to paragraph 2, that registration "shall not take place until the treaty or international agreement has come into force ...".[67] The registration of a document, however, does not amount to an acknowledgement by the United Nations that the registered document is a treaty. The unilateral Egyptian declaration on the Suez Canal

---

[64] See, e.g., K. Widdows, "What is an Agreement in International Law?", 50 *BYIL* (1979), 117-149 at 143, see also D.N. Hutchinson, "The Significance of the Registration or Non-Registration of an International Agreement in Determining Whether or Not It Is a Treaty", 46 *Current Legal Problems*, Vol. 11 (1993), 257-290, at 265-266.

[65] In Interpretation of the Treaty of Neuilly, 1924 PCIJ (Series A), No. 4, the Court did not take notice of the fact that the compromis in that case was not registered.

[66] This chapter deals only with registration from the point of view of defining what constitutes an international treaty. There are, however, many other problems, such as whether a treaty in breach of international law may be registered by the Secretary-General. On this point and on the history of this Article see M. Brandon, "Analysis of the Terms 'Treaty' and 'International Agreement' For Purposes of Registration Under Article 102 of the United Nations Charter", 47 *AJIL* (1953), at 49-69. See also S. Rosenne, "United Nations Treaty Practice", 86 *Recueil des Cours* (1954-II), at 771-443.

[67] UNGA Res. 97 (I), Yearbook of the United Nations (1946-1947).

was registered,[68] though it is plainly not a treaty. The practice of the UN Secretariat is undoubtedly to lean in favour of registration.[69]

Although all members of the UN have a duty to register a treaty, very often treaties are not registered at the time they are concluded, or at all. This is the case with certain bilateral agreements,[70] lump sum agreements[71] and secret agreements. Thus, it can be said that registration (or non-registration) of a treaty does not have any evidentiary value. On one hand, not all treaties are registered; on the other, the UN Secretariat registers almost all documents submitted to it, including unilateral declarations. This was also the finding of the Court in the *Qatar/Bahrain* case, in which registration was held not to be decisive as to the character of the document in question. Bahrain submitted an argument that Qatar's late registration of the Minutes both with the UN Secretariat (under Article 102 of the UN Charter) and with the General Secretariat of the League of Nations (under Article 17 of the Pact of the League of Arab States) indicated that Qatar did not accord to this document binding force. The Court emphasized, however, that non-registration of a treaty has no bearing on its validity; it remains valid as between the parties.[72]

Non-registration with the United Nations[73] or non-publication is not a reliable indicator of the parties intentions, or lack thereof, to be bound by a treaty. In particular, the duty to publish in the *United Nations Treaty Series*

---

[68] 265 UNTS 299.

[69] M. Tabory, "Recent Developments in the United Nations Treaty Registration and Publication Practices", 76 *AJIL* (1982), at 357-358. It is submitted that Art. 102 expresses an absolute obligation on UN members and does not have a discretionary character. Parties who are not UN members are not bound by it. See also Art. 81 of the 1986 Vienna Convention which establishes an obligation to register a treaty for all the Parties, also for those who are not members of the UN. Of importance is also Art. 4, para. 1, of the Regulations which stipulates that all agreements to which the UN is a Party; or where the UN has been authorized by the treaty or agreement to effect registration; or where the UN is the depositary of a multilateral treaty or agreement are registered by the UN Secretariat ex officio. B. Simma (ed.), *The Charter of the United Nations, A Commentary* (2002), at 1282-1283.

[70] For the reasons of non-registration see Hutchinson, *supra* note 64, at 277; the same author is of the view that the Court did not ascertain whether the process of registration was completed, at 279.

[71] R.B. Lillich, "The Obligation to Register Treaties and International Agreements with the United Nations", 65 *AYIL* (1971), at 771-773.

[72] Maritime Delimitation and Territorial Questions between Qatar and Bahrain (Qatar *v.* Bahrain), Jurisdiction and Admissibility, Judgment of 1 July 1994, *supra* note 8, paras. 28 and 29.

[73] An example was the non-registration by Iraq of the 1963 "agreed minutes" (Iraq and Kuwait), which Iraq later invoked as proof that it had not intended to be legally bound. See M. Mendelson and S. Hulton, "The Iraq-Kuwait Boundary: Legal Aspects", 23 *Revue Belge de Droit International* (1990), 293-332, at 294.

rests with the UN Secretariat, not with the parties,[74] and non-publication in the *Series* cannot be evidence of the intention of parties not to be bound by it.

The element of intent was discussed within the Commission, and it was eventually decided that it should not be included in the final Draft.[75] It was stated explicitly that intent was already contained in the notion "governed by international law".[76] Some members of the Commission were of the view that there are agreements that by their very definition are governed by international law, notwithstanding the intention of the parties, such as territorial arrangements. According to this view, the intention of the parties is of no importance, whether it is spelled out or not, since it is only international law that may be employed in cases of such agreements. The extensive discussion which arose in connection with the notion of "governed by international law" during the Diplomatic Conference was mostly provoked by uncertainty as to the legal character or legal consequences of instruments such as "agreed minutes"; or declarations as, for example, the Yalta and Potsdam Agreements. [77]

The 1933 Harvard Draft Convention on the Law of Treaties had taken into account as one of the elements of international treaties their subjection to international law.[78] Its Article 1(a) (Use of the Term 'Treaty') included the following definition: "[a] treaty is a formal instrument of agreement by which two or more States establish a relation under international law between themselves". Similarly to the later drafts of the ILC, the Harvard Commentary stresses the necessity for a treaty to be governed by

---

[74] See W.K. Geck, "Treaties, Registration and Publication", 7 *Encyclopaedia of Public International Law* (1984), 490-496, at 492; C.A. Fleischhauer, "The United Nations Treaty Series", in Y. Dinstein and M. Tabory (eds.), *International Law at a Time of Perplexity: Essays in Honour of Shabtai Rosenne* (1989), at 131-148.

[75] YILC (1962), Vol. I, 638th meeting, at 52. See also the Official Records of the United Nations Conference on the Law of Treaties (1968), UN Doc.A/Conf.39/II/ Add.2, para. 6, at 9.

[76] *Supra n*ote 75, YILC (1962), Vol. I, 638th meeting, at 52.

[77] The Official Records of the United Nations Conference on the Law of Treaties (1968), Summary Records of the Plenary Meetings and of the Meetings of the Committee of the Whole, at 227-228: for example, the United Kingdom representatives, Sir R. Vallat and Sir I. Sinclair, were of the view that many 'agreed minutes' and 'memoranda of understanding' were not international agreements subject to the law of treaties because there was no intention to create legal rights and obligations, or a legal relationship. The view was also expressed as to the difference between international agreements concluded with the intention to create rights and obligations and some political statements which set out only policy objectives and/or agreed views; on the other hand, the representative of the Soviet Union argued that instruments, such as the Atlantic Charter of Potsdam or Yalta Agreements, provided for rights and obligations, *id.*, at 226.

[78] Harvard Research in International Law, "Draft Convention on the Law of Treaties", 29 *AJIL* (Supplement 1935), at 693-695.

international law. Thus "[t]he law governing the validity, binding force, interpretation, application and termination of treaties between States cannot be the municipal law of any of them; it is well settled by the doctrine, practice, and jurisprudence that this law is international law".[79] The draft mentioned loan agreements and the purchase of buildings, *inter alia*, as examples of "treaties" that would be excluded by this definition.

2.8 Conclusions

The definition of a treaty, as enshrined in the VCLT, does not reflect all the varied forms under which a treaty may appear. This is best illustrated by the jurisprudence of the PCIJ and the ICJ, which provides examples of some of the difficulties that may arise in connection with determining whether an instrument constitutes a treaty,[80] notwithstanding its designation. The ICJ has never relied exclusively on the VCLT to determine the nature of an instrument, but in each and every case has focused rather on the legal content of the instrument in question.

The following conclusions may be drawn at this stage:

(i) the ILC (generally) was of the view that it is the content of the legal obligation that distinguishes a legally binding agreement from a political one;

(ii) the formal definition of a treaty, as contained in Article 2(a) of the VCLT, does not reflect the development of multifaceted forms (both formal and substantive) of co-operation between States;

(iii) in determining the status of an instrument, the nature of the tranaction, the text and the circumstances of its conclusion must be taken into consideration (the *Aegean Sea* and *Cameroon/Nigeria* cases);

(iv) interdependence of mutual obligations does not necessarily create a bilateral engagement, and, therefore, not all interdependent obligations are treaties (the *Eastern Greenland* case);

(v) binding treaties must enumerate commitments to which parties have consented in order to create rights and obligations in international law for the parties (the *Qatar/Bahrain* case).[81]

---

[79] *Id.*, 693.

[80] Klabbers, *supra* note 2, at 64.

[81] However, difficulties arise in cases of non-legally binding instruments, some of which contain fairly detailed provisions resembling the treaty in form. In instances of this kind, the element of intention of the parties appears to be one of the factors to be taken into consideration (see section 3 below).

3. Informal Arrangements and "Soft Law"

3.1. Preliminary Considerations: The Role of the Intention of the Parties

The crucial element in distinguishing between formal and informal instruments is the element of intention, i.e., whether parties to a treaty intended to be bound by it or not. The element of intention of the parties has at least three different roles. The first is its role as one of the elements of the concept of the treaty, which distinguishes binding instruments from non-binding ones. The second is its role within the canons of treaty inter-pretation, as suggested by, for example, Sir Hersch Lauterpacht[82] and Lord McNair.[83] The third is its role in determinations of the expression of the will of the parties to a dispute to subject themselves to adjudication or not. To some extent this is similar to the second role; intention may be used in interpreting the "agreement" between the parties to ascertain the existence and the scope of the will of parties to seize an international court or tribunal.

In the *Qatar/Bahrain* case, Bahrain advanced an argument resting on intention, claiming that the signatories never intended to conclude an internationally binding agreement. The Foreign Minister of Bahrain had stated that by signing the Minutes in 1990 he had never intended to commit Bahrain to a legally binding agreement, and that, according to the Constitution of Bahrain, treaties affecting the territory of a State may only come into effect after their positive enactment as a law. Thus, having been aware of these strict requirements, he could not have legally bound his State, and had only treated the signing of the Minutes as a political statement. The Court refused to investigate further the intentions of the representatives of the two governments. It found that in this particular case the objective evidence was clear enough not to necessitate recourse to any further means, such as the *travaux préparatoires*:

---

[82] H. Lauterpacht, "Restrictive Interpretation and the Principle of Effectiveness of Treaties", 26 *BYIL* (1949) at 73. Sir H. Lauterpacht held a very strong the view on this matter: "[t]he intention of the parties – express or implied – is the law. Any considerations – of effectiveness or otherwise – which tend to transform the ascertainable intention of the parties into a factor of secondary importance are inimical to the true purpose of interpretation".

[83] Lord McNair, *The Law of Treaties* (1961), at 366: "[m]any references are to be found ... to the primary necessity of giving effect to the "plain terms" of a treaty, or construing words according to their "general and ordinary meaning" or their natural signification and so forth and of not seeking aliunde for a meaning "when the terms are clear". But this so-called rule of interpretation like any others is merely a starting-point, a prima facie guide, and cannot be allowed to obstruct the essential quest in the application of treaties, namely to search for the real intention of the contracting parties in using the language employed by them".

[t]he Court does not find it necessary to consider what might have been the intentions of the Foreign Minster of Bahrain or, for that matter, those of the Foreign Minister of Qatar. The two Ministers signed a text recording commitments accepted by their Governments, some of which were to be given immediate application. Having signed such a text, the Foreign Minister of Bahrain is not in a position to say that he intended to subscribe only to a 'statement recording a political understanding', and not to an international agreement.[84]

That finding was confirmed in the 1995 *Qatar/Bahrain* case.[85] According to Klabbers:

[t]he *Qatar v Bahrain* decision is important for two reasons. First, it unequivocally makes clear that any commitment is a legal commitment. Second, it establishes something of a methodology for ascertaining the true nature of an international instrument: first and foremost are its actual terms. If the text of an instrument allows the ascertainment of commitments, then it is a legal text and the discussion is effectively closed. It is only where the text itself is ambiguous that recourse to other indicators appears justified.[86]

Klabbers applies this statement to the general concept of a treaty. However, the judgment of the Court may lend itself to a different interpretation. It may be argued that the Court applied this only to the issue at hand, namely the establishment of its jurisdiction. Support for this claim may be found in the dissenting opinion of Judge Schwebel, who was strongly critical of the findings of the Court, but referred only to the issue of the Court's jurisdiction. He said:

[i]n the jurisprudence of this Court, jurisdiction may be conferred upon it only by the common intention of both parties to the case...But if that common intention is lacking, if the intention to submit to the Court's jurisdiction is that

---

[84] Qatar *v.* Bahrain, Judgment of 1 July 1994, *supra* note 8, 121-122, para. 27. The necessity of intention of the parties to submit themselves to the Court's jurisdiction was always maintained by the Court, see Aegean Sea case (*supra* note 7) where the Court said: "[r]egard must be paid to the intention of the Greek Government at the time when it deposited its instrument of accession to the General Act; and it was with that jurisprudence in mind that the Court asked the Greek Government to furnish any available evidence of explanations of the instrument of accession given at that time", at 29, para. 69. It was also confirmed by the Court, e.g., in the Fisheries Jurisdiction case (Spain *v.* Canada), Jurisdiction, Judgment of 4 December 1998, 1998 ICJ Rep., para. 49.

[85] The judgment was not without controversy. In particular, it was subject to severe criticism by Judge Schwebel, who emphasized the failure of the Court to take into account travaux préparatoires to ascertain the true intention of the parties. Dissenting Opinion of Judge Schwebel, Qatar *v.* Bahrain, Judgment of 15 February 1995, *supra* note 8, at 25-39.

[86] Klabbers, *supra* note 2, at 215.

of one but not both parties, the Court is without jurisdiction to decide the
merits of the dispute.[87]

In any event, it could be said that the Court, having examined the content of
the legal obligation included in the instrument in question, decided that it
laid down very clearly the parties' rights and obligations and therefore
constituted an agreement, the existence of which could be stated without the
necessity of recourse to the intentions of the parties.

3.2 Memoranda of Understanding

International relations call for numerous arrangements and understandings
between States, which may be recorded in ways which, in terms of formality,
fall short of what is generally considered as constituting a treaty.[88] Such an
arrangement may, nevertheless, constitute a legally binding agreement if the
parties to it so desire.[89] However,[90] for a number of reasons, States in
practice frequently prefer that such arrangements between them do not give
rise to legal rights and obligations enforceable under international law. Such
arrangements, and the documents in which they are recorded, have been
referred to variously as, for example, "gentlemen's agreements",
"memoranda of understanding" or "informal instruments". The reasons for
this preference, and the uses which these agreements serve, as well as the
non-legal effects they may have, lie rather in the purview of the diplomatist
or political scientist than of the lawyer. The issues that are, strictly speaking,
relevant to the lawyer, are, firstly, how to distinguish those arrangements
which do constitute legally binding agreements from those which do not;

---

[87] Dissenting Opinion of Judge Schwebel, Qatar v. Bahrain, Judgment of 15 February 1995,
supra note 8, at 27-28.

[88] R.R. Baxter, "International Law in Her Infinite Variety", 29 *ICLQ* (1980), at 549-66; O.
Schachter, "The Twilight Existence of Nonbinding International Agreements", 71 *AJIL*
(1977), at 296-304; F. Roessler, "Law, De Facto Agreements and Declarations of Principle in
International Economic Relations", 21 *GYIL* (1978) at 27-59; C. Lipson, "Why are some
international agreements informal?", *International Organisation* (1991), at 495-538; F.
Münch, "Comments on the 1968 Draft Convention on the Law of Treaties", 29 *ZaöRV*
(1969), at 1-11; P.M. Eiseman, "Le gentlemen's agreement comme source du droit
international", 106 *Journal du Droit International* (1979), at 326-348; J. Klabbers, *supra* note
2, at 121-56.

[89] YILC (1966), Vol. II, Report of the ILC to the General Assembly on the work of its
eighteenth session, UN Doc.A/CN.4/191, at 188: In its 1966 Commentary to Draft Articles
the ILC, explained that "very many instruments in daily use such as an "agreed minutes" or a
"memorandum of understanding", could not appropriately be called formal instruments, but
they are undoubtedly agreements subject to the law of treaties. A general convention on the
law of treaties must cover all such agreements...".

[90] See above, Section I.2(c).

and, secondly, whether, notwithstanding that the arrangements themselves are not directly binding on the parties, they may have some secondary or indirect legal effect.[91]

With regard to the first of these issues, the decisive factor distinguishing binding treaties from non-binding instruments is the intention of parties, that is, whether the instrument in question was intended to create international rights and obligations between the parties. In this respect, there are no special rules relating to the type of informal instrument here under consideration.

As mentioned earlier, the ILC considered that the element of the intention of the parties was included in the phrase "governed by international law".[92] The ICJ confirmed the importance of intention of the parties in defining the character of any given international instrument and emphasized its independence of the form taken by the treaty. It observed that "... the question of form ... is not a domain in which international law imposes any special or strict requirements",[93] and that "[w]here ... as is generally the case in international law, which places the principal emphasis on the intention of the parties, the law prescribes no particular form, parties are free to choose what form they please provided their intention clearly results from it".[94]In the literature, the role of the intention of the parties in determining whether an obligation is binding is also treated as important. For example, Fawcett considered that an essential element of a legally binding international agreement (in contradistinction to political obligations such as treaties of alliance) is the intention of the parties to create legal obligations between them.[95] *Oppenheim's International Law* also relies upon the intention of the parties: "[i]t is suggested that the decisive factor is still whether the instrument is intended to create international legal rights and obligations between the parties – an element which the International Law Commission regarded as embraced within the phrase "governed by international law"".[96]

---

[91] The only possible legal effect of non-binding agreements would seem to arise by way of estoppel and in relation to the doctrine of good faith. Discussion of these difficult doctrines is beyond the scope of this chapter, but see A. Aust, "The Theory and Practice of Informal International Instruments", 35 *ICLQ* (1986), at 807-812, and A. Aust, *Modern Treaty Law and Practice* (2000), at 45-46.

[92] *Id.*, para. 6, at 189.

[93] Nuclear Tests cases, *supra* note 10, 267-268; Temple of Preah Vihear case, *supra* note 31, at 31-32.

[94] Temple of Preah Vihear case, *supra* note 31, at 31. The Court was consistent in stressing that the designation of a treaty was not the decisive factor in defining its legal character; South West Africa cases, *supra* note 1, at 331.

[95] Fawcett, *supra* note 4, at 385-386.

[96] Sir R. Jennings, Sir A. Watts (eds.), *Oppenheim's International Law*, Vol. 2 (1996), at 1202; Lord McNair, *supra* note 83, at 15; S. Rosenne, *Developments of the Law of Treaties* 1945-1986 (1989), at 85-123.

It also seems well established as a general rule that the nature of the parties' intentions is to be ascertained from all the circumstances of each case, no particular factor necessarily being decisive, though it seems to emerge from the jurisprudence of the ICJ that substantial priority is accorded to the actual terms of the agreement. There is no reason to distinguish memoranda of understanding from any other form of agreement in this respect.[97]

As noted above, the judgment of the ICJ in the *Qatar/Bahrain* case raised the question of the existence of informal agreements, as well as the question of the possibility of using objective criteria to determine the legal character of an instrument. Klabbers, for example, puts forward an interesting but controversial argument which denies the possibility of the existence of instruments which resemble treaties but are not treaties: "[t]hey are drafted in similar ways, concluded in similar ways, complied with or violated in similar ways, and often even terminated in similar ways".[98] He argues that the practice of States is inconsequential and insufficient, stating that "…it is doubtful whether States can simply conclude treaties and nevertheless agree that those treaties are not treaties but something else".[99] However, in modern practice, States often employ instruments that have the form of treaties, but are not treaties in substance. We cannot disregard what States do in respect of treaty-making and conclude that if the practice does not confirm the theory, States have no right to act in a certain manner.

On the other hand, an issue raised by Klabbers relates to the possibility of informal instruments having binding effect on the parties by way of workings of good faith and/or estoppel. He denies such a possibility on the ground that these are non-legally binding instruments, which, therefore, can contain no legal obligations at all. He relies on the judgment of the ICJ in the *Nicaragua v Honduras* case in which it said that good faith "is not in itself a source of obligation where none would otherwise exist".[100] The same view has also been expressed by other writers, such as Bothe, who said that: "[g]ood faith is a legal concept, and basing respect for non-legal obligations on a legal concept would not seem to be appropriate".[101] Nonetheless, another view has been expressed to the effect that, for example in cases in which the nature of the legal obligation is unclear, "it is believed that, the determination of the extent of the obligation of a State, although lying within

---

[97] For a discussion of some possible relevant circumstances in the context of memoranda of understanding etc., see Aust, *Modern Treaty Law and Practice*, *supra* note 91, at 27-30.
[98] Klabbers, *supra* note 2, at 131.
[99] *Id.*, at 130.
[100] Border and Transborder Armed Actions (Nicaragua *v.* Honduras), Jurisdiction and Admissibility, Judgment of 20 December 1988, 1988 ICJ Rep. 69, at 105.
[101] M. Bothe, "Legal and Non-legal Norms – a Meaningful Distinction in International Relation", 11 *NYIL* (1980), 65-95, at 95.

the competence of the interested State, must take place in accordance with legal duty to act in good faith".[102]

According to Keller, Klabbers' main arguments are based on the premises that "international relations are fully enclosed within the normative framework of international law to the extent that law is the only possible normative language of international politics and that ... there are simply no alternative normative systems, such as morality, courtesy or politics on which one might found such an agreement, even if international law could be excluded."[103] But as Keller points out, there is no rule of international law that would prohibit the creation of non-legally-binding agreements, and States and international organizations are free to do so provided that they do not breach any legal obligation in the process. Keller is further of the view that:

> [i]n seeking alternative 'normative systems' Klabbers seems to overstate what is actually required. For it is not clear why, in the rough and ready world of international politics, considerations of mutual advantage, trust and reputation should be deemed to be an insufficient source of obligations, if parties concerned take them to be sufficient for their particular purposes. Indeed these extra-legal considerations play an equally important role in the fulfillment of treaty obligations.

and further:

> ... principles on which a non-legally binding agreement might operate, concepts of breach and invalidity are easily adapted from the law of treaties to flesh out the expectations of the parties. That the treatment of these matters would be still less certain or predictable would apparently be a risk the parties are prepared to accept.[104]

Similarly, Sir I. Sinclair, stated that in the practice of States, it often happens that for reasons of expediency it is necessary to produce a text that "will, in order to satisfy claimed political imperatives, simultaneously bear the appearance of a treaty instrument without in fact constituting one".[105]

In conclusion, the judgment of the Court in the *Qatar/Bahrain* case, taken at face value, could support the general views expressed by Klabbers. The Court rejected the argument of Bahrain based on the lack of intention to be bound by the 1990 Minutes. The Court based its test of binding force of the document on objective considerations. A close analysis of the judgment, however, indicates that the Court did not base its decision to determine the character of the Minutes on its form or on the intention of the Parties but on

---

[102] Jennings and Watts, *supra* note 96, at 1202.

[103] See the review of J. Klabbers' book by P. Keller, in 47 *ICLQ* (1998), at 241.

[104] *Id.*

[105] See the review of J. Klabbers' book by Sir I. Sinclair, in 97 *AJIL* (1997), at 749. See also Aust, *Modern Treaty Law and Practice, supra* note 91, at 41.

the commitment and the corresponding consent of the parties as to the content of the obligation at hand. It is worth noting that, while the Court did define the 1990 Minutes as an agreement, the real emphasis of the Judgment was on the binding nature of the obligation they contained. From this it may be inferred that non-binding instruments (the Court did not address this matter) may include binding obligations. A different view may be expressed that there was already, agreed by Parties, a general obligation arising from previous dealings, so that the Doha Minutes were not the only self-standing instrument in question.[106] Indeed, the Court is very explicit in stressing that:

> ... the 1990 Minutes include a reaffirmation of obligations previously entered into; they entrust King Fahid with the task of attempting to find a solution to the dispute during a period of six months; and, lastly, they address the circumstances under which the Court could be seized after May 1991. Accordingly, and contrary to the contention of Bahrain, the Minutes are not a simple record of a meeting, similar to those drawn up within the framework of a Tripartite Committee, they do not merely give an account of discussions and summarize points of agreement and disagreement. They enumerate commitments to which Parties have consented. Thus they create rights and obligations in international law for the Parties. They constitute an international agreement.[107]

> It follows that in order to determine the character of an international instrument, the content of the obligation therein must be scrutinized, on a case-by-case basis. It is, thus, impossible (and indeed not even in accordance with State practice) to assume an all-encompassing view that all international instruments are binding. Once again it has to be reaffirmed that the designation of an instrument cannot serve as an indicator as to the nature of the legal obligation therein. The following view reflects the position adopted by the Court: "[t]he fact that the interested State is the judge of the existence of the obligation is, although otherwise of considerable importance, not of decisive relevance for the determination of the legal character of the instrument".[108]

Another problem also considered by Klabbers[109] is the question of so-called administrative agreements concluded between governmental agencies or departments. The main problem of interest here is whether these agreements bind States or only departments of the government. This question concerns not only the law of treaties but also that of State responsibility. It raises questions, such as which actions of which organ are binding on the State, which is an abstract entity that is not capable of an independent action, and

---

[106] A view expressed by Professor J. Crawford in discussion with one of the authors.
[107] Qatar v. Bahrain, Judgment of 1 July 1994, *supra* note 8, para. 25.
[108] Jennings and Watts, *supra* note 96, at 1202.
[109] Klabbers, *supra* note 2, at 97-104.

which can act only through its agents.[110] The starting point to the answer is Article 2 of the 2001 ILC Articles on State Responsibility.[111] This Article lists as one of the two necessary elements of a wrongful act its attributability to the State under international law (the second element being a breach of an international obligation of a State). The Articles define attribution to the State of the conduct of its organs in a broad manner. Of special importance in the context of administrative agreements is Article 4 (Conduct of Organs of State), which reads as follows:

> (1) The conduct of any State organ shall be considered an act of that State under international law, whether the organ exercises legislative, executive, judicial or any other functions, whatever position it holds in the organisation of the State, and whatever its character as an organ of the central government or of a territorial unit of the State; (2) An organ includes any person or entity which has that status in accordance with the internal law of the State.

Against this background, Klabbers wonders whether administrative agreements concluded by State agencies may generate State responsibility for the State by creating international legal obligations that are binding on it, or whether they do not create international legal obligations for the State but only bind the respective agency. In the latter case, State responsibility would not arise in the event of their breach. Klabbers believes that the fact that individual departments or agencies may legally bind themselves under international law should not be understood as according them with international legal personality (or in other words treating them as international law subjects capable of bearing international rights and obligations), and he rejects this hypothesis. He also rejects the possibility that there is a third legal order (apart from the national and international orders), "which could for all practical purposes be called international agency law". He concludes rightly that providing that administrative agreements generate legal rights and obligations, they become the "onus of the State".[112]

The practice of States supports this view, expressed by many authors. Lord McNair was of the opinion that these administrative agreements do bind States: "[w]hat is important is that this practice must not be allowed to obscure the fact that the real contracting parties are States"; and according to him, "[i]t is necessary to insist upon this point, because any notion that an Agreement expressed to be made between Governments or Government Departments binds only those Governments might have a tendency to impair

---

[110] YILC (1973), Vol. II, Report of the ILC to the General Assembly on the work of its twenty-fifth session, UN Doc. A/9010/Rev.1, at 169. See also Certain Questions Relating to Settlers of German Origin in the Territory Ceded by Germany to Poland (Advisory Opinion), (1922-1924) PCIJ (Series A), no. 6, at 22. See also Klabbers, *supra* note 2, at 100.

[111] Available at http://www.law.cam.ac.uk/rcillLCR/DrafArts98.htm; Crawford, note 10, commentary, at 94-99.

[112] Klabbers, *supra* note 2, at 101 and 103.

the binding character of such agreements by encouraging the subsequent Governments, perhaps of a political complexion completely different from the Government which made the agreement, to repudiate them".[113] The possibility of a separate, third legal order must also be rejected. The relations between States are contained in two legal orders: national and international.[114] Thus, the conclusion to be drawn is that the legal obligations created by the administrative agreements bind the State as a whole, and not the agency or a department in question, since the latter are not subjects of international law.[115]

3.3 "Soft law" Instruments

The phenomenon of so-called "soft law" is the result of the varied relationships between States. As has been said, the "subtlety of the processes by which contemporary international law can be created is no longer adequately captured by reference to the orthodox categories of custom and treaty".[116]

According to Dupuy, it was Lord McNair who coined the term "soft law".[117] There are many proponents of the view that there are some kinds of "arrangements" or "undertakings" constituting "soft", "fragile" or "weak" law that are generally complied with, but which are free from the pressures of the principle *pacta sunt servanda,* as well as from the rules of customary international law. Perhaps not surprisingly, many of these undertakings are drawn up under the auspices of international organizations. These arrangements are made intentionally ambiguous by their drafters, and it has been observed that this results in a corresponding lack of clarity in the way

---

[113] Lord McNair, *supra* note 83, at 20.

[114] Klabbers, *supra* note 2, at 102; J. A. Barberis, "Nouvelles Questions Concernant la Personnalité Juridique Internationale", 97 *Recueil des Cours* (1983-I), 145-304, at 176.

[115] E.W. Vierdag, *Spanningen tussen recht en praktijk in bet verdragenrecht,* Preadvies Nederlands Vereniging voor Internationaal Recht (1989), at 49-52.

[116] A. Boyle, "Some Reflections on Relationship of Treaties and Soft Law", in V. Gowland-Debbas (ed.), *Multilateral Treaty-making: The Current Status of Challenges to and Reforms Needed in the International Legislative Process* (2000), at 25; On the issue of the legal character of non-binding UNGA Resolutions see the fundamental work of K. Skubiszewski, in Vol. 61-I, *Annuaire de l'Institute de Droit International* (1985), Helsinki Session. In particular, as to their possible treaty-making character, see the Rapport Provisoire, at 136-149, paras. 12-13.

[117] R.J. Dupuy, "Declaratory Law and Programmatory Law; From Revolutionary Custom to 'Soft Law'", in R. J. Akkerman, P. J. Krieken and C. O. Pannenborg (eds.), *Declaration on Principles, A Quest For Universal Peace, Liber Amicorum Discipulorumque Professor dr. B. V.A. Röling* (1979), 247-257, at 252.

they are discussed or written about.[118] The ambiguity of such "arrangements" or "undertakings" is widely admitted in doctrine.

Sir Robert Jennings observed that the same provisions are used as evidence by opposing parties before international tribunals in support of their conflicting claims, since each party can give ambiguous provisions its own slant.[119] He points out that the tests applicable to ascertaining the existence of a norm of customary law or a treaty are irrelevant since much of the new "law" is not custom, and "it is recent, it is innovatory, it involves topical political decisions, and it is often the focus of contention".[120] Since soft law instruments are, thus, highly susceptible to varying interpretations, they provide for their drafters a great deal of freedom in arguing their way out of compliance with such instruments. It may be said that "soft law" may occur in any circumstances where States wish to accord significance to something agreed upon but which is plainly intended to amount to less than an expression of intention to be bound by it.[121]

Supporters of the concept of "soft law" believe: that, with its flexible character, it is a helpful technique in situations where States want to act collectively, but at the same time "do not want to fetter their freedom of action".[122] Examples of "soft law" can be found especially in environmental law. International economic "soft law" is also common.[123] In fact, it was first used in this field of law, in particular in dealing with economic issues that were thought to be within the sovereign power of States.[124] The nature of soft law was perfect for uses such as combining collective regulations and restraint in economic dealings with flexibility and freedom to manoeuvre as and when changed circumstances required.

International economic relations had to accommodate almost irreconcilable differences between the approaches of different legal systems and the different goals of a highly diverse and vastly enlarged international community. Thus, States were faced with the problems of achieving an agreement on universally acceptable rules and an unwillingness to undertake legal obligations. As a rule, States are willing to take legal obligations when they expect to fullfil them.[125] It may happen that States try to avoid legally

---

[118] R.R. Baxter, *supra* note 88, at 556-557.

[119] R.Y. Jennings, "What is International Law and How do We Tell It When We See It?", 37 *Annuaire Suisse* (1981), 59-88, at 67.

[120] *Id.*

[121] G.M. Borchardt and K.C. Wellens, "Soft Law in the European Community Law", 14 *European Law Review* (1989), 267-321, at 269.

[122] P. Birnie, "Legal Techniques of Settling Disputes: The Soft Settlement Approach", in W. Butler (ed.), *Perestroika and International Law* (1990), 175-185, at 184.

[123] I. Seidl-Hohenveldern, *International Economic Law* (1989), at 42-45.

[124] G. Schwarzenberger, "The Principles and Standards of International Economic Law", *Recueil des cours* (1966-I), 5-89, at 27-29.

[125] Bothe, *supra* note 101, at 91.

binding obligations because of formal requirements necessary to creating and terminating them.[126]

Other authors reject the concept of "soft law" and claim that either law is binding or it is not law at all.[127] This view is maintained by many who regard "soft law" as detrimental to the system of international law. Lysén states that "one legal rule cannot be more legal than another".[128] Others find this approach unjustified because "[soft law] has great strength as a conflict resolution device ...".[129] Yet other authors deny even the existence of "soft law", because "it is not supported by either State practice or judicial practice"; and "it lacks plausible theoretical underpinnings and even justifications, and most importantly, its application falls victim to the same binary way of thinking which traditionally characterised law".[130] The term "soft law" is viewed by some as unfortunate since it suggests a source of law of inferior value. The concept of "soft law" escapes the traditional rules of legal classification, and attempts to explain the nature of "soft law" have not been entirely successful or persuasive. Some scholars believe that both legal and non-legal norms may be created within the realm of "soft law" instruments, while others restrict it to containing only non-legal norms.[131] Others see the term "soft law" as referring to two things, the first being the "soft" content (language) of instruments which are otherwise hard in nature, that is, formally binding in law (for example, treaty provisions), and the second being the "soft" nature of certain international instruments themselves (for example, joint declarations; joint communiqués; various acts of international organizations).[132] Some other writers do not attempt to coin a

---

[126] T. Gruchalla-Wesierski, "A Framework for Understanding Soft Law", 30 *McGill Law Journal* (1984), 38-88, at 41.

[127] P. Weil, "Towards Relative Normativity in International Law?", 77 *AJIL* (1983), 413-442, at 416-417. See also J. Klabbers, who argues for the redundancy of the concept of 'soft law'. He observes that the division of law into 'hard' and 'soft' leads to a confusion as to the consequences of breach of a norm of soft law, and begs the question whether the breach of a soft law norm leads to international wrongfulness, "The Redundancy of Soft Law", 65 *NJIL* (1996), at 167. See also R. Bilder, "Beyond Compliance: Helping Nations to Cooperate", in D. Shelton (ed.), *Commitment and Compliance, The Role of Non-Binding Norms in the International Legal System* (2000), at 65-73, at 72 ("[b]y blurring the traditional distinction between law and non-law, such usage threatens to damage a valuable normative tool which states have long used an relied on, and, in effect, depreciate the currency of law"). See also O. Elias and C.L. Lim, *The Paradox of Consensualism in International Law* (1998), at 230-232.

[128] G. Lysén, "The Joint Declaration by the EEC and the CMEA", *North Carolina Journal of International Law and Commercial Regulations* (1989), 369-389, at 376.

[129] Birnie, *supra* note 122, at 183.

[130] Klabbers, note 2, at 164.

[131] M. Virally, below note 135, Rapport provisoire, at 166-257; Rapport definitive, at 328-352.

[132] J. Sztucki, "Reflections on International 'Soft Law'", in *Festchrift Till Lars Hjerner, Studies in International Law* (1990), at 549-575.

definition of this phenomenon but satisfy themselves by observing that "soft law" gives an impression that "something is missing in the legal binding nature of law as we know it from the daily life, and even international life".[133]

The legal effects, if any, of instruments of "soft law" are as unclear as those that may be attached to informal instruments. It is sometimes noted that "soft law" instruments may have legal effects arising from estoppel.[134] According to Virally, for instance, the principle of estoppel results from the general principle of *bona fides*, on which political obligations are based.[135] The same considerations, which apply to informal agreements in this respect, also apply to "soft law" instruments. In our view, however, the applicability of the principle of estoppel (which is an institution with specific independent legal effect, unlike good faith) to a non-binding instrument, is doubtful. As to the general principle of good faith, from which estoppel results, its usefulness may also be considered of limited value if we adhere to the concept that it is not itself an independent legal principle. It must also be observed that the very link between estoppel and the principle of good faith is disputed by some authors. MacGibbon, for example, sees estoppel as an independent ground for evaluating legal relationship, distinct from good faith.[136]

On the basis of an examination of certain international environmental law declarations relating to regional co-operation between the Baltic Sea States concerning environmental issues, our conclusion that if any legal effects can be attributed to these "soft law" declarations, it is only the principle of good faith. On the basis of this principle, concerned States pledge to take all appropriate measures to comply with the contents of these declarations. But this is as far as it goes, and the principle of estoppel, to the best of our knowledge was never even considered by the States concerned. All the interviewed lawyers and diplomats were in any event very doubtful about attaching any significant legal effects to such declarations, and treated them

---

[133] A.J.P. Tammes, "Soft Law", in *Essays on International and Comparative Law in Honour of Judge Erades* (1983), at 187.

[134] Y. van der Mensbrugghe, "Legal Status of International North Sea Conferences", in D. Freestone and T. IJlstra (eds.), *The North Sea: Perspective on Regional Environmental Cooperation, International Journal of Estuarine and Coastal Law* (1990), Special Issue, at 21.

[135] M Virally, "La distinction entre textes internationaux ayant une portée juridique dans les relations mutuelles entre leur auteurs et les textes juridiques qui en sont dépourvus" (rapport définitive), Vol. 60-I *Annuaire de l'Institute de Droit International* (1983), Session de Cambridge, at 356: "[e]n conséquence, il est soumis aux obligations juridique résultant de l'estoppel, lorsqu'il a crée les apparences d'un engagement juridique auxquelles une autre partie s'est fiée et que les conditions auxquelles le droit international subordonne l'apparition de telles obligations sont remplies."

[136] I. McGibbon, "Estoppel in International Law", 7 *ICLQ* (1958), 468-513, at 513 .

as an indication of certain future aspirations, which indeed resulted in conclusion of the 1992 Helsinki Convention.[137]

The legal workings of "soft law" were scrutinized closely by jurists in relation to various declarations, in particular in the field of international environmental law, such as the 1972 Stockholm Declaration and the 1992 Rio Declaration. For example, the Baltic Sea was the subject of many such declarations (for instance the 1988 Ministerial Declaration[138] and the 1990 Baltic Sea Declaration).[139] Similarly, numerous declarations were adopted in connection with the North Sea (the Bremen Declaration, the London Declaration; and the Hague Declaration). Y. van der Mensbrugghe examined the North Sea Declarations, concluding that their legal status is "controversial".[140] Indeed, they have an imprecise and ambiguous legal nature and purpose: some are intended only to supply information, some to express an agreed policy, and some actually attempt to impose legal obligations. According to the same author, they are regarded with suspicion by classical international lawyers. Declarations may be unilateral, bilateral or multilateral. It would be an oversimplification to claim that only environmental law has given rise to a significant number of declarations: for example, mention must be made also of the 1978 Bonn Declaration on Hijacking. On the international level, the above-mentioned declarations were not registered in accordance with Article 102 of the UN Charter. However, at the national level, at least in relation to the Baltic Sea Declarations, the practice of States has varied. The declarations were not published in any way in the former communist States. In Sweden, Denmark, and the Federal Republic of Germany ("FRG"), the declarations were published in official journals. In the FRG, the Ministerial Declarations were in fact translated into the national legal order by way of a declaration of the Minister of the Environment.[141] Moreover, in the summer of 1988, the Minister of the Environment of the FRG presented a 10-point catalogue for strengthening efforts to protect the Baltic Sea as a response to the Ministerial Declaration. The plan presented detailed requirements for reducing nutrient inputs from sewage treatment plants. In relation to the reduction of dangerous substances, the Minster announced a state-of-the-art limitation of hazardous substances in industrial waste. In 1989, the FRG Parliament approved the

---

[137] Helsinki Convention on the Protection of the Marine Environment of the Baltic Sea Area, 13 *ILM* (1974), at 546.

[138] Baltic Sea Environmental Proceedings, No. 26 (Baltic Sea Marine Environment Protection Commission (HELCOM) 1988), at 30-36.

[139] Ronneby, Sweden, 1990, Conference on the Baltic Sea Environment <http://www.helcom.fi/helcom/declarations/1990.pgf>.

[140] Van der Mensbrugghe, note 134, at 15-22.

[141] Bekanntmachung einer Ministerdeklaration und der Empfehlungen der Baltic Sea Marine Environment Protection Commission-Helsinki, HELCOM 9/ibis 9/II.

programme. In Sweden, Denmark and Finland, the Declaration was included in the long-term Action Plan on the Protection of the Environment, and approved by their Parliaments. In the former Soviet Union a programme based on the Ministerial Declaration was set up for the Baltic Sea region for the period up to 1996, which took into account about five hundred of the most significant sources of pollution of the sea and provided, in expenditure, up to 1.5 billion roubles for the construction of a cleaning system. Furthermore, in order to implement the Ministerial Declaration, cleaning plants for municipal sewage were provided for in the main cities in the period 1992-1993.[142] In Poland, in contrast, no action whatsoever was taken to implement this Declaration.

The question arises whether the canons of interpretation of the VCLT can be used to interpret the content of these types of instruments. It appears, in the light of the ICJ's interpretation of the 1990 Minutes in the *Qatar/Bahrain* case, that the answer should be in the affirmative. In our view, however, the application of the VCLT rule of interpretation to non-binding instruments is not straightforward, since other principles of the law of treaties are not applicable, such as those relating to termination or registration. In fact, as noted above, these requirements are often the reason that States prefer to rely on "soft law" instruments in order to avoid strict procedural rules attached to treaties. Therefore, the question may be asked why one particular set of rules (on interpretation) is applicable with the exclusion of all other rules.[143]

On a closer look at the Ministerial Declaration, the language indicates that the undertakings intended by the signatories are generally policy-oriented. Thus, the Ministers of the Environment of the Baltic States declare their intention to "establish"; "intensify efforts"; "take appropriate action"; "develop methodologies"; "respect relevant recommendations"; "promote" and "co-operate". The Declaration does not have any annexes which would specify how these goals are to be achieved. The only section in the whole of the Declaration which describes somewhat more specific goals refers to the general need to reduce the load of pollutants, especially heavy metals and toxic or persistent organic substances and nutrients as soon as possible, but no later than 1995. Furthermore, it states that a reduction of, "for example", 50 per cent in such discharges would be desirable. Even the wording of these more detailed undertakings is rather imprecise and, undoubtedly, further legal acts will be required to transform these political into specific

---

[142] J. J. Kolbasov, "Provovyje Mery Okhrany Moriia Ot Zgrazieniia S Sushi" (Legal Measures for the Protection of the Sea from Land-Based Pollution), a paper presented at the International Conference on Ecology and Law in the Baltic Sea Region: Sources and Developments, held in Riga, Latvia, 1990, at 9 (on file with the authors).

[143] But see Schachter, *supra* note 88, at 302-303, argues that it would be convenient and reasonable to apply the rules for the interpretation of treaties, in so far as they are not at variance with the non-binding nature of such instruments.

commitments, capable of being implemented, for example, though national legislation.

The Declaration was merely intended as a political act which was (emphatically and explicitly) non-binding. Indeed, the intention of the Baltic States was to diminish the pollution of the Baltic Sea without the use of any legally binding instruments. This was considered significant in and by itself, and, in view of the circumstances present at that time, more important than a commitment to fulfill obligations with clearly defined objectives. Thus, the Declaration, as evidenced by further practice, served as a common ground for further discussions, particularly as the Participating States had undertaken to report on their progress in its implementation. Finally, it was believed that the non-binding nature of the Declaration would guarantee a more sincere approach in determining generally the needs of the Baltic Sea and compliance with the Declaration.

The Bonn Declaration on Hijacking[144] was signed by seven industrialized countries that reached an agreement to boycott air traffic of any countries offering sanctuary to hijackers. This Declaration appears to make a very strong statement of intent. Under thorough analysis, however, it seems that this Declaration also is non-binding in nature. The language is imprecise and weak ("intensify", "will initiate", and "should take"), and although the goals seem to be clearly defined, the means for achieving these goals are not clearly spelled out.[145] The language used in this Declaration to express obligation suggests the imposition of moral rather than legal duties, and it is suggestive of a document of a political, not a legal, nature.[146] Although the Declaration was signed by the Prime Ministers of, for example, Italy, the United Kingdom and Canada, the Presidents of the United States and France and the Chancellor of the Federal Republic of Germany, the weak, ill-defined and imprecise language, different from the one employed in treaties, indicates that the Declaration does not contain any binding obligations.[147]

---

[144] The Declaration reads as follows: "The heads of State and Government concerned about the terrorism and taking of hostages, declare that their Governments will intensify their efforts to combat international terrorism. To this end, in cases where a country refuses extradition or prosecution of those who have hijacked an aircraft and/or not returned such aircraft, the heads of State and Government should take immediate action to cease all flights to that country. At the same time, their Governments will initiate action to halt all incoming flights from that country or from any country by the airlines of the country concerned. The heads of State and Government urge other Governments to join them in this commitment." (Canada, the Federal Republic of Germany, France, Italy, Japan, the United Kingdom, the United States), 17 *ILM* 1285 (1978).

[145] J.J. Busutill, "The Bonn Declaration on International Terrorism: A Non-binding Agreement on Aircraft Hijacking", 31 *ICLQ* (1982), 474-487, at 485.

[146] *Id.*, at 487; van der Mensbrugghe, *supra* note 134, at 18.

[147] Of historical value is at present the character of the EEC-CNIEA Joint Declaration. Both Lysén and Bloed erroneously conclude from the language of the Declaration and the manner

Another question is how the Ministerial Declaration on the Baltic Sea compares with the Bremen, London and the Hague Declarations on the North Sea.[148] The text of the Baltic Sea Declaration is even more vague and imprecise than the wording of these instruments. Moreover, other Declarations have annexes which are sometimes very precise in requiring specific action to be taken "in the framework of the existing bodies, conventions and programmes", despite the fact that the intention of the parties was to make them non-binding.[149] The London Declaration, for example, contains some rather concrete provisions, such as one requiring the parties "to take steps to minimise by no less than 65 per cent the use of marine incineration by 1 January 1991" (Article XVI, paragraph 24b) and to "phase out such operations by 31 December 1994, and to seek agreement to such a date within the Oslo Convention by 1 January 1990" (Article XVI, paragraph 24.(c)). It, thus, appears that the wording used is sufficiently well hedged in order to allow avoidance of duties without being seen to violate the Declaration. Thus, the Declaration appears to record political decisions, which would have to be made more precise prior to their implementation for them to constitute legal obligations.

The Bremen and London Declarations similarly indicate "objectives" which have to be further pursued, along the lines set out in the relevant documents. The general language used in both Declarations is similar to that of the Ministerial Declaration. The Ministers decide "to confirm", "to ensure", "to accept the principle", "to take or intensify measures", "to invite the appropriate international bodies". The Hague Declaration is not very different from the Bremen and London Declarations. Despite the fact that it contains a comprehensive set of annotations and annexes, with certain concrete aims, the legal obligations imposed by the Declaration remain rather vague. The preamble of the Declaration lists the two main tasks of the Conference from which it arose: to assess whether previously adopted measures will be met, and "decide ... which further initiatives needed to be taken". In the context of these "future initiatives", the Declaration records the participants' decision to adopt a comprehensive set of "common actions" to reduce inputs of hazardous substances. Some of the goals of these actions

---

of its negotiation and approval by the EC that the Parties clearly intended the Declaration to be legally binding between them and that it was a 'simple' agreement on the establishment of official relations between the two parties. See Lysén, *supra* note 128, at 388. A. Bloed, *The External Relations of the Council for Mutual Economic Assistance* (1989), at 198. The language of the Declaration is vague and ill-defined. Therefore, it is difficult to see how it can give rise to treaty obligations. The language used was clearly indicative of political obligations.

[148] Text of Declarations in: D. Freestone and T. IJlstra (eds.), *The North Sea Basic Legal Documents on Regional Environmental Co-Operation* (1991), at 3-40.

[149] Van der Mensbrugghe, *supra* note 134, at 20.

are policy-oriented and vague,[150] while others are more specific.[151] Despite this specificity, however, the document as a whole is a blueprint for the desirable future and does not record the signatories' agreement to implement the actions listed through national laws, but rather expresses their desire that such actions be taken. Even the operative language used in this Declaration suggests its policy-oriented character. Thus, the parties are "urged" to "take initiatives", "exchange information", "take measure" and "co-operate".

The view has been expressed that although the documents are non-binding, the parties must act in good faith when attempting to carry out such Declarations by transforming them into legal instruments.[152] In our view, this Declaration, like the one discussed above, was not binding. Its language was policy-oriented, vague and ill-defined. The States, having adopted this Declaration, did not implement it even to the extent they have done in respect to the Ministerial Declaration. However, these two documents gave rise to the 1992 Convention on the Protection of the Marine Environment of the Baltic Sea Area ("Helsinki Convention"). Many of the postulates included in the Declarations were better defined and made more precise in this Convention, such as rules on the reduction of hazardous waste and on the principles of mutual co-operation. The role of "soft law" instruments in such a process was defined by Boyle as "significant, only because they are the first step in a process eventually leading to a conclusion of a multilateral treaty".[153] Although, as indicated above, the character of "soft law" – whether "law" or "non-law"– is not at all clear, its main features (as to which there is some degree of consensus in the doctrine) may be summarized as follows: "soft law" is not binding; "soft law" consists of general norms or principles but not rules; and "soft law" is not readily enforceable through binding dispute resolution mechanisms.[154]

Developments in recent years may have slightly changed the generally negative attitude towards "soft law". As Professor Boyle argues, "soft law" does fulfill a very useful role in the contemporary law-making process because it has several attractive features that makes it a useful alternative to treaties. For example, it is easier to reach an agreement in the case of a "soft

---

[150] One of these common actions is "to agree" (presumably sometime in the future) that discharges of substances that are persistent, toxic, and liable to bioaccumulate should, before the year 2000, be reduced to levels "that are not harmful to man or nature".

[151] The Declaration noted the desirability of achieving a significant reduction between 1985 and 1995 (of 5 per cent or more) of inputs via river estuaries for each of the substances in Annexe IA, and atmospheric emissions by 1995 of the substances specified in Annex IA, if achievable by applying the best available technology. Similar provisions were adopted in relation to substances causing a major threat to the environment, and to substantial reductions in the quantities of pesticides.

[152] Van der Mensbrugghe, *supra* note 134, at 21.

[153] Boyle, *supra* note 116, at 29.

[154] *Id.*, 31-38, as cited in Boyle, at 28.

law" instrument than a treaty, the consequences of non-compliance being less severe; States may avoid the need to subject the instrument to a domestic ratification process, and escape democratic accountability within that process; and "soft law" instruments are more susceptible to amendment than treaties. The usefulness of a treaty as a law-making instrument, on the other hand, may be greater in the event of new law-making. It cannot be denied, however, that the "soft law" instruments are good evidence of State practice and *opinio juris* in support of customary law.[155] They may not be binding but they may be an element in the process of the formulation of the uniform conviction of States that certain principles are law, such as, in our view, the 1992 Rio Declaration, which assists the ongoing (not yet completed) process of crystallization of the principle of sustainable development.[156] It has been noted that "[b]oth treaties and soft law instruments can be vehicles for focusing consensus on rules and principles, and for mobilising a consistent, general response on the part of States".[157] It simply depends on given circumstances which type of instrument will fulfill a more useful role. The 1992 Rio Declaration on Environment and Development ("Rio Declaration"), Boyle observes, has gained general support precisely because it was drafted in the form of a non-binding, "soft law" instrument, containing rules that partly codify existing environmental law and new rules.

"Soft law" instruments also play a versatile role in the multilateral treaty-making process. They may start a treaty-making process, in the form of non-binding guidelines; they may serve as mechanisms for authoritative interpretation or amplification of the terms of a treaty; they may provide detailed rules and technical standards required for implementation; and they may be incorporated into the terms of a treaty by implied reference.[158] For example, standard-setting in the International Labour Organization ("ILO"), although often effected by non-binding recommendations, is of paramount importance and encompasses a broad range of activities ranging from the

---

[155] As stated by the ICJ in relation to the UN General Assembly Resolutions and intergovernmental declarations in, e.g., the Military and Paramilitary Activities in and against Nicaragua case (Nicaragua *v.* US), Merits, Judgment of 27 June 1986, 1986 ICJ Rep. 14, at 98-104, paras 187-195; Legality of the Use of Nuclear Weapons, 1996 ICJ Rep. 241, 254-255, paras. 70-73; Gabčikovo-Nagymaros case, *supra* note 10, at 7.

[156] See the comments on the possibility of sustainable development complying with the standards of the 1969 North Sea Continental Shelf cases in relation to the formation of customary law in V. Lowe, "Sustainable Development and Unsustainable Arguments", in A. Boyle and D. Freestone (eds.), *International Law and Sustainable Development, Past Achievements and Future Challenges* (1999), at 23-24 and 31-36.

[157] Boyle, *supra* note 116, at 28.

[158] *Id.*, 30-31.

actual standard setting to supervision, assistance and promotion.[159] According to the ILO Committee on Legal Issues, recommendations

> ... have the potential to supplement existing Conventions, thus enhancing their impact; or they may pave the way to the adoption of a new Convention through a maturing process. ... [they] can also clear the way for the ratification of existing Conventions by promoting their principles either on an individual basis or through a consolidation, possibly around the four strategic objectives; and they include details that would be unwieldy in a Convention but which provide additional reference points for national law in practice.[160]

Finally, it may be noted that "soft law" has led to the emergence, in particular in recent years, of different "soft" procedures of dispute avoidance mechanisms within the, treaty context, which are based on assistance rather than classical dispute resolution procedure.

Thus, the legal nature of "soft law", and equally its relationship with treaties, is far from clear. In particular, the expansion in recent years of certain types of treaties (for example, in the field of environmental protection) has given rise to international agreements, which contain not only specific obligations, but also vague provisions of an ambiguous nature which do not impose "hard" (absolute) obligations on States. As Boyle has explained, some treaties may generate only principles but not rules, which do not have the strength of hard law. Such a treaty "may be potentially normative, but still "soft" in character, because it articulates "principles" rather than "rules" ". They should, however, "not be confused with "non-binding" law".[161] As an example of this he cites the 1992 UN Framework Convention on Climate Change ("Climate Change Convention"), where such principles are included in a treaty (for example, Article 3 (Principles)).[162]

As Boyle states, the elements of Article 3 are drawn directly from the (non-binding) 1992 Rio Declaration. These principles are not only a part of the Climate Change Convention, but also reflect principles which are emerging at the general level, common to environmental law in general, but which have not achieved the status of customary law. They are couched in

---

[159] International Labour Office, Governing Body, Committee on Legal Issues and International Labour Standards, Possible Improvements in the Standard-Setting Activities of the ILO, 277th Session, Geneva March 2000, at 3. GB.277/LILS/2, available from the ILO website, at: http://www.ilo.org/public/english/standards/relm/gb/docs/gb277/index.htm#LILS.
[160] *Id.*, at 2, para. 10.
[161] Boyle, *supra* note 116, at 32.
[162] Art. 3 (Principles): "[i]n their actions to achieve the objective of the Convention and to implement its provisions, the parties shall be guided, inter alia, by the following: 1. The Parties should protect the climate system for the benefit of present and future generations of humankind, on the basis of equity and in accordance with their common but differentiated responsibilities ... 2. The Parties should take precautionary measures to anticipate, prevent, or minimise the causes of climate change and mitigate its adverse effects ... 3. The Parties have a right to, and should, promote sustainable development ...".

an aspirational manner, for instance through use of the word "should". Their content is not certain and precise. They are, however, "relevant to interpretation and implementation of the Convention as well as creating expectations relating to matters that must be considered in good faith in the negotiation of further instruments".[163] Finally, it may be said that:

> [s]ustainable development, intergenerational equity, or the precautionary principle, are all more convincing seen in this sense: not as binding obligations which must be complied with, but as principles, considerations or objectives to be taken account of–they may be soft, but they are still law.[164]

The legal character of "soft law", thus, remains ambiguous, especially if considered in the context of the problem of what constitutes a binding international obligation. This phenomenon has been analyzed by political scientists, who offer an answer to the question of how to treat legal obligations with a varied normative content included in the same instrument. The importance which States attach to international obligations is not exclusively conditioned by the legal nature of these obligations: "[t]he schematic distinction between those obligations that are and those that are not legally binding does not necessarily offer insight in the constraint obligations imposed on states".[165] Rather, practice in this regime makes clear that this is a much more diffuse process:

> ... the principle of sustainable development has induced expectations as to the conduct of States, can be used to claim from other States that they adjust their policies and indeed had begun to act as a *de facto* constraint on policy-makers. This is no way dependent on its recent inclusion in the legally binding 1992 Helsinki and Paris Conventions. In the continuous assessments States make as to which of the large number of prescriptions for preventive action are import-ant and are complied with, the legal nature is only one of the relevant factors. The relevance of the legal nature cannot be taken for granted and can only be assessed on a case by case basis.[166]

Finally, it has been rightly observed that "soft law":

> may be used deliberately solely to steer conduct in a desired direction to achieve generalized 'soft law' rather than 'hard' goals, and this may in given cases be more effective over a long term, especially in the case of developing states. This is the case in situations where there are uncertainties of a

---

[163] Boyle, *supra* note 116, at 33.
[164] *Id.*, especially at 34.
[165] A. Nollkaemper, *The Legal Regime for Transboundary Water Pollution: Between Discretion and Constraint* (1993), at 252.
[166] *Id.*

scientific, Technological, economic or social nature, but when some immediate change of behaviour is required.[167]

In our view, the nature of so-called "soft law" has not been fully explored. In particular, there is a confusion between completely non-binding declarations (such as the Baltic Sea Declaration) and soft provisions of binding treaties (such as the above cited Climate Change Convention) that according to Boyle contain "soft" principles that are non-binding obligations, but nevertheless are aspirational and constitute law at least to a certain degree. If we take up this distinction further, there appear to be three types of possible situations: non-binding instruments; binding law; "soft" but potentially normative principles contained in treaties that constitute, nevertheless, some law. According to Lowe:

> the real differences between hard law and soft law lie in the processes by which the rule is articulated and in the consequences of its breach. The essential natures of the normativity of hard law and of soft law are not different ... The distinction between 'hard' law and 'soft' law is not great. In terms of strength of the expectations of compliance, there is no necessary distinction between the categories of 'hard' and 'soft' law, though there are, of course, great differences in relation to the various norms within each category.[168]

We agree with the view expressed above that one of the most important legal problems concerning "soft" law are the legal consequences of non-compliance with "soft" law provisions (or principles). Again we have to differentiate between "soft" law *sensu stricto* and the "soft" principles contained in treaties. In the first case, there is a theoretical, yet completely unexplored and never tested, possibility of invoking the principle of estoppel.

What are the legal consequences, however, of non-compliance with a "soft" principle contained in a treaty? The question arises as to whether such non-compliance is to be treated as a breach of an international obligation (a breach of a treaty rule), or whether there are some other (unspecified) legal consequences attached to a breach of such a "soft" principle contained in a treaty, which differ from general rules applicable in instances of a breach of "hard" obligation?

In our view, attaching any legal consequences (including the principle of estoppel) to non-binding provisions is incorrect. Non-binding instruments have no legal effects and therefore their breach is without legal consequences. The breach of a treaty provision of a "soft" character should

---

[167] P. Birnie, "The Status of Environmental 'Soft Law': Trends and Examples with Special Focus on IMO Norms", in H. Ringbom (ed.), *Competing Norms in the Law of Marine Environmental Protection, Focus on Ship Safety and Pollution Prevention* (1997), at 39.
[168] Lowe, in A. Boyle and D. Freestone (eds.), *supra* note 156, at 30.

be treated as a breach of a legal obligation, thus resulting in the possibility of the invocation by an injured State of rules of State responsibility.

There is yet another complication, namely that the wording of the provision in question must be taken into account in determining the content of the obligation. "Soft" provisions could only serve as guidance for the parties and employ the word "should" (for example, "should strive to); or they could be couched in more imperative terms demanding concrete action, which nevertheless remain weak as to the scope and the nature of the obligation. For example, Article 4, paragraph 4(b), of the 1992 Climate Change Convention states the following: "[p]arties shall communicate information on their policies and measures to review green house emissions with the aim of returning individually or jointly to their 1990 emissions levels". Although this provision uses the word "shall", the only real obligation contained in this provision is to provide information on measures adopted by the Party. Admittedly, States are not likely to litigate exclusively on the basis of a breach of a provision of such a general and "soft" character. We with Boyle that "soft" rules contained in treaties, however, may lay down parameters that affect the way courts decide issues.[169]

4. Conclusions

This chapter started with the definition of a treaty under the VCLT and then proceeded to examine different legal phenomena which might or might not be treaties. One conclusion is that – the VCLT does not encompass all possible varieties of contemporary law-making. Some of the current developments, such as "soft law", do not lend themselves to easy classification. Some "soft law" documents, as illustrated above, may look like treaties, from the point of view of their content, and they may be even signed by the governments. As pointed out above, the 1988 Ministerial Declaration which covered the Baltic Sea was "ratified" by the Parliament of the Federal Republic of Germany. This resulted in a situation where a "soft law" instrument was enacted as a "hard" law instrument at the municipal level, but remained "soft" at the international level. The Declaration was even treated as hard by the FRG at both levels.

The case law of the ICJ has focused mainly on the question of what constitutes a *compromis,* an agreement to submit the case to the Court's jurisdiction. In the *Qatar v Bahrain* case that the Court made important statements as to the nature of treaty obligation and the minimal relevance of the intention of the parties. The findings of the Court in this case "... serve only to blur further the grey twilight zone between binding and non-binding

---

[169] Boyle, *supra* note 116, at 32.

international agreements".[170] As observed elsewhere in this chapter, the Court's decision may lead to the conclusion that a non-binding instrument may contain binding obligations. Conversely, as is sometimes asserted, a binding instrument may contain non-binding obligations.

Therefore, due to this variety of legal forms of international co-operation, defining what is a treaty only according to the VCLT is a daunting task. It therefore appears that it is up to international courts and tribunals to decide in each case that arises before them the nature and the scope of a given obligation. Further difficulty is caused by the fact that in contemporary international relations, a clear division between the formal sources of obligations for States cannot always be upheld, at least in relation to treaties, soft law and unilateral acts (as seen in the classic *Eastern Greenland* case).

The only feature of "soft law" norms in relation to which there is agreement in international law doctrine is its uncertain character. Although widely used by States, "soft law" does not fall squarely within the ambit of the international normative system or within classical sources of international law. As Chinkin notes, it "facilitates international co-operation by acting as a bridge between the formalities of law-making and the needs of international life by legimating behaviour and creating stability."[171] It is also clear, however, that "soft law" has its negative side. The same author stated: "[s]oft law may maintain the fiction of a universal international law, while in reality leading to its destruction though the formulation of relative standards."[172]

---

[170] Chinkin, *supra* note 8, at 247.
[171] C. Chinkin, "Normative Development in the International Legal System", *supra* note 127, at 42.
[172] *Id.*

CHAPTER TWO

Actors and Factors in the Treaty-Making Process*

1. Introduction

Who are the contemporary lawmakers in the international context? The answer to this question depends as well on the definition of the law-making process. For example, in the case of the international treaties, how far, if at all, do we take the pre-negotiations stage into consideration? Do we assess both direct and indirect influences in the formation of treaties as being equally important? Do we accord the same importance to the views expressed in the treaty-making process by entities other than States? And how can we tell if and to what degree participation of various actors at different stages of the treaty-making process have contributed to and have been reflected in the final result?

As Professor Franck put it:

> [i]nternational law has matured into a complete legal system covering all aspects of relations among states, and also, more recently, aspects of relations between states and their federal units, between states and persons, between persons of several states, between states and multinational corporations, and between international organisations and their state members ... Only a few decades ago, international law applied exclusively to states. Today, it is an intricate network of laws governing a myriad of rights and duties that stretch across and beyond national boundaries, piercing the statist veil even while it sometimes pretends that nothing has changed ... At a purely functional level,

---

* This chapter is an updated and revised version of M. Fitzmaurice, "The Actors and Factors in the Evolution of Treaty Norms (An Empirical Study)", 4 *Austrian Review of International and European Law* 1999, at 1-84, and reprinted with kind permission of Kluwer Law International/Brill Academic Publishers. Reprinted with kind permission of the Publisher.

the expansion results from an immense increase in the number and diversity
of organizations and conferences engaged in law-making.[1]

These issues are related to other fundamental problems of international law,
such as sovereignty and recognition.[2]

This chapter will investigate the actors and factors exerting influence on
the evolution of treaties and on their adaptability to changed circumstances.
The manner in which actors behave in the treaty-making process is
conditioned by, but not limited to political, scientific, technical and
economic factors. The factors, which influence the development and
evolution of treaties, are (mostly) of an extra-legal character. This begs the
question whether international law is comprised only of legal rules, devoid
of any extra-legal content, or whether policy considerations are also
contained within the body of international law. After all, such policy
considerations may be considered an integral part of the process we call
international law. It may also be considered that the assessment of so-called
extra-legal considerations is *part of the legal process,* in the same way as is
the reference to the accumulation of past decisions and current norms. Put in
another way, "there is no avoiding the essential relationship between law and
politics."[3] However, the view that the law is autonomous is familiar.[4]

If extra-legal factors are taken into account as important influences on the
evolution of international law, then a further question arises, namely whether
consideration of such "extraneous" factors requires a new form of treaty-
making. Treaties, as living instruments, are subject to pressure from States

---

[1] T. Franck, *Fairness and International Law and Institutions* (1995), at 5-6.

[2] As Professor Franck has observed: "[s]overeignty has historically been a factor greatly
overrated in international relations ... [n]ever, however, have notions of sovereignty
demanded as much cautious rethinking as now. ... we shall see many instances of national
sovereignty being overridden by international law and international or regional regimes". And
further, the same author states: "[t]he impossibility of reconciling the notions of sovereignty
which prevailed even as recently as fifty or sixty years ago with the contemporary state of
global interdependence signals the profound transformation of international law which has
occurred during the second half of this century", *id.,* at 3-4.

[3] R. Higgins, "Integrations of Authority and Control, Trends in the Literature of International
Law and International Relations", in W. M. Reisman and B. H. Weston (eds.), *Toward World
Order and Human Dignity* (1976), 79, at 85; R. Higgins, *Problems and Process, International
Law and How We Use It* (1994), at 2-16; M. McDougal, H. D. Laswell, and W. M. Reisman,
"The World Constitutive Process of Authoritative Decision", 19:3 *Journal of Legal Education*
(1966-1967), at 253.

[4] "We are not unmindful of, nor we are insensible to, the various considerations of a non-
judicial character, social, humanitarian and other ... but these are matters for the political
rather than for the legal arena. They cannot be allowed to deflect us from our duty of reaching
a conclusion strictly on the basis of what we believe to be the correct legal view", South-West
Africa (Ethiopa *v.* South Africa; Liberia *v.* South Africa), Preliminary Objections, Judgment
of 21 December 1962, 1962 ICJ Reports 319, Joint Dissenting Opinion of Judges Fitzmaurice
and Spender, at 466.

and other actors, both within and outside the treaty regime, and to the influence of the institutions, if any, created by the treaty régimes (as well as to the influence of regional developments). A further issue to be addressed, therefore, is the identification of the actors influencing the dynamic evolution of treaty régimes. The present chapter will scrutinize the role of the following actors: States, non-State actors consisting of intergovernmental organizations ("IGOs"), or more precisely civic society, and a large and amorphous group to which belong non-governmental organizations ("NGOs"), associations and corporations.

The focus of this chapter is on the actors and factors which contribute to the emergence of a treaty (through negotiations) and which influence further changes (through amendments). The treaty-making process is a predominantly political one which is focused on the pursuit by the parties of their own conflicting and competing interests with a view toward achieving maximum benefit for themselves, tempered by the need to find an acceptable compromise. The present chapter will attempt to illustrate various political factors as used by different types of actors that participate in the treaty-making process. However, the chapter is not based on political science theories concerning the legal process, such as régime theory. Nonetheless, régime theory has been used recently to illustrate environmental law making,[5] and some of its postulates may be discernible in the chapter, in particular, in relation to negotiations.

This chapter will not deal with theories underlying international law-making or, for that matter, with the question of the theoretical basis of the participation of non-State actors in normative processes.[6] These are subjects

---

[5] See, e.g., in general: A.M. Slaughter-Burley, "International Law and International Relations Theory: A Dual Agenda", 87 *AJIL* (1993), 205-239; O.R. Young and G. Osherenko, "Testing Theories of Regime Formation: Findings from a Large Collaborative Research Project", in V. Rittberger and P. Mayer (eds.), *Regime Theory and International Relations* (1993), at 223-251; S.D. Krasenr (ed.), *International Regimes* (1983); R.O. Keohane, *After Hegemony, Cooperation and Discord in the World Political Economy* (1984). Generally, on politics see: O.R. Young and G. Osherenko (eds.), *Polar Politics: Creating International Environmental Regimes* (1993); O.R. Young, *International Cooperation: Building Regimes for Natural Resources and the Environment* (1989); O.R. Young, *International Governance, Protecting Environment in a Stateless Society* (1994); M. List and V. Rittberger, "Regime Theory and International Environmental Management", in A. Hurrell and B. Kingsbury (eds.), *The International Politics of the Environment* (1992), at 85-109. On the interdisciplinary approach (international law and international relations theory), see A.M. Slaughter, A.S. Tulumello and S. Wood, "International Law and International Relations Theory: A New Generation of Interdisciplinary Scholarship", 92 *AJIL* (1998), 367-397. Also, M. Byers, "Taking the Law out of International Law: A Critique of the 'Iterative Perspective'", 38 *Harvard International Law Journal* (1997), at 201; O.R. Young, *International Governance, Protecting Environment in a Stateless Society* (1994).

[6] See, e.g., K. Raustiala, "The 'Participatory Revolution' in International Environmental Law", 21 *Harvard Environmental Law Review* (1997), at 537-586.

that have recently received much attention, in particular, by international relations scholars.[7] The aim of this study is simply to survey the practice of contemporary treaty-making.[8] The purpose of the study is to illustrate the interaction between the different factors, as applied by three groups of actors that play a role in relation to treaties. Thus, the approach adopted in this study is not that of the régime theorist, nor is the method adopted that of the political scientist. The intention is not to construct a comprehensive régime theory on the basis of the present survey, but rather to present an empirical study of certain legal and, predominantly, extra-legal factors which influence the treaty-making process and which derive from States, IGOs, and non-State actors, which includes corporations, associations, and NGOs of different kinds, such as those involved in the fields of human rights and environmental protection, as well as individuals and groups of individuals.[9] However, it may be noted that there is no legal definition of a NGO.[10]

We are witnessing at present an expansion of the role of NGOs. As Alkoby observes, the reasons for this expansion are linked to the phenomenon of "globalization" which has eroded the notion of "the modern sovereign state."[11] He states that there are three economic and political factors of globalization which contributed to this state of affairs. First, he mentions the collapse of the communist régimes, which divided the world and the disappearance of which contributed to the change of concerns of States from security issues to matters of global commons, being matters which require collective action in order to solve shared problems, as exemplified by international environmental law. Second, there is a growing interdependence of financial markets which makes viable the manufacturing of products in various locations. Third, increasing "fragmentation" within States contributes to the establishment of "cross-border links and the decrease of nationalism". He states that all these developments are assisted by a global communications network. Furthermore, he concludes that

---

[7] On the subject of various theories underlying the participation of NGOs, see A. Alkoby, "Non-State Actors and the Legitimacy of International Environmental Law", 3 *Non State Actors and International Law* (2003), at 23-98.

[8] However, as Alkoby stated: "[a] comprehensive theoretical enquiry, examining how the rise of global civil society has changed the character of the international system, and addressing issues such as the evolution of norms at the international level; the way in which they influence actors' behavior; and the potential effects of creating (or empowering) multiple sources of legitimate influence, is still lacking.", *supra* note 7, at 25.

[9] Raustiala, *supra* note 6, asserts that there are two types of private non-State actors in international environmental law: the regulated parties represented by business firms and the beneficiaries of the regulation-represented by the environmental NGOs, at 557.

[10] J.K. Gamble and Ch. Ku, "International Law – New Actors and New Technologies: Center Stage for NGOs?", 31(2) *Law and Policy in International Business.* (2000), 221-262, at 227-229.

[11] Alkoby, *supra* note 7, at 28.

"[u]nder these conditions of interdependent interactions, the international system can no longer maintain clear boundaries between domestic and international law."[12]

2. The Stages in the Treaty-Making Process Considered

For the purpose of this chapter, and in order to identify the factors that influence treaty-régimes, the preliminary issue that will be considered is whether the initial stages of the treaty-making process (such as initiating the process and negotiating the text) should be taken into consideration, or whether the focus should be limited to those factors that influence the dynamic evolution of treaties after their adoption. The former factors are arguably as important as the latter factors. It is clear that one of the most important initial stages that influence a treaty as a dynamic instrument are the negotiations, since these initiate the basic framework of the proposed treaty and mould it in a manner relevant to its further legal development. Negotiations constitute a stage of treaty making that combines legal and extra-legal elements; prevalent are political factors that constitute the essence of the negotiations. Extra-legal factors, which may not be codified within the treaty régime, may nonetheless influence the text of the treaty and consequently to some extent the final form of the treaty as a living instrument. That part of the treaty-making process that is political must, however, be distinguished from the legal-technical treaty-making procedures that aim to bestow a formal structure on the treaty.[13] The New Haven School emphasizes negotiations and actor expectations in the context of the general social process within which legal normativity resides, and within which power is established through the process of authoritative decisions.[14] Without having to go so far, it may be assumed that "... treaty-making means – by necessity – learning from the past successes and failures".[15] The final form of a treaty will depend on the interplay between three main actors: States,

---

[12] Alkoby, *supra* note 7, at 29, and see as well at 28.
[13] There are several excellent publications that are devoted to this topic; for example P. Reuter, *Introduction to the Law of Treaties* (1995), chapter 2.
[14] M. McDougal and H.D. Laswell, "The Identification and Appraisal of Diverse Systems of Public Order", in R. Falk and S. H. Mendlovitz (eds.), *The Strategy of World Order, Vol. 2: International Law* (1966), at 45-54.
[15] W. Lang, "Diplomacy and International Environmental Law-Making: Some Observations", 3 *YIEL* (1993), 108-122, at 110.

IGOs, and NGOs (see below). Of these, States are the most powerful actors in negotiating a treaty.[16]

Further, this chapter will investigate, both from the legal and non-legal points of view, influences on amendments, revisions and modifications of the primary text of a treaty.[17] These influences vary and many factors may contribute to change. Such change may stem from pressure from international organizations or non-State actors; new technological and scientific discoveries; from political circumstances; or issues related to economic factors within the structure of sustainable development. Often there is a combination of these elements. For example, an organization may exert pressure on States to review a treaty from the point of view of amending or revising it due to new political circumstances or scientific and technological advancements.

3. The Actors

3.1 States

It may be said that States are the leading actors in the treaty-making process, both in negotiations and at the later stages of treaty-making. Political scientists have devoted many in-depth studies to the role of the State in negotiations. This is perceived as a two-level process operating at the national level, where the negotiators are subject to pressure from domestic groups pursuing their policies, and at the international level where "national governments seek to maximize their own ability to satisfy domestic pressures, while minimizing the adverse consequences of foreign developments".[18] This chapter will be devoted, however, to scrutinizing the factors that prompt States to exert certain pressures to conclude a treaty at a certain time or to introduce changes to it.

---

[16] Putman presents an interesting view on negotiations from the political scientist's perspective, R.D. Putman, "Diplomacy and Domestic Politics: The Logic of Two-level Games", 42:3 *International Organization* (1988), at 427-460.

[17] Brownlie treats amendments to an existing treaty text as basically a political process but admits that procedural aspects are of lawyers' concern. I. Brownlie, *Principles of Public International Law* (6th ed., 2003), at 601. See M.J. Bowman, "The Multilateral Treaty Amendment Process – Case Study", 44 *ICLQ* (1995), 540-559; see also the 1969 Vienna Convention on the Law of Treaties, Articles 39-41.

[18] Putman, *supra* note 16, at 434.

3.2 Inter-governmental Organizations ("IGOs")

The role of IGOs in the multilateral treaty-making process has a long history. However, this role has changed enormously since the 19th century due to an expanded international community and the emergence of organizations, which strive for universal membership.[19] Four organizational patterns for treaty-making in international organizations have been identified: "(1) [IGOs] especially U.N. sponsored treaty making conferences; (2) expert treaty making bodies; (3) "managerial" forms of treaty-making; or (4) ..."treaty making with strings attached".[20] Regarding the first type, Alvarez gives an example of the 1998 "massive" Rome negotiations to establish the International Criminal Court. This pattern follows certain well-developed and accepted rules, such as work conducted in plenary and in forums of specialized bodies, as well as a division into formal and informal sessions, and reliance on well-tested United Nations ("UN") rules and encouragement of package deals and the use of the IGO secretariats to "conduct advance preparations", "to encourage reliance on final standard clauses as with respect to reservations and entry into force," and its staff "serve as legitimating conduits for proposals made by unpopular or isolated states".[21] The United Nations Environment Programme ("UNEP"), for example, has dealt successfully with many environmental problems, such as regional seas, ozone depletion and climate change, due to its apolitical approach. It has been argued that international organizations have become leaders in international negotiations – "a development that makes it appropriate to speak of them as architects of the institutional arrangements emerging from these negotiations".[22]

The second pattern is based on experts, such as the UN Commission on Trade Law ("UNCITRAL"); the International Civil Aviation Organization's ("ICAO") legal committee; and the International Law Commission ("ILC"). These bodies follow well-tested procedures and "produce large volumes of information, as with respect to the current practices and opinions of states."[23] Further, Alvarez says, "usually working in tandem with U.N. conferences, these institutionalized experts produce drafts that, at their best, achieve technocratic legitimacy because of their source and quality."[24] Such an example is the International Atomic Energy Agency ("IAEA"), which acted

---

[19] J. Alvarez, "The New Treaty Makers", 25 *Boston College International and Comparative Law Review* (2002), 213-234, at 218-220.
[20] *Id.*, at 220.
[21] *Id.*, at 220-221.
[22] See O.R. Young, International Governance, *supra* note 5; P.H. Sand, *Lessons Learned in Global Environmental Governance* (1990), World Resource Institute.
[23] Alvarez, *supra* note 19, at 221.
[24] *Id.*

as a forum for the 1986 conference on negotiating the Vienna Convention on Notification and on Assistance in Case of Nuclear Accident and a Convention on Nuclear Safety. The IAEA only has a mandate in relation to the establishment and adoption of safety standards. Its General Conference can discuss any question within the statute and to make recommendations to the Member States.[25]

The third "managerial" pattern is based on the premise that the conclusion of a treaty is the first step, while the ultimate goal is to "secure the benefits of institutionalization on an on-going basis…".[26] The structural framework is established with various bodies, which, amongst others, monitor and set standards. The "framework [environmental] conventions establish "living" treaty regimes and offer "the prospect of a virtually continuous legislative enterprise".[27]

The fourth pattern is exemplified by the International Labour Organization (the "ILO") and involves "treaty making that is constitutionally sanctioned, even mandated, under the charter of a formal full-fledged [IGO] that tries to pressure its members to ratify the treaties produced by the regime."[28] As Alvarez describes, the ILO Constitution attaches strings to its legal instruments, requiring action by the ILO members and involving strict monitoring. The increasing role of IGOs in the in the treaty-making process has enabled less powerful States to be more meaningfully involved in the treaty-making process; it has enabled wider participation of NGOs in various forms of diplomacy reserved previously for States; changed the role of the State (on one the hand, we witness the increase of power of other actors and civil society; on the other hand, IGOs "remain vehicles for the assertion of state power"[29]); and finally, IGOs have increased the volume of available information to treaty initiators.[30]

The importance of IGOs cannot be underestimated in the international treaty-making process. The confusion relates rather to the exact role, the extent of the involvement, and the relationship between all the actors engaged in the process. This is partly due to the fact that organizations differ to a considerable degree. It has been said that "[t]he role which international law plays in an organisation will vary, in nature and scope, depending on whether the organisation concerned is engaged primarily in resolving political problems and issues or is concerned essentially with the

---

[25] Article 111(A), paragraph 6.
[26] Alvarez, *supra* note 19, at 221.
[27] *Id.*, citing G. Handl, "Environmental Security and Global Challenge: The Challenge of International Law," in H. Neuhold, W. Lang, K. Zemanek (eds.), *Environmental Protection and International Law* (1991), at 59-89.
[28] *Id.*, at 222.
[29] *Id.*, at 228.
[30] *Id.*

establishment or development of norms and standards."[31] However, the participation of IGOs, as Young aptly observes, may sometimes constitute obstacles in the formulation of international régimes. He submits the example of the World Bank, which initially obstructed the building of environmental régimes for Third World States (for which States the question of reconciliation of development and environment is of crucial importance). The Bank relied on economic theories which did not take environmental exigencies sufficiently into account. Thus, we may say that IGOs sometimes, in a fashion similar to States, promote their own interests, which are not always best for a particular régime.[32]

Finally, the role of IGOs as actors in the treaty-making process is very complicated due to their dual character. On the one hand, they may be viewed as a forum where the representatives of Member States express views which are the views of the governments they represent. On the other hand, we may say with certain simplification, without touching upon the doctrines relating to international personality of organizations, that they enjoy a separate international personality which is distinguishable from that of their Member States, and that an IGO is a separate entity that is qualitatively and quantitatively different from the simple summation of Member States.[33]

3.3 Non-Governmental Organizations ("NGOs")

3.3.1 NGOs in general, including the treaty-making process (with special reference to their role within the UN system)

NGOs, associations and corporations are amongst the most important actors in international negotiations. It is admitted that these organizations exert an important influence over negotiations, on the domestic and international

---

[31] T. Mensah, "The Practice of International Law in International Organisations", in Bin Cheng (ed.), *International Law: Teaching and Practice* (1982), 146-163, at 147.

[32] Young, *International Governance*, *supra* note 5, at 171.

[33] There is a wealth of literature on the subject of the legal personality of international organizations. To mention a few: C.F. Amerasinghe, "International Personality Revisited", 47 *Austrian Journal of Public International Law* (1995), at 123-145; J.A. Barberis, "Nouvelle questions concernant la personalité juridique internationale", 179 *RCADI* (1983-I), 145-304; C. Brölmann, "The 1986 Vienna Convention on the Law of Treaties: The History of Draft Article 36 Bis.", in J. Klabbers and R. Lefeber (eds.), *Essays on the Law of Treaties, A Collection of Essays in Honour of Bert Vierdag* (1998), at 120-140. In particular, at 122-127; R. Higgins, *supra* note 2, "Problems and Process", at 46; J. Klabbers, *An Introduction to International Institutional Law* (2002), at 52-59.

levels.[34] It is at present universally recognized that in the field of international human rights law NGOs play a leading role at all stages of treaty-making – i.e. also at the stage of negotiations and pre-negotiations – by influencing the domestic decision-makers who are the participants. Corporations, for example, enter into contracts with capital-importing States, and the international legal personality of multinational enterprises can be based on this consideration. Nevertheless, multinational enterprises or transnational corporations may still lobby the treaty-making powers, whose legal personality and legal competence in those respects are accepted under international law. Finally, the interests of such multinational enterprises are "reflected" in international law, for example in the terms of bilateral investment treaties and in the Trade Related Intellectual Property Rights Agreement ("TRIPS") resulting from the Uruguay Round of trade negotiations. On the other hand, there is a view that multinational enterprises shape international law in a more direct fashion, for example, by asserting their views in relation to treaty interpretation, with the result that those views have become a form of material evidence in international law. It may be that "international law" presents too limited a picture, because many of the legal activities of multinational enterprises may be said to generate a certain kind of "proto-law."

The complicated issues relating to the forms of NGO participation in the treaty-making process (direct or indirect influence) are exacerbated by the absence of universally accepted classifications of the types of NGOs. Furthermore, public-private partnerships involve a multitude of types and forms.[35] Even authors, such as Börzel and Risse, who present a sophisticated

---

[34] For a comprehensive study on the participation of NGOs in the environmental field, see ECOLOGIC/FIELD, S. Oberthür, M. Buck, S. Müller, S. Pfahl, R. Tarasofsky, J. Werksman, A. Palmer, *Participation of Non-Governmental Organisations in International Environmental Governance: Legal Basis and Practical Experience* (2002) ("ECOLOGIC/FIELD Report"), see internet site: <http://www.pacinst.org/inni/NGOParticipation/NGOParticipationStudy. pdf>. See also P. T. Muchlinski, "Global Bukowina' Examined: Visiting the Multinational Enterprise as a Transnational Law-Making Community", in G. Teubner (ed.), *Global law Without a State* (1997), at 79 generally, but especially, at 88-89 (contrast between a foreign investor and a host State and the paradox of the self-validating contract), at 90-91 (lobbying activists of the MNEs and evidence of 'protection' by home States), 93 (BITs), and at 96 (TRIPs); D. Otto, "Nongovernmental Organisations in the United Nations System: The Emerging Role of International Civil Society", 18 *HRQ* (1996), at 106-141; D. Shelton, "The Participation of Non-Governmental Organizations in International Judicial Proceedings", 88 *AJIL* (1994), at 611-642; O.A. Elias and C.L. Lim, *The Paradox of Consensualism in International Law* (1998), chapters XI and XII.
[35] T. Börzel and T. Risse, "Public-Private Partnerships: Effective and legitimate Tools of International Governance?", in Edgar Grande and Louis W. Pauly (eds.), *Complex Sovereignty: On the Reconstitution of Political Authority in the 21st Century* (forthcoming); available at <http://www.fu-berlin.de/atasp/texte/021015_ppp_risse_boerzel.pdf>. These authors describe four distinct types of public-private partnerships (PPPs): cooptation,

system of classification, note that "... the distinctions are not as clear-cut as they look like. There is a lot of overlap in these functions."[36] NGOs and public-private partnerships evolve all the time, change their function(s), and grow in importance; and today's classification may be obsolete tomorrow. There are more fundamental problems which relate to theses types of partnerships that have not yet been explored and analyzed sufficiently, such as the role of public-private partnerships in international governance, and whether and to what extent such partnerships contribute to democracy and to the legitimacy of international governance. The same authors admit that there is a lack of empirical knowledge to address these questions and that they should be answered on the basis of conditions and actors within a particular régime, some of which will be considered in this chapter.[37]

Within the UN system, Article 71 of the UN Charter envisaged the possibility of NGOs[38] having a role within the UN structure. Article 71 provides that

> [t]he Economic and Social Council may make suitable arrangements for consultation with non-governmental organizations which are concerned with matters within its competence. Such arrangements may be made with international organizations and, where appropriate, with national organizations after consultations with the Member of the United Nations concerned.

According to Resolution 1296 (XLIV) (1968)[39] of the Economic and Social Council ("ECOSOC"), the areas encompassed are international, economic, social, cultural, educational, health, scientific, technological and related matters and human rights. ECOSOC has defined the requirements in relation to the internal structure and international scope with which NGOs must comply in order to acquire consultative status. Once approved by ECOSOC, the status of an NGO is subject to a regular review procedure, from the point of view of appropriateness of the designated category and with respect to the organization's continuing adherence to its statutory requirements. ECOSOC structures the 'NGO consultative status' on three levels: (a) NGOs having a basic interest in most ECOSOC activities: i.e. NGOs with so-called "general status" fall within Category I (for example, the International Council of Women) belong to Category I;[40] (b) NGOs with specific interests, such as

---

delegation, co-regulation, self-regulation in the shadow of hierarchy. For the purposes and function in terms, they distinguish: rule and standard setting, rule implementation, and service provision, at 5.

[36] *Id.*, at 5, note 3.

[37] *Id.*, at 18.

[38] It appears that ECOSOC uses the term 'NGOs' as a generic term to cover all non-State actors.

[39] ESC Res. 1296 (XLIV) B, UN, ESCOR, Article 1.

[40] In 1996, 69 NGOs qualified for this status.

human rights or the environment constitute Category II;[41] and (c) all other NGOs with such fields of interest as allow them to be consulted only occasionally are granted "Roster status".[42] All NGOs with consultative status may send observers to any public meeting of ECOSOC or of the subsidiary bodies. Categories I and II are permitted to submit written statements for circulation at the above-mentioned meetings, and Category I NGOs, in addition, may make oral statements.[43]

In 1996, ECOSOC adopted a Resolution updating the 1968 Resolution.[44] According to the Chairman of the Working Group, that carried out the review, there were four main reasons for the review: the participation of thousands of NGOs in the United Nations Conference on Environment and Development ("UNCED"); the growth of human rights NGOs and the participation of thousands of human rights advocates in the UN Conference on Human Rights; the contribution of NGOs to humanitarian assistance in world crises; and the strengthening of the international women's movement. This Resolution introduced new principles, namely, that national, regional, and sub-regional organizations may request consultative status and that NGOs from all areas and regions of the world should be involved equitably, effectively and genuinely.

One of the most welcome developments of the 1996 review is that it established the eligibility of national NGOs for consultative status, including national affiliates of international NGOs. Many national NGOs are based in developing countries and represent the interests of the "South". In general, the new arrangements retain the categories of consultative status which distinguish between different types of NGOs, and those which are included on an ECOSOC roster are those which do not have consultative status.

Specifically, the status of privileges of these NGOs may be described as follows:

(i) *NGOs with general status* are able to consult with officers from the Secretariat on matters of interest to the NGO; allowed to make oral statements based on recommendations by the Committee on Non-Governmental Organizations (the "Committee"); allowed to submit brief written statements; may designate representatives to sit at the meetings of ECOSOC and its subsidiaries; have the right to place items on the agendas of ECOSOC and its subsidiaries;

---

[41] In 1996, 436 NGOs qualified for this status.
[42] In 1996, 563 NGOs qualified for this status.
[43] Over 1,500 NGOs have consultative status with the Council, see *NGO & ECOSOC - The United Nations and Civil Society*, <http://www.un.org/partners/civil_society/ngo/n-ecosoc.htm>.
[44] ESC Res. 1996/31,51 sess., UN Doc. A 15113 (Part II) (1996).

(ii)*NGOs with special status*: able to consult with officers from the Secretariat on matters of interest to the NGO; allowed to make oral statements based on recommendations by the Committee; allowed to submit written statements; may designate representatives to sit at meetings of ECOSOC and its subsidiaries;

(iii)*NGOs with Roster status*: able to consult with officers of the Secretariat on matters of interest to the NGO; may designate representatives to attend meeting in the NGOs field of competence.

The Secretary-General is authorized to offer facilities to NGOs with consultative status including: access to UN grounds and facilities; arrangement of informal discussion on matters of special interest to groups and organizations; access to UN press documentation services; accommodation for conferences or smaller meetings of consultative organizations on work of ECOSOC; and appropriate seating arrangements and facilities for obtaining documents during public meetings.[45] As the above indicates, privileges granted to NGOs with a consultative status are not very extensive. According to ECOSOC Resolution 1006/31, an NGO enjoying such a status is subject to periodical review by the Committee. If the Committee decides that the NGO under review has not met the requirements for consultative status, it may recommend to ECOSOC its suspension or exclusion.

The participation of NGOs in the work of the UN was a controversial matter, which caused many negative responses from certain States, such as those of the Soviet Union and Argentina during the 1970s. This negative attitude did not, however, stop the expansion of NGO participation within the system of the UN. There are several reasons for this continuing expansion. Firstly, certain NGOs, which already existed before the establishment of the UN, expanded at a later stage and became global NGOs meriting their inclusion in Categories I and II. Secondly, certain other NGOs which were initially suspicious that the UN's work was at odds with their aims, became acquainted with, and came to approve of, the UN's work. Thirdly, new NGOs are being established as new areas of economic activity emerge. Finally, some existing NGOs have gained more skills and experience and want to move onto the global agenda.[46]

Several benefits stem from the broad participation of NGOs. These include, for example, technical expertise; new ideas for politicians from with

---

[45] Information from: *NGOs & Economic and Social Council*, ECOSOC, The United Nations Department of Social Affairs (DESA), at: <http://www.un.org/esa/coordination.ngo/pdf.guidelines.pdf>.
[46] P. Willetts, "Introduction", in P. Willetts (ed.), *The Conscience of the World, The Influence of Non-Governmental Organisations in the U.N. System* (1996), 1-14; and also "Consultative status for NGO's at the United Nations", 31-62, at 37.

non-bureaucratic channels; assistance for governments to secure ratification or implementation of new treaties; voicing of interests of people not well represented in policy-making; representing interests of future generations; enhancing the accountability of international organizations and governments by monitoring negotiations and strengthening of international agreements by monitoring governmental compliance.[47]

NGOs have developed networks of co-operation, both between themselves and with various organizations such as the ILO (International Labour Organization),[48] UNESCO (the United Nations Educational, Scientific and Cultural Organization); UNICEF (the United Nations Children Fund); WHO (the World Health Organization); FAO (the Food and Agriculture Organization); the Council of Europe; OAS (the Organization of American States); OAU (the Organization of African Unity); and LAS (the League of Arab States). The participation of NGOs in the work of particular organizations is either regulated by these organizations' rules of procedure or is very often developed during the practice of an organization.

According to Charnowitz, a new period of extensive relationships between NGOs and international organizations has been entered as a result of the broad participation of NGOs in the preparatory committee for UNCED itself. He points out that "NGOs in this current period are gaining access to more international organizations and exerting greater influence in multilateral negotiations".[49]

NGOs participate in diverse ways in the UN conferences that formulate global policies, such as in the case of the protection of the ozone layer. However, NGOs do not have the right to vote during these conferences. They can, nevertheless, influence the decision-making process through (for example) their input in respect of reports and committee work; through taking part in plenary debates (though the time allocated to them is rather limited) and through lobbying. The last means of influence is often informal since, on the one hand, lobbying mars the image of NGOs as apolitical, while, on the other hand, diplomats strive to preserve the premise that they obey only their governments.

3.3.2 NGOs beyond the treaty process

The present chapter concerns factors and actors influencing treaty evolution. In international practice, however, the involvement of NGOs is much more extensive than just participation in the treaty-making process. As indicated above, a survey of the activities of NGOs in general exceeds the framework

---

[47] S. Charnovitz, "Two Centuries of Participation: NGOs and International Governance", 18(2) *Michigan Journal of International Law* (1997), 183-286, at 274-275.
[48] See ECOLOGIC/FIELD Report, *supra* note 34, at 79-80.
[49] Charnovitz, *supra* note 47, at 265.

of this article. However, simply by way of example, many international financial organizations have developed closer links with non-State actors. The best example of such an organization is the International Bank for Reconstruction and Development ("IBRD" or the "World Bank"), and the International Development Association ("IDA").[50] The World Bank has a very well developed process of formal co-operation with other international organizations. Nevertheless, the participation of NGOs was often relatively inextensive and informal. The basis for co-operation with IGOs is set out in Article V, section 8 of the IBRD Articles of Agreement and Article V, section 4 of the Articles of Agreement of the IDA. On the basis of these provisions, the World Bank is empowered to co-operate with general international organizations and public international organizations which perform tasks in areas relevant to the Bank's activities. The IDA has co-operated with public international organizations which provide technical and financial assistance to less developed areas in the world. This co-operation is effected on the basis of agreements.

The degree of co-operation with NGOs improved in 1981 when a special NGO-World Bank Committee was set up. Generally speaking, this Committee was set up in order to enable the collaboration between NGOs and the World Bank on project operation. In the late 1980s, however, NGOs participating in this Committee were criticized by other NGOs, in particular for their lack of accountability to the wider NGO community and for being "token" NGOs. Lack of transparency at the World Bank, especially in granting loans, was also criticized, as well as lending, which led to environmental destruction. The World Bank shifted its attitude to permit more extensive collaboration with NGOs. In particular, it called for increased staff resources to liaise with NGOs; the establishment of a funding window for NGOs operations; stronger NGO-Bank operational collaboration; the improvement of NGO-government co-operation by educating governments on their role in development; the establishment of sector committees covering key-issues of NGO concern; interdepartmental decision-making to ensure that the Bank's response to public criticism is admitted by the relevant Bank departments; and strengthening of the existing NGO Unit.[51] It has accordingly been said that "NGOs have successfully

---

[50] See I.F.I. Shihata, "The World Bank and Non-Governmental Organisations", 25 *Cornell IL.J* (1992), at 623-641. See also I.F.I. Shihata, "The World Bank's Contribution to the Development of International Environmental Law", at 631-657 in G. Hafner, G. Loibl, A. Rest L. Sucharipa-Berhman, K. Zemanek (eds.), *Liber Amicorum for Professor I. Seidl-Hohenveldern* (1998), at 631-659; see also G. Loibl, "The World Group and Sustainable Development", in F. Weiss, E. Denters, P. de Waart (eds.), *International Law with a Human Face* (1998), at 513-532.

[51] All information, see S. Cleary, "The World Bank and NGOs", in Willetts, *supra* note 46, at 63-97, see in particular at 91.

influenced the World Bank since the beginning of the 1980s. ... The influence of NGOs can be expected to increase in the short- and medium-term. But one should not overestimate the extent of this influence."[52]

Despite some criticisms, it must be noted that the World Bank has acknowledged a decisive role for these organizations in developing States. It has passed several Operational Policy Notes and Operational Policy Directives in which, among other things, are listed the fields of its activities in which co-operation with the non-State actors has become absolutely indispensable [53]

One of the most recent developments in the World Bank, connected to its collaboration with civil society, is the establishment of a Joint Facilitative Committee in October 2003. It is a Bank-civil society working group, the task of which is exploring transparent and effective mechanisms of dialogue and engagement between civil society and the World Bank at the global level.[54] The Bank has three forms of cooperation with civil society – facilitation, dialogue and consultation and partnership.[55] Facilitation takes place when the Bank provides technical and financial assistance, including guidance and encouragement to client governments collaborating with civil society organizations in their countries on Bank supported activities. Both dialogue and consultations are conducted on the bilateral level.=Dialogue takes place in relation to a country strategy, sector studies, specific projects and programmes. This dialogue occurs between the Bank and civil society, and includes local governments and other donor agencies.[56] Consultation involves "certain expectations that the process will influence decision-making and result in more consensual policies, programmes and projects." [57] Civil society organizations ("CSOs") are consulted by the Bank at all levels: global, regional and domestic. At the global and regional levels, the Bank formally consults on the major policies in, e.g., the areas of forest management, information disclosure, indigenous peoples and resettlement,

---

[52] *Id.*, at 94.

[53] See <http://web.worldbank.org/WBSITE/EXTERNAL/TOPICS/CSO/0,,pagePK:220469~theSitePK:228717,00.html>.

[54] Dialogue with Civil Society, see internet at: <http://web.worldbank.irg.WBSITE/EXTERNAL/TOPICS/CSO/O,,content....228717,00.htm>.

[55] The Discussion Paper *Issues and Options for Improving Engagement Between the World Bank and Civil Society Organizations* distinguish three types of the civil society organizations. October 2003, Civil Society Team, External Vice- Presidency, Environmentally and Socially Sustainable Development, Vice-Presidency, The World Bank, see internet at: <http://sitersources.worldbank.org/CSOResources/CSPaper.pdf>.

[56] See below note 60. Recent examples of dialogues: World Bank – Civil Society February Lunch Discussion on "Setting a New Developments Path in Brazil", 23 February 2004; World Bank and Civil Society Discussion on Poverty Reduction and Governance.

[57] See internet at: <http://web.worldbank.irg.WBSITE/EXTERNAL/TOPICS/CSO/O,,content....228717,00.htm>.

poverty reduction strategies. At the country level, the Bank consults civil society organizations on Country Assistance Strategy, sector studies and individual Bank-funded development projects. Often consultations encompass civil society organizations, governments, businesses and other donor agencies.[58] Partnerships involve cooperation in the area of operational and/or advocacy partnerships at the national (e.g. education, environment, health and rural development); regional (e.g. Pakiv European Roma Fund, a Joint Programme of the Bank, European NGOs, foundations and governments to promote the development of Roma people); and transnational levels (e.g. the Global Alliance for Vaccines; the Global Development Gateway).

In 2002, the World Bank created a team, comprising of 120 civil society specialists working across the institution.[59] They are mostly social scientists and communication officers qualified to work with the civil society sector. At the country level there are over 80 Civil Society Country Staff working in 70 Bank country offices worldwide to promote the civil society organizations in the participation in Bank funded projects and programs. At the regional and departmental levels, the Civil Society Group comprises of 40 staff that work at the World Bank Headquarters in Washington in various units, geographic regions, funding mechanisms and with specific constituencies. At the global level, the Civil Society Team sets out institutional strategy, providing advice to senior management, doing research and dissemination and reaching out to CSOs at the global level.

One of the most interesting cooperative initiatives by the Bank is partnership with civil society organizations.[60] They vary from formal agreements and large multi-stakeholder programmes to informal cooperation and capacity-building within the country-level projects. The examples of such partnerships include forest conservation, AIDS vaccines, eradication of polio, rural poverty, micro-credit and internet development.

In conclusion, it can be said that the World Bank's policy towards civil society is much changed and that the Bank's involvement with civil society is increasing and became more collaborative. As to the role of civil society in the treaty-making process, it reflects, in our view, the general (diversified and oblique) nature of public-private partnerships. It may involve a formal agreement or just be confined to direct or even indirect influence at the negotiations stage, through the official partners to negotiations. It appears

---

[58] See below note 62.
[59] World Bank Staff working with Civil Society, see internet at: <http://web.worldbank.org/WBSITE/EXTERNAL/TOPICS/CSO/0,,contentMDK:20093777~menuPK:225317~pagePK:220503~piPK:220476~theSitePK:228717,00.html#>.
[60] Partnerships with Civil Society, see internet at: <http://web.worldbank.org/WBSITE/EXTERNAL/TOPICS/CSO/0,,contentMDK:20093777~menuPK:225317~pagePK:220503~piPK:220476~theSitePK:228717,00.html#>.

that at this stage of the development of relationships between the World Bank and civil society, the informal, indirect type is more realistic.

The increasing role of civil society is also visible in the UN agencies such as the World Health Organization ("WHO"). Relations between civil society and the WHO are regulated by the 1987 Principles Governing Relations with Non-Governmental Organizations ("1987 Principles").[61] In light of the 1996 ECOSOC Resolution (see above), the UN agencies also reviewed their own policies.

In 2001, a review was undertaken of the principles governing the WHO's relationship with NGOs. The existing cooperation between the WHO and civil society can be formal and informal. The prerequisite for formal cooperation is to enter into initial contacts, establishing a plan of work and joint activities. After this initial period, the official application may be submitted. Admissibility is assessed by the Executive Board. As of July 2002, there were 180 NGOs in official relations with the WHO. This involves participation without a vote in the WHO governing body meetings, such as the Health Assembly and the Executive Board and making statements at these meetings. The formal and informal cooperation includes a multitude of forms, such as joint events, campaigns and consultations, participation of NGOs in WHO consultations and expert groups and contribution by NGOs in policy-making, standard setting and emergency operations.[62]

The review conducted by the Director-General identified several drawbacks in the system of cooperation between the WHO and civil society. The review pointed out that the current 1987 Principles were inadequate to meet the needs of WHO and the needs and aspirations of civil society. The Director-General proposed that the existing state of affairs should be replaced by a two-fold policy of accreditation and collaboration. The first of these elements would govern the participation of NGOs in Governing Body meetings, while the second would enhance working relations between civil society and the WHO. As to the involvement of NGOs in the treaty-making process, the WHO has a fairly standard procedure. A good example is the recent 2003 Framework Convention for Tobacco Control. This Convention was negotiated within the Intergovernmental Negotiating Body. NGOs participated in negotiations (such as the Medical Women's International Association, International Alliance of Women, Commonwealth Medical Association),[63] but only by way of a rather limited right to make

---

[61] Resolution WHA40.25; see also Report by the Director-General, "Policy for relations with non-governmental organizations," 14 April 2003, UN Doc. A56/46, Fifty-sixth World Health Assembly, EB113/24, ANNEX ("the Report").

[62] The Report, paragraphs 7-11, note 67.

[63] See internet at: <http://www.who.int/gb/fctc>.

statements.[64] According to paragraphs 14-16 of the Provisional Rules adopted during the negotiating process of the 2003 Framework Convention for Tobacco Control, in order to speak a NGO must be invited or make a request to speak and this request must be accepted. According paragraph 15, "Organisations wishing to avail themselves of this privilege, should address their request to the Chair, through a Secretary of the Negotiating Body or to the relevant working group. The request should refer to the item number and title and provide a legible statement, along with seven copies, in either in English or French. The request should be handed in at the NGO Liaison Office, Room E131. Organizations should call or visit the Office to verify that their request has been accepted." Paragraph 16 of the Rules provide that statements should be succinct and address the issue being discussed, and that, as a general rule, speaking time is no more than three minutes.

It appears that NGOs that are "allowed" to speak or invited to do so for three minutes, must go to a deal of effort in order to do so. Accordingly, NGOs can influence the text of a treaty only to a very limited extent, since their participation in the treaty-making process within the framework of the WHO is not very extensive.

4. Negotiation and Amendment of Conventions

4.1 The Law of the Sea Convention

4.1.1 Introduction

The negotiations on the 1982 Convention on the Law of the Sea ("UNCLOS" or the "1982 LOS Convention") provides a very good example of the interplay of divergent interests of States. One of the tasks of the UNCLOS First Committee was to translate the doctrine of the "common heritage of mankind" – in itself controversial – into the régime of deep-seabed mining. From the point of view of the interests involved, three main groups of States may be distinguished during negotiations: first, a group consisting of the industrialized countries (the future major importers of the metals to be recovered from manganese nodules); secondly, a group consisting of the majority of developing States (which had an interest in sharing the revenues from the resources in question); and, thirdly, a group consisting of land-based producers and exporters of metals (a group which

---

[64] World Health Organisation, Intergovernmental Negotiating Body on the WHO Framework Convention of Tobacco Control, Fifth Session, A/FTCT/INB5/DIV/4. 20 August 2002, "Participation of Nongovernmental Organizations and Provisional Relations with WHO in the Intergovernmental Negotiating Body on the WHO Framework Convention on Tobacco Control."

included some developed and some developing countries).[65] However, the most fundamental differences of opinions were between a different grouping of States, namely between the "Group of 77" (which consisted of almost all developing States) on the one hand, and the developed States on the other.

One of the main points at issue was the system of exploitation of the deep-sea area and the role of the International Seabed Authority ("ISA"). Developed States were represented by, *inter alia*, the United States of America, (which voiced the most extreme views, see below), the European Community countries and Japan. During the course of the negotiations, the US, the EC countries and Japan continued to present proposals that the only operators should be State-owned and private companies.[66]

The US government has not yet ratified UNCLOS. In the words of one author "[s]o vehement in fact were the objections by the Reagan administration that as early as January 1982 the United States hinted at its refusal even to sign the Convention, much less to endorse it to the Senate for ratification".[67] This situation has changed since the adoption of the regime on the deep sea-mining in 1944 (see below).

There were also other elements of the 1982 LOS Convention which made it unacceptable for the Reagan administration to endorse its contents. One of the most controversial issues was the international bureaucracy established by this treaty to ISA, the "Council" and the "Enterprise". As Joyner assessed it, "in general, the US government was philosophically antagonistic toward the principle of the common heritage of mankind enshrined in Part XI of the Convention".[68] This principle was viewed as a form of international socialism — detrimental to technologically advanced States and companies

---

[65] Yuwen Li, *Transfer of Technology for the Deep Sea-Bed Mining, The 1982 Convention and Beyond* (1994). Sanger points out that "UNCLOS-3 will be remembered for the number of groups – negotiating groups, drafting groups, special interest groups – that crowded into the arena. There was method, not madness, in this multitude. ... There were the traditional groups based on areas and blocs – the East Europeans, the West Europeans and Others (including the US, Canada, Japan, Australia and New Zealand) and the Group of 77 with its three regional sections of Asia, Africa and Latin America. There were groups that were formed officially by the conference's president, ranging from negotiating groups with long-term task to other groups that were assembled at a moment of crisis, like the Committee of 12 (knows also as 'the Good Samaritans') during the final session. There were also semi-official groups, the most notable being the 'Evenson Group', first formed by the Norwegian lawyer as an informal drafting group in the last days of the Seabed Committee", C. Sanger, *Ordering the Oceans, The Making of the Law of the Sea* (1987), at 29.

[66] UN Doc. A/Conf.62/C.1/L.6 (United States), in Off. Rec. Vol. III., at 1690172; UN Doc. A/CONF.62/L.8(EE Countries), in Off. Rec.Vol. III, at 173-175; UN Doc. A/CONF.62/L.9(Japan), in Off. Rec., Vol. III, at 175-177.

[67] C.C. Joyner, "The United States and the New Law of the Sea", 27 *ODILA* (1996), 41-58, at 42; see also J. Charney, "U.S. Provisional Application of the 1994 Deep Seabed Agreement", 88(4) *AJIL* (1994), at 705-714.

[68] Joyner, *supra* note 67, at 43.

and beneficial for developing States. It was also viewed as a precedent for the introduction of a similar régime with economic implications in relation to the moon, other celestial bodies and the South Polar Region. The main focus of concern was the ISA, which was to be financed by United Nations funds and was seen by the US administration in 1982 as especially designed to propagate international socialism and monopolistic international bureaucracy and to serve the interests of developing States by promoting the so-called "New Economic Order". The bureaucracy proposed was also appraised as being both awkward and cumbersome.

4.1.2 Negotiation of the 1982 Convention on the Law of the Sea

As mentioned above, during the negotiations phase of UNCLOS, the interests of developing States were presented by a group of like-minded States, namely, the Group of 77. This Group rejected unconditionally the licensing system of exploitation proposed by developed States. The Chairman of the Group of 77 stated, *inter alia*, that the Group "did not believe the claims that equitable distribution of the profits derived from the exploitation of the common heritage of mankind could be effected through the use of a method which was typical of an era of paternalism and dependence".[69] Several papers, including one referred to as the "Informal Single Negotiating Text" in 1975 ("1975 ISNT"), which attempted to reconcile the interests of developing and developed States were presented.[70] They were, however, rejected by one or other of the groups on the basis that there was not enough control bestowed on the ISA (according to the developing States)[71], and in the case of the 1975 ISNT on the ground that too much power and control was granted to the ISA (according to the developed States). The Group of 77 was adverse to the system of exploitation (the "parallel system") as being contradictory to the principle of common heritage of mankind. The division of the deep-seabed area (the "Area") between States and their companies, on the one hand, and the "Enterprise" (the executive arm of the ISA), on the other, would result (according to developing States) in depriving the Enterprise of access to the necessary technology and financial capability to operate on its own.

Thus, Article 151 paragraph 2 of UNCLOS (as drafted in the 1977 Informal Composite Negotiating Text ("ICNT")) reflected an uneasy compromise between these two groups of States. The US administration was

---

[69] Yuwen Li, *supra* note 65, at 68 citing R. Platzöder, Third United Nations Conference on the Law of the Sea, Volumes I-XVIII, 1982, (1988), Vol. III, at 452-453.
[70] For a survey, see Yuwen Li, *supra* note 65, at 68-74.
[71] Pinto's (Chairman of the Working Group of the First Committee) paper "Basic Conditions of Exploration and Exploitation". Pinto's paper did not grant control over the whole area to the ISA.

of the view that the wording of this Article did not ensure guaranteed access to the Area by operators other than the Enterprise. The US had several other remaining objections against the ICNT (see above), such as issues of transfer of technology; mandatory joint ventures; financial arrangements; production limitations; and the review conference.[72] The US objections resulted in the revision of Article 151 and its incorporation into Article 153 of the draft document ICNT/Rev. 1 in 1979, which eventually became Article 153 of the 1982 LOS Convention.

As may be observed from the above survey of the difficult negotiations relating to deep-seabed mining, Article 153 of UNCLOS attempted to reconcile divergent views presented by developed and developing States. The final legal text of the Article was the result of profound non-legal concerns, economic and political. Article 153 failed to accommodate all (or at least most) expectations and, thus, lent itself to revision. The initial US proposals, if accepted, would have established a parallel legal system of deep-seabed mining. This system would have been characterized by two completely separate legal regimes covering two areas. One area would have been under the exclusive control of the ISA and governed by international law; and the other would have been accessed by States and their companies and governed by national laws. The parallel system which was finally adopted by the Convention reflected only partially the United States' proposal. The 1982 LOS Convention opted for a parallel system under the full control of the ISA and governed exclusively by international law. As was correctly stated "[t]he basic feature of the parallel system is that the ISA on behalf of mankind as a whole will control activities in the Area and conduct mining through the Enterprise".[73]

Yuwen Li is of the view that although imperfect, the system adopted by UNCLOS "reflects a balance of the bargaining powers which was achieved at the beginning of the 1980s … [and] is a more equitable system than either the original single ISA system advocated by developing countries, or the simple licensing system favoured by major industrialized countries".[74] This view is difficult to sustain. Even Yuwen Li admits[75] that after the conclusion of the Convention, the deep-seabed mining system was criticized by some governments of industrialized countries, by scholars and by representatives of the mining industry. From the outset, developed countries were not satisfied with the final result. They resented the concessions they had made and considered the relevant provisions outdated. Developing countries were aware of the negative feelings prevalent among developed States and

---

[72] B.H. Oxman, "The Third United Nations Conference on the Law of the Sea: The Seventh Session (1978)", 73 *AJIL* (1979), 1-41.

[73] Yuwen Li, *supra* note 65, at 86.

[74] *Id.*

[75] *Id.*

mindful of the fact that certain concessions towards the developed States were necessary in order for the system to work. It has been aptly put that "[t]he reality is that UNCLOS III, which lasted for nine years, simply did not produce a universally acceptable legal framework for future deep-seabed mining. This is not due to any shortcomings of UNCLOS III, but because the issue is closely linked to other political, economic and financial factors, all of which are in a continuous state of flux. Any law which aims to establish a framework for future business activities cannot be made too far ahead of practice."[76]

4.1.3 The initiatives of the UN Secretaries-General

The signing of UNCLOS did not put an end to the controversies which dogged the whole process of its negotiation. It became obvious that UNCLOS as it stood would not be universally signed or ratified unless some modification of its provisions in respect of Part XI were made. Resolution I of the Third UN Conference on the Law of the Sea established the Preparatory Commission for the ISA and the International Tribunal for the Law of the Sea ("Prepcom"). It was clear from the outset that Prepcom was ill equipped to deal with the controversial matters which related to deep-seabed mining and which remained following the signing of UNCLOS. In 1993, it was decided that Prepcom would no longer convene. Moreover, in the late 1980s it became obvious that due to the fall in metal prices world-wide, manganese nodule mining was unlikely to take place during this century and that it may not be able to produce sufficient profits to compete with terrestrial resources.[77] However, it may be said that "[t]he practical significance of Part XI in the Convention as a whole may have diminished, but its significance in ideological terms or as a precedent remains".[78]

Following the unsuccessful attempts of Prepcom, the initiative to remedy the situation was taken up in 1990 by the then UN Secretary-General (Mr. Perez de Cuellar).[79] He convened informal negotiations with some 25 representatives of key signatory and non-signatory States to define the outstanding issues. On the basis of the proposal of the representative of the

---

[76] *Id.*
[77] See D.H. Anderson, "Efforts to Ensure Universal Participation in the United Nations Convention on the Law of the Sea", 42 *ICLQ* (1993), 654-664 generally, and at 657; on the same topic see also D.H. Anderson, "Further Efforts to Ensure Universal Participation in the United Nations Convention on the Law of the Sea", 43 *ICLQ* (1994), at 886-893; D.H. Anderson, "LOS Convention, Status and Prospects", 18 *Marine Policy* (1994), at 494-497; D.H. Anderson, "Legal Implications of the Entry into Force of the UN Convention on the Law of the Sea", 44 *ICLQ* (1994), at 312-326; J. Stevenson and B. H. Oxman, "The Future of the United Nations Convention on the Law of the Sea", 88 *AJIL* (1994), at 488-499.
[78] Anderson, "Efforts ...", *supra* note 77, at 657.
[79] *Id.*, at 657-664.

United Kingdom and Germany, a list of nine topics was drawn up. These were: (1) costs to State parties; (2) the enterprise; (3) decision-making; (4) the review conference; (5) transfer of technology; (6) production limitation; (7) a compensation fund; (8) financial terms of contracts; and (9) the environment.

The industrialized countries explained that the costs of ISA and that of funding the Enterprise and its first mining site were too high, especially in view of the price of technology and the high-commercial risk of the operation. Also objectionable was the establishment of the equivalent system of a nationalized industry on an international level in relation to seabed mining in a period when industry was generally being privatized. As to the benefits for developing countries, they could profit for example from royalties. Another arguable issue concerned the system of decision-making in the ISA, in particular in relation to financial matters, in which majority voting could mean exclusion of the major industrialized countries from the decision-making process (Articles 160-161 of UNCLOS). Yet another problem was posed by Article 155 which dealt with a review conference. This provision envisaged the possibility that the amendments to the mining system could be adopted and could enter into force for all parties, in some cases without the specific consent of all parties. This provision posed a particular problem for those parties whose written constitutions provided for an explicit decision expressing the consent of a State by its appropriate constitutional organ. A serious controversy was caused by the provisions on the compulsory transfer to the ISA and the Enterprise of technology which could have been obtained in commercial markets. Moreover, the governments did not have the means to force private companies to transfer future technology to the authority. In addition, Article 151, which concerned limitation of production, no longer reflected reality due to changes in the metal markets and metal consumption which occurred in the 1980s. Anderson states that the idea of limiting production and establishing a "compensation fund" for the benefit of land-based producers was viewed as contrary to the principle of free competition and markets; and that "[o]ther obstacles, such as the review conference, can be seen as being of a more technical nature".[80]

During the next stage of the Secretary-General's consultation, the issues in contention were discussed individually, in order to decide which of them required immediate attention and which could be considered at a later stage, when more was known about the economic implications of deep-seabed mining. These consultations were successful in that agreement was reached on the key issues (listed above). Upon entry into force of UNCLOS only certain institutions were to be established and they were to be cost effective.

---

[80] *Id.*, at 658-659.

The cost of the first mine site was to be met by a joint venture contract with the capital provided by a private sector partner. In relation to decision-making, it was agreed to establish a system of chambers with representation of parties with common interests (such as producers, consumers, and investors in deep-seabed mining). Substantive decisions were to be taken by a two-thirds majority of those present and voting, providing that these decisions were not opposed by a majority in any of the chambers. It was also agreed that a Financial Committee should be created, separate from both the Council and the ISA. As to the review conference, it was agreed that the procedures of the VCLT should be followed as much as possible. Wide support for any changes was to be secured, as well as wide participation in the provision for the entry into force of an amended text. The principle of transfer of technology was shaped by the new operational system of the Enterprise, which was to operate through joint ventures. The technology was to be acquired on a commercial basis from its private sector partners. Finally, in relation to financial assistance for the creation of a compensation fund, existing financial institutions would be used. Environmental issues were not seen as an obstacle to universal participation in the 1982 LOS Convention and were left for later consideration. The successor of Mr. Perez de Cuellar as the UN Secretary-General, Mr. Boutros Boutros Ghali, proceeded with consultations, acknowledging that that "it was clear that the Convention would be severely damaged if it should enter into force without participation of the industrialised States since they were the major users of the sea as well as the heaviest polluters".[81] The character of consultations changed in that all interested States were able to participate. The number of participants rose from 30 to 75. The consultations were held in January 1993 on the basis of the note of Legal Counsel, Dr. Fleischhauer. This note summarized the position as at that time on the eight key issues, (the consideration of environmental issues having been postponed). The note adopted similar divisions to those previously adopted. The issues in contention were divided into two groups, the first group constituting issues in which some agreement was emerging, the second comprising issues which could be deferred for later consideration. The first group of issues comprised costs to the States parties, the Enterprise, decision-making, the review conference and transfer of technology. The issues proposed for later consideration included production limitation, the compensation fund and financial terms of contract. The view was taken that these issues would better be discussed when commercial production began and until then their

---

[81] *Id.*, at 661.

shape was to remain only broadly defined. The progress in consultations prompted the Clinton administration to participate."[82]

4.1.4 The drafting of the Implementation Agreement

From April 1993, informal negotiations were held between developed and developing States to find an acceptable compromise which was "not based precisely on any of the options contained in the Information Note of April 1993". A new approach was established which was based on dealing individually with eight topics which were identified at the beginning of the consultation process as obstacles to the signing and ratification of the LOS Convention by industrialized States.[83] It has been said that "[t]his approach remained true to the offer made by the Group of 77 in August 1989 to address specific concerns expressed by industrialised States."[84] An important informal Group (known as the "Boat Group") was formed which consisted of representatives of both industrialized and developing States, namely, Australia (French); Fiji (Nandan); Indonesia (Djallal); Italy (Treves); Jamaica (Rattray); Nigeria (Sani Mohamed); Germany (Koch); United Kingdom (Anderson); United States (Scholtz). The task of the Group was to prepare a draft Resolution for adoption by the General Assembly and the text of an agreement on the Implementation of Part XI of the LOS Convention.

The consultations with the Secretary-General remained informal until the moment at which he could submit the report prepared by the Boat Group (known as "the Boat Paper") to the General Assembly. This report was to contain a draft resolution and a text of a draft agreement for consideration. On 16 November 1993 Guyana submitted a 60th instrument of ratification which, in accordance with Article 308, triggered the entry into force of the LOS Convention twelve months later. This event hastened up consultations which were held in January/February, April and May/June 1994. It was proposed that the new implementation agreement would be applied provisionally, on an interim basis pending its entry into force, by States which so agreed and with effect from 16 November 1994. The initial

---

[82] There were several proposals as to the form of the future amendment: a contractual instrument such as a Protocol establishing agreed amendments to Part XI of the Convention; an interpretative agreement containing understandings on the interpretation and application of Part XI and taking into account developments in international relations and the mining industry since 1982; an interpretative agreement for an interim regime, i.e. an arrangement according to which new ratifying States could exclude the application of most of Part XI, accepting only the principle of the common heritage of mankind; some interim arrangements until mining was about to begin and an obligation to attend a Conference at that time to establish a definite regime; and an agreement additional to the Convention. These proposals were contained in the Information Note by Dr. Fleishhauer of 8 April 1993.

[83] Anderson, "Further Efforts …", *supra* note 77, at 887-893.

[84] *Id.*, at 887.

position in regard to the financing of the ISA was modified, to the effect that during the interim period the costs of running the ISA would be borne from the regular budget of the United Nations (rather than by the other States) subject to the consent of the General Assembly. Industrialized States were permitted to attend meetings of the ISA on condition that they consented to the provisional application of the new implementation agreement.

The Agreement on the Implementation of Part XI of the Convention ("the Implementation Agreement") was adopted by the General Assembly on 28 July 1994. The Implementation Agreement and Part XI are interpreted and applied together as a single instrument. In the event of differences the Agreement prevails. "[I]n other words, the Agreement modifies in effect the terms of Part XI".[85] The Implementation Agreement significantly modified all controversial issues.[86] It may also be noted that the 1994 Agreement has taken a different approach to deep-seabed mining, namely, an evolutionary and functional approach towards establishment of the ISA and the Enterprise and the modification of provisions which were strongly opposed by the US and other industrialized countries. On the other hand, the Agreement stipulates that the Area and its resources constitute the common heritage of mankind. The ISA will play a strong role in organizing and controlling the use of minerals in this area and, most importantly, will guard the interests of developing States and land-based producers. In addition, "[n]o state may claim or exercise sovereignty or sovereign rights over any part of the area or its resources; ... [t]he Area shall be open to use exclusively for peaceful purposes by all states; ... [and] [a]ctivities in the Area shall be carried out for the benefit of mankind as a whole, irrespective of the geographical location of states, whether coastal or land-locked, and taking into consideration the interests and needs of other states".[87] Many States, however, viewed the 1994 Implementation Agreement as a political compromise rather than a final settlement of deep-seabed mining.

The position of the ISA is quite difficult at present in the light of the limited role of the Enterprise. Under these new conditions, the ISA should give priority to finding ways and means to place the Enterprise in a position to participate in joint ventures and engage in commercial activities. It is assumed that the joint venture model is an acceptable means by which to implement the principle of common heritage of mankind, because it encourages investment by the mining industry in co-operation with the Enterprise and because the problem of transfer of technology is easily solved within the joint venture structure. The joint venture is a very common form

---

[85] Anderson, "Legal ...", *supra* note 77, at 317.
[86] See Anderson, *supra* note 77, at 317-319; on the contents of the Implementation Agreement see for example authors enumerated in note 77.
[87] L.D.M. Nelson, "The New Deep Sea-Bed Mining Regime", 10(2) *IJMCL* (1995), 189-203, at 203.

of commercial co-operation, very familiar to both developed and developing countries. Joint ventures are also generally acceptable as a political compromise that allows developing countries to fulfil their aspirations, at least to a certain degree, under the protection of an internationally supervised régime. On the other hand it is in the interest of developed countries and potential mining operators to utilize mineral resources under a universally accepted system. For the sake of securing political and economic stability, industrialized countries have a duty to share their technology with developing countries within a mutually agreed régime, as opposed the complete absence of an international régime. It appears that the 1994 Agreement achieved this task.[88] As one author points out "[t]o what extent this new regime can be said to put the general interests of the world community ahead of the special interests of any state or group of states is a question which remains unanswered".[89] Moreover, despite the support for the Implementation Agreement by the Clinton administration, there remain some conservatives in the current US administration who oppose the ratification of UNCLOS on ideological grounds.

4.2 The Straddling Stocks Convention

4.2.1 Background

The negotiation of the 1995 Agreement for the Implementation of the Provisions of the United Nations Convention on the Law of the Sea of 10 December 1982 relating to the Conservation and Management of Straddling Fish Stocks and Highly Migratory Fish Stocks ("Straddling Stock Convention")[90] provides yet another excellent example of the interplay of

---

[88] Yuwen Li, note 65, at 253-254, 256-257.

[89] Nelson, note 88, at 203.

[90] UN Doc. A/CONF.164/37 (1995); on the topic see, e.g., D.A. Balton, "Strengthening the Law of the Sea: The New Agreement on Straddling Fish Stocks and Highly Migratory Fish Stocks", 27 *ODILA* (1996), at 125-151; A. Tahindro, "Conservation and Management of Transboundary Fish Stocks: Comments in Light of the Adoption of the 1995 Agreement for the Conservation and Management of Straddling Fish Stocks and Highly Migratory Fish Stocks", 28 *ODILA* (1997), at 1-58; L. Juda, "The Post-UNCLOS-III System" in L. Juda, *International Law and Ocean Use Management: The Evolution of Ocean Governance* (1996), at 255-314; L. Juda, "The 1995 United Nations Agreement on Straddling Stocks and Highly Migratory Fish Stocks: A Critique", 28 *ODILA* (1997), at 147-166; M. Hayashi, "The 1995 Agreement on the Conservation and Management of Straddling and Highly Migratory Fish Stocks: Significance for the Law of the Sea Convention", 29 *Ocean and Coastal Management* (1995), at 51-69; D. Freestone and Z. Makuch, "The New International Environmental Law of Fisheries: The 1995 UN Straddling Stock Convention", 7 *YIEL* (1996), at 3-51; P.G.G. Davies and C. Redgwell, "The International Legal Regulation of Straddling Fish Stocks", 67 *BYIL* (1996), at 199-275.

different factors in the process of treaty making. Both States and NGOs were major actors in relation to the negotiation of the Straddling Stock Convention. However, in this part of the chapter, only the position of States will be reviewed.

The UN High Seas Fishing Conference was preceded by the FAO Technical Consultation on High Sea Fishing in September 1992 and by a meeting of "like minded States", hosted by Canada in St. John's, in 1993. On 29 January 1993, the 47th session of the General Assembly adopted a resolution approving the convening of an intergovernmental conference on straddling and migratory stocks.[91] The Conference ("the UN Fish Conference") met at the UN Headquarters from 19 to 23 April 1993, 12 to 30 July 1993, and 14 to 31 March 1994.

The organizational session of the UN Fish Conference in April 1993 elected S. Nandan, Ambassador of Fiji to the United Nations, as its Chairman. He prepared a paper on relevant issues as a guide.[92] States were asked to submit their comments on this paper and ten did so. The "'like-minded States', Argentina, Canada, Chile, Iceland and New Zealand urged the Conference to recommend a new global fisheries convention".[93] The Conference began in July with days of general statements from about 96 countries, some international organizations and about twenty-four NGOs.

The UN Conference was the result of growing international tension (due to conflicting interests between States) in relation to fisheries. Many economic and political factors contributed to an unsatisfactory situation. One of these was the establishment of the 200 nautical mile Exclusive Economic Zone ("EEZ") which imposed artificial limitations on living resources management. These limitations particularly affected States, such as Canada and Argentina, with a broad continental margin extending outside the above limit. In addition, EEZs were facing over-exploitation due, in some cases, to mismanagement. In turn, this resulted in expansion of long-distance fishing and directly affected so-called "straddling fish stocks" – i.e. those which are not confined to a 200 mile limit in their life cycle. The greatest tension was thus observed between long distance fishing nations and coastal States.[94] Further, many areas were in dispute, including the Northwest Atlantic, Northeast Atlantic, and the Pacific and Bering Seas. Developments in technology, such as the use of drift nets also played a contributory role in escalating the conflict. Straddling and migratory stocks account for about 10

---

[91] UN General Assembly, 47th Session, Resolution 47/192/ 29 January 1993.

[92] UN Doc. A/CONF. 164/10.

[93] C. Higginson, "The UN Conference on High Seas Fishing", 2:3 RECIEL (1993), 237-243, at 240.

[94] It exceeds the framework of this chapter to comment on the Estai incident. There are many excellent publications on the topic such as P.G.G. Davies, "The EC/Canadian Fisheries Dispute in the Northwest Atlantic", 44 ICLQ (1995), 927-939, at 933-938.

per cent of world food supply. Finally, a conference on straddling and highly migratory fish stocks was also recommended in Agenda 21 adopted at UNCED.[95]

The Straddling Stock Convention constitutes the elaboration of Part VII, section 2, Articles 116-120 of UNCLOS (high seas) and Articles 63 paragraph 2, and 64-67 deal with the conservation and management of living resources (coastal States).

4.2.2 The UN Fish Conference

In his excellent account of the Conference, Barston points out that during the UN Fish Conference three main groups of States could be distinguished: the extreme coastal States group (Chile, Colombia, Ecuador, Peru) which was linked with the activist coastal States (Canada, Argentina, Norway), the high seas fishing group (Japan, Korea, Poland and China), and the moderate reformist coastal States (Australia and New Zealand). The same author singles out a further two sub-groups. The first of these sub-groups included the Russian Federation, the United States and the European Union, a group with diversified interests. The second sub-group was the very large group of developing States, not organized, on behalf of which Indonesia and India spoke.[96]

The first group comprised States with different interests in respect of straddling and migratory stocks, both within the EEZ and beyond it. By the way of example, the group comprised, on the one hand, Canada (which was caught in a dispute with the European Union over straddling stocks in the Grand Banks area) and, on the other hand, the Latin American States, led by Chile, which promoted the concept of the so-called "presencial sea". Nonetheless, these States had some general interests in common. These common interests included agreement as to the character of rights of coastal States within the EEZ over living resources (that is, sovereign rights), a claim as to some rights in relation to the management of the living resources outside this area and the competence as to inspection and arrest of foreign flag vessels by coastal States on the basis of an agreement. A contrasting position was assumed by long distance fishing States. The position of this group was based on the principle of "due regard" for the interests of both flag and coastal States.

The members of this group advocated that the powers of specialist international organizations should have priority over those of coastal States, including the right of inspection and arrest. The third (moderate) group

---

[95] UN Conference on Environment and Development (UNCED), 1992, Agenda 21, section 17-49, 17-56, section 17-50.
[96] R. Barston, "United Nations Conference on Straddling and Highly Migratory Fish Stocks", 19(2) *Marine Policy* (1996), at 159-166.

approach the problem of fisheries from the point of view of maintaining the biological unity of stocks, as well as ensuring effective enforcement. The US promoted a policy of balancing the interests of coastal States and those of long distance fishing States, whilst the Russian Federation, referring to the experience in relation to the Bering Sea, proposed special provisions in connection with enclosed and semi-enclosed seas. Developing States did not form a unified group at this Conference.

The various groups of States at the UN Straddling Stocks Conference submitted documents on different issues relating to a future Agreement. During the third session of the Conference, the Chairman prepared a review of the negotiating text. As summarized by Barston, there were ten pertinent issues of negotiations during the third session (14 to 31 March). These were the coherence and compatibility of conservation and management measures within and outside of national jurisdiction, general principles of fisheries co-operation and management, regional and sub-regional organizations, flag State duties, port State responsibilities, action with regard to non-parties, enclaves, special requirements of developing countries, compulsory dispute settlement, and review procedures.[97]

During the fourth session, the most controversial issue related to determining the factors to be considered in establishing a regional management and conservation structure. The European Community advocated a limited interpretation and suggested that the term "biological unity" should be used, rather than "biological characteristics". On the other hand, Canada supported the term "biological characteristics" due to the fact that the characteristics of stocks vary to a great degree, so that any one of several characteristics might be regarded as forming a biological unity. Great disagreement was also caused by the proposed expansion of the rights of coastal States in comparison with those of States fishing on the high seas. Long distance fishing States, such as Poland, challenged the idea that conservation and protection measures on the high seas should be no less stringent than in coastal areas. The issue of a strict regional regulation was a source of concern for larger developing States and newly industrialized States (such as Thailand, India, Indonesia, Chile and Mexico) since it was assumed that these regulations would have a limiting effect on their freedom to develop commercially. Other points of disagreement concerned potential problems arising from a lack of sufficient EEZ fisheries data and likely differences between data on straddling and migratory species deriving from the national assessments in relation to EEZ and those from regional organizations. Japan, on the other hand supported the proposal that regional organizations should have a mandate to recommend quotas even if they differed from those set by States.

---

[97] *Id.*, at 162.

The most controversial issue was that of enforcement. As quoted by Barston, the Canadian Fisheries Minister, P. Tobin, expressed the general feeling that without effective enforcement even the best conservation measures would be without teeth.[98] On this issue States were mainly divided into two groups: those which wanted to give coastal States the primary responsibility for enforcement, and those States (Chile, Ecuador, Peru) which preferred to see the enforcement of conservation measures effected through regional organizations with a varying degree of power. As to the detention and arrest of ships, the high seas fishing States (Poland, Korea, Panama and some of the European Union States) were of the view that this would require consent of the flag State.

After the March 1994 session, Mr. Nandan issued a "Revised Negotiating Text"[99] and thereafter a "Draft Agreement for the Implementation of the Provisions of the United Nations Convention on the Law of the Sea of 10 December 1982 Relating to the Conservation and Management of Straddling Fish Stocks and Highly Migratory Fish Stocks" (the "Draft Agreement") for further consideration at later sessions. In order to make a future agreement effective, the Revised Negotiating Text gave a slight jurisdictional advantage to coastal States. The intention was that "distant water fishing nations [would] have an incentive to reach agreement".[100] The Draft Agreement introduced a radically new solution – the States fishing in the waters adjacent to the EEZ have to comply with conservation and management regulations established by the coastal State for the adjacent areas until a given dispute is peacefully settled and so long as these rules were equivalent to those applied the EEZ .

Although focused on limiting over-fishing, the Draft Agreement proposed different legal structures to those contained in the earlier Revised Negotiating Text. Its main theme was a duty of co-operation between coastal States and distant water fishing States in order to achieve the objective of long-term conservation and sustainable use of straddling and highly migratory fish stocks (Article 2 of the Draft Agreement). This aim was to be reached through direct negotiations or through the appropriate mechanism for co-operation (Article 7 paragraph 1 of the Draft Agreement). Article 7 paragraph 2 of the Draft Agreement introduced a very important provision, namely that the conservation measures taken on the high seas and those taken under national jurisdiction "shall be compatible to ensure conservation

---

[98] *Id.*, at 164.

[99] United Nations Conference on Straddling Fish Stocks and Highly Migratory Fish Stocks, Revised negotiating text (Prepared by the Chairman of the Conference), UN Doc. A/CONF/164/13/Rev.1 (20 March 1994) (RNT).

[100] J.M. Van Dyke, "Modifying the 1982 Law of the Sea Convention: New Initiatives on Governance of High Seas Fisheries Resources: The Straddling Stocks Negotiations", 10(2) *IJMCL* (1995), 219-227, at 221.

and management of stocks overall". This provision appears to give priority to coastal States in the matter of conservation of straddling and highly migratory fish stocks.

The difference between the Revised Negotiating Text and the Draft Agreement is that the Draft Agreement substituted the provision that empowered the coastal State to enforce observance of its conservation regulations in the area beyond the 200-mile limit with the above provision. It has been said that "… it achieves more or less the same result by substituting rigid requirements for binding dispute resolution designed to promote early agreement on terms that are "compatible" with the coastal state's regulation of its own citizens in its own zone".[101] Article 30 paragraphs 2 and 3 of the Draft Agreement contained an encouragement for fishing States to join regional fishing organizations and to participate in negotiations held, aimed at preservation of high seas fish stocks. The Draft Agreement empowered coastal States to enforce conservation rules by policing their own vessels and prohibiting vessels from unauthorized fishing (Article 17 paragraph 3-b-iv of the Draft Agreement). Flag States must prohibit their vessels from fishing in areas under the jurisdiction of an international organization (Article 32 paragraph 2 of the Draft). According to Article 21 port States are also authorized to enforce the rules on vessels that use their facilities.

In summary, one of the most important aims of the negotiations leading to the conclusion of the Agreement was to ensure the establishment of internationally agreed minimum standards for the conservation and management of straddling and highly migratory fish stocks and to provide for effective enforcement of these standards through flexible but binding dispute resolution procedures.[102] The Agreement was adopted without vote on 4 August 1995.[103]

4.2.3 Evaluation

How has the Agreement accommodated the divergent approaches expressed during the negotiations to the regulation of the conservation of straddling fish stocks and highly migratory fish stocks? As mentioned above, one of the controversies related to Article 7, which introduced the so-called compatibility principle - that is, the compatibility of conservation and management measures within and outside areas of national jurisdiction (Article 7 paragraph 2). The Straddling Stocks Agreement emphasizes the

---

[101] *Id.*, at 223.

[102] Closing Statement by Ambassador S.N. Nandan, Fourth Session of the United Nations Conference on Straddling Stocks and Highly Migratory Fish Stocks, 26 August (1994).

[103] Unlike the Implementation Agreement to Part XI of LOS Convention, it is not necessary to be a party to UNCLOS in order to become a party to the Straddling Stock Agreement, but "there is clearly a close link between them" Davies and Redgwell, note 90, at 258-259.

duty of co-operation between coastal and fishing States with respect to straddling stocks, so that agreement may be reached upon necessary measures for the conservation of the stocks in the adjacent high seas (Article 7 paragraph 1). Such co-operation may be direct or may be effected through the co-operation procedures contained in the Agreement (Articles 8-16 (part III)). This duty to cooperate also extends to ensuring compatibility of conservation and management measures specified in Article 7 paragraph 2. That provision imposes an obligation to take into account measures adopted within the scope of national jurisdiction and an obligation to ensure that measures adopted on the high seas do not undermine the effectiveness of such measures (Article 7, paragraph 2a). Thus, to accommodate the objections expressed by Poland and Korea during the negotiations, the requirement that the measures taken on the high seas be no less stringent than national measures was deleted from Article 7 as it stands in the Straddling Stocks Agreement. Nonetheless, on balance, the interests of coastal States were accommodated to a higher degree than those of fishing States. According to Davies and Redgwell, "[f]urther evidence of the priority accorded [to] coastal State interests is found in the obligation to take into account the biological unity of the stocks (a clear application of an ecosystem approach)..."[104] (Article 7, paragraph 2b). According to the same Article, consideration must be given to the extent to which the stocks occur and are fished in areas under national jurisdiction (Article 7, paragraph 2 e and f). Other provisions stress further the duty to co-operate within the framework of the regional fishing organizations ("RFO"), which under the Straddling Stocks Agreement, play a crucial role in granting access to fishing.

The crux of all these provisions is to ensure that no party is exonerated from acting in accordance with the obligations under the Straddling Stock Agreement, nor is any party permitted to fish unilaterally and without restriction for straddling and highly migratory fish stocks without being a member of the relevant RFO, participating in the relevant regional arrangements, or agreeing to apply regional measures. The view has been expressed that

> [a] serious question remains whether these provisions are consistent with the freedom of fishing on the high seas, and the extent to which the Agreement's further elaborations of the duty to co-operate is reflected in customary international law on the point. Such an assessment may become pertinent for distant water fishing nations unhappy with the balance of rights and interests in the Agreement and searching for alternatives to participation therein.[105]

---

[104] Davies and Redgwell, note 90, at 263.
[105] *Id.*, at 265.

Compliance and enforcement were the most controversial subjects during the negotiations (see above). Although Article 19 of the Straddling Stocks Agreement bestows the main responsibility in relation to compliance and enforcement on the flag State, the role of coastal States is strongly defined. With the authorization of the flag State, coastal States may board and inspect a vessel on the high seas which is suspected of having been engaged in unauthorized fishing within an area under the jurisdiction of a coastal State (Article 20, paragraph 6). There must be reasonable grounds for that suspicion, and there is no absolute obligation on the flag State to grant permission. The flag State has an obligation to co-operate with the coastal State in taking appropriate enforcement action and speedily and fully investigate any such allegation of unauthorized fishing when so requested by a coastal State. Article 21 grants an extensive new right to coastal States which permits them to take enforcement action in relation to violations of RFO conservation and management measures on the high seas. A State party to the Agreement, as well as a member of a RFO, may enforce the conservation provisions of that RFO against a fishing vessel of another party to the Agreement even if that party is not a member of the RFO in question. Article 21 paragraph 1 gives a right to duly authorized inspectors of the inspecting State to board and inspect a fishing vessel flying the flag of another State party to the Straddling Stock Agreement, in order to ensure compliance with applicable RFO measures. Article 22 specifies the consequences of such an inspection which differ in relation to serious and non-serious violations. In the case of serious violations and in case involving lack of response from the flag State – that is, a failure by the flag State to take necessary investigatory and enforcement action – an inspecting State may retain its investigators on board to collect further evidence and may request the vessel to be escorted to the nearest port. Nonetheless, the flag State retains its investigatory and enforcement powers at any stage (Article 21 paragraph 12).

As far as port State enforcement powers are concerned, Article 23 paragraph 3 permits measures in relation to vessels that are voluntarily in a port. These powers may include inspection of gear and record books, and prohibition of landing and shipment of catch in cases in which it has been established that the catch has taken in a manner which undermines the effectiveness of sub-regional, regional or global conservation and management measures on the high seas. These provisions of the Straddling Stocks Agreement are modelled on Articles 218-220 and 226-228 of the 1982 LOS Convention in relation to port State powers in the field of environmental protection.

In conclusion, it may be said that the Straddling Stock Agreement is a victory for coastal States, but not a total defeat for fishing States. For example, in effect, the formulation of Article 7 of the Agreement accommodates the vision of coastal States but also "attempts to reduce or eliminate conflicts which may arise between measures taken within an EEZ and those which apply in the adjacent high seas area through strategy based on co-operation".[106] On the one hand, fulfillment of the interests of the coastal States in reality amounted to a restriction on freedom of fishing in the high seas, even though it has been done through international arrangements. On the other hand, the ambitions of States introducing unilateral management regulations (such as Canada) have been to some extent ameliorated by the Agreement. The introduction of innovative measures such as granting inspection rights to non-flag States on the high seas were a necessary, if not overdue, measure.[107]

4.3 The Baltic Sea Area

4.3.1 Introduction

There are numerous examples in the law of the sea that illustrate the influence of extra-legal factors on the negotiating process. One that may be mentioned is regional co-operation in the Baltic Sea area ("the Baltic region"). The Baltic region is a microcosm of continuous interaction between all actors (including the European Union) and all factors. For these reasons special and broader attention will be accorded to this case study of the negotiating process in the Baltic region.

4.3.2 The original conventions

During the 1970s, in which the two Baltic Sea Conventions were concluded – namely the Convention on Fishing and Conservation of the Living Resources in the Baltic Sea and the Belts ("the Gdansk Convention")[108] and the 1974 Convention on the Protection of the Marine Environment of the Baltic Sea ("the Helsinki Convention")[109] (collectively, "the Baltic Conventions"), the economic and political situation in this region was extremely diversified. Political factors were the most important contributing reasons for the lack of extensive legal regulation in the region. At the time of the conclusion of these Baltic Conventions, the coastal States were members of various economic and political organizations. The Federal Republic of Germany ("FRG") and Denmark were members of the

---

[106] Freestone and Makuch, note 90, at 28.

[107] *Id.*, at 50.

[108] See M. Fitzmaurice, "The Legal Regime of the Baltic Sea Fisheries", 29 *NILR* (1982), at 174-251.

[109] See M. Fitzmaurice, *International Legal Problems of the Environmental Protection of the Baltic Sea* (1992).

European Economic Community; the German Democratic Republic ("GDR"), Poland and the Soviet Union were members of the Council of Mutual Economic Assistance ("CMEA"), while Finland and Sweden belonged to the European Free Trade Association ("EFTA"). Furthermore, the Soviet Union, Poland, and the GDR were members of the Warsaw Pact, while the FRG and Denmark were members of NATO. The status of Finland was special in that, whilst not a member of CMEA, it had concluded an agreement in 1948 on co-operation with the Soviet Union; and in 1973, an agreement on co-operation with the CMEA.

The conclusion of the Helsinki Convention on protection of the Baltic Sea environment, as in the case of the Gdansk Convention, resulted from a relaxation of the political climate during the 1970s. The political situation in the Baltic region, in particular the position of the GDR, had been the major factor preventing the conclusion of regional arrangements involving all the States in the region ("the Baltic States"). The FRG was concerned to avoid the possible consequence that by signing a treaty with the GDR it would be regarded as having indirectly recognized the GDR itself. The conclusion of the Baltic Conventions was only made possible by the amelioration of the political climate in the 1970s, especially due to the establishment of "Ostpolitik" by the FRG, which marked the commencement of a new period of mutual relations among the Baltic States. The decisive events were the signing of the treaties between the Soviet Union and the FRG on 12 August 1970; between Poland and FRG on 7 December 1970; and between FRG and GDR on 21 December 1970.

This improved political climate ("détente") prompted the Polish Government to submit a proposal aimed at the conclusion of an international agreement on the protection of the living resources of the Baltic Sea and subsequently on the Protection of the Baltic Sea Environment. It may be stated categorically that only the political treaties between the FRG, the GDR, Poland and Russia enabled conclusion of the specific treaties on fisheries and environmental protection.

4.3.3 Amendment of the Helsinki Agreement

In contrast, the 1992 Convention on the Protection of Marine Environment of the Baltic Sea Area ("the Helsinki Convention") is an excellent example of how States negotiate a new agreement, having taken into consideration scientific developments and progress of knowledge in certain areas. It became obvious that the 1974 Convention (see above) was no longer adequate as a proper framework for the environmental protection of the Baltic Sea. In the words of the Swedish Minister for the Environment and Natural Resources, Mr. Olof Johansson:

> [t]he group, which prepared the new Helsinki Convention, has worked
> efficiently to bring the convention with annexes in line with the developments
> since 1974. I welcome the introduction in the convention of the precautionary
> principle as well as implementation of the concepts of best environmental
> practice and best available technology to reduce pollution. I see with
> satisfaction that the Convention covers nature conservation and biodiversity.
> One of the important novelties is the enlargement of the new convention to
> cover the coastal waters of the Baltic Sea.[110]

The 1992 Helsinki Convention conforms with all the exigencies of modern
approaches to environmental protection. It embodies the above-mentioned
"precautionary principle", the "polluter pays principle", the concepts of
"Best Environmental Technology" and "Best Environmental Practice",
environment impact assessment, information disclosure and notification on
pollution incidents. The provisions of the 1992 Helsinki Convention are
similar to those of the new 1992 Convention for the Protection of the
North-East Atlantic, which will replace the Paris and Oslo Conventions. At
the same time as the 1992 Convention was signed, the States-party signed a
Joint Comprehensive Environment Action Programme which identified
132 "hot spots", that is, the points in the Baltic Sea area which require
immediate attention.

The same strong political factors that played such an important role
during the time of the conclusion of the 1974 Convention were also present
in 1992. Three Baltic republics, Lithuania, Latvia and Estonia, became
parties to the new convention. The Diplomatic Conference served as a forum
for strong political statements. For example Mr. Elvades Vebra of Lithuania
said:

> [a]s you know, Lithuania was an independent country before World War 2,
> however, Soviet occupation in 1940 interrupted its normal development ... An
> alien totalitarian centralised management system ruined Lithuania's economy,
> devastated its environment and imposed on the Lithuanian people a *Homo
> Sovieticus* attitude towards all human values.[111]

Thus, the negotiation of environmental treaty gave States the opportunity to
make political statements that were only loosely linked with the subject-
matter at hand. However, the political factors that surrounded the conclusion
of the 1974 Convention were in fact different from those pertaining to the
conclusion of the 1992 Convention. In the case of the former, they were a
conditio sine qua non for the conclusion of the treaty, whilst in relation to
the latter, they were of secondary importance and in fact the conclusion of a
treaty became a source of political opportunity.

---

[110] Diplomatic Conference on the Protection of the Marine Environment of the Baltic Sea
Area, 9 April 1992, Helsinki.
[111] Statement of the Head of the Delegation of the Republic of Lithuania at the Diplomatic
Conference on the Protection of Marine Environment of the Baltic Sea Area, 9 April 1992.

4.3.4 Amendment of the Gdansk Convention

The Gdansk Convention provides a very good example of the influence of non-legal factors on the process of amendment of an existing treaty which was instigated by State actors. At the time of the signing of the Gdansk Convention, the waters under the jurisdiction of the Baltic States consisted of internal waters and territorial seas, and in the case of Poland, Sweden and Denmark also included exclusive fisheries zones up to 12 nautical miles. Thus, the only one multilateral convention in force between all the Baltic States was concluded before the extension of exclusive fisheries (economic) zones beyond the 12-mile limit. The "Final Act" relating to the Gdansk Convention anticipated the necessity of an accommodation of the working of the Convention, in particular of the International Baltic Sea Fisheries Commission ("IBSFC"), upon the extension of exclusive fisheries (economic) zones.

A basis for such an amendment was first put forward by Sweden in a memorandum ("the Memorandum") at the Third Session of the IBSFC in 1977. While confirming the necessity of continued co-operation amongst the Baltic States within the framework of the Gdansk Convention, the Memorandum proposed amendments of the Gdansk Convention to accommodate the imminent extension of exclusive fishing (or economic) zones. In particular, the Memorandum proposed the following amendments to the Gdansk Convention: recommendations related to the exclusive fisheries zones of the Baltic States should be taken only with the approval of interested States; a new system for the allocation of the Total Allowable Catch ("TAC") should be established for the extended zones; the IBSFC should fix TAC for the whole area of the Baltic Sea – the States having an obligation to conduct mutual consultations within the IBSFC, whilst themselves ultimately fixing their national quotas. In the case of an area in the Baltic Sea being claimed by more than one State as a result of extension of fisheries (economic) zones, an international agreement should be concluded, pending which the States concerned should refrain from exercising jurisdiction over the disputed area; should the potential catches in the extended fisheries zones exceed a State's harvesting capacity, other States' fishing vessels should be permitted to conduct fishing activities in that zone on the basis of bilateral agreements; there should be an annual session of the IBSFC instead of biannual sessions; there should be a shorter period to lodge an objection against its recommendation; and the "joint enforcement system" should be abolished and be replaced by an obligation to consult within the framework of the IBSFC on means of control over the implementation of the binding recommendations of the IBSFC.

Between 1977 and 1978, the anticipated extension of exclusive zones took place, making amendments to the Gdansk Convention necessary. Draft amendments to the Gdansk Convention, based on the Swedish proposal, were submitted for discussion. The main proposed amendments were as follows: States would acquire a "veto" over recommendations affecting their own fisheries; a State would be able, by notification to the IBSFC, to withdraw at any time its acceptance of any recommendation of the IBSFC which affected its own exclusive fisheries zone, such withdrawal becoming effective 90 days after notification; after a year had elapsed from entry into force of any recommendation, any State would be able to notify the IBSFC of termination of its acceptance of that recommendation, in which case the recommendation would cease to be binding on that State after 12 months from the notification; and a recommendation which ceased to be binding on one State could be renounced by any other State, and would cease to be binding on it days after notification thereof to the IBSFC. It was obvious that the proposed amendments would affect the Commission's independent law-making capacity and role would evolve into that of a co-ordinator.

Another factor that contributed to the Convention's amendment was the introduction of the EC common fisheries policy that affected individual participation of the then FRG and Denmark (see below). It should also be noted in this context that, as the EU has the sole competence to represent the Member States in the international fishery organisations, the 2004 accession countries (Poland, Latvia, Estonia and Lithuania) to the European Union, at the 30th session of IBSFC, are required to withdraw from the Convention.[112]

In 1982, a major Protocol[113] ("the Protocol") of amendments to the Gdansk Convention was concluded. These amendments were the result of the extension of exclusive fisheries (economic) zones and the introduction of the EC Common Fisheries Policy.

Some of the amendments to the Gdansk Convention resulted in changes to the system of the IBSFC opting-out procedure and generally in modified the functions of the IBSFC. The amendments shortened the period of notification by any party concerning the objections to the recommendation from 60 days to 30 days. Another change was the provision specifying the period of time after which a recommendation ceases to be binding on a contracting party, namely one year from the date of notice by that party of its termination of acceptance of the recommendation, provided such notice of termination had not been previously withdrawn (Article XI, paragraph 4(a) of the Protocol).

The amendments to the Gdansk Convention also resulted in changes to the Fisheries Rules. (The Fisheries Rules covered a range of matters including the standardization of information to be included in the fishing logs, gear regulation, closed seasons, fish size regulation, mesh size

---

[112] See www.ibsfc.org.
[113] The Protocol amending the Gdansk Convention was signed on 11 November 1982, OJ 1983, L 277, at 5, and entered into force on 10 February 1984.

regulation, by-catch regulation, and a special conservation regulation for salmon.) The IBSFC adopted new Fisheries Rules in 1984. Under the new Rules, the International Council for Exploration of the Sea ("ICES") was to continue to give advice as to the TAC, not for individual zones but for the whole of the Baltic Sea. For individual zones TAC was to be allocated by the IBSFC within the general quota submitted by ICES. Unfortunately, since the extension of the exclusive fisheries (economic) zones in the Baltic Sea, allocation is based on the individual needs of the respective States, rather than on biological data. In short, the TAC recommended for the Baltic States exceed the figures recommended by the ICES, and some of the fish species in the Baltic Sea have thereby become endangered.[114]

The extension of the EEZs in the Baltic region has resulted in the impairment of the effectiveness of the IBSFC. The most important factor, which diminished the effectiveness of the Commission, was the abolition of the Joint Enforcement System. Control over compliance with those recommendations of the IBSFC which have been accepted is now left to the States. This has proved to be a less than wholly successful solution, since States tend to overlook the necessity of long-term management based on scientific advice. The powers of the IBSFC suffered further impairment due to the introduction of the right of veto of each member in relation to recommendations concerning the area under its jurisdiction.

5. Inter-Governmental Organizations

In this section, the work and role of IGOs generally in the fields of international shipping and the protection of human rights will be discussed. See also section 5.2 below for a discussion on NGOs in context of IGOs.

5.1 The Law of the Sea: The International Maritime Organisation

The International Maritime Organization ("IMO")[115] is one of the main actors in the development of the law of the sea, both as a participant in negotiations and as an initiator of changes in an existing treaty. The status of IMO is defined in many articles of UNCLOS as "the competent international organization" in respect of setting rules and standards for the protection of the marine environment from vessel-source pollution and in connection with safety of navigation. According to the Convention, the States have "to conform to" "to give effect to" "to implement" "to take account of" various

---

[114] See www.ibsfc.org.
[115] Previously named the Inter-Governmental Maritime Consultative Organization (IMCO).

regulations and standards set by the "competent international organization" (namely, IMO). As Birnie observes, there is a variety of formulations which describe the law-making activity of IMO and which lead to some degree of confusion. Examples of such formulations include " 'the applicable international rules and standards', or 'generally accepted international standards', or 'generally accepted international regulations', ..., or 'applicable international regulations', or 'generally accepted international regulations', or 'global and regional rules, standards and recommended practices and procedures' ", etc.[116] IMO presently has in force about 27 Conventions with protocols and adopts various specific codes of practice and guidelines. It has 170 members and over 50 NGOs have observer status at the IMO.

According to Article 1 of the IMO Convention, IMO was set up to provide a machinery for co-operation for governments in the field of governmental regulation and practices relating to technical matters affecting shipping engaged in international trade. In addition, IMO was established to encourage the adoption of the highest possible standards in matters of maritime safety and efficiency of navigation, to encourage the removal of discriminatory action and unnecessary restrictions by governments affecting shipping concerns, and to provide for consideration by IMO of any matters concerning shipping, which may be referred to it by any organ or specialized agency of the United Nations, and to provide for exchange of information among governments on matters under consideration by IMO. According to Article 2, the Organization has a consultative and advisory character. The views were expressed that the actions of IMO influenced the scope of its activities. It has been argued despite its all-embracing character, IMO's main functions relate to questions of technical character (which enjoy the unanimous consent of its members). For this perspective, economic and commercial considerations, the general problems of the international law of the sea, as well as fishing and exploitation of the deep-seabed are of no concern to this organization.[117] This restrictive assessment of IMO's functions and its contribution to the general law of the sea is only partially true. For example, its participation in the development of the general marine environmental protection law is enormous and undisputed.

The law-making functions of IMO are extremely complicated and widespread. They include instruments of "soft law" and "hard law" character, although an attempt to draw a sharp distinction between these is

---

[116] P. Birnie, "The Status of Environmental 'Soft Law': Trends and examples with Special Focus on IMO Norms", in H. Ringbom (ed.), *Competing Norms in the Law of Marine Environmental Protection – Focus on Ship Safety and Pollution Prevention* (1997), 31-57, at 35-36.

[117] B.O. Okere, "The Technique of International Maritime Legislation", 30 *ICLQ* (1981), 513-536, at 514.

difficult.[118] The better approach is to distinguish them into treaty instruments and non-treaty instruments that relate to a plethora of forms, such as guidelines and the IMO codes. Although some non-binding instruments are regarded by IMO as of equal importance to treaties, and to be incorporated by States into their national legislation,[119] the focus here will be on IMO's role in the treaty-making process.

To this effect, the Maritime Safety Committee ("MSC"), decided to assist States in defining criteria, which would help to identify which instruments are mandatory and which were not. One of the problems is inconsistent wording in the Convention on Protection of Pollution from Ships ("MARPOL 73/78") and the SOLAS Conventions. A Special Working Group was established to assist deliberations and to draw up a list of relevant expressions. As a general rule, it was stated that the expressions such as "shall comply with"; "in accordance with"; "in compliance with"; "not inferior to" reflected mandatory character, whilst the expressions "taking into account"; "having regard to"; "based on" were indicative of recommendations only. According to the suggestions expressed by the Working Group,[120] in order to bestow mandatory character on certain acts, the procedure adopted in SOLAS should be used. Non-binding instruments must be referred to expressly in the text of the convention, regulation must be prescribed in the text of the convention, and the procedure for their amendment must follow the procedure for amendment of the convention. Regulations in the nature of recommendations should be listed in a footnote and their character should be clearly specified as non-binding.

Other IGOs also actively participate in negotiating treaties in context of the law of the sea. These IGOs concluded agreements on co-operation with the IMO. The total number is 36. Not all of them (as is the case with non-State actors, see below) participate to the same degree in the development of shipping conventions. The most active are: the International Hydrographic Organization ("IHO"), the Organization for Economic Co-operation and Development ("OECD"), the Commission of the European Union ("EU"),

---

[118] See Birnie, note 116, at 44-49.

[119] Birnie divides "international instruments establishing standards for world shipping adopted by IMO into two classes: [the first (and the more important of the two)] establishing technical standards and procedures on construction and operation of ships, and those promoting uniform rules and procedures concerning legal issues, which may take the form of conventions, or other binding treaty instruments incorporating technical regulations, and [(secondly)] non-binding instruments regarded by IMO as of equal importance for states to incorporate into their national legislation."; the first category is further classified by the same author into "'technical' instruments and treaties on legal issues", id., at 44-45.

[120] IMO Doc. MSC 66/WP2, 10 May 1966; Consideration and Adoption of Amendments to Mandatory Instruments; Report of the drafting group of uniform wording for referencing IMO instruments, IMO Doc. MSC66/WP 10/Add. 4 June 1966. MSC Session, Agenda Item 3. The proposal will be discussed at the MSC's 67th Session.

the International Oil Pollution Compensation Fund ("1971 Fund"), the Commission established by the Convention for the Prevention of Marine Pollution by Dumping from Ships and Aircraft ("Oslo Commission"), the Commission established by the Convention for the Prevention of Marine Pollution from Land ("Paris Commission"), the Baltic Marine Environment Protection Commission ("Helsinki Commission"), and the International Oil Pollution Compensation Fund ("1992 Fund").

IMO provides an excellent example of the interaction between all three types of actors – States, IGOs and NGOs – because IMO demonstrates perfect co-operation between them. Each and every convention has been drafted by IMO as a result of very close mutual co-operation. This co-operation is manifested in two ways – by written submission presented before the diplomatic conference and by way of participation in diplomatic conferences. There are very few organizations that could match IMO in its role of actively shaping and influencing the treaty-making process among States.

IMO's role of this is widely recognized and appreciated. For example, Mr. Müller of Switzerland, the Chairman of the Committee as a Whole II during the negotiations of the 1989 International Convention on Civil Liability for Oil Pollution Damage ("CLC") noted that the Committee which was instructed to draft the CLC was able to do so only as a result of the efforts made by IMO (IMCO) during the previous two years. The Committee worked on the basis of the draft prepared by the Legal Committee of IMO. The text of the proposal contained several alternatives. The Chairman acknowledged that the completion of the draft was possible only due to the effort of the Secretariat and its Executive Secretary, Mr. Mensah.[121]

5.2 IGOs and NGOs in the Field of Human Rights

It cannot be forgotten that the work of IGOs often involves the participation of NGOs, however (in)extensive that participation may be in particular cases. Women's NGOs – such as the Women's International League for Peace and Freedom ("WILPF"), the International Council for Women, the International Federation of Business and Professional Women, and the World Union of Catholic Women's Organizations – participated in drafting of the two 1966 Covenants on Human Rights (Civil and Political Rights; and Economic, Social and Cultural Rights) (collectively the "Human Rights Covenants"). The WILPF opposed the division of rights into two instruments, as well as the reiteration in Article 3 of both Covenants of the

---

[121] Inter-governmental Maritime Organization, Official Records of the International Legal Conference on Marine Pollution Damage, 1969, at 99.

non-discrimination guarantee in the Universal Declaration of Human Rights. According to this NGO, the inclusion of Article 3 (which accords equal enjoyment of rights for men and women) would serve no purpose as the Universal Declaration already accorded such right, and was preferable to await the result of the implementation of those rights in the Universal Declaration.[122]

In context of an IGO influencing treaty-making, the Commission on the Status of Women ("CSW"), established by the UN Economic and Social Council in 1946,[123] has succeeded in influencing the formulation of Article 3 of both Covenants (namely, explicit reference to sexual equality) and in the formulation of Article 23 of the Covenant on Civil and Political Rights which guarantees equality of rights within the family, reflecting a request by CSW that this Article should be based on Article 16 the Universal Declaration.

During the UN's Women's Decade, which ended in 1985 in Nairobi, the 1979 Convention on the Elimination of All Forms of Discrimination against Women ("the Women's Convention") was concluded. The basis of the Convention was the 1967 Declaration on Elimination of Discrimination against Women. The drafting of the Convention was postulated by the CSW and was later approved by the resolution of the Mexico Conference. It was the CSW which drafted the Women's Convention – and, in fact, presented a working paper with four draft Conventions. The first draft was based on replies from governments and on a report of the original working group established by the CSW. The remaining drafts were submitted by Benin, Indonesia, and the All African Women's Conference (an NGO). A draft was presented by Belgium. The draft was prepared by the CSW, with some additions in the light of the Belgian draft, formed the basis of the discussion. By the end of 1976, the Drafting Committee had completed its task, and further work was continued within the Working Group of the Whole of the General Assembly's Third Committee. Within this body, drafting was done by States. The Women's Convention was submitted to signature on 1 March 1980, and came into force on 3 September 1981.

---

[122] See also section 6.2 below J. Connors, "NGOs and the Human Rights of Women at the United Nations", in P. Willetts (ed.), note 46, 147-180. Generally on various forms of participation of NGOs in the field of human rights see C.M. Eya Nchama, "The role of non-governmental organizations in the promotion and protection of human rights", 9 *Human Rights Bulletin* (1991), at 50-83. The above author gives for example an exhaustive account of the negotiations leading to the conclusion of the 1951 Convention On the Status of Refugees and Stateless Persons. During the negotiations of this Convention several NGOs participated such as the World Jewish Congress; the International Union for Child Welfare; the League of Red Cross Societies. They all submitted comments on almost all aspects of the question of refugees (at 75-78).

[123] <http://www.un.org/Conferences/Women/PubInfo/Status/Scrn5.htm>.

6. NGOs and Associations[124]

This section is divided into three distinct case studies dealing with the participation of NGOs and associations in the making and shaping of treaty norms in the fields of (1) environmental law; (2) human rights protection; and (3) the international regulation of the shipping industry.

6.1 Environmental Protection

In international environmental law, especially after the 1980s, the leading environmental NGOs, such as the World Wildlife Fund ("WWF") and the Union for Conservation of Nature ("IUCN") were joined by other NGOs in an attempt to change political attitudes (domestic, regional or international), and to disseminate research findings. It is undisputed that NGOs help ensure the legitimacy and the quality of decision-making.[125] One of the most important examples of their role in treaty forming and development is their participation in the International Whaling Commission or in respect of the London Convention. In addition, NGOs "of genuinely international character" played a crucial role during the 1992 Earth Summit in Rio de Janeiro (the "Rio Conference"). The Secretary-General of the United Nations said that these organizations were directly involved with the subject-matter of the Rio Conference.[126] The IUCN was involved in the immediate preparation for Rio in 1992 and, even more significantly, it assisted in drafting Agenda 21, one of the least binding of the documents adopted at Rio. NGOs contributed, in particular, to sections on biodiversity; forests; oceans and seas; population and resources; environmental education; and environmental law. NGOs influenced negotiations both directly and indirectly, through networking.[127] It was said that networking was a key ingredient of implementation (at the national level) of the Rio Conference instruments. It has been said elsewhere that:

> … NGOs appear to have influenced global environmental politics in two important ways. The first relates to their contribution to the building up of an accessible, international knowledge base which, … is a prerequisite for taking appropriate internationally agreed action. The second relates to their ability to

---

[124] On the history of NGOs, see S. Charnowitz, note 47, at 183-286. See also ECOLOGIC/FIELD Report, note 34, generally.

[125] See K. Stairs and P. Taylor, "Non-Governmental Organizations and the Legal Protection of the Oceans: A Case Study", in A. Hurrell and B. Kingsbury (eds.), *The International Politics of the Environment: actors, interests, and institutionst* (1992), at 134.

[126] UN Doc. A/Conf.48/PC.11.

[127] S. Morphet, "NGOs and the Environment", in Willetts, note 46, at 116-146.

influence major UN bodies (all run by governments) or governments separately to take appropriate actions.[128]

The role of NGOs is not, however, absolutely undisputed. It may be noted that (for example) at the Rio Conference, the US government did not allow the representatives of NGOs to participate directly in negotiations.[129] The view was taken that NGOs educate the governmental delegations and provide a link between them.

NGOs also participate in numerous other treaty negotiations especially in the fields of human rights (see below) and the environment. It would be impossible to describe NGOs involvement in all these instances; however, a few examples will be sufficient to illustrate the point.

6.1.1 The Straddling Stocks Convention

The first example pertains to the participation of the NGOs in the negotiations leading to the Straddling Stocks Agreement (see above). The participation of NGOs in these negotiations was pronounced, due to the rules of procedure adopted at the organizational session.[130] Greenpeace International ("Greenpeace") stressed its presence by bringing one of its Rainbow Warrior vessels onto the East River in New York outside the conference room and by distributing parts of illegal driftnets seized in the Mediterranean. More substantively, Greenpeace and other main NGOs brought technical expertise to the discussion and contributed to media awareness of the issues under discussion. NGOs participated in the negotiations in their own right and as members of governmental organizations. The impact of NGOs on negotiations was even more meaningful since they attempted to speak with one voice. Sometimes, however, NGOs were not admitted to informal meetings and had to glean information from official delegations. Nonetheless, NGOs played a crucial rule in these negotiations and "ensured that 'real' issues and problems were dealt with, rather than mere abstractions".[131]

6.1.2 The Helsinki Convention

The 1992 Helsinki Convention also serves as an illustration of the increasing role of NGOs. During the Diplomatic Conference held in Helsinki, 5-6 April

---

[128] *Id.*, at 141.
[129] P. Waak, "Shaping a Sustainable Planet: The Role of Non-governmental Organisations", 6:2 *Colo. .I. Int't Envtl'L.& Pol'y* (1995), at 353.
[130] For an account of NGO participation, see A.C. de Fontaubert, "The Politics of the United Nations Conference on Straddling Fish Stocks and Highly Migratory Fish Stocks", 29 *Ocean and Coastal Management* (1995), Special Issue, at 79-91.
[131] *Id.*, at 83.

1992, representatives of 23 NGOs from Baltic Sea countries were present. They were grouped in the Coalition for a "Clean Baltic" ("the Coalition"). At that stage, the participation, was limited to commenting on the text of the new Convention. The Coalition made pronouncements on the future role of NGOs in the environmental protection of the Baltic region. It said:

> [t]he role of NGOs and grass root activities should be given higher priority in the Joint Programme ... The possible future contribution in the structures responsible for the implementation of actual projects should be recognized ... The role of local communities, scientists and authorities cannot be enough emphasized, because implementation will not be possible without active local participation.[132]

Thus, strictly speaking, NGOs did not play a role in negotiating the 1992 Helsinki Convention or the Joint Action Programme (programme for the Implementation of the Helsinki Convention). Nevertheless, the participation of NGOs described above made possible their future active participation in developing the provisions of the 1992 Helsinki Convention. For example, HELCOM has decided to grant observer status to several NGOs.[133] The Commission further decided to apply the same rules for co-operation with all observer organizations, intergovernmental and non-governmental.

However, NGOs have come to play a more active role than just that of observers. Recently, they started to participate in the implementation of HELCOM Programmes, such as the HELCOM Programme Implementation Force. This Programme was particularly designed to implement the Joint Action Programme (see above). This programme consists of several elements which are headed by a "lead-party". NGOs are the lead parties for many of these programme elements, such as those on institutional strengthening and human resource development (management programmes for coastal lagoons and wetlands (WWF); public awareness and environmental education (the Coalition).

The question arises whether the participation of NGOs (as described above) had any influence on the development of the Helsinki Convention. Certainly, they had at least an indirect effect resulting (for example) in amendments to the Annexes attached to the Convention. (According to Article 29 of the 1992 Helsinki Convention, the Annexes are an integral part of the Convention.) Those annexes which deal with different sources of pollution are subject to a periodical review process. NGOs accredited to the Helsinki Convention have very well defined views on the problems of

---

[132] NGO Statement on the Protection of the Environment of the Baltic Sea Region, Diplomatic Conference, Helsinki, 5-6 April 1992.
[133] For example, the International Council for Local Environmental Initiatives (ICLEI); Union for the Baltic Cities (UBC); EUROCHLOR; European Union for Coastal Conservation (EUCC); WWF.

environmental protection of the Baltic Sea (which do not always correspond with the views of the parties to the Convention). NGOs may influence States to propose amendments to the Annexes, for example during the meetings of HELCOM, or through participation in the Joint Implementation Programme.

6.1.3 The Climate Change Convention

NGOs initially played a very significant role in the 1992 Framework Convention on Climate Change (the "Climate Change Convention"). The Climate Change Convention expressly mentions non-State actors assisting the Conference of the Parties ("COP") (Article 7 paragraphs 2-1 and 6).[134] NGOs that participated in meetings of the Conference of the Parties (COP) of the Climate Change Convention may be grouped in three categories: environmental NGOs; business corporations; and local communities. The Climate Change Convention refers to NGOs in Articles 4 paragraph 2 (i), & paragraphs 2 (1) and (6).

There were numerous non-State actors accredited to the COP of the Climate Change Convention. There are networks of particular types of non-State actors to assist them in communicating with one another. For example, the environmental NGOs' network was the Climate Action Network; the business corporations' network was the Global Climate Coalition; and the local communities' network was the International Council for Local Environmental Institutions. As Alkoby observes, that marked presence of business entities was a special feature of the Climate Change Convention negotiations.[135] At the time leading to the Kyoto negotiations, Alkoby notes that many of the business NGOs "used the same methods of action in their attempts first to thwart the chances of reaching an agreement and then to

---

[134] It states "the Conference of the Parties to this end shall ... seek and utilise, where appropriate, the services and cooperation of, and information provided by, competent international organisations and intergovernmental and non-governmental bodies" (Article 7 paragraph 2-1); "The United Nations, its specialised agencies and the International Atomic Energy Agency, as well as any State member thereof or observers thereto not Party to the Convention, may be represented at sessions of the Conference of the parties as observers. Any body or agency, whether national or international, governmental or non-governmental, which is qualified in matters covered by the Convention, and which has informed the secretariat of its wish to be represented at a session of the Conference of the Parties as an observer, may be so admitted unless at least one-third of the Parties present object. The admission and participation is subject to the rules of procedure adopted by the Conference of the Parties". See on the subject: D. Tolbert, "Global Climate Change and the Role of International Non-Governmental Organisations", in R. Churchill and D. Freestone (eds.), *International Law and Global Climate Change* (1991), at 95; D. Wirth, "Public Participation in International Processes: Environmental Case Studies at the National and International Levels", 7 *Colo.J.Intl'lEnvtl.L.& Pol'y* (1996), 1; see also Alkoby, note 7, at 36-43.

[135] *Id.*, at 37.

influence the form and content of the commitments."[136] He notes that the business community was grouped in three groupings: "grey" (focused on the economic impacts of the agreement); the "light green" (consisting of renewable energies, cogeneration, natural gas and other energy efficient industries); and the "green" (representing insurance companies – related to the progressive industry forces on the issues of climate change). The interaction with the business community remains informal. He further states that it was the first time that the successful implementation of a treaty is dependent upon the participation of non-State actors. He identifies "two related but distinct functions";[137] one is a potential participation of business enterprises (and other NGOs) in "the Kyoto Protocol's market-based mechanisms and the disputes arising from these mechanisms. The second is the possible function of NGOs as monitors of state obligations under the agreement".[138]

However, wide participation of non-State actors in the COP has not guaranteed them as much influence on treaty-forming as in the case of the IMO (see below). Most recently, the participation of non-State actors in the work of COP has been restricted to presenting their views from the floor. Non-State actors, in their respective groupings, had to be allocated slots to take the floor. Since 1995, in order not to disrupt the proceedings, non-State actors are not permitted to approach the delegates during the sessions and may only distribute materials. Overall, the extent of their participation is left to the discretion of the chairman. Some delegations include members of the environmental NGOs. These members present to other members of the delegation (who represent the government) the views of NGOs on matters under discussion.

The influence of NGOs on the Climate Change Convention is, therefore, indirect and limited. Some NGOs assist States in preparing their national "in-depth" reports and share their technical expertise with governments. They also provide independent comments on the data submitted by governments. For example, the Global Industrial and Social Progress Research Institute ("GISPRI"), which is an environmental NGO, has participated in many meeting of the COP and subsidiary bodies and assisted the Japanese delegation in those meetings. The same body has been organizing the research committee on "Joint Implementation" ("JI") to study criteria for JI for the purpose of giving advice to the Japanese Government. GISPRI published a preliminary Report results of were reflected in the Japan Programme for Activities Implemented Jointly under the Pilot Phase. GISPRI worked as a Technical Unit of the IPPC WG 2 Sub-group 2. In

---

[136] *Id.*
[137] *Id.*, at 38.
[138] *Id.*, at 38-39.

connection with the work of the COP, GISPRI will be one of the core groups of the AD Japan Forum. It will also continue the activities of the research committee on "joint implementation" to study international criteria pertinent to JI. GISPRI will conduct studies on other climate change related areas such as trade and the environment, possible technology transfer in Asia and possible research and development into mitigation technologies. GISPRI will also work with the Japanese Government to prepare and assess national communications, especially in regard to policy measures.

On the other hand, the NGO Resource Analysis, a corporate body, was assigned to a project by the Government of the Netherlands to formulate country studies on climate change in Bangladesh, Bolivia, Costa Rica, Ecuador, Ghana, Senegal, and Surinam. It is involved in numerous projects in the field of climate change including: brainstorming sessions on the implementation of the UN Framework Convention on Climate Change in Central and Eastern Europe; developing climate policy in Hungary; policy analysis and development support of the Netherlands Government Climate Change Group (1989-1993); the development of national implementation strategies in co-operation with the Ministry of Housing Spatial Planning and the Environment.

As mentioned above, some of these NGOs promote research in climate change by sharing their expertise. An example of such an NGO is "START". This is a system of interconnected regional research networks. The fundamental purpose of this system of networked regional research centres is to promote regional research through training and fellowship programmes, to encourage indigenous scientific capacity to engage in focused research on critical regional environmental issues of global importance.

In general, it may be said that due to recent developments (see above), the NGOs accredited to the Climate Change Convention, although high in numbers, do not play a very significant role in its shaping. The reasons are twofold – first, the role of the NGOs was deliberately limited; in addition, some NGOs are merely of a technical, consultative type (such as START). Due to their nature, these NGOs focus on assistance in technological matters, rather than on active participation in the treaty-forming process. The most common types of such NGOs are those that assist in the preparation of national communications. This activity may have some effect on the future shape of a treaty; nonetheless the link is rather tenuous.

6.1.4 Some Conclusions

In fact, the only way in which these organizations appear to actively influence the text of the Convention is through statements made during the sessions, distribution of materials, through informal lobbying and membership in official State delegations. The latter form of active participation in the treaty-making process seems to be the most effective, since in the end the final treaty product depends on the political will of States.

6.2 Human Rights

6.2.1 The Women's Convention

As mentioned in above section 5.2, NGOs often participate in the activities of IGOs. However, it may be said that the womens' rights NGOs have concentrated their efforts on the work of the Commission on the Status of Women ("CSW"). About 30 womens' rights NGOs with consultative status, together with women's organizations without such status, participated on a regular basis in the work of the CSW. According to Connors, the "[d]rafting of the Convention was, by and large, the work of the Member States, although established non-governmental organisations dedicated to issues of women contributed".[139]

Another NGO involved in the drafting of the Women's Convention was the International Confederation of Free Trade Unions ("ICFTRU"). Article 11 of the Convention the work of women was partly drafted by the ICFTRU. The ICFTRU opposed too swift a revision of the ILO Convention concerning night work, expressing its unease as to the application of standards protecting women in the Women's Convention which, it was felt, disregarded the maternal function of women. The ILO asserted that the issues relating to pensions, retirement, and maternity protection belong to its sphere of regulation.

In 1982, in accordance with Article 17 of the Women's Convention, the Committee on the Elimination of Discrimination against Women ("CEDAW") was elected. Unlike the 1989 Convention on the Rights of the Child ("The Rights of the Child Convention"), the Women's Convention did not establish a system whereby NGOs would monitor and would supply information as to the State's national implementation of provisions of the Convention. At present, however, CEDAW is engaged in a programme of examining individual articles of the Convention or themes which have bearing on the whole Convention. "This work forms the basis of further general examination of the States parties' reports and input for the secretariat, specialized agencies and other UN organizations, as well as NGOs".[140] The preliminary background papers on issues selected by the

---

[139] Note 126, at 160-161. The organizations were: The Council of Social Democrat Women, the International Federation of University Women, the World Young Women Christian Association, the International Planned Parenthood Federation and the All African Women's Conference.
[140] *Id.*, at 165.

Committee is prepared in consultations, *inter alia,* with NGOs and submitted for comments. This procedure gives an opportunity for NGOs to be involved in the implementation of the Convention.

It must be stressed that the drafting of the Declaration against Discrimination (the "Discrimination Declaration"), which was the basis for the Women's Convention, involved active participation of women's NGOs. Governments, specialized agencies of the UN, and NGOs were *equally* invited to submit comments and proposals on the text of the Declaration. The drafting of the Declaration was undertaken on a basis of a memorandum by the CSW, which was prepared from replies from 34 governments, 15 NGOs and four specialized agencies. NGOs, unlike States, were unified in their responses that a declaration would be particularly useful in highlighting world-wide discrimination against women. They suggested that the concerns of the declaration should encompass family and criminal law, discrimination against single women and female heads of household, prostitution, employment and education.[141] Along with the governments, 22 NGOs participated actively in the drafting of the Discrimination Declaration. The final article summoned women's organizations to initiate a campaign to inform women and men about the principles of the Declaration and those on women's equality in the UN Charter and the Universal Declaration. The Article called on governments, individuals and NGOs to promote implementation of the above-mentioned principles. The CSW monitored the implementation of the Declaration. The national reports were submitted by States, specialized agencies and NGOs. However, not many reports were submitted (14 NGOs submitted reports).

6.2.2 Convention on the Rights of the Child

Human rights NGOs also played a crucial role in the drafting of the Rights of the Child Convention.[142] The Convention in question was, in one view, the result of the activities of Save the Children Union ("SCIU"), an NGO. The 1924 Declaration of Geneva by the SCIU inspired the United Nations to issue a Declaration of the Rights of a Child in 1959. In honour of the twentieth anniversary of this Declaration, 1979 was proclaimed by the United Nations as the Year of the Child, the same time the General Assembly of the United Nations authorized the Commission on Human Rights (the "Human Rights Commission") to draft a convention on children's rights.

---

[141] *Id.,* at 156.

[142] For extensive treatment, see: G. Van Bueren, *The International Law on the Rights of the Child* (1995); see also: Yo Kubota, "The Protection of Children's Rights and the United Nations", 58 *Nordic Journal of International Law* (1994), 7-23; M. Longford, "NGOs and the Rights of the Child", in P. Willetts, note 46, 214-240.

The Commission set up a Working Group in 1979. As of 1981, NGOs that had earned consultative status with ECOSOC were listed as present in its attendance of Human Rights Commission records each year. The early years were marked, however, by the lack of sufficient organization and the lack of a joint approach on the part of NGOs. In the first live years of the negotiations, the influence of NGOs was not as significant as in later years, when the approach by NGOs became more structured. NGOs tended to make statements that were emotional "whereas [as it has been put] they needed to be more carefully prepared".[143] Forty-one NGOs attended one or more of the meetings on the Working Group (five were classed in the first category; 27 in the second and nine were on the Roster). This period of drafting was nonetheless characterized by the inability of NGOs to convey their views.

The situation changed with the adoption of the common stand. About ten NGOs presented a joint paper, which commented on Articles of the Polish draft convention proposal. The crucial year was 1983 when 23 NGOs formed an alliance-based NGO Ad Hoc Group on the Drafting of the Convention on the Rights of the Child (the "NGO Group"). This Group published a Report on Informal Consultations Among Non-Governmental Organizations (the "NGO Group Report"). This group elected Defence for Children International ("DCI") to act as their Secretariat. DCI is an international organization "which is both non-confessional and non-political".[144] The NGO Group continued their active participation throughout other sessions of the Working Group and continued to submit reports. These reports focused either on the possible alterations of the Draft Articles or presented drafts of new articles. The NGOs were mainly involved in the drafting of articles concerning substantive matters. The year 1984 was marked by the emergence of NGOs as an active and positive force in the Working Group. According to Cantwell, NGO participation in the drafting of this Convention was "quite unprecedented in degree and particularly useful and constructive."[145] The NGO Group identified about fifteen articles of the Convention for which they were primarily responsible, a similar number in formulation of which they had a substantial impact and two articles in relation to which NGO proposals were used for the Working Group as a basic text. NGOs did not succeed, however, in convincing governments on the participation of children aged 15-17 in armed conflicts (Article 38 of the Convention).

Of interest (from the point of view of treaty-making) are the reasons listed by Cantwell as to why NGOs were so effective in relation to the Rights of the Child Convention. Their reasons are as follows: the members

---

[143] N. Cantwell, "Non-governmental Organizations and the United Nations Convention on the Right of the Child", 9 *Human Rights Bulletin* (1991), at 17.
[144] Longford, note 142, at 222.
[145] *Supra* note 143, at 222.

of the NGOs groups were often better briefed on children's matters than the governmental representatives; a constructive, even friendly, relationship existed within the NGO community; the representatives of NGOs became skilled negotiators, familiar with UN practice, and thereby formed a very effective group; the establishment of the Secretariat became a focal point for governments enabling them to receive information on NGOs; UNICEF assisted members of NGOs to make the most of social events to meet representatives of governments and the Working Group Chairman; and finally, the amicable atmosphere within the Working Group helped drafting.[146]

The reasons for the successful participation of NGOs in the Right of a Child Convention are enumerated below. Cohen[147] suggests that in relation to the NGO Group working on the Rights of the Child Convention, three typical models of individual NGO activities may be distinguished: activities in which an individual NGO's interests were not supported by the Group; activities in which an individual NGO's interest extended beyond that of the Group; and activities in relation to which outside individual NGOs came to the NGO Group for support and assistance.

According to Longford,[148] the attitudes of NGOs and national groups during the discussion in the Working Group "were fairly predictable": Eastern bloc States were more enthusiastic about economic than political rights, while the United States was not a proponent of any right which may be construed to support the notion of a welfare state; Roman Catholic States supported the rights of the unborn child; Islamic States rejected anything which did not conform to Islamic religious laws; and developing States stressed their economic problems. In particular, the latter issue influenced the formulation of Article 4 of the Convention (the parties to the Convention will undertake measures "with regard to economic, social and cultural rights ... to the maximum extent of their available resources").

It must be stressed that NGO influence on the Convention was enormous, and none of what has been said should be construed (too) negatively. The parts of the Convention owing to NGO efforts include several articles modifying the original Polish draft, and the Convention also contains a set of articles which owe their existence purely to NGO initiatives. The latter include protection of the child against sexual and other exploitation, traffic, torture, and armed conflicts. One of the most significant achievements was the formulation of the concept of juvenile criminal justice, which confirmed all the major criminal justice guarantees included in the Covenant of Civil and Political Rights as being applicable as well to children. During the

---

[146] *Id.*, at 224-225.
[147] C.P. Cohen, "The Role of Non-governmental Organizations in Drafting of the Convention on the Rights of the Child", 12 *HRQ* (1990), 137-147, at 141-142.
[148] Longford, note 142, at 226.

period of the drafting of the Convention, NGOs – both as a group and individually – influenced the representatives of States by meetings within the Working Group and outside it. Nonetheless, as has been said, not all NGO initiatives met with success. Examples include proposals on the rights of illegitimate children, as well as an attempt to raise the minimum age of children participating in an armed combat from fifteen to eighteen, were unsuccessful.[149]

Notwithstanding some failures suffered by NGOs during the drafting stage of the Convention, it may be assessed that "[t]here is agreement, however, in governmental and non-governmental circles, that the contribution of the NGO community to the drafting and promotion of the Convention on the Rights of the Child has broken significant new ground."[150] Moreover, the whole drafting process was a harmonious one. In the words of Javier Perez de Cuellar:

> [t]he drafting of the Convention was not an easy task. In the years since the Declaration of the Rights of the Child was adopted, many perceptions have changed and many concerns evolved, and the Convention has had to he shaped accordingly. The process of its drafting was a model of how our organisation can and should strive to achieve common goals. Unproductive political confrontations were set aside while delegates from countries with different social and economic systems, representing the various cultural, ethical and religious approaches to life, worked together with non-governmental organisation in a spirit of harmony and mutual respect and the best interests of the child as their paramount objective.[151]

6.2.3 Shipping

There are 54 NGOs with consultative status at IMO. In order to be granted this status, organizations must complete a questionnaire in which they state their interest in the purposes of IMO and the manner in which they may be of assistance to IMO's work. The IMO Council adopts the decision to grant consultative status on the basis of a recommendation by any of the Committees. Non-State actors participating in the work of IMO are subject to a periodical review process. Those who fail to participate in the work of the organization may be deprived of such consultative status by the decision of the Council taken upon the recommendation of one of the Committees. The accredited non-State actors enjoy the possibility of participating in the sessions of the IMO Assembly. They are allowed to take the floor – following the States and IGOs – and may express their opinions on the matters under consideration. On the request of IMO they prepare drafts of

---

[149] *Id.*, at 214-240.
[150] Cantwell, note 143, at 16.
[151] Cited in Longford, note 142, at 229-230.

conventions, such as in the case of the 1989 Convention on the International Law of Salvage ("Salvage Convention").[152] The Rules of Procedure of the International Conference on Liability and Compensation for Damage in Connection with the Carriage of Certain Substances by Sea, the International Conference on the Revision of the 1969 Civil Liability Convention, and the 1971 Fund Convention specify that the observers from NGOs invited to the Conference may, upon the invitation of the President or the Chairman of the Conference, take part without vote in the deliberations of all the bodies of the Conference.

NGOs participating in the work of IMO form a very varied group consisting of such diverse actors as Greenpeace and the International Union of Marine Insurance ("IUMI"). Not all of them are equally active. Among those with significant presence in the work of the IMO may be mentioned the following: the International Chamber of Shipping ("ICS"), the International Union of Marine Insurers ("IUMI"), the International Confederation of Free Trade Unions ("ICFTU"), the International Maritime Committee ("IMC"), the International Association of Classification Societies ("IACS"), the European Council of Chemical Manufacturers' Federation ("CEFIC"), Friends of the Earth International ("FOEI"); the International Salvage Union ("ISU"), the International Association of Independent Tanker Owners ("INTERTANKO"), the International Group of P & I Associations ("P & I"); the International Tanker Owners' Pollution Federation ITD ("ITOPF"), the Advisory Committee on the Protection of the Sea ("ACOPS"), the Society of International Gas Tankers and Terminal Operators Limited ("SIGTTO"), Greenpeace International, the International Association of Dry Cargo Shipowners ("INTERCARGO"). These non-State actors exercise a considerable degree of influence on the text of a treaty – by producing draft texts, and by participating in negotiations.

An example of the first means of influence is the International Salvage Convention, a working draft of which was presented by the International Maritime Committee ("IMC"). The Salvage Convention is a good example how pressure from bodies other than the IMO resulted in reform of the law of salvage. The main groups that consistently exerted pressure for a change in salvage law are coastal States (with an interest in protection of coastal environment) and salvors (with and interest in increasing rewards for their services). The Salvage Convention resulted from the dissatisfaction of salvors with traditional principles of salvage. These principles have been codified in the 1910 Convention for the Unification of Certain Rules of Law Relating to Assistance and Salvage at Sea (the "Brussels Convention").)[153] The principles contained the Brussels Convention were inadequate to

---

[152] C. Redgwell, "The Greening of Salvage Law", 14 *Marine Policy* (1990), at 142-150.
[153] Text in C. Parry, *The Consolidated Treaty Series* (1983), Vol. 212, at 178.

accommodate changed circumstances. In particular, "salvors were confronted with the double hurdle of the 'no cure, no pay' principle and potential interference of the coastal State to protect its coastal environment".[154] According to Redgwell, there were additional factors that prompted salvors to exert pressure for the conclusion of a new international instrument. These additional factors were the reduction of salvage reward due to a growing tendency to "write off" the damaged vessel, the increase in salvors' costs due to advances of technology and additional costs resulting from failure to avert or minimize pollution damage. Redgwell also points out that all these factors resulted in three events – changes to Lloyd's Standard Form; the 1981 International Maritime Comity Draft Convention; and the 1989 IMO Convention on the Law of Salvage.

The role of the IMC was of the utmost importance in influencing the legal form of the 1989 Convention. The IMC took under consideration the modified Lloyd's Open Forum ("LOF80") and brought the provisions of the Draft in line with it. The IMC established an international subcommittee to prepare a draft convention that was discussed at the 1981 Montreal Conference. The draft convention received an approval of 31 out of 32 national maritime law associations present. This Draft formed the basis the 1989 Salvage Convention. The final text is a compromise between salvors, insurers, shipowners and coastal States. It must be stressed that the role of the IMO was that of a moderator between all these groups.

7. The European Union

7.1 Introduction

The status of the European Union ("EU") as an actor in the treaty-making process, whether as a negotiator or a factor instigating changes to the text of an existing treaty, is a formidable issue for any inquiry. It exceeds the framework of this chapter and is, in any case, already the subject of many learned studies.[155] This chapter will only outline the possible legal issues

---

[154] Redgwell, note 152, at 144.

[155] See, for example, M. Cremona, "The Doctrine of Exclusivity and the Position of Mixed Agreements in the External Relations of the European Community", 15 *European Law Review* (1990), at 393-428; D. O'Keefe and P. Twomey (eds.), *Legal Issues of Maastricht Treaty* (1994), in particular: M. Cremona, "The Common Foreign and Security Policy of the European Union and the External Relations Power of the European Community", at 247-258; N. Emiliou, "The Allocation of Competence between the EC and its Member States in the Sphere of External Relations", in N. Emiliou and D. O'Keefe (eds.), *The European Union and World Trade Law, After GATT Uruguay Round* (1996), at 31; S. Weatherill, "Beyond Pre-Emption? Shared Competence and Constitutional Change in the European Community?", in

relating to the EU's influence in treaty-making. Two case studies (dealing with fisheries and environmental protection) will be presented to illustrate some of the problems that arise.

The EU may present itself as a legal or a political entity. In both these forms, it may exert a direct or an indirect influence on the treaty-making process. For example, as a legal entity, the EU is a party (exclusively or together with its Member States) to international agreements such as those on fisheries or on environmental protection. This EU's dual character presents considerable difficulties in comprehending the legal aspects of its nature and activities. The present chapter will mainly concentrate on the factors that are exerted by the EU on third States party to the same treaty system.

The external role of the EU as a legal entity vis-à-vis other States in the treaty-making process (i.e. as a sole actor or sharing competence with its Member States) is conditioned by its extremely complicated internal law. The lack of proper understanding of all the intricacies of the system have led to many misunderstandings and a sense of insecurity for non-Member States.

As a legal entity, the EU is taking a very active stand in international relations. For example in the law of the sea, it participates in the IMO (see above); HELCOM and PARCOM; the Memorandum of Understanding on Port State Control; and is a party to UNCLOS.[156] In 1993, the EU announced its plan to extend its activities in the field of the law of the sea and to replace individual State action by co-ordinated EU action.[157]

The EU's ambitious plans for further future expansion beg certain questions not only in regard to the position of third States, but also among the EU members themselves. For example, what is the division of competence between the EU and its members? What is the scope of the doctrine of parallelism? Are the Member States allowed to act individually? Do they have to arrive at a common position? What are the circumstances justifying pre-emptive action by the EU?[158]

O' Keefe and Twomey (eds.), *supra*, at 13-33; A. Nollkaemper, "The External Competence of the Community with Regard to the Law of Marine Environmental Protection: The Frail Support for Grand Ambitions", in Ringbom (ed.), note 116, at 165-186; D. McGoldrick, *International Relations Law of the European Union* (1997).

[156] A. Koers, "Participation of the European Economic Community in a New Law of the Sea Convention", 73 *AJIL* (1979), at 426-443.

[157] "A Common Policy on Safe Sea. Communications from the Commission", COM (93) 66 final. The Council adopted the Communication in Council Resolution on a common policy on safe seas, *OJ* 1993, C 271/1.

[158] See, e.g., J.T. Lang, "The Ozone Layer Convention: A New Solution to the Question of Community Participation in 'Mixed' International Agreements", 23 *CMLR* (1993), at 157-176; M. Hession and R. Macrory, "The Legal Framework of European Community Participation in International Environmental Agreements", 2 *New European Law Review* (1994), at 59-136; J. Scott, *EC Environmental Law* (1998), especially Chapter 1, at 3-24; A.

The case-law of the European Court of Justice (the "ECJ") concerning the competence of the EU in relation to its external relations is vast. While fundamental principles have been established, there are still areas in which doubt remains.[159] One such area is the realm of marine environmental protection. Without doubt, the EU is competent to pursue an external policy in this field. There are, however, a number of questions to which no answers may as yet exist, such as, whether and when the EU has the exclusive power to act to the exclusion of its Member States. Also, what precisely are the obligations of the Member States when the Community does not have exclusive authority? These problems "continue to bewilder practitioners and scholars".[160] The EU Council has failed to lay down clear rules on allocation of competence and the ECJ's case-law has proved to be ambiguous in the field of marine environmental protection.

Another problem that may be puzzling for third States relates to the competence to negotiate a treaty on behalf of the EU in cases of concurrent powers. Does it lie with the Community or with Member States? According to the case-law of the ECJ, "in so far as it has been established that the substantive provisions of the Convention come within the Community competence, the Community is also competent to undertake commitments for putting those provisions into effect" (Opinion 2/91, paragraph 28). Further, in cases of shared competence, the Member States are entitled, but not required, to use the institutions of the Community (case C-316/91).[161]

The legal situation is more complicated in cases where the subject-matter of an agreement falls in part within the exclusive competence of the EU and in part under the competence of Member States. According to (the above-mentioned) Opinion 2/91, institutions of the Community and Member States should co-operate both in "the process on negotiations and conclusion and in fulfilment of the obligations entered into" (paragraph 36). This follows from the "requirement of unity in the international representation of the Community". However, the case-law leaves many issues ambiguous, such as that relating to the scope and nature of the obligation to co-operate.

Manau, "The Implied External Competence of the European Community After the ECJ Opinion 1/94 -Towards Coherence Diversity", *Legal Issues of European Integration* (1995), at 11-129; J.H.J. Bourgeois, "The EC in the WTO and Advisory Opinion 1/94: an Echernach Procession", 32 *CMLR* (1995), at 763-787.

[159] Case 22/70, *Commission v Council* [1971] ECR 263, para, 16 (ERTA case); Cases 3, 4 & 6/79 *et al.*, [1776] ECR 1279, paras. 19-20; Opinion 1/76 [1977] ECR 741; Opinion 741; Opinion 2/91 [1993] 3 CMLR 800, paras, 7-9; Opinion 1/94 (re WTO Agreements) [1994] ECR I-5267.

[160] Nollkaemper, note 155, at 167.

[161] Case C-316/91, *European Parliament v Council* [1994] ECR 1-625, paras. 26 and 34.

7.2 The EU and the GATT/WTO

The EU Member States have divergent views on many issues, and the practice of co-ordinating meetings, which has recently developed in the EU, has not always been successful.[162] A good example of this problem is the "buy Europe" clause.[163] The Commission proposed a system favouring bids advantageous to the EU. The EU did not enjoy such preferential treatment in the context of certain agreements such as GATT. There was disagreement among the Member States as to this proposal, i.e. whether the proposed system would best serve reciprocal encouragement of procurement. Germany, the Netherlands, Denmark, and the UK agreed to accept a "watered down" clause in relation to future agreements with third States. Spain, France, and Italy, however, were in favour of a more stringent clause in order to protect the EU, which would, in any case, be a tougher negotiating strategy. In relation to the external relations of the EU, there was disagreement as to whether inclusion of the clause should be made conditional upon the outcome of pending negotiations with GATT. In the end the directive was accepted as proposed originally by the Commission.

The adoption of this clause had important effects on the conduct of international negotiations.[164] After entry in force of this directive, this clause resulted in reciprocal treatment for EU companies from the USA. EU companies were prohibited from bidding for federal government contracts. Negotiations between the EU and the US followed, supplemented by negotiations between Delors and President Clinton. The result of these was a partial agreement – a Memorandum of Understanding in 1993 that would terminate in May 1995 upon the conclusion of the Multilateral Agreement on Government Procurement, which at this time was being negotiated by the members of the WTO.

In order to implement the Memorandum of Understanding, the EU had to take legislative measures on the basis of Article 113 of the Treaty of Rome. This resulted in legal action brought by the European Parliament ("EP") before the ECJ. The decision of the ECJ would have, inter alia, a great consequence for the future conduct of trade negotiations. The issue was whether the EU had an exclusive competence to negotiate and conclude trade agreements, in which case Member States would lose their freedom to

---

[162] See R. Frid, *The Relations between the EC and International Organisations: Legal Theory and Practice* (1996).

[163] The Commission proposed as follows: "the rejection of a tender where more than half of the value of the contract was represented in goods produced or services provided outside of the EU, and discrimination in favour of EU companies which submitted tenders for a price no greater than 3 per cent above that on non-EU tender", in K. A. Armstrong, S. J. Bulmer, *The Governance of the Single Market* (1988), at 135.

[164] *Id.*, at 135.

adopt bi-lateral agreements. In the end this issue was decided by Opinion 1/94 (see above), which elucidated that only the free movement of goods and certain aspects of services fall under exclusive competence of the EU. Moreover, the Court upheld the view of the EP that Article 113 could not have been the only basis of the Council Decisions. The consequence of this is that there is no sole legal basis and no sole decision-making procedure for implementation of international trade agreements.

In 1994, a new Multilateral Procurement Agreement was agreed upon and annexed to the 1994 World Trade Organization ("WTO") Agreement. Although it covered a wide range of services, telecommunications (which was left out of the Memorandum of Understanding) was not included in it.[165]

7.3 The EU and the Basel Convention

The Basel Convention on the Prohibition of Transboundary Transport of Hazardous Wastes (the "Basel Convention") provides another example of the problems surrounding the role of the EU as an actor on the international scene. The problem which arose related to the general definition of "hazardous waste". There was a tension between the call for total prohibition on the transboundary shipment of hazardous waste, on one hand, and the permission of shipment of waste (for recovery) as a raw material, on the other. This issue led to certain disagreements between the Member States. Initially, the views were divided. Some States, such as Denmark, proposed to the Council that a total ban should be imposed, while the Netherlands, France, Germany, the UK did not support this position.

The Convention parties agreed in Decision II/12 to the total ban of all exports of hazardous waste from OECD countries to non-OECD countries ("Decision II/12"). Decision II/12 was to have an immediate effect in relation to hazardous waste for disposal, and was to be effective from 1 January 1998 in relation to waste for recovery. It was necessary for any formal amendment to be submitted to the Basel Secretariat by 18 March 1995. In the period between Decision II/12 and the deadline for the formal submission, the Council reopened the debate over the export of hazardous waste. Yet again States were divided in their views on the issue. Some States expressed concern that the lack of a global definition of "hazardous waste" would result in a policy that would be either damaging for trade or for the environment. Denmark received support from Austria, Finland and Sweden (which at that time had acceded to the EU).

---

[165] *Id.*, at 136-137. See further S. Arrowsmith, J. Linarelli, D. Wallace Jr., *Regulating Public Procurement, National and International Perspectives* (2000).

Under the provisions of the Basel Convention, amendments to that Convention can be proposed either by the EU, as one entity, or by the individual members, except within the system of shared competence. Denmark and the new members wished to pursue a separate proposal. The Commission reacted by issuing a warning letter in which it was stated that the regulation of hazardous waste required EU action. Ultimately, the EP voted in favour of a resolution banning export of all hazardous waste to non-OECD countries, and the Commission proposed an amendment to Regulation 259/93 implementing the second part of the above-mentioned Decision, i.e. a ban on hazardous waste for recovery. Commissioners Bangemann and Brittan voted against this amendment. This supports the view that "the economic DGs have often appeared to be working to a different agenda from that of DG XL."[166] The Council in 1995 authorized the Commission to negotiate with the Convention parties for the incorporation of the second part of Decision II/12.

7.4 Some General Conclusions

Certain tentative conclusions may be drawn as to the role of the EU as an international actor in relation to third States. The complicated internal EU structure (and process) is triggered by its participation in international agreements. It has been demonstrated in many cases that the unclear rules that govern the interplay between the EU and the Member States are often a reason for internal conflicts. Such internal conflicts, in turn, reflect on the relationship between third States and the EU during treaty negotiations and in the case of treaty amendments. In the words of Hession and Macrory "[t]he involvement of the Community and the Member States, their obligations to each other under Community law, the agreement to be signed, and their obligations to Third States, create a gordian knot of obligations impossible to unravel in a sensible way".[167] Thus, the uncertain legal position between the EU and its Member States as to their competence makes it difficult for third parties to participate with full confidence and comprehension as equal partners in the treaty-making process. This is in particular true in cases of shared competence, such as in the case of environmental treaties.

An indirect influence on treaty making is exerted through the second EU pillar, i.e. the Common Foreign and Security Policy ("CFSP"). The framework of the CFSP was established by the Treaty on European Union ("TEU") and later the ECJ in the *Centro-Com* case, which established the

---

[166] Note 163, at 221-222.
[167] Hession and Macrory, note 158, at 183; see also N.A. Neuwahl, "Shared Powers or Combined Incompetence? More on Mixity", 33 *CMLR* (1996), at 667-687.

relationship between Member States and EU institutions in cases of national foreign and security policy and Common Commercial Policy.[168] The CFSP has been defined by Article J.1 of the Title V, which provides as follows: "[t]he Union and its Member States shall define and implement common foreign and security policy, governed by the provisions of this Title and covering all areas of foreign and security policy".

Article J.1 paragraph 2, enumerates the following objectives: (1) to safeguard the common values, fundamental interests and independence of the Union; (2) to strengthen the security of the union and its members in all ways; (3) to preserve peace and strengthen international security, in accordance with the principles of the United Nations Charter, as well as the principles of the Helsinki Final Act and the objectives of the Charter of Paris; (4) to develop and consolidate democracy and the rule of law and respect for human rights and fundamental freedoms.

Since the Treaty does not have a definition of CFSP, its scope has developed in practice. The question of interest relates to the instruments of CFSP. The view expressed in doctrine is that these are neither treaties nor legal tools of the EU.[169] Broadly speaking, the EU has at its disposal two means of pursuing the CFSP, namely adoption of a "common position", and "joint action". The differences between those two measures are not clear-cut. It may be said that the first of these measures is found (for example) in Political Declarations and the second is used in cases in which "member States have important interests in common".[170] The common position is governed by Article 12 of the TEU. Member States have the duty to "inform and consult one another within the Council on any matter of foreign and security policy of general interest in order to ensure that their combined influence is exerted as effectively as possible by means of concerted and convergent action". A common position has been developed on issues such as the sanctions against the former Yugoslavia, arms imports to former Yugoslavia, East Timor, Nigeria and the situation in Angola. Joint action is governed by Article J3 of the TEU and, as was indicated above, is applicable in cases of "important interests in common". The recognition of new States belongs to this category although it is, in the final analysis, a unilateral act of

---

[168] Case C-124/95, The Queen ex parte: Centro-Com Srl *v* HM Treasury and Bank of England, Judgment of 14 January 1997 ("Centro-Com case").

[169] McGoldrick, note 155, at 149; N. Neuwahl "Foreign and Security Policy and the Implementation of the Requirements of "Consistency" under the Treaty on European Union", in O'Keefe and Twomey (eds.), note 155, at 227-246.

[170] McGoldrick, note 155, at 150.

State.[171] In accordance with Article J3 paragraph 4, both types of measure require unanimous support.

In conclusion, the second pillar of the EU has no direct bearing on the treaty-making process. Nevertheless, in an indirect way, through adoption of an EU common stand in the international sphere, CFSP influences the formation of treaties. In many ways, the general guidelines for common action adopted by the European Council will result, or have already resulted, in the adoption of a treaty, such as, for instance, in strengthening existing co-operation on issues of international interest such as the fight against arms proliferation, terrorism, and traffic in illicit drugs.[172] The general issue of the participation of the EU in the treaty-making process is part of the broader problem concerning the international legal personality of the EU and the EC. This complicated problem, however, exceeds the framework of this study which is devoted primarily to the role of (some of) the actors and factors in influencing the process of treaty-formation.

7.5 The EU and Fisheries

7.5.1 The Common Fisheries Policy

As pointed out above, one of the reasons for amendments to the Gdansk Convention was the accession of the European Community (EC) to that Convention.[173] The accession of the EC was a direct result of the introduction of the Common Fisheries Policy ("CFP"). The accession of the EC was proposed in response to the conflict of interests for FRG and Denmark, both parties to the Treaty of Rome and to the Gdansk Convention. The conflict arose with the introduction of the CFP. The introduction of the CFP, and in particular the transfer of their national competence by the EC Member States to the EC as an entity, gave rise to a number of problems. One problem concerned the IBSFC allocation of TAC to the FRG and Denmark, in light of the provisions of the CFSP. Two further issues also arose, namely the application of the EC (as a separate entity) to become a party to the Gdansk Convention and the inhibiting effect of the transfer of national competence (by the EC States to the EC) on the adoption of amendments to the Convention.[174]

---

[171] C. Wabrick, "Recognition on States", 41 *ICLQ* (1992), 473-482; McGoldrick, "Yugoslavia - The Responses of the International Community and International Law", 49(2) *Current Legal Problems* (1996), at 375-394.

[172] See MacGoldrick, note 155, at 154-155.

[173] For extensive treatment, see M. Fitzmaurice, "Common Market Participation in the Legal Régime of the Baltic Sea Fisheries", 33 *GYIL* (1990), at 214-235.

[174] Among the EC members the Common Fisheries Policy originated in Regulation 2141/70 and 2142/70 now codified as EEC No. 100/76 OJEC 19, L 20 (28 January 1976) which

The Common Fisheries Policy is based on Article 3 paragraph D and
Article 38 to Article 47 of the Treaty establishing the EEC and the Single
European Act.[175] The CFP has internal and external aspects. The ECJ has
ruled that the EC has competence to adopt conservation measures, including
TAC and national quotas, and to negotiate and conclude agreements which
concern fishing on the high seas. On 3 November 1976, the Council adopted
a set of resolutions on both the external and internal aspects of the CFP. As a
result, the Commission was authorized to negotiate fisheries agreements
with third States and with international fisheries organizations such as the
IBSFC and the North-East Atlantic Fisheries Commission ("NEAFC").[176]
The external policy in relation to CFP came into effect on 1 January 1977. In
short, the main aspect of the external policy is that the EC members lost their
independent right to negotiate and conclude international agreements on
fisheries as well as to hold membership of international fisheries
organizations. These powers now belong to the EC which acts as one entity
towards third States.

7.5.2 The EU and the Gdansk Convention

Following the introduction of the CFP, the Embassies of the Federal
Republic of Germany and Denmark submitted an official proposal to the
Polish Government (Depositary of the Gdansk Convention), in relation to the
accession of the EC to the Gdansk Convention. The proposal described
amendments that were necessary to enable the EC to become a party to the
Convention.[177]

However, the parties to the Gdansk Convention expressed very different
views on the proposed accession. Sweden and Finland were in favour of
accession, while Poland, the Soviet Union and the GDR initially opposed EC
participation, on the grounds that its accession to the Gdansk Convention
would result in the exertion of influence by non-Baltic EC Member States in
respect of matters relating to the Baltic Sea. In order to clarify matters, two
meetings were convened in Warsaw. At the first meeting of the Parties to the

---

entered in force at the beginning of 1971. The external effect of the CRP (transfer of
competence to third States in fisheries matters by the EEC member States to the EEC) became
effective in 1977. On the CFP see for example: A. Koers, "The External Authority of the EEC
in regard to Marine Fisheries", 14 *CMLR* (1977), at 269-301; R. Churchill, "Revision of the
EEC Common Fisheries Policy, Part I and Part II", 5 *European Law Review* (1980), Nos. 1
and 2, 3-37 and 95-111.

[175] Treaty establishing the European Economic Community (EEC), 25 March 1957, entered
into force 1 January 1958, 23 *UNTS*, Single European Act, 17 and 28 February 1986 *OJ*,
1987, L. 169, 25 *ILM* (1986), at 506-518.

[176] Bulletin of the European Community, 10, 1976, points 1503-1505.

[177] See sections 4.3.3 and 4.3.4 above, regarding the accession of Poland, Estonia, Latvia and
Lithuania to the EU in 2004.

Gdansk Convention (22-26 June 1981), the Soviet Union, Poland and the GDR maintained their opposition to EC accession. In September, the EC presented a memorandum in which it elucidated its legal position *vis-à-vis* the Gdansk Convention. During the second meeting of the parties to the Gdansk Convention (which was held in Warsaw on 9-11 November 1982) the States that had previously opposed EC accession expressed their approval.

Three steps were taken to effect the EC accession to the Gdansk Convention. Firstly, the Gdansk Convention was amended so as to allow the participation of the EC (since originally the Convention was only open to States). In addition, the present Parties to the Convention, namely, Denmark and the FRG withdrew their participation in it. Finally, the EC acceded to the Gdansk Convention. Thus, this procedure followed that taken in relation to other fisheries commissions, such as the North West Atlantic Fisheries Organization ("NAFO"); and NEAFC. The accession of the EC to the IBSFC meant that there were then five (rather than six) State members of the IBSFC (the EC having replaced the FRG and Denmark). The Appendix also provides that the EC had been invited by all Contracting Parties to accede to the Convention in Article XVII, states that as from the date of accession, the EC takes over from the two States all rights and obligations in respect of their participation in the Convention. The Appendix further states that the EC is invited by all Contracting Parties to accede to the Convention to replace the FRG and Denmark, and that the participation of these two States will cease the moment the Convention entered into force for the EC.

As a result of the amendments to the Gdansk Convention, a new paragraph was added to the Convention. That paragraph made clear that, in addition to States interested in the preservation and national exploitation of the living resources of the Baltic Sea and the Belts, economic IGOs to which competence in matters regulated by the Gdansk Convention has been transferred may become parties to this Convention, providing they were so invited (Article XVII, paragraph 2, as amended of the Gdansk Convention). It was also made clear that any reference in the Gdansk Convention to a "Contracting State" applies *mututatis mutandis* to such an organization (Article XVII, paragraph 3, as amended of the Gdansk Convention). Finally, it was specified that in the event of a conflict between the obligations of an inter-governmental organization under the Agreement that established it, and its obligations under the Gdansk Convention, the latter will prevail (Article XVIII, paragraph 4, as amended).[178]

---

[178] This provision gave rise to many contradictory interpretations (see also the ECJ Judgments as for example in *Hageman v Belgium* case (30 April 1974, ECR, 449)). See also A. Th. S. Leenen, "Participation of the EEC in International Environmental Agreements", 10 *Legal Issues of European Integration* (1984), Special Issue, Vol. 1, at 93-111. This topic, however, exceeds the framework of this chapter.

In conclusion, it may be said that EC efforts to accede to the Gdansk Convention were successful. The EC became a party to the Convention despite active opposition from the (then) communist States (which were traditionally not in favour of the EC in general). It may be observed that the EC benefited from the strong support of Sweden and Finland (prior to their accession to the EC). Given that that these States played a leading role as parties to the Gdansk Convention, their attitude was of paramount importance for the success of the EC's endeavours in this regard.[179]

7.5.3 The Spanish/Canadian Fisheries Dispute

Another very topical example of EU influence on treaties in the field of fisheries relates to the dispute between Spain (and, thus, the EU) and Canada.[180] However, this example does not relate directly to the internal law of the EU, but rather illustrates the behaviour of the EU as an international actor dealing with the interests of its Member States within in an IGO. The present example is the reverse of that described above (in which non-EU Member States had to change their policy following pressure from the EU). In the present example, the EC policy within NAFO was based on vetoing NAFO decisions. In the period between 1986 and 1995, the EU opted out of 53 NAFO decisions. All eleven remaining Member States lodged only five objections.

On 1 March 1995, the EU opted out of the quota established by NAFO and set its own quota, which was five times as high. Canada responded by extending its Act by a Regulation of 3 March, specifically to cover vessels of Portugal and Spain fishing for halibut in Greenland. Canada prohibited any fishing by Spain and Portugal for this stock from 3 March to 31 December in any year. Further developments involved the conclusion of the Fisheries Agreement between Canada and the EU (the "EU/Canada Fisheries Agreement"); Spain's initiation of proceedings in the ICJ against Canada; and the signing of the 1995 Highly Migratory and Straddling Stocks Convention (see above).

The EU/Canada Fisheries Agreement has been accepted by NAFO. Annex I to this Agreement contains very stringent new conservation and enforcement measures which are applicable to all fishing vessels of Member States of NAFO. (Even before the entry into force of this Agreement, the EU and Canada agreed on the provisional application of those measures). Following these developments, Canada has amended its Regulations to its new promulgated Fisheries Act. Vessels flying the flag of Spain and Portugal were removed from the list of countries whose vessels were subject

---

[179] See note 177 above.
[180] See P. Davies, note 94, at 927-939.

to Canadian measures. Despite the above-mentioned developments, Spain brought the case against Canada before the ICJ.

This case is an example of the interplay between treaty law, municipal law and EU law. Related provisions deriving from all these sources of law interact and influence each other. The Canadian Fisheries Act influenced provisions of the EU/Canada Fisheries Agreement. The EU had to accept these strict provisions in order to exclude vessels flying the Spanish and/or Portuguese flags from the list of those this were subject to Canadian measures. The conservation policies of NAFO also contributed to the final form of the EC/Canada Fisheries Agreement. These events undoubtedly influenced the negotiations and final text of the Straddling Stocks Convention. It can be presumed that the Straddling Stock Convention will influence the text of future treaty instruments in relation to the notions of conservation, enforcement and freedom of the high seas, that is, areas in which revolutionary concepts were introduced.

7.6 The EU and Environmental Treaties: the 1992 Helsinki Convention

The new 1992 Helsinki Convention[181], provides for the accession of the EC. In contrast to the Gdansk Convention, EC participation in the Helsinki Convention did not provoke protest from the other parties. Due to changes in the political climate, especially the collapse of communism, the accession of the EC to the Helsinki Convention was uncontroversial.

Under Article 35 of the 1992 Convention, the EC shall, in matters within its competence, exercise on its behalf the rights and fulfil the responsibilities that the Convention would otherwise attribute to the Member States. Member States are prohibited from exercising these rights individually. In voting within the Helsinki Commission ("HELCOM"), again in relation to matters within the EC's competence, the EC has the same number of votes as its Member States who are contracting Parties. The legal position of the EC in the Helsinki Convention is the same as it was under the old 1974 Convention for the Prevention of Marine Pollution from Land-Based Sources (the "Paris Convention").[182] Unlike the case of the Gdansk Convention, the role of the EC in the Helsinki Convention has so far been rather inconspicuous. Whereas with the Gdansk Convention, the EC is an equal party implementing the treaty and shaping its development, in the Helsinki Convention its role is rather that of a "silent partner". This

---

[181] See note 109 above.
[182] See now the 1992 Convention for the Protection of the Marine Environment of the North-East Atlantic (the OSPAR Convention), 32 *ILM* 1068.

difference in role derives from differences in its legal status under both Conventions. In the Gdansk Convention the EC is the sole party to the exclusion of its Member States, but in the Helsinki Convention (as in the Paris Convention) the EC is a party together with its Member States. This differentiated status has caused many problems and misunderstandings as to the role of the EC in relation to its Member States in respect of the above Conventions, particularly as to the division of competence between them. For example, in respect of the Paris Commission ("PARCOM"), there has been a history of refusal by the EC Commission to agree to the adoption of measures covering standards for particular substances where the standards in question were more stringent than those existing under EC regulations. This was despite the fact that all other PARCOM members (EC Member States) were in favour of more stringent standards. The result has been actually to prevent the adoption of any standards whatsoever by PARCOM in relation to PCBs.[183] Prompted by the conduct of the EC Commission, the chairman of PARCOM wrote to the Commission, demanding some explanation as to the division of powers between the EC and its Member States. The EC response was that the division of power was an internal Community matter. At the same time, the EC specifically prevented the adoption by PARCOM of a binding resolution on PCBs.

It has been said that, as a general rule, the EC attempts to decelerate the process of PARCOM in cases where EC legislation is less advanced than that proposed PARCOM.[184] However, as a general rule, the EC Commission has been active in PARCOM, for example in relation to questions as to its competence and in seeking a negotiating mandate in respect of Paris Commission measures, this state of affairs is due to many factors, such as the enlargement of the EU and the shift of emphasis in PARCOM towards the concepts and principles of "best available technology" and "best environmental practice" (which influence industries and products). The Commission examines all draft measures that are to be presented to PARCOM. It also claims shared or exclusive competence on behalf of the European Union and, as a consequence, seeks a negotiating mandate.[185] On the other hand, the role of the EU in HELCOM has (so far) been less pronounced in comparison with its role in PARCOM. In fact, its Commission never played an independent role and it has never claimed competence, either shared or exclusive, to do so. However, this state of

---

[183] "Polychlorinated Biphenyls". See, e.g., S. Saetvik, *Environmental Co-operation Between the North Sea States, Success or Failure?* (1988).

[184] T. IJlstra, "L'action communautaire dans les Commissions de Paris et Oslo", in J. Lebullenger and D. Lemorvan (eds.), *La Communauté Européenne et la mer* (1990), at 381-403.

[185] S. Sadovski, "Protection of the Marine Environment of the North Sea: the 'Russian Doll' Effect", in Ringbom, *supra* note 116, at 109-119.

affairs is also changing. The recommendations adopted during the March 1998 proceedings stipulate that "[m]easures should be taken to fully utilise the increased support of the European Union in the HELCOM process".[186] The reasons given in support of this new approach were the increased importance of the EU's environmental legislation in this region, the accession process, the evolving role of the EU as a major source of support in relation to investment activities and the broad implications of the EU policies, directives and programmes for agriculture, energy and transport. In co-ordinating its activities with the EU, HELCOM members should support the dialogue on the implementation of EU directives in respect of a (now enlarged) number of countries. In the circumstances, EU influence can be expected to expand to a considerable degree in the implementation and development of the Helsinki Convention.

8. Concluding Remarks

The chapter has examined the role played by the main actors States and non-State actors (IGOs, NGOs, associations, and corporations) engaged in the treaty-making process (including negotiations and subsequent changes to the treaty text) and scrutinizing the factors (legal and extra-legal) which influence the behaviour of the actors. The case studies in this chapter were selected from the fields of the law of the sea, human rights, international economic law, the law of the EU, environmental law and shipping. The study took into account actors operating on a global level and those operating on a regional level (such as in the Baltic Sea). The case studies clearly indicate that States are still the most effective and influential actors in relation to the treaty-making process. Notwithstanding the growing participation of non-State actors, States still play the most prominent role in any treaty process. This prominent role is as much visible in relation to treaties which are negotiated and amended only between States, as it is in relation to treaties which are sponsored by an IGO (such as the IMO) and to treaties which generate a certain organizational structure, such as a Secretariat or working groups (for example, the 1992 Climate Change Convention). Ultimately, States dictate the final form of a treaty and of amendments to a treaty.

IGOs play a very useful role as actors that initiate the treaty-making process. They provide a first draft of a treaty or propose amendments to it, they serve as a meeting place for the representatives of governments to exchange views and, on the basis of the discussion between the representatives of the governments, submit a final draft of a treaty (for

---

[186] Baltic Sea Environment Proceedings, No. 72, March 1998.

example the IMO). Thus, it may be said that IGOs, as actors influencing the evolution of treaties, play a "forum role" in the main, and act as "facilitators" for States to reconcile controversies and achieve mutually acceptable results. They should not be viewed as independent and influential bodies enjoying a separate will, acting on a par with States.[187]

The most unexpected findings were those in relation to the role of NGOs and corporations in the treaty-making process. In contrast they do not play an equally prominent role in all fields. Indeed, in some fields, they do not play an influential role at all. Their most pronounced presence is in the field of human rights (for example the 1989 Rights of the Child Convention). In the field of environmental protection, on the other hand, while undoubtedly NGOs do have a significant influence at the regional level, it is surprising to find that, at the global level, they do not yet, on the whole, exert a substantive influence on treaty making (for example Climate Change Convention). Although a large number of non-State actors are present during negotiations, their participation is confined to limited lobbying, and is thus deprived of significant influence. The only meaningful manner in which they may influence indirectly – the development of a treaty, in the context of the Climate Change Convention, is in the form of assistance accorded to Member States in the preparation of national reports and in lobbying at the national level.[188] Even in fora in which they enjoy a more pronounced status, their participation is subject to rigorous regulations which define their status in great detail (for example the IMO). In comparison with other NGOs, shipowners' associations at the IMO have the strongest position and exert the most meaningful influence on the treaty-making process in comparison with other NGOs (as demonstrated in the context of the Salvage

---

[187] For example, at IMO the discussion on the definition of pollution damage clearly shows that IGOs are not in any way treated differently from NGOs; neither is their input as observers more substantial. Representatives of both of these groups asked for "clarifications" (see Director of the International Oil Pollution Compensation Fund asked for clarification of the concept of "pollution damage"); "express concern" (representative of the EC Commission); "support" (the observer from the International Group of P & I Associations supported the demand for a clear definition of the concept of pollution damage); Official Records of the International Conference on Liability an Compensation for Damage in Connection with the Carriage of Certain Substances by Sea, 1984 and the International Conference on the Revision of the 1969 Civil Liability Convention and the 1971 Fund Convention, 1992, IMO London 1993.

[188] Putnam states: "[t]he polities of many international negotiations can be usefully conceived as a two-level game. At the national level, domestic groups pursue their interests by pressuring the government to adopt favourable policies, and politicians seek power by construing coalitions among these groups. At the international level, national governments seek to maximise their own ability satisfy domestic pressures, while minimizing the adverse consequences of foreign developments. Neither of the two games can be ignored by central decision-makers, so long as their countries remain independent, yet sovereign", R.D. Putnam, note 16, at 434.

Convention). However, this position derives from the special character of shipping, which is focused to a great extent on the transnational private sector. In fact, the present research has shown that there are very few established rules which govern the participation of NGOs in the treaty-making process. As a result, the influence of NGOs in this process depends on a variety of factors – the particular forum, the success with which NGOs are able to mobilize their skills so to achieve greater influence may be achieved (such as the negotiations on the Rights of the Child Convention) and finally, on human factors, as well such as the attitude of a Conference Chairman towards NGOs.

At present, it appears that NGOs hold an uncertain position in some fields, in particular in the case of environmental protection, partly due to an uneasy relationship between NGOs and State actors.[189] Generally speaking, there is a mutual lack of trust between NGOs and States. On the one hand, NGOs and corporations are disillusioned about the true intentions of States, which ultimately define the scope of the involvement of NGOs. On the other hand, States become irritated by interference with the treaty-making process, which in the majority of cases they see as ignoring their particular interests as States. This uneasy relationship may also be seen in relation to the collaboration between the World Bank and NGOs. One point that emerges from this study, is that it appears that in order to achieve equal partnership with States and to influence them more effectively in the treaty-making process, NGOs must exhibit a high level of professionalism rather than apply emotional arguments. They must also present a uniform and well-organized front. Too much diversification weakens the proposals of NGOs. Another problem is that States are sometimes suspicious as to their intentions, claiming that NGOs are, at the end of the day, political creatures. However, the negotiation and drafting of the Rights of the Child Convention exemplifies how NGOs can achieve success. They have shown profound knowledge of the problem; they co-operated fully with each other; they co-operated with States. It has to be pointed out, however, that as indicated above, the Chairman of the Working Group during the drafting of this Convention, Professor Adam Lopatka of Poland, had an enormous impact on the NGO participation. "[I]n the opinion of many who took part, the eventual success of the Working Group in producing an acceptable draft Convention is due in no small measure to the personal qualities of Adam Lopatka. ... [W]hen he presided over meetings, he was fair and polite to each participant, and never refused permission to anyone who wished to speak ... [t]he

---

[189] Another area in the field of international law in which NGOs may have some influence, if not yet a direct role, is that of international litigation, in particular in relation to the advisory jurisdiction of the International Court of Justice, see R. Higgins, "Remedies and the International Court of Justice: An Introduction", in M. Evans (ed.), *Remedies in International Law: the Institutional Dilemma* (1998), at 1-10.

Chairman was scrupulously fair in allowing anyone who wanted to speak to take the floor."[190] Generally speaking, in more classical fora, such as the United Nations, the role of the above actors and the scope of their participation in the treaty-making process is defined by States.

Turning to the factors which influence the actors in the treaty-making process, this study has revealed that these factors are mostly of an extra-legal character; not only in relation to the negotiations of a treaty (which by definition is a political process), but also in relation to the introduction of amendments to a treaty. This observation is applicable in equal measure within the global (for example UNCLOS) and the regional contexts (such as in case of the Baltic Sea region). The sole example of true legal factors influencing the status quo of a treaty lies within the realm of EU law. The examples provided above clearly indicate that considerations that have their roots in the European legal order have compelled changes to certain treaties. Interestingly, these changes, originating from the internal law of the EU – have affected in a profound manner the treaty relationship with non-EU members.

Finally, this study suggests that the existing forms of international law-making are able to accommodate various factors. A very good example is that in the Baltic Sea region where political, economic and legal factors played a crucial role in the creation of the initial treaty régime and contributed further to revision of the treaty. As to the involvement of NGOs, it may equally be concluded that existing forms serve their purpose. As the process of treaty-making continues, in most cases, to be dominated by States, new forms of treaty-making are not warranted. Even the most effective participation of NGOs in the cases studied above has not interfered with, or influenced the final outcome to such a degree as to indicate that radical changes to the classical procedures for treaty-making are warranted.

Treaty-making using existing methods is sufficiently flexible to allow consideration of the interests of all actors by using existing methods. A good example is that of the IMO in which States, IGOs, and NGOs have collaborated successfully, using legal tools which are of a traditional character. Ultimately, the form of a treaty is not of critical importance, provided that the treaty reflects an agreement that was achieved by the actors concerned.

---

[190] Longford, *supra* note 142, at 220-221.

CHAPTER THREE

Aspects of the Law Relating to Material Breach of Treaty[*]

1. Introduction

1.1 General Remarks

Breach of treaty obligations raises several important questions. In particular, one such issue is the question of "material" breach of treaty, which remains one of the most challenging and complicated issues of the law of treaties. The issues raised include the following: what makes a breach material; the relationship between the law of state responsibility (countermeasures) and the law of treaties (material breach); the applicability of the principle of proportionality in termination and suspension of treaties as a consequence of a material breach; the severability of treaty provisions as a consequence of material breach; and the legal position of the "injured state", including the situation where the breached treaty involves "integral" or "interdependent", rather than simply "reciprocal", obligations. These issues will be the focus of this chapter.

The central provision here is Article 60 of the VCLT, on "termination or suspension of the operation of a treaty as a consequence of its breach", which provides as follows:

> 1. A material breach of a bilateral treaty by one of the parties entitles the other to invoke the breach as a ground for terminating the treaty or suspending its operation in whole or in part.

---

[*] This chapter is an updated and significantly revised version of M. Fitzmaurice, "Material Breach of a Treaty – Certain Legal Issues", published in 6 *Austrian Review of International and European Law* 2001, at 3-44 and reprinted with kind permission of Brill Academic Publishers.

2. A material breach of a multilateral treaty by one of the parties entitles:

(a) the other parties by unanimous agreement to suspend the operation of the treaty in whole or in part or to terminate it either:

(i) in the relations between themselves and the defaulting State, or

(ii) as between all the parties;

(b) a party specially affected by the breach to invoke it as a ground for suspending the operation of the treaty in whole or in part in the relations between itself and the defaulting State;

(c) any party other than the defaulting State to invoke the breach as a ground for suspending the operation of the treaty in whole or in part with respect to itself if the treaty is of such a character that a material breach of its provisions by one party radically changes the position of every party with respect to the further performance of its obligations under the treaty.

3. A material breach of a treaty, for the purposes of this article, consists in:

(a) a repudiation of the treaty not sanctioned by the present Convention; or

(b) the violation of a provision essential to the accomplishment of the object or purpose of the treaty.

4. The foregoing paragraphs are without prejudice to any provision in the treaty applicable in the event of a breach.

5. Paragraphs 1 to 3 do not apply to provisions relating to the protection of the human person contained in treaties of a humanitarian character, in particular to provisions prohibiting any form of reprisals against persons protected by such treaties.

The drafting of what became Article 60 of VCLT was subject to much criticism. Simma, in his seminal article, said as follows:

[a]rticle 60 constitutes one of the provisions [of the Vienna Convention] with regard to which – aside from the procedural shortcomings – the limited scope of the Vienna Convention on the Law of Treaties will be felt most clearly and painfully. While Article 60 and its related provisions carefully and equitably regulate the application of the reactions to breach having their *sedes materiae* in the law of treaties, any examination of the breach situation limited to an analysis of the rules of the Vienna Convention will, due to the exclusion of the similar reactions having their *sedes materiae* in the law of international responsibility provide the observer with an incomplete picture.[1]

---

[1] B. Simma, "Reflections on Article 60 of the Vienna Convention on the Law of Treaties and its Background in General International Law", 20 *ÖZÖRV* (1970), 5, at 83.

The inherent right of the suspension or of the termination of a treaty due to material breach also entered the case-law of the ICJ, e.g., in the 1971 *Namibia Advisory Opinion*,[2] in which the Court said as follows:

> The silence of a treaty as to the existence of such a right cannot be interpreted as implying the exclusion of a right which has its source outside of a treaty, in general international law, and is dependent on the occurrence of circumstances which are not normally envisaged when a treaty is concluded.[3]

The consideration of the material breach issue will be discussed in the context of the law of treaties as laid down in the VCLT and in the light of the relevant provisions in the field of state responsibility, as set forth in the ILC State Responsibility Articles, taking into account the existing case-law.[4]

1.2 The Requirement that the Breach be Material: the "Object and Purpose" Test

The distinction between "material" as distinct from "non-material" breach was also one of the issues raised by many international lawyers. For example, Lord McNair was of the view that only the breach of an essential, or important, or material provision, not just any breach, of the treaty entitles the other party to denounce the whole treaty. He wrote as follows:

> The question is controversial. There are some writers who maintain that it is only the breach of an 'essential' or 'important' or 'material' term of a treaty that entitles the other party to denounce the whole treaty; others hold that the breach of any term justify the other party in denouncing the whole treaty because it is impossible to say whether or not that term was one which induced him to conclude the treaty although he accepted the rest of the treaty with reluctance. In our submission, the balance of common sense,

---

[2] Legal Consequences for States of the Continued Presence of South Africa in Namibia (South-West Africa) Notwithstanding Security Council Resolution 276 (1970), Advisory Opinion of 21 June 1971, 1971 ICJ Rep. 16. By Resolution 2145, the United Nations General Assembly terminated the mandate in respect of Namibia (South-West Africa) conferred by the League of Nations on the United Kingdom and exercised on its behalf by the Republic of South Africa. The mandate was terminated because South Africa had "failed to fulfil its obligations" under the mandate and had "disavowed the mandate". The Court applied the rules as to material breach of a treaty, i.e., the mandate.

[3] *Id.*, at paragraph 96.

[4] The work of the ILC in relation to material breach was a subject of many learned discussions and publications. To mention a few: S. Rosenne, *Breach of Treaty* (1985); S. Rosenne, *The Law of Treaties: A Guide to the Legislative History of the Vienna Convention* (1970); Simma, *supra* note 1; D.W. Greig, "Reciprocity, Proportionality, and The Law of Treaties", 34 *VJIL* (1994), 295-403; M.M. Gomaa, *Suspension or Termination of Treaties on Grounds of Breach* (1996).

practical convenience, and judicial authority supports the former of those two contrasted views.[5]

Article 60(3)(b) of the VCLT provides that a "violation of a provision essential to the accomplishment of the object and purpose of the treaty" constitutes a material breach. The problems of interpretation of the above provision are related to inherent difficulties in defining the object and purpose of a treaty.[6] The issue of the meaning of "object and purpose" of a treaty has always been puzzling international lawyers, in particular since the rendering by the Court of the 1951 *Genocide* Advisory Opinion.[7] In that case, the dissenting Judges in their joint opinion voiced their doubts as to the nature of "object and purpose". They submitted as follows:

> Moreover, we have difficulty in seeing how the new rule can work. When a new rule is proposed for the solution of disputes, it should be easy to apply and calculate to produce final and consistent results. [...] What is the 'object and purpose' of the Genocide Convention? To repress genocide? Of course; but is it more than that? Does it comprise any or all of the enforcement articles of the Convention? That is the heart of the matter.[8]

As has been observed, the ICJ's references to object and purpose "reveal little of the process by which the [Court] arrived at the determination of the object and purpose of a given treaty".[9] The "ILC" has not been very helpful either in elucidating the issue. Former Special Rapporteurs on the law of treaties avoided the problem by referring to the "nature" of certain types of treaties (Brierly),[10] or to its "original purpose"; or to an "essential aspect of its original purpose (Lauterpacht)",[11] while Sir Gerald Fitzmaurice[12] and Sir Humphrey Waldock referred to object(s) and purpose(s).[13] Prompted by the *Genocide* Advisory Opinion, the ILC was, however, mindful of the inherent difficulties involving the use of the concept of the "object and purpose". It was observed that

---

[5] Lord McNair, *The Law of Treaties* (1961), at 478.

[6] For a survey of views, see, e.g., I. Buffard and K. Zemanek, "The 'Object and Purpose' of a Treaty: An Enigma?", 3 *ARIEL* (1998), 311-343; J. Klabbers, "Some Problems Regarding the Object and Purpose of Treaties", *8 FYIL* (1997), 138-160.

[7] Reservations to the Convention on the Prevention and Punishment of the Crime of Genocide, Advisory Opinion of 28 May, 1951 ICJ Rep. 15 ("Genocide Advisory Opinion").

[8] *Id.,* at 44.

[9] Buffard and Zemanek, *supra* note 6, at 317.

[10] J.L. Brierly, Report on the Law of Treaties, YILC (1950), Vol. II, 222, at 223; *id.,* Second Report on the Law of Treaties, YILC (1951), Vol. II, 70, at 73.

[11] Sir Hersh Lauterpacht, First Report on the Law of Treaties, YILC (1953), Vol. II, 90, at 126; *id.,* Second Report on the Law of Treaties, YILC (1954), Vol. II, 123, at 133.

[12] Sir G. Fitzmaurice, Report on the Law of Treaties, YILC (1956), Vol. II, 104; *id.,* Second Report on the Law of Treaties, YILC (1957), Vol. II, 16.

[13] Sir H. Waldock, First Report on the Law of Treaties, YILC (1962), Vol. II, 27; *id.,* Third Report of the Law of Treaties, YILC (1962), Vol. II, 27.

it was said – and rightly – that in any given case the question of the compatibility or incompatibility of a particular reservation with the object and purpose of a treaty depends to a considerable extent on the conclusion reached as to exactly how much of the subject-matter of a treaty is to be regarded as representing the 'object and purpose of a treaty' and as to exactly which provisions are to be regarded as material for achievement of the 'object and purpose.' But these are questions on which opinions of the parties themselves may well differ, so that the principle applied by the Court is essentially subjective and unsuitable [...] as a general test for determining whether a reserving State is or is not entitled to be considered a party to a multilateral treaty. [...] The Special Rapporteur believes these criticism of the Court's criterion to be well-founded. [...] Nevertheless, the Court's criterion of 'compatibility with the object and purpose of the Convention' does express a valuable concept to be taken into account both by States formulating a reservation and by States deciding whether or not to consent to a reservation that has been formulated by another State. [..] Accordingly, the Special Rapporteur has tentatively inserted in paragraph 2 (a) for the Commission's consideration a provision stating the Court's concept as a general principle to be taken into account, without however attaching any sanction to it [...].[14]

Despite these doubts within the ILC, the notion of "object and purpose" was quite liberally included in many Articles of the VCLT.[15]

A further issue is the criterion of "object and purpose" of a treaty as it relates to Article 60(3)(b) of the VCLT. Simma observes that this article implies that "the violation of a provision essential to the accomplishment of the object or purpose of a treaty" is a material breach.[16] It may also be noted that the ILC understood by the object and purpose "any object and purpose". It was stated in the comments of the ILC in relation to former draft Article 57(3)(b) - which was to become Article 60(3)b) - that "[t]he other and more general form of material breach is that in sub-paragraph (b), and is there defined as a violation of a provision essential to the accomplishment of any object and purpose of the treaty".[17] F. Kirgis, while in principle in agreement with this reasoning, adds that common sense would suggest the solution that a relatively minor violation of an essential provision of a treaty would not constitute a material breach.[18] It is obvious that the inherent problems

---

[14] Waldock, First Report on the Law of Treaties, *supra* note 13, at 65-66.

[15] See the list in Buffard and Zemanek, *supra* note 6, at 321.

[16] Simma, *supra* note 1, at 61; see also F.L. Kirgis, "Some Lingering Questions about Article 60 of the Vienna Convention on the Law of Treaties", 22 *Cornell ILJ* (1989), 549, at 552; M. Gomaa, *supra* note 4, at 33.

[17] YILC (1966), Vol. II, at 255.

[18] Kigris, *supra* note 16, at 552. See also the same author with regard to the argument that the admission to the ILO of an entity (Palestine) lacking the attributes of a State is a material breach of the organisation's constitution; F.L. Kirgis, "Admission of 'Palestine' as a Member of a Specialized Agency and Withholding the Payment of Assessment in Response", 84 *AJIL* (1990), 218-230, at 224.

relating to the definition of object and purpose affect the notion of the breach as well.

Klabbers is of the view that the formulation of the notion of the object and purpose of a treaty in Article 60 of the VCLT is an example of the indeterminacy of this concept, since States generally "adopt conceptions of a treaty's object and purpose as they see fit".[19] This is exemplified by the *Namibia* opinion and the *Air Services Agreement* case.[20] Klabbers notes that in the *Namibia* opinion, the United States submitted that South Africa's refusal to recognize the authority of the United Nations, its systematic rejection of the recommendations of the General Assembly and the Security Council, and its application of apartheid policies, all constituted material breaches. He continues:

> If so, it must mean either the Mandate had three distinct objects and purposes (establishing UN supervision, establishing UN authority, and pursuance of human rights standards) or one object and purpose of such a general nature as to subsume various acts contrary to it as material breaches.

> In addition, other governments held that South Africa had lost its status as mandatory partly as a result of violating other instruments such as the United Nations Charter and the Universal Declaration of Human Rights, which appears to imply that a treaty's object and purpose is not limited to the treaty itself but can also be derived from extraneous sources.[21]

In the *Air Services Agreement* case, the US argued that the losses suffered by one of the aircraft carriers was evidence that France had materially breached the treaty under consideration by suspending the flights. Klabbers assumes that this would mean that the object and purpose of the air services agreement was to provide air services. However, elsewhere, the US submitted that the "fundamental objective" was to provide cheap air travel. This argument proves, according to Klabbers, that the "notion of object and purpose turns out to be employed in substantiation of various distinct arguments.[22] The same author presents yet another case to prove his point. In the *Rainbow Warrior* arbitral award,[23] the arbitral tribunal defined all breaches of France as "material" without specifying, however, the object and purpose of the treaty in question, or indicating whether the breaches related to provisions essential for the accomplishment of the treaty's object and purpose.

---

[19] Klabbers, *supra* note 6, at 142.
[20] Case Concerning the Air Service Agreement of 27 March 1946 (United States *v.* France), ("Air Services Agreement case") Award of 9 December 1978, 54 ILR 338 (1979).
[21] Klabbers, *supra* note 6, at 142-143.
[22] *Id.*, 143.
[23] Rainbow Warrior Arbitration (New Zealand *v.* France), Award of 30 April 1990, 82 ILR 499 (1990).

These observations as to the nature of "object and purpose" of a treaty only prove the general confusion surrounding this problem. In the words of Buffard and Zemanek:

> With regret one must conclude at the end of the enquiry that the object and purpose of a treaty are indeed something of an enigma. The method for clarification suggested in the hypothesis provides an objective determination only in respect of a specially structured convention. While it was in all cases possible to establish the "purpose" of a convention beyond doubt from the language of its preamble, the "object" remained elusive in the testing [...] with the exception of [...] conventions with a [...] definite object. Generally, indications of the object may be found in most preambles but they are rarely exhaustively formulated. One is thus required to discover the object by interpreting the provisions of the respective treaty as a whole [...]. One thing is, however, clear: the consideration of treaty provisions to determine which of them are essential for achieving the purpose of the treaty, and are, therefore, its "object", and which of them are not, is a considerable challenge for States, even when undertaken in good faith. If the separation of "essential" and "unessential" is not undertaken with the help of formal criteria, like classifying final causes as unessential, the views of States as to the essential core of a treaty will nearly inevitably be subjective, particularly in espect of provisions concerning a judicial competence to decide disputes over the implementation of the treaty.[24]

Likewise, Greig analyses the difficulties of specifying and defining the "purpose and object" in relation to a material breach. He states:

> ... in the process of defining a sole object and purpose of a multifaceted treaty, the degree of abstraction in the definition will also increase. Ultimately, the right of termination may be lost because no single provision would be essential to the achievement of the treaty's object and purpose.

> To avoid this dilemma, article 60(3)(b) might be regarded as applying to the *principal* object and purpose. There are practical difficulties, however, with establishing a hierarchy of objects or purposes, apart from artificiality of the process (individual parties may have quite different objectives in mind or at least different priorities). Some objects or purposes would be demoted to a second-class status. [...]

> If materiality were equivalent to proportionality this difficulty could be circumvented. A treaty could have several significant purposes, and a breach sufficiently inimical to any of them would be material, but only with respect to that particular object and purpose. [...]

> With regard to the second proposition, if a broader meaning of "object or purpose" were accepted, materiality would have a second task to perform, namely that of limiting termination or suspension to the relevant parts of the treaty. But if materiality were equivalent of proportionality, or, indeed, if materiality were an expression of customary international law, which requires

---

[24] Buffard and Zemanek, *supra* note 6, at 342-343.

a degree of proportionality between the reaction and the wrongful act in question, would article 60(3) not have to be worded differently? Curiously enough, the answer seems to be both yes and no.[25]

Yet another issue that remains unclear is the problem of the breach itself. As Gomaa notes, the "literal interpretation of paragraph 3 (b) of Article 60 'material breach' depends exclusively upon the *character* of the violated *provisions* and does not take into consideration the degree or gravity of the *breach* itself".[26] According to the same author, close analysis of the commentary of the ILC on what became Article 60 appears to indicate "that the breach, and not only the breached provision, is significant in constituting a material breach." The ILC has stated that according to their unanimous decision "the right to terminate or suspend must be limited to cases where the breach is of a *serious* character",[27] This pronouncement of the ILC corresponds with the Arbitral Award in the *Tacna-Arica Arbitr*ation[28] (which in fact was analyzed by the Commission). The Arbitrator in the case stated "[i]t is manifest that if abuses of administration could have effect of terminating such an agreement, it would be necessary to establish such serious conditions as the consequence of administrative wrongs as would operate to frustrate the purpose of the agreement, and, in the opinion of the Arbitrator, a situation of such gravity has not been shown".[29]

During its work on material breach, the ILC saw the articles pertaining to this institution primarily as, on the one hand, recognizing the right of a party to a treaty to invoke the breach of a treaty as a ground for terminating it or suspending its operation; and on the other hand, it regarded these articles as providing for procedural safeguards against arbitrary denunciation of a treaty (in particular as contained in Article 65 of the VCLT and the preservation of stability of treaties). One of the issues discussed was the question of the kind of breach which may give rise to a right to terminate or suspend a treaty. It was decided that the breach had to be of a serious character. The discussion of the Commission was focused as well on an exact definition of the breach in question: i.e., fundamental or material. The "fundamental" breach was favoured by Fitzmaurice; however, the ILC preferred the description of a breach as "material". The Commission was of the view that the word "fundamental" might be understood to mean that only the violation of a provision directly touching upon the central purposes of the treaty could constitute a valid ground for the other party terminating it.[30] The Commission also recognized that other provisions which a party assumed to be

---

[25] Greig, *supra* note 4, at 353-354.
[26] Gomaa, *supra* note 4, at 32 Gomaa, note 4, at 32.
[27] Cited in Gomaa, *supra* note 4, at 33, YILC (1996), Vol. II, at 255.
[28] Tacna-Arica Question (Chile *v.* Peru), 2 RIAA (1925) 921.
[29] YILC (1966), Vol. II, at 943-944.
[30] YILC (1966), Vol.II, at 255.

essential for the effective implementation of a treaty may have been very material to the treaty, even though these provisions may be of ancillary character. The ILC stated that a repudiation of a treaty not sanctioned by any of the provisions of Article 60 would automatically be a material breach of the treaty (para. 3(a)). Material breach of a treaty would also be a violation of a provision essential to the accomplishment of any object and purpose of the treaty.

In conclusion, it may be observed that "[t]he history of the Convention as a whole, and of the provision relating to material breach, confirms that State practice upholds the extremely conservative approach of the different special rapporteurs who themselves had examined *doctrine* and State practice with considerable care. Breach of treaty does not bring that treaty to an end either for the party in breach or for the party injured by the breach, unless they both agree to regard the treaty as terminated ..."[31]

2. The Relationship Between Material Breach and State Responsibility

2.1 The Problem

The starting point of scrutinizing the relation between material breach of treaty and the law of State responsibility[32] is Article 73 of the VCLT which reads as follows: "The provisions of the present Convention shall not prejudice any question that may arise in regard to a treaty [...] from the international responsibility of a State[...]". The prevailing view in doctrine is that there is a clear distinction between taking countermeasures by a State and denunciation or suspension of a treaty.[33] This view was adhered to by Waldock, who stated that the right to denounce or suspend the operation of a treaty does not influence the other rights of the injured State as regards reprisals.[34] Similarly, Rosenne observed:

> Material breach of treaty, which alone has its *sedes materiae* in the law of treaties, may entitle the injured party to take steps to protect interests in the continued performance of the treaty by both parties. Breach by itself, that is breach whether or not it is a material breach, is not treated in the law of

---

[31] Rosenne, "Breach of Treaty", *supra* note 4, at 24.

[32] For an extensive overview on the subject until 1984, see Rosenne, "Breach of Treaty", *supra* note 4.

[33] L.-A. Sicilianos, "The Relationship Between Reprisals and Denunciation or Suspension of a Treaty", 4 *EJIL* (1993), 341.

[34] Sir H. Waldock, Second Report on the Law of Treaties, YILC (1963), Vol. II, at 76, paragraph 14.

treaties itself: its *sedes materiae* is to be found elsewhere, in the law of State responsibility.[35]

The purposes of countermeasures (reprisals) and of the means available under Article 60 of the VCLT are different. As Sicilianos points out, "[a]lthough in most cases reprisals have a coercive character, denunciation and suspension of the application of a treaty generally have a corrective aim, which is called for by an imbalance caused by the breach in the complex of reciprocal rights and obligations of the parties".[36] The fundamental difference between Article 60 on material breach and the law of State responsibility (countermeasures) was explained by Special Rapporteur Crawford in his third Report on State Responsibility.[37] He argued as follows:

> [I]t is clear that there is a legal difference between the suspension of a treaty (or a severable part of a treaty) and the refusal (whether or not justified) to comply with the treaty. The suspension of a treaty (or of a severable part of a treaty), if its legally justified, places the treaty in a sort of limbo; it ceases to constitute an applicable legal standard for the parties while it is suspended and until action is taken to bring it back into operation. By contrast, conduct inconsistent with terms of a treaty in force, if it is justified as a countermeasure, does not have the effect of suspending the treaty; the treaty continues to apply and the party taking countermeasures must continue to justify its non-compliance by reference to the criteria for taking countermeasures (necessity, proportionality, etc.) for as long as its non-compliance lasts. Countermeasures are no more ground for suspension of a treaty than necessity.[38]

He further explained:

> There is a clear distinction between action taken within the framework of the law of treaties [...], and conduct raising questions of State responsibility [...]. The law of treaties is concerned essentially with the content of primary rules and with the validity of attempts to alter them; the law of responsibility takes as given the existence of the primary rules (whether based on treaty or otherwise) and is concerned with the question whether conduct inconsistent with those rules can be excused and, if not, what the consequences of such conduct are. Thus it is coherent to apply Vienna Convention rules as to materiality of breach and the severability of provisions of a treaty in dealing with issues of suspension, and the rules proposed in the Draft articles as to proportionality etc., in dealing with countermeasures.[39]

---

[35] Rosenne, *supra* note 4, at 24.
[36] Sicilianos, *supra* note 33, at 345.
[37] J. Crawford, *Third Report on State Responsibility*, UN Doc. A/CN.4/507/Add.3 (1999).
[38] *Id.*, paragraph 324.
[39] *Id.*, paragraph 325.

The differentiation between means available to States under Article 60 and under the system of State responsibility and their substantive legal nature was noted by Riphagen – even before he became a Special Rapporteur.[40] He stated:

> Individual 'countermeasures' in relation to the treaty can go no further than the suspension of the operation of the treaty in relations between the defaulting state and the state 'specially affected by the breach.' Such suspension does of course relate to the obligation to perform the treaty, but (article 72) 'does not otherwise affect the legal relations between the parties established by the treaty' and in particular does not release the parties from the obligation 'to refrain from acts tending to obstruct the resumption of the treaty'. A state party, not 'specially affected by the breach' may also take the 'countermeasure' of suspension but only 'if the treaty is of such character that a material breach of its provisions by one party radically changes the position of every party with respect to the further performance of its obligation under treaty.[41]

Riphagen also expressed the view that the provisions of Article 60 safeguard the stability of treaties, protecting a treaty from a complete breakdown as a result of a breach. He says that this purpose of Article 60 "seems to be relevant also within the context of allowed countermeasures. [...] The extra-state interests thus created by the treaty make the breach and the countermeasures a matter which regards the group of states parties to the treaty as a whole".[42] However, Riphagen used the term "countermeasures" in relation to the means available under Article 60. As already noted, the difference between countermeasures and the measures envisaged in Article 60 was maintained by Crawford, the last Special Rapporteur on State responsibility. One of the fundamental underlying premises of the Articles on State Responsibility that has a bearing on the essential differentiation between the framework of material breach under Article 60 and countermeasures is the distinction of the rules on State responsibility between primary and secondary rules, a division introduced by Roberto Ago and upheld as the basis of the final Articles.[43]

This division also has practical advantages. Crawford in his First Report on State Responsibility submitted that this distinction "allows some general rules to be restated and developed without having to resolve a myriad of issues about the content of application of particular rules, the breach of

---

[40] His views, however, were to a great extent reflected in his drafts as Special Rapporteur of the Commission on State responsibility.

[41] W. Riphagen, "State Responsibility: New Theories of Obligation in Interstate Relations", in R. St. J. Macdonald and D. M. Johnston (eds.), *The Structure and Process of International Law: Essays in Legal Philosophy, Doctrine and Theory* (1983), 581-625, at 601.

[42] *Id.*, 601.

[43] YILC (1970), Vol. II, at 306, paragraph 66 (c).

which may give rise to responsibility".[44] According to the ILC, the starting point is the establishment of the existence of a primary rule that creates an obligation under international law for a State, and the assumption that a question has arisen as to whether that State has complied with the obligation. Having ascertained that these two conditions are present, a number of issues of a general character arise which belong to the realm of the secondary rules of State responsibility.[45] In other words, the Articles deal with the consequences that flow from the commission of an internationally wrongful act as such. For these reasons, the Articles exclude, *inter alia,* consequences of a breach for the continued validity or binding effect of a primary rule, such as the right of an injured State to terminate or suspend a treaty for material breach, as enshrined in Article 60 of the VCLT. The ILC was clear as to the necessary distinction between the termination or suspension of treaty relations on account of the material breach on the one hand and countermeasures on the other. Countermeasures concern conduct justified by its proportionality and necessity, taken in derogation from subsisting treaty obligations, in response to an internationally wrongful act of a State against which they are taken. By their nature they are temporary measures, adopted to achieve a required effect that loses its justification once this effect is achieved.[46] Greig, very critical as to Article 60, noted the conflict between Articles 42(2) ("the termination of a treaty, its denunciation or the withdrawal of a party, may take place only as a result of the application of the provisions of the treaty or of the present Convention. The same rule applies to suspension of the operation of a treaty") and Article 73 ("the provisions of the present Convention shall not prejudice any question that

---

[44] J. Crawford, *First Report on State Responsibility,* UN Doc. A/CN.4/490 (1998), at paragraph 16.

[45] These issues include: a) the role of international law as distinct from the internal law of the State concerned in characterising conduct as unlawful; b) determining in what circumstances conduct is to be attributed to the State as a subject of international law; c) specifying when and for what period of time there is or has been a breach of an international obligation; d) determining in what circumstance a State may be responsible for the conduct of another State which is incompatible with an international obligation of the latter; e) defining the circumstances in which wrongfulness of conduct under international law may be precluded; f) specifying the content of State responsibility, in terms of cessation of the wrongful act, and reparation for an injury done; g) determining any procedural or substantive preconditions for a State to invoke the responsibility of another State, and the circumstances in which the right to invoke responsibility may be lost; h) laying down the conditions under which a State may be entitled to respond to a breach of an international obligation by taking countermeasures designed to ensure the fulfilment of the obligations of the responsible State under these rules. see Report of the ILC on the work of its fifty-third session (23 April - 1 June and 2 July - 10 August 2001), GAOR Supplement No. 10 (A/56/10), paragraph 77(3).

[46] Crawford, *First Report on State Responsibility, supra* note 44, at paragraph 326.

may arise in regard to a treaty ... from international responsibility of a State"):

> On its face, article 42 (2) seems to give the Convention regime priority with regard to the continued existence of the treaty or the primary rights it creates, despite the fact that the Convention is not to affect the international responsibility of states under article 73. The difficulty with this interpretation is that the Convention regime is incomplete. For example, non-material breaches are, by virtue of article 73, left to the rules concerning the responsibility of states. However, articles 60 and 42 imply that the rules in question should not impinge upon the Convention restrictions. The problem is that principles of reciprocity and proportionality are the hallmarks of the customary system of state responsibility.[47]

The law of State responsibility accepts the existence of the primary rules, regardless of their source, and its purpose is to find an answer to the question whether conduct inconsistent with those rules can be excused and, if not, to the question of the consequences of such conduct.[48] The law of State responsibility and as a result, the Articles presented by the Commission, are not, therefore, conceptually concerned with the consequences of a breach for the continued validity or binding effect of the primary rule, such as the right of an injured State to terminate or suspend a treaty for material breach, as set out in Article 60 of the VCLT.[49]

Evidence of the confusion surrounding material breach and countermeasures can be seen in the fact that Article 60 is often viewed in the context of proportionality of remedies available, despite the doctrinal differences between these two concepts. As a general rule, confirmed by the arbitral award in the *Air Services Agreement* case, a remedy must exhibit "some degree of equivalence with the alleged breach."[50] In the light of this award, Greig to express criticism regarding the absence in Article 60 of true proportionality which, in relation to the law of treaties, may be translated as "reciprocity".[51] In his view, the provisions of Article are defective in a number of ways and do not reflect the state of international law as it stands at present. First, he argues that this Article 60 grants a power to the innocent party to terminate or suspend a treaty, in whole or in part, in response to a breach, which appears to disregard the role that the principle of proportionality plays in limiting this power. The second objection relates to the consideration that Article 60 defines materiality in terms of the importance of the provision breached and not in terms of the gravity of

---

[47] Greig, *supra* note 4, 357.

[48] Crawford, *First Report on State Responsibility, supra* note 44, at paragraph 325.

[49] Report of the International Law Commission, 53rd Session (23 April to 1 June; 2 July to 10 August 2001), 56 UNGAOR, Supplement No. 10 (A156/10) ("ILC Report 2001").

[50] Air Services Agreement case, *supra* note 20, at 443, paragraph 83.

[51] Greig, *supra* note 4, at 342; *id.,* 343. See text accompanying note 18 above.

breach; but this, he argues, implies that "a minor breach of an important provision can give rise to the right of termination, whereas a serious breach of a provision not essential to the accomplishment of the object and purpose of the treaty does not do so".[52] A further objection relates to the equation in Article 60 of suspension and termination of treaties in cases of breach; but suspension implies the willingness of the party concerned to resume the relationship, which is impossible in case of termination.

A closer look at Article 44, dealing with the separability of treaty provisions, and in particular paragraphs 2 and 3, of the VCLT does not justify the assumption that it can be applicable in cases of material breach.[53] Greig explains that Article 44(3) and Article 60 on the wording of Article 44(2) are "equal exceptions".[54] From this it follows that Article 44(3) has no priority over Article 60. In fact, Articles 60(3)(b) and 44(3) operate in different circumstances. The former concerns the violation of a provision essential to the accomplishment of the object and purpose of a treaty, while Article 44(3) is relevant only to clauses that are "not an essential basis of the consent of the other party or parties to be bound by a treaty as a whole." Greig argues that the formula adopted by the VCLT did not reflect international customary law on material breach as applied by the ICJ in the *Namibia* opinion.[55] Greig suggests that "[i]t would have been more in keeping with state practice for the International Law Commission to have drafted article 60 simply as a limit to the course of conduct open to a party affected by a breach".[56] This solution, he continues, would allow formulating Article 60 as granting to a party a right to terminate a treaty in whole or in part only if, first, the breach is material and, second, performance or satisfaction by a party in breach is not forthcoming. Judicial practice, as evidenced by the *Air Services Agreement* case, suggests, in contrast to Article 42(2) of the VCLT, that the right of suspension exists under the

---

[52] *Id.*, 343.

[53] The relevant paragraphs of Article 44 read as follows:

"(2) A ground for invalidating, terminating, withdrawing from or suspending the operation of a treaty recognized in the present Convention may be invoked only with respect to the whole treaty except as provided for in article 60.

(3) If the ground relates solely to particular clauses, it may be invoked only with respect to those clauses where: (a) the said clauses are separable from the remainder of the treaty with regard to their application;

(b) it appears from the treaty or is otherwise established that acceptance of those clauses was not an essential basis of the consent of the other party or parties to be bound by the treaty as a whole; and (c) continued performance of the remainder of the treaty would not be unjust."

[54] Greig, *supra* note 4, at 345.

[55] Legal Consequences, *supra*, note 2 and accompanying text.

[56] Greig, *supra* note 4, at 368, see also at 369.

general law of responsibility. Article 60, in Greig's view, fails to embody the concepts of reciprocity (*inadimplenti non est adimplentum*) and proportionality that were the cornerstones of the *Air Services Agreement* case.

However, these critical remarks of Greig regarding Article 60 are not shared by Gomaa, who is of the view that "proportionality is pre-built into the mechanism of Article 60, and it is automatically applied when measures contained therein are activated." This is achieved "essentially by virtue of the combined effect of the relation of paragraphs 1 and 2 with paragraph 3". Gomaa also submits that the grounds laid down in Article 60(3) are sufficiently significant "to render termination or suspension not a disproportionate response".[57]

The above discussion illustrates the problems and the confusion surrounding the uneasy relationship between Article 60 and the rules of State responsibility. This is particularly discernible in relation to available countermeasures within the paradigm of State responsibility and the measures adopted under Article 60. There are several contrasting, if not mutually exclusive, approaches to this question which also include the interpretation of the principle of *inadimplenti non est adimplentum.* There appears to be disagreement regarding the distinction between those measures that have their source in the law of treaties and those derived from State responsibility.

2.2 Judicial and Arbitral Decisions

In general, the position has not been clarified in judicial and arbitral decisions.

The pleadings of the United States in the *Air Services Agreement* case indicate that it considered termination or suspension of the treaty as the ultimate response to breach of a treaty: "[i]f a trivial or nonmaterial breach gave the aggrieved party an excuse to terminate all treaty obligations, the rule of *pacta sunta servanda* would be seriously impaired. However, where the sanction to be invoked is a simple reciprocal withdrawal of rights, the rule of proportionality provides an adequate safeguard."[58] The United States appears to have considered the use of countermeasures as applicable to lesser breaches of international law, but did not exclude the possibility of recourse to suspension or termination in case of material breach. Thus, it appears that in the above view, the notion of reciprocity does not exclude the latter

---

[57] Gomaa, *supra* note 4, at 120-121.
[58] Air Services Agreement case, *supra* note 20; see also, L.F. Damrosch, "Retaliation or Arbitration – Or Both? The 1978 United States-France Aviation Dispute", 74 *AJIL* (1980), 785-807.

possibility, but rather limits the affected State's response. While both the United States and France, in their pleadings, attempted to differentiate rigorously between the measures rooted in the law of treaties and those belonging to the law of State responsibility,[59] there was some confusion as to the precise legal nature of the adopted measures. In fact, both States appeared to apply to material breach the legal attributes that are characteristic of State responsibility. It may be inferred from the pleadings that neither of the parties took into account the division between primary and secondary rules of international law, which is of fundamental importance for the law of State responsibility. Had they done so, measures under material breach and measures under the régime of State responsibility would be clearly defined and separated.

The Decision of the Arbitral Tribunal did not dwell on the legal differences stemming from material breach and countermeasures. The Tribunal focused on two questions: the principle of legitimacy of countermeasures and the limits of such measures in the light of either the existence of a machinery for negotiations or a mechanism of arbitration or judicial settlement.[60] The Tribunal confirmed the legality of countermeasures under international law: "If a situation arises which, in one State's view, results in the violation of an international obligation by another State, the first State is entitled, within the limits set by general rules of international law pertaining to the use of armed force, to affirm its rights through 'counter-measures'."[61]

What is interesting is that the Tribunal expressly stated that it was of no importance – at least to the case at hand – to "introduce various doctrinal distinctions and adopt a diversified terminology dependent on various criteria, in particular whether it is an obligation allegedly breached which is the subject of the countermeasures or whether the latter involve another obligation, and whether or not all obligations under consideration pertain to the same convention".[62] Likewise, the Tribunal found that the source of the measures – the law of treaties or the law of State responsibility - adopted by the US was not important. The Tribunal confirmed that countermeasures must be "equivalent" or "proportionate".[63] Further, the Tribunal explained that the state of present international law did not endorse the belief that when the party enters negotiations, it is automatically prohibited from adopting countermeasures, "especially where such counter-measures are accompanied by an offer for a procedure affording the possibility of accelerating the

---

[59] Air Services Agreement case, *supra* note 20, at paragraph 18.
[60] *Id.*, paragraphs 80-99.
[61] *Id.*, paragraph 81.
[62] *Id.*
[63] *Id.*, paragraph 83.

solution of the dispute".[64] Equally, the agreement to resort to judicial settlement does not prevent parties from taking countermeasures. It is only the actual setting-up of an arbitral tribunal or actual recourse to judicial proceedings that leads to disappearance of the possibility of applying countermeasures.

The principle of reciprocity was, to a limited extent, the subject of pleadings before the Court in the *Oil Platforms* case.[65] However, the Court did not refer to this question in its Judgment. In particular, the notion of reciprocity in this case related to non-performance. Counsel for the United States, Mr. Mathias, pleaded that breach of reciprocal obligations by a State (in this case the alleged breach by Iran of the 1955 Treaty) quashes the possibility for that State to object to corresponding non-performance.[66]

The *Rainbow Warrior* arbitral award is equally inconclusive as to the relationship between countermeasures, Article 60 and the *pacta sunta servanda* principle. The breached agreement in question related to the detention of two French officers on an island in the Pacific Ocean. They were detained there to complete their prison sentence, which was imposed on them by a Criminal Court in New Zealand for the bombing of the "Rainbow Warrior" in the harbour of Auckland.[67] France claimed that both officers had to be transferred due to medical emergency. The arguments of the parties to the dispute were focused, on the one hand, on the law of treaties (New Zealand), i.e., on the view that the act of France should be analysed in the light of the provisions relating to a fundamental change of circumstances, as enshrined in the VCLT.[68] France, on the other hand, looked to the Draft Articles on State Responsibility. France's pleadings were based on the principle of the universal applicability of the circumstances of *force majeur* and distress to all breaches of an international obligation – irrespective of its source.[69] Although the Tribunal took notice of the provisions of Article 60 and of the *pacta sunta servanda* principle, it was primarily concerned with the question whether there was a breach of an international obligation, and not with the extent of the breach. The Tribunal explained that the alleged breach of the obligation which had its roots in the law of treaties did not preclude the application of the rules of States responsibility, which relate to all breaches of international obligations,

---

[64] *Id.*, paragraph 91.
[65] See, e.g., public sitting held on Wednesday, 5 March 2003, at 3 p.m. at the Peace Palace, in the case concerning Oil Platforms (Islamic Republic of Iran *v.* United States of America), verbatim record, CR 2003/18. <http://www.icj-cij.org/icjwww/idocket/iop/iopcr/iop_icr2003-17_20030305.PDF>.
[66] *Id.*
[67] See note 23.
[68] *Id.*, 549.
[69] *Id.*

regardless of their source, "since in the international law field there is no distinction between contractual and tortuous responsibility, so that any violation by a State of any obligation, of whatever origin, gives rise to State responsibility and consequently, to the duty of reparation".[70] It follows that the existence of circumstances precluding wrongfulness in this case should be ascertained in the light of the customary law of State responsibility, without prejudice to the terms of the agreement between the parties and the relevant provisions of the VCLT.

2.3 The *Gabčikovo-Nagymaros* case

The issue of the relationship between material breach and the law of State responsibility has been recently addressed in the *Gabčikovo-Nagymaros* case decided by the ICJ on 25 September 1997.[71] Since the relationship between the material breach and the law of State responsibility featured extensively in this case, it merits broader discussion. First, the issue of material breach will be discussed, followed by the issue of State responsibility and, finally, it will be shown how these problems are inexorably connected with each other.

The *Gabčikovo-Nagymaros* case involved the construction and operation of installations in the Bratislava-Budapest section of the Danube River which was going to be affected by the 1977 Treaty Concerning the Construction and Operation of the Gabčikovo-Nagymaros System of Locks (the "1977 Treaty").[72] The portion in question of the Danube River formed the frontier between Hungary and the Slovak Republic, with Cunovo and Gabčikovo situated on the Slovak territory and Nagymaros situated on the Hungarian territory. The substantive provisions of the 1977 Treaty provided for the construction and operation of a system of locks by the parties as a joint investment. The system's objective was to achieve "the broad utilization of the natural resources of the Bratislava-Budapest section of the Danube river for the development of water resources, energy, transport, agriculture and other sectors of the national economy of the Contracting Parties".[73] The project's aims were the following: production of electricity; improvement of navigation; protection against flooding. The parties were mindful of the requirements of the protection of nature and of the upholding of the water quality in the Danube, while erecting the system of locks.

---

[70] *Id.*, 599.
[71] Gabčikovo-Nagymaros Project (Hungary *v.* Slovakia), Judgment of 25 September, 1997 ICJ Rep. 7 ("Gabčikovo-Nagymaros case"). See chapter 10 below for further discussion of other aspects of the law of treaties arising in this case.
[72] Reprinted in 32 *ILM* 1247 (1993).
[73] Preamble to the 1977 Treaty, *id.;* Gabčikovo-Nagymaros Project, *supra* note 71, at 17-18.

Article 1 (2) of the Treaty provided for the building of two systems of locks: one situated on the territory of Czechoslovakia and the other in the territory of Hungary. The entire system was very complicated and consisted of a dam, a power plant, and a bypass canal. The whole system was supposed to constitute "a single and indivisible operational system of works".[74] The work was based upon the principle of joint management and financing in which both parties participated in equal measure. Hungary committed itself to control the sluices at Dunakiliti and the works at Nagymaros, and Czechoslovakia was to control the works at Gabčikovo. The work on the project started in 1978. In 1983, however, upon the request of Hungary, the parties signed a Protocol to slow down the project and to postpone putting into operation the power plants. By the Protocol of 1989, the parties decided to speed up the project. In 1989, only the work in the Czechoslovak sector was very well advanced. The collapse of the communist regime prompted growing negative attitudes towards the project. The foremost doubts were expressed as to its economic viability and the effects of the completion of the project on the environment. This resulted in the decision of the Hungarian Government to suspend the project in 1989. In view of the actions taken by Hungary, Czechoslovakia adopted a unilateral solution which became known as "Variant C". This entailed a unilateral diversion of the Danube by Czechoslovakia on its territory, upstream of Dunakiliti. "Variant C" included the erection of the construction at Cunovo of an overflow dam and a levee connecting that dam to the south bank of the bypass canal. The provisional solution was followed by a decision to continue the construction of the Gabčikovo project. In 1991, the work was started on the "Variant C". In 1992, the Hungarian Government transmitted a *note verbale* to the Czechoslovak Government terminating the 1977 Treaty. In 1992, Czechoslovakia proceeded to dam the river. In 1993, Slovakia became the Slovak Republic, an independent State. In 1993, Hungary and the Slovak Republic signed a Special Agreement to submit the dispute to the ICJ.[75]

2.3.1 Material Breach

Hungarys contended that Czechoslovakia had violated Articles 15, 19 and 20 of the 1977 Treaty by refusing to enter into negotiations with Hungary to adopt the Joint Contractual Plan to new developments in environmental protection. These Articles were specifically designed to oblige the parties to take appropriate measures necessary for the protection of water quality, of

---

[74] 1977 Treaty, *infra* note 85, at 1247.
[75] Special Agreement between the Republic of Hungary and the Slovak Republic for Sub-mission to the International Court of Justice of the Differences between them concerning the Gabčikovo-Nagymaros Project, note 71, at 11. The text is also reproduced 32 *ILM* 1291 (1993).

nature and of fishing interests jointly on a continuous basis. The Court was of the view that while both parties indicated in principle a willingness to undertake further research, Czechoslovakia refused to countenance a suspension of the works at Dunakiliti, and at a later stage of the implementation of "Variant C". Hungary then asked for suspension as a prior condition for environmental research. It claimed that continuation of works would prejudice the outcome of negotiations. The Court found that suspension of the works by Hungary at Nagymaros and Dunakiliti was a contributory factor to creating a situation that was not favourable for conducting negotiations.[76] Hungary relied mainly on the construction of "Variant C" by Czechoslovakia as the basis for invoking material breach of the 1977 Treaty. The Court found that Czechoslovakia only violated the 1977 Treaty when it diverted the waters of the Danube into the bypass canal in October 1992. However, in constructing the works which lead to the operation of "Variant C", Czechoslovakia did not act unlawfully. The Court held that the notification of termination by Hungary in 1992 was premature, and that Czechoslovakia had not yet breached the 1977 Treaty. This lead the Court to conclude that Hungary was not entitled, at the time that it did, to invoke any such breach of the 1977 Treaty as a ground for terminating it. Moreover, the Court took the view that Hungary's declaration (issued on 6 May 1992 with effect as from 25 May 1992) terminating the 1977 Treaty was not in accordance with the principle of good faith. In fact, both parties were in agreement that Articles 65 to 67 of the VCLT, if not codifying customary law, at least generally reflect it, and contain certain procedural principles that are based on good faith. The Court concluded that by its own conduct, Hungary prejudiced its right to terminate the 1977 Treaty. The Court quite forcefully stated that "this would still have been the case even if Czechoslovakia, by the time of the purported termination, had violated a provision essential to the accomplishment of the object or purpose of the Treaty".[77] The Court applied the rules and procedures relating to material breach in a very rigorous manner, in requiring the observance of procedural as well as substantive obligations. The Judgment indicates that the Court supported the principle of stability of treaties and approached all rules concerning the possibility of unilateral termination, including those relating to material breach, with due caution.

It will be noted that in this respect, the Court's approach is in line with its approach in the *ICAO* case, where the Court assumed a limited view as to material breach as a ground for termination.[78] Although the statements of the Court on that matter were in relation to jurisdictional clauses, nonetheless, it

---

[76] Gabčíkovo-Nagymaros Project, note 71, at 66, paragraph 107.

[77] *Id.*, at 67, paragraph 110.

[78] Appeal Relating to the Jurisdiction of the ICAO Council (India *v.* Pakistan), Judgment of 18 August 1972, 1972 ICJ Rep. 46 ("ICAO case"), at 38.

must be recalled that "[m]uch of the rationale advanced by the Court to restrict claims of unilateral right under general international law to terminate or suspend jurisdictional treaties for breach would appear to have cogency in relation to all treaties, whether or not they contain jurisdictional clauses".[79]

2.3.2 State Responsibility and Material Breach

The Court in the *Gabčikovo-Nagymaros* case made several *obiter dicta* on the relationship between the law of treaties and the law of State responsibility that further elucidated this complicated issue. In particular, the Court stated, in line with the approach of the ILC:

> A determination of whether a convention is or is not in force, and whether it has or has not been properly suspended or denounced, is to be made pursuant to the law of treaties. On the other hand, an evaluation of the extent to which the suspension or denunciation of a convention, seen as incompatible with the law of treaties, involves the responsibility of the State which proceeded to it, is to be made under the law of State responsibility.[80]

The pleadings of Hungary appear to assimilate to a certain extent the arguments based on the law of State responsibility with that of the law of treaties. It pleaded one of the grounds of termination of the 1977 Treaty as constituting a state of necessity. The Court rejected this argument:

> In this respect, the Court will merely observe that, even if a state of necessity is found to exist, it is not a ground for the termination of a treaty. It may only be invoked to exonerate from its responsibility a State which has failed to implement a treaty. Even if found justified, it does not terminate a Treaty; the Treaty may be ineffective as long as the condition of necessity continues to exist; it may in fact be dormant, but – unless the parties by mutual agreement terminate the Treaty – it continues to exist. As soon as the state of necessity ceases to exist, the duty to comply with the treaty obligations revives.[81]

In addition, Hungary argued in its memorial that the termination of the 1977 Treaty operated as a countermeasure in response to the unilateral modification and application by Slovakia.[82] A further argument by Hungary was that the termination of the 1977 Treaty was not only justified by the plea of material breach by Slovakia, but also permissible on the grounds of the

---

[79] H.W. Briggs, "Unilateral Denunciation of Treaties: The Vienna Convention and the International Court of Justice", 68 *AJIL* (1974), 51, at 60-61.
[80] Gabčikovo-Nagymaros Project, note 71, at paragraph 47.
[81] *Id.*, at 84, paragraph 101.
[82] See the Declaration of Hungary concerning the termination of the 1977 Treaty, 32 *ILM* 1259 (1993), at 1285-1288; see also extensively R. Lefeber, "The Gabčikovo-Nagymaros Project and the Law of State Responsibility", 11 *LJIL* (1998), 608-623, in particular at 618-620.

violation of environmental obligations by Slovakia under general international law.[83] The Court, however, held as follows:

> As to that part of Hungary's argument which was based on other treaties and general rules of international law, the Court is of the view that it is only a material breach of the treaty itself, by a State party to that treaty, which entitles the other party to rely on it as a ground for terminating the treaty. The violation of other treaty rules or rules of general international law may justify the taking of certain measures, including countermeasures, by an injured State, but it does not constitute a ground for termination under the law of treaties.[84]

2.4 Conclusion

According to one view, the question of material breach as formulated in Article 60 of the VCLT is subsumed under the rule of stability of treaties expressed in Article 26 of the VCLT, i.e., *pacta sunt servanda*. This approach was indeed the core of the foundation of the work of the ILC in relation to material breach. The ILC, in formulating Article 60, was concerned with avoiding *Sportpalast-Diplomatie* - the blatant and illegal breaches of international treaty obligations.[85] The Commission indeed adopted a cautious approach towards material breach, asserting that it "was agreed that a breach of a treaty, however serious, does not *ipso facto* put an end to the treaty, and also that it is not open to States simply to allege a violation of a treaty and pronounce the treaty at an end. On the other hand, it considered that within certain limits and subject to certain safeguards the right of a party to invoke the breach of a treaty as ground for terminating it or suspending its operation must be recognized".[86] As Waldock explained at the Diplomatic Conference, the intention of the Commission was to strike a balance between the need to uphold the stability of treaties and the need to ensure reasonable protection of the innocent victim of the breach of the treaty.[87]

The view has been expressed that the ability to terminate or suspend a treaty is not a legal consequence of material breach,[88] but that "[f]or the sake

---

[83] See the Memorial of the Republic of Hungary, Vol. I, at 316-317, 317-319.

[84] Gabčikovo-Nagymaros Project, note 71, at paragraph 106.

[85] Rosenne, "Breach of Treaty", *supra* note 4, at 11.

[86] YILC (1966), Vol. II, at 225.

[87] Official Records of the United Nations Conference on the Law of Treaties, First Session, Vienna, 6 March 1968, UN Doc. A/CONF-39/11, at 335.

[88] R. Mazzeschi, "Termination and Suspension of Treaties for Breach in the ILC Works on State Responsibility", in M. Spinedi and B. Simma (eds.), *United Nations Codification of State Responsibility* (1987), at 57.

of legal security and treaty stability [...] termination or suspension have been subjected to many restrictive conditions and limitations to curb any possible abuse".[89] It was asserted that it is a form of non-violent self-help, which is a measure taken as a lawful response to a breach deriving from the law of treaties and not from State responsibility. Therefore, the above view seems to circumvent the uneasy relationship between termination of a treaty under Article 60 and countermeasures by assessing it from a different point of view, namely, the principle *pacta sunt servanda*. According to this theory, the guiding principle appears to be the stability of treaties, not the idea of a penalty inflicted on the erring State.

In our view, the transposition of institutions of the law of State responsibility to the law of treaties cannot be justified. Such reasoning ignores the doctrinal differentiation between measures having their source in the law of treaties and those that have their source in the law of State responsibility, but the purpose and legal effects of both areas of the law are different. As the ILC explained:

> Countermeasures are to be clearly distinguished from the termination or suspension of treaty relations on account of the material breach of a treaty by another State, as provided for in article 60 of the Vienna Convention on the Law of Treaties. Where a treaty is terminated or suspended in accordance with article 60, the substantive legal obligations of the States parties will be affected, but this is quite different from the question of responsibility that may already have arisen from the breach. Countermeasures involve conduct taken in derogation from a subsisting treaty obligation but justified as a necessary and proportionate response to an internationally wrongful act of the State against which they are taken. They are essentially temporary measures, taken to achieve a specified end whose Justification terminates once the end is achieved.[90]

The confusion between the material breach and State responsibility is possibly rooted in the issue of sources of a breach of an international obligation, as defined by Article 12 of the Articles on State Responsibility. This Article reads as follows: "There is a breach of an international obligation by a State when an act of that State is not in conformity with what is required of it by that obligation, regardless of its origin and character". These sources may be, e.g., customary law, a treaty, a unilateral act, or a judgment of an international tribunal. In other words, "[t]he formula 'regardless of origin' refers to all possible sources of international obligations, that is to say, to all processes for creating legal obligations recognized by international law".[91] Equally, there does not exist in international law a

---

[89] Gomaa, *supra* note 4, at 184.
[90] ILC Report 2001, *supra* note 49, Introductory commentary to Part Three, Chapter II, paragraph (4).
[91] *Id.,* commentary to Article 12, paragraph (3).

division between responsibility *ex delicto* and *ex contractu*.[92] Thus, the confusion as to material breach and the law of State responsibility has its origin in the lack of proper differentiation between the source of a breach of an international obligation (that indeed is not based on a classification of origin of a breach) and measures adopted in connection with the suspension of a treaty (the material breach) and the refusal to comply with a treaty (the adoption of countermeasures). The assimilation of State responsibility with the law of treaties also blurs the difference between primary and the secondary rules.[93] With regard to this distinction, which is supported in doctrine,[94] Lefeber observes:

> The objective of Article 60 of the Vienna Convention is to regulate the *long-term* future treaty relationship between the parties to a treaty following a material breach of the treaty by one of the parties, and not legal consequences of an internationally wrongful act. The right of a state to suspend or terminate a treaty in response to a material breach of that treaty by another party is clearly distinct from the right to resort to countermeasures. The latter right enables a state to secure cessation and/or reparation for an internationally wrongful act and does not provide a state with a legal instrument to regulate a long-term relationship. For this reason, it cannot be assumed too lightly that the termination of a treaty can be justified by the right to resort to countermeasures, if at all. The material breach of a treaty may not even have amounted to an internationally wrongful act, as the wrongfulness of such act may have been precluded by one of the circumstances precluding wrongfulness recognized in the law of state responsibility. Yet, in such a case, a state has the right to suspend or terminate a treaty in response to a material breach by another state, but surely not the right to resort to countermeasures.[95]

In our view, the term countermeasures must be used in a strict manner, i.e., as an institution that belongs to the field of State responsibility. Countermeasures are measures that may be taken by an injured State to vindicate its rights as a consequence of the commission of a wrongful act by another State and further to restore the legal relationship with the responsible State that has been disrupted by the wrongful act. We are aware of the contrasting view according to which suspension or termination of a treaty under Article 60 of the VCLT is considered to be a countermeasure of a more flexible,[96] generic type, whose legal nature is not strictly defined but

---

[92] This was confirmed by the *Rainbow Warrior* arbitration; see text accompanying notes 23 and 67.

[93] Crawford, *supra* note 37, at paragraph 325.

[94] W. Riphagen, *Fourth Report on the Content, Forms and Degrees of State Responsibility* (Part 2 of the Draft Articles), YILC (1963), Vol. II, Part I, at 17, paragraph 2.

[95] R. Lefeber, "The Gabčikovo-Nagymaros Project and the Law of State Responsibility", 11 *LJIL* (1998), 608-623, at 611-612.

[96] G. Abi-Saab, "General Course of Public International Law", 207 *RCADI* (1987-VII), 15-463.

depends on circumstances in which these instruments operate. However, this type of reasoning adds more confusion and in some ways blurs the necessary distinction between the law of treaties and that of State responsibility. Finally, it must be noted that the ILC, during its codification of the law of treaties, was aware of the possible confusion that might have arisen between the law of treaties and the law of State responsibility. The role of Article 73 of the VCLT was considered to "prevent any misconception from arising as to the interrelation between rules governing [the law of State responsibility] and the law of treaties".[97]

3. Breach of Treaty and the Different Types of Treaty Obligations: The Legacy of Fitzmaurice's Classification

The issue of the classification of international treaty obligations of states arose in connection with Sir Gerald Fitzmaurice's work on the termination of treaties and the conflict between successive treaties. This question was dealt with first in his Reports and subsequently, in the Draft Expository Code in which Fitzmaurice provided several definitions of such obligations.[98] During his work on the codification of law of treaties, Sir Gerald Fitzmaurice, as Special Rapporteur, introduced a classification of the obligations of States within the structure of the law of treaties. The category of obligations he described as integral obligations[99], which appears to be gaining a certain degree of currency,[100] will be the focus of this Section. The importance of Fitzmaurice's classification for contemporary law of treaties and the law of State responsibility will be highlighted in this Section and the one following.

Fitzmaurice identified and distinguished between three types of treaty obligations, namely the reciprocal type, and the non-reciprocal types, i.e.: interdependent obligations and integral obligations. These types of obligations will be discussed below, first, in relation to termination of

---

[97] Commentary to Draft Article 69 of the 1966 Draft Articles on the Law of Treaties, YILC (1966), Vol. II, at 267, paragraph I.

[98] See, e.g., Articles 18 and 19 of the Draft Code, Fitzmaurice, "Second Report", YILC (1957), Vol. II, at 30-31, and 35; see also "Third Report", YILC (1958), Vol. II, at 27 (Article 18.

[99] The role of "integral" and "interdependent" obligations in the context of conflicts of environmental treaties is considered in chapter 9 below.

[100] See, e.g., J. Crawford, *The International Law Commission's Articles on State Responsibility: Introduction, Text and Commentary* (2002), at 257-260, 270 (on invocation of responsibility by an "injured" state); see further J. Pauwelyn, *Conflict of Norms in Public International Law: How WTO Law Relates to other Rules of International Law* (2003), at 52-88 (on the role of integral obligations in the context of treaty interpretation in WTO law in particular and international law in general).

treaties containing them and, then, in relation to the conflict of successive treaties.

Reciprocal obligations are obligations, which are held individually by each party to a treaty towards each of the parties to the treaty, individually. Under bi-lateral treaties, these obligations are inevitably reciprocal in nature, and under multi-lateral treaties they may be of this nature. The interdependent obligation type are obligations which, by reason of the character of a given treaty, are necessarily dependent upon the corresponding performance by all other parties (Article 19 paragraph 1(ii)(b)). An example of such obligation is contained in disarmament treaties (Article 61 of the Code).

Integral obligations, in contrast, and as the name suggests, require absolute and integral performance (Article 18 paragraph 1), and are to be found in treaties "where the juridical force of the obligation is inherent, and not dependent on a corresponding performance by the other parties to the treaty", as in the cases of treaties containing interdependent or reciprocal obligations. Integral obligations are "of a self-existing character, requiring absolute and integral application and performance under all conditions..." (Article 19 paragraph 1 paragraph iv). An example is contained in the Convention on the Prevention and Punishment of the Crime of Genocide where "the obligation of each party was altogether independent of performance by any of the others, and would continue for each party even if defaults by others occur" (Commentary to Article 61 of the Code). Human rights treaties also fall into this category, as do treaties imposing obligations to maintain certain labour standards, to ban certain practices in implementation of the International Labour Conventions or under the maritime conventions as regards safety at sea. The same principles underlie the treatment of prisoners as expressed in the 1949 Geneva Convention (see, e.g, Article 60(5) of the VCLT), as well as those imposing international obligations to maintain a certain régime or system in a given area, such as the régime of the sounds and belts at the entrance of the Baltic Sea, as enshrined by the 1857 of Treaty Copenhagen and the 1857 Treaty of Washington (Commentary to Article 84 of the Code). Disarmament treaties, as explained by Fitzmaurice, illustrate the difference between integral and interdependent/reciprocal obligations. In principle, the obligation of each party to disarm, or to respect certain levels of armaments, or not to manufacture certain types of weapons, is "necessarily dependent on a corresponding performance of the same thing by all the other parties, since it is of the essence of such treaty that the undertaking of each party is given in return for a similar undertaking by others. Particular breaches by one party, amounting to a repudiation, would ensure for all practical purposes an end of the treaty, but this would come to pass from force of circumstances rather than from a juridical act of the parties declaring the end of the treaty.

Therefore, the case would in some ways be more akin to that of the tacit acceptance by parties of an illegal repudiation of the treaty on the part of them..." (Commentary to Article 84).

3.1 Termination of Treaties on Grounds of "Fundamental" Breach Depending on the Type of Obligation

According to Article 18 of the Draft Code, "fundamental" (i.e. material) breach operates as a ground giving right to the other party to declare the termination of the treaty in relation to bilateral and not to multilateral treaties (Article 18(1)(i)). Therefore, no matter how serious the breach of a multilateral treaty by one party, this does not give the other parties a right to terminate the treaty.

More specifically, in the case of reciprocal obligations, their fundamental breach may result in justification by other parties to refuse performance in the relation to the defaulting party, of any obligations of the treaty, which consists of a mutual and reciprocal grant or interchange between the parties of rights, benefits concessions or advantages, or of the right of particular treatment in respect to a particular matter (Article 19(1)(ii)(a)). In the case of interdependent obligations, their fundamental breach may justify the cessation of performance of any obligation in a treaty that has been subject to that breach (Article 19(1)(ii)(b). Further, with respect to a treaty of the interdependent type, when a party commits a general breach of the entire treaty in such a way as to constitute a repudiation of it, or a breach in so essential or particular a manner as to be tantamount to a repudiation, the other parties may treat it as terminated, or any of them may withdraw from further participation. In contrast, the fundamental breach of an "integral" obligation, by one party will never constitute a ground for termination or withdrawal of other parties (Article 19(1)(iv)(a) and cannot even (to the extent to which otherwise might be relevant or practicable) justify non-performance of the obligations of the treaty in respect of the defaulting party or its nationals or vessels (Article 19(1)(iv)(b).

Article 29 of the second Report and Article 94 of the Code deal with the legal effects of termination of treaties regarding different types of obligation. Again, Fitzmaurice distinguished between bilateral and multilateral treaties. In context of the bilateral treaties, "termination is necessarily of the treaty itself and for both parties..." (Article 29(1)(i). However, in the case of multilateral treaties the legal effect depends on the type of treaty obligation. Where the treaty contains an integral obligation, the treaty itself will not be terminated, nor will the participation of any other party. Due to the legal character of the treaty, although the party in question will cease to be bound by the obligations of the treaty as such, the remaining parties will continue to be fully bound in order to implement it, even though, as a result, the party whose participation has ended, its nationals, vessels, continue to enjoy the benefits of the treaty (Article 29(1)(ii)). In the case of reciprocal (or concessionary types) of obligation, the treaty itself will not be terminated, nor will the participation of any other party, but the remaining parties will be entitled to refuse to carry out its obligations towards the party which ceases to participate and to stop according to such party any of the rights or benefits pertaining under the treaty (Article 29 paragraph 1 (iii)). In the case of the fully interdependent obligations, "where the participation of all the parties is a condition of the obligatory force of the treaty, the remaining parties will, by reason of the character of the treaty, be released from their own obligations, and the treaty will accordingly come to an end" (Article 29(1)(iii)).

The groundbreaking division of obligations introduced by Fitzmaurice was reflected to some extent in the VCLT (see below).[101] The VCLT does not contain any provisions that are directly descriptive of the reciprocal type of obligation. However, it is apparent that the drafters of the treaty were aware of the distinction between the different kinds of obligation introduced by Fitzmaurice from the wording of Article 41, which limits the right of a group of some (but not all) of the parties to a multilateral treaty to modify its terms as between themselves, to a modification which:

> (i)does not affect the enjoyment by the other parties of their rights under the treaty or the performance of their obligations;
>
> (ii)does not relate to a provision, derogation from which is incompatible with the effective execution of the object and purpose of the treaty as a whole;.[102]

The VCLT does not contain any provision in the same terms as the various provisions in Fitzmaurice's Draft Code relating to the "integral" obligation. But, again, the VCLT does appear to recognize a type of treaty in which the effect of breach is basically the same as that ascribed by Fitzmaurice to the integral type of obligation. Article 60(5) provides that paragraphs 1 to 4 of the same Article, which set out the rights of the other parties in multilateral treaties to breach of obligations by one party, and in particular rights such as to suspend the operation of the treaty in relations between themselves and the defaulting party "do not apply to provisions relating to the protection of the human person contained in treaties of a humanitarian character, in particular to provisions prohibiting any form of reprisals against persons protected by such treaties". This provision certainly covers the same ground

---

[101] Waldock, who succeeded Fitzmaurice as Special Rapporteur on the law of treaties, upheld to a certain degree the classification of obligations introduced by Fitzmaurice, in spite of certain misgivings. "The Second Report" on the Law of Treaties, YILC (1964), Vol. II, at 59, paragraphs 25-32; see also YILC (1966), Vol. II, at 217, paragraph 13.
[102] Article 41(1)(b)(i) of the VCLT.

as the reference to treaties on human rights in the passage from the Fitzmaurice commentary quoted above. Existence of the other forms of treaty he cites may be controversial; but as stated above, both on the analogy of "conventions as regards standards of safety at sea" and of the concept of an "international obligation to maintain a certain régime or system in a given area" (of which, elsewhere, Fitzmaurice cites the Antarctic treaties as an example), many environmental treaties could fall within the description of "integral obligations".[103]

3.2 Solidarity Obligations

The classification of international obligations by Fitzmaurice may, to a certain degree, be reflected in what is called solidarity obligations, a notion which is relevant to breaches of multilateral treaties.[104] The notion of solidarity obligations is based on the premise that breaches of a multilateral treaty may affect to a certain (but to a different) degree all the parties to it, and therefore "broaden the number of States which are entitled to react to breaches of multilateral treaties". In particular, it has been often argued that all the parties to such a treaty should be recognized as enjoying the right, in the name of 'solidarity', to take at least some action against a State which breaches its obligations thereunder".[105] Depending on the extent of the right to take an action against a State that infringed the rights, Hutchinson distinguishes solidarity *sensu stricto* and *lato sensu*.[106] The directly injured State party to a multilateral treaty has an undisputed right ("first level right") of action against the wrongdoing State. However, apart from this first level

---

[103] See Fitzmaurice Draft Code, note 98, Article 18 and commentary thereto in "Third Report", YILC (1958), Vol. II, at 27 and 42.

[104] See D. N. Hutchinson, "Solidarity and Breaches of Multilateral Treaties", 59 *BYIL* (1988), 151-215, at 155; see also B. Simma, "Reflections on Article 60 of theVienna Convention on the Law of Treaties and Its Background in General International Law", 20 *ÖZÖRV* (1970), 5, at 49; P. Reuter, "Solidarité et divisibilité des engagements conventionnels", in Y. Dinstein and M. Tabory (eds.), *International Law at a Time of Perplexity: Essays in Honour of Shabtai Rosenne* (1989), 623; see also K. Sachariev, "State Responsibility for Multilateral Treaty Violations: Identifying the 'Injured State' and its Legal Status", 35 *NILR* (1988) 273; C. Annecker, "Part Two of the International Law Commission's Draft Articles on State Responsibility", 37 *GYIL* (1994) 206; A. de Hoogh, *Obligations Erga Omnes and International Crimes: A Theoretical Inquiry Into the Implementation and Enforcement of the International Responsibility of States* (1996); B. Simma, "Bilateralism and Community of Interest in the Law of State Responsibility", Dinstein and Tabory (eds.), above, at 821; B. Simma, "From Bilateralism to Community Interest in International Law", 250 *RCADI* (1994-IV), 221-384, at 349; M. Ragazzi, *The Concept of International Obligations Erga Omnes* (1997).

[105] Hutchinson, *id.*, at 156-157.

[106] *Id.*, 157-174.

of rights, there is a second level, which belongs to all other parties to a treaty, which gives them limited right of action, under certain circumstances, in cases of a breach of a right of one of the parties to the treaty that is necessary to uphold the existence of a multilateral treaty.[107] Hutchinson noted an important feature of the second level rights: they are "not auxiliary to first-level rights: they are not conferred on the parties to a treaty with the sole purpose of enabling them to assist those of their number whose first-level rights are infringed by a breach in the enforcement of their rights. On the contrary, each party is vested with them in recognition of its own individual and independent interest, severable from that of every other party, in upholding the legal regime which the treaty creates. This interest still exists even if the holder of a first-level right decides not to take steps at all to enforce its rights against the wrongdoing State."[108]

Hutchinson distinguishes solidarity (following the classical distinction in international law) in relation to "non-serious" breaches and "serious" breaches. In relation to the first type of solidarity, the same author reaches the conclusion, fully supported by practice, that "…the parties enjoy none of the rights which have been described above as rights by way of solidarity *lato sensu* and which might enable them to protest the treaty against erosion and amendment."[109] The lack of a possibility of an action based on the law of treaties does not deprive the State to take an action based on the law of State responsibility, i.e. countermeasures. The measures based on the law of treaties and the law of State responsibility derive from different sources and their legal character is entirely different, as argued in Section 2 above.

In the event of a serious breach of a treaty, Article 60 provides for a redress of both solidarity *sensu stricto* and *lato sensu*.

There is a link between the concept of solidarity and Fitzmaurice's classification of international obligations. Although the concept of solidarity is couched within terms of a right to remedies in case of a breach of a multilateral treaty obligation, it is clear that the extent of the solidarity right depends on the type of obligations breached: reciprocal, interdependent or integral. Article 60 of the Vienna Convention, if not explicitly, adopts such a classification, in which materiality of a breach is linked to a definition of an injured State and a right to a remedy. Article 60(2)(a)(i) and 60(2)(b) correspond to the concepts of a reciprocal and interdependent obligation, whilst Article 60(5) corresponds to the concept of an integral obligation. Article 60(2)(b), grants "a right severally in each 'specially affected' State, empowering it to make its own independent decision whether to suspend its treaty relations with the wrongdoer".[110] Article 60(2)(a)(i) grants this right to

---

[107] *Id.*, note 9.
[108] *Id.*, at 171.
[109] *Id.*, at 184.
[110] *Id.*, at 189.

a group of States, which act collectively, upon a decision adopted unanimously. As Hutchinson notes, the exercise of such a right may cause problems.[111] This leads us to consideration of a the question of the rights of parties affected by a material breach of a treaty.

4. The Notion of the "Injured State" and the Law of Treaties

Following on from the discussion in the previous section, special consideration must be given to the relationship between Article 60(2) of the VCLT and the relevant provisions in the ILC Articles on State responsibility in relation to the question of an injured State. The question of the rights and obligations of an injured State, both from the point of view of Article 60(2) of the VCLT and the relevant Articles on State Responsibility are pivotal not only in the context of available remedies, but also in the context of *locus standi* before international courts and tribunals. The main considerations in this section will be based on Article 42 and 48, adopted by the ILC on second reading at its 53rd Session in 2001. Within the framework of this section we are, in particular, interested in the definition of an "injured State" and how it relates to Article 60. As described above, this relationship is far from clear, both in academic opinion and in the relevant case-law.

4.1 Definition of the "Injured State"

The definition of an "injured state" is inexorably linked with other taxing issues of State responsibility, such as obligations *erga omnes* and serious breaches of obligations under peremptory norms of general international law. Although the *problematique* of obligations *erga omnes* and of serious breaches of obligations under peremptory norms of international law do not constitute the primary subject-matter of this essay, it may be observed that the ILC was divided over these issues. As is well-known, the ILC was very divided as to the content, the extent and, generally, the purpose of the inclusion of Article 19 on what was termed "international crimes" in the Draft. The differences of opinion were exacerbated by the lack of uniform understanding of the interrelated, but not identical concepts of international crimes, obligations *erga omnnes* and *ius cogens* norms, as well as the underlying concept of a procedural right based on the *actio popularis*, and, of course, the notion of injured state.

Some members of the ILC submitted during the second reading of the Draft Articles that the category of obligations *erga omnes* should be

---

[111] *Id.*

applicable to fundamental human rights stemming from general international law, not only from a particular treaty régime, as suggested by the Court in the *Barcelona Traction* case. Likewise, it was argued that these obligations could not necessarily be equated with fundamental obligations, peremptory norms or norms *ius cogens*. The discussion eventually led to the adoption of Articles 42 concerning the invocation of responsibility by an injured State and Article 48 dealing with the invocation of responsibility by a State other than an injured State. They read as follows:

Article 42

A State is entitled as an injured State to invoke the responsibility of another State if the obligation breached is owed to:

(a) that State individually; or

(b) a group of States including that State, or the international community as a whole, and the breach of the obligation:

    (i) specifically affects that State; or

    (ii) is of such a character as radically to change the position of all the other States to which the obligation is owed with respect to the further performance of the obligation.

Article 48

1. Any State other than an injured State is entitled to invoke the responsibility of another State in accordance with paragraph 2 if:

    (a) the obligation breached is owed to a group of States including that State, and is established for the protection of a collective interest of the group; or

    (b) The obligation breached is owed to the international community as a whole.

2. Any State entitled to invoke responsibility under paragraph 1 may claim from the responsible State:

    (a) Cessation of an internationally wrongful act, and assurances and guarantees of non-repetition in accordance with article 30; and

    (b) Performance of the obligation of reparation in accordance with the preceding articles, in the interest of the injured State or of the beneficiaries of the obligation breached.

3. The requirements for the invocation of the responsibility by an injured State under Articles 43, 44 and 45 apply to an invocation of responsibility by a State entitled to do so under paragraph 1.

One of the main issues on which the discussion within the ILC and the comments received from States focused was how to crystallize and define the "injured State". Some governments observed that such a definition should strike an appropriate balance between the notions of "injured State", "wrongdoing State", and a State with a "legal interest". A question that has intrigued international lawyers for a long time was the vindication of a collective or general interest. On the one side, it was argued that common interests can only be protected by the means of collective action.[112] On the other, it was considered that States, other than those with an interest of their own, have *locus standi* on behalf of a treaty community or the community of States as a whole, in order to protect common interests. The difficulties with accommodating the public interest are inherent in those fields "where the law does not have as its purpose the creation of synallagmatic rights and obligations".[113] The ICJ encountered these problems in the *South West Africa (Second Phase)* cases in 1966. The case concerned the administration of the mandate over South-West Africa by South Africa and was brought before the Court by Ethiopia and Liberia. The jurisdiction of the Court was based on a compromissory clause which referred disputes between the League of Nations members arising under mandate to the PCIJ. Instrumental in granting the jurisdiction of the Court was Article 37 of its Statue which transferred the jurisdiction from the PCIJ to the ICJ, thus enabling Ethiopia and Liberia to bring the case before the Court based on the League of Nations mandate system. The case essentially involved a matter of public interest. In the first Judgment in 1962,[114] the majority of the Court was of the view that both Ethiopia and Liberia had *locus standi* before the Court, notwithstanding the fact that the applicant States brought the case in the public interest, not in their individual interest. The public interest concerned the management of the mandate under the League of Nations system.

The Court's ruling was challenged in its decision in 1966,[115] when the Court, by the casting vote of its President, Judge Spender, decided against the admissibility of the claim exactly on the grounds of the lack of individual legal interest of Ethiopia and Liberia. According to the Court, these States were not in the position to defend the public interest which was based on their general membership of the League of Nations. The matter at hand, according to the Court, was within the realm of supervisory and political organs, now defunct, of the League of Nations, not of the Court. The

---

[112] C. Gray, *Judicial Remedies in International Law* (1987), 214-125; see also Separate Opinion of Judge Morreli, in South West Africa (Ethiopia/Liberia v. South Africa), Second Phase, Judgment of 15 July 1966, 1966 ICJ Rep. 59, at 64-65.

[113] J. Crawford, "The Standing of States: A Critique of Article 40 of the ILC's Draft Articles on State Responsibility", in M. Andenas (ed.), *Liber Amicorum in Honour of Lord Slynn of Hadley: Judicial Review in Perspective* (2000), Vol. II, at 24.

[114] South West Africa (Ethiopia/Liberia v. South Africa), First Phase, Judgment of 21 December 1962, 1962 ICJ Rep. 339.

[115] South West Africa (Ethiopia/Liberia v. South Africa), Second Phase, Judgment of 18 July 1966, 1966 ICJ Rep. 6.

Court, while denying the possibility of the *locus standi* in this case to protect the public interest, equally did not acknowledge the existence of an *actio popularis* within the paradigm of international law.

The *Wimbledon* case[116] appears to provide some support for the theory that the Court allows the possibility of the protection of collective rights stemming from an international treaty. The dispute in this case was triggered by Germany's denial of passage, on the grounds of neutrality of the Kiel Canal, *vis-à-vis* the S.S. Wimbledon, a ship that was commissioned to deliver weapons to Poland, then at war with the Soviet Union. The claim against Germany for the breach of Article 380 of the 1919 Treaty of Versailles was brought not only by France, but also by Great Britain, Italy and Japan. The Court granted *locus standi* to all these States, holding that "each of the four Applicant Powers has a clear interest in the execution of the provisions relating to the Kiel Canal, since they all possess fleets and merchant vessels flying their respective flags. They are, therefore, even though they may be unable to adduce a prejudice to any pecuniary interest an interested Power", entitled to bring the dispute before the Court. The Court, however, interestingly stressed that although the breach of the provision in question was against France, other States have their own interests in the action, which derive from the use which may be made of the canal by vessels flying the flag of these States. The Court, in fact, made a theoretically important distinction between a direct legal interest (that of France) and an indirect legal interest (that of the Great Britain, Italy and Japan), which, while deriving from the same multilateral treaty, does not encompass the protection or vindication of the same right.

In the *Barcelona Traction* case,[117] the ICJ attempted to reverse the standpoint it had adopted in the *South West* Africa case and made a statement which, though often cited, is nevertheless somewhat unclear:[118]

---

[116] The SS "Wimbledon" (France/Great Britain/Italy/Japan *v.* Germany), Judgment of 1 August 1923, 1923 PCIJ (Series A), No.1, at 20.

[117] Barcelona Traction, Light and Power Company Limited (Belgium *v.* Spain), Second Phase, Judgment of 5 February 1970, 1970 ICJ Rep. 3.

[118] "[A]n essential distinction should be drawn between the obligations of a State towards the international community as a whole, and those arising *vis-à-vis* another State in the field of diplomatic protection. By their very nature the former are the concern of all States. In view of the importance of the rights involved, all States can be held to have a legal interest in their protection; they are obligations *erga omnes.* Such obligations derive, for example, in contemporary international law, from the outlawing of acts of aggression, and of genocide, as also from protection from slavery and racial discrimination. Some of the corresponding rights of protection have entered into the body of international law (Reservations to the Convention an the Prevention and Punishment of the Crime of Genocide, Advisory Opinion, 1951 ICJ Rep. 23); others are conferred by international instruments of a universal or quasi-universal character. Obligations, the performance of which is the subject of diplomatic protection, are not of the same category. It cannot be held, when such an obligation in particular is in

With regard more particularly to human rights, to which reference has already been made in paragraph 34 of this Judgment, it should be noted that these also include protection against denial of justice. However, on the universal level, the instruments which embody human rights do not confer on State the capacity to protect the victims of infringements of such rights irrespective of their nationality. It is therefore still on the regional level that as solution to this problem has had to be sought: thus, within the Council of Europe, of which Spain is not a member the problem of admissibility encountered by the claim in the present case has been resolved by the European Convention on Human Rights, which entitles each State which is a party to the Convention to lodge a complaint against any other contracting State for violations of the Convention, irrespective of the nationality of victims.[119]

As Crawford points out, the statement of the ICJ in this paragraph is unclear; on the one hand, the Court recognizes obligations *erga omnes*; on the other, it appears to go against the truly *erga omnes* character such obligations. He considers two possible explanations. One is that the Court, in referring to "the principles and rules concerning the basic rights of human person", limited itself to those principles and rules which were clearly recognized by general international law as obligations *erga omnes* in 1970. A second possible explanation is that the Court envisaged the existence of obligations *erga omnes* in international law, but without States having any corresponding rights of protection. As Crawford observes:

Such an interpretation would in turn deprive the Court's earlier pronouncement of its significance. The contrast drawn in this passage between the instruments and the European Convention is also baffling. The relevant provision of the Covenant on Civil and Political Rights (Article 4) is not limited by reference to considerations of the nationality of claims, any more than Article 24 of the European Convention was.[120]

Finally, the same author admits the possibility that perhaps these two passages could be reconciled on the basis of the distinction between remedies available for claims brought within the framework of diplomatic protection and those brought in relation to human rights. This interpretation would result in the possibility in general international law of the recognition of an obligation not to deny justice to a person before national courts and would not produce the result of assimilating two fields, or equating remedies available to an interested State for a breach of human rights obligations, to those which may be used by States whose own rights have been infringed by a denial of justice to their nationals.

---

question, that all States have a legal interest in its observance. In order to bring a claim in respect of a breach of such an obligation, a State must first establish its right to do so". *Id.*, paragraph 32, 33-35 [paragraph breaks suppressed].

[119] *Id.*, at 47, paragraph 91.

[120] Crawford, *supra* note 113, at 26-27.

There is indeed a plethora of different views to support the contention that the obligations *erga omnes* may in fact give the right of *locus standi* before the Court. Some of these views are based on the analysis of the content of the obligation in question. Lefeber, for example, claims that the content of the obligation may be such as to render the right to bring the claim before the Court conditional on demonstration by the applicant State of an individual substantive interest, i.e., nationality in the ease of denial of justice; "[t]o substantiate the claim, it will not be sufficient for the claimant state to demonstrate that a legal interest has been affected by the act of another state; ... [but] it is necessary and sufficient that a right pertaining to the claimant state has been infringed".[121] Thus, this reasoning brings us back to the (classical) bi-lateralization of the relationships between States which by their legal nature belong to the multilateral context.

As evidenced by the above considerations, i.e., problems of *locus standi* regarding such obligations, the question of the injured State, and responsibility for the breach-remained in the centre of unresolved issues in the law of treaties and the law of State responsibility. The imprecise wording of Article 60 of the VCLT gave rise to many conflicting interpretations and left unanswered questions relating to the relationship between the rules laid down in this Article with the corresponding ones in the realm of State responsibility (including the rather confusing Article 40 of the 1996 Draft).

4.2 Integral Obligations in International Law

The similar problem of a State's redress for a breach of an international obligation in a multilateral context exists within the realm of State responsibility. This was a question on the agenda of the ILC during the codification of the Articles on State Responsibility. This problem was linked with a notion of the 'injured' State. Riphagen, a Special Rapporteur proposed several remedial measures available to an injured State.[122]

---

[121] R. Lefeber, *Transboundary Environmental Interference and the Origin of State Liability* (1996), at 117.

[122] See in particular Special Rapporteur Riphagen Sixth Report, YILC (1985), Vol. II, Part 2, paragraph 3 of the commentary, also, at 9. He proposed several remedial measures: such a restoration to a previous state, payment of money, guarantees on non-repetition and countermeasures that, according to Riphagen, were of a different character from remedial measures. A State was free (according to the Rapporteur, adoption of countermeasures is not a claim-right but they are governed by freedom of election) to adopt them *vis-à-vis* a State in breach. The State, which adopts them, was obliged to fulfil certain acts (the State in breach had a correlative right to demand its implementation). Having elected to adopt a countermeasure, a State is freed from the fulfilment of these acts and the State in breach loses its right to demand it. Riphagen, *Sixth report*, draft articles 8 and 9, at 10 and 11.

It should be reiterated that the realm of application of the law of treaties and that of State responsibility are different and that any similarities, such as the formulation of an injured State in Articles on State Responsibility and Article 60 of the VCLT,[123] or the recourse to countermeasures, as contrasted with the invocation of the material breach of a treaty, do not change the difference between these two fields of international law.[124]

It was an initial draft of the article on the injured State proposed by Riphagen that gave rise to consideration of the solidarity issue within the

---

[123] Crawford, the Special Rapportuer, explains as follows: "(4) The definition in article 42 is closely modelled on article 60 of the Vienna Convention on the Law Treaties, and although the scope and purpose of the two provisions is different. Article 42 is concerned with any breach of an international obligation of whatever the character, whereas article 60 is concerned with the breach of treaties. Moreover article 60 is concerned exclusively with the right of a State party to a treaty to invoke a material breach of that treaty by another party as a grounds for its suspension or termination. It is not concerned with a question of responsibility for breach of the treaty. This why article 60 is restricted to "material" breaches of treaties. Only a material breach justifies termination or suspension of the treaty, whereas, in the context of State responsibility, any breach of treaty gives rise to responsibility irrespective of its gravity. Despite these differences, the analogy with article 60 is justified. Article 60 seeks to identify the State parties to a treaty which are entitled to respond individually and in their own right to a material breach by terminating or suspending it. In the case of a bilateral treaty, the right can only be that of the other State party, but in the case of a multilateral treaty article 60 (2) does not allow every other State to terminate or suspend the treaty for material breach. The other State must be specially affected by the breach, or at least individually affected, in that the breach necessarily undermines or destroys the basis for its own further performance of the treaty." (footnotes omitted), see Crawford, *supra* note 2, at 256-257.

[124] Crawford comments further as follows: "But it is clear that there is a legal difference between suspension of a treaty. The suspension of a treaty (or a severable part of a treaty), if it is legally justified, places the treaty in a sort of limbo; it ceases to constitute an applicable legal standard for the parties while it is suspended and until action is taken to bring it back into operation. By contrast conduct inconsistent with terms of a treaty in force, if justified as a countermeasure, does not have the effect of suspending the treaty; the treaty continues to apply and the party taking countermeasures must continue to justify its non-compliance by reference to the criteria for taking countermeasures...for as long as its non-compliance lasts. Countermeasures are no more a ground for the suspension of a treaty than is necessity (paragraph 324). There is thus a clear distinction between action taken within the framework of the law of treaties (as codified in the Vienna Convention), and conduct raising questions of State responsibility (which are excluded from the Vienna Convention). The law of treaties is concerned essentially with the content of primary rules and with the validity of attempts to alter them; the law of responsibility takes as given the existence of the primary rules (whether based on a treaty or otherwise) and is concerned with the question whether conduct inconsistent with these rules can be excused and, if not, what the consequences of such conduct are. Thus it is coherent to apply Vienna Convention in dealing with issues of suspension, and the rules proposed in the Draft articles as to proportionality etc, in dealing with countermeasures." Third Report on State Responsibility, by James Crawford, Special Rapporteur, *supra* note 37.

ambit of State responsibility.[125] In 1966, the ILC adopted the text of draft articles on its first reading.[126] Article 40 concerned the injured State.[127] Drafting of Article 40 was not satisfactory.[128] Generally speaking, Article 40

---

[125] Sixth Report, Article 6. See also Article 5 in 1985, Part Two of the Commission's Draft Articles on State Responsibility. See Hutchinson, *supra* note 104, at 152-156.

[126] YILC (1996), Vol. II, Part 2, at 58, UN Doc.A/CN.4/SER.A/1966.add.1 (Part 2), see internet at: <http://www.un.org/law/ilc/index.htm>.

[127] Article 40 provides as follows:

> 1. For the purposes of the preset articles, 'injured State' means any State a right of which is infringed by the act of another State, if that act constitutes, in accordance with Part One, an internationally wrongful act of that State.
>
> 2. In particular, 'injured State' means:
>
> (a) if the right infringed by the act of a State arises from a bilateral treaty, the other State party to the treaty:
>
> (b) if the right infringed by the act of a State arises from a judgement or other binding dispute settlement decision of an international court or tribunal, the other State or States parties to the dispute and entitled to the benefit of that right;
>
> (c) if the right infringed by the act of a State arises from a binding decision of an international organ other than an international tribunal, the State or States, in accordance with the constituent instrument of the international organisation concerned, are entitled to the benefit of that right;
>
> (d) if the right infringed by the act of a State arises from a treaty provision for a third State, that third State;
>
> (e) if the right infringed by the act of a State arises from a multilateral treaty or from a rule of customary international law, any other State party to the multilateral treaty or bound by the relevant rule of customary international law, if it is established that:
>
> (i) the right has been created in public favour;
>
> (ii) the infringement of the right by the act of State necessarily affects the enjoyment of the rights or the performance of the obligations of the other States parties to the multilateral treaty or bound by the rule of customary international law; or
>
> (iii) the right has been created or is established for the protection of human rights and fundamental freedoms;
>
> (f) if the right infringed by the act of a State arises from a multilateral treaty, any other State party to the multilateral treaty, if established that the right has been expressly stipulated in that treaty for the protection of the collective interest of the States parties hereto.
>
> 3. In addition, 'injured State' means, if the internationally wrongful act constitutes an international crime, all other States."

[128] See J. Crawford, P. Bodeau, J. Peel, "The ILC's Draft Articles on State Responsibility: Toward Completion of a Second Reading", 94 *AJIL* (2000), 660.

defined some of the cases where a State or group of States might be eligible to claim a "right correlative to the obligation breached",[129] in a bilateral or multilateral context. Article 40 paragraph 3 included international crimes and, in such a case, all other States were injured and were entitled to act. As Crawford, Bodeau and Peel explain, there were many difficulties with Article 40, in particular, "[t]he conversion from the language of obligation to the language of right was premature, and appeared to imply that all responsibility can be assimilated to classical bilateral right-duty relations"; it did not distinguish properly between different categories of an injured State, and ignored the difference in the legal position between bilateral and multilateral obligations; it differentiated for no reason between treaty and other obligations; stipulated wrongly that the regimes of common interest can be only established through explicit stipulation in multilateral treaties; and mentioned specifically human rights treaties in a awkward and imprecise manner.[130]

Article 40 although clumsily drafted, and as Dupuy noted, based on 're-bilateralization' of rights having its roots in a multilateral treaty "to give its bearer an interest in an action for responsibility",[131] included some solidarity rights (or communitarian) concepts. There are some echoes of Fitzmaurice's classification in Article 40, such as, for example, Article 40 paragraph 40 b (ii) that reminds to a certain degree of so-called interdependent obligation (see above);[132] and a special place granted to the protection of human rights and fundamental freedoms (however, drafted in a rather meaningless manner) is reminiscent of Fitzmaurice's integral obligation.

Article 40 led Crawford to classify types of multilateral obligations from the point of view of the notion of an injured State. Three types can be distinguished: (i) obligations *erga omnes*, i.e. owned to the international community as a whole, in which all States would have a legal interest in their compliance (as introduced by the Court in the *Barcelona Traction* case); (ii) obligations owned to all parties to a particular regime (*erga omnes partes*), i.e. it refers to "an international regime in the maintenance and implementation of which all the States parties have the common interest".[133] These obligations included matters that are of common interest of the

---

[129] *Id.,* at 665.

[130] *Id.,* at 666.

[131] P.-M. Dupuy, "A General Stocktaking of the Connections between the Multilateral Dimension of Obligations and Codification of the Law of Responsibility", 13 *EJIL* (2002), 1053-1081, at 1069.

[132] Professor Crawford gives it as an example of an "integral" obligation, Third Report on State Responsibility, International Law Commission , Fifty-second session, Geneva 1 May to 9 June, 10 July to 18 August 2000, A/CN.4/507, at 41. This question will be further commented on.

[133] *Id.,* at 49.

parties. They are of collective character and concern, e.g. environmental matters, such as climate change or biodiversity, and disarmament; and (iii) obligations to which some or many State are parties, but in respect of which particular States or groups of States are recognised as legally interested. These multilateral obligations, regardless of whether they are *erga omnes* or not, may concern particular States or sub-groups of States. It may be inferred from Article 60(2)(b) that a "State specially affected" by a breach of a multilateral obligation should have the right "to invoke responsibility of the State concerned in respect to the breach".[134] These obligations do not apply to relations specifically between two States. In relation to this classification, Professor Dupuy calls for caution in distinguishing according to the source of the obligation, i.e. whether it is based on a treaty and established only among the parties (*erga omens partes),* or it has its source in a rule of general international law, therefore is of a character *erga omnes.*[135]

Unsatisfactory drafting of Article 40, resulted in its a complete re-drafting and in its replacement with the new Article 42 and 48. Article 42 is similar in its construction to Article 60 of the VCLT. As explained by Crawford, Article 42 contains three types of obligations, as does Article 60 of the VCLT. Article 42(a) sets out an obligation that is owned "to that State individually" (an obligation in a bilateral context); Article 42(b)(i) establishes an obligation to which a State is a party and by breach of which a "State may be specially affected," although it cannot be asserted that that the obligation is owned by that State individually; and thirdly, Article 42(b)(ii) deals with an obligation, breach of which changes radically the position of all other States, since "the performance of this obligation by a responsible State is a necessary condition of its performance by all other States".[136] The Rapporteur further explains that: "[i]n each of these cases, the possible suspension or termination of the obligation or of its performance by the injured State may be of little value to it as a remedy. Its primary interest may be in the restoration of the legal relationship by cessation and reparation."[137]

Fitzmaurice's classification is partly reflected in Article 42, as are solidarity or communitarian interests. It may be said that paragraph (b)(ii) reflects so-called "interdependent" obligations. This is different from the approach of Crawford who appears to assimilate "interdependent" or "integral" obligations. He explained in a footnote that this term gave rise sometimes "to confusion, being used to refer to human rights or environmental obligations that are not owed on an "all or nothing" basis. The term "interdependent obligations may be more appropriate.".[138] Sicilianos

---

[134] *Id.,* at 50.
[135] Dupuy, *supra* note 131.
[136] Crawford, *supra* note 100, at 257.
[137] *Id.*
[138] *Id.*

adopts the same view as Crawford.[139] Dupuy, however, submits that the type of obligation dealt with in Article 42(b)(ii) is interdependent in character and the breach of an integral obligation "... is to be found in Article 48, in two kinds, restricted and general, of obligations *erga omnes partes* and obligations *erga omnes* absolutely, ...with the first having their origin in treaties, the latter in customary obligations."[140]

Sicilianos however correctly observes that Article 48, embodying the obligations *erga omnes partes* has no counterpart in Article 60 of the VCLT. These are obligations of a collective kind, implying that States other than a directly injured State (Article 42) may invoke State responsibility. Dupuy makes an interesting observation that a State can only invoke responsibility if it has been injured. The injury does not have to be in the shape of physical damage; it may just be a legal harm, due to the fact of being members of a limited contractual community (*erga omnes partes* obligations) and of the international community (obligations *erga omnes*). It appears that this reasoning may be applicable in relation to solidarity rights, i.e. in relation to the second level of rights, where entitlement for redress may stem from the fact of belonging to certain community with interdependent rights, the direct breach of such a right, resulting in the breach of legal rights of other interrelated States. As in solidarity rights, the states affected not individually, do not act in redress of their own interests but rather on behalf and in the interests of "the subjects that have been directly injured."[141]

Sicilianos also notes that an interdependent obligation of the kind found in disarmament treaties is a different one to that found in environmental or human rights treaties. He is right in explaining that the obligations concerning disarmament agreements

> ...can certainly not be brought under a bundle of bilateral relations; they are nonetheless dominated by a sort of global reciprocity in the sense that each state disarms because the others do likewise. One can, therefore, easily understand that breach of this sort of obligation might 'radically change' the situation of all other states as to the further performance of, for example, their own disarmament obligation. The case is different for obligations relating to environmental protection or human rights. These tend to promote extra-state interests, are not of a synallagmatic nature and fall outside the interplay of reciprocity. A breach of human rights by state A, however serious it may be, in no way changes the position of other states regarding compliance with their own obligations in the same area. It follows that the 'interdependent' obligations and those laid down for the purposes of protecting a collective

---

[139] L.-A. Sicilianos, "The Classification of Obligations and the Multilateral Dimension of the Relations of International Responsibility", 13 *EJIL* (2002), 1127-1145, at 1134.

[140] Dupuy, *supra* note 131, at 1072.

[141] Sicilianos, *supra* note 139, at 1140.

interest, or (better) an extra-state interest, cannot be identified with each other.[142]

In the view of the present authors, this second type of an interdependent obligation is an integral obligation as formulated by Fitzmaurice. The impact of Fitzmaurice's classification on this area of the law is patent.[143]

4.3 Consequences of Breach

What, then, are the legal consequences of the breach in relation to each and every category of States to which the obligation breached was owed? According to Article 60(2)(b), a party specially affected by the breach is entitled to invoke it as a ground for suspending the operation of a treaty in whole or in part in the relations between itself and the defaulting State. As to the position of States, which are not specially affected (States with a *per se* interest in material breach), these are entitled to invoke the breach as a ground for suspending the operation of the treaty in whole or in part they can do so with respect to themselves if the treaty is of such a character that a material breach of its provisions by one party radically changes the position of every party with respect to the further performance of its obligations under the treaty. This applies only where a material breach results in a radical change in the nature of the treaty as a whole *vis-à-vis* the position of each and every party to it. Thus, the rule contained in Article 60(2)(a) of the VCLT refers in principle to the content of a treaty, not to a classification of a breach of the treaty (as a material or non-material breach).

Article 60(2)(c) deals with the rights of States who are not directly affected by the breach, but who may invoke the breach as a ground for suspending the operation of the treaty as a whole or in part with respect to themselves if the treaty is of such a character that a material breach changes the position of every party with respect to further performance of its obligations under the treaty. The procedural requirement to terminate or suspend a treaty in such circumstances is unanimous agreement of all the parties to the treaty in relation between themselves and the defaulting State, or as between all the parties.

Articles 65 to 68 of the VCLT, which set up the procedure with respect to invalidity, termination, withdrawal from or suspension of the operation of a

---

[142] *Id.*, at 1135.

[143] Fitzmaurice's classification gave rise to a typology of obligations not only contained in Article 60 of the VCLT, but in the broader context of State responsibility. He was a pioneer of the solidarity or communitarian approach to international obligations, fully reflected in the concepts underlying Article 42 and, especially, Article 48 of responsibility, going outside the traditional framework of bilateralism in international relations. See Dupuy, *supra* note 131, at 1072.

treaty, are to be followed in relation to material breach as well. According to Rosenne, this procedure is based on two principles: firstly, giving formal notice of the claim, including relevant details, through diplomatic channels; and secondly, the resolution of any consequent dispute not otherwise settled through compulsory recourse to a form of non-binding conciliation machinery specified in the Annex to the Convention. According to Rosenne, the first element is the result of the common "revulsion against *Sportpalast* diplomacy;" and the "second element reflects the ambiguity, the generality, and the open-endedness of Article 33 of the Charter of the United Nations".[144] The same author emphasizes the other weakness of the procedure of the Vienna Convention, which, in his view, is an overly legalistic and does not reflect "general diplomatic experience or the diplomatic temperament".[145] However, he concludes that new conceptions are evolving that are characterised by a blurred line between purely political and purely legal approaches. Rosenne sees this new evolution going in the direction of establishing new machinery of monitoring and reporting "aiming at the systematic and organizational mobilization of informed public opinion (including governmental opinion)" to support "what is commonly believed to be the intention of the drafters of the treaty, deviation from which, endorsed by such monitors, attracts to the government concerned charges (which no government likes to hear) of treaty-breaking.".[146] We agree with Rosenne that

> [t]he restriction of article 60 of the Vienna Convention to a narrowly defined concept of "material breach" is an indication that the international community is not prepared to go very far in admitting that a breach of a treaty, however grave, operates in itself to put the treaty to an end. At the most it is a ground, if duly established, for an injured party to terminate the treaty in an orderly way. In that sense, article 60 has an important role in performing the function of preserving the juridical relations created by the treaty and not allowing them to be arbitrarily disturbed, whatever be the political and legal strains under which they may have come.[147]

The International Law Commission, in its 2001 Report, elucidated the relationship between peremptory norms of international law and the obligations towards the international community as whole. The Report states as follows:

> Whether or not peremptory norms of general international law and obligations to the international community as a whole are aspects of a single basic idea, there is at the very least substantial overlap between them. [...] But there is at least a difference in emphasis. While peremptory norms of general international law focus on the scope of priority to be given to a certain number

---

[144] Rosenne, "Breach of Treaty", *supra* note 4, at 35.

[145] *Id.*, at 36.

[146] *Id.,* at 40.

[147] *Id.*, 43.

of fundamental obligations, the focus of obligations to the international community as a whole is essentially on the legal interest of all States in compliance – i.e., in terms of the present Articles, in being entitled to invoke the responsibility of any State in breach. Consistently with the difference in their focus, it is appropriate to reflect the consequences in two distinct ways. First, serious breaches of obligations arising under peremptory norms of general international law can attract additional consequences, not only for the responsible State but for all other States. Secondly, all States are entitled to invoke responsibility for breaches of obligations to international community as a whole. The first of these propositions is the concern of the present chapter; the second is dealt with in article 48.[148]

The link between Article 42 and Article 60 of the VCLT is visible. In fact, Article 42 was modeled on Article 60, "although the scope and purpose of these two provisions is different. Article 42 is concerned with any breach of an international obligation of whatever character, whereas article 60 is concerned with breach of treaties".[149] The main difference is that Article 60 is not concerned with the issue of responsibility for breach of a treaty. Under the law of State responsibility, any breach of a treaty incurs State responsibility. The legal construction of Article 42 resembles the structure of Article 60. The latter article is structured on the basis of the right of the other party to suspend or terminate the treaty (in a bilateral context), and the State specially affected by the breach, or at least individually affected by the breach in that the breach necessarily renders further performance of a treaty impossible (in a multilateral context). In line with the structure of Article 60 of the VCLT, Article 42 may be operational in three instances. First, in order to invoke the responsibility of another State as an injured State, a State must have an individual right to the performance of an obligation, in the way that a party to a bilateral treaty had in relation to the other State party (sub-paragraph (a)). Secondly, it may be invoked by a State specially affected by the breach of an obligation to which it is party, even though the obligation in question is not owed to it individually (sub-paragraph (b)(i)). Thirdly, it may be invoked when performance of the obligation by the responsible State is a necessary condition of its performance by all other States (sub-paragraph (b)(ii)). This is the so-called "integral" or "independent" obligation. This obligation may be defined as a breach that necessarily affects enjoyment of the rights by the performance of the obligations of other States parties. In case of such an obligation, each State is treated as individually injured by the breach of an integral obligation.[150]

The ILC explained that sub-paragraph (a) of Article 42 differs from Article 60 in that it also covers cases where the performance of an obligation

---

[148] See note 49, introductory commentary to Part Two, Chapter III, at paragraph 7.
[149] *Id.*, paragraph 4.
[150] J. Crawford, *supra* note 37, at paragraph 91.

under a multilateral treaty or customary international law is owed to one particular State. Article 60 (1) of the VCLT which is based on a formal criterion aims at bilateral, as opposed to multilateral, treaties. According to the ILC, although a multilateral treaty will characteristically set up a structure or rules applicable to all States parties, in certain cases its performance in a particular situation may involve a relationship of bilateral character between two parties. The Report refers to such treaties as a "bundle of bilateral relations".[151]

Article 42(b) relates to injury arising from violations of collective obligations, i.e., obligations that apply between more than two States and whose performance in a particular case is not owed to one State individually, but to a group of States or even the international community as a whole. The breach of these obligations only injures a particular State if additional requirements are met. The term "group of States" refers to a considerable number of States in the world that may be considered as forming for that purpose a "community of States of a functional character."[152] Sub-paragraph (b)(i) is concerned with injury of a "specially affected" State by the violation of a collective obligation. This formulation mirrors the one used in Article 60(2)(b) of the VCLT. These rules cover the cases in which the legal effects of an internationally wrongful act extend by implication to the whole group of States bound by the obligation or to the international community as a whole, but the wrongful act has particular adverse effects on one State or on a small group of States.[153] In analogy to Article 60(2)(b) of the Vienna Convention, sub-paragraph (b)(i) of Article 42 does not define the nature or extent of the special impact that a State must have sustained in order to be considered "injured". This has to be assessed in each and every case separately, in consideration of the primary obligation breached; and further, such State must be affected by the breach in such a way as to be distinguishable from the generality of other States to which the obligation is owed. Sub-paragraph (b)(ii) deals with a special category of obligations, whose breach affects every State to which the obligation is owed. This rule is parallel to Article 60(2)(c) of the VCLT. Finally, the Report reiterates that the articles deal with obligations regardless of the

---

[151] See note 49, at 298; Hutchinson, *supra* note 104, at 151; C. Annacker, "The Legal Régime of Erga Omnes Obligations", 46 *Austrian Journal of Public & International Law* (1994), 131, 136.

[152] See note 49, commentary to Article 42, paragraph 11.

[153] The Report gives an example of pollution of the high seas in breach of Article 194 of the 1982 Law of the Sea Convention. Pollution may impact one or several States whose beaches may be polluted by toxic residues or closed. In that case, independently of any general interest of the States parties to this Convention in the preservation of the marine environment, these coastal States parties should be considered as injured by the breach; *id.*, commentary to Article 42, paragraph (12).

source. In practice, interdependent obligations envisaged in sub-paragraph (b)(ii) will usually arise under treaties establishing particular regimes. The Commission observed that even under such treaties, it may not be the case that just any breach of the obligation has the effect of impairing the performance of other States. Therefore, the sub-paragraph is narrow in scope. Accordingly, a State is assumed to be injured under sub-paragraph (b)(ii) if the breach is of such a character as radically to affect the enjoyment of the rights or the performance of the obligation of all the other States to which the obligation is owed.[154]

Article 48, as mentioned above, is complimentary to Article 42. It is concerned with the invocation of responsibility by States other than the injured State, acting in the collective interest. It will be apparent that Article 48 has its roots in the concept of obligations *erga omnes* and in the closely related norms of *ius cogens*.[155] The State entitled to invoke responsibility under this article is acting not in exercise of its individual right as an injured State, but as a member of the group of States to which the obligation is owed, or a member of the international community as a whole. However, the term "legal interest" is not a basis for a distinction between articles 42 and 48, since the injured State in the sense of Article 42 also has legal interests. Article 48 is structured in the following manner: paragraph 1 defines the categories of obligations that give rise to the wider right to invoke responsibility; paragraph 2 sets out the forms of responsibility that may be claimed by States other than an injured State; and paragraph 3 applies the requirements of invocation contained in Articles 43, 44 and 45 to the invocation of responsibility under Article 45 paragraph 1. In its commentary, the ILC explains that States other than the injured State do not have to act together; and that the entitlement of these other States will coincide with that of an injured State in relation to the same internationally wrongful act in those cases where a State suffers individual injury from a breach of an obligation to which Article 48 is applicable.

Article 48(1) defines the categories of obligations breach of which may entitle States other than the injured State to invoke responsibility. The first type of obligations, i.e., obligations owed to a group of States and established to protect a collective interest of the group, may be invoked by States other than the injured State if two conditions are met: the obligation whose breach has given rise to responsibility must have been owed to a group to which a State invoking responsibility belongs, and the obligation must have been established to protect a collective interest, regardless of the source of obligation (multilateral treaty or customary law). This type of obligation is referred to as "obligations *erga omnes partes*". These collective

---

[154] *Id.*, commentary to Article 41, paragraph (13).
[155] See the quotation accompanying note 112.

obligations must apply between a group of States and have been established is some collective interest, such as the environment and assume the form of multilateral arrangements. The second type of community obligation is governed by paragraph (1)(b), States other than an injured State may invoke responsibility if the obligation in question was owed "to the international community as a whole." Although by their nature they are what the ICJ called obligations *erga omnes* in the *Barcelona Traction* case, the Article avoids this term in order to avoid that these obligations are confused with those simply owed to all parties to a treaty.

Article 48(2) defines the categories of claims that States may make when invoking responsibility under Article 48, The list is exhaustive, and the main principle is that invocation of responsibility under this Article results in a more restricted scope of rights than those granted under Article 42. Paragraph 2 (b) envisages the possibility that a claim for reparation may be made on behalf of the injured State, if any, or the beneficiaries of the obligation breached. As the ILC explained, this measure involves an element of progressive development, which aims to protect the community or collective interests at stake.[156] Furthermore, the formulation in sub-paragraph 2(b) "performance of the obligation of reparation in accordance with the preceding paragraphs" indicates that the States under Article 48 may not demand reparation where the injured State could not do so.[157]

---

[156] *Id.,* commentary to Article 48, paragraph (12).

[157] See further J. Crawford, *Third Report on State Responsibility*, UN Doc. A/CN.4/507 (2000), who provides two very useful tables (below) of States entitled to invoke responsibility in respect of multilateral obligations, as well as the extent to which States may invoke responsibility:

1. States entitled to invoke responsibility in respect of multilateral obligations

Category of multilateral obligations	States entitled to invoke responsibility	Extent of application
Obligation erga omnes	All states	Applies to obligations erga omnes in the sense of the Barcelona Traction case
Obligation erga omnes partes	All States parties	Applies to legal regimes involving public interest of all States parties, including in particular integral obligations
Material obligation generally	Unless otherwise provided, any State "specially affected by the breach" or regarded as having a "special interest"	Applies to all obligations which are multilateral in provenance and to which a specially affected State is a party; does not apply in legal contexts (e.g., diplomatic protection) recognized as pertaining specifically to the relations of two States inter se

2. The extent to which differently affected States may invoke the legal consequences of the responsibility of a State:

	Bilateral obligations		Multilateral obligations	
	Injured State	"Specially affected" State	Obligation erga omnes partes	Obligation erga omnes
Cessation & assurances & guarantees)	Yes	Yes	Yes	Yes
Restitution	Yes	Yes	On behalf of the victim/ specially affected State; otherwise by agreement between the States parties	On behalf of the victim/ specially affected State; otherwise by agreement between the States parties
Compensation & satisfaction	Yes	Yes	On behalf of the victim/ specially affected State; otherwise by agreement between the States parties	On behalf of the victim/ specially affected State; otherwise by agreement between the States parties
Counter-measures	Yes	Yes	On behalf of the victim/ specially affected State; otherwise by agreement between the States parties	On behalf of the victim/ specially affected State; otherwise by agreement between all States; but individually in case of well-attested gross breaches

5. Concluding Remarks

Kirgis observed in 1989 that there were still many "opaque" relationships between Article 60 and some other articles of the VCLT, such as Articles 42, 44, 65, 72 and 73, and a "hazily-defined relationship between the treaty law of material breach and the more general law of state responsibility".[158] In view of the present author, the most interesting (and generating the most discussion) is the relationship between material breach and the law of State responsibility. As shown above, the problem of identifying the injured State is part and parcel of the same relationship. The confusion between the two institutions (in particular between material breach and countermeasures) stems from the assimilation of the primary rules (the law of treaties) and secondary rules (the law of State responsibility). The measures adopted in response to material breach have their roots in *sedes materiae* of the law of treaties, internal to the provisions of the treaty in question. The measures that may be adopted following material breach alter and affect substantive legal obligations of the States parties. They are, however, different from countermeasures. The latter constitute a response of a State to an internationally wrongful act, regardless of origin and hence external to the treaty in question. Their character is temporary, and their aim is to restore the previous legal relationship between the States involved. Article 60 only concerns the right of a party to invoke material breach of that treaty as a ground for termination or suspension of that treaty; it is not concerned with the question of responsibility. Only "material" breach is a justifiable ground for termination or suspension, whereas in the context of State responsibility any breach of a treaty gives rise to responsibility, irrespective of gravity. In relation to material breach, the principle of reciprocity does not apply.

Furthermore, it is true that the structure of Article 42 mirrors that of Article 60(2) of the VCLT. It is however only a formal resemblance. The structure of Article 60(2) is particularly useful in relation to a position of an injured State within the framework of multilateral relations that constitute a nexus of multifaceted rights and obligations of States. As said above, the parallel features of Articles 60 and 42 are as follows. In the first instance, in order to invoke the responsibility of another State as an injured State, that State must have an individual right to the performance of the obligation breached. Secondly, a State may be specially affected by the breach of an obligation to which it is a party, even though this obligation is not owed to it individually. Thirdly, it may be that performance of the obligation by the responsible State is a necessary condition of its performance by all other States (as in the case of an "integral" obligation). To equate Article 42 and Article 60(2) substantively, however, would be an error. The scope and the

---

[158] Kirgis, *supra* note 16, at 572.

purpose of both articles is different. Likewise, drawing parallels between Articles 42 and 48 would be a mistake. Article 42 adopts a more traditional model in relation to responses to a breach of an international obligation, whereas Article 48 addresses the problem of responses by States not individually injured by a breach, within the framework of obligations *erga omnes partes* and obligations protecting more general, even universal, community interests. The Articles on State Responsibility (and the Commentary by the ILC) followed and developed the line of reasoning adopted by the ILC during both the codification of the law of treaties and the law of State responsibility in maintaining that material breach and countermeasures taken by a State belong to different legal categories and serve different legal aims.

CHAPTER FOUR

The Doctrine of Fundamental Change of Circumstances Revisited

1. Introduction

The doctrine of fundamental change of circumstances (sometimes called the doctrine *rebus sic stantibus*), pursuant to which a party to a treaty may be entitled to a release from its obligations under a treaty as a result of changes in the circumstances that existed at the time of the conclusion of the treaty that constituted an essential basis for the conclusion of the treaty, remains a difficult one in the law of treaties. The idea behind the doctrine is well-known, and it has a counterpart in the law of contract in the municipal law of many countries. As will be seen in sections 2 and 3 below, the International Law Commission (the "ILC" or the "Commission") and the International Court of Justice (the "ICJ") have had occasion to pronounce on this doctrine, and a great deal has been written about it.[1] Nevertheless the conditions of its

---

[1] Perhaps the most thorough consideration of the doctrine is to be found in A. Vamvoukos, *Termination of Treaties in International Law: the Doctrine of Stantibus Sic Rebus and Desuetude* (1985). See also, e.g., I. Sinclair, *The Vienna Convention on the Law of Treaties* (1984), at 192-196; Lord McNair, *The Law of Treaties* (1961), at 681-691; O. Lissitzyn, "Treaties and Changed Circumstances (*rebus sic stantibus*)", 61 *AJIL* (1967), at 895-922; E. Stein and D. Carreau, "Law and Peaceful Change in a Subsystem: 'Withdrawal' of France from the North Atlantic Treaty Organization", 62 *AJIL* (1968), 577 at 614-622; T.O. Elias, *The Modern Law of Treaties* (1974), at 119-128; G. Haraszti, "Treaties and the Fundamental Change of Circumstances", 146 *Recueil des cours* (1975-III), at 1-94; E. Zöller, "The 'Corporate Will' of the United Nations and the Rights of the Minority", 81 *AJIL* (1987), 610, at 626-629; R. Jennings and A. Watts (eds.), *Oppenheim's International Law* (1992), at 1304-1309; and the excellent paper by R. Müllerson, "The ABM Treaty: Changed Circumstances, Extraordinary Events, Supreme Interests and International Law", 50 *ICLQ* (2001), at 509.

applicability and its constituent elements remain problematic in a number of important respects.

This chapter will be devoted to the review of a number of aspects of the doctrine of fundamental change of circumstances, with a view to identifying the exact role played by the doctrine and the consequences of its invocation. Reference will be made to the recent withdrawal of the United States from the 1972 Treaty between the United States of America and the USSR on the Limitation of Anti-Ballistic Missile Systems ("the ABM Treaty").[2] It will be suggested that in spite of the recognition of the existence of the principle, fundamental problems still exist regarding its place in the law of treaties.

2. The International Law Commission and the Codification of the Doctrine of Fundamental Change of Circumstances[3]

The doctrine of fundamental change of circumstances was codified in Article 59 of the 1966 ILC Draft Articles.[4] In its discussions, the ILC noted that "[a]lmost all modern jurists, however reluctantly, admit the existence in international law of the principle with which this Article is concerned and which is commonly spoken of as the doctrine of *rebus sic stantibus*",[5] and that the idea behind the principle is known in municipal law systems. However, the Commission noted the need to confine the operation of the doctrine within clear limits, given the obvious risks to the security of treaties embodied in the doctrine.

---

[2] See 23 UST 3435, TIAS No. 7503. Signed May 26, 1972, in force 3 October, 1972; terminated 13 June 2002. The text of the treaty is also available at <www.state.gov/www/global/arms/treaties/abm/abm2.html>.

[3] *Report of the International Law Commission on the Work of the Second Part of its Seventeenth Session*, Monaco, 2-28 January 1966, Vol. II, UN Doc. A/6309/Rev.1, at 256-260.

[4] Article 59 reads: "Fundamental Change of Circumstances: 1. A Fundamental change of circumstances which has occurred with regard to those existing at the time of the conclusion of a treaty, and which was not foreseen by the parties, may not be invoked as a ground for terminating or withdrawing from the treaty unless: (a) the existence of those circumstances constituted an essential basis of the consent of the parties to be bound by the treaty; and (b) the effect of the change is radically to transform the scope of obligation still to be performed under the treaty. 2. A fundamental change of circumstances may not be invoked: (a) As a ground for terminating or with drawing from the treaty establishing a boundary; (b) If the fundamental change is the result of a breach by the party invoking it either of the treaty or of a different international obligation owed to the parties to the treaty." See Lossitzyn, note 1, for a critique of Article 59.

[5] See note 3, at 257.

The Commission observed that, in the past, the principle had been considered to be based on a tacit condition implied in every "perpetual" treaty, one which would permit withdrawal from or termination of a treaty in the event of a fundamental change of circumstances. However, the Commission noted that the tendency today was to consider the implied term as only a fiction by which it was attempted to reconcile the dissolution of treaties with the principle of the principle *pacta sunt servanda*. This fiction was considered by the ILC as an undesirable one since it increased the risk of subjective interpretation and abuse. This was the reason why the Commission decided to reject the implied term theory and formulated the principle as one based on an objective rule of law by which, on grounds of equity and justice, a fundamental change of circumstances may, under certain conditions, be invoked by a party as grounds for terminating the treaty. The Commission, in order to stress the objective character of the rule, decided that it would be better not to use the term *rebus sic stantibus*, either in the text of the Article or even in the title, and by doing so to avoid the doctrinal implication of that term.[6]

The Commission also recognised that, in the past, the application of this principle was limited to so-called perpetual treaties, i.e. to treaties not making any provision for their termination. The Commission did not, however, find this approach convincing, and stated that the doctrine "should not be limited to treaties containing no provision regarding their termination, though for obvious reasons it would seldom or never have relevance for treaties of limited duration or which are terminable upon notice".[7] As to the conditions of the invocation of such a principle, the Commission "attached great importance to the strict formulation of these conditions", and decided "to emphasize the exceptional character of this ground for termination or withdrawal by framing the article in negative form".[8]

The Commission concluded that a treaty establishing a boundary should be considered an exception to the doctrine, because the rule, instead of being an instrument of peaceful change, might become a source of dangerous tensions if applied in that context. The Commission was also of the view that a fundamental change may not be invoked if it had been brought about by a breach of a treaty by the party invoking it or by that party's breach of international obligations owed to the other parties to the treaty, in accordance with the general principle of law that a party cannot take advantage of its own wrong-doing.[9]

---

[6] See note 3, at 258. For criticism of the ILC's rejection of the "implied term" approach, see Lissitzyn, note 1, at 912-922, who stresses the paramountcy of the shared intentions and expectations of the parties.

[7] See note 3, at 258.

[8] *Id.*, at 259. See the Gabčikovo-Nagymaros case, section 3.3 below.

[9] See Case Concerning the Factory in Chorzów, 1927 PCIJ (Series A), No. 9, at 31.

The Commission clarified that a subjective change in the attitude or policy of the Government could never be invoked as a ground for terminating, withdrawing or suspension of the operation of a treaty. The Commission considered that the definition of a "fundamental change of circumstances" should exclude abusive attempts to terminate the treaty on that basis. Furthermore, and quite importantly, the Commission noted that the proper function of codification was to minimize the risks posed to the security of treaties by the doctrine of fundamental change of circumstances by strictly defining and circumscribing the conditions under which recourse may properly be had to this principle, especially when those conditions are coupled with strict procedural safeguards relating in general to invoking of grounds for invalidity or termination of treaties.[10]

The doctrine of fundamental change of circumstances was again considered at the Diplomatic Conference on the Law of Treaties, where the work of the ILC was taken as a basis.[11] There was general agreement among the participants that the application of this doctrine should be based on the general principles of equity and justice. In the context of the potential threat to the security of treaties, an interesting discussion took place concerning the relationship between the doctrine of fundamental change of circumstances and the principle of *pacta sunt servanda*. Some of the delegates were of the view that despite the commonly held conviction, the clause *rebus sic stantibus* was not the counterpart of the principle of *pacta sunt servanda*. It was said that: "[o]nce a treaty came into existence, it had to be executed in good faith; otherwise it remained a dead letter. But whether or not the treaty remained binding, despite a fundamental change of circumstances, was an entirely different matter. It was a practical problem and could not be solved merely by referring to the logical principle of good faith."[12]

Many delegates stressed the potentially dangerous character of this doctrine. The participants were in agreement that it was essential to make this doctrine as restrictive as possible to safeguard against abuse and to emphasise that its application in practice should be exceptional, and that the stability of treaties should be maintained. In the event, the doctrine was

---

[10] See note 3, at 269.

[11] The United Nations Conference on the Law of Treaties, Official Records (New York, 1969), first Session Vienna, 26 March –24 May 1968, (UN Doc. A/CONF.39/11.Add.1); Summary Records of the Plenary Meeting and Meeting of the Committee of a Whole; Second Session, Vienna 9 April –22 My 1969, Summary Records of Plenary Meeting and Meeting of Committee of the Whole (UN Doc. A/CONF.39/11/Add.1).

[12] Mr Stuyt, the Netherlands, First Meeting, at 367. See also Vamvoukos, *supra* note 1, at 216: "*Pacta sunt servanda* means that treaties are inviolable, but it does not mean that treaties cannot be terminated or modified. Where it is established by lawful procedure that a rule for the termination or revision of the treaty applies, the rule of *pacta sunt servanda* ceases to operate. The sphere of its application begins where that of the doctrine of *rebus sic stantibus* begins."

codified in Article 62 of 1969 the Vienna Convention on the Law of Treaties ("VCLT"), which provides as follows:

> 1. A fundamental change of circumstances which has occurred with regard to those existing at the time of conclusion of a treaty, and which was not foreseen by the parties, may not be invoked as a ground for terminating or withdrawing from the treaty unless: (a) the existence of those circumstances constituted an essential basis of the consent of the parties to be bound by the treaty; and (b) the effect of the change is radically to transform the extent of obligations still to be performed under the treaty.
>
> 2. A fundamental change of circumstance may not be invoked as a ground for terminating or withdrawal from the treaty; (a) if the treaty established a boundary; or (b) if fundamental change is the result of a breach by the party invoking it either of an obligation under the treaty to any other international obligation owed to any party to the treaty.
>
> 3. If, under the foregoing paragraphs, a party may invoke a fundamental change of circumstances as a ground or terminating or with withdrawing from a treaty it may also invoke the change as a ground for suspending the operation of a treaty.

Thus, the VCLT specifies the following conditions for the termination or withdrawal from a treaty on the grounds of a fundamental change of circumstances: firstly, the change must be of circumstances existing at the time the treaty was made; secondly, the change of circumstances must be "fundamental"; thirdly, the change must not have been foreseen by parties; fourthly, the existence of these circumstances must have constituted an essential basis of the consent of the parties to be bound by the treaty in the first place; fifthly, the effect of the change must be radically to transform the "extent" of obligations still to be fulfilled under the treaty. The VCLT does not provide much guidance as to what is "fundamental", nor does it make it precise what is the "extent" of obligations still to be performed; [13] but it is clear that all of these conditions are to be fulfilled for a successful invocation of the doctrine from a legal point of view, confirming the policy of maintaining the security of treaty relations.

---

[13] As noted recently by F. Kirgis, "Proposed Missile Defenses and the ABM Treaty", *ASIL Insights*, May 2001, at <www.asil.org/insights/insigh70.htm>. The same author notes that the word "extent" in the English text of Article 62 is in the French "*portée*", which could be translated as "impact". See also Lissitzyn, note 1, at 915.

3. Some Decisions of International Courts on the Doctrine of Fundamental Change of Circumstances

The doctrine of fundamental change of circumstances has been considered judicially in several cases, but it has been remarked that "in almost all cases in which the doctrine has been invoked before an international tribunal, the latter, while not rejecting it in principle, has refused to admit that it could be applied to the case before it".[14] The operation of the doctrine of fundamental change of circumstances has arisen in a number of cases before the World Court, and recently before the European Court of Justice. The parts of the judgments that are relevant for this discussion will be considered in this section, with a view to shedding light on the elements of Article 62.

3.1 The *Free Zones* case[15]

In this case, the French Government invoked the principle of *rebus sic stantibus*, although it stressed that the principle does not allow unilateral denunciation of a treaty claimed to be out of date.[16] Switzerland argued on the other hand that there was a difference of opinion as regards this doctrine, and disputed the existence in international law of a right that could be enforced through the decisions of a competent tribunal to the termination of a treaty because of changed circumstances. Switzerland argued that in any event, (a) the circumstances alleged to have changed were not circumstances on the basis of whose continuance the parties could be said to have entered into the treaty; (b) in any event, the doctrine does not apply to treaties creating territorial rights; and (c) France had allowed too long a period to pass after alleged changes of circumstances had manifested themselves before raising the plea.[17]

For its part, the Permanent Court of International Justice ("PCIJ") found that the facts did not justify the application of the *rebus sic stantibus*

---

[14] Jennings and Watts, *supra* note 1, at 1307, where reference is made to a considerable amount of international case law on the doctrine of fundamental change of circumstances at note 8. See also Vamvoukos, *supra* note 1, Chapter 4, at 152-185, for a discussion of case law that includes decisions of municipal courts.

[15] Case of the Free Zones of Upper Savoy and the District of Gex (France *v.* Switzerland), 1932 PCIJ (Series A/B), No. 46, at 158.

[16] Case of the Free Zones of Upper Savoy and the District of Gex (France *v.* Switzerland), 1932 PCIJ (Series C), No. 58, at 578-579, 109-146 and 405-415, see also Case Concerning the Factory in Chorzów, Jurisdiction, 1927 PCIJ (Series A), No. 9, at 31; Case of the Free Zones of Upper Savoy and the District of Gex (France *v.* Switzerland), 1929 PCIJ (Series C), No.17/1, at 89, 250, 256, 283-284.

[17] *Id.,* at 463-476.

principle. It stated that "[a]s the French argument fails on the facts, it becomes unnecessary for the Court to consider any of the questions of principle which arise in connection with the theory of the lapse of treaties by reason of changed circumstances, such as the extent to which the theory can be regarded as constituting a rule of international law, the occasions on which and the method by which effect can be given to the theory if recognised, and the question whether it would apply to treaties establishing rights" such as those that were the subject of the case.[18] The ILC, with this and other cases in mind, stated that "[t]he evidence of the principle of customary law is considerable, but the International Court has not yet committed itself on the point."[19]

3.2. The *Fisheries Jurisdiction* Case[20]

This case was the first dealing with the topic following the codification of the principle of fundamental change of circumstances in the VCLT. The ICJ considered whether certain provisions of an agreement concluded in 1961 between the United Kingdom and Iceland had come to an end as a result of a fundamental change of circumstances relating to fishing techniques and international law relating to fisheries. The Court noted that the principle and the conditions and exceptions to which it is subject had been "embodied" in Article 62 of the VCLT, "which may *in many respects* be considered as a reflection of existing customary law on the subject".[21] First, regarding the argument concerning changes in fishing techniques, the Court found that the alleged changes could not affect the relevant provision for the purposes of the case, namely the compromissory clause that provided for reference to the Court in the event of a dispute. The Court found the relevant obligation, i.e. the obligation to submit the case to adjudication, did not meet the conditions for the applicability of the principle. This was set out in the following statement:

---

[18] Free Zones case, *supra* note 15, at 158.
[19] ILC Report, *supra* note 3, at 258. For the view that the Court's reasoning is supportive of the doctrine, see Haraszti, *supra* note 1, at 40-41.
[20] Fisheries Jurisdiction cases, (United Kingdom v. Iceland and Federal Republic of Germany v. Iceland), (Jurisdiction), Judgments of 2 February 1973, 1973 ICJ Reports, at 4 and 49 respectively. The references to the judgment in this chapter will be to the United Kingdom case. See H. Thirlway, "The Law and Practice of the International Court of Justice", 64 *BYIL* (1993), at 75-81, for comment on this case, as well as the treatment of the doctrine in dissenting opinions in the Right of Passage over Indian Territory (Portugal v. India), Merits, Judgment of 12 April 1960, 1960 ICJ Rep. 6.
[21] Paragraph 36 of the Judgment (our emphasis).

in order that a change of circumstances may give rise to a ground for invoking the termination of a treaty it is also necessary that it should have resulted in a radical transformation of the extent of the obligations still to be performed. The change must have increased the burden of the obligations to be executed to the extent of rendering the performance something essentially different from that originally undertaken.[22]

The Court found that the dispute, insofar as it related to the continued validity of the compromissory clause, was exactly of the character anticipated by the parties, and since the change in circumstances was foreseen, it did not have the effect of terminating the obligation. Secondly, regarding the change in international legal opinion on fisheries jurisdiction, the Court recognised that "changes in the law may under certain conditions constitute valid grounds for invoking a change of circumstances affecting the duration of a treaty".[23] However, it found that while recognition of the 12-mile fisheries zone that Iceland secured by entering into the 1961 agreement was no longer in issue as a result of changes in the law ("although some of the motives which induced Iceland to enter into the 1961 agreement might have become less compelling or have disappeared altogether"),[24] the same could not be said of all parts of the 1961 agreement, especially the compromissory clause, the purpose of which remained unchanged. The Court did not find it necessary to pronounce upon the applicability of the principle of fundamental change of circumstances to other parts of the treaty, stating that those would be dealt with at the merits stage; the only pertinent change at this jurisdictional stage concerned the compromissory clause.

Two important issues regarding the operation of the principle can be identified in the Court's Judgment. First, the Court underscored the importance of the non-foreseeability criterion embodied in Article 62(1) of the VCLT – the doctrine of fundamental change does not operate where the change in question was foreseen by the parties at the time of the agreement. Secondly, the Court may be seen to be suggesting that if the "motives" that induced one party (Iceland) to enter into the agreement had become "less compelling" or had "disappeared altogether",[25] the principle of fundamental change could operate. Of course, this is somewhat speculative, as the Court did not find that there was any change in the circumstances as far as the compromissory clause was concerned; the suggestion referred to here was not relevant for the Court's decision. In any event, it would be difficult to sustain the argument that the "disappearance" of one party's motives alone could justify the operation of the principle. This is confirmed by the importance attached by the Court to the "procedural complement to the

---

[22] Paragraph 43 of the Judgment.
[23] Paragraph 32 of the Judgment.
[24] Paragraph 34 of the Judgment.
[25] *Id.*

doctrine of changed circumstances", i.e. "the requirement that a State invoking a fundamental change of circumstances should be prepared to allow a third party to determine whether the conditions for the operation of the doctrine are present",[26] which complement was already included in the compromissory clause. This "procedural complement" is of the first importance if the security of treaties is to be guaranteed. The Court cannot, therefore, properly be considered to have sanctioned the view that the disappearance of one party's motives as a fundamental change of circumstances constituting grounds for the termination of a treaty.

Briggs, commenting on the Court's Judgment in this case, stated that "[i]t should also be noted that in the *Icelandic Fisheries* cases, the Court, while recognising the rules set forth in the Vienna Convention and in customary international law with regard to denunciation of treaties for duress or changed conditions, found that the rights were surrounded in each case by substantive conditions limiting their application. The contentions of Iceland were rejected not because the Court refused to recognise the rules invoked but because Iceland refused to meet the conditions and limitations which were an intrinsic part of the rules and essential for their application. In this connection, it was not the procedural provisions of the Vienna Convention which the Court considered applicable; but its concern with procedures for dealing with unilateral claims to terminate treaties is clear. For example, the Court regarded what it termed 'the procedural complement to the doctrine of changed circumstances' as an essential part of the doctrine."[27]

3.3. The *Gabčikovo-Nagymaros* Case[28]

The 1977 Treaty Concerning the Construction and Operation of the Gabčikovo-Nagymaros System of Locks (the "1977 Treaty")[29] between Hungary and Czechoslovakia provided for the construction and operation of a system of locks by the Parties as a "joint investment". The joint investment was essentially aimed at the production of hydroelectricity, the improvement of navigation on the relevant sectors of the Danube and the protection of the areas along the banks against flooding. At the same time, by the terms of the

---

[26] Sinclair, *supra* note 1, at 195; see paragraphs 44 and 45 of the Judgment.

[27] H.W. Briggs, "Unilateral Denunciation of Treaties: The Vienna Convention and the International Court of Justice", 68 *AJIL* (1974), at 68.

[28] Case Concerning the Gabčikovo-Nagymaros Project (Hungary v. Slovakia), Judgment of 25 September 1997, 1997 ICJ Reports, at 3. See chapter 10 below for a discussion of other aspects of the law of treaties in this case.

[29] 1977 Treaty Between Hungarian's People's Republic and the Czechoslovak Socialist Republic Concerning the Construction and Operation of the Gabčikovo-Nagymaros System of Locks, signed in Budapest on 16 September 1977 reproduced in 31 *ILM* 1247 (1993).

treaty, the parties undertook to ensure that the quality of water in the Danube was not impaired as a result of the Project and that the obligations for the protection of nature arising in connection with the construction and operation of the system of locks would be fulfilled.

Before the Court, Hungary identified several "substantive elements" that it alleged had changed fundamentally by the date it gave notification of termination of the treaty: the notion of "socialist integration" for which the Treaty had originally been a "vehicle", but which had since disappeared; the "single and indivisible operational system", which was to be replaced by a unilateral scheme; the fact that the basis of the planned joint investment had been frustrated by the sudden emergence of both States as market economies; the attitude of Czechoslovakia that had turned the "framework treaty" into an "immutable norm"; and, finally, the transformation of a treaty consistent with environmental protection into "a prescription for environmental disaster". Slovakia argued that the changes identified by Hungary had not altered the nature of the obligations under the Treaty from those originally undertaken, so that no entitlement to terminate it arose from those changes.[30]

The Court again reaffirmed that Article 62 of the VCLT reflected customary law, albeit with the same qualification – "in many respects" – that it employed in the *Fisheries Jurisdiction* case.[31] It found that while the political situation was "of relevance" to the conclusion of the 1977 Treaty, a joint investment programme for the production of energy, the control of floods and the improvement of navigation on the Danube were not so closely linked to political conditions as to render these an essential basis for consent of the parties which, in changing, radically altered the extent of the obligations still to be performed.[32] The change of circumstances of the conclusion of the 1977 Treaty i.e. the collapse of the communist regime and the obsolete stated aim of strengthening communist economic cooperation (within the framework of the Council for Mutual Economic Assistance), was not viewed by the Court as sufficiently fundamental to constitute grounds for termination of the treaty. The Court took into consideration the content of the obligation in both cases and decided that it was not affected by any change of circumstances. The Court further concluded that even if the estimated profitability of the project had diminished by 1992, it had not done so to such an extent as to "radically" transform the parties' obligations. Likewise, new developments in the state of environmental knowledge and of environmental law were not completely unforeseen – Articles 15, 19 and 20 of the 1977 Treaty allowed the Parties, as the Court found, to take account of

---

[30] Paragraph 95 of the Judgment.
[31] Paragraph 46 of the Judgment. See note 21 above.
[32] Paragraph 104 of the Judgment.

these changes and to accommodate them when implementing the provisions of the 1977 Treaty. The Court, having analysed arguments submitted by both parties, stated that

> [t]he changed circumstances advanced by Hungary are, in the Court's view, not of such a nature, either individually or collectively, that their effect would radically transform the extent of the obligations still to be performed in order to accomplish the project. A fundamental change of circumstances must have been unforeseen; the existence of circumstances at the time of the Treaty's conclusion must have constituted an essential basis of the consent of the parties to be bound by the Treaty. The negative and conditional wording of Article 62 of the Vienna Convention on the Law of Treaties is a clear indication moreover that the stability of treaty relations requires that the plea of fundamental change of circumstances be applied only in exceptional cases.[33]

Thus, according to the Court, the termination of treaties as a result of a fundamental change of circumstances is the exception and the stability of treaties the rule. In both the *Fisheries Jurisdiction* and the *Gabčikovo-Nagymaros* cases, the Court adopted a restrictive approach to the interpretation of this doctrine. The threshold for what amounts to a fundamental change is high, as is evident from the wording of Article 62 or the VCLT.

3.4 *Racke* v. *Haupzollamt Mainz* [34]

This is one case in recent times that stands out because the plea of fundamental change of circumstances was apparently upheld exceptionally by an international court. The case arose out of the suspension in 1991 by the Council of the European Communities ("EC") of the operation of the Cooperation Agreement between the EC and Yugoslavia following the outbreak of hostilities in the Former Yugoslavia. An importer of Yugoslav wines who became liable to higher import duties as a result of the suspension, commenced litigation in the German courts which led to a request to the European Court of Justice ("ECJ") for a preliminary ruling as to the validity of the suspension. The ECJ found that two conditions were to be satisfied for a successful invocation of fundamental change of circumstances. Regarding the first condition, namely that the existence of the fundamental change of circumstances upon which the suspension of the

---

[33] *Id.*

[34] Case C-162/96 (1998) *ECR*-I-3655. See J. Klabbers, "Re-inventing the Law of Treaties: The Contribution of the EC Courts", 30 *NYIL* (1999), 45, at 57-59, and O. Elias, "General International Law in the European Court of Justice: From Hypothesis to Reality", 31 *NYIL* (2000), 3, at 17-22.

treaty was based must have constituted an essential basis of the consent of the parties, the ECJ found that it was necessary that "the maintenance of a situation of peace in Yugoslavia, indispensable for neighbourly relations, and the existence of institutions capable of ensuring implementation of the co-operation envisaged by the Agreement throughout the territory of Yugoslavia" subsisted; but it found that this was not the case on the facts. Regarding the second condition, namely that the changed circumstances must have had the effect of radically transforming the extent of the obligations assumed by the parties under the treaty, the ECJ ruled that it was sufficient that no purpose was served by continuing to grant preferences with a view to stimulating trade where Yugoslavia was breaking up, since "customary international law does not require an impossibility to perform obligations". Accordingly, the plea was upheld, provided that no "manifest error of assessment" existed in the Council's appreciation of the situation and its invocation of the plea.[35]

It has been noted that this was a rather more lenient version of the doctrine of fundamental change of circumstances than is implicit in Article 62 of the VCLT, as reflected in the cases before the ICJ considered earlier.[36] However, it has been suggested that it is probable that the fact of war in a neighbouring country, which persisted in spite of a ceasefire agreement and which had been determined to constitute a threat to international peace and security by the Security Council in its resolution 713 (1991), led the ECJ and the Council to adopt the position it did.[37] It has also been suggested that it should be remembered that in this case, the primary issue before the ECJ was whether individuals within the EC could rely on customary international law in order to challenge the validity of EC law:

> [T]his focus on the individual's position, tuning the Court's mind to the needs and interests of individuals, may have caused the Court to misconstrue the case as one in which the trader invoked the *rebus sic stantibus* doctrine ... it transpires that the opening up of international actors may well have consequences for the application of the law of treaties. One may wonder whether the Court would have come up with such a relaxed version of *rebus sic stantibus* had the case been brought by one of the Community institutions, for instance; and it seems questionable that the Council would have argued it with such fervour had Yugoslavia complained against the suspension.[38]

This appreciation of the case finds some support in the view that "the Court approached the matter as one of judicial review, and the Article 62 point was not dealt with in much depth. The Court said, in effect, that the Council had not been clearly wrong; it did not say the Council had been right to apply the

---

[35] Paragraphs 53-57 of the Judgment.
[36] Klabbers, *supra* note 34, at 59.
[37] See Klabbers and Elias, both at note 34 above.
[38] Klabbers, *id.*, at 59.

principle".[39] In other words, the extent to which reliance is to be placed on this case as clear authority for the operation of the doctrine of fundamental change of circumstances is limited by the circumstances of the case, illustrated by the Court's own statement that

> [b]ecause of the complexity of the rules in question and the imprecision of some of the concepts to which they refer, judicial review must necessarily, and in particular in the context of a preliminary reference for an assessment of validity, be limited to the question whether, by adopting the suspending regulation, the Council made manifest errors of assessment concerning the conditions for applying the rules.[40]

4. Fundamental Change of Circumstances and the ABM Treaty

In this section, the applicability of the doctrine of fundamental change of circumstances as grounds for withdrawing from a treaty will be considered in relation to the withdrawal of the United States from the 1972 ABM Treaty. The conditions for the invocation of the doctrine as developed in the previous section will be examined in relation to the circumstances of this treaty, and as will be seen, this situation highlights several important features of the doctrine of fundamental change of circumstances.

4.1 The Withdrawal of the United States from the Treaty

The ABM Treaty was a bilateral treaty concluded between the United States and the former Soviet Union, and since the break up of the latter, both the United States and the Russian Federation continued to regard themselves as bound by the treaty. The following Statement by the White House Press Secretary on December 13, 2001, the day on which President Bush announced the withdrawal of the United States from the Treaty, reflects the pertinent considerations on which the decision to withdraw was based. The Statement reads:

> The circumstances affecting US national security have changed fundamentally since the signing of the ABM Treaty in 1972. The attacks against the US homeland on September 11 vividly demonstrate that the threats we face today are far different from those of the Cold War. During that era, now fortunately in the past, the United States and the Soviet Union were locked in an

---

[39] A. Aust, *Modern Treaty Law and Practice* (2000), at 242. See also Elias, *supra* note 34, at 18-20.

[40] Paragraph 52 of the Judgment.

implacably hostile relationship. Each side deployed thousands of nuclear weapons pointed at the other. Our ultimate security rested largely on the grim premise that neither side would launch a nuclear attack because doing so would result in a counter-attack ensuring the total destruction of both nations.

Today, our security environment is profoundly different. The Cold War is over. The Soviet Union no longer exists. Russia is not an enemy, but in fact is increasingly allied with us on a growing number of critically important issues. The depth of the United States-Russian co-operation in counter-terrorism is both a model of the new strategic relationship we seek to establish and a foundation on which to build further co-operation across the broad spectrum of political, economic and security issues of mutual interest.

Today, the United States and Russia face new threats to their security. Principal among these threats are weapons of mass destruction and their delivery means wielded by terrorists and rogue states. A number of such states are acquiring increasingly longer-range ballistic missiles as instruments of blackmail and coercion against the United States and its friends and allies. The United States must defend its homeland, its forces and its friends and allies against these threats. We must develop and deploy the means to deter and protect against them, including through limited missile defense of our territory.

Under the terms of the ABM treaty, the United States is prohibited from defending its homeland against ballistic missile attack. We are also prohibited from cooperating in developing missile defenses against long-range threats with our friends and allies. Given the emergence of these new threats to our national security and the imperative of defending against them, the United States is today providing formal notification of its withdrawal from the ABM treaty. As provided in Article XV of that Treaty, the effective date of withdrawal will be six months from today".[41]

The withdrawal of the United States took effect six months later in accordance with Article XV(2) of the Treaty on 13 June 2002.[42] However, regardless of the express provision for this method of termination in the treaty, and separate from the apparent choice of the United States to follow this procedure as set out in Article XV(2), there was a clear reference in this statement to the doctrine of fundamental change of circumstances as a basis for the decision of the United States to withdraw; and it has been suggested that, taking account of "political, military-strategic and even ideological changes in the world since the ABM Treaty was concluded with changes referred to by States when resorting to *rebus sic stantibus* arguments, current

---

[41] Text available at <http://www.state.gov/t/ac/rls/fs/2001/6848.htm>.

[42] Article XV(2) provides that "Each Party shall, in exercising its national sovereignty, have the right to withdraw from this Treaty if it decides that extraordinary events related to the subject matter of this Treaty have jeopardized its supreme interests. It shall give notice of its decision to the other Party six months prior to withdrawal from the Treaty. Such notice shall include a statement of the extraordinary events the notifying party regards as having jeopardized its supreme interests".

changes are of such a magnitude and character that if *rebus sic stantibus* can ever be justifiably used this may be one of such cases".[43] This justifies consideration of the role of the principle in relation to the ABM Treaty.

4.2 The Conditions for the Applicability of the Doctrine

The conditions for the applicability of the doctrine in international law as set out in Article 62 of the VCLT will now be considered. Any reading of Article 62 will indicate that these conditions are cumulative – all of them must be satisfied, which shows the need to keep the operation of the doctrine within strict limits. It should also be noted that there is obviously some overlap between these conditions.[44]

4.2.1 The requirement that the change relate to circumstances existing at the time of the conclusion of the treaty

Firstly, the requirement that the change must have occurred with regards to the circumstances that existed at the time of the conclusion of the treaty is satisfied here. This condition does not refer to the quality of the changes, but rather to the temporal issue; and the argument of the United States was precisely that the circumstances that led to the conclusion of the treaty no longer exist.

4.2.2 The requirements that the change must be fundamental and that the changes were changes to the circumstances that constituted an essential basis of the consent of the parties to be bound by the treaty

Secondly, the change in circumstances must be "fundamental". Article 62 does not define what the term "fundamental" means, and it must indeed be that the answer to the question whether a change is fundamental or not would depend on the particular circumstances in question. In this context,

---

[43] See Müllerson, *supra* note 1, at 530. The same writer also states that "although emerging ballistic missile threats from 'rogue' regimes referred to by the United States are part of the changed circumstances, the latter notion is obviously much wider. It includes the disappearance of the bipolar world, military strategic parity between the US and the USSR (Russia), struggle between capitalist and communist ideologies and transformation of other political, military-strategic and ideological factors. Changes of such magnitude may indeed nullify the very *raison d'être* of the ABM Treaty, i.e. its very object and purpose even without new threats from 'rogue' regimes"; *id.*, at 512-513. The article contains very useful information, replete with references, regarding the relevant political considerations.

[44] See text accompanying note 13, especially the views of Lissitzyn on the ambiguity of the main conditions for the application of the doctrine.

the end of the Cold War and the apparent emergence of new threats from "rogue" states would be the main "fundamental" changes.

In the *Gabčikovo* case, the ICJ confirmed that the change in ideological-political circumstances was "of relevance", and while they did not suffice to justify termination of the treaty on grounds of fundamental change of circumstances, the possibility that such factors could indeed justify such a change in appropriate circumstances was left open;[45] it would indeed be difficult to conceive of a ruling to the effect that a change in political circumstances could indeed not be relevant. In that case, the collapse of the Communist regime and the obsolescence of the aim of strengthening communist economic cooperation within the framework of the Council for Mutual Economic Assistance were not viewed as being sufficiently fundamental, and neither was the consideration that the project was no longer as profitable as anticipated at the time of the conclusion of the treaty.

In the context of the ABM Treaty, it would appear that the changed political-ideological circumstances that formed the basis of the decision of the United States to withdraw were more "fundamental"as those circumstances were more obviously directly relevant to the conclusion of the Treaty. Thus, it can be said that there are stronger grounds for arguing that the requirement that the change be fundamental was satisfied in this case. The same applies to the related further requirement that the existence of these circumstances must have constituted an essential basis of the consent of the parties to be bound by the treaty in the first place.

A number of considerations should however be noted in this context. In the first place, the basic issue here is that statements made by both Parties and discussions between them at the political-diplomatic level are of a very different character from legal arguments that would be made, for example, in the more legally focused and more formal setting, such as that to be found in the context of international judicial or other proceedings where the issue is submitted to a third party for determination. The manner in which arguments are formulated and the particular facts and circumstances that are highlighted by the parties in the latter kind of setting will be of the first importance in the reasoning and conclusion of any such third party, even if, as is likely to be the case, they may not necessarily determine absolutely the outcome of the case. The point is that the appreciation of the political facts – the changed circumstances that would be in issue in such a case – may be appreciated by such a third party decision-maker in a way that is different from the way these issues would be appreciated in a less formal setting; and the positions expressed by commentators or even the parties to a treaty themselves may not necessarily provide a resolution on the basis of law. One only needs to compare the fact that the doctrine of fundamental change has extremely

---

[45] See note 28, at paragraph 104 of the Judgment.

rarely been invoked successfully before international judicial bodies with the conclusions reached by some commentators that state practice outside the international judicial context supports the existence of the doctrine.[46]

In the light of the above considerations, the views of Russia, "the State that in legal terms is somewhere between a successor State to the former USSR and its legal continuation",[47] are instructive in relation to the withdrawal of the United States from the ABM Treaty. Russia clearly expressed its desire to maintain the ABM Treaty. In response to the announcement by President Bush that the United States would withdraw from the treaty in accordance with Article XV(2) of the Treaty, President Putin stated that, while the decision was not unexpected, Russia considered it a "mistake" that could destroy the existing nuclear balance and create a new arms race.[48] Accordingly, in Russia's view, the *rebus sic stantibus* argument as such was not compelling, and the difficulties considered by the United States to have subsided continued to be real enough. Suggestions have been made as to the reasons why Russia held or expressed these views,[49] but it is clear that it did.[50] The point, however, is that the political issues involved

---

[46] See, e.g., Vamvoukos, *supra* note 1, Chapter 3; Lissitzyn, *supra* note 1, at 902-912.

[47] See Müllerson, *supra* note 1, at 516. As to the arguments put forward by certain United States officials to the effect that the dissolution of the USSR brought with it an end to the Treaty, he states, correctly, in our view, that such views "completely misinterpret some elementary points of international law concerning continuity and succession of States especially as applied in cases of fundamental changes which took place in the former USSR and Central and Eastern Europe"; *id.*, at 511, *supra* note 8.

[48] <http:news.bbc.co.uk/1/hi/americas/1707812.stm>. According to the same BBC report, the Russian Prime Minister Mikhail Kasyanov stated that while Washington was "within its rights" (probably referring to the fact that Article XV(2) of the ABM Treaty allowed such unilateral withdrawal, rather than an acceptance of the operation of the principle of *rebus sic stantibus* as being applicable in this case), the decision was a cause of annoyance" for Moscow. On the Russian position, see further Müllerson, *supra* note 1, at 521-524. See also "Russia's anxieties over missile defence", <http://news.bbc.co.uk/1/hi//world/Europe/1994338.stm>.

[49] Müllerson states that "Russia is today opposing any possible US withdrawal from or even modification of the ABM Treaty, not because it would affect any concrete Russian strategic interests, but because, having lost the empire (i.e. the Soviet Union) and not yet found its role in the world, Russia is constantly trying to box above its weight", *id.*, at 523. However, he also refers to the Decree of the President of the Russian Federation, No. 24, 10 January 2000, where it is stated that "Russia opposes all attempts at a creation of the structure of international relations based on the dominance in international relations of developed Western countries led by the United States"; *id.*, at 524.

[50] Should the case fall to a third party legal decision-maker, such suggestions would argue for a conclusion to the effect that Russia did not mean what it said, or, to put it differently, that a political policy expressed by a sovereign state, which it may legally express and adopt to the extent permitted by international law, is not realistic and therefore that the alleged threat was not real, and that therefore, circumstances had changed. One may speculate as to whether this kind of judicial pronouncement would indeed ever be made, or if it was made, whether it

here make it difficult to speak meaningfully, outside a formal legal context, of the legal effect to be attributed to the opposed position of the parties to the treaty regarding a plea by one party of a fundamental change of circumstances. A third party decision-maker might be inclined to take a wider view and consider that withdrawal from the treaty could indeed pose a threat to international peace and security, that the changed circumstances did not remove the ultimate threat that was addressed by the ABM Treaty. But as stated above, all of this is speculation,[51] and much would depend on the way the legal arguments were formulated and analyzed in a formal setting. In sum, it is difficult to anticipate the result of the more objective consideration of this kind of political-factual dispute by a third party applying international law.

The most that can be said with certainty is that the grounds for saying that circumstances have changed in such a fundamental way as to affect the basis for the consent of the parties to the treaty seem to be stronger in the case of the ABM Treaty than they were, for example, in the *Gabčikovo* case. Whether they would be strong enough to constitute grounds for termination is a different matter, in view of the strict limits of the doctrine as reflected in the VCLT and ICJ's judgment in that case.

In determining whether a change is fundamental and affects the consent of the parties to the treaty, it is also worth posing the question as to "would the parties consider the conclusion of such a treaty in the changed circumstances?". It has been stated that "[t]here is no doubt that today the United States and Russia would not even contemplate the conclusion of such a treaty".[52] While this may constitute a rule of thumb in some cases – and no more than a rule of thumb – it is unlikely that it would provide a useful guide to the application of the *rebus sic stantibus* doctrine. For example, Iceland in the *Fisheries Jurisdiction* case and Hungary in the *Gabčikovo* case, simply by virtue of seeking release from the relevant treaties in the face of changed circumstances, clearly would not contemplate entering into such treaties at the time that they made the plea of fundamental change of circumstances, and they certainly would *say*, were it up to them, that they would not have concluded the treaty. But the approach of the ICJ makes it clear that this is

---

would be proper to do so. In such a case, it is probable that a third party decision-maker would be inclined to either take the policy seriously, even if it finds for other reasons that circumstances have indeed changed. It would be odd for a third party to pronounce as to whether a sovereign state really means what it says and has said consistently on many occasions.

[51] It is important to remember the words of Lissitzyn: "[t]he ambiguities residing in expressions 'fundamental change', 'not foreseen by the parties', 'an essential basis of the consent of the parties', and radically to transform the scope of the obligation' are patent"; *supra* note 1.

[52] See Müllerson, note 1, at 531.

not the test, as the plea was rejected in both cases.[53] Such a formulation of the purport of the doctrine would clearly be inimical to the stability of treaty relationships, the maintenance of which is paramount. This consideration is relevant to the requirement that the change must not have been foreseen by the parties, which is considered in the following section.

4.2.3 The requirement that the change must not have been foreseen by the Parties in the light of express provision for other grounds for termination included in a treaty

In the *Fisheries Jurisdiction* case,[54] the ICJ dealt with this requirement in the context of the compromissory clause in the 1961 Agreement between Iceland and the United Kingdom. It found that, at least as regards the agreement to submit the case to the ICJ, it could not be said that there had been a fundamental change of circumstances that justified termination of that part of the treaty, whose object and purpose remained unchanged; the resolution of the kind of dispute that had arisen between the parties was indeed the reason for the inclusion of the compromissory clause. More importantly, in the *Gabčíkovo* case[55], the ICJ found that, contrary to Hungary's arguments, the changes in environmental law and the changes in the state of environmental knowledge were not "completely" unforeseen, finding that Articles 15, 19 and 20 of the 1977 Treaty provided for the Parties to take account of these changes and to accommodate such changes when implementing the provisions of the 1977 Treaty.

Did the US and the USSR foresee that the Cold War might end one day, or that threats might arise from quarters other than the other party? In this context it is necessary to look at the terms of the treaty. Relevant here is Article XIII of the ABM Treaty, which provides that

> 1. To promote the objectives and implementation of the provisions of this Treaty, the Parties shall establish promptly a Standing Consultative Commission, within the framework of which they will: ...

> (d) consider possible changes in the strategic situation which have a bearing on the provisions of this Treaty; ...

This Standing Consultative Commission was established by a Memorandum of Understanding of December 21, 1972, and it was a main forum regularly used by both Parties for various purposes,[56] including the five-year periodic

---

[53] See Sections 3.2 and 3.3 above.
[54] See Section 3.2 above; paragraph 43 of the Judgment.
[55] See Section 3.3 above.
[56] <www.state.gov/www/global/arms/treaties/abm/abm2.html>.

review of the Treaty, as provided for in Article XIV(2).[57] Together, Articles XIII and XIV(2) would seem to contemplate changes of the kind that have indeed arisen and have allegedly given rise to the issue of fundamental change of circumstances – namely changes in the strategic situation, and that strategic situation is clearly at the heart of the bases for the conclusion of the ABM Treaty, if it was not itself *the* basis. Furthermore, there is Article XV(2), pursuant to which the United States withdrew from the Treaty.[58] This Article, it will be recalled, permits each Party, "in exercising its national sovereignty", to withdraw from the Treaty "if it decides that extraordinary events related to the subject matter of this Treaty have jeopardized its national interests". Again, the thrust of the United States' argument for withdrawing from the treaty was the threat to its security posed by rogue states and the restrictions and constraints imposed by the terms of the ABM Treaty itself. On the basis of these provisions, and recalling the Court's ruling as to foreseeability in the *Gabčikovo* case, would seem difficult to argue that the changes were not foreseen by the Parties. Not only were they foreseen, provision was also made for them in the treaty, allowing the parties to both modify (Article XIII/XIV(2)) and terminate (Article XIV) the treaty.[59]

In this context, there is a further issue to be considered, namely the effect on the applicability of the plea of fundamental change of circumstances of express provision for the possibility of denunciation (such as that contained in Article XV of the ABM Treaty), or other grounds for termination or

---

[57] Article XIV(2) provides that "Five years after the entry into force of this Treaty, and at five-year intervals thereafter, the Parties shall together conduct a review of this Treaty.

[58] See note 42 for the text of Article XV(2).

[59] Lissitzyn, *supra* note 1, at 914-922, identifies a difficulty with the approach of the ILC, which ended up in the VCLT, which attempts to adopt an "objective rule of law" approach at the expense of his preferred "shared expectations of the parties" approach. He states that "'Not foreseen' can have several meanings. 'Foreseeing' a future event may mean expecting it as inevitable, or thinking of it as possible but not likely. In most cases ... 'foreseeing' an event is more likely to be imputed rather than shown as a fact. ... It is apparent that [the VCLT] results in a piling up of subjectivities rather than their diminution ... The decision maker must not only establish the shared intentions and expectations of the parties in order to determine what circumstances constituted 'an essential basis of the consent of the parties,' but must also choose between the various meanings that can be attributed to the ambiguous terms ...". The extent to which this amounts to a real problem is not clear, since this is in many ways what is expected of a third-party decision-maker: see O.A. Elias and C.L. Lim. *The Paradox of Consensualism in International Law* (1998), Chapter X (esp. Section 2.2), and the ICJ's treatment of the doctrine does not appear to have been the cause of doctrinal controversy, as seen above. In any event, in the context of the provisions of the ABM Treaty discussed here, the ambiguity appears to have been minimized by the anticipation of the change of circumstances and provision for the dealing with them.

withdrawal. It has been stated, relying on the *Racke* case,[60] that the scope of applicability of both methods of termination is different, and that the two methods are independent. On the other hand, the view has been expressed, albeit in a qualified manner, that the doctrine of fundamental change is residual in character and may not be invoked where there are other grounds recognized by international law.[61] It is submitted first that the *Racke* case may not be a reliable precedent, for reasons given in section 3.4 above. Secondly and more importantly, it is submitted that the existence of other grounds for termination or withdrawal should preclude the operation of the doctrine if a distinction is drawn between the express provision of such grounds in the treaty on the one hand and the existence of those other grounds for termination that are applicable by operation of the law. This is because the relations between the parties should be governed first and foremost by what they have expressly agreed. Where the specific circumstances are anticipated by the parties and are provided for in the treaty, and there is nothing in the way of the operation of those specific provisions laid out in the treaty for dealing with those circumstances, it is submitted that the invocation of other grounds should be precluded. The situation would be different if the foreseen circumstances are different from the unforeseen change in circumstances, and in such a case the independence of the grounds for termination can be upheld. Where they are identical or where they do overlap, as in the case of the ABM Treaty, it is submitted that, at best, the fundamental change of circumstances would operate as a secondary argument which has no immediate legal effect, but which can be raised in support of the bargaining position of the party seeking to rely on the plea. In fact, in the case of Article XV(2) of the ABM Treaty, it would seem that the express provision regarding grounds for withdrawal, referring as they do to national sovereignty, extraordinary events and supreme interests, are wider than the scope of any fundamental change of circumstances argument, which provides further reason to argue that the latter is excluded.[62] The role played by the doctrine of fundamental change in the context of the ABM Treaty itself is not clear, and the degree of reliance placed on it by the United States is dubious.

---

[60] See Müllerson, *supra* note 1, at 530, note 78, pointing out that the EC Council, in terminating the treaty in that case, had not observed the procedure for termination set out in that treaty, but that the European Court of Justice had not struck down the Council's invocation of the doctrine of fundamental change.

[61] See Vamvoukos, *supra* note 1, at 200-206.

[62] As Müllerson puts it, the "US would hardly resort to the *rebus sic* stantibus clause to withdraw from the ABM Treaty", but could use it in combination with Article XV "in order to convince Russia ... as well as other interested States, of the legitimacy of its cause", *supra* note 1, at 530.

Be that as it may, the point made in this section is that it appears difficult to maintain that the requirement that the change must not have been foreseen has been satisfied in the case of the ABM Treaty. Furthermore, the existence of provision in the treaty would have at least evidentiary value as establishing the fact that the change was indeed foreseen.

4.2.4 The requirement that the effect of the change must be radically to transform the "extent" of obligations still to be fulfilled under the treaty

Some of the circumstances pertinent to a consideration of this requirement have already been considered in relation to the other conditions. One issue that has not been covered, and which is relevant under this heading, is the issue of whether the situation in which the United States found itself in 2001 was so radically different from what was the case in 1972. In this context, much has been written about whether the perceived threats to the United States could not be adequately dealt with in ways that would not infringe the ABM Treaty, let alone require its termination. For example, following the announcement of the decision to withdraw, the Chairman of the United States Senate Foreign Relations Committee criticized the Bush administration's priorities, stating that the United States should be more worried about terrorists with weapons of mass destruction than countries with long-range ballistic missiles (the implication being that the terrorist attacks of September 11, in 2001, which provided further impetus for the decision to withdraw, would not have been prevented or averted by the existence of missile defences), while the Bush administration's response appeared conditional – the argument was that the terrorists and States that support them against the United States if *would* use them if they acquired them.[63] More significantly, it has been said that the actual threat posed by rogue states acquiring missiles that could reach the United States is not real, that the threat would not materialize for years, that several of the current threats can be dealt with by technologies and systems that do not infringe the ABM Treaty, and that diplomacy rather than abrogating the ABM Treaty is the better way to deal with the problem of missile proliferation.[64] If these prove to be correct, serious questions would be raised about the decision to withdraw in so far as it is based on a fundamental change of circumstances argument. But, as noted in Section 4.2.2 above, it is difficult to reach any meaningful conclusions on the basis of anything other than full information provided by the parties ideally before an independent third party (a situation that was hardly likely to occur). Thus, any conclusions drawn on the issue in

---

[63] See <http://archives.cnn.com/2001/ALLPOLITICS/12/12/rec.bush.abm>.

[64] See, e.g., <http://news.bbc.co.uk/1/hi/americas/2044034.stm>; <www.ucsusa.org/security/ift7.html>; and also <http://www.rmbowman.com/ssn/ ABMTreaty2.htm>

the context of this chapter would be speculation. What is clear, however, is that the party seeking to rely on a fundamental change of circumstances will have to discharge the burden of explaining its reasons to other parties, and it would presumably have to explain whether abrogation of the treaty is a necessary result of the changed circumstances or whether other measures could be taken instead.

4.2.5 Conclusion

In conclusion, there would seem to be sufficient reason to question the applicability of the doctrine of fundamental change of circumstances in the context of the termination of the ABM Treaty. The outcome of legal disputes in general tends to be very heavily influenced by the facts of the dispute,[65] and this is particularly true in the context of the ABM Treaty. The nature of the issue indicates that a conclusive answer to the applicability of the doctrine would depend on the information available, which is particularly difficult given the "supreme" national security interests involved. The invocation of the plea of fundamental change of circumstances thus poses even greater problems in the context of such a treaty than it otherwise does. It is precisely for this reason that the subject of the next subsection is of fundamental importance.

4.3 The Procedural Requirements for the Application of the Doctrine in the VCLT

Article 65 of the VCLT provides in pertinent part as follows:

> 1. A party which, under the provisions of the present Convention, invokes ... a ground for impeaching the validity of a treaty, terminating it, withdrawing from it or suspending its operation, must notify the other parties of its claim. The notification shall indicate the measure proposed to be taken with respect to the treaty and the reasons therefor.
>
> 2. If, after the expiry of a period, no party has raised any objection, the party making the notification may carry out ... the measure which it has proposed.
>
> 3. If, however, objection has been raised by any other party, the parties shall seek a solution through the means indicated in article 33 of the Charter of the United Nations.[66]

---

[65] See Elias and Lim, *supra* note 59, Chapter IX, esp. Sections 1.13 and 1.14.

[66] Article 66 provides that if no solution is reached under Article 65(3) within twelve months, any party to the dispute *may* refer the case to the ICJ or to the Secretary-General of the United Nations in order to set into operation the conciliation procedures set out in the Annex to the Convention.

It will be recalled that, in the *Fisheries Jurisdiction* case, the ICJ attached importance to what it called the "procedural complement to the doctrine of changed circumstances", without expressly saying that the obligation to submit to a third party was based on customary law, and Briggs considers that the Court considered it "an essential part of the doctrine".[67] The importance of this element cannot be overestimated, even if only subparagraph 2 alone, and not subparagraph 3, had been included in Article 65. It is the need to involve the other party (in the case of a bilateral treaty), contained in subparagraph 2 that shifts the nature of the doctrine from the purely subjective/auto-interpretative to the more objective legal sphere.[68] At the subjective/auto-interpretative end of the spectrum, a State seeking to withdraw from the treaty is the sole arbiter of whether a fundamental change has occurred, and an announcement to that effect would suffice, and the other party would have no part to play in the termination of the treaty. This is clearly not desirable from a legal point of view, and such licence to unilaterally terminate on the basis of auto-determination presents a direct affront to the stability of treaty relationships. At the other legal/judicial extreme, there would be a third-party decision-maker to whom the matter would be submitted for a decision as to whether the alleged change of circumstances is sufficient to entitle the other party to withdraw from the treaty. Again, desirable as this may be from a legal point of view, judicial resolution of disputes such as those in the context of the ABM treaty is extremely rare in the international legal system. The provisions of Article 65, therefore, present a sensible working compromise, one which, it is submitted, *must* be an essential part of the doctrine of fundamental change of circumstances in particular and the termination of treaties in general, if the doctrine is to be regarded as being *legal* in character.

In the *Racke* case, the ECJ stated that Article 65 was not binding on the Council, which had not complied with its requirements, on the basis that these procedural requirements did not form part of customary law, and the EC was not a party to the VCLT.[69] The USSR acceded to the VCLT on 29 April 1986, while the United States is not a party, and in any event, as stated in Article 4 of the VCLT, it does not apply to treaties such the ABM Treaty that entered into force before the VCLT. The status as customary law of the requirements to submit the case to a third party in Article 65(3) is questionable, in spite of the ICJ's apparent approval in the *Fisheries*

---

[67] See Section 3.2 above, in particular the comments of Briggs.
[68] See B. Cheng, "The Future of State Practice in a Divided World", in R. St. J. MacDonald and D. Johnston (eds.), *The Structure and Process of International Law: Essays in Legal Philosophy, Doctrine and Theory* (1983), at 513.
[69] See Müllerson, *supra* note 1, at 530, note 8.

Jurisdiction case.[70] What is clear is that the other party, even as a matter of customary law, must at a minimum comply with *some* of the requirements reflected in Article 65(2).

There is, for example, consensus in the literature that a plea of fundamental change of circumstances entitles a party to a legal right to demand that either the parties or a competent international tribunal should declare the treaty terminated or its operation suspended, or that the parties should negotiate for its revision in good faith with a view to resolving the dispute.[71] It has been suggested that where the right to negotiate or submit to third party adjudication is invoked, the other party or parties to the treaty are under a corresponding obligation, and if they do not fulfil that obligation, the State invoking the plea is entitled to terminate or suspend the operation of the treaty.[72] However, if there is no conventional obligation on the parties to submit the case to the ICJ or other third party (arising either from being a party to the VCLT or other agreement), it would appear that negotiations in good faith are the only requirement. The question that then arises is what the legal position is where those negotiations do not produce a solution, either in the form of an agreement that the treaty should be terminated or an agreement to modify it, both of which would appear to be consensual solutions, rather than any separately and distinctly identifiable consequence of the legal operation of the plea of fundamental change of circumstances. In the case of the ABM Treaty, it appears that some "negotiations" did indeed take place, but these did not produce agreement as to the existence a fundamental change of circumstances.[73] It can hardly be said, therefore, that the termination of the ABM Treaty is an illustration of the operation of the doctrine of fundamental change of circumstances as grounds for the termination of treaties in international law. The fact is that Russia has acquiesced in the withdrawal of the United States in accordance with Article

---

[70] The editors of *Oppenheim's International Law*, for example, go only as far as saying that a party "was not, however, entitled simply to declare that because the change of circumstances rendered the treaty's obligations unbearable it could no longer consider itself to be bound by the treaty: the proper course was considered to be for it first to approach the other party (or parties) with a request to agree to the abrogation of the treaty, *perhaps coupling the request with an offer to submit any disputed issue to judicial determination*" (our emphasis); *supra* note 1, at 1304-1305. However, in the Gabčikovo case (Section 3.3 above), the Court noted, at paragraph 109, that "Articles 65 to 67 of the Vienna Convention on the Law of Treaties, if not codifying customary law, at least generally reflect customary international law and contain certain procedural principles which are based on an obligation to act in good faith".

[71] See, e.g. Vamvoukos, *supra* note 1, at 206-214.

[72] *Id.*

[73] See, e.g., N. Sokov, "US Withdrawal from the ABM Treaty: Post-Mortem and Possible Consequences", at <http://cns.miis.edu/pubs/reports/2abm.htm> (Center for Nonproliferation Studies); <http://www.acronym.org.uk/54abm.htm>; <http://www.cdi.org/russia/johnson/5503-1.cfm>.

XV(2) of the treaty, in spite of its objections.[74] What is clear is that the United States followed the procedure in Article XV(2) for withdrawing from the treaty as agreed by the parties. What is not clear is the role – if there is such a role – played here by the doctrine of fundamental change of circumstances, properly so-called.

Of course, where the parties do indeed agree that there has been a fundamental change of circumstances and that the treaty should accordingly be terminated or modified, it would be possible to identify an independent role for the doctrine. But the facts here do not appear to indicate that the official Russian position was that there had indeed been a fundamental change of circumstances. In addition, the fact that the United States acted in conformity with the express provisions of that treaty (which did not appear to require agreement or acceptance of the reasons for withdrawal by the other party) makes it difficult to draw any conclusions as to the operation of the doctrine in this case. The same observation can be made in relation to the various examples of state practice that have been cited by some writers as indicating the operation of the doctrine.[75] While such examples may indeed indicate how States perceive the issue in cases in which they are interested in terminating a treaty, the most that they can indicate are the perceptions of the State seeking to rely on the doctrine, and the fact that the doctrine is indeed recognized in state practice. What is as important, however, is the reaction of the other parties to the treaty, and not merely the unilateral perceptions of the states making the plea. If most examples of the illustration of the application of the doctrine are similar to the case of the ABM Treaty, it will be difficult to identify the exact role played by the doctrine. The achievement of the VCLT is that in contains provisions for the resolution of the issues by adjudication or conciliation if negotiations do not produce a solution.

5. Concluding Remarks

The question then is exactly what role there is for the doctrine of fundamental change of circumstances. As formulated in the VCLT, it appears to be the basis of a right of the invoking party to have the matter resolved by negotiation or submitted the dispute to a third party for resolution. Only where that obligation is not complied with by the other parties can the doctrine entitle the invoking party to withdraw or terminate the treaty. But (1) where the negotiations are conducted in good faith and do not yield a result, and the parties do not agree to termination or modification

---

[74] See, e.g., <http://www.whitehouse.gov/news/releases/2001/12/20011213-8.html>.
[75] See note 46. See also Müllerson, *supra* note 1, at 524-531, especially with respect to the 1871 London Conference.

– which would be the most illuminating scenario – the principle does not seem to provide a solution prescribed by law. The obligation imposed by the law is to negotiate in good faith, not to reach a solution;[76] and (2) where the negotiations do yield a solution and the parties agree to revision or termination, it is difficult to argue that the plea itself, rather than agreement between the parties, that produced the solution and resulted in termination or revision of the treaty. In other words, in the most usual scenario where one party alleges a fundamental change of circumstances, i.e. where negotiations do take place as to whether circumstances have changed and if so what to do about it, there does not seem to be any identifiable role for the doctrine. Either the parties agree, in which case the case is resolved by mutual consent, rather than by way of a fundamental change, or they do not agree, in which case the principle does not provide a resolution. It is only where the other party or parties to the treaty refuse to negotiate or to submit the dispute to a third party that the doctrine can be said to have a role to play. This is a role of limited scope indeed, one that can be avoided by negotiating in good faith.

With respect to the ABM Treaty, one could even go so far as to question the legal nature of the treaty itself. In the context of a bilateral treaty regulating national security and defence, provision is made for unilateral withdrawal on the basis of "national sovereignty", "supreme" interests and "extraordinary events", where no provision is made for third-party adjudication or a right to reject the statement of reasons given by the other party, the *legal* character of the entire agreement may well be questioned. It has been written that, in the context of the ABM Treaty, "withdrawal is primarily a political and not a legal issue".[77] Reference to the role of fundamental change of circumstances based on the operation of law would seem somewhat otiose in this context. It is little wonder that there was little reference to the niceties of international law in the statements made in the context of withdrawal from this treaty.

If the doctrine of fundamental change of circumstances is truly of legal character, the best scenario for testing the legal nature of the operation of the principle as constituting independent legal grounds for terminating or withdrawing from a treaty is to have objective third party pronouncement to that effect. That is precisely what is lacking with respect to the plea of fundamental change of circumstances, a problem which the VCLT addresses squarely by including provisions for settlement of disputes of this nature, which also apply to all grounds for invalidity, termination or suspension of treaties – after all, the problem posed by unilateral termination for the

---

[76] And the question whether negotiations in good faith did take place is itself one that can be the grounds for dispute, especially if a refusal or failure to negotiate amounts to grounds for termination.

[77] D. Sloss, "Reply to Response", <www.asil.org/insights/insigh70.htm>.

stability of treaties is similar in all these cases. The difference is that fundamental change of circumstances allows for even greater subjectivity and unilateralism than other grounds for termination or invalidity, since it does not require any particular conduct (such as breach) on the part of either party and, as seen in the case of the ABM Treaty, depends on subjective appreciation of circumstances outside the treaty itself. As Lissitzyn puts it:

> In the absence of adjudication, the actual outcome of controversies will continue to be determined more by political than by legal considerations.[78]

So much for the legal character of the doctrine of fundamental change of circumstances. In our view, it is right and proper that the application of the doctrine be restricted as it is in the VCLT, as interpreted by the ICJ.

---

[78] Note 1, at 922. The same writer states that the risk posed to the stability of treaties by the doctrine "can be exaggerated ... Great political issues are not decided by international law". We may also recall Klabbers' statement that the doctrine is "the one and only doctrine that manages to arouse the interest of non-lawyers".

CHAPTER FIVE

Optional Clause Declarations and the Law of Treaties[*]

1. Introduction

This chapter focuses on a number of issues concerning the relationship between the law of treaties and the Optional Clause system as they arise in theory and in the jurisprudence of the ICJ, with particular emphasis placed on the *Bakassi Peninsula* case,[1] and the *Fisheries Jurisdiction* case.[2] The issues, which are discussed below, focus mainly on the question of the legal character of Optional Clause declarations and the applicability of the general rules of interpretation of treaties to them; to a certain extent on the legality of certain reservations to these declarations; as well as the applicability of other aspects of the law of treaties in the context of the Optional Clause system. Sections 2 and 3 of this chapter provide a theoretical background to the issues involved and outline the main characteristics of Optional Clause declarations, while Section 4 examines the jurisprudence of the PCIJ and the

---

[*] This chapter is co-authored by Dr Maria Vogiatzi and is an updated and revised version of M. Fitzmaurice, "The Optional Clause System and the Law of Treaties: Issues of Interpretation in Recent Jurisprudence of the International Court of Justice", 20 *Australian Year Book of International Law* (1999), 127-160. Reprinted with kind permission of the Australian Year Book of International Law.

[1] Case Concerning Land and Maritime Boundary between Cameroon and Nigeria (Cameroon v. Nigeria), Preliminary Objections, Judgment of 11 June 1998, 1998 ICJ Rep. 275, ("Bakassi Peninsula case").

[2] Fisheries Jurisdiction (Spain v. Canada), Jurisdiction of the Court, Judgment of 4 December 1998, 1998 ICJ Rep. 432, ("Fisheries Jurisdiction case").

ICJ, and in particular the two most recent cases mentioned above, followed by conclusions.[3]

Article 36 provides as follows:

> 1. The jurisdiction of the Court comprises all cases which the parties refer to it and all matters specially provided for in the Charter of the United Nations or in treaties and conventions in force.
>
> 2. The states parties to the present Statute may at any time declare that they recognize as compulsory ipso facto and without special agreement, in relation to any other state accepting the same obligation, the jurisdiction of the Court in all legal disputes concerning:
>
>> a. the interpretation of a treaty;
>>
>> b. any question of international law;
>>
>> c. the existence of any fact which, if established, would constitute a breach of an international obligation;
>>
>> d. the nature or extent of the reparation to be made for the breach of an international obligation.
>
> 3. The declarations referred to above may be made unconditionally or on condition of reciprocity on the part of several or certain states, or for a certain time.
>
> 4. Such declarations shall be deposited with the Secretary-General of the United Nations, who shall transmit copies thereof to the parties to the Statute and to the Registrar of the Court.
>
> 5. Declarations made under Article 36 of the Statute of the Permanent Court of International Justice and which are still in force shall be deemed, as between the parties to the present Statute, to be acceptances of the compulsory

---

[3] This chapter will not attempt to cover all aspects of Optional Clause declarations. Many excellent publications are already available on the topic. See, e.g., S. Oda, "Reservations in the Declarations of Acceptance of the Optional Clause and the Period of Validity of Those Declarations: The Effect of the Schultz Letter", 19 *BYIL* (1998), 1; S. Oda, "The Compulsory Jurisdiction of the International Court of Justice: A myth?", 49 *ICLQ* (2000), 251; L. Lloyd, "A Springboard For the Future: A Historical Examination of Britain's Role in Shaping the Optional Clause of the Permanent Court of International Justice", 79 *AJIL* (1985), 28; M. Vogiatzi, "The Historical Evolution of the Optional Clause", 2 *Non State Actors and International Law* (2002), 41; N. Kebbon, "The World Court Compulsory Jurisdiction under the Optional Clause", 58 *Nordic Journal of International Law* (1989), 257; E.J. de Arechaga, "The Compulsory Jurisdiction of the International Court of Justice Under the Pact of Bogotá", in Y. Dinstein and M. Tabory (eds.), *International Law in A Time of Perplexity, Essays in Honour of Shabtai Rosenne* (1989), 335; C.H.M. Waldock, "The Decline of the Optional Clause", 32 *BYIL* (1955-56), 244; J.G. Merrills, "The Optional Clause Today", 50 *BYIL* (1980), 87; J.G. Merrills, "The Optional Clause Revisited", 64 *BYIL* (1993), 197; D.W. Greig, "Nicaragua and the United States: Confrontation Over the Jurisdiction of the International Court", 62 *BYIL* (1991), 119.

jurisdiction of the International Court of Justice for the period which they still have to run and in accordance with their terms.

6. In the event of a dispute as to whether the Court has jurisdiction, the matter shall be settled by the decision of the Court.

In this chapter, the term "Optional Clause" refers to Article 36(2) and (3) itself; the term "Optional Clause declaration" refers to a declaration made by a State pursuant to paragraph 2 of Article 36; and the term "Optional Clause system" refers to the whole system arising under the Optional Clause, which includes the Optional Clause itself (in its context as an Article of the Statute of the ICJ, an integral part of the Charter of the United Nations) and the individual Optional Clause declarations of States and the relations between declarant States, which arise as a result of them. The issues that arose in the *Bakassi Peninsula* case and the *Fisheries Jurisdiction* case concern, principally, the declarations themselves and the consensual relations between the declarant States. However, the *Bakassi Peninsula* case, which followed the rationale of the *Right of Passage* case,[4] also involves issues relating to the interpretation of parts of the Optional Clause itself.

It may be added that the term "reservation" is used to describe the conditions or limitations that States, as a matter of common practice, place upon their acceptance of the Court's jurisdiction in Optional Clause declarations. The use of the term "reservation" in this context has become so commonplace that the authors consider that it would probably be confusing to refrain from its use in this particular context. However, the authors wish to emphasize that no conclusions there from should be drawn as to the "treaty" nature of Optional Clause declarations, or that the treaty rules relating to reservations apply to the conditions in Optional Clause declarations. The term "condition" would, arguably, be more appropriate and is, indeed, the word used in paragraph 3 of the Optional Clause.

2. The Main Characteristics of the Optional Clause System

2.1 The Voluntary Nature of Submission and the Legal Content of Optional Clause Declarations

Under the Statute of the ICJ, the Optional Clause system, inherited from the PCIJ, was devised as a compromise between, on the one hand, States desiring true compulsory jurisdiction of the ICJ, in the sense that any State party to the Statute would have the right by way of unilateral application to

---

[4] Right of Passage over Indian Territory (Portugal *v.* India), Preliminary Objections, Judgement of 26 November 1957, 1957 ICJ Rep. 125 ("Right of Passage case").

bring before the Court any dispute it had with another State party, and, on the other hand, States wishing to retain the traditional consensual character of international adjudication. Article 36(2) is commonly referred to as providing for the "compulsory jurisdiction" of the Court. However, the definition "compulsory" is not accurate as States are under no general obligation to submit to the Court's jurisdiction. If they choose to do so, this submission is ultimately the product of their own consent. Therefore, and in this sense, it is correct to say that the jurisdiction of the ICJ remains very much voluntary. As early as 1923, the World Court stated that "[i]t is well established in international law that no state can, without its consent, be compelled to submit its disputes with other States either to mediation or to arbitration, or to any other kind of pacific settlement."[5] This principle has been reaffirmed time and again. In fact, in most cases involving jurisdictional issues, the Court has stated in unequivocal terms that consent is the basis of the Court's jurisdiction.[6] The supremacy of the principle of consent is firmly rooted both in the Court's practice, as well as in the UN Charter and the Statute of the ICJ.

True compulsory jurisdiction would mean that any State member to the Statute could institute unilateral proceedings against another member. Being a party to the Statute of the ICJ would, thereby, be the only requirement.[7] The lack of true compulsory jurisdiction relating to the ICJ has frequently been cited as one of the main shortcomings of the World Court. It has been criticised as jeopardizing the ICJ's authority and, over the years, numerous suggestions have been put forward aiming to remedy this so-called defect.[8]

---

[5] Eastern Carelia Advisory Opinion, 1923 PCIJ (Series B), No 5, at 27. See also Chorzow Factory case, 1927 PCIJ (Series A), No. 9, at 32: "When considering whether it has jurisdiction or not, the Court's aim is always to ascertain whether an intention on the part of the Parties exists to confer jurisdiction upon it".

[6] See among others: Corfu Channel (UK v. Albania), Preliminary Objections, Judgment of 25 March 1948, ICJ Rep. 15, at 27: "... consent of the parties confers jurisdiction on the Court"; Anglo-Iranian Oil Company (UK v. Iran), Judgment of 22 July 1952, 1952 ICJ Rep. 93, at 102-103: "[T]he jurisdiction of the Court to deal with and decide a case on the merits depends on the will of the Parties. Unless the Parties have conferred jurisdiction on the Court in accordance with Article 36, the Court lacks such jurisdiction"; Monetary Gold Removed from Rome in 1943, (Italy v. France, UK, US), Judgment of 15 June 1954, 1954 ICJ Rep. 19, at 32: "[the principle that] the Court can only exercise jurisdiction over a state with its consent is a well established principle of international law embodied in the Court's Statute".

[7] H. Kelsen, *The Law of the United Nations: A Critical Analysis of Its Fundamental Problems* (1950), at 522–523.

[8] G. Fitzmaurice, "Enlargement of the Contentious Jurisdiction of the Court", in L. Gross (ed.), *The Future of the International Court of Justice,* Vol. II (1976), at 461; J.K. Gamble and D.D. Fischer, *The International Court of Justice – An Analysis of a Failure* (1976); R. Falk, *Reviving the World Court* (1986); L.F. Damrosch (ed.), *The International Court of Justice at A Crossroads* (1987).

The main characteristic of Article 36(2), as contrasted to *ad hoc* or *post hoc* jurisdiction, is that certain classes of disputes, pre-defined in an abstract and general manner, are labelled as suitable for submission to the Court. Article 36(2) sets out that States can accept, by depositing a declaration with the Secretary-General of the United Nations, the jurisdiction of the Court in advance and for an undefined number of disputes with respect to four broad categories mentioned therein.[9] Once a dispute arises, no special agreement to submit to ICJ jurisdiction is necessary, as consent is deemed pre-existing and the scope of the ICJ's jurisdiction is delineated by the combination of the declarations of the parties. The element of compulsion is found in the States' prior agreement to submit to the Court potential disputes falling within the categories mentioned under Article 36(2). As the Court has stated:

> The characteristic of this compulsory jurisdiction is that it results from a previous agreement which makes it possible to seise the Court of a dispute without a Special Agreement, and that in respect of disputes subject to it, the Court may be seised by means of an Application by one of the parties.[10]

The difference between jurisdiction accepted under Article 36(1) (special agreements and compromissory clauses) and that accepted under Article 36(2) is first and foremost that jurisdiction based on Article 36(1) is the immediate product of treaty negotiations, whereas jurisdiction established on the basis of Article 36(2) is the product of declarations formulated unilaterally. A further difference is that the scope of potential cases, which are based on compromissory clauses, is in a way limited and predefined because it depends on the particular subject matter of the treaty, whereas jurisdiction accepted under Article 36(2), allows States to "pick and mix" in an abstract and general manner the types of disputes they are willing to submit before the Court, should the opportunity so arise. As Judge Higgins aptly described, in accepting jurisdiction under the Optional Clause "a State effectively signs a blank cheque", as it does not know with certainty either

---

[9] Article 36(2) of the Statute of the ICJ reads as follows:
"The states parties to the present Statute may at any time declare that they recognize as compulsory *ipso facto* and without special agreement, in relation to any other state accepting the same obligation, the jurisdiction of the Court in all legal disputes concerning:
a. the interpretation of a treaty;
b. any question of international law;
c. the existence of any fact which, if established, would constitute a breach of an international obligation;
d. the nature or extent of the reparation to be made for the breach of an international obligation."
[10] Nottebohm (Liechtenstein *v.* Guatemala), Preliminary Objections, Judgment of 18 November 1953, 1953 ICJ Rep. 111, at 122.

the exact subject matter of a future dispute, or the other party to that dispute.[11]

To conclude, Article 36(2) embodies a legally binding obligation, into which States are free to enter. States are afforded great flexibility in defining the extent and content of the obligation they assume under the Optional Clause. It is for this reason that States will often argue on the substance and scope of the obligation they have assumed under Article 36(2), but very rarely will they dispute the actual binding nature of their declarations.

2.2 Freedom to append reservations

Neither the drafting history of the Statue or the Statue itself contemplate the possibility of accepting the jurisdiction of the Court with reservations. Article 36(3) allows only for two specific reservations: (a) those referring to the right of States to "choose partners" in relation to which State(s) they accept the compulsory jurisdiction of the Court; and (b) those referring to time limits of declarations. However, from the very beginning of the Court's function it became commonplace for States to appended declarations containing numerous and varied reservations.[12] The League of Nations recognized and endorsed this practice in an effort to facilitate acceptance of the Optional Clause. In 1924, a resolution was adopted by the League Assembly urging states to accept the compulsory jurisdiction of the Court even "with the reservations which they regard as indispensable"; and again, in 1928, suggesting that states could adhere to the Optional Clause with "appropriate reservations limiting the extent of their commitments both as regards duration and as regards scope".[13]

The practice of States to accept the Optional Clause with reservations was firmly upheld at the San Francisco Conference. The Conference deemed the practice so well established that it was considered unnecessary to modify Article 36(3) in order to include an express reference to the right of States to append all different types of reservations.[14] This practice means that States accepting the compulsory jurisdiction of the Court have great freedom in regulating almost all aspects of their acceptance. However, as explained

---

[11] R. Higgins, *Problems and Process: International Law and How We Use It* (1994), at 191.

[12] The first declaration of acceptance containing a reservation was submitted by the Netherlands in 1921.

[13] "Resolution concerning Arbitration, Security and Reduction of Armaments of 2 October 1924", *League of Nations Official Journal*, Special Supplement No. 21, at 21; "Resolution concerning the Optional Clause of Article 36 of the Statute of the Permanent Court of International Justice", *League of Nations Official Journal*, Special Supplement No. 68, at 183.

[14] "Report of Subcommittee D to Committee IV/1 on Article 36 of the Statute of the International Court of Justice", *Documents of the United Nations Conference on International Organisation*, Vol. 13, at 559.

above, this freedom is balanced by the principle of reciprocity, which allows States to invoke each others' reservations. The more far-reaching reservations a State includes in its declaration, the more it potentially restricts its own ability to bring another State before the Court, since the defendant State has the right to rely on reservations made by the applicant State. On the other hand, reciprocity could also be viewed as a factor which multiplies the effects of reservations, since it allows States that have not included a particular reservation in their declaration to invoke it if it is included in the declaration of their adversary.

The freedom of States to accept the compulsory jurisdiction with reservations has been strongly affirmed in the jurisprudence of the Court, even though it has rarely been directly challenged. In upholding the right of states to qualify their declarations as they see fit, the Court has strongly emphasised the unilateral element of Optional Clause declarations.

In the *Nicaragua* case, the Court remarked in relation to a temporal reservation by the United States, which allowed for termination after six months' notice:

> Declarations of acceptance of the compulsory jurisdiction of the Court are facultative, unilateral engagements, that States are absolutely free to make or not to make. In making the declaration a State is equally free either to do so unconditionally and without limit of time for its duration, or to qualify it with conditions or reservations.[15]

In the *Fisheries Jurisdiction* case, which concerned the interpretation of a reservation made by Canada relating to conservation measures, the Court made a number of important pronouncements in relation to the freedom of States to qualify their acceptance. It stated clearly that the right to append reservations is not an exception, but the rule and concluded that reservations are an indispensable part of declarations, since acceptance of compulsory jurisdiction is based on an opt-in, rather than an opt-out system:

> It is for each State, in formulating its declaration, to decide upon the limits it places upon its acceptance of the jurisdiction of the Court: "This jurisdiction only exists within the limits within which it has been accepted" (*Phosphates in Morocco, Judgment 1938, PCIJ., Series A/B, No. 74*, p.23). Conditions or reservation thus do not by their terms derogate from a wider acceptance already given. Rather, they operate to define the parameters of the State's acceptance of the compulsory jurisdiction of the Court.[16]

---

[15] Military and Paramilitary Activities in and Against Nicaragua (Nicaragua *v.* United States of America), Jurisdiction and Admissibility, Judgment of 26 November 1984, 1984 ICJ Rep. 392, at 418 (the "Nicaragua case").

[16] Fisheries Jurisdiction case, *supra* note 2, at 453.

The same conclusion had been reached by Judge McNair in the *Anglo-Iranian Oil Company* case when he stated explicitly that the mechanism of Article 36(2) "is that of 'contracting-in' not 'contracting-out' " and further explained that a State "being free either to make a declaration or not, is entitled, if it decides to make one, to limit the scope of its Declaration in any way it chooses, subject always to reciprocity".[17] It was in this context that the Court referred to the unilateral origins of Optional Clause declarations in particularly strong terms and emphasized not only the freedom of States to accept the jurisdiction of the Court under the Optional Clause, but also the freedom to determine the limits of their acceptance: "A declaration of acceptance of the compulsory jurisdiction of the Court, whether there are specified limits or not, is a unilateral act of State sovereignty."[18] In the same decision, in an effort to further emphasize the control that States have over the formulation of their declarations, the Court also repeated the statement from the *Nicaragua* case quoted above.[19]

In the few occasions that the freedom to append reservations beyond the strict confines of Article 36(3) has been challenged directly, the Court has ruled overwhelmingly in favour of the established practice. For example, in the *Aerial Incident of 10 August 1999* case, where Pakistan argued that a reservation contained in the declaration made by India, which excluded from the jurisdiction of the Court disputes arising in connection to members of the British Commonwealth (known as the "Commonwealth reservation"), the Court held that this was extra-statutory because it was not expressly mentioned in Article 36(3).[20]

In order to support its argument, Pakistan relied on what the Court deemed to be an erroneous interpretation of the phrase "*on condition of reciprocity on the part of several or certain states*" in Article 36(3). Pakistan stated that a correct reading of this phrase permitted reservations *ratione personae*, such as the Commonwealth reservation. Furthermore, Pakistan argued that State practice had not amended Article 36(3) and that such "extra-statutory" reservations could not be invoked against States that refused to accept them.[21] The judgment once again stressed the liberty of

---

[17] Individual Opinion of Judge McNair, Anglo-Iranian Oil Company case, *supra* note 6, at 116.

[18] Fisheries Jurisdiction case, *supra* note 2, at 453.

[19] *Id.*, at 455-456.

[20] Aerial Incident of 10 August 1999 (Pakistan v. India), (Jurisdiction of the Court), Judgment of 21 June 2000, 2000 ICJ Rep. 12.

[21] Memorial of the Government of Pakistan, Aerial Incident of 10 August 1999, Section D; Oral Arguments of Pakistan, Aerial Incident of 10 August 1999, (CR 2000/1), 3-4-2000, Argument of Mr. Munshi, paragraphs 20 (a) and 21-27: "[the Commonwealth] reservation is inconsistent with the terms of the Statute and, therefore, cannot be invoked by India against Pakistan ... Pakistan is entitled to reject it as being incompatible with the terms of Article 36, paragraph 3. The Indian reservation goes beyond the range of reservations permitted by that

States in defining the terms of their declarations and included detailed references to its pronouncements in the *Nicaragua* and in the *Fisheries Jurisdiction* cases. The Court also referred to the resolutions of the League Assembly and the report of the San Francisco Sub-Committee, dismissed Pakistan's assertions and stated:

> The Court would further observe that paragraph 3 of Article 36 of its Statute has never been regarded as laying down in an exhaustive manner the conditions under which declarations might be made ... the Court cannot accept Pakistan's argument that a reservation such as India's Commonwealth reservation might be regarded as "extra-statutory", because it contravened Article 36, paragraph 3, of the Statute.[22]

2.3 Reciprocity and the Relationship between Articles 36(2) and 36(3)

The principle of reciprocity is one of the fundamental characteristics of the Optional Clause. According to Article 36(2) States accept the compulsory jurisdiction of the Court "in relation to any other State accepting the same obligation", whereas Article 36(3) stipulates that "declarations can be made unconditionally or on condition of reciprocity on the part of several or certain states or for a certain time".[23]

It is generally accepted that reciprocity is a logical consequence stemming directly from two facts: firstly, that the jurisdiction of the Court, including its compulsory jurisdiction, is based on consent and, secondly, that States are free to delimit their acceptances by means of reservations and other conditions as they see fit. Although the drafters of the PCIJ Statute did not envisage the right to append reservations to declarations of acceptance, they did allow States the choice of accepting the compulsory jurisdiction of the Court in all or any of the four specified categories of legal disputes mentioned in Article 36 of the PCIJ Statute. This created the possibility that

---

paragraph and therefore is not opposable to any State that does not, in one way or another, accept it. Pakistan does not accept it." Both available from: <http://www.icj-cij.org/icjwww/idocket/ipi/ipiframe.htm>.

[22] Aerial Incident of 10 August 1999 case, *supra* note 20, at 29-30. See also J. G. Merrills, "The Aerial Incident of 10 August 1999, (*Pakistan v. India*), Judgment of Jurisdiction", 50 *ICLQ* (2001), at 657-662.

[23] The pertinent part of Article 36(2) reads: "The States Parties to the present Statute may at any time declare that they recognize as compulsory *ipso facto* and without special agreement, in relation to any other State accepting the same obligation, the jurisdiction of the Court in all legal disputes concerning ...".

Article 36(3) reads: The declarations referred to above may be made unconditionally or on condition of reciprocity on the part of several or certain States, or for a certain time.

States might accept the jurisdiction of the Court for different types of disputes, hence the insertion of the words accepting the same obligation in Article 36. Although Article 36(2) of the ICJ Statute does not allow a similar choice between the four categories of disputes therein mentioned, the widespread practice of appending reservations to declarations of acceptance has had the same effect, i.e. in practice declarations do not necessarily coincide. Since declarations do not coincide, in order for the Court to exercise its jurisdiction, "it is necessary to find their common element, that common element being the joint definition of the scope of the jurisdiction in the concrete case".[24] As the use of different types of reservations became gradually widespread, questions of reciprocity have arisen mainly in relation to them. Broadly speaking this has been translated to mean that States have the right to invoke reservations contained in each others declarations.[25]

A disputed issue is whether reciprocity is an inherent characteristic of declarations, or whether States have to specify that their acceptance is subject to it. The confusion seems to stem from the fact that although Article 36(2) appears to describe quite clearly the concept of reciprocity, the actual word is used only in Article 36(3) as an alternative to the unconditional acceptance of the Optional Clause. The question becomes all the more relevant since nearly all declarations ever deposited under Article 36(2) contain the statement that they are made on condition of reciprocity.

The problem originates from the drafting of Article 36. What became Article 36(3) was initially part of a proposal submitted by the Brazilian delegate R. Fernandez, aiming to establish two different versions of Article 36, one of which would provide for true compulsory jurisdiction. As he considered it undesirable for States to accept compulsory jurisdiction, unless at least some of the Great Powers did so, he included the following provision:

> ... [States] may adhere unconditionally or conditionally to the Article providing for compulsory jurisdiction, a possible condition being reciprocity on the part of a certain number of Members, or of certain Members, or, again, of a number of Members including such and such specified Members.[26]

---

[24] S. Rosenne, *The Law and Practice of the International Court 1920-1996*, Vol. II-Jurisdiction, (1997), at 762; E. Brown-Weiss, "Reciprocity and the Optional Clause", in L. F. Damrosch (ed.), *supra* note 8, 82, at 83; H. Thirlway, "Reciprocity in the Jurisdiction of the International Court of Justice", 15 *NYIL* (1984), 97-138; J.A. Frowein, "Reciprocity and Restriction Concerning Different Optional Clauses", in N. Ando, E. McWhinney and R. Wolfrum (eds.), *Liber Amicorum Judge Shigeru Oda*, Vol. I, (2002), at 397-417.

[25] See, however, Kelsen, *supra* note 7, at 526-527 who took the view that reciprocity should not apply to reservations. According to him reciprocity meant that parties needed to subscribe to the same categories of disputes but could not invoke each others reservations.

[26] League of Nations, *The Records of the First Assembly-Meetings of the Committees, Minutes of the Third Committee* (1920), Geneva, Annex 11, 553. The Brazilian Declaration of

Although Fernandez's proposal was rejected, as a compromise the phrase *on condition of reciprocity on the part of several or certain states* was included in Article 36. From the above it is evident that paragraph (3) does not embody a "condition of reciprocity" but rather a condition *ratione personae*, aiming to make a declaration of acceptance operative only when a specific number of States or certain States have subscribed to the Optional Clause system. According to one view, Article 36(3) makes it possible for States to accept the jurisdiction of the Court "without the condition of reciprocity".[27] This assertion, however, takes the word reciprocity in paragraph (3) out of context, since, as explained above, it should be read in conjunction with the phrase *on the part of several or certain states.*

The majority of writers believe that reciprocity is embodied in the words *accepting the same obligation* found in Article 36(2) and is an inherent characteristic of the Optional Clause system that applies to every declaration, whether specifically invoked therein or not.[28] Waldock characterised reciprocity as "a basic constitutional provision of the Statute applying to every declaration" even those made "unconditionally".[29] Indeed this is the only conclusion afforded by the drafting history and the *rationale* behind Optional Clause declarations.

3. Legal Character of Optional Clause Declarations and Principles of Interpretation

This chapter mainly concerns the issue of the legal character of Optional Clause declarations and the principles to be applied in their interpretation. These two issues will be treated separately and successively. This order is

---

Acceptance, deposited in 1921 contained the following sentence: "... we declare to recognize as compulsory, in accordance with the said resolution of the National Legislature, the jurisdiction of the said Court for the period of five years, on condition of reciprocity and as soon as it has likewise been recognized as such by two at least of the Powers permanently represented on the Council of the League of Nations".

[27] E. Hambro, "Some Observations on the Compulsory Jurisdiction of the International Court of Justice", 25 *BYIL* (1948), 133, at 136-137, concludes that "it is possible for a State to accept the jurisdiction of the Court without reciprocity, but that such unconditional acceptance cannot be presumed"; J.H.W. Verzijl, *The Jurisprudence of the World Court: A Case by Case Commentary*, Vol. II, (1965-1966), at 266.

[28] H.W. Briggs, "Reservations to the Acceptance of the Compulsory Jurisdiction of the International Court of Justice", 93 *Recueil des Cours* (1958-I) 229, at 237; M.O. Hudson, *The Permanent Court of International Justice 1920-1942, A Treatise* (1943), at 465; S.A. Alexandrov, *Reservations in Unilateral Declarations Accepting the Compulsory Jurisdiction of the International Court of Justice* (1995), at 30; D.W. "Greig, Reciprocity, Proportionality and the Law of Treaties", 34 *VJIL* (1994), 295, at 306.

[29] Waldock, *supra* note 3, 255.

logical in the sense that, in the ordinary course one might anticipate that the principles of interpretation to be applied would follow from the legal character ascribed to Optional Clause declarations. However, in practice, it is found that the World Court is somewhat ambiguous in its findings concerning the legal character of Optional Clause declarations. The Court has tended to be rather clearer in its formulation of principles to be applied to their interpretation. Thus, but only to a certain extent, one often finds oneself reversing this natural order of analysis, and looking to the applicable principles of interpretation to obtain an insight into the true legal character of the declarations.

The foundations of the jurisprudence regarding the character of the Optional Clause had been laid already before the present Court was set up, partly through decisions of the PCIJ and partly through Strate practice within the League of Nations. In particular, two aspects were already established which essentially provide the basis for the development of ICJ jurisprudence in relation to the Optional Clause system: firstly, the relationship of Optional Clause declarations and the law of treaties; and, secondly, their relationship to unilateral acts. These two aspects, and their implications on issues of interpretation, are described briefly in this section.

3.1 The Relationship between Optional Clause Declarations and the Law of Treaties

The particular issue that has been consistently at the heart of the debate concerning the legal character of Optional Clause declarations, and one that has been fundamental to the arguments before the Court, is the extent to which Optional Clause declarations are, or form part of, a treaty.

Optional Clause declarations may be seen as having a treaty character in two ways: (i) they are documents originating from a treaty system (the Charter of the United Nations and the Statute of the ICJ, which is an integral part of the former); and (ii) it has long been part of the jurisprudence of the Court concerning Optional Clause declarations that they give rise to a consensual relationship between those declarant States between which there exists, in accordance with the terms of their respective declarations, reciprocity in relation to their submission to the jurisdiction of the Court in accordance with the terms of Article 36, paragraph 2, of the Statute.

During the drafting of the VCLT, the International Law Commission ("ILC") took varied approaches towards the issue of the legal character of Optional Clause declarations. However, finally the ILC veered strongly in favour of their "contractual" nature . A proposal was made relating to the definition of a treaty in the Draft Articles on the Law of Treaties to include unilateral declarations and other instruments of a unilateral nature, which give rise to international agreements between States.[30] The ensuing discussion in the ILC can generally be summarized as taking the position that "... such declarations could not be regarded as anything other than agreements or treaties within the meaning of the definition in Article 2, paragraph (a), of the draft".[31] It should be noted, however, that in the end, although the ILC did not oppose the characterization of the Optional Clause as a treaty relation, it did not openly endorse that definition either by including an express mention in the VCLT.

A point to bear in mind, when analysing the views of the ILC, is the influence of the then recent (1952) *Anglo-Iranian Oil Company* case (see below for more detail). Here, it will suffice to say that the Commission invoked the pronouncements of the Court in order to support the view that despite their predominantly contractual nature, Optional Clause declarations possessed a minimum element of unilateral character, which could not and should not be overlooked. Although views varied regarding the exact interpretation of the judgment, the influence of the above case proved crucial when assessing whether explicit reference to the Optional Clause should be included in the draft Articles. Under the light of the Court's findings it was decided to err on the side of caution and avoid direct pronouncements regarding the legal character of declarations under Article 36(2) of the ICJ Statute.

In his first report on the Law of Treaties, Lauterpacht was a supporter of the treaty theory.[32] He considered Optional Clause declarations to be acts of accession or acceptance of an already established instrument, presumably one formed by the different declarations already deposited, and as such to constitute a treaty. The decisive point for him was that the various declarations formed part of a network of common rights and obligations, which, in their turn, gave rise to a treaty relationship.[33]

Fitzmaurice recognized the existence of a unilateral element in relation to Optional Clause declarations, but emphasized also their substantive, contractual nature. He included them in the type of legal phenomena, which he named "unilateral declarations that are unilateral in form but not in substance".[34] He explained that, generally, this type of declaration:

> is unilateral in form but contractual in substance, either because it is one of two or more similar Declarations intended to be interdepended or interlocking,

[30] Sir G. Fitzmaurice, *Fourth Report on the Law of Treaties,* YILC (1959), Vol. II, 37, at 94, UN Doc. A/CN.4/120.

[31] 638th Meeting, YILC (1962), Vol. I, 54, at 56.

[32] H. Lauterpacht, *First Report on the Law of Treaties,* YILC (1953), Vol. II, 90, at 101, UN Doc. A/CN.4/63.

[33] *Id.*, at 103.

[34] Sir G. Fitzmaurice, *The Law and Procedure of the International Court of Justice,* Vol. I (1986), at 363.

or because it is linked to the action of another State, which either forms the *quid pro quo* for it, or in respect of which it is itself the *quid pro quo*.[35]

Then, in relation specifically to Optional Clause declarations, he said:

> the interlocking, and hence basically contractual nature of these Declarations arises directly from the condition of reciprocity attached to nearly all of them, the general effect of which is to limit the obligation of the defendant State to go before the Court under the Declaration to cases in which, were it plaintiff, it could itself take the other party to the Court under the corresponding Declaration made by that party.[36]

Waldock was of a similar view. He stressed the contractual nexus between the parties to Optional Clause declarations and their striking similarities to treaties. He said that:

> The origins and the treaty character of the Optional clause declaration, the role of the Secretary-General of the United Nations in receiving and registering notices of declarations under the Optional clause, the practice of States in making their declaration, and the jurisprudence of the Court, it is considered to leave no real doubt as to the consensual nature of the juridical bond established between states by their declarations.[37]

At the same time he noted that the above considerations did not nullify the unilateral character of declarations *per se,* mainly because their making was not a matter of negotiation with other States already party to the Optional Clause system. Careful consideration of the following passage, however, reveals that the term "unilateral" was employed in a very limited sense, signifying little more than an act of accession. He was equally cautious when assessing the multilateral and bilateral element involved in declarations of acceptance and considered declarations under Article 36(2) as a "multilateral act of a special character".[38]

Waldock accepted the existence of a multilateral element on the basis that such declarations were not autonomous, but required adherence to the Statute of the Court (i.e. a multilateral treaty) and that they resulted in relations with a number of States. However, he argued that the emphasis of the Optional Clause mechanism was on relations between two States, i.e. the two litigant parties, upon which former or subsequent acts of acceptance of the Optional Clause by other States had little bearing.[39] He believed that although the Statute of the Court was the cornerstone of the whole Optional Clause system, Article 36(2) was envisaged to function on a bilateral level.

---

[35] *Id.,* 364.

[36] *Id.,* 365.

[37] Waldock, *supra* note 3, at 254.

[38] *Id.* "... this is not to deny the unilateral character of the act by which a State gives its adherence to obligations of the Optional Clause".

[39] *Id.,* at 254.

He was right in saying that the declarations, or any other later acts of accession to the Optional Clause system, did not affect the obligations of the two States as between themselves. Furthermore, that they had little bearing on the actual obligation to accept the Court's jurisdiction, since there "is little mutuality among the collective body of States adhering to the Clause".[40] Nonetheless, Waldock stated that relationship is not entirely bilateral since the States, while adhering to the Optional Clause, submit themselves to the whole Statute of the ICJ. Thus, States with a legal interest under Article 62 may participate in a process with a multilateral aspect. However, the unclear relationship between multilateral, bilateral and unilateral elements of the Optional Clause declaration led Waldock to suggest that: "[t]he easiest course is, perhaps, to call it a consensual relation which is *sui generis*".[41]

A similar view was later expressed by the former President of the ICJ, Sir Robert Jennings, who, in the 1984 *Nicaragua* case (on jurisdiction), adhered to the same opinion as expressed by Waldock, when he said:

> The discussion in the oral proceedings of whether or not the legal character of declarations under the Optional Clause is, or is not, governed by the law of treaties, I found not entirely helpful and in any event inconclusive. The fact of the matter must surely be that the Optional Clause regime is *sui generis*. Doubtless some parts of the law of treaties may be applied by useful analogy; but so may the law governing unilateral declarations; and so, most certainly, may be the law deriving from the practice of States in respect of such declarations.[42]

3.2 The Relationship between Optional Clause Declarations and Unilateral Acts of States

The position that Optional Clause declarations are, in essence, unilateral acts seem to be less widely accepted in the doctrine. It should be noted, that the few authors that have adopted opinions favouring the unilateral nature of declarations made under Article 36(2) have always stopped short from actually endorsing the view that such declarations are unilateral acts not only in form, but also in substance. Instead, they have tended to emphasize the unilateral origins of declarations of acceptance, which they consider as a defining element and one that should be duly considered in all aspects of legal issues that might arise in relation to them.

---

[40] *Id.*
[41] *Id.*
[42] Separate Opinion of Judge Jennings in the Nicaragua case, *supra* note 15, at 546.

The opinions analysed in this section centre on the notion of reciprocity in context of the Court exercising its jurisdiction only where the relevant declarations of acceptance coincide. Whereas, authors who subscribe to the "contractual nature" of Optional Clause declarations, tend to view this coinciding as establishing a bilateral contractual relationship between declarant States, authors favouring the "unilateral nature" of declarations, while acknowledging the importance of reciprocity, attribute to it a different meaning and seem to perceive it, instead, as a facilitative tool enabling the Court to exercise its jurisdiction. They do not regard it as the foundation of a contractual relationship between States.

According to Torres-Bernardez, it is the very nature of compulsory jurisdiction under Article 36(2), as opposed to jurisdiction based on *compromis* and treaties in force, which implies that coinciding Optional Clause declarations do not create treaty relationships. He started from the premise that as far as *ad hoc* agreements or treaties are concerned, States give their express consent at the moment of signature of the relevant agreement, which in turn results in a clear contractual bond amongst the parties. He concluded that it is this lack of clear agreement, which advocates against the contractual character of the Optional Clause. Thus, he considered that the function of reciprocity is not to establish contractual bilateral relationships between declarant States, but to allow the Court to exercise its jurisdiction by identifying the common ground between two declarations:

> ... it is always possible to start from the premise that said states have been *ad idem*, at least at the moment of the singing of the relevant agreement, treaty or convention. In the system of 'compulsory jurisdiction' as has been set forth in the Statute, the consent of the states is expressed in unilateral declarations formulated by each state. These declarations cannot be considered, either notionally or legally, as bilateral or multilateral instruments, not even with respect to the area of coincidence of the various consents.[43]

Torres-Bernardez further explained that although some degree of interconnection might exist between coinciding declarations, the moment a specific dispute arises, this interconnection cannot be assimilated to a contractual bilateral obligation because declarations of acceptance are drafted unilaterally, in a general and abstract manner, with complete freedom to append reservations, and are not addressed to, nor accepted by other States:

---

[43] S. Torres-Bernardez, "Reciprocity on the System of Compulsory Jurisdiction and in Other Modalities of Contentious Jurisdiction Exercised by the International Court of Justice", in E.G. Bello and B.A. Ajibola (eds.), *Essays in Honour of Judge Taslim Olawale Elias,* Vol. I., *Contemporary International Law and Human Rights* (1992), 291 at 293, 305. However, see his dissenting Opinion in the Fisheries Jurisdiction case, *supra* note 2, at 639, where he adopted a position favouring the contractual character of Optional Clause declarations.

> The declarations are unilateral acts that each declarant state performs prior to the birth of the dispute, drafted in a general and abstract manner, independently from any other declarant states (and usually on different dates which may be far distant in time from each other), and which may have a widely varying material content and scope, in light of the authorization of 'reservations' *ratione materiae, ratione personae* and *ratione temporis,* which the declarant state also drafts unilaterally.[44]

Villagran-Kramer also favoured the view that Optional Clause declarations are unilateral. His position, however, is not entirely clear. Although he acknowledged that declarations of acceptance give rise to a certain type of agreement between States, he states that the moment a specific case is brought before the Court (and that the Court's Statute, where declarations of acceptance ultimately emanate from, is a conventional instrument) such declarations cannot be attributed with contractual character. Instead, they are characterised as *parallel unilateral acts.*[45] He elaborated further on the reciprocal effects of declarations of acceptance by explaining that the sole aim of the coinciding, or (as he terms it) the "parallelism", of declarations was to provide the Court with the opportunity to exercise its jurisdiction by discovering the common ground covered by two declarations.[46] Although Villagran-Kramer did not further explain his view, it could be argued that in using the word "parallel" he implies that the reason why coinciding declarations of acceptance do not result in the formation of a contractual bond, is the lack of any element of direct or indirect engagement between the various States accepting the compulsory jurisdiction of the Court.

It is interesting to note that the ILC, in its recent and ongoing study on the topic of unilateral acts of States (see below), has so far refused to classify Optional Clause declarations as falling within the ambit of unilateral acts. In his fifth report, Special Rapporteur Rodriguez-Cedeño stated clearly that Optional Clause declarations belonged within the realm of treaty relationships, despite the fact that certain characteristics, such as the latitude of States to append reservations might contravene that conclusion:

> Some unilateral declarations raise doubts about their place in the Vienna régime or in the context of unilateral acts; this is the case, for example, of declarations accepting the compulsory jurisdiction of the International Court of Justice formulated by States pursuant to article 36 of the Statute, which the Commission has examined previously. The Special Rapporteur, concurring with some legal scholars, has affirmed that such declarations belong within

---

[44] *Id.,* at 305.
[45] F. Villagran-Kramer, "Les Actes Unilatéraux Dans Le Cadre De La Jurisprudence International", in *International Law on the Eve of the Twenty-First Century-Views from the International Law Commission* (1997), 137, at 140.
[46] *Id.,* at 141. "La coïncidence des déclarations n'établit pas un accord entre deux Etats ayant fait des déclarations unilatérales. Le parallélisme se maintient et c'est seulement dans une aire commune que la Cour trouve l'espace nécessaire pour exercer sa juridiction".

treaty relationships However, as the Court itself has recognized, their specific characteristics can make them appear different from what are clearly treaty declarations.[47]

3.3 Principles of Treaty Interpretation

Although it is evident that the purpose of treaty interpretation is to elucidate the meaning of treaty provisions that are considered obscure by establishing the common will of the parties in relation to them,[48] the method and means for establishing that common will can vary significantly. To this end, there exist three main schools of interpretation, which can be classified as follows: (i) the objective approach, which advocates the supremacy of the text of the treaty, (ii) the subjective approach which places strong emphasis on the intentions of the parties and (iii) the teleological approach which emphasizes the object and purpose of the treaty. Some authors consider that the most difficult part lies in the reconciliation of the objective and subjective elements, and they believe that the question of recourse to preparatory work (*travaux préparatoires*) helps to distinguish the proponents of the objective from the proponents of the subjective school. This is so in the sense that the former would be more reluctant, whereas the latter would be more liberal, in permitting recourse to preparatory work in order to discover the true intentions of the parties.[49]

It should be noted, however, that the above is perhaps a simplified representation that exaggerates the differences between the three schools of interpretation. The positions mentioned above are not considered mutually exclusive. This view is adopted not only by the majority of writers, but also by the VCLT, which, although in favour of the textual approach, does not rule out the application of either the subjective or the teleological method.

The work of the ILC on the law of treaties[50] was largely influenced by the work of Fitzmaurice on treaty interpretation. Fitzmaurice identified six principles of interpretation, which are based upon the jurisprudence of the World Court and which are frequently mentioned and applied by various international courts and tribunals.[51] As they have also been invoked in

---

[47] V. Rodriguez–Cedeño, *Fifth Report on Unilateral Acts of States*, UN Doc. A/CN.4/52, paragraph 73 available at: <http://www.un.org/law/ilc/index.htm>.

[48] R.Y. Jennings and A. Watts (eds.), *Oppenheim's International Law*, Vol. I (1992), at 1266.

[49] M. Koskenniemi, *From Apology to Utopia: The Structure of the Legal Argument*, (1989), at 298-299; Sir I. Sinclair, *The Vienna Convention and the Law of Treaties* (1984), at 116.

[50] Sir H. Waldock, *Third Report on the Law of Treaties*, YILC (1964), Vol. II, 5, at 55, UN Doc.A/CN.4/167 and Adds.1-3, stated clearly that his draft articles took their inspiration from Fitzmaurice's major principles of interpretation.

[51] Fitzmaurice, *supra* note 34, at 50-51 and 344-346.

relation to the interpretation of Optional Clause declarations, a brief description will be given here. The six principles are as follows:

1. *Principle of actuality or textuality*: meaning that treaties are to be interpreted as they stand, on the basis of their actual texts;

2. *Principle of the natural and ordinary meaning*: meaning that, subject to the principle of contemporaneity (see below Principle VI), particular words and phrases are to be given their usual meaning in the context which they occur. Only when there is direct evidence that the terms used are to be understood in a different manner than the natural and ordinary one, or if interpretation leads to manifestly unsound and absurd results, can this principle be displaced;

3. *Principle of integration*: treaties are to be interpreted as a whole, and particular parts and chapters are to be interpreted also as whole.

Subject to the above three principles are:

4. *Principle of effectiveness (ut res magis valeat quam pereat)*: This principle has a double meaning. Firstly, that treaties are to be interpreted with due regard to their declared or apparent object and purposes, in a manner that enables them to achieve their objective; and, secondly, that particular provisions are to be interpreted in a manner that reason and meaning can be attributed to every part of the text;

5. *Principle of subsequent practice*: Recourse to the subsequent conduct and practice of the parties is allowed, as affording the most convincing evidence derived from how the treaty has been actually interpreted; and

6. *Principle of contemporaneity*: The terms of a treaty must be interpreted according to the meaning they possessed at the time when the treaty was originally drafted.

Most of the above principles were incorporated in the ILC's proposals, which were adopted virtually without change by the Vienna Conference as Articles 31-32 of the VCLT.

The general rule of treaty interpretation is contained in Article 31 of the VCLT.[52] In its commentary, the ILC stressed that the title "general rule" in

---

[52] Article 31 of the VCLT: General Rule of Interpretation:
(1) A treaty shall be interpreted in good faith in accordance with the ordinary meaning to be given to the terms of the treaty in their context and in the light of its object and purpose.
(2) The context for the purpose of the interpretation of a treaty shall comprise, in addition to the text, including its preamble and annexes: (a) any agreement relating to the treaty which was made between all the parties in connexion with the conclusion of the treaty; (b) any instrument which was made by one or more parties in connexion with the conclusion of the treaty and accepted by the other parties as an instrument related to the treaty.

the singular tense was chosen, in order to emphasize that the process of treaty interpretation was a unity and that the various elements included in Article 31, i.e. the text, the context and the object and purpose of the treaty, formed a "single, closely integrated rule" and did not lay down a legal hierarchy of norms of interpretation of treaties.[53]

Although the ILC took the position that the "starting point of interpretation is the elucidation of the meaning of the text, not an investigation *ab initio* into the intentions of the parties" and that "the text must be presumed to be the authentic expression of the intentions of the parties", it further explained that the enumeration of the various elements of interpretation in Article 31 represents a logical progression, in the sense that one starts with the text, then progresses to the context and, finally, to subsequent materials (additional agreements, practice) related to the treaty.[54] Article 31(1) also refers to the principle of good faith, which the ILC considers as an intrinsic characteristic of treaty interpretation that applies to the entire process described therein and, by consequence, any interpretation that violates this principle cannot stand.

The ILC also mentioned the principle of effectiveness (above under IV) and stated that, although it was not included in a separate provision, it was nonetheless incorporated in Article 31(1), which required that a treaty be also interpreted in the light of its object and purpose: "[w]hen a treaty is open to two interpretations one of which does and the other does not enable the treaty to have appropriate effects, good faith and the objects and purposes of the treaty demand that the former interpretation should be adopted".[55] The ILC continued, however, by warning that this should not be construed as endorsing an "extensive" or "liberal" interpretation going beyond or against the terms of the treaty under question.[56] Thus, although the general rule of Article 31(1) incorporates both the textual and the teleological methods of interpretation, it seems to give precedence to the textual approach.[57]

---

(3) There shall be taken into account, together with the context: (a) any subsequent agreement between the parties regarding the interpretation of the treaty or the application of its provisions; (b) any subsequent practice in the application of the treaty which establishes the agreement of the parties regarding its interpretation; (c) any relevant rules of international law applicable in the relations between the parties.
(4) A special meaning shall be given to a term if it is established that the parties so intended."
[53] *Report of the ILC on the Work of its Eighteenth Session,* YILC (1966), Vol. II, 172, at 220, UN Doc. A/CN.4/191.
[54] *Id.*; See also M. Fitzmaurice, "The Practical Working of the Law of Treaties", in M.D. Evans (ed.), *International Law* (2003), at 186.
[55] *Report of the ILC on the Work of its 18th Session, supra* note 53, at 219.
[56] *Id.*
[57] For a comprehensive survey regarding the principle of effectiveness see H. Gutierrez-Posse, "Le maxime *ut res magis valeat quam pereat*", 23 *ZÖR* (1972), 229-254. See also I.

Article 32 refers mainly to *travaux préparatoires*, which it characterizes as supplementary means of interpretation.[58] It makes clear that recourse to the *travaux préparatoires* is acceptable in order to aid interpretation governed by the principles enshrined in Article 31 and that they are "neither autonomous nor alternative means of interpretation."[59] Resort to the *travaux préparatoires* is strictly regulated and permitted only in two occasions: (i) in order to confirm the meaning resulting from the application of Article 31, or (ii) when such application produces ambiguous, obscure or manifestly absurd results. Other supplementary means of treaty interpretation can be found in various principles and maxims derived mainly from domestic law.[60] Some of the most commonly used principles and maxims: (i) *lex specialis derogat legi generali*: a specific rule prevails over a general one; (ii) *lex posterior derogate legi priori*: the more recent rule prevails over the older rule; (iii) *expressio unius est exclusio alterius*: express mention of a certain situation excludes other situations not mentioned; and (iv) *contra proferentem*: if two meanings of a provision are possible, then the meaning that should be adopted is the one less favourable to the party that proposed that provision, or for whose benefit that provision was inserted. This last principle has been unsuccessfully invoked in relation to the interpretation of Optional Clause declarations (see below, the *Anglo-Iranian Oil Co.* case and *Fisheries Jurisdiction* case, Part II).

Finally, it should be noted that the canons of the VCLT regarding the interpretation of treaties are considered beyond doubt as customary international law.[61] The Court confirmed this in a number of instances. For example, in the *Libya/Chad* case it stated:

> The Court would recall that, in accordance with customary international law, reflected in Article 31 of the 1969 Vienna Convention on the Law of Treaties, a treaty must be interpreted in good faith in accordance with the ordinary meaning to be given to its terms in their context and in the light of their object and purpose. Interpretation must be based above all upon the text of the treaty.

Buffard and K. Zemanek, "The Object and Purpose of a Treaty: An Enigma?", 3 *ARIEL* (1998), 311-343.

[58] Article 32 of the VCLT: Supplementary Means of Interpretation:

> "Recourse may be had to supplementary means of interpretation, including the preparatory work of the treaty and the circumstances of its conclusion, in order to confirm the meaning resulting from the application of article 31, or to determine the meaning when the interpretation according to article 31: (a) leaves the meaning ambiguous or obscure; or (b) leads to a result which is manifestly absurd or unreasonable."

[59] *Report of the ILC on the Work of its 18th Session, supra* note 53, at 223.

[60] For a detailed analysis of various principles and maxims see R.Y. Jennings and A.Watts (eds.), *Oppenheim's International Law, supra* note 48, at 1277-1282.

[61] Sinclair, *supra* note 49, 153.

As a subsidiary measure recourse may be had to means of interpretation such as the preparatory work of the treaty and the circumstances of its conclusion.[62]

3.4 Unilateral Acts and the Question of Restrictive Interpretation

The question of the interpretation of unilateral acts, though not yet settled, has been briefly discussed by the ILC during its ongoing consideration of the topic of unilateral acts of States. In his fourth and fifth reports submitted in 2001 and 2002, respectively, Special Rapporteur Rodriguez-Cedeño considered that the rules of the VCLT could constitute a valid reference in the elaboration of rules of interpretation for unilateral acts, adapted, however, to reflect the special characteristics and nature of such acts. For this reason he submitted that unilateral acts, on the basis that they create self-imposed limitations on sovereignty, ought to be interpreted restrictively, i.e. in a manner imposing the least possible limitations.[63] In order to support this assertion he quoted the *Nuclear Tests* cases, where the Court pronounced that when interpreting unilateral acts, ascertaining the intention of the declaring State is of paramount importance and that in case of doubt a restrictive interpretation was called for:

> Of course, not all unilateral acts imply obligation; but a State may choose to take up a certain position in relation to a particular matter with the intention of being bound-the intention is to be ascertained by interpretation of the act. When States make statements by which their freedom of action is to be limited, a restrictive interpretation is called for.[64]

Although the restrictive criterion was not mentioned explicitly in the draft ILC Articles the accompanying commentary stated quite clearly the preponderance of a restrictive interpretation as far as unilateral acts were

---

[62] Territorial Dispute (Libyan Arab Jamahiriya/Chad), Judgment of 3 February 1994, 1994 ICJ Rep. 6, at 19-20. Similar statements are also included in the Maritime Delimitation and Territorial Question between Qatar and Bahrain (Qatar v. Bahrain), Jurisdiction and Admissibility, Judgment of 15 February 1995, 1995 ICJ Rep. 6, at 18; Oil Platforms (Islamic Republic of Iran v. US), Preliminary Objections, Judgment 12 December 1996, 1996 ICJ Rep. 803, at 812; and more recently in Kasikili/Sedudu Island (Botswana/Namibia), Judgment of 13 December 1999, 1999 ICJ Rep. 1045, at 1051.

[63] V. Rodriguez-Cedeño, *Fourth Report on Unilateral Acts of States,* UN Doc. A/CN.4/519, at: <http://www.un.org/law/ilc/index.htm> paragraph 112, at 126-127: "... as the Court itself pointed out in the *Nuclear Tests* case referred to above, such [unilateral] acts should be interpreted restrictively. In accordance with the case law and the doctrine, there is no doubt whatever that the restrictive criterion predominates in this context"; idem *Fifth Report on Unilateral Acts of States*, Addendum 1, note 47, paragraph 128.

[64] Nuclear Tests (Australia v. France; New Zealand v. France), Judgments of 20 December 1974, 1974 ICJ Rep. 253, at 267 and 1974 ICJ Rep. 457, at 473.

concerned.[65] Despite certain misgivings, especially relating to *travaux préparatoires* (which some considered problematic to resort to in the context of unilateral acts), a restrictive interpretation of unilateral acts appears to be the method favoured by the majority of the ILC.[66]

In this respect, it is interesting to note that Special Rapporteur Rodriguez-Cedeño mentioned Optional Clause declarations as prime examples of acts suitable for restrictive interpretation.[67] This assertion, however, cannot be accepted. The method of restrictive interpretation in relation to declarations of acceptance of the Court's compulsory jurisdiction is not endorsed either in theory or in the practice of the Court.

The *rationale* behind the principle of restrictive interpretation, the origins of which can be traced back to arbitration agreements, is that due to the voluntary nature of the Court's jurisdiction all international engagements purporting to confer jurisdiction on it, particularly declarations under Article 36(2), should be interpreted restrictively in order to avoid extending the consent of States. This means that there should always be a presumption against, rather than in favour of, jurisdiction. This position seems to stem from well-known *dicta* as set out in the *Chorzow Factory* case. In this case, the Court stressed the need to take a cautious approach as regards questions of jurisdiction in that the Court stated that jurisdiction should be affirmed only in the absence of any doubts.[68] Although the Court accorded great importance to the intentions of the parties when deciding questions of jurisdiction, it did not consider that recourse to a restrictive interpretation should be automatic, but should only take place in exceptional circumstances. The same conclusion was reached in the *Phosphates in Morocco* case where the Court stated clearly:

> the terms on which the objection *ratione temporis* submitted by the French Government is founded, are perfectly clear ... In these circumstances, there is no occasion to resort to a restrictive interpretation that, in case of doubt, might

---

[65] V. Rodriguez-Cedeño, *Fifth Report on Unilateral Acts of States*, Addendum 1, note 47, paragraph 134.

[66] *Report of the ILC on the Work of its Fifty-third Session*, UN Doc. A/56/10, at: <http://www.un.org/law/ilc/reports/2001/2001report.htm>, paragraphs 244 and 245; *Report of the ILC on the Work of its Fifty-fourth Session*, UN Doc. A/57/10, at: <http://www.un.org/law/ilc/reports/2002/2002report.htm>, paragraphs 403-404, at 426-427.

[67] V. Rodriguez-Cedeño, *Fourth Report on Unilateral Acts of States*, *supra* note 63, paragraph 127.

[68] Chorzow Factory case, *supra* note 5, at 32: "It has been argued repeatedly in the course of the present proceedings that in case of doubt the Court should decline jurisdiction. It is true that the Court's Jurisdiction is always a limited one, existing only in so far as States have accepted it; consequently, the Court will, in the event of an objection – or when it has automatically to consider the question – only affirm its jurisdiction provided that the force of the arguments militating in favour of it is preponderant."

be advisable in regard to a clause which must on no account be interpreted in
such a way as to exceed the intention of the States that subscribed to it ...[69]

The position adopted in the *Anglo-Iranian Oil Company* case, where the
Court rejected an *a priori* application of restrictive interpretation. It
proceeded, instead, from the premise of the textual approach supplemented
by the intentions of the declarant State. This left little room for doubt that the
restrictive interpretation is not a tool, which is regularly employed within the
analysis of Optional Clause declarations .[70]

Conversely, it is true that the Court has been very cautious in its
interpretation of Optional Clause declarations. This, however, has been so as
specific factors, which limited the Court's jurisdiction, already existed at the
time of the drafting of the relevant declarations . It was not due to the Court
considering that the need for a restrictive interpretation was inherent in
Optional Clause declarations. The same view has been adopted by the
majority of doctrine. Sir G. Fitzmaurice for instance, stated that the issue at
hand was the reality of consent given and not that of a restricted
interpretation. Furthermore, he said that in order to avoid injustice being
done to either party to a dispute, what was required was "neither restricted
not liberal interpretations of jurisdictional clauses, but *strict proof* of
consent".[71] A similar position has also been expressed by Rosenne, who
stated clearly that in light of the above mentioned pronouncements of the
Court "a theory which holds that *a priori* the declarations are given to a
restrictive interpretation is singularly unconvincing".[72]

4. The Jurisprudence of the PCIJ and the ICJ

Notwithstanding that theory generally tends to favour the treaty character of
the Optional Clause, and despite arguments by judges (including in strong
dissenting judgments and, arguments presented by parties in their
submissions) the Court's jurisprudence does not reflect this approach.
According to the jurisprudence of the World Court, Optional Clause
declarations consistently appear to have dual characteristics. As will be
discussed below, the Court has emphasized, over the years and in equal

---

[69] Phosphates in Morocco (Italy *v.* France), Preliminary Objections, Judgement of 14 June
1938, 1938 PCIJ (Series A/B), No. 71, 10, at 23-24.
[70] Anglo Iranian Oil Company case, *supra* note 6 and *infra* Part II.
[71] Sir G. Fitzmaurice, "The Law and Procedure of the International Court of Justice 1951-54",
34 *BYIL* (1985), 1 at 86-87.
[72] Rosenne, *supra* note 24, at 814. A similar opinion was also adopted by C. De Visscher,
Problèmes d'Interprétation Judiciaire en Droit International Public (1963), at 261; H.
Lauterpacht *The Development of International Law by the International Court* (1958), at 344-
347.

measure, both the unilateral and the contractual elements of Optional Clause declarations. On the question of their interpretation, the Court has adopted a similarly equivocal position.

4.1 Two PCIJ Cases

The position that Optional Clauses are unilateral in nature was first adopted in the *Phosphates in Morocco* case[73]. In this case, the PCIJ pointed out that the actual declaration was a unilateral act and *that this factor should play a decisive role in setting the principles of its interpretation*. Although it did not adopt a restrictive interpretation, the PCIJ placed strong emphasis on the intentions of the declarant State and exhibited great caution in evaluating a French reservation:

> The Declaration of which the ratification was deposited by the French Government on April 25th, 1931, is a unilateral act by which that Government accepted the Court's compulsory jurisdiction. This jurisdiction only exists within the limits within which it has been accepted. In this case, the terms on which the objection *ratione temporis* submitted by the French Government is founded, are perfectly clear ... In these circumstances, there is no occasion to resort to a restrictive interpretation that, in case of doubt, might be advisable in regard to a clause which must on no account be interpreted in such a way as to exceed the intention of the States that subscribed to it ... it is necessary always to bear in mind the will of the State which only accepted the compulsory jurisdiction within specified limits, and consequently only intended to submit to that jurisdiction [specific] disputes ...[74]

Although the above passage, and in particular the opening phrase, points quite explicitly towards the unilateral nature of declarations of acceptance, there exists some doubt as to whether the PCIJ referred to Optional Clause declarations as unilateral acts only for purposes of interpretation, or whether it endorsed that they possess a truly unilateral character. Both views have been advanced.[75] However, the proper position seems to be that the above pronouncements of the PCIJ were made in relation to interpretation. This view is reinforced by the fact that the same judgment also stressed the reciprocal nature of obligations embodied in Optional Clause declarations. Furthermore, it seemed, to a certain extent, to adopt a rather ambivalent position relating to their legal character, by, on the one hand, emphasising

---

[73] See note 69, at 22.
[74] *Id.,* at 23-24.
[75] Waldock, *supra* note 3, at 252; F. Villagran-Kramer, "Les Actes Unilatéraux Dans Le Cadre De La Jurisprudence International", in *International Law on the Eve of the Twenty-First Century-Views from the International Law Commission* (1997), 137, at 141.

their unilateral nature for purposes of interpretation and, on the other hand, their contractual nature derived from the principle of reciprocity.

The *Electricity Company of Sofia* case further developed this position.[76] Therein, the PCIJ implied strongly that the submission of Optional Clause declarations resulted in the establishment of a contractual obligation. The relevant remarks by the PCIJ resulted from the invocation by Belgium of two equal heads of the Court's jurisdiction: (i) a general treaty of arbitration with Bulgaria; and (ii) the declarations of the two States made under Article 36(2) of the Statute of the PCIJ . The Court emphasized that the legal obligations, which resulted from the acceptance of the compulsory jurisdiction of the Court, were of a similar legal nature as those stemming from a general arbitration agreement. In other words, they were treaty obligations.[77] The view, that the submissions of unilateral declarations gave rise to an agreement between the declarant States, was fully supported in assenting opinions.[78]

4.2 The *Anglo-Iranian Oil Company* Case

The first case in which the the ICJ examined the legal character of Optional Clause declarations was the *Anglo-Iranian Oil Company* case.[79]

At the centre of this dispute was the exact meaning to be given to a reservation of the Iranian declaration, which stated that Iran recognized the Court's jurisdiction "in any disputes arising after the ratification of the present declaration, with regard to situations or facts relating directly or indirectly to the application of treaties or conventions accepted by Persia *and subsequent to the ratification of this declaration*".[80] [Emphasis added]. It is evident that the above reservation is grammatically capable of resulting in two different meanings: (i) firstly, and as adopted by the United Kingdom, that the phrase "subsequent to the ratification" refers to "situations and facts"; and (ii) secondly, one as adopted by Iran, that it refers to "treaties and conventions accepted by Persia". Strictly speaking, the issue before the Court was the interpretation of the wording of Iran's declaration, rather than of its legal character. However, it was soon evident that the position taken as regards the general question of the legal classification of Optional Clause

---

[76] Electricity Company of Sophia and Bulgaria (Belgium *v.* Bulgaria), Preliminary Objection, Judgment of 4 April 1938, 1939 PCIJ (Series A/B), No. 78, at 64.

[77] *Id.*, at 76, 81.

[78] Separate Opinion of Judge Anzilloti, *id.*, at 87; Dissenting Opinion of Judge Urrutia, *id.*, at 103; Dissenting Opinion of Judge Hudson, *id.*, at 121, who said that by the acceptance of compulsory jurisdiction Belgium and Bulgaria were bound *per se.*

[79] See note 6.

[80] *Id.*, at 102.

declarations, underlay the question of their interpretation . Both parties expressed views on the legal nature of the Optional Clause in order to advance their preferred interpretation.

The United Kingdom took the position that Optional Clause declarations were, in fact, treaties: they called for the application of the principle of effectiveness, since this was the only interpretation that would give meaning to all the words included in the Iranian declaration; and, alternatively, for the application of the *contra proferentem* rule.[81] Iran, on the other hand, took the position that declarations under Article 36(2) were not treaties. It rejected both the applicability of the principle of effectiveness and the *contra proferentem* rule, which it considered suitable only in context of bilateral relations and not in context of unilateral declarations. Instead, quoting from the *Phosphates in Morocco* case, Iran placed strong emphasis on the intentions of the Iranian Government and proposed a restrictive interpretation, which would guarantee the respect of such intentions.[82]

The Court adopted a position close, but not identical, to the one supported by Iran. It rejected an *a priori* restrictive interpretation of Optional Clause declarations. Instead, it started from the premise that such declarations were subject to the general rules of textual treaty interpretation, providing that: such a textual interpretation would have due regard to the intentions of the declarant State in order not to surpass the scope of the jurisdiction to which that State had consented. Although the Court considered that "[t]his declaration must be interpreted as it stands having due regard to the words actually used",[83] it qualified this assertion by stating that:

> the Court cannot base itself on a purely grammatical interpretation of the text. It must seek the interpretation which is in harmony with a natural and reasonable way of reading the text, having due regard to the intention of the Government of Iran at the time when it accepted the compulsory jurisdiction of the Court.[84]

The Court then proceeded to explore the intentions of Iran as they emerged from various extraneous materials, such as the circumstances surrounding the denunciation by Iran of various treaties of capitulation, satisfying itself

---

[81] Observations and Submissions of the UK, Anglo-Iranian Oil Company case, *supra* note 6, at 335-336.

[82] Observations Préliminaires de l'Iran, *id.,* at 295; Oral Arguments of Iran, *id.,* 9-6-52, Plaidoirie du Professeur Rolin, at 449: "Je n'ai pas besoin de vous dire, Messieurs, qu'il n'y a pas d'intention commune et il ne peut pas y avoir d'intention commune. Le mécanisme de l'article 36 du Statut ... est que chaque déclaration est élaborée en toute indépendance, isolement par chaque Etat ... Vous n'avez donc pas de concours de consentement, vous avez une succession de consentements"; *id.,* at 449: "... l'interprétation restrictive est l'interprétation la plus conforme à l'intention du Gouvernement d'Iran.".

[83] Anglo-Iranian Oil Co. case, *supra* note 6, at 105.

[84] *Id.,* at 104.

that "it was the manifest intention of the Government of Iran" to exclude from the jurisdiction of the Court treaties accepted before the ratification of its declaration.[85]

The decision of the Court rejected the application of the principle of effectiveness. In this context it indirectly made certain ambivalent comments with respect to the legal character of Optional Clause declarations. Although it considered that an interpretation attributing a meaning to every word of the text was valid as far as treaties texts were concerned, it added:

> But the text of the Iranian Declaration is not a treaty text resulting from negotiations between two or more States. It is the result of unilateral drafting of the Government of Iran, which appears to have shown a particular degree of caution when drafting the declaration. It appears to have inserted, *ex abundanti cautela*, words which, strictly speaking, may seem to have been superfluous.[86]

The above pronouncement can be interpreted in two ways, one favouring the unilateral character of declarations, the other favouring their contractual nature. Lauterpacht and Fitzmaurice opted for the latter interpretation and read the above passage as meaning that Optional Clause declarations were treaty instruments resulting from unilateral drafting (and not treaty instruments resulting from negotiations).[87]

Despite the above pronouncements of the Court, the contractual nature of the Optional Clause was fully endorsed in the dissenting opinions of Judges Read and Alvarez. Judge Read, taking the view that declarations of acceptance gave rise to contractual relationships, supported the application of all rules of treaty interpretation[88] and Judge Alvarez, adopting a similar approach, concluded that:

> the Declaration is a multilateral act of a special character; it is the basis of a treaty made by Iran with the States which had already adhered and with those

---

[85] *Id.,* at 106.

[86] *Id.,* at 105

[87] H. Lauterpacht, *First Report on the Law of Treaties, supra* note 32; *idem, supra* note 72, at 345-346: "There ought to be no difficulty in considering the text of Article 36(2) of the Statute of the Court ... as the text of a treaty to which the declaring State gives its adherence"; Fitzmaurice, *supra* note 34, at 366.

[88] Dissenting Opinion of Judge Read, Anglo-Iranian Oil Company case, supra note 6, at 142: "I am unable to accept the contention that the principles of international law which govern the interpretation of treaties cannot be applied to the Persian declaration. Admittedly it was drafted unilaterally. On the other hand, it was related, in express terms to Article 36 of the Statute, and to the declarations of other States which had already deposited, or which might in the future deposit, reciprocal declarations. It was intended to establish legal relationships with such States, consensual in their character, within the régime established by the provision of Article 36."

that which would subsequently adhere to the provisions of Article 36, paragraph 2, of the Statute of the Court.[89]

Thus, it can be concluded that, although the Court did not explicitly state that Optional Clause declarations possess a unilateral legal character, its pronouncements regarding the interpretation of declarations leave little doubt as to the importance the Court accorded to the subjective element of the intentions of the parties. This is an approach that would not have been accepted in the interpretation of a regular treaty text. Although the Court's starting point was the method of textual interpretation, it accorded much greater importance to the intentions of the declarant State and it was more permissive in allowing recourse to extraneous elements, such as *travaux préparatoires*. In this respect, the method of interpretation followed was closer, but not identical, to that of unilateral acts.

The dilemmas inherent in this approach may be solved (and explained) through the approach adopted by Rosenne.[90] This author supports the view that in the interpretation of Optional Clause declarations, "a clear distinction has to be maintained between the canons of interpretation and the nature and process of interpretation".[91] As to the canons of interpretation, generally speaking, the Court applies to other acts including declarations, the same rules as to the interpretation of treaties, that is to say, it establishes what words mean in their context (providing it does not lead to absurd results). If, however, this starting point results in an unsatisfactory outcome, then the Court's attention "is focused not on what the words mean in their context but on allied questions of who used them and for what purpose."[92] Rosenne explains that in the context of declarations, this involves establishing whether the case before the Court is comparable with the terms of jurisdiction, accepted unilaterally by each of the parties. Another explanation is provided by Fitzmaurice in the following commentary on the judgment in the *Anglo-Iranian Oil Company* Case in which he said:

> ... The conclusion seems to be that, in the Court's view ... extraneous elements constitute a more important element, and can more legitimately be resonated to, in the interpretation of unilateral, or rather unilaterally formulated, instruments, than in the case of bilaterally of multilaterally formulated ones, in respect of which the textual element will predominate.[93]

---

[89] Dissenting Opinion of Judge Alvarez, *id.*, at 125. Although Judge Alvarez considered that rules of treaty interpretation should apply, he had a very different understanding of these rules. Under his theory of a "new international law", he advanced a strongly teleological approach, where the object and purpose of a treaty was not considered static but evolving in accordance with the changing conditions surrounding a treaty, at 126.

[90] Rosenne, *supra* note 24, at 809-815.

[91] *Id.*, 810.

[92] *Id.*, 811.

[93] Fitzmaurice, *supra* note 34, 366.

4.3 The *Nicaragua* Case

In the *Nicaragua* case, the Court made several pronouncements on the legal nexus between the Optional Clause system and treaty rules. In his admirable study on this matter, Professor Greig said: "[t]he Court has been ambivalent as to the nature of the bond created by declarations under Article 36, or by the combined effect of such declarations when an application has been made to the Court thus identifying particular declarations between which the necessary nexus must exist to found the Court's jurisdiction".[94] He concentrated in particular on the issue of good faith and the rules governing the termination of treaties. On the issue of good faith, the Court was of the view that no matter the type of international obligation, whether a unilateral obligation or a bilateral or multilateral obligation, it is subject to the basic principle of good faith.[95] It was with respect to declarations under which a state accepted the Court's jurisdiction with "indefinite duration" that the Court made an explicit analogy with the law of treaties. It said as follows: "[I]t appears from the requirements of good faith that they should be treated by analogy, according to the law of treaties, which requires a reasonable time for withdrawal from or termination of treaties that contain no provision regarding the duration of their validity".[96]

According to Professor Greig, the particular character of Optional Clause declarations appears to indicate that although in many ways they create agreements, "it is also true that many of the conventional rules are inapplicable to the way in which declarations are made to operate".[97] Thus,

---

[94] Greig, *supra* note 3, 176.

[95] Nicaragua case, *supra* note 15, at 418. In this case the Court fell back on the statements concerning good faith made in the Nuclear Tests case, *supra* note 64, at 267-268. In this case the Court made an exhaustive statement as to the legal character of unilateral declarations and the principle of good faith: "[I]t is well recognised that declarations made by way of unilateral acts, concerning legal or factual situations, may have the effect of creating legal obligations. Declarations of this kind may be, and often are, very specific. When is the intention of the State making the declaration that it should become bound according to its terms, that intention confers on the declaration the character of legal undertaking, the State being henceforth legally required to follow a course of conduct consistent with the declaration." The Court went on to say: "One of the basic principles governing the creation and performance of legal obligations, whatever their source, is the principle of good faith. Trust and confidence are inherent in international co-operation, in particular in an age when this co-operation is becoming increasingly essential. Just as the very rule *pacta sunt servanda* in the law of treaties is based on good faith, so also is the binding character of an international obligation assumed by unilateral declaration. Thus interested States may take cognisance of unilateral declarations and place confidence in them, and are entitled to require that the obligation thus created be respected."

[96] Nicaragua case, *supra* note 15, at 420.

[97] Greig, *supra* note 3, at 179.

the practice of States may diverge from the rules contained in Article 56 of the VCLT.[98]

Professor Greig is correct in stating that the assessment of the issue of the notice period contained in the United States Declaration and the Schultz letter (attempting to modify the original Declaration) depends in part on classification. The closer it was to a treaty in character, the more the United States had to follow the prescribed notice period; the closer it was in nature to a unilateral declaration, the less stringent the requirements were relating to the notice period (the alternative which seems to be supported by state practice). However, whatever the character of such a declaration, there is an undisputed duty to act in good faith, at least in respect of its termination. Thus,

> Some respect was due to the period of notice which the United States had promised to give other declarant States in the way it had framed its own declaration accepting the Court's jurisdiction, and by this promise at least the United States was bound.[99]

When considering the Court's decision in the *Nicaragua* case, it is important to bear in mind the dual nature of the Optional Clause system. In this case, the Court considered the consensual relationship which had resulted from the declarations of the two States concerned. The Court's decision, in so far as it applied aspects of treaty law, related to this aspect. As will be explained below, the Court subsequently distinguished the position of declarations in their unilateral aspect and, in particular, in relation to the formalities required by the ICJ Statute relating to the making of an Optional Clause declaration. For example, in the *Bakassi Peninsula* case, the Court refused to apply these provisions of treaty law (i.e. the duty of good faith).

4.4 The *Right of Passage* doctrine

In the *Right of Passage* case,[100] which was heard before the Court in 1957, raised other issues relating to the Optional Clause declarations relevant to the two recent cases. Indeed, the Court's judgment in this case has become a *locus classicus* in relation to various aspects of the Optional Clause system.

---

[98] See also Sir H. Waldock, *Second Report on the Law of Treaties*, YILC (1963), Vol. II, 36, at 68, UN Doc.A/CN.4/156 and Adds.1-3: "[t]aken as a whole, State practice under the Optional Clause declaration, and especially the modern trend toward Declarations terminable upon notice, seem only to reinforce the clear conclusion to be drawn from the treaties of arbitration, conciliation and judicial settlement, that these treaties are regarded as essentially of terminable character". See also the same view taken by Judge Schwebel in his Dissenting Opinion in the Nicaragua case, *supra* note 15, at 621.

[99] Greig, *supra* note 3, at 181.

[100] Right of Passage case, *supra* note 4.

In particular, this case involved an extensive analysis of paragraph 4 of the Optional Clause.[101] This provision outlines the formalities required in relation to the submission of Optional Clause declarations and is of considerable practical importance since it pertains to the point in time from which reciprocal obligations of States arising from Optional Clause declarations come into existence. In the *Right of Passage* case, the Court interpreted paragraph 4 of the Optional Clause as containing two separate, unrelated elements: the deposit of a State's Optional Clause declaration with the Secretary-General of the United Nations, on the one hand, and the duty of the Secretary-General of the United Nations to forward the declaration to the parties to the ICJ Statute and to the Registrar of the ICJ, on the other hand.[102] In the *Right of Passage* case, the Court explicitly asserted that the date from which reciprocal obligations of States arise is the date when the declaration is deposited with the Secretary-General of the United Nations.[103]

---

[101] Article 36(4) of the ICJ Statute: "Such declarations shall be deposited with the Secretary-General of the United Nations, who shall transmit copies thereof to the parties to the Statute and to the Registrar of the Court."

[102] Right of Passage Case, *supra* note 100, 147: The Court said as follows: "It has been contented ... that Article 36 requires not only the deposit of the Declaration of Acceptance with the Secretary-General but the transmission by the Secretary-General of a copy of the Declaration to the parties to the Statute, the Declaration of the Acceptance does not become effective until the latter obligation has been discharged. However, it is only the first of these requirements that concerns the State making the Declaration. The latter is not concerned with the duty of the Secretary-General or the manner of fulfilment. The legal effect of a Declaration does not depend upon a subsequent action or inaction of the Secretary-General. Moreover, unlike some other instruments, Article 36 provides for no additional requirement, for instance, that the information by the Secretary-General must reach the Parties to the Statute, or that some period must elapse subsequent to the deposit of the Declaration before it can become effective. Any such requirement would introduce an element of uncertainty to into the operation of the Optional clause system. The Court cannot read into the Optional clause any requirement of that nature." The Court further ascertained that any changes to the Declarations must be notified to the parties to the Statute in the same manner, *id.*, at 143.

[103] *Id.*, 145-147: The Court said as follows: "By the deposit of its Declaration of Acceptance with the Secretary-General, the accepting State becomes a Party to the system of the Optional Clause in relation to the other declarant States, with all the rights and obligations deriving from Article 36. The contractual relation between the Parties and compulsory jurisdiction of the Court resulting therefrom are established "*ipso facto* and without special agreement" by the fact of the making of the Declaration. Accordingly, every State which makes a Declaration of Acceptance must be deemed to take into account the possibility that, under the Statute, it may at any time find itself subjected to the obligations of the Optional clause in relation to a new signatory as the result of the deposit by that Signatory of a Declaration of Acceptance. A State accepting the jurisdiction of the Court must accept than an Application may be filed against it by a new declarant State on the same day on which that State deposits with the Secretary-General its Declaration of Acceptance. For it is on that day that the consensual bond, which is the basis of the Optional clause, comes into being between the States concerned."

The Court's decision in this case turned essentially upon the interpretation of paragraph 4 of the Optional Clause itself, rather that on any other consideration of the underlying legal character of the Optional Clause system generally, or of Optional Clause declarations in particular. Thus, in itself it might be thought to lie somewhat outside the main theme of the present chapter. However, though not directly an issue, certain attitudes towards the issue of the relationship of between the Optional Clause system and the law of treaties are implied by the Court's judgment. In this respect, the Court may be seen as reinforcing the ambivalence relating to the legal character of Optional Clause declarations, which was inherent in the basic jurisprudence relating to the issue already developed by the PCIJ. On the one hand, the decision that the question of the time of the coming into force of Optional Clause declarations depended solely upon a proper interpretation of paragraph 4 of the Optional Clause may be seen (certainly in comparison to some arguments put forward by Nigeria in the *Bakassi Peninsula* case, in which precisely the same issue was before the Court, as will be discussed below) as reinforcing the argument that declarations are purely unilateral in nature. However, the Court firmly reinforced the importance of the consensual bond which comes into existence between declarant States within the Optional Clause system. Indeed, the Court describes this as "the consensual bond, which is the basis of the Optional Clause ...".[104]

When we consider the *Bakassi Peninsula* case below, we shall consider the implications of this part of the judgment in the *Right of Passage* case, as well as the substantial criticisms of the *Right of Passage* doctrine contained not only in the arguments of Nigeria in the *Bakasssi Peninsula* Case, but also in powerful dissenting opinions in that case and as contained in commentary on the case by certain authors.

4.5 The *Bakassi Peninsula* Case[105]

On 29 March 1994, Cameroon filed an application to institute proceedings against Nigeria, relating to the question of sovereignty over the Bakassi Peninsula and to the delimitation of their maritime boundary. By way of additional application of 6 June 1994, the Court was to consider the delimitation of the frontier between Cameroon and Nigeria from Lake Chad to the sea. Additionally, Cameroon claimed for monetary compensation for the material and non-material damage allegedly caused by Nigeria due to its unlawful acts in relation to the disputed areas. Nigeria filed several

---

[104] See the passage quoted above in note 102.
[105] See note 1.

Preliminary Objections arguing against the ICJ's jurisdiction and the admissibility of the Cameroon's application.

This chapter will only focus on the first of Nigeria's Preliminary Objections. Nigeria's preliminary objection was based, broadly speaking, on Cameroon's alleged lack of good faith in the implementation of the procedure on relation to the Optional Clause. The essence of Nigeria's objection lay in the timing as between Cameroon's deposit with the Secretary-General of the United Nations of its Optional Clause declaration and the date of its commencement of proceedings against Nigeria. Nigeria itself had accepted the Court's jurisdiction on 14 August 1965, with due observance of all formalities. Cameroon accepted the Court's jurisdiction on 3 March 1994 and on the copies of its Optional Clause declaration were submitted to the Secretary-General of the United Nations. The Secretary-General, in turn, submitted the copies of Cameroon's declaration to, *inter alia*, Nigeria, but only about ten and half months later. In the meantime, Cameroon had already instituted proceedings before the Court against Nigeria on 29 March 1994. Nigeria claimed that it had had no knowledge of Cameroon's Optional Clause declaration until it was notified by the Registrar of the Court that Cameroon had instituted proceedings. It was this short period of time between acceding to the Optional Clause system and the filing of the case, and the fact that, allegedly, Nigeria had no knowledge of Cameroon's submission to the Court's jurisdiction at the time when Cameroon instituted proceedings, which was the basis of Nigeria's First Preliminary Objection. The objection was phrased as follows:

> 1. ... Cameroon, by lodging the Application of 29 March 1994, violated its obligations to act in good faith, acted on abused of the system established by Article 36, paragraph 2, of the Statute, and disregarded the requirement of reciprocity established by Article 36 paragraph 2, of the Statute and the terms of Nigeria's Declaration of 3 September 1965; 2. That consequently the conditions necessary to entitle Cameroon to invoke its Declaration under Article 36, paragraph 2, as basis for the Court's jurisdiction did not exist when the Application was lodged; and 3. Accordingly, the Court is without jurisdiction to entertain the Application.[106]

The relevant facts relating to Nigeria's first preliminary objection were, thus, not really distinguishable from those in the *Right of Passage* case and Cameroon's principal argument against Nigeria's objection was simply that there was no reason for the Court not to follow its earlier decision. The Court effectively accepted this contention, and dismissed the objection. In the first place, the Court strongly re-affirmed the principles of the *Right of Passage* case, by stating:

---

[106] *Id.,* 284-285.

> The conclusions ... reached by the Court in 1957 reflected the very essence of the Optional Clause providing for acceptance of the Court's compulsory jurisdiction. Any State party to the Statute, in adhering to the jurisdiction of the Court in accordance with Article 36, paragraph 2, accepts the jurisdiction of the Court in its relations with States previously having adhered to that clause. At the same time, it makes a standing offer to the other States party to the Statute which have not yet deposited a declaration of acceptance. The day one of those States accepts that offer by depositing in its turn its declaration of acceptance, the consensual bond is established and no further condition needs to be fulfilled.[107]

Having further noted that that principle had been affirmed in subsequent cases (the *Temple of Preah Vihear*[108] and *Nicaragua* case*)* the Court would have applied it in the present case without further consideration. However, before doing so, the Court had to consider a number of arguments made by Nigeria. These arguments, the terms of the Court's dismissal of them, as well as strong support for some of them by dissenting Judges in the case and the comments of certain authors on them, are all relevant to the question of the relationship between the Optional Clause system and the law of treaties.

A number of Judges disagreed with the judgment of the majority in relation to their affirmation of the principle in the *Right of Passage* case itself. In general, the dissenting Judges did not endorse the interpretation of the Court in both the *Right of Passage* and in the present case of the provisions contained in Article 36, paragraph 4. Judge Weeramantry persuasively explained that the classical interpretation of this Article presented by the Court in the *Right of Passage* case was incorrect in that it treated the two requisites contained in paragraph 4 separately, although both of them are expressed in imperative terms. Moreover, he pointed out that the basic rule of interpretation requires that "all words in the instrument under interpretation should, as far as possible, be given full efficacy".[109] Similar concerns were voiced by Judge Koroma.[110]

Another issue in respect of the original interpretation in the *Right of Passage* case, and in the judgment under consideration, was the assertion by the Court in the *Right of Passage* case that one factor in support of their interpretation of paragraph 4 of the Optional Clause was the element of uncertainty, which would have been introduced into the Optional Clause system by an additional requirement "that information transmitted by the Secretary-General must reach the Parties to the Statute, or that some period must elapse subsequent to the deposit of the Declaration before it can

---

[107] *Id.*, 291.
[108] Temple of Preah Vihear case, (Cambodia *v.* Thailand), Preliminary Objections, Judgment of 26 May 1961, 1961 ICJ Rep. 17, at 31; Nicaragua case, *supra* note 15, 412.
[109] Dissenting Opinion of Vice-President Weeramantry, *supra* note 1, at 365.
[110] Dissenting Opinion of Judge Koroma, *id.*, at 386.

become effective".[111] This assertion was, of course relied upon by Cameroon,[112] and was reaffirmed by the Court in its judgment.[113]

Nigeria alleged that Article 78 of the VCLT[114] applied to Optional Clause declarations. In its judgement, the Court made it quite clear that the regime provided for depositing and transmitting of declarations is "distinct from the regime envisaged for treaties under the Vienna Convention".[115] For that reason the VCLT may "*only* be applied to declarations *by analogy*" [italics added].[116] Furthermore, the Court found that, in any event, to the extent that there was an analogy between the regime for Optional Clause declarations and the VCLT, this did not apply with respect to Article 78 of the Convention, which "is only designed to lay down the modalities according to which notifications and communications should be carried out",[117] but with respect to Articles 16 and 24 of the VCLT,[118] which govern "the conditions in which a State expressed its consent to be bound by a treaty and those under which a treaty comes into force."[119]

This concept of two analogous processes, governed by different regimes, is somewhat elusive, and some confusion has arisen as to whether, in pointing to the analogy, the Court was not effectively applying the provisions of the VCLT to Optional Clause declarations. For instance, Judge Koroma in his Dissenting Opinion argued that the approach of the Court towards the application of the law of treaties to declarations was contradictory. He stressed the fact that the Court initially adhered to the view that Article 36 paragraph 4 was distinct from the regime of the VCLT, later, however, it took the view that the general rule relating to treaties applied to unilateral declarations. It is submitted that the wording of the judgment quoted above does not bear this interpretation and that this view is further supported by the Court's consideration of the ILC's treatment on the matter.

---

[111] Right of Passage case, *supra* note 4, at 146-147.

[112] *Verbatim* Record of the Proceedings, text on: <http://www.icj-cij.org/icjwww/idocket/icn/icnframe.htm>

[113] See note 1, at 292.

[114] Article 78: "Except as the treaty or the present Convention otherwise provide, any notification or communication to be made by any State under the present Convention shall ... (c) if transmitted to a depositary, be considered as received by the State for which it was intended only when the latter State has been informed by the depositary."

[115] See note 1, at 293.

[116] *Id.*

[117] *Id.*

[118] Article 16: "Unless the treaty otherwise provides, instruments of ratification, acceptance, approval or accession establish the consent of a State to be bound by a treaty upon: ... (b) their deposit with the depositary'. Article 24 further provides that '[w]hen a consent of a State to be bound by a treaty is established on a date after the treaty has come into force, the treaty enters into force for that State on that date, unless the treaty otherwise provides."

[119] See note 1, at 293.

The Court quoted the following important passages from the ILC's Report in which it had stated, firstly, as follows:

> In the case of the deposit of an instrument with a depositary, the problem arises whether the deposit by itself established the legal nexus between the depositing State and other contracting States, or whether the legal nexus arises only upon their being informed by the depositary.[120]

The ILC then continued in the following terms:

> The Commission considered that the existing general rule clearly is that the act of deposit by itself establishes the legal nexus ... This was the view taken by the International Court of Justice in the *Rights of Passage over Indian Territory* (preliminary objections) case in the analogous situation of the deposit of instruments of acceptance of the optional clause under Article 36, paragraph 2, of the Statute of the Court ... Therefore, the existing rule appears to be well-suited.[121]

The Court itself, having quoted these passages, then stated:

> Thus the rules adopted in this sphere by the Vienna Convention correspond to the solution adopted by the Court in the case concerning the *Right of Passage over Indian Territory*. That solution should be maintained.[122]

It appears, therefore, that the Court pointed to the ILC's adoption of the Court's solution in the *Right of Passage* case when discussing the framing of the VCLT as support for the correctness of that decision. In the *Bakassi Peninsula* case, the Court did not apply, by way of analogy, the solution provided by the VCLT in context of Cameroon's the Optional Clause declaration .

Nigeria relied on a further argument, which arose as a result of the Court's decision in the *Nicaragua* case. In that case, the Court said:

> It appears from the requirements of good faith that they [that is to say, Optional Clause declarations] should be treated, by analogy, according to the law of treaties, which requires a reasonable time for withdrawal from or termination of treaties that contain no provision regarding the duration of their validity.[123]

Nigeria alleged that the requirement for a time period, thus established by the Court with respect to the withdrawal of declarations, should, equally, apply in relation to their coming into force. The Court rejected this argument, saying that the conclusion in the *Nicaragua* case "in respect of the

---

[120] *Report of the ILC on the Work of its Eighteenth Session*, YILC (1966), Vol. II, at 172, 201, UN Doc. A/CN.4/191, quoted in the Judgment of the Bakassi Peninsula case, *supra* note 1, at 293-294.
[121] *Id.*
[122] Bakassi Peninsula case, *supra* note 1, at 294.
[123] Nicaragua case, *supra* note 15, at 420.

withdrawal of declarations under the Optional Clause is not applicable to the deposit of declarations.". The Court continued by way of explanation:

> Withdrawal ends existing consensual bonds, while deposit establishes such bonds. The effect of withdrawal is therefore purely and simply to deprive other States which have already accepted the jurisdiction of the Court of the right they had to bring proceedings before it against the withdrawing State. In contrast, the deposit of a declaration does not deprive those States of any accrued right.[124]

An interesting challenge to the correctness of this part of the Court's decision is provided by Elias and Lim.[125] They oppose the concept of accrued rights as being applicable in the context of the Optional Clause declaration. The very function of such a clause is, they say, to ensure the jurisdiction of the Court. They argue that we are not dealing here with any rights, but simply with certain jurisdictional issues, which are subject to a challenge in the event of a dispute.[126] In the event, however, that there is such a right, it may be assumed that this right gives rise to another State's obligation. This was the position taken by Nigeria, which claimed to be deprived of its rights by the deposit of Cameroon's declaration. Due to its lack of knowledge as to the existence of Cameroon's declaration, it argued, it was not aware that certain concessions were made, that this could have impaired its position before the Court, the authors conclude: "the distinction between withdrawal and deposit thus appears to be one difficult to sustain, and the reason for allowing a reasonable period to elapse in the one case would appear to apply equally to the other".[127] In this respect, however, it has to be noted that the Court's view in relation to the *Nicaragua* case was not really based on the issue of the desirability, or fairness, in relation to a requirement for a reasonable time to elapse between the deposit and the coming into effect of Optional Clause declarations. Rather, the Court was persuaded by the lack of the juridical basis requiring such a time period, which did exist in relation to their withdrawal.

The third argument submitted by Nigeria was that the conduct of Cameroon in relation to their acceptance of the Court's jurisdiction, and filing of the suit, "infringes upon the principle of good faith that today plays a larger role in the case-law of the Court than before ...".[128] The Court, in this respect, confirmed its existing jurisprudence, according to which the principle of good faith, while well established, was not in itself a source of obligation in international law, generally, but was a principle which had to

---

[124] Bakassi Peninsula case, *supra* note 1, at 295.
[125] O. Elias and C. Lim, "The *Rights of Passage* Doctrine Revisited: An Opportunity Missed", 12 *LJIL Law* (1999), 231, at 235-238.
[126] *Id.,* at 237-238.
[127] *Id.,* 238.
[128] Bakassi Peninsula case, *supra* note 1, at 296.

be applied in context of the implementation of exiting obligations.[129] Since Cameroon did not infringe any right of Nigeria in the absence of a legal duty to inform Nigeria about its intention to bring proceedings before the Court, Nigeria could not rely solely on the principle of good faith in support of its claim.[130] Furthermore, the Court emphasized that the deposit of Cameroon's declaration was published in the Journal of the United Nations. Thus, Nigeria must be taken to have known about it. It has to be stated, however, that several Judges expressed their concern at the issue of lack of good faith on the part of Cameroon.[131]

The final argument raised by Nigeria in favour of its support of its contention that the Court should not apply the doctrine in the *Right of Passage* case related to the question of reciprocity within the workings of the Optional Clause system. The definition of reciprocity, as applied by the Court in this case, was the classical one derived from several previous cases, for example the *Norwegian Loans* case[132] and the *Nicaragua* case.[133] Nigeria, however, put forward a wider interpretation of reciprocity. It maintained that on the date when Cameroon filed its Application, it (Nigeria) was not aware of Cameroon's acceptance of the Court's compulsory jurisdiction and that:

> [a]ccordingly, it could not have brought an application against Cameroon. There was an absence of reciprocity on that date. The condition contained in the Nigerian Declaration was operative; consequently, the Court does not have jurisdiction to hear the Application.[134]

---

[129] Fitzmaurice, *supra* note 34, Vol. II, at 609-618; H. Thirlway, "The Law and Procedure of the International Court of Justice 1960-1989", 63 *BYIL* (1990), at 7.

[130] Bakassi Peninsula case, note 1, at 297.

[131] E.g. Dissenting opinion of Judge *ad hoc* Ajibola, at 399.

[132] Certain Norwegian Loans (France v. Norway), Merits, Judgment 6 July 1957, 1957 ICJ Rep. 9, at 23: "[r]eciprocity in the case of Declarations accepting the compulsory jurisdiction of the Court enables a Party to invoke a reservation to that acceptance which it has not expressed in its own Declaration but which the other party has expressed in its Declaration ... Reciprocity enables the State which has made the wider acceptance of the jurisdiction of the Court to rely on the reservation laid down by the other Party. There the effect of reciprocity ends.".

[133] Nicaragua case, *supra* note 15, at 419: "the notion of reciprocity is concerned with the scope and substance of the commitments entered into, including reservations, and not with the formal conditions of their creation, duration or extinction. It appears clearly that reciprocity cannot be invoked in order to excuse departure from the terms of a State's own declaration, whatever its scope, limitations or conditions.".

[134] Bakassi Peninsula case, *supra* note 1, at 298. Nigeria recognised the compulsory jurisdiction of the Court "as compulsory *ipso facto* and without special agreement, in relation to any other State accepting the same obligation, that is to say, on the sole condition of reciprocity, the jurisdiction of the International Court of Justice in conformity with Article 36(2) of the Statute of the Court".

This interpretation was opposed by Cameroon as being wrong, both in fact and in law. Nigeria denied the applicability of the precedent in the *Right of Passage* case in which it was said that the notion of reciprocity and that of equality were not "abstract conceptions. They must be related to some provision of the Statute or of the Declarations".[135] Nigeria argued that the definition of reciprocity expressed in its 1965 Declaration was more explicit through the addition of the words "and that is to say on the sole condition of reciprocity". Those words, according to Nigeria, indicated that they supplemented the concept of "coincidence" required by Article 36 paragraph 2 by the element of mutuality inherent by the concept of reciprocity. Nigeria sought to mitigate the effects of the doctrine of the *Right of Passage* case "by creating an equality of risk and precluding that proceedings be brought before the Court by surprise".[136] This interpretation, however, was rejected by the Court. It was of the view that the expression "on the sole condition of reciprocity" "must be understood as explanatory and not adding any further conditions" and not "as a reservation *ratione temporis*".[137] It added that "the principle of reciprocity is not affected by any delay in the receipt of copies of the Declaration by the Parties to the Statute".[138]

This particular statement of the Court prompted Judge Koroma to refer to what he termed "jurisdictional equality", which must be ensured by the Court in its interpretation of the principle of reciprocity under the Optional Clause. Judge Koroma explained that:

> To the extent that an application had been filed against a Party, but one which was not in a position to invoke the jurisdiction of the Court had it felt the need to do so – to that extent, the jurisdictional equality which should exist between the two Parties had not existed.[139]

Thus, the claim of Nigeria was not about the delay in the receipt, but about its lack of knowledge of the actions taken by Cameroon. Similar concerns were voiced by Judge Weeramantry when he said:

> I note the prejudice the *Rights of Passage* case may cause to a party. A ruling which in effect confirms that the filing of a declaration becomes operative the very next moment after it filed could be an embarrassment to a State which is in the process of negotiation with another. Unknown to itself, it could have the ground surreptitiously cut from under its feet, perhaps after it has made some vital concession, in the belief that the matter is still under consideration.[140]

---

[135] Right of Passage case, *supra* note 4, at 145.

[136] Bakassi Peninsula case, *supra* note 1, at 299.

[137] *Id.*, at 300.

[138] *Id.*, at 299, quoting from the Right of Passage case, *supra* note 4, at 145.

[139] Dissenting Opinion of Judge Koroma, *supra* note 1, at 389.

[140] Dissenting Opinion of Judge Weeramantry, *supra* note 1, at 375.

The *Bakassi Peninsula* case indicates clearly that the legal character of the Optional Clause system, generally, and of the Optional Clause declarations, in particular, still remains very much a mystery. The main point at issue is the applicability of the general law of treaties to declarations. The Court strongly endorsed the importance of the consensual basis of the Optional Clause system in the *Right of Passage* case when it said that the deposit of a State's Optional Clause declaration brought into existence the "consensual bond, which is the basis of the Optional clause".[141] On the other hand, the Court held that that bond, or at least those aspects of it included in the deposit of declarations, were not governed by the regime of the VCLT. The principles of treaty law contained in the VCLT, and generally, were applicable to the Optional Clause system and Optional Clause declarations, if at all "only by analogy". It is not entirely clear, however, what this term implies, or to what extent this analogy is applicable. States, at least, appear to have a somewhat selective approach towards particular provisions of the VCLT in the context of declarations. For example, Nigeria pleaded the applicability of Article 78 paragraph (c), but not of Articles 16-24 of the VCLT.[142] This case evidenced the lack of agreement as to the understanding of the fundamental notions, procedural and substantive, of the Optional Clause system. Procedural issues, such as the legal character of the notification by the Secretary-General of the Untied Nations and the time when the Optional Clause declaration takes effect, remain unsolved. Procedural issues in turn have an effect on the substantive issues, such as the role of good faith and the rights and obligations of States-participants in the Optional Clause system.

4.6 The *Fisheries Jurisdiction* Case

While the *Bakassi Peninsula* case, in so far as it is relevant to this chapter, largely involved consideration and reaffirmation of the principles adopted in the *Right of Passage* case, the *Fisheries Jurisdiction* case[143] involved consideration and reaffirmation of the principles in relation to the legal character and the interpretation of Optional Clause declarations (as formulated in the *Anglo-Iranian Oil Company* case and in the *Phosphates in Morocco* case).[144] The *Fisheries Jurisdiction* dispute arose in relation to the

---

[141] Right of Passage case, *supra* note 4, at 143. For quotation see note 103.

[142] See note 114.

[143] See note 2.

[144] See, e.g., B. Kwiatkowska, "Fisheries Jurisdiction *(Spain v Canada)*", 93 *AJIL* (1999), at 502; A.P. Linares, "The ICJ Canada-Spain Fishing Dispute", 8 *RECIEL* (1999), at 215; L. de la Fayette, "The Fisheries Jurisdiction Case *(Spain v. Canada)*, Judgment on Jurisdiction of 4 December 1998", 48 *ICLQ* (1999), at 664.

1994 amendment of the *Canadian Coastal Fisheries Act,* amendments to the regulations implementing the Act, and to an incident which occurred in implementation of this Act.[145] This incident, which took place on 9 March 1995, involved the pursuit, boarding and seizure on the high seas by Canada of the Spanish fishing vessel *Estai.*

Both Canada and Spain had accepted the compulsory jurisdiction of the Court. Canada originally accepted the compulsory jurisdiction of the Court in 1985. Bill C-29 amended the *Coastal Fisheries Protection Act* in order to prevent foreign vessels from fishing straddling fish stocks in the regulatory area of the Northwest Atlantic Fisheries Organization ("NAFO"). This geographical area stretches beyond the Canadian exclusive economic zone ("EEZ"). On the same day that Bill C-29 was adopted, Canada, filed a new Optional Clause declaration, which included a reservation specifically aimed at the exclusion from the jurisdiction of the Court of disputes, which might arise in relation to measures taken by Canada pursuant to the amended *Coastal Fisheries Protection Act.* The relevant parts of the Canadian Declaration read as follows:

> (2) ... the Government of Canada accepts as compulsory *ipso facto* and without special convention, on condition of reciprocity, the jurisdiction of the International Court of Justice, in conformity with paragraph 2 of Article 36 of the Statute of the Court, until such time as notice may be given to terminate acceptance, over all disputes arising after the present declaration with regard to situations or facts subsequent to this declaration, other than ...

> (d) disputes arising out of concerning conservation and management measures taken by Canada with respect to vessels fishing in the NAFO regulatory Area, as defined by the Convention on Future Multilateral Co-Operation in the Northwest Atlantic Fisheries, 1978, and the enforcement of such measures.

Following the *Estai* incident, on 28 March 1994, Spain brought the case before the Court. Spain raised the following points: that the legislation of Canada, insofar as it claimed to exercise jurisdiction over ships flying a foreign flag on the high seas, outside the EEZ of Canada, was not applicable to Spain; that Canada was bound to refrain from any repetition of the acts complained of, and to offer Spain the reparation that was due, in the form of an indemnity the amount of which should cover all damages and injuries occasioned; and that the boarding on the high seas of the Spanish ship, the measures of coercion and the exercise of jurisdiction over the ship and over its captain constituted a concrete violation of the principles and norms of

---

[145] On 12 May 1994, following the adoption of Bill C-8, Canada also amended Section 25 of its Criminal Code relating to the use of force by police officers and other peace officers enforcing the law. This section applied as well for fisheries protection officers, since their duties incidentally included those of peace officers. On May 1994, the Coastal Fisheries Protections Regulations were amended. They were further amended on 3 March 1994.

international law.[146] The case, as a whole, concerned a large number of international law issues. In this chapter, however, the point which will be discussed is that of jurisdiction.

The Court made a number of very important statements concerning the legal character of Optional Clause declarations and of reservations attached to them. Firstly, it said that a declaration of acceptance of the compulsory jurisdiction of the Court "whether there are specified limits set to that acceptance or not, is a unilateral act of State sovereignty".[147] That statement, through the addition of the words "act of State sovereignty" reaffirms in even stronger terms the unilateral nature of Optional Clause declarations originally enunciated in the *Phosphates in Morocco* case. The words "whether there are specified limits" are also significant in relation to the emphasis that the Court placed upon the freedom of States in relation, not only to whether they submit to the Court's jurisdiction within the Optional Clause system at all, but also with respect to the terms upon which they do so. In this respect, the Court stated:

> It is for each State, in formulating its declaration, to decide upon the limits it places upon its acceptance of the jurisdiction of the Court: 'This jurisdiction only exists within the limits which it has been accepted' (*Phosphates in Morocco*, Judgment, 1938, *PCIJ Series A/B*, No. 74, at 23)[148]

The Court then quoted and approved the following passage from the *Nicaragua* case, stressing the unilateral character of Optional Clause declarations:

> Declarations of acceptance of the compulsory jurisdiction of the Court are facultative unilateral engagements that States are absolutely free to make or not to make. In making the declaration, a State is equally free either to do so unconditionally and without limit of time for its duration, or to qualify it with conditions or reservations.[149]

The Court also observed:

> Conditions or reservations thus do not by their terms derogate from a wider acceptance already given. Rather, they operate to define the parameters of the State's acceptance of the compulsory jurisdiction of the Court.[150]

The above passages take Optional Clause declarations very far from the notion of a treaty instrument. The Court was quite explicit in stating that Optional Clause declarations resemble neither a multilateral treaty to which declarant States adhere, subject to reservations, nor exhibit any (but in the

---

[146] Fisheries Jurisdiction case, note 2, at 437.
[147] *Id.*, 453.
[148] *Id.*
[149] *Id.*, at 455 and Nicaragua case, *supra* note 15.
[150] Fisheries Jurisdiction case, *supra* note 2, at 453.

most general sense) mutual intentions as between the different declarant States. On the other hand, the Court also affirmed the consensual aspect of the Optional Clause system as enunciated in the *Bakassi Peninsula* case and the *Right of Passage* case:

> At the same time it [an Optional Clause declaration] establishes a consensual bond and potential jurisdictional link with the other states which have made declarations pursuant to Article 36, paragraph 2, of the Statute, and 'makes a standing offer to other States party to the Statute which have not yet deposited a declaration of acceptance'.[151]

Turning now to the question of interpretation, it will be seen that the main jurisdictional problems in this case centered on the interpretation of sub-paragraph (d) of the Canadian declaration. In particular, the issue at hand was not so much the actual meaning of the words included in the Canadian declaration, but the manner of their interpretation. The question before the Court was whether the Canadian reservation should be interpreted in a manner that did not undermine the system of compulsory jurisdiction established under Article 36 and consequently the Canadian reservation could not be understood to exclude from the Court's jurisdiction acts contrary to basic norms of international law; or whether the interpretation of Canada, that demanded that the Court give full effect to the intentions of the declarant State when interpreting Optional Clause declarations in order not to exceed the limits of the State's consent, should prevail.

Spain claimed that the Canadian reservation was invalid or inoperative, due to its incompatibility with the Statute of the Court, the Charter of the United Nations and with international law in general.[152] Spain further asserted that reservations to Optional Clause declarations should not be interpreted in such a manner as to allow reserving states "to undermine the system of compulsory jurisdiction" and advocated the application of the principle of effectiveness to the interpretation of reservations by explaining that reservations should be interpreted by reference to the object and purpose of the declaration, which was ultimately the acceptance of the compulsory jurisdiction of the Court.[153] Furthermore, Spain claimed that though it did not support a "restrictive interpretation" of Optional Clause declarations, it was a proponent of the most limited scope permitted in the context of the general rules laid down by Article 31 of the VCLT.[154] As to the other rules of interpretation, Spain was in favour of the *contra proferentem* rule. According to this rule an ambiguous text must be construed against the party which drafted it. In the view of Spain, this manner of interpretation was of

---

[151] *Id.*, at 453 and Bakassi Peninsula case, *supra* note 1, at 291.
[152] *Id.*, at 451-452.
[153] *Id.*, 452.
[154] *Id.*

particular importance in relation to unilaterally drafted instruments, such as Optional Clause declarations and reservations to them. Finally, Spain claimed that a reservation to an Optional Clause declaration must be interpreted according to the Statute of the Court, the Charter of the United Nations and general international law.[155]

Canada on the other hand, underlined the unilateral elements of Optional Clause declarations and relied heavily on the rules of interpretation for the Optional Clause already laid down in the *Anglo-Iranian Oil Company* case where it was stated that declarations under Article 36(2) and reservations thereto have to be interpreted in an natural way, in their context and with particular regard for the intention of the declarant State.[156]

The Court rejected the arguments of Spain, and reasserted the principles of interpretation of Optional Clause declarations enunciated in the *Anglo-Iranian Oil Company* case.[157] The Court went on to say, also in accordance with the principles in *Anglo-Iranian Oil Company*, that the intention of a State may not only be deduced from the text of the relevant clauses, but also from the context in which the clause is to be read, and from the examination of evidence connected with its preparation and the purposes intended to be served. For that reason it also took into account Canadian ministerial statements, parliamentary debates, legislative proposals and press communiqués.[158]

The emphasis on the importance on the object and purpose intended to be served by the Optional Clause, brings us to the issue of the principle of effectiveness, with respect to which the judgment involves an important further affirmation of the unilateral and voluntary nature of Optional Clause declarations. Spain had argued in favour of the applicability of the principle of effectiveness on the basis of the object and purpose of the declaration being acceptance of the compulsory jurisdiction of the Court. However, though the Court affirmed the validity of the principle of effectiveness as a principle suitable for treaty interpretation, it rejected its application to the Optional Clause:

> Certainly, this principle has an important role in the law of treaties and in the jurisprudence of this Court; however, what is required in the first place for a reservation to a declaration made under Article 36, paragraph 2, of the Statute, is that it should be interpreted in a manner compatible with the effect sought by the reserving State.[159]

---

[155] *Id.*

[156] *Id.*

[157] *Id.*, at 454.

[158] *Id.* It may be noted that in support of this, the Court cited its jurisprudence relating to the law of treaties in Aegean Sea Continental Shelf (Greece *v.* Turkey), Judgment of 19 December 1978, 1978 ICJ Rep. 3, at 29.

[159] *Id.*, at 455.

Similarly, as far as the *contra proferentem* rule is concerned, the Court recognised its validity as a possible tool for the interpretation of contractual instruments, but stated clearly that this principle was not a suitable tool for the interpretation of unilateral declarations under Article 36(2).[160]

Despite the above pronouncements emphasizing the unilateral nature of declarations made under the Optional Clause, the Court repeated certain statements made in the *Bakassi Peninsula* case, and concluded that the regime relating to Optional Clause declarations was not identical with that of treaties under the VCLT, and that the provisions of that convention "may *only apply analogously* to the extent compatible with the *sui generis* character of the unilateral acceptance of the Court's jurisdiction".[161]

Finally, the Court clarified another important question regarding the interpretation of reservations. It explained that:

> There is a fundamental distinction between the acceptance by a State of the Court's jurisdiction and the compatibility of particular acts with international law. The former requires consent. The latter question can only be reached when the Court deals with merits, after having established its jurisdiction and having heard full legal argument by both parties.[162]

Thus, the Court rejected the contention of Spain that reservations have to be interpreted according to the principle of legality, in the sense that a declarant State should be precluded from excepting from its submission to the jurisdiction of the Court cases concerning actions contrary to international law. The decision of the Court, taking into account the above considerations, concluded that the dispute was within the terms of the Canadian reservation, and for that reason the Court did not posses jurisdiction in this case.[163]

The Court's judgment included a number of dissenting opinions.[164] The main disagreement related to the decision of the Court that the issue of the legality of the actions of Canada was a matter to be considered as part of the merits, and not an issue of jurisdiction. To that end, judges criticized the general method of interpretation adopted by the Court relating to Optional Clause declarations and argued in favour of an interpretation closer to the one adopted by Spain. According to Judge Weeramantry, the Court failed to accord the requisite importance to the principle of effectiveness,[165] whereas Judges Ranjeva, Vereshchetin and Torres-Bernandez criticised what they considered as an excessive emphasis on the subjective criterion of the

---

[160] *Id.*, at 454-455.

[161] *Id.*, at 453.

[162] *Id.*, at 456.

[163] *Id.*, at 457.

[164] The following judges attached dissenting opinions: Vereshchetin; Vice President Weeramantry; Ranjeva; Bedjaoui and Judge *ad hoc* Torres Bernardes.

[165] Dissenting Opinion of Judge Weeramantry, *id.*, at 508.

intentions of the author State and on the unilateral nature of declarations of acceptance of the Court's compulsory jurisdiction.[166]

In conclusion, the *Fisheries Jurisdiction* case is yet another example of the difficulties facing States, and the Court itself, in attempting to find a uniform understanding of the legal (and extra-legal) aspects of Optional Clause declarations and reservations. Firstly, they must be treated as one unity, in accordance with the principle of integration. Further, both declarations and reservations must be interpreted within their ordinary meaning ("natural and reasonable"). Owing, however, to their special characteristics as unilateral acts, the intentions of States must be taken into account and the relevant circumstances under which they were formulated taken into consideration. The Court accepted the application of the VCLT rules to declarations, but only by way of analogy, and only to the extent to which they were compatible with the *sui generis* character of Optional Clause declarations. Most importantly, however, the Court made it clear that in order to ascertain its jurisdiction, consent to jurisdiction and not the legality of the subject matter of a particular reservation, is what mattered. As the Court stated in the Judgment:

> The Court has already indicated that there is no rule of interpretation which requires that reservation be interpreted so as to cover only acts compatible with international law ... [T]his is to confuse the legality of the acts with consent to jurisdiction ...[167]

5. Concluding Remarks

As evidenced in the *Bakassi Peninsula* case and the *Fisheries Jurisdiction* case, the main issue which keeps the determination of the legal character of Optional Clause declarations so elusive, is their relationship with treaties. As

---

[166] Dissenting Opinion of Judge Ranjeva, *id.*, at 568-569: "In endorsing a unilateral interpretation of the reservation ... the Court has failed to appreciate the nature of the network of relationships constituted by the various declarations of acceptance under Article 36, paragraph 2,of the Statute. The relations between the litigant parties come into being at the time when the condition formulated by the respondent -including any reservation- are accepted by the applicant when it files its application. From that point in time, we are no longer dealing with a single, unilateral intention, that of the respondent, but with the common intention of the two parties, as formed at the moment when the intention of the author of the reservation and meets that of the applicant State, an event which creates the jurisdictional link between the litigant parties. Consequently, when faced with a common intent concealing an underlying divergence of views ... the Court cannot lightly lay aside the traditional rules for the interpretation of treaties"; Dissenting Opinion of Judge Vereshchetin, *id.*, at 575-580; Dissenting Opinion of Judge *ad hoc* Torres-Bernardez, *id.*, at 639-644.

[167] Fisheries Jurisdiction case, *supra* note 2, at paragraph 79.

pointed out elsewhere in this chapter, neither the Court nor international lawyers have yet produced a clear-cut and uniform definition of what an Optional Clause declaration is and how it relates to treaties. Thus, the *Fisheries Jurisdiction* case emphasized the unilateral nature of Optional Clause declarations – and the absolute freedom of States to define the parameters of their acceptance of the jurisdiction of the Court within the Optional Clause system – more strongly than ever, while still putting forward the consensual relationship to which they give rise. At the same time, the Court again stated that, whether consensual or not, the Optional Clause system does not fall directly under the régime of the VCLT, the provisions of which may be applicable in relation to Optional Clause declarations, and if at all, only by analogy, and only to the extent compatible with their unilateral character.

Faced with this ambiguity relating to the definition of the legal characteristics of the Optional Clause system, generally, and of Optional Clause declarations, in particular, it is legitimate to analyse the Court's decisions in relation to the interpretation of Optional Clause declarations and to compare these with the principles of interpretation of normal treaty documents as a key to their legal character. In this respect, one may say of the canons, or rules, of interpretation relating to normal treaty documents, and which go beyond the text of the treaty documents themselves, that they, broadly speaking, exist for the purposes of establishing the terms of the treaty as they may be deemed to have been mutually agreed. They are so "deemed to have been" because, in cases of a dispute, the position almost by definition is that there is no real accord as to the terms of the treaty and the Court has in effect to some extent to construct this "accord" itself. The result of this process will not necessarily, or indeed, normally embody the actual subjective intentions of both parties, and may well actually embody the subjective intentions of neither, or none, of them. The position, however, adopted by the Court in relation to Optional Clause declarations is very different. Here, in perhaps the most stark expression of the principle involved, the Court (in a passage which has been quoted above, but which bears repetition) stated in the *Fisheries Jurisdiction* case:

> What is required in the first place for a reservation to a declaration made under Article 36, paragraph 2 of the Statute, is that it should be interpreted in a manner compatible with the effect sought by the reserving State.[168]

One aspect of the distinction is, of course, that unlike treaties, Optional Clause declarations do not result from negotiations. In addition, it is suggested that the distinction actually goes beyond, or deeper, than this. The question that seems to arise quite forcefully is: if Optional Clause declarations are treaty documents in any sense at all, what kind of treaty

---

[168] *Id.*, at 455.

documents are they? One possible answer might have been that they are at least analogous to documents which relate to the adherence to a multilateral convention. However, that interpretation, which might have been possible on the basis of Article 36 of the Statute as originally conceived (and which has not been without support subsequently, for instance among some of the dissenting Judges in the *Anglo-Iranian Oil Company* case) really ceased to be tenable at all when, as developed in practice and endorsed in the Court's jurisprudence, States were allowed total latitude in the imposition of conditions, limitations or "reservations" upon their acceptance of the Court's jurisdiction within the Optional Clause system. In the absence of that latitude, that is to say, were States' ability to make reservations been as restrictive as appears to have been intended by the original drafters of the ICJ Statute, there would have been a common régime of submission to the jurisdiction of the Court within the system, to which, it could have been said, States were adhering to by deposit of their Optional Clause declarations; and the interpretation of those declarations would have been made with references to that common régime.

In such a case, the application of the principle of effectiveness put forward by Spain in the *Fisheries Jurisdiction* case might have been valid. However, of course, it was specifically in rejection of that application that the Court made the statement of the effect to be achieved in interpreting an Optional Clause declaration. If, one accepts that there is no analogy with a multilateral convention and that the nature of the consensual relationship between declarant States within the Optional Clause system is bilateral, one is still left with a problem as to what kind of treaty document, in relation to that bilateral relationship, an Optional Clause declaration is.

The Court has, on a number of occasions (*Right of Passage* case, *Bakassi Peninsula* case and the *Fisheries Jurisdiction* case) used the concept of offer and acceptance to illustrate the nature of Optional Clause declarations. The validity of this illustration is questionable. An offer document, whether addressed to a particular party or to the world at large is intended to directly engage the mind of another party which accepts it. Whereas, an acceptance is an acceptance of one particular offer. Jointly, they form a contract, and will, in general, be interpreted or construed together as a whole (in accordance with the principle of integration) to arrive at the terms of the contract between the parties. This is not at all the case with Optional Clause declarations. Although an Optional Clause declaration may be deposited with a particular party, or dispute, in mind (this indeed was the case in connection with Cameroon's Optional Clause declaration, which was the subject matter of the *Bakassi Peninsula* case), this is not generally the case. Furthermore, in no case can an Optional Clause declaration really be said to be intended to engage directly the mind of any counterparty, with a view to obtaining an acceptance of that declaration. The fact is that, the more one analyses the issue, the more tenuous the connection between Optional Clause declarations and the law relating to treaties seems to become.

Rosenne focuses on this point. According to him, reliance on principles of general international law in relation to Optional Clause declarations is only relevant in the event of a State's amendment or withdrawal of its declaration when there is no specified time limit on the declaration, or express reservation providing for withdrawal.[169] He further observes that the problem which arises is to what extent the law of treaties fills the *lacuna* in respect of those aspects of unilateral declarations which have not yet been covered by relevant practice in the system of compulsory jurisdiction. To this effect the VCLT becomes relevant. Firstly, a State which is party to the Optional Clause system has bound itself by way of an obligation, which is not unlike other international obligations, and must, therefore be interpreted and implemented in good faith. This obligation, however, lacks precision and works only in relation to other States which accept the same obligation. The scope of this obligation is defined by the principle of reciprocity.[170] This approach was endorsed by the Court, which in the *Nicaragua* case said as follows:

> In fact, declarations, even though they are unilateral acts, establish a series of bilateral engagements with other States accepting the same obligation of compulsory jurisdiction, in which the conditions, reservations and time-limit clauses are taken into consideration. In the establishment of this network of engagements, which constitute the Optional Clause system, the principle of good faith plays an important role.[171]

Rosenne further explains the substantive differences between treaties and unilateral declarations. He argues that such difference is not just due to the unilateral character of declarations, since "interlocked unilateral acts undoubtedly can constitute a form of international treaty".[172] Rather, the difference is to be found in: (i) the notion of the function of reservations to treaties, which are entirely different to reservations to Optional Clause declarations; and (ii) in the fact that declarations may be modified or terminated unilaterally. The first of these two points is underlined by the description of the function of "reservations" to Optional Clause declarations contained in the Court's judgment in the *Fisheries Jurisdiction* case, which read:

---

[169] Rosenne, *supra* note 24, at 822-823.

[170] *Id.*, 823.

[171] Nicaragua case, *supra* note 15, at 418.

[172] Rosenne, *supra* note 24, 825, citing Maritime Delimitation and Territorial Questions between Qatar and Bahrain (Qatar *v.* Bahrain), Jurisdiction and Admissibility, Judgment of 1 July 1994, 1994 ICJ Rep. 6, at 130.

Conditions or reservations thus do not by their terms derogate from a wider acceptance already given. Rather, they operate to define the parameters of the State's acceptance of the compulsory jurisdiction of the Court.[173]

Having scrutinized all legal characteristics of compulsory jurisdiction, Rosenne came to the conclusion "that the true treaty element is provided only by the integral Charter and Statute" . This combined instrument establishes a system available on a voluntary basis to all States party to the Statute. He states further that this system contains three elements common to all parties to the ICJ Statute, regardless of whether they have accepted the compulsory jurisdiction, namely: (a) recognition of the power of the Court to settle any matter of its own jurisdiction ; (b) recognition of the binding force and finality of the judgments by the Court; (c) acknowledgment of the obligation of compliance with the decisions of the Court deriving from Article 94 of the Charter and of the powers of the Security Council relating to that.[174] According to Rosenne, by submitting an Optional Clause declaration, a State makes a general offer to other States with similar declarations, on terms which coincide with one another. However, this declaration cannot be deemed as accepted by any other States until a relevant State relies on it in context of a specific case: "It it only then that latent obligations are perfected".[175]

Undoubtedly, the transaction between States under the Optional Clause system is unique. It is, as Rosenne warns, unwise and uncautious to attempt to apply the principles of the law of treaties *en bloc* to it.[176] He further accepts the view, expressed as well by Waldock and Jennings, that the system of compulsory jurisdiction is *sui generis,* and that obligations which flow from it are also *sui generis.* Thus, they should not be assimilated with the type of obligations which are regulated by the law of treaties since "it is not on all fours with them."[177] This ultimately is the view taken by Elias and Lim, when they concluded on the question of the analogy between Optional

---

[173] Fisheries Jurisdiction case, *supra* note 2, at 453.

[174] Rosenne, *supra* note 24, 837.

[175] *Id.,* 828.

[176] *Id.,* 830: "This unique bond existing between two states engaged upon litigation when both have or may be deemed to have accepted the compulsory jurisdiction, and the extreme difficulty of pinning down exactly what this bond is, who are its other parties, and when it arose (except in relation to the date of the institution of the proceedings) otherwise than in the context of an actual case, impose the maximum of caution before applying *en bloc* the general law of international treaties to that part of the transaction which supplies the consensual basis of the jurisdiction. The significance of *dicta* of the Court drawing attention to the unilateral character of a declaration accepting the compulsory jurisdiction and stressing that such a text is not a treaty text resulting from negotiations between twp or more States lies precisely in their warning not to be so quick in applying the general law of treaties to a declarations accepting the compulsory jurisdiction."

[177] *Id.,* 831.

Clause declarations and the law of treaties in relation to the dispute in the *Bakassi Peninsula* case*:*

> It is submitted that the analogy with the treaties is of very limited utility. Declarations under the Optional Clause are not treaties and the analogy is unreliable in the context of jurisdictional skirmishes of the sort herein encountered.[178]

The problem is that with the principles of interpretation, as developed in relation to treaties and adopted by the VCLT, being applicable to Optional Clause declarations only to a limited extent, and being subject to being overruled by other principles stemming from the unique of undertakings within the Optional Clause system (in particular the unilateral and voluntary nature of Optional Clause declarations), the way is open for case-by-case decision-making. This does not contribute to the stability of international transactions. Alternatively, it is proposed that the Court will fall back on its own jurisprudence (such as in the *Right of Passage* case*)*, which will cause States to claim that the Court does not take into consideration the changes in international law during the passage of time, and in some cases, as in the *Bakassi Peninsula* case, will result in a feeling of injustice done to parties to the dispute.

The *Fisheries Jurisdiction* case calls for one more comment concerning the refusal of the Court to interpret Canada's reservation in the light of the legality in international law regarding the matters, which the reservation sought to exclude from Canada's submission to the jurisdiction of the Court. Although it is understandable that certain judges expressed concern as to the content of the reservation, it would be difficult to reconcile the Court's scrutiny as to the legality of certain reservations with the overriding principle of the consent of States to the Court's jurisdiction. One has to agree with the Court's judgment when it said:

> In point of fact, reservations from the Court's jurisdiction may be made by States for a variety of reasons; sometimes precisely because they feel vulnerable about the legalityof their position or policy. Nowhere in the Court's case-law it has been suggested that interpretation in accordance with the legality under international law of the matters exempted from the jurisdiction of the Court is a rule that governs the interpretation of such reservations.[179]

Thus, both the *Bakassi Peninsula* case and the *Fisheries Jurisdiction* case clearly indicate that the legal character of declarations and the canons of their interpretation have retained a good deal of their mystique. This results in the situation whereby:

---

[178] Elias and Lim, *supra* note 125, 241.
[179] Fisheries Jurisdiction case, *supra* note 2, at 455-456.

A substantial proportion of the Court's hearings and judgments were directed not towards the substantive issues of international law at the heart of a case, but at issues concerning its own jurisdiction. With declining emphasis on the Optional clause declaration and the increased use of *ad hoc* referrals to the Court, this necessary preoccupation with jurisdictional issues is receding somewhat – another healthy trend.[180]

---

[180] R. Higgins, *supra* note 11, at 191.

CHAPTER SIX

Methods of Expression of Consent to be Bound by a Treaty*

1. Introduction

The issue of consent to be bound has recently gained some currency. This has been the result of what has been termed "creative legal engineering",[1] pursuant to which some departure has been made in the practice of certain international organisations from the basic principle of international law that a State cannot be bound by a treaty without its consent.[2] This trend can be

---

* An expanded version of this chapter will appear in a forthcoming issue of the *Nordic Journal of International Law* (2005), published by Brill Academic Publishers.

[1] See R. Lefeber, "Creative Legal Engineering", 13 *LJIL* (2000), at 1. See also R. Churchill and G. Ulfstein, "Autonomous Institutional Arrangements in Multilateral Environmental Agreements: A Little-Noticed Phenomenon in International Law", 94 *AJIL* (2000), at 623-659; J. Brunnée, "COPing with Consent: Law-Making Under Multilateral Environmental Agreements", 15 *LJIL* (2002), at 1-52; N. Lavranos, "Multilateral Environmental Agreements: Who Makes the Binding Decisions", *European Environmental Law Review*, February 2002, at 44-50; G. Loibl, "Conference of Parties and the Modification of Obligations: the Example of International Environmental Agreements", (to be published, on file with authors).

[2] Article 11 of the VCLT reads as follows: "[T]he consent of a State to be bound by a treaty may be expressed by signature, exchange of instruments constituting a treaty, ratification acceptance, approval or accession, or by other means so agreed". States are free to choose the means of expressing consent to be bound by treaties, and in general, there are few major issues relating to the question of consent to be bound as set out in Article 11. One of these issues relates to the problem of supremacy of either ratification or signature, which has only occasionally arisen in practice; see, e.g., chapter 11 below, at section 3.1. On this subject see, e.g., Lord Arnold McNair, *The Law of Treaties* (1961), at 131-155; Hans Blix, "The Requirement of Ratification", 30 *BYIL* (1953), at 352-379; G.G. Fitzmaurice, "Do Treaties

---

seen to have its roots in the introduction of tacit consent and/or "opting-out" procedures, as noted in the decision-making procedures of some United Nations specialised agencies, such as the International Civil Aviation Organisation,[3] and later in other organisations, in particular fisheries commissions (such as the Northeast Atlantic Fishery Commission, the Northwest Atlantic Fisheries Organisation, and the International Baltic Sea Fishery Commission, and also within some multilateral environmental agreements.[4]

The essence of these tacit consent/opting-out procedures is that decision-making acts are adopted by a majority vote, but Parties may lodge objections and thus avoid being bound by the act. This means that a member state is automatically bound by the act of the organisation unless it takes specific action to avoid being so bound (i.e. by "opting out").[5] The intention of this system is to combine the principle of sovereignty (the right of a member state to lodge an objection) whilst, by making it politically unattractive to lodge an objection, encouraging the creation of universally applicable rules and standards for all parties to the treaty in question.

This raises issues of consent to be bound by a treaty as well as the issue of the law-making or rule-making acts of international organisations. The law-making power of organisations has its roots in the constituent treaty of the organisation, so that one might refer to a "derivative treaty obligation",[6] i.e., although the organisation legislates directly for States, its legal power to do so is ultimately founded in the treaty establishing the organisation. There is a difference of opinion as to the theoretical basis of the acts of international organisations operating under the opting-out system. The question is whether these acts have an independent law-making character, or whether they constitute, in effect, an agreement analogous to an agreed amendment to the treaty between the states concerned.[7] On the one hand, the

---

Need Ratification?", 5 *BYIL* (1934), at 113-137. This chapter will not dwell on the classical law relating to the methods of expression of consent to be bound by a treaty as codified in Articles 11-17 of the VCLT, but the main focus of this chapter will be on "other means so agreed", as stated in Article 11.

[3] See F. Kirgis, "Specialised Law-Making Processes", in O. Schachter and C. Joyner (eds.), *The United Nations Legal Order* (1995), at 66-76.

[4] These are described by Churchill and Ulfstein, *supra* note 1, as "autonomous institutional arrangements".

[5] On the subject see in particular: K. Skubiszewski, "A New Source of the Law of Nations Resolutions of International Organizations", in *Receuil d'études de droit international en hommage à Paul Guggenheim* (1968), at 508-520.

[6] P. Szasz, "International Law-Making", in E. Brown-Weiss (ed.), *Environmental Change and International Law: New Challenges and Dimensions* (1992), 41-74, at 65.

[7] R. Ago, "Die Internationalen Organizationen und Ihre Funktionen im inneren Tätigkeitsgebiet der Staaten", *27 Rechtsfragen der Internationalen Organisation* (1955), at 20-38; H. Blix, *Treaty Making Power* (1960), at 293-296; H. Kelsen, *Principles of*

view has been expressed by some authors that such acts, having been taken by a majority vote of the organisation concerned, and becoming binding on the Member tates without their explicit agreement (as was traditionally always required for the formation of an international treaty), do have law-making character independent of the will of the Member states.[8] If this is the case, then there would seem to be no real occasion, *at the time of its adoption*, for expressing consent to be bound by the new provision or rule.[9] On the other hand, there is the view that "opting-out" is simply a system developed for the purpose of accelerating and simplifying the process of concluding or amending a treaty, since all acts of the organisation are based upon agreement (that is, upon bringing the will of the States into accord) and not upon any unilateral legislative powers of the organisation concerned.[10] In this case, the consent of the parties to the new provision is expressed by their omission to opt out of it – and this tacit expression of consent, or expression by omission, is indeed a new means of expression of consent to be bound which lacks one of the characteristics of traditional means enumerated in Article 11 of the VCLT. In the case of the true opting-out procedure, the latter interpretation is probably the true one, though it can be said that, whatever the theoretical nature of the acts of an international organisation within the "opting-out" system may be, the adoption of majority voting within the organisation, coupled with absence of a requirement for express acceptance by a member state, tends, in practice, to emphasise the law-making nature of the acts of the organisation.

The "opting-out" procedure could be considered as the precursor of the new developments relating to the issue of the expression of consent to be bound. Further changes to the absolute requirement of consent have taken place most visibly in certain multilateral environmental agreements in which can be observed the expansion of legislative power of Conferences or Meetings of the Parties ("COPs" or "MOPs") can be observed.[11] This

---

International Law (1952), at 365-367. See also J. Sommer, "Environmental Law-Making by International Organisations", 56 *ZaöRV* (1996), at 268.

[8] K. Skubiszewski, *Uchwaly Prawotworcze Organizacji Miendzynarodowych Przeglad Zagadnien I Analiza Wstepna* (Law-making Resolutions of International Organisations. Survey of Problems and preliminary Analysis) (1965), at 69.

[9] Churchill and Ulfstein express a similar view and treat the opting-out procedure as genuine law-making by COPs (as opposed to indirect law-making as in the event of e.g. the adoption of protocols); *supra* note 1, at 638-640.

[10] G.J.Tunkin, *Theory of International Law* (1974), at 106 (translated and with introduction by W. Butler).

[11] Such as for example, the 1985 Vienna Convention on the Protection of Ozone Layer (the "Vienna Convention of the Protection of Ozone Layer") and the 1987 Montreal Protocol on the Substances that Deplete the Ozone Layer (the "Montreal Protocol"); the 1992 United Framework Convention on Climate Change (the "Climate Change Convention"); and the 1997 Kyoto Protocol (see section 3 below).

phenomenon is aptly described by Churchill and Ulfstein as "autonomous institutional arrangements", which they believe "... marks a distinct and different approach to institutional collaboration between States, being more informal and flexible, and often innovative in relation to norm creation and compliance".[12]

In order to facilitate the sometimes difficult treaty adoption and amendment procedure in international law, the structure of most MEAs is three-tiered. The first tier is a framework convention; the second a protocol to the convention, which is an independent treaty, creating more detailed obligations for the parties (not all parties to the framework convention are parties to the protocol); and the third, annexes and/or appendices containing technical data, such as the list of controlled substances, by either the framework convention or a protocol.[13] COPs and MOPs are the bodies set up under framework conventions and protocols respectively, consisting of representatives of the parties. They have regulatory powers to adopt fundamental decisions, relating to all aspects of the treaty regime and also its annexes and appendices. These powers of the COPs/MOPs also extend to so-called adjustment procedures, which have the effect of amending the obligations of States under the treaties. These will be discussed below, as in some cases (such as the 1987 Montreal Protocol), they present new legal structures that differ from the traditional approaches to the question of expression of consent to be bound.[14]

These growing powers of COPs and MOPs raise questions of sovereignty, efficiency and legitimacy.[15] An example is the decision relating to the Basel Convention, on the prohibition of transboundary movement of hazardous wastes originating in OECD countries and directed to non-OECD

---

[12] Churchill and Ulfstein, *supra* note 1, at 625. According to these same authors "a special feature of many MEAs is that they establish an institutional framework of what we have called autonomous institutional arrangements, in form of COPs, subsidiary bodies, and secretariats to develop and control their parties' environmental commitments, rather than setting up informal IGOs of the traditional kind ... In spite of their formal denomination we nevertheless conclude that these self-governing, treaty-based AIAs [autonomous institutional arrangements] of MEAs may be considered IGOs, albeit of a less formal, more *ad hoc* nature than traditional IGOs"; *id.*, at 658.

[13] Lavranos, *supra* note 1, at 45.

[14] *Id.*, at 44-45; see also, G. Loibl, *supra* note 1.

[15] J. Brunnée, *supra* note 1, at 10, argues that "[w]hatever the approach, it is in the relevant decision-making processes that the sovereignty-efficiency tension appears to come to a head. The need for quick responses to a new or changing threat would seem to militate in favour of binding decision-making directly by a COP rather than subject to the consent of States, and in favour of majority rather than consensus decision-making by COPs. Yet, treaty adaptation will be meaningful only if majority requirements are set so as to ensure that large number of parties, including at least some of the key players, are on board. Therefore, some observers suggest that consensus decision-making ultimately is one of the most efficient way to bring about a text that will have key states' buy-in".

countries, adopted by the COP-2, by consensus, without any formal objection from the Parties. There were doubts voiced by some countries as to the binding force of such a decision, since it modified the treaty obligations significantly. Therefore, it was argued, the Convention should be subject to a formal amendment procedure. As a result, the COP-3 proposed a formal amendment, according to which the ban will enter into force after three-quarters of the Contracting Parties have ratified it and it will bind only those States that ratified it.[16]

2. The Montreal Protocol

An early example of such an expansion of the powers of COP/MOP is the Montreal Protocol on Substances that Deplete Ozone Layer. The Montreal Protocol on Substances That Deplete the Ozone Layer ("Montreal Protocol")[17] together with the Vienna Convention for the Protection of the Ozone Layer [18] ("Vienna Convention") constitute a legal framework to protect the ozone layer.[19] These two instruments "represent a swift and substantive response to relatively new and controverted scientific information, despite the involvement of parties with strongly opposed views".[20] The legal structure of both these instruments is fairly complicated and its detailed description exceeds the confines of this chapter. Briefly, the Vienna Convention and the Montreal Protocol each have one main decision-making organ, namely the Conference of the Parties (under the Vienna Convention) and the Meeting of the Parties (under the Montreal Protocol). Each party has one vote within each of these bodies. The main body adopts rules and takes most decisions by consensus. The law-making body of both the Vienna Convention and the Montreal Protocol has the duty to review and assess control measures on the basis of available scientific, technological,

---

[16] Lavranos, *supra* note 1, at 46, Decision II/12, COP-2, 1994; Decision III/1, COP-3, 1995, inserting new article 4A. This amendment is yet to be ratified by all the Parties.

[17] The Montreal Protocol on Substances which Deplete the Ozone Layer signed on 16 September 1987, 26 *ILM* 1550 (1989), entered into force on 22 September 1988.

[18] The Vienna Convention for the Protection of the Ozone Layer, signed on 22 March 1985, 26 *ILM* 1529 (1987), entered into force on 1 January 1989.

[19] See, e.g., A. Gallagher, "The 'New' Montreal Protocol and the Future of International Law for Protection of the Global Environment", 14(2) *Houston Journal of International Law* (1992), at 267-361; D. Hurblut, "Beyond the Montreal Protocol: Impact on Nonparty States and Lessons for Future Environmental Protection Regimes", 4 *Colo. J. Int'l Envtl.L&Pol'y* (1993), at 345-368.

[20] Thomas Nuruddin, "Saving the Ozone: Monitoring and Ensuring Compliance under the Vienna Convention and the Montreal Protocol Conference on Administrative and Expert Monitoring of International Legal Norms" (1996), Centre for International Studies (text unpublished on file with the author).

environmental and economic information. Such assessment may lead to the activation of the amendment and adjustment procedures; and as will be seen below, the adjustment procedure is an example of the trend departing from the traditional requirement of expression of consent to be bound.

The amendment procedure is set out in Article 9(2) of the Vienna Convention. This procedure involves a traditional means of expression of consent to be bound. After their adoption, the amendments are submitted to the parties for ratification, approval or acceptance. Ratification, approval or acceptance of amendments is notified to the Depositary in writing. Amendments enter into force between the Parties who accepted them on the ninetieth day after the receipt by the Depositary of notification of their ratification, approval or acceptance by at least two-thirds of the parties concerned, except as may be otherwise provided. Thereafter, the amendments enter into force for any other Party on the ninetieth day after that Party deposits its instrument of ratification, approval or acceptance of the amendments. The above-described procedure is a classical procedure, which relies on the principle of full consent of a state to be bound by a treaty. Even in the case of majority voting (in the event of the failure to achieve consensus), in order to adopt an amendment to the Vienna Convention and to protocols, States express their consent to be bound by them thereafter, by ratification, acceptance or approval of the adopted amendment (i.e., by modes which are all listed in Article 11 of the VCLT).[21]

The procedure for adjustments set out in Article 2(9) of the Montreal Protocol, in contrast, is not traditional. This procedure was designed to implement a process of assessments, which was provided for in Article 6 of the Montreal Protocol.[22] Parties to the Montreal Protocol decide whether adjustments regarding substances with ozone-depleting potential should be made, and, if so, what the adjustments should be. They further decide what adjustments and reductions of production or consumption of the controlled substances from 1986 levels should be undertaken, and, if so, what the scope, amount and timing of any such adjustments and reductions should be. Proposals for such adjustments must be communicated to the Parties by the

---

[21] So far, there have been four amendments to the Montreal Protocol: the London Amendment of 1990, the Copenhagen Amendment of 1992, the Montreal Amendment of 1997 and the Beijng Amendment of 1999.

[22] Article 6: "Any party not operating under Article 5, [i.e. *developed countries*] that has facilities for the production of controlled substances under construction, or contracted for prior to 16 September 1987, and provided for in national legislation prior to 1 January 1987, may add the production from such facilities to its 1986 production of such substances for the purposes of determining its calculated level of production for 1986, provided that such facilities are completed by 31 December 1990 and such production does not raise that party's annual calculated level of consumption of the controlled substances above 0.5 kilograms per capita".

secretariat at least six months before the meeting at which they are to be proposed for adoption. The basic procedure for the adoption of such decisions is consensus. If consensus and consequently agreement cannot be reached, such decisions, as a last resort are adopted by a two-thirds majority of the Parties present and voting, representing at least fifty percent of the total consumption by the Parties of the controlled substances. The decisions are binding on all parties. The decisions adopted in such a manner are communicated to all Parties by the Depositary. Unless otherwise provided, the decisions enter into force on the expiry of six months from the date of the circulation of the communication by the Depositary. Generally, the adjustments that were adopted revised the time guidelines for reductions and accelerated the schedule.[23]

The consequence of this procedure for the adoption of adjustments is that they bind States that voted against them. As amended in London, the Montreal Protocol provides that any party may withdraw from it at any time after four years of assuming the obligations of reducing the consumption of controlled substances.[24] The withdrawal takes place one year after giving notice. Whilst, as we have seen, it is not difficult in the opting-out procedure to interpret the *omission* to opt-out as constituting a tacit expression of consent to be bound by a new provision or rule to which the right to opt-out applies. It is much more difficult to so interpret the arrangements under this adjustment procedure. Thus, in the case of opting-out procedures, the parties retain the option to consent, by omitting to opt-out, to the treaty with the new provision or rule, or they can elect to reject the new provision or rule, while remaining bound by the treaty as it originally stood. But under the adjustment procedure under the Montreal Protocol, the parties have no such choice; it appears that the only manner in which States Parties to the Protocol may avoid being bound by the adjustments is to withdraw from the Protocol. As a result of a majority decision to adopt the new rule, the option of the treaty as it originally stood is effectively denied to the parties.[25] In

---

[23] The procedure has been further used in 1995. Report of the Conference of the Parties to the Basel Convention on the Control of Transboundary Movements of Hazardous Wastes and their Disposal, 10 February 2003, UNEP/CHW.6/40, at 46.

An important change to the procedure was made by the London Amendment to the Montreal Protocol. The words "representing at least fifty per cent of the total consumption of the controlled substances" were deleted from the original text and were replaced by the words "representing a majority of the parties operating under paragraph 1 of Article 5 present and voting and a majority of Parties not so operating present and voting". This provision effectively changed the decisive role of the developed countries and granted the right of veto to both developed and developing countries.

[24] London Amendment, *supra* note 21, Annex II section X.

[25] The importance of changes to treaty obligations under the adjustment procedure should not be underestimated. As Lavranos observes, certain technical adjustments significantly affect companies that deal with the affected substance; see, e.g., Lavranos, *supra* note 1, at 46.

these circumstances, it is difficult to say that there is a new expression of consent to be bound relating to the new provision. It would seem, rather, to be the case that the only expression of consent to be bound was that given in respect of the original entry into force of the treaty. This system has indeed been subject to some criticism regarding the absence of a true opportunity to consent to the specific content of new rules or provisions introduced under it. As one author points out "[i]f treaty standards can be modified without formal amendment, governments cannot be sure of the treaty obligations they assume at the moment of signature and ratification – what is effective compliance today may be either irrelevant or non-compliance tomorrow".[26]

An important question in this context relates to the authorisation in the treaty itself to adopt decisions with binding effect on the parties – i.e. the so-called "enabling clauses". Loibl describes them as "in general giving a specific mandate to the Conference of the Parties (or another organ or institution established under an international environmental agreement) to elaborate (more detailed) rules in a particular area without providing for a specific amendment procedure."[27] One of the first of such enabling clauses was included in the 1987 Montreal Protocol, Article 8 of which states that "[t]he Parties, at their first meeting, shall consider and approve procedures and international mechanisms for determining non-compliance with the provisions of this Protocol and for treatment of Parties found to be in non-compliance". This became a standard procedure in other environmental treaties, most notably in the 1997 Kyoto Protocol. The according of extensive legislative powers to the COPs/MOPs has however also taken place within certain treaty regimes, even without enabling clauses.[28] An example of this is the Basel Convention, which established a non-compliance procedure at the sixth meeting of its COP, even though the Convention does not include any enabling clause authorising the creation of such a procedure.[29]

---

[26] P.H. Sand, "Institution-Building to Assist Compliance with International Environmental Law: Perspectives", 53 *ZaöRV* (1996), 774-795, at 790-791.

[27] Loibl, *supra* note 1.

[28] The powers of the MOP under the Montreal Protocol to enact adjustments are not based on enabling clauses. Therefore, authors such as Loibl differentiate between these two types of the expansion of the powers of COPs and MOPs, i.e. dividing them into amendment of a treaty and legislation based on enabling clauses. However, the issue here is to illustrate the growing trend of States being bound without their explicit consent by the decisions of autonomous institutional arrangements in certain multilateral environmental agreements, so that this accurate observation is not material for present purposes.

[29] Report of the Conference of the Parties to the Basel Convention on the Control of Transboundary Movements of Hazardous Wastes and their Disposal, 10 February 2003, UNEP/CHW.6/40, at 46.

3. The Kyoto Protocol

The Kyoto Protocol[30] ("the Protocol") is a protocol to the 1992 United Nations Framework Convention on Climate Change.[31] The Protocol was adopted in 1997 at the Conference of the Parties to the Climate Change Convention. Even before its entry into force, certain of its provisions have been given some effect through an informal procedure that involves their adoption in meetings of the Parties to the Climate Change Convention. In particular, this procedure has been adopted in connection with the compliance mechanism under the Kyoto Protocol. The setting up of a compliance mechanism is envisaged in Article 18 of the Protocol itself, which provides as follows:

> The Conference of the Parties ... serving as the meeting of the Parties to this Protocol shall, at its first session, approve appropriate and effective procedures and mechanisms to determine and to address cases of non-compliance with the provisions of the Protocol, including through the development of an indicative list of consequences, taking into account the cause, type, degree and frequency of non-compliance. Any procedures and mechanisms under this Article entailing binding consequences shall be adopted by means of an amendment to this Protocol.

The Kyoto Protocol is an example of the expanding role of COP based on so-called "enabling clauses".[32] The enabling clause in Article 18

---

[30] Kyoto Protocol to the United Nations Framework Convention on Climate Change ("Climate Change Convention"), 37 *ILM* 22 (1998); see also http://unfccc.int. UNCCC, Conference of the Parties, 3rd. Sess., UN Doc. FCCC/CP/1997/L.7/Add.1 (1998). According to Article 25, it "shall enter into force on the ninetieth day after the date on which not less than 55 Parties to the Convention, incorporating Parties included in Annex I which accounted in total for at least 55 per cent of the total carbon dioxide emissions for 1990 of the Parties included in Annex I, have deposited their instruments of ratification, acceptance, approval or accession ..." As of 2 February 2005, 141 Parties and regional economic integration organizations have deposited instruments of ratifications, accessions, approvals or acceptances, which account for 61.6 per cent emissions, source: <http://unfccc.int/essential_background/kyoto_protocol/status_of_ratification/items/2613.php>. The Kyoto Protocol entered into force on 16 February 2005.

[31] United Nations Framework Convention on Climate Change, opened for signature on 4 June 1992, entered into force on 21 March 1994, 31 *ILM* 849 (1992).

[32] On the history of the negotiations of the compliance procedure under the Kyoto Protocol see R. Lefeber, "From The Hague to Bonn to Marrakesh and Beyond: A Negotiating History of the Compliance Regime Under the Kyoto Protocol", *The Hague Yearbook of International Law* (2001) 25. See also J. Brunnée, "A Fine Balance: Facilitation and Enforcement in the Design of a Compliance Regime for the Kyoto Protocol", 13 *Tulane Environmental Law Journal*, 223 (2000); See M. Fitzmaurice and C. Redgwell "Environmental Non-Compliance Procedures and International Law, *NYIL* (2000), at 35. On legal issues arising from such mechanisms in relation to the law of treaties and the law of State responsibility; G. Loibl,

distinguishes between those procedures and mechanisms adopted under this Article that have binding effect and those that do not, so that, for example, the consequences of non-compliance that would entail penalty payments for the Parties for non-compliance would have to be adopted by the way of amendments. Penalty payments under the non-compliance system of the Kyoto Protocol distinguish it from other non-compliance regimes. The Kyoto Protocol envisages the establishment of certain mechanisms: Joint Implementation (Article 8); Article 12 (Clean Development Mechanisms); and Article 17 (emissions trading). The COP is authorised to elaborate on these mechanisms. The COP has the powers to suspend a Member state from participating in the above-mentioned mechanisms, as is the case (admittedly on a smaller scale) with the non-compliance procedure of the Montreal Protocol[33] and other non-compliance regimes.

However, in every case, the rules on the basis of which elaboration of these procedures and mechanisms are effected use different terms. Article 8 speaks of "guidelines"; Article 12 of "modalities", and "procedures", and Article 17 of "principles", "modalities", "rules" and "guidelines". As Loibl observes, none of these provisions specify the legal character of the rules adopted in the fulfilment of the relevant enabling clauses.[34] He further

---

"Environmental Law and Non Compliance Procedures: Issues of State Responsibility", in: M. Fitzmaurice and D. Sarooshi (eds.), *Issues of State Responsibility Before International Judicial Institutions* (2004), at 201.

> *"Recognizing* the need to prepare for the early entry into force of the Kyoto Protocol,
>
> *Also recognizing* the need to prepare for the timely operation of the procedures and timely operation of the procedures and mechanisms relating to compliance under the Kyoto Protocol,
>
> *Noting* that it is the prerogative of the Conference of the Parties serving as the meeting of the Parties to the Kyoto Protocol to decide on the legal form of the procedures and mechanisms relating to compliance,
>
> 1. *Decides* to adopt the text containing the procedures and mechanisms relating to compliance under the Kyoto Protocol annexed hereto;
>
> 2. *Recommends* that the Conference of the Parties serving as meeting of the Parties to the Kyoto Protocol, at its first session, adopt the procedures and mechanisms relating to compliance annexed hereto in terms of Article 18 of the Kyoto Protocol."

[33] Adopted by Decision IV/5 of the 4th Meeting of the Parties and revised by Decision X/10 (10th Meeting of the Parties).

[34] Similar issues are raised by the enabling clauses in Articles 7(4) and 18(2)(a) of the Cartagena Protocol on Biosafety, 39 *ILM* 1027 (2000). Under these Articles, decisions adopted by the COP/MOP may have significant effects on the Parties. The Cartagena Protocol does not specify the manner in which the decisions adopted on the basis of these Articles will bind the Parties. Therefore, arguably, the Parties to be bound by these decisions could have

explains that although the legal status of the rules was not determined during negotiations, Parties treated them as having binding effect on the Parties. Annex I Parties (developed countries) only ratified the Kyoto Protocol once the rules on the mechanisms were agreed. Loibl argues "this would strengthen the argument that the "enabling provisions" for the mechanisms authorise the COP/MOP to adopt "rules" which have legal effect for the Parties".[35]

4. The International Maritime Organisation

Interesting treaty-making techniques have been developed by the International Maritime Organisation ("IMO"). The IMO has broad powers relating, inter alia, to the safety of shipping and the protection of the environment from shipping activities.[36] In order to achieve this, the IMO elaborates agreements, drafts and manages them, makes recommendations and convenes conferences.[37] It has adopted a number of non-binding codes, which contain provisions that reflect rapidly changing safety and other requirements concerning shipping. In order to make these codes binding and to update existing treaties, the IMO has incorporated them into conventions by means of a procedure for the amendment of conventions that simplifies the process but also binds the minority without its express consent.

For example, on 27 May 1999, the voluntary 1993 International Code for the Safe Carriage of Packaged Irradiated Nuclear Fuel, Plutonium and High-

---

requested their ratification. However, thus far, no Party brought forward such a request. It may be assumed therefore that the Parties are prepared to comply with the decisions of the COP/MOP. See Loibl, *supra* note 1.

[35] *Id.*

[36] As enumerated by Birnie, these include; "(i) to provide an effective machinery for technical, legal and scientific co-operation among governments in this field in relation to pollution from ships and related activities, and for mitigation of environmental effects and compensation; (ii) to adopt practicable international standards in matters concerning safety and prevention and control of such sources of pollution: (iii) to encourage the widest acceptance and effective implementation of these standards at the global level; (iv) to strengthen national and regional capacities for national and regional action to prevent, control, combat and mitigate marine pollution and to promote technical cooperation to this end; and (v) to cooperate fully with other organisations within the UN system as well as relevant international regional and non-governmental organisations to ensure a coordinated approach and avoid duplication". See P. Birnie, "The Status of Environmental 'Soft Law': Trends and Examples with Special Focus on IMO Norms", in H. Ringbom (ed.), *Competing Norms in the Law of Marine Environmental Protection* (1997), 31, at 42.

[37] *Id.*, at 44.

Level Radioactive Waste on Board Ships ("INF Code")[38] became mandatory on 1 January 2001, pursuant to an amendment adopted under Chapter VII (Carriage of Dangerous Goods) of the Safety of Life at Sea Convention ("SOLAS")[39] at the 71st session of the Maritime Safety Committee (the "MSC")[40]. The INF Code was adopted by the MSC at the same session (Resolution 88(71)) by way of amendment to SOLAS, in accordance with its Article VIII (b), which provides that amendments shall be deemed to have been accepted on a particular date unless, prior to that date, more than one third of the Contracting Governments to SOLAS, or Contracting Governments the combined merchant fleets of which constitute not less than 50 percent of the gross tonnage of the world's merchant fleet, have notified their objection to the amendment.

This procedure is noteworthy for two reasons. Firstly, the MSC, not the Parties, suggests the proposed amendments to SOLAS. Secondly, and more importantly, the amendments are approved if adopted by a majority (if less than one third of the Contracting Parties or less than 50 percent of gross tonnage of the world's merchant fleet, objects) and they thereby bind the minority of Parties that may disagree. This mechanism of consent to be bound differs from the traditional freedom enjoyed by States in accepting treaty obligations. It is also different from the classical opting-out procedure. It may be said that these are only treaty obligations of a technical nature, and that this mechanism is "in order" as the new obligations do not unduly burden States, who have already consented to be bound by the convention in question (in this case, SOLAS) under the less strict procedure. However, the amendments described above, which were applicable as of 1 January 2001 to all ships, regardless of size, engaged in the carriage of packaged irradiated nuclear fuel, plutonium and high-level radioactive waste, are far-reaching. Ships are required to hold a valid International Certificate of Fitness, which, for ships registered in the United Kingdom, is issued by the Maritime and Coastguard Agency on behalf of the Secretary of State, certifying that they have been constructed to certain standards, including such matters as strength stability, fire protection, securing of cargo, temperature control and integrity of power supplies.[41]

---

[38] 1993 International Code for the Safe Carriage of Irradiated Nuclear Fuel, Plutonium and High-Level Radioactive Wastes in Flasks on Board Ships ("INF Code") was renamed the International Code for the Safe Carriage of Packaged Irradiated Nuclear Fuel, Plutonium and High-Level Radioactive Waste on Board Ships; see full text at: <http://www. admiraltylawguide.com/conven/infcode1999.html>.

[39] 1974 International Convention on the Safety of Life at Sea ("SOLAS"), London, 1 November 1974, entered into force 25 May 1980; 1184 *United Nations Treaty Series* 2.

[40] See MSC 87 (71).

[41] In the UK, the "INF Code amendment" was adopted under the Merchant Shipping Regulations 2000 of 7 December 2000 (No. 3216).

5. The 1994 UNCLOS Implementation Agreement

The 1994 Implementation Agreement to the 1982 United Nations Convention on the Law of the Sea[42] is an example of ingenious and pragmatic treaty making, the purpose of which was to speed up the process of the entry into force of UNCLOS.[43] This Agreement modified Part XI of the LOS Convention on deep sea-bed mining, in order to make these provisions acceptable to the industrialised nations within the LOS Convention system.[44] The Agreement provides for flexible methods of expression of consent to be bound. Article 4(1) and (2), entitled "consent to be bound", provide, respectively, that

> After the adoption of this Agreement, any instrument of ratification or formal confirmation of or accession to [UNCLOS] shall also represent consent to be bound by this Agreement;

and

> No State or entity may establish its consent to be bound by this Agreement unless it has previously established or establishes at the same time its consent to be bound by [UNCLOS].

Article 4(3) provides that a State or entity referred to in Article 3 may express its consent to be bound by the Implementation Agreement by (a) signature not subject to ratification, formal confirmation or other procedure set out in Article 5; (b) signature subject to ratification or formal confirmation, followed by ratification or formal confirmation; (c) signature subject to the procedure set out in Article 5; or (d) accession. Furthermore, it is stated that formal confirmation by the entities referred to in Article 305, paragraph 1 (f) of the Convention, shall be in accordance with Annex IX of the Convention. The instruments of ratification, formal confirmation or accession shall be deposited with the Secretary-General of the United Nations.

Article 5 introduces a simplified procedure regarding States that expressed their consent to be bound by UNCLOS before the date of the adoption of the Implementation Agreement. Article 5(1), states that a state or entity that has deposited before the date of adoption of the Implementation

---

[42] 1982 United Nations Convention on the Law of the Sea ("UNCLOS" or "LOS Convention"), 10 December 1982, entered into force 16 November 1994, See text at <http://www.oceanlaw.net/texts/losc.htm>.

[43] 1994 Agreement relating to the Implementation of Part XI of the United Nations Convention on the Law of the Sea ("Implementation Agreement"), 28 July 1994, entry into force 28 July 1996; See text at: <http://www.un.org/Depts/los/convention_agreements/texts/unclos/closindxAgree.htm>.

[44] R. Churchill and V. Lowe, *The Law of Sea* (1999), at 20-21.

Agreement an instrument of ratification or formal confirmation or of accession to UNCLOS and which has signed this Implementation Agreement in accordance with Article 4, paragraph 3 (c), shall be considered to have established consent to be bound by the Implementation Agreement 12 months after the date of its adoption, unless that state or entity notifies the depositary in writing before that date that it is not availing itself to the simplified procedure set out in this article. In the event of such notification, consent to be bound by the Implementation Agreement shall be established in accordance with Article 4(3)(b).

It is obvious from these provisions regarding the procedure for expression of consent to be bound adopted by the Implementation Agreement that it was dictated by the requirements of the widest possible participation in UNCLOS, as modified by the Implementation Agreement. The draftsmen of the Implementation Agreement adopted a mechanism that combines the classical methods of the consent to be bound with a simplified procedure, in order to make participation in the modified UNCLOS agreeable to all States.

6. Concluding Remarks

From its humble beginnings in the form of the opting-out procedure, the trend resulting in modification of the traditional requirement of express consent has matured into (or at least is moving into a direction of) granting of far reaching rule-making powers of the organs (COPs/MOPs) established by certain treaty regimes, most notably in the sphere of international environmental law. However, even the opting-out procedure, based on tacit consent, was viewed as and classified as a departure from traditional treaty-making mechanisms, with a strong rule-making role for the organs set up by a treaty. Procedures such as opting-out were assessed as "going far beyond traditional sources of international law", which require "orthodox ratification" before obligations are created for parties.[45] Mechanisms and procedures being developed under more recent MEAs (such as the Montreal Protocol, the Kyoto Protocol and also the IMO) go even further. The case of the 1994 Implementation Agreement to the 1982 LOS Convention is slightly different. The flexible mechanism of consent to be bound provided for by the Agreement was to facilitate the universal acceptance of the 1982 LOS Convention, the entry into force of which was imminent. This ingenious solution was purely pragmatic and is specially tailored for this particular case. It shows, however, the infinite flexibility of the law of treaties and provides confirmation, if it is needed, that treaties are living instruments.

---

[45] Kirgis, *supra* note 3, at 90.

In some cases this particular type of international rule-making is adopted on the basis of majority decision, such as the system of adjustments under the 1987 Montreal Protocol, or the practice of the IMO. Such majority rule-making was considered rather exceptional and confined to a narrow area of technical and very specialised cooperation.[46] One may wonder whether it is still the case and whether international law (at least its fast expanding branch of international environmental law) will not see the increased adoption of such an approach. It is a practical and efficient manner of dealing with rapidly changing environmental standards.

This "specialised international law-making"[47] is based on what may be called "derived" consent, i.e. consent derived from consent to the treaty that set up the structure. Parties, therefore, give a general consent to the mechanisms and regimes which would be adopted on the basis of the decisions of the organs so empowered by the relevant treaty. However, there is no agreement as to the legal character of this "derived" rule-making. Is it a new treaty, a secondary treaty obligation based on a constituent treaty or an act of organ adopted in the course of discharging its duties? It may even be asked in bolder terms whether the different systems of standard-setting by international organisations constitute a new category of sources of international law.[48] Whatever the case, the position regarding the expression of consent of States to be bound in these contexts appears to depart further and further from the classical structures enshrined in the VCLT. It is interesting to note that in the case of the Kyoto Protocol, the limit of consent to be bound appears to be set by Article 18, under which, in the event of mechanisms and procedures entailing "binding consequences", amendment to the Protocol is necessary.

These new ways of expressing consent to be bound give rise to the question whether rule-making in the fora described above is evolving into what may be called "equivalent of global legislation".[49] This phenomenon has raised questions relating to the legitimacy of the MEA-based law. The extensive powers bestowed on organs involved in this collective law-making can be seen as a threat to State sovereignty, a problem which perhaps in international environmental law is less pronounced due to its "consensual processes".[50] One of the possible solutions would be the departure from the formal traditional international law and recourse to the so-called

---

[46] See G. Danilenko, *Law-Making in the International Community* (1993), at 67-68; C. Brölmann, "Limits of Treaty Making" (manuscript on file with the authors).
[47] See C. Alexandrowicz, *The Law-Making Functions of Specialised Agencies of the United Nations* (1973), at 40-69, and E. Klein, "United Nations, Specialised Agencies", 5 *EPIL* 1983, at 349-368.
[48] See Brölmann, *supra* note 46, and V. Degan, *The Sources of International Law* (1997), at 6.
[49] Brunnée, *supra* note 1, at 4.
[50] *Id.*, at 10 and 7-15.

"interactional law" approach. This is based on the work of Lon Fuller and constructivist international relations theory, according to which international law derives from "a mutually generative process" in which actors in a continuous law-making process reach a common understanding through mutual interaction and which is characterised by a fluidity between binding and non-binding norms.[51] This approach would broaden the legislative role of COPs (and would include non-binding decision-making) based on a continuous interactional processes within the structures of COPs and their subsidiary bodies. It may be said that "[t]hrough the construction and reconstruction of the normative framework, law-makers must attend to law's internal legitimacy requirements and the inclusiveness of the law-making process ... The greater the extent to which the requirements are met, the greater the legitimacy of the norms or legal regime, and its power to promote adherence. At the same time, the more the law-making meets international tests of legitimacy and occurs through inclusive process, the more it will be able to constrain political expediency and power that might otherwise direct the evolution of an MEA regime."[52] This interactional approach would divert attention from formal concerns, such as the method of law-making, and direct focus to "promoting inclusive interactional processes and to nurturing the prerequisites for legitimate law-making."[53] Whether one agrees with these remarks or not, it is clear that the changing world of consent to be bound by the treaties under consideration raises interesting and important questions, some of which relate to fundamental issues of sovereignty and legitimacy.

In our view, these developments clearly indicate that the problem of consent to be bound is an evolving and living part of the law of treaties. Apart from the procedures in place that modify the fundamental principle of consent to be bound, other practical and necessary *ad hoc* solutions are adopted by States (such as the Part XI to the Law of the Sea Convention). Therefore, far from being staid, interesting and thriving developments are to be found in this area of the law of treaties.

---

[51] *Id.*, at 33-50. See also J. Brunnée and S. J. Toope, "International Law and Constructivism: Elements of an Interactional Theory of International Law", 39 *Colum.J. Transnat'L L* (2000), at 19.

[52] Brunnée, *supra* note 1, at 51.

[53] *Id.*, at 52.

CHAPTER SEVEN

The Law of Treaties and the Relationship Between the Security Council and the International Criminal Court[*]

1. Introduction

The relationship between the International Criminal Court ("ICC") and the Security Council of the United Nations has been the subject of a great deal of consideration, often regarding the matter of the consequences of the overlap between their respective functions.[1] However, less attention has been

---

[*] This chapter is co-authored by Anneliese Quast, and will also appear in M. Fitzmaurice and M. Craven (eds.), *Interrogating the Treaty: The Law of Treaties in Review* (2005), forthcoming, to be published by Wolf Legal Publishers.

[1] O. Elias and A. Quast, "The Relationship between the Security Council and the International Criminal Court in the Light of Resolution 1422 (2002)", 3 *Non-State Actors and International Law* (2003), at 165; L. Condorelli and S. Villalpando, "Referral and Deferral by the Security Council", and "Relationship of the Court with the United Nations", both in A. Cassese, P. Gaeta and J. Jones (eds.), *The Rome Statute of the International Criminal Court* (2002), Vol. I, at 219 and at 627, respectively (containing a useful bibliography at 654); P. Gargiulo, "The Controversial Relationship between the International Criminal Court and the Security Council", in F. Lattanzi and W. Schabas (eds.), *Essays on the Rome Statute of the International Criminal Court,* Vol. I (1999), at 67, esp. 85-91; M. Bergsmo and J. Pejić, "On Article 16", in O.Trifftterer and C. Rosbaud (eds.), *The Rome Statute of the International Criminal Court* (2000), at 373; M. Arsanjani, "The Rome Statute of the International Criminal Court", 93 *AJIL* (1999) 22; A. Cassese, "The Statute of the International Criminal Court: Some Preliminary Reflections", 10 *EJIL* (1999); V. Gowlland-Debbas, "The Relationship between the Security Council and the Projected International Criminal Court", 3 *Journal of Armed Conflict Law* (1998), at 97; V. Gowlland-Debbas, "The Role of the Security Council in the New International Criminal Court", in V. Gowlland-Debbas and L. Boisson de Chazournes (eds.), *The International Legal System in Quest of Equity and Universality/ L'Ordre juridique international, un système en quête d'équité et d'universalité, Liber*

paid to the legal nature of that relationship.[2] This chapter is a speculative examination of the possibility of considering the legal relationship between the ICC and the Security Council as a treaty relationship. Thereafter, some of the implications of such a characterization will be considered.

A number of links exist between the ICC and the Security Council. Some of these links are found in the Statute of the ICC,[3] namely Articles 13(b) (concerning the power of the Security Council to refer cases to the ICC), 16 (concerning the power of the Security Council to defer prosecutions by the ICC), 87(5b) and 87(7) (both concerning cases referred to the ICC by the Security Council in which a State fails to co-operate with the ICC). Another link between the United Nations and the Security Council is the Relationship Agreement, which is not yet in force.[4] While this Relationship Agreement clearly establishes a treaty relationship between the ICC and the United Nations, including the Security Council, it is less simple to characterize the relationship between the ICC and the Security Council as a treaty relationship on the basis of the provisions of the ICC Statute.

This chapter will focus, somewhat speculatively, on Article 16 of the ICC Statute in particular as a possible basis for an "agreement" between the ICC and the Security Council. We referred elsewhere, with some diffidence,[5] to the possibility that Article 16 could be so construed, and this chapter is a further exploration of that suggestion. Article 16 can be considered as a conferral of a right by the States Parties to the ICC Statute on the Security Council, according to the principles reflected in the VCLT 1986,[6] with a

---

Amicorum Georges Abi-Saab (2001), at 629; D. Sarooshi, "Aspects of the Relationship between the International Criminal Court and the United Nations", 32 *NYIL* (2001), at 27; F. Berman, "The Relationship between the International Criminal Court and the Security Council", in H. von Hebel, J. Lammers, J. Schukking (eds.), *Reflections on the International Criminal Court* (1999), at 173; N. Elaraby, "The Role of the Security Council and the Independence of the International Criminal Court", in M. Politi and G. Nesi (eds.), *The Rome Statute of the International Criminal Court* (2002), at 43; E. Wilmshurst, "The International Criminal Court: the Role of the Security Council", in M. Politi and G. Nesi (eds.), *The Rome Statute of the International Criminal Court* (2002), at 39; L. Yee, "The International Criminal Court and the Security Council: Article 13 (b) and 16" in R. Lee (ed.), *The International Criminal Court* (1999), at 143.

[2] Notable exceptions include L. Condorelli and S. Villalpando, *supra* note 1, at 220, 228; D. Sarooshi, *supra* note 1, at 38-44.

[3] UN Doc. A/CONF.183/9, 17 July 1998 ("Rome Statute"), as corrected by *procès-verbaux* of 10 November 1998, 12 July 1999, 30 November 1999, 8 May 2000, 17 January 2001 and 16 January 2002. The Statute entered into force on 1 July 2002.

[4] ICC-ASP/1/3, Assembly of States Parties to the Rome Statute of the International Criminal Court, First Session New York, 3-10 September 2002, Official Records, at 243; see <www.un.org/law/icc/asp/1stsession/report/english/part_ii_g_e.pdf>.

[5] Elias and Quast, *supra* note 1, at 179-181.

[6] 25 *ILM* 243 (1986). The VCLT 1986 is not yet in force, and, for reasons discussed below, its provisions may not apply to the particular kind of agreement which are the subject of this

corresponding obligation on the ICC to defer cases where the Security Council validly requests deferrals. The question addressed here relates to the extent to which the law of treaties can be said to apply to the legal mechanism underlying such a conferral.

The analysis will touch on a number of issues in the law of treaties, including (a) treaties between international organisations (and their effects on the organs of that international organisation); (b) the question whether a right in favour of a third party is created simply by the provisions of the treaty between the parties to that the treaty – i.e. a unilateral act, a *"stipulation pour autrui"* – or whether the right is created by a separate collateral agreement between, on the one hand, the parties to the treaty and, on the other hand, the third party, i.e. the consent of the third party is required for the creation of the right; (c) the relationship between the international organisation and its constituent instrument; and (d) whether the conferral of a right, particularly within the "collateral agreement" analysis, can properly be considered to result in a "treaty" relationship.

After considering these issues, the discussion will turn to the question of a possible problem, if it can be said that there is an agreement or some other "treaty" relationship. This problem would arise from the fact that one of the parties in this "treaty" relationship is a judicial body, one capable, in principle, of pronouncing authoritatively on the exercise of rights against itself by the other party. The ICC, as does any judicial institution, has the competence to determine its own jurisdiction, and since a Security Council resolution requesting a deferral in accordance with Article 16 of the ICC Statute directly affects the jurisdiction of the ICC, the ICC would appear to have the power to pronounce upon the lawfulness of any such resolution, in order to determine whether its prosecution of a case is to be deferred in accordance with that resolution. In other words, this chapter will consider some of the possible implications of the law of treaties on the relationship between the ICC and the Security Council, and the extent to which "constitutional" issues can raise questions of "contractual" (treaty law) questions.

---

chapter. Nevertheless, the following analysis is based on the principles underlying its Articles 36 and 37, which, as will be seen in the following discussion, exist outside the VCLT 1986. Speaking in relation to the Vienna Convention on the Law of Treaties of 1969 ("VCLT"), it has been observed that "[t]he definition of a treaty, as enshrined in the VCLT, does not reflect the varied forms under which a treaty may appear ... The ICJ has never relied exclusively on the VCLT to determine the nature of an instrument, but in each and every case has focused rather on the legal content of the instrument in question"; see M. Fitzmaurice, "The Identification and Character of Treaties and Treaty Obligations between States in International Law", 73 *BYIL* (2002) 141, at 164.

2. Does Article 16 of the ICC Statute Create a "Treaty" Relationship Between the ICC and the United Nations?

The ICC Statute is clearly a treaty between the States Parties to it ("States Parties"). The issue is whether a "treaty" relationship exists between the States Parties and the Security Council on the basis of Article 16. Article 16 of the ICC Statute reads as follows:

> No investigations or prosecutions may be commenced or proceeded with under this Statute for a period of twelve months after the Security Council, in a resolution adopted under Chapter VII of the Charter of the United Nations, has requested the Court to that effect; that request may be renewed by the Council under the same conditions.

If a right is conferred by the States Parties on the Security Council via Article 16, in the form of a collateral agreement rather than a "*stipulation pour autrui*", this could imply a "treaty" relationship between them regarding that right in form of a "collateral agreement".

Central to this analysis is Article 36 of the VCLT 1986, which deals with the conferral of a right on a third party as follows:

> (2) A right arises for a third organization from a provision of a treaty if the parties to the treaty intend the provision to accord that right either to the third organization, or to a group of international organizations to which it belongs, or to all organizations, and the third organization assents thereto. Its assent shall be governed by the rules of the organization.

> (3) A State or an international organization exercising a right in accordance with paragraph 1 or 2 shall comply with the conditions for its exercise provided for in the treaty or established in conformity with the treaty.

The provisions of Article 16 of the ICC Statute and Article 36 of the VCLT 1986 will now be examined.

2.1 The Conferral of a Right

The first question which arises is whether there is a right to be conferred in Article 16. In this provision, the States Parties enable the Security Council to defer investigations or prosecutions from the Court. In spite of the term "request", there is no doubt about the binding character of a valid Security Council resolution with regard to the ICC. The binding effect may not stem from Chapter VII of the United Nations ("UN") Charter, which would appear to provide for the creation of obligations on Member States of the UN only,[7] but from the interaction of Chapter VII of the UN Charter and Article 16 of the ICC Statute.[8] Furthermore, although the Security Council "requests" the deferral, there is nothing to suggest that acceptance of that request by the ICC is necessary. The ICC is not granted any discretion as to whether to defer or not, nor does Article 16 provide for any exceptions to the power of the Security Council to defer cases. The wording of Article 16 also supports this view: "*no* investigation or prosecution shall be commenced or proceeded with". It should also be recalled that it was intended that the primary responsibility of the Security Council with regard to international peace and security under Article 24 of the UN Charter was to be maintained.[9] However, if an Article 16 resolution was not binding upon the ICC, the ICC could interfere or decide freely to proceed with its prosecution of a case, and, thereby, interfere with or compromise measures or actions of the Security Council in maintaining or restoring international peace and security, which would undermine the primary responsibility granted to the Security Council. Finally, if the drafting history of Article 16 is considered, it will be recalled that the final version reflects a compromise reached after extensive discussions.[10] An earlier draft prohibited the ICC from commencing a prosecution "arising from a situation which is being dealt with by the Security Council as a threat to or breach of the peace or an act of aggression under Chapter VII of the Charter, unless the Security Council otherwise decides".[11] In the final version, the position is reversed so that the ICC can commence prosecution in such cases *unless* a deferral is requested by a Chapter VII resolution. It is difficult to imagine, in view of the balance struck in Article 16 between the roles of the Security Council and the ICC, that such a resolution is not binding on the ICC. Accordingly, it would appear that Security Council resolutions passed pursuant to the powers vested in it by Article 16 and Chapter VII of the UN Charter were meant to be binding upon the ICC, i.e. preventing it from dealing with a case under the conditions stipulated in Article 16.[12] Therefore, the binding character of

---

[7] See Sarooshi, *supra* note 1, at 40-41, and Stahn, *supra* note 1, section 4.B.1. Bergsmo and Pejić (*supra* note 1, article 16, paragraph 23) disagree and explain that the chapter VII resolution establishes a legal duty on the Court.

[8] Condorelli and Villalpando, *supra* note 1, chapter 17.2, at 646; According to Stahn, *supra* note 1, section 4.B.1, the obligation to implement such a resolution flows solely from Article 16 of the Rome Statute.

[9] Bergsmo and Pejić, *supra* note 1, article 16, paragraph 7; R. Lee, *supra* note 1, Introduction, at 36; D. Sarooshi, *supra* note 1, at 39; see also L. Condorelli and S. Villalpando, *supra* note 1, chapter 17.2, at 653.

[10] See Elias and Quast, *supra* note 1, at 166-169.

[11] Draft Statute for an International Criminal Court, *Report of the International Law Commission on the Work of its 46th Session*, UN Doc. A/49/355, 21 February 1997.

[12] See Bergsmo and Pejić, *supra* note 1, article 16, paragraph 10; Condorelli and Villalpando, *supra* note 1, at 647-8; Stahn, *supra* note 1, section 4.B.1.

an Article 16 resolution would appear to express the intention of the States Parties to the ICC Statute to create a right in favour of the Security Council.[13]

Article 16 empowers the Security Council to defer cases, but it would appear that the proper beneficiary of the right of power, strictly speaking, is the United Nations. It is the United Nations that is the legal person on whom the right is conferred, and the Security Council is the organ responsible for exercising that right.[14] The identity of the third party is also important for the purposes of the VCLT 1986, paragraph 2, which provides that supplementary to the intention of the parties to the treaty to create a right in favour of a third organization, there needs to be an assent to the conferral of the right, and that the assent shall be governed by the rules of that organisation. For present purposes, the question of third party assent is important because it would place the arrangement conferring the right on the third party on the level of an agreement. The question then becomes whether that agreement is one which would fall within the proper scope of the law of treaties.

There is no specific provision in the UN Charter dealing with the assent of the UN to the conferral of a right.[15] However, the Security Council, shortly after the entry into force of the ICC Statute on 1 July 2002, adopted a Chapter VII Resolution[16], in which it requested a deferral, "consistent with the provisions of Article 16 of the Rome Statute". The UN (for present

---

[13] In Hohfeldian terms, the effect of the valid resolution could be described as a power on the part of the Security Council, corresponding to a disability on the part of the ICC. See W. N. Hohfeld, *Fundamental Legal Conceptions as Applied in Judicial Reasoning and Other Legal Essays* (1919).

[14] B. Simma *et al.* (eds.), *The Charter of the United Nations: A Commentary* (2002), at 762; see also J. Klabbers, *An Introduction to International Institutional Law* (2002), at 287-291.

[15] Sir F. Berman, *supra* note 1, at 176 states that such a conferral is neither legally nor politically possible because it was not for the ICC Statute, as a legal instrument, to "confer" such a right. His view relates to the question of the extent to which a third party can alter the legal capacity of an international organization. However, it is the case that Article 16 serves to create a direct obligation on the ICC flowing from a Security Council resolution, an obligation which, as stated above, could be difficult to establish otherwise since UN resolutions, strictly speaking, bind only those States Parties which are party to the UN Charter. Accordingly, the UN is itself not being conferred with any "new" rights in the sense that such rights were not provided for in the Charter. It is the effect of the exercise of the right *on the ICC* that is "new" – there is nothing new in the ability of the UN Security Council to adopt a Chapter VII resolution in the name of international peace and security. If we adopt Hohfeld's analysis, the obligation on the ICC – which in any event is a new legal person – merely means that the corresponding right is that of the Security Council, in relation to the ICC, arising from its existing responsibilities under the Charter. There is, to be sure, no real question of there being a modification of the UN Charter to allow the Security Council to exercise new functions not envisaged therein.

[16] UN Doc. S/RES/1422 (2002); see Elias and Quast, *supra* note 1.

purposes the Security Council) exercised the power conferred upon it in Article 16 of the Rome Statute. The exercise of that power would amount to (implicit) acceptance by the UN of the right conferred pursuant to Article 16 of the ICC Statute. At this point, all three conditions set out in Article 36 (2) VCLT 1986 are met. The important question for our purposes, however, is whether this acceptance or assent was necessary for the conferral of a right. If it is not, then there is no role for the law of treaties in an analysis of the relationship between the ICC and the Security Council based on Article 16 of the ICC Statute. It is to this issue that we will now turn.

2.2 The Legal Mechanism underlying the Conferral of a Right on a Third Party

The mechanism by which rights are conferred on third parties has been the subject of doctrinal debate.[17] According to one approach, the creation of a right is a unilateral act of the parties of a treaty, i.e. a *"stipulation pour autrui"*.[18] As States can bind themselves acting individually, there is no reason why they cannot do so jointly.[19] Then, the assent of the third party on whom the right is conferred would only have, at best, declaratory effect – it would not be needed for the creation or conferral of a right. According to this approach, Article 16 of the ICC Statute cannot be considered to create a treaty relationship between the States Parties to the ICC Statute and the Security Council. It is merely a common unilateral act of the States Parties with respect to the Security Council. According to the opposing approach, the mechanism for the creation/conferral of a right on the third party is a collateral agreement between the parties to the treaty, on the one hand, and the third party, on the other hand.[20] According to this approach, the provision in favour of the third party is an offer, or a benefit, which turns into a right once the third party assents to it. In this case, the consent of the third party is constitutive and not merely declaratory. The right is created and conferred

---

[17] For a brief summary of the doctrinal differences (in the context of the VCLT), see YILC (1966), Vol. II, at 228-229.

[18] I. Sinclair, *The Vienna Convention on the Law of Treaties* (1980), at 103; E. Jiménez de Aréchaga, "Treaty Stipulations in Favour of Third States", 50 *AJIL* (1956), at 338 (developed further in his "International Law in the Past Third of a Century", 159 *Recueil des Cours* (1978), at 50-55); G. Fitzmaurice, Special Rapporteur, Fifth Report, YILC (1960), Vol. II, at 102-105.

[19] G. Fitzmaurice, *id.*, at 102, paragraph 83.

[20] D. Anzilotti, *Corso di Diritto Internazionale* (transl. Lehrbuch des Völkerrecht) (1929), at 324-327; P. Reuter, *Introduction to the Law of Treaties* (1995), at 104, paragraph 158; C. Rousseau, *Principes Généraux du Droit International Public*, at 477; G. Scelle, *Précis de Droit des Gens*, deuxième partie (1932), at 368; Separate Opinion of Judge Negulesco in the Free Zones of Upper Savoy and Gex case, PCIJ Reports, (Series A), No. 22, at 36-37.

by means of a "collateral" agreement separate from the original treaty. According to this view, Article 16 of the ICC Statute creates a (separate) treaty relationship between the States Parties and the Security Council.

The wording of the penultimate sentence of Article 36(2) of the VCLT 1986 requires the intention of the parties to the original treaty for conferral of the right as much as it requires the assent of the third party. Nevertheless, this does not indicate *ipso facto* that Article 36 adopts the "collateral agreement" approach rather than the "unilateral act" approach. As will be discussed below, it was stated that it was not intended to make a choice between the two approaches.[21]

Doctrine does not provide much guidance with regard to the debate.[22] One argument that has been put forward in support of the "unilateral act" approach is state practice with regard to the conferral of rights on third parties.[23] Jiménez de Aréchaga[24] argued that the assent of the third party is usually not registered with the UN Secretary General, contrary to the provisions of Article 102 of the UN Charter,[25] which obliges the Member States of the UN to register with the UN Secretariat every treaty and agreement which is entered into by a Member State after the UN Charter comes into force. The conclusion that Jimenez de Aréchaga seems to draw from the States' practice not to register the acceptance, is that the acceptance does not constitute an agreement.

However, the registration of an international agreement with the UN Secretariat has never been one of the defining characteristics of a treaty. Furthermore, it is not mentioned in the definition of a treaty in Article (2)(1)(a) of both the 1969 and 1986 VCLTs,[26] even though the drafters did have Article 102 of the UN Charter in mind in both cases (see Articles 80 and 81 of both VCLTs, respectively). Furthermore, the term "international

---

[21] YILC (1966), Vol. II, at 229 ; P. Reuter, *supra* note 20.

[22] Reference is often made in this context to the dictum of the Permanent Court of International Justice ("PCIJ") in the Free Zones case, *supra* note 20, which has been used by writers on opposing sides of the debate to support their positions. The Court stated that "It cannot be lightly presumed that stipulations favourable to a third state have been adopted with the object of creating an actual right in its favour. There is however nothing to prevent the will of sovereign States from having this object and effect. The question ... is therefore one to be decided in each particular case: it must be ascertained whether the States which have stipulated in favour of a third State meant to create for that State an actual right which the latter has accepted as such". See Sinclair, *supra* note 18, at 100-101.

[23] Sir G. Fitzmaurice, Special Rapporteur, Fifth Report, YILC (1960), Vol. II, at 103, paragraph 85; YILC (1966), Vol. II, at 228.

[24] Jimenez de Aréchaga, *supra* note 18 (1956), at 353.

[25] Article 102: "Every treaty and every international agreement entered into by any Member of the United Nations after the present Charter comes into force shall as soon as possible be registered with the Secretariat and published by it."

[26] See Fitzmaurice, *supra* note 1, at 161.

agreement" as referred to in Article 102 of the UN Charter seems to include unilateral acts of an international character, and the view of the Technical Committee at San Francisco, that they should be treated as international agreements, was accepted and followed in subsequent state practice.[27] Thus, for present purposes, the conclusions drawn by Jimenez de Aréchaga, based on the practice of non-registration of arrangements pursuant to which rights are conferred on third parties, are not conclusive. Jimenez de Aréchaga also argued that the "collateral agreement" approach is based on an "extremely overdrawn fiction", as the exercise of the right cannot constitute the acceptance of the offer of the conferral of a right by the third party – the right, he argued, must be acquired prior to its exercise.[28] However, there does not appear to be any fundamental objection to the basic idea underlying the "collateral agreement" approach, as the idea of acceptance of a contract by conduct is well-known in national legal systems.[29]

The discussion of this issue has sometimes attached importance to the question the modification or revocation of the right conferred.[30] Article 37(2) of VCLT 1986 provides that

> [w]hen a right has arisen for a third State or a third organization in conformity with article 36, the right may not be revoked or modified by the parties if it is established that the right was intended not to be revocable or subject to modification without the consent of the third States or the third organization.

Different views have been expressed regarding the importance of the third party's ability to revoke or modify the right conferred. However, it would appear that Article 37 does not allow for an unequivocal conclusion. If, as the wording of Article 37 suggests, the right may be revoked unless it is established that it was not intended to be revoked, the implication is that the general position is that the right can be revoked. Article 37, therefore, appears to contemplate the possibility of rights that are both revocable and those that are not. It, therefore, does not necessarily stipulate the nature of the source of the right acquired under Article 36. The question turns on the circumstances of the particular case, and the intention of the parties to the

---

[27] B. Simma *et al.* (eds), *supra* note 14, at 1280; L. Goodrich, E. Hambro, A. Simons (eds), *Charter of the United Nations* (1969), at 612.

[28] E. de Aréchaga, *supra* note 18, at 352.

[29] Regarding German law, see Jauernig, BGB *Kommentar* (2004), §151 Rn. 1; *Münchener Kommentar zum BGB* (2001), § 151 Rn. 55, Kramer; Palandt, *BGB* (2004), § 48 Rn. 2, Heinrichs. In English law, the leading case of *Carlill* v *Carbolic Smoke Ball Co.* [1892] 2 Q.B. 484, establishes that the requirement for the communication of the acceptance of an offer to the offeror is waived in certain circumstances, including, pertinently, so-called unilateral contracts where the need for acceptance is waived or is implied by conduct, such as the actual performance of the obligation under the contract.

[30] Reuter, *supra* note 20, paragraphs 158-160; Sinclair, *supra* note 11, at 103; Sir G. Fitzmaurice, Special Rapporteur, Fifth Report, YILC (1960), Vol. II, at 103, paragraph 89.

conferring treaty. Article 37 could be taken to mean that there is no collateral agreement as such, but simply a unilateral conferral of a right. At the same time, it could be taken to mean that the third organization, since its assent appears to be required by the wording of Article 36, has consented to a system, an agreement whereby its right may be revoked or modified without its consent, or one whereby its right may not be revoked without its consent, as the case may be. Thus, Article 37, does not provide a conclusive answer to the question of the mechanism underlying the conferral of a right on a third organization under Article 36.

It is also said, in favour of the "unilateral act" approach, that "there is nothing in international law to prevent two or more States from effectively creating a right in favour of another State by a treaty if they so intend".[31] However, it may also be asked why in international law two or more States should be able, through a treaty concluded between themselves, to alter the legal position of a third party without its consent. There could be reasons, political or otherwise, why a third state may not wish to be the beneficiary of a right to which it has not assented, even if such occasions are rare. An approach that insists on the conferral of such a right would attach more weight or value to the intention of the states conferring the right than to the intent of the third party, and it is not apparent why that should be the case. In any event, there would seem to be very little to be gained in not acknowledging the importance of the choice that should be open to the third party. Nothing is lost by requiring the assent of the third party. In other words, it is not obvious why the law should do away with the requirement of that assent. In this respect, it is noteworthy that Article 36 both the VCLT (dealing with rights conferred on third states) and the VCLT 1986 (dealing with third organizations) refer to the requirement of the assent (presumed in the case of the VCLT) of the beneficiary of the right arising from a treaty to which it is not party.

As already mentioned above, the VCLT 1986 intended to not make a choice between the different doctrinal approaches. The reason for this position was, that "the two doctrines would be likely to produce different results only in very exceptional cases".[32] In other words, the practical relevance of the difference between the two doctrinal approaches is not likely to be substantial.[33] Nevertheless, the fact remains that Article 36 states that a right arises for a third organization if the conferring parties agree *and* the third organization assents thereto. In other words, the assent of the third organization is required. The further point arising from the wording of Article 36 is that, while it did not mean to make a choice between the two

---

[31] YILC (1966), Vol II, 228; I. Sinclair, note 18, at 100.
[32] YILC (1966), Vol. II, at 229
[33] *Id.*, at 228.

approaches, the compromise position it adopts still requires the assent of the third organization. Accordingly, since Article 36 is also meant to account for the "unilateral act" approach, it can be said that, even under the "unilateral act" approach, i.e. that the right conferred on the third party comes into existence without its assent, there still needs to be an acceptance of that right by the third organization. Thus, should the third organization reject the right, the right would cease to exist. Once the assent is given (even if impliedly, e.g. by the exercise of that right), there is a collateral agreement about the (continuing) existence of the right. The plain meaning of Article 36 requires the acceptance of the third organization.

Article 36, as seen earlier, was intended to be silent as to the legal effect of the assent of the third party. Two reasons why the assent of the third party is required in Article 36, regardless of its precise legal effect for present purposes, is the desirability of the third party being able to decide for itself about its own legal position in relation to the right being conferred.[34] Even if it is a right (as opposed to an obligation) which is being conferred, this conferral may not necessarily be in the interests of the third party. This desirability is expressed in the requirement of the third organization's assent in Article 36(2). The second, and more important reason, is, as stated by the International Law Commission, the clear requirement of the assent of a third international organization, as distinct from the presumed assent in the case of a third state in the VCLT, "is justified by the fact that the international organization has not been given unlimited capacity and that consequently, it is not possible to stipulate that its consent shall be stipulated in respect of a right". The requirement of assent is therefore strict, in the case of an international organization.[35]

In any event, even if, as the "unilateral act" approach would have it, the right was created by a unilateral act of the parties to the original treaty, the assent given subsequently by the third party would complete the "collateral agreement" *at the point when that assent is given*. The "unilateral act" approach does not exclude the possibility of there being a subsequent agreement when the assent of the third party is given. It simply states that such an agreement is not necessary for the creation of the right. With regard to Article 16 of the ICC Statute, the Security Council can be seen to have accepted the right, or the power, by its adoption of Resolutions 1422 (2002) and 1487 (2003), pursuant to which the Security Council exercised the right of deferral provided for in Article 16 and even referred explicitly to it in the preambles of both resolutions. At this point, the agreement can be said to have been concluded" between the States Parties and the Security Council with regard to Article 16 of the ICC Statute.

---

[34] *Id.*
[35] YILC (1982), Vol. II, Part Two, at 43. See the point made by Berman, *supra* note 15.

2.3   Would the Collateral Agreement Created by Article 36 Constitute a Treaty?

Article 2 of the VCLT 1986, and the VCLT, provides that

> [f]or the purposes of the present Convention, (a) "treaty" means an international agreement governed by international law and concluded in written form: (i) between one or more States and one or more international organizations; or (ii) between international organizations, whether that agreement is embodied in a single instrument or in two or more related instruments and whatever its particular designation.

The characteristic feature of a legal agreement is that it is legally binding[36] as opposed to morally or politically binding. It is legally binding when the parties to the agreement intend it to have legal effect[37], for instance to create rights and obligations[38] or at least a relationship governed by (international) law[39]. The phrase "governed by international law" stipulates that not only must the actors involved have treaty-making capacity under international law, they must also apply this capacity with regard to the "agreement" in question.[40] For instance, if there are legal obligations created by the "agreement", they must be binding under and regulated by public international law as opposed to any chosen private law.[41] There is no doubt that both the UN and the ICC fulfil the requirements of Article 2, as they both possess treaty-making capacity in international law, and that the subject of this "agreement" is a matter regulated by public international law. In addition, if it is argued that this cannot be a true agreement because it is one-sided, in favour of the UN/Security Council, it should be remembered that the wording of Article 16 is a compromise, reached after well-known and lengthy deliberations, between the respective roles and powers of the ICC and the Security Council regarding international peace and security.[42] Furthermore, even if the agreement were "one-sided", the common law

---

[36] A. McNair, *The Law of Treaties* (1961), at 6; Reuter, *supra* note 20, paragraph 64 and 74; Fitzmaurice, *supra* note 6, at 146 and 164.

[37] Reuter, *supra* note 18, paragraphs 64 and 74.

[38] McNair, *supra* note 36; J.L. Brierly, YILC (1950), Vol. II, at 226; H. Lauterpacht, YILC (1953), Vol. II, at 90

[39] J.L. Brierly, *id.*; G. Fitzmaurice, YILC (1956), Vol. II, at 104 and 107.

[40] On this see Fitzmaurice, *supra* note 6, at 160-161.

[41] McNair, *supra* note 36, at 4-5; Fitzmaurice, *supra* note 6, at 160 *ff*; H. Waldock at the Vienna Diplomatic Conference on the Law of Treaties (1968), UN Doc. A/Conf.39/11/Add.2, paragraph 6, at 9. The observations of these authors were made in relation to treaties between states, but the observations apply, *mutatis mutandis*, to treaties to which international organizations are party.

[42] For further details on this compromise, see Elias and Quast, *supra* note 1, at 166-169, and references therein.

doctrine of consideration "never met with general acceptance"[43] and is not a part of the requirements for the existence of a treaty. In addition, it is immaterial whether the "collateral agreement" is concluded in written form or not. Article 3 of VCLT 1986 itself provides that the

> fact that the present Convention does not apply ... to international agreements not in written form between one or more States and one or more international organizations, or between international organizations; or shall not affect the legal force of such agreements or the application to them of any of the rules set forth in the present Convention to which they would be subject under international law independently of the Convention.

For these reasons, the collateral agreement can be considered to satisfy the criteria in order to be classified as a treaty.[44]

2.4 Who Would be the Parties to the "Treaty" Emanating from the "Collateral Agreement"?

The analysis thus far has proceeded on the assumption that the States Parties to the ICC Statute confer a right on the Security Council and a corresponding obligation upon themselves. However, the reality is that the ICC Statute is the constituent treaty of an international organization. As a result, the States Parties to the ICC Statute in fact confer the right on the Security Council with a corresponding obligation upon the ICC – the organization created in the treaty – and not upon themselves, as such. The question is whether this fact has consequences for the preceding analysis.

With respect to the existence of a treaty, the only difference is that the identity of one of the parties to this "treaty" is changed. The fact that the ICC itself, and not the States Parties, is subject to the obligation created by this treaty does not change the fact that a relationship between two subjects of international law exists, which is legally binding under and governed by international law. The question is how to characterize the position of the ICC in this "treaty" arrangement. It is submitted that the international organization, in this case the ICC, upon the entry into force of its constituent treaty, assumes the rights and obligations set out in that constituent instrument. In the present case, the ICC assumes the rights and obligations vis-à-vis the Security Council by way of the provisions of the ICC Statute. The entire point of the treaty, i.e. the ICC Statute, is to set out the legal

---

[43] J. Klabbers, *The Concept of Treaty in International Law* (1996), at 86.

[44] For what it is worth, it may be concluded that the doctrinal differences between the "unilateral act" analysis and the "collateral agreement" approach do not have any material consequences on the foregoing analysis of Article 16 of the ICC Statute under the law of treaties. As seen above, the "unilateral act" approach does not exclude the possibility that an agreement between the parties and the third party may be concluded subsequently.

position governing the organization created, the ICC, and the extent of its international legal capacity. Article 16 of that Statute confers on the Security Council rights in relation to the international organization, which those States Parties create by means of the treaty. After the entry into force of that constituent treaty and the establishment of the organization, the role of the States Parties ceases, as such, with respect to those rights and obligations which are created for the international organization, rather than the States Parties, unless the contrary is indicated. At that point, the organization, the ICC, assumes the rights and obligations that were set out for it in the treaty, its Statute. This is precisely what Article 16 reflects: the desire of the States Parties to create an organization with particular rights and duties vis-à-vis the Security Council.

The problem concerns the relationship between the international organization, an independent legal person, and the States Parties to the instrument creating that organization. This relationship is, to say the least, a close one, as the States Parties conclude an agreement to pursue a common purpose through the establishment of the organization. The aims of the organization are also the aims of the States Parties to its constituent treaty. Despite this close relationship, the organization is, however, not the same legal person as the States Parties to its constituent treaty. The organization has separate legal personality from the States Parties to the constituent treaty. It could be said that the relationship between them is a relationship of principal and agent or representative. It is, however, difficult to consider the States Parties to the treaty establishing the organization as being agents or representatives of the organization, as the organization does not exist prior to the entry into force of the treaty. It is for this reason that it is preferable to view the organization as merely having assumed the rights and obligations created for it by the States Parties to the constituent treaty. There could of course be obligations which remain the obligations of the States Parties after the organization is created, such as those relating to financial contributions to the organization. However, there are also rights and obligations which are exclusively those of the organization.

For this reason, based on the special relationship between an international organization and the States Parties to its constituent instrument, it is submitted that the ICC is a party to the agreement with the Security Council.

We will return to the potential consequence of this conclusion in Section 4 below.

3. The Relationship Agreement Between the UN and the ICC

Article 2 of the ICC Statute provides that the ICC "shall be brought into relationship with the United Nations through an agreement to be approved by the Assembly of States Parties to this Statute and thereafter concluded by the President of the Court on its behalf".[45] The accordant Relationship Agreement[46] is intended to regulate the working relationship between the ICC and the UN by establishing a legal basis for their co-operation within their respective mandates. According to the preamble of the ICC Statute[47], the ICC was established in order to put an end to impunity for the perpetrators of crimes, which threaten the peace, security and well-being of the world. Accordingly, the ICC will be acting in the domain of international peace and security, a domain in which, according to Article 24 of the UN Charter, the UN Security Council has primary responsibility. Therefore, Article 13 of the ICC Statute establishes a possibility for the Security Council to trigger the jurisdiction of the ICC by referring specific situations to the Prosecutor. Article 16 of the ICC Statute allows the Security Council to preserve its main responsibility on international peace and security by deferring situations from the ICC's jurisdiction.[48] It is this same field of action[49] which calls for co-operation between those entities. The ICC is an independent international institution which was established, according to the preamble of its Statute, "in relationship with the United Nations system". The Relationship Agreement, like the provisions of the ICC Statute itself, therefore reflects a balance between the need to co-operate on the one hand and the independence of both bodies on the other.

Evidently, a more obvious treaty relationship, other than the one based on Article 16 of the ICC Statute, will be established by the proposed Relationship Agreement, as this agreement is a treaty. This Relationship Agreement is not the focus of this essay, as it will only cover certain aspects of the overall relationship between the ICC and the UN, while the issues raised in this chapter relate to the role of the Security Council vis-à-vis the ICC, which are covered explicitly in the ICC Statute. Nevertheless, it is important with respect to the foregoing analysis of Article 16, in the following way: The negotiations in the drafting of Article 16 (referred to above)[50] taken together with the spirit of the numerous references in both the draft Relationship Agreement[51] and the preamble to the ICC Statute, indicate a mutual recognition and understanding of the respective roles of the ICC and the UN. This could provide support, in a more general way, for the

---

[45] The Relationship Agreement entered into force upon approval of the UN General Assembly and of the Assembly of States Parties on 13 September 2004.

[46] *Supra* note 3.

[47] At paragraphs 3-5.

[48] Bergsmo and Pejić, *supra* note 1, article 16, paragraph 7; Sarooshi, *supra* note 1, at 39; see also Condorelli and Villalpando, *supra* note 1, at 653.

[49] Condorelli and Villalpando, *supra* note 1, at 221; Wilmshurst, note 1, at 39.

[50] Elias and Quast, *supra* note 42.

[51] See the preamble and articles 1-3 of the draft Relationship Agreement, *supra* note 3.

analysis of Article 16 as being the basis for a treaty relationship between the two organizations. The negotiations and mutual recognition of their respective roles buttress the notion of an "agreement", an understanding, between the two bodies, particularly since Article 16 is the one of the provisions, if not *the* provision, of the ICC Statute with regard to which disputes or conflicts of responsibilities between the UN and the ICC might arise. Any reading of Article 16 is to be considered in the context of this "agreement", this understanding. The importance of the notion of an agreement or mutual understanding will be developed further in the next Part.

4. The Problem of *Compétence de la Compétence*. The ICC as a Party to an Agreement and as a Judge with Respect to that Agreement

The competence of international courts and tribunals to determine their own jurisdiction over a case is universally recognized in international law.[52] This competence is supplementary and temporally prior to questions of the competence of the court or tribunal to deal with the merits of the case. In contemporary international law, the jurisdiction of a court or tribunal to determine its jurisdiction, or *la compétence de la compétence*, or *Kompetenz-Kompetenz*, is an inherent, incidental power of a court,[53] which is independent from any explicit expression in the constitutive document of the Court.[54] By exercising its *Kompetenz-Kompetenz*, a court decides whether a case falls within its jurisdiction. In the case of the ICC, Article 19 of the ICC Statute provides that the ICC shall satisfy itself that it has jurisdiction in any case brought before it. It is, therefore, within the ICC's inherent jurisdiction to determine whether a Chapter VII resolution requesting a deferral of a case is valid in law and, therefore, binding on it, as such resolutions prevent the

---

[52] C.F. Amerasinghe, *Jurisdiction of International Tribunals* (2002), at 141. See also the Decision on the Defence Motion for Interlocutory Appeal on Jurisdiction by the Appeals Chamber of the International Criminal Tribunal for the Former Yugoslavia ("ICTY") in Prosecutor *v.* Dusko Tadić, IT-94-1, AR72, 2 October 1995, ("*Tadić* case") <http://www.un.org/icty/tadic/appeal/decision-e/51002.htm>, paragraphs 14-41.

[53] Regarding the suggestion that in the first half of the 20th century, in public international law there was some discussion as to whether *Kompetenz-Kompetenz* is based upon the will of the parties to a case, in consequence, be withdrawn from a court, see Amerasinghe, *supra* note 52, at 126 ff.

[54] *Tadić* case, *supra* note 52; O. Trifterer, *Commentary on the Rome Statute of the International Criminal Court: Observers' Notes, Article by Article* (1999), at 407.

ICC from exercising its jurisdiction over that case (albeit for a limited period of time).[55]

According to the analysis in the preceding sections, a collateral agreement, giving rise to a "treaty relationship" between the ICC and the United Nations can be said to exist based on Article 16 of the ICC Statute and the overall relationship between the two bodies, which creates a right for the Security Council to "request" the deferral of cases and a corresponding obligation on the part of the ICC to defer such cases. The problem that arises in this context is the following. If the ICC exercises its *Kompetenz-Kompetenz* with regard to Article 16 of the ICC Statute, i.e. if it reviews the legality of a Security Council Resolution based on Chapter VII of the UN Charter and Article 16 of the ICC Statute in order to ensure that the requested deferral of its jurisdiction is valid in law, it will be acting in two different capacities. On the one hand, it would be taking a decision as to whether the resolution meets the criteria set out in Article 16 of the ICC Statute, i.e. (i) it will be acting as a court. Simultaneously, it would be pronouncing authoritatively on its own obligation to defer the case of deferral, an obligation it has towards the Security Council stemming from the "treaty" relationship, i.e. (ii) it will also be a party to an agreement.[56]

This would appear to pose a problem of conflict of interest on the part of the Court. As Amerasinghe puts it, "[b]ecause ... the tribunal ... may have an interest in preserving its own jurisdiction and it makes the decision on the issue, it is possible to postulate an inherent conflict of interest".[57] With regard to Article 16 of the ICC Statute, the ICC as a judicial body would be in a position to pronounce authoritatively about the existence of one of its own obligations under the "treaty". This is why the possible conflict of interest is more tangible in a decision of the ICC relating to Article 16 of the ICC Statute, than in other decisions courts take with regard to their own jurisdiction. For example, in the *Tadić* case the issue was whether the ICTY could validly review an act of the Security Council, the organ which established the ICTY.[58] The possibility of the International Court of Justice reviewing resolutions of the Security Council has also been the subject of

---

[55] Condorelli and Villalpando, *supra* note 1, chapter 4.3, at 221 and chapter 17.2, at 648 and 650; W. Schabas, *An Introduction to the International Criminal Court* (2004), at 84; Stahn, *supra* note 1, 4B1 at the end; See also Sarooshi, *supra* note 1, at 44 with regard to a referral resolution, article 13 (b) RS; A. Zimmermann and H. Scheel, "Zwischen Konfrontation und Kooperation", 50 *Vereinte Nationen* (2002), at 137, 140; Elaraby, *supra* note 1, at 43 and 45-46, seems to exclude the possibility of the review of an article 16 of the ICC Statute by the Court: "The compliance with such a resolution [i.e. article 16 of the ICC Statute] is not subject to the discretionary power of the ICC. The Council is the ultimate authority." See also Elias and Quast, note 1, at 182-185.

[56] Elias and Quast, *supra* note 1, at 180-181.

[57] Amerasinghe, *supra* note 52, at 159.

[58] *Supra* note 52, and references cited in the decision of the Tribunal.

discussion in the literature.[59] In none of these examples was there a contractual relationship between the party to an agreement, which also had the inherent judicial power to pronounce authoritatively on the content of that agreement, including its own obligations. The International Court of Justice, the Security Council and the ICTY are all organs of the United Nations and they are not separate legal persons where the judicial organs are in a "contractual" relationship with the non-judicial organs. This differs from the situation of the ICC and the Security Council. In the case of the proposed Relationship Agreement between the ICC and the UN, the dispute resolution provision in Article 22, provides that the UN and the ICC "agree to settle any dispute related to the interpretation or application of the present Agreement by appropriate means". Here there is a treaty relationship, but it is not stated that it is for the ICC to resolve such disputes. It is this "treaty" relationship based on Article 16 which distinguishes the ICC and the UN from other instances, and which presents the problem of the conflict of interest in a more acute way.

Does this conflict of interest mean that the ICC is to relinquish its competence to determine jurisdictional issues arising from Article 16, and that a third party, such as the International Court of Justice ("ICJ"), should resolve such disputes?[60] Although, during the *travaux préparatoires*, suggestions were made to establish a mechanism allowing the ICC to request advisory opinions of the ICJ,[61] they were neither included in the ICC Statute nor in the draft of the Relationship Agreement.[62]

The argument could be put forward that, to the extent that there is a treaty relationship between the ICC and the Security Council, the inherent power of the ICC to determine its own jurisdiction should be maintained in spite of this conflict of interest. This would not simply be based on the fact that the power is inherent, as that would simply beg the question. Rather, the reason for this would be that, after all, to the extent that there is as real an "agreement" as has been suggested in the preceding sections of this chapter

---

[59] See, e.g., D. Akande, "The International Court of Justice and the Security Council: Is there Room for Judicial Control of Decisions of the Political Organs of the United Nations?", 46 *ICLQ* (1997), 309-343.

[60] The only reference made to the International Court of Justice in the ICC Statute with regard to dispute settlement is contained in Article 119(2). However, this relates to the settlement of disputes not concerning the judicial function of the ICC only, which excludes disputes between the ICC and the Security Council about the legality of a Security Council resolution based on Article 16 of the ICC Statute.

[61] See Condorelli and Villalpando, *supra* note 1, at 231, referring to paragraph 23 of the *Report of the Preparatory Committee on the Establishment of an International Criminal Court*, Vol. I, UN Doc.A/51/22 (13 September 1996).

[62] It could however be argued that the International Court may not be the most suitable body for this purpose, as it is itself an organ of the United Nations Organization, its principal judicial organ.

between the ICC and the UN, an agreement which is the basis of this "conflict of interest", it could be said that the Security Council has assented, albeit implicitly to the competence of the ICC to determine whether its Article 16/Chapter VII resolutions had been validly adopted. The ICC Statute does not contain any limitations on the competence of the ICC to determine its own competence nor any alternative method of dispute resolution relating to the interpretation of the Statute in disputes between itself and the ICC.

However, it could be that the occasion for the kind of dispute under discussion is unlikely to arise in practice. The "review" of the resolutions of the Security Council would probably be limited to the manner of their adoption, as it would be difficult, given the spirit of co-operation, which is supposed to govern the relationship between the ICC and the UN, for the ICC to enter into a review of the reasons according to which the Security Council would adopt the resolution requesting deferral.[63] It may also be a challenge to rule authoritatively that the Security Council will fail to comply with the rather generous rules that have been developed through its own practice over a long period of time. At the same time, much would depend on the particular resolution at hand, and, as has been pointed out elsewhere, there could be other *substantive* grounds for impeaching the legal effect of Article 16 resolutions.[64]

5. Conclusion

To summarize, it will be apparent that the foregoing speculations test the limits of the concept of a "treaty". It may well be that a treaty analysis is not the obvious means of characterizing or analyzing the relationship between the ICC and the United Nations in terms of their respective roles in the maintenance of international peace and security, as this is more obviously a constitutional matter. Even in that event, the foregoing analysis is of interest as an enquiry into the nature and possible roles played by the notion of a treaty in contemporary international relations, particularly with regard to the situation of international organizations.

---

[63] For further discussion of the prospects of review of an article 16 resolution by the Security Council, see Elias and Quast, *supra* note 1, at 182-185.
[64] *Id.*, at 184; and Stahn, *supra* note 1, generally.

CHAPTER EIGHT

The Kyoto Protocol Compliance Regime and the Law of Treaties

1. Introduction

1.1 The Kyoto Protocol and its Compliance Mechanism

The Kyoto Protocol[1] ("the Protocol") is a protocol to the 1992 United Nations Framework Convention on Climate Change (referred to in this essay as the "Climate Change Convention").[2] The Protocol was adopted in 1997 at the Conference of the Parties to the Climate Change Convention. The Kyoto Protocol entered into force on 16 February 2005. Even before its entry into force, certain of its provisions have been given some effect through an informal procedure that involves their adoption in meetings of the Parties to the Climate Change Convention. In particular, this procedure has been adopted in connection with the compliance mechanism under the Kyoto Protocol. The setting up of a compliance mechanism is envisaged in Article 18 of the Protocol itself, which provides as follows:

> The Conference of the Parties ... serving as the meeting of the Parties to this Protocol shall, at its first session, approve appropriate and effective procedures and mechanisms to determine and to address cases of non-compliance with the provisions of the Protocol, including through the development of an indicative list of consequences, taking into account the cause, type, degree and frequency of non-compliance. Any procedures and

---

[1] Kyoto Protocol to the United Nations Framework Convention on Climate Change, 37 *ILM* 22 (1998); see also http://unfccc.int, UNCCC, Conference of the Parties, 3rd. Sess., UN Doc.FCCC/CP/1997/L.7/Add.1 (1998).

[2] United Nations Framework Convention on Climate Change, opened for signature 4 June 1992, entered into force 21 March 1994, text in: 31 *ILM* 849 (1992); see also <http://unfccc.int>.

mechanisms under this Article entailing binding consequences shall be
adopted by means of an amendment to this Protocol.

In 2001, the Conference of the Parties to the Climate Change Convention
adopted a text laying down the "procedures and mechanisms relating to
compliance under the Kyoto Protocol."[3] The first Meeting of the Parties to
the Protocol that will formally adopt this compliance mechanism has not
taken place, and the amendment to the Protocol envisaged in Article 18 (see
above) has, therefore, not yet been effected.

1.2 The Scope of this Chapter

This chapter will focus on certain issues arising from the relationship of the
Climate Change Convention, the Kyoto Protocol, and its compliance regime
with certain provisions of the law of treaties as codified in the 1969 Vienna
Convention on the Law of Treaties (the "VCLT"). Three issues will be
raised in relation to the possible operation of the VCLT:

(a) What is the nature of the treaty relationship between the Parties to the
Kyoto Protocol? This question has to be viewed not only in relation to the
relevant provisions of the Kyoto Protocol, but also to Article 30 of the VCLT

---

[3] Decision 24/CP.7, FCC/CP/2001/13/Add.3, Procedures and Mechanism Relating to
Compliance under the Kyoto Protocol, 8th Plenary Meeting, 7th Session 2001. The Decision
stated, *inter alia*, the following:

"*Recognizing* the need to prepare for the early entry into force of the Kyoto
Protocol,

Also recognizing the need to prepare for the timely operation of the
procedures and timely operation of the procedures and mechanisms relating to
compliance under the Kyoto Protocol,

Noting that it is the prerogative of the Conference of the Parties serving as the
meeting of the Parties to the Kyoto Protocol to decide on the legal form of the
procedures and mechanisms relating to compliance,

1. *Decides* to adopt the text containing the procedures and mechanisms
relating to compliance under the Kyoto Protocol annexed hereto;

2. *Recommends* that the Conference of the Parties serving as meeting of the
Parties to the Kyoto Protocol, at its first session, adopt the procedures and
mechanisms relating to compliance annexed hereto in terms of Article 18 of
the Kyoto Protocol."

On the history of the negotiations of the compliance procedure under the Kyoto Protocol see
R. Lefeber, "From The Hague to Bonn to Marakesh and Beyond: A Negotiating History of
the Compliance Regime Under the Kyoto Protocol", *Hague YIL* (2001) 25. See also J.
Brunnée, "A Fine Balance: Facilitation and Enforcement in the Design of a Compliance
Regime for the Kyoto Protocol", 13 *Tulane Environmental Law Journal* (2000), at 223.

(concerning the application of successive treaties relating to the same subject matter).[4]

(b) What, if any, were the obligations of signatories to the Kyoto Protocol with respect to the implementation of its provisions, prior to its entry into force? As will be described below, this issue arises because certain provisions of the Protocol have been implemented through the medium of the Meeting of the Parties to the Climate Change Convention, even though the Protocol has not yet entered into force. Here, we must ask what role Article 18 of the VCLT might play (concerning the obligation not to defeat the object and purpose of the treaty prior to its entry into force).[5]

(c) Is suspension of a State-Party under compliance regimes generally, and under the Kyoto Protocol compliance regime in particular, governed by the suspension norms of the law of treaties (namely, the rule in Article 60 of the VCLT) or by the law of state responsibility (specifically, the countermeasures rule)?[6]

1.3 Compliance Regimes

Compliance regimes are designed to provide a softer approach to treaty non-compliance than the traditional, classic system of dispute settlement under international law.[7] The main purpose of compliance procedures (at least in their facilitative form, on which see further, below) is to encourage a non-complying State to return to compliance without accusing it of wrongdoing, or holding it to account for the consequences that entail from wrongdoing. In general, it may be said that the non-compliance regime "lacks complexity; it has a non-confrontational and transparent character; it leaves the competence for decision-making on the Contracting Parties to each Convention; and it includes a transparent and revolving reporting system and procedures."[8]

---

[4] See Section 3.1 below.

[5] See Section 3.2 below.

[6] See Section 3.3 below.

[7] The Group of Legal Experts under the Montreal Protocol has stated that a non-compliance procedure "allows and encourages the parties to assist each other in the implementation of the control measures agreed by them and to a certain degree to prevent them from referring cases of breaches of the Protocol directly to confrontational settlement of disputes procedure." Ms. C. Brojoklund, who was the first President of the Montreal Protocol Implementation Committee, described the Montreal Protocol NCP as "an assisting rather than dispute solving body which is to act as a new forum outside the traditional judicial framework." Cited in: I. Rummel-Bulska, "Implementation Control: Non-Compliance and Dispute Settlement", in: W. Lang (ed.) *The Ozone Treaties and Their Influence on the Building of International Legal Regime; Special Issue: Österreichische aussenpolitische Dokumentation*, 1996.

[8] Paragraph 23.1 of the 1993 Lucerne ECE Declaration, Environment for Europe, <http://www.unece.org/env/europe/>. See also on the character of non-compliance regimes: G. Handl, "Controlling Implementation of Compliance with International Economic

The compliance regime under the Kyoto Protocol is just one of many compliance regimes currently operating in the environmental field. Other examples include the regime of the 1987 Montreal Protocol on Substances that Deplete the Ozone Layer ("Montreal Protocol"),[9] and also the Aarhus Convention.[10] Compliance mechanisms establish multilateral fora that provide for discussion of compliance problems before they develop into formal disputes. They allow for the resolution of these problems without recourse to international adjudication. In fact, the entire mechanism upon which such procedures are based is fundamentally different from dispute settlement. Access to compliance procedures is much broader and is established in a different way. For example, the compliance procedure established by the Montreal Protocol is designed to assist in securing compliance rather than to punish non-compliance. To that end, one of the ways in which the compliance mechanism can be set in motion is through a submission by the non-complying Party itself.[11] Alternatively, a concerned party may invoke the procedures in question or the Secretariat may report cases of apparent non-compliance.

Commitments: The Rocky Road from Rio", 5 *Colorado JEL&P* (1994), 329; J. Brunnée, "The Kyoto Protocol: Testing Ground for Compliance Theories?", in 63 *Zeitschrift für Ausländisches öffentliches Recht und Völkerrecht*, (2003), at 255-280; see also R. Wolfrum, "Means of Ensuring Compliance with and Enforcement of International Environmental Law", 272 *RCADI* (1998) 56 *et seq.*; G. Loibl, "Dispute Avoidance and Dispute Settlement in International Law-Some Reflections on Recent Developments", XXIV *Curso Del Derecho Internacional* (1997), 101.

[9] Adopted in 1992 by the Copenhagen Amendment, see Report of the Fourth Meeting of the Parties to the Montreal Protocol on Substances that Deplete the Ozone Layer, UNEP/OzL.Pro.4/15 25 November 1992. See also Review of the Non-Compliance Procedure of the Montreal Protocol Pursuant to Decision IX/35 of the 9th Meeting of the Parties, Ad Hoc Group of Legal and Technical Experts of Non-Compliance with the Montreal Protocol, First Session, Geneva, 3-4 July 1998.

[10] The 1998 Convention on Access to Information, Public Participation in Decision-Making and Access to Justice in Environmental Matters ("Aarhus Convention"), signed on 25 June 1998 in Aarhus (Denmark) and entered into force on 30 October 2001, full text see <http://www.unece.org/env/pp/documents/cep43e.pdf>; First Meeting of the Parties, Luca, 21-23 October 2002, decision I/7, Structure and Functions of the Compliance Committee and Procedures for the Review of Compliance.

[11] Paragraph 4 of the non-compliance procedure under the Montreal Protocol: "[w]here a Party concludes that despite having made its best, *bona fide* efforts, it is unable to comply fully with its obligations under the Protocol, it may address to the Secretariat a submission in writing, explaining, in particular, the specific circumstances that it considers to the cause of its non-compliance. The Secretariat shall transmit such submissions to the Implementation Committee which shall consider it as soon as practicable." Adopted by Decision IV/5 and Annexes IV and V of the Fourth Meeting of the Parties to the Montreal Protocol, UNEP/ Ozl.Pro.4/15, 25 November 1992, 32 *ILM* 874 (1993).

The 1989 Basel Convention,[12] for example, demonstrates the facilitative character of non-compliance procedures.[13] Article 1 of the "Mechanism for Promoting Implementation and Compliance" therein, adopted at the sixth meeting of the Conference of the Parties to the Basel Convention, states that:

> The objective of the mechanism is to assist Parties to comply with their obligations under the Convention and to facilitate, promote, monitor and aim to secure the implementation of and compliance with the obligations under the Convention.[14]

Article 2 in turn states further that:

> The mechanism shall be non-confrontational, transparent, cost-effective and preventive in nature, simple, flexible, non-binding and oriented in the direction of helping parties to implement the provisions of the Basel Convention. It will pay particular attention to the special needs of developing countries and countries with economies in transition, and is intended to promote cooperation between all Parties. The mechanism should complement work performed by other Convention bodies and by the Basel Convention Regional Centres.[15]

Indeed, the latest mechanism under the Basel Convention represents a further softening of the approach usually taken to non-compliance in that it only contains a facilitative procedure and no enforcement procedure. In particular, it contains no provision allowing for the suspension of a non-complying Party. The facilitation procedure set out in Article 19 of the mechanism provides only for the establishment of a *voluntary* "compliance action plan." If compliance remains an issue after the establishment of such a compliance action plan, the most that Article 20 allows the administering Committee is (a) to consider further support, and (b) to issue a cautionary statement and to "provide" advice regarding future compliance in order to help the Parties implement the provisions of the Basel Convention and to promote cooperation between all Parties.[16]

Unlike traditional dispute settlement procedures, compliance mechanisms also do not require the consent of the interested states. There need not be an "injured State" in order to invoke the procedure. This differs from the traditional stance under the rules of state responsibility, even taking into

---

[12] The 1989 Convention on the Control of Transboundary Movements of Hazardous Wastes and Their Disposal ("Basel Convention"), signed 22 March 1989, entered into force 5 May 1992, 28 *ILM* 657 (1989).

[13] See Monitoring The Implementation of and Compliance with the Obligations Set Out by the Basel Convention, Geneva, December 9-13, 2002.

[14] UNEP/CHW.6/40, *Report of the Conference of the Parties to the Basel Convention on the Control of Transboundary Movements of Hazardous Wastes and their Disposal, 6th Meeting, Geneva,* 9-13 December 2002, <http://www.basel.int/COP6/ENGLISH/Report40e.doc>.

[15] *Id..*

[16] *Id..*

consideration that the International Law Commission in its Articles on State Responsibility has broadened the universe of States that, in principle, may invoke the responsibility of another State.[17] Compliance procedures are designed to ensure continuing participation in a cooperative treaty regime and fulfilment of obligations that are not always reciprocal in nature. The underlying logic here is that failure to fulfil these obligations will affect the achievement of the common goals of a treaty, such as a treaty which has the protection of the environment as its principal aim. These treaty regimes are designed to protect the environment in such areas where the pace, magnitude and irreversibility of environmental damage render *inter partes* enforcement, in any event, ineffective (as in the case of the Montreal and Kyoto Protocols).

Not only are compliance procedures designed to prevent harmful activities, they are also meant to induce the cessation of continuing harm, such as harm to the environment. That preventive element is reflected in provisions dealing with assessment (Article 6 of the Montreal Protocol), monitoring (Article 9 of the 1979 Convention on Long- Range Transboundary Air Pollution Treaty, the "LRTAP")[18] and verification of compliance (Article 19 of the 1989 Basel Convention[19] and Article 21 of the 1995 Straddling Stocks Agreement[20]).

Facilitative measures are typically linked with the compliance regime. For example, in the context of ozone layer and climate change, the system of reporting and data collecting provides the data needed to make the compliance mechanism work. Such facilitative measures make it possible to verify whether, and to what degree, States comply with their treaty obligations.[21] Even though facilitative measures could stand alone, it is useful to combine them with compliance procedures. For our purposes, these two elements of compliance regimes, *sensu largo*, are reflected in the two "branches" of the Compliance Committee, the facilitative and the

---

[17] Draft Articles on State Responsibility of States for Wrongful Acts, Articles 42 and 48, in *Report of the International Law Commission on the Work of its Fifty-third Session*, UNGAOR, 56th Sess., Supp.No.10, at 43, UN Doc. A/56/10 (2001), *available at* <http://www.un.org/law/ilc>. The Articles are also annexed to GA Res. 56/83, para.2 (Dec.12, 2001). See also J. Crawford, *The International Law Commission's Articles on State Responsibility: Introduction, Text and Commentary* (2002).

[18] Signed 13 November 1979, entred into force 16 March 1983, see UNECE website for full text of LRTAP: <http://www.unece.org/env/lrtap/full%20text/1979.CLRTAP.e.pdf>.

[19] *Supra* note 13.

[20] The 1995 Agreement on Straddling and Highly Migratory Fish Stocks ("Straddling Stocks Agreement"), signed 4 December 1995, entered into force 11 December 2001, 34 *ILM* 1542 (1995).

[21] C. Chinkin, "International Environmental Law in Evolution", in: T. Jewel and J. Steele (eds.), *Law in Environmental Decision-Making, National, European, and International Perspectives* (1998), at 292-265.

enforcement branches, set up under the Kyoto Protocol (see Section 2.2 below).

2. The Kyoto Protocol and Its Compliance Regime

2.1 General Structure

The Climate Change Convention acknowledges in its Preamble that climate change and its adverse effects are a common concern of mankind. Article 2 outlines the main purpose of the Convention, which is to achieve the stabilisation of greenhouse gas concentrations in the atmosphere at a level that would prevent dangerous anthropocentric interference with the climate system. The parties to the Climate Change Convention are divided into Annex I countries (developed countries and countries with economies in transition) and non-Annex I countries (developing countries). Annex I countries are obliged to return, by the year 2000, to their 1990 levels of greenhouse emissions.[22] They have also committed themselves to financial mechanisms and technology transfer obligations in order to enable developing countries to achieve the "effective implementation" of the regime.[23] Brunnée points out that: "The dichotomy between Annex I and non-Annex I party commitments also underpins the Kyoto Protocol. It contains no new commitments for non-Annex I parties, only a series of soft, highly qualified, policy-related commitments, and the language neither envisages future emission-related commitments by developing countries nor provides for their creation."[24]

The main provisions of the Kyoto Protocol are contained in Articles 3 (imposing legally-binding emissions reductions and limitations by the Annex I parties),[25] 5 and 7 (monitoring and reporting commitments). Furthermore, Annex I parties, in order to discharge their commitments, are accorded

---

[22] Article 4.2 (a) of the Climate Change Convention.

[23] Articles 4.1 and 12.1 of the Climate Change Convention.

[24] Brunnée, *supra* note 3, at 230.

[25] Article 3 (1): "The Parties included in Annex I shall, individually or jointly, ensure that their aggregate anthropocentric carbon dioxide equivalent emissions of the greenhouse gases listed in Annex A do not exceed their assigned amounts, calculated pursuant to their quantified emission limitation and reduction commitments inscribed in Annex B and in accordance with a view to reducing their overall emissions of such gases by at least 5 percent below 1990 levels in the commitment period 2008 to 2012." Individual parties' "quantified emission limitation and reduction commitments" ("QELRCs") are included in Annex B of the Protocol and their resulting "assigned amounts" range from eight percent reductions to ten percent increases.

flexibility in employing the various mechanisms.[26] These mechanisms help countries to meet their targets, for example, by the trading of emissions. Architecturally, the two central features of the Kyoto Protocol are that (1) all the mechanisms are subject to Article 3.1 (the core provision of the Protocol) and (2) the several mechanisms are themselves interrelated. For example, the transfer or acquisition of reduction units between the Parties, for the purpose of Article 3, is subject to compliance by the Parties with their obligations under Articles 5 and 7. Non-compliance would entail the Parties losing their eligibility for such transactions.

The key provision is Article 18, which sets up the system of non-compliance under the Kyoto Protocol.[27] A major prerequisite of any effective non-compliance system is transparency amongst the Parties. A sound national reporting system is critical. The Climate Change Convention had already introduced a reporting obligation on all Parties,[28] and the Kyoto Protocol is based on a system of in-depth reporting on the general compliance of the Parties with Article 3.[29] There is, furthermore, a system of expert assessment of the implementation of the commitments of the Parties (Article 8.3). These in turn lead to expert reports to the Conference of the Parties which serves as a meeting of Parties to the Protocol (hereafter,

---

[26] Other significant provisions are contained in Article 4 (joint fulfilment), Article 6 (joint implementation), Article 12 (use of clean development mechanism – the "CDM"), and Article 17 (international emission trading).

[27] "The Conference of the Parties serving as the meeting of the Parties to this Protocol shall, at its first session, approve appropriate and effective procedures and mechanisms to determine and to address cases of non-compliance with the provisions of this Protocol, including through the development of an indicative list of consequences, taking into account the cause, type, degree and frequency of non-compliance. Any procedures and mechanisms under this Article entailing binding consequences shall be adopted by means of an amendment to this Protocol." The Procedures and mechanisms relating to compliance under the Protocol were adopted by Decision 24/CP.7 at the 8th plenary meeting of the COP, 10 November 2001. See note 3 above. See further section 3 of Chapter 6 above.

[28] Article 12.1.

[29] Article 7: "1. Each Party included in Annex I shall incorporate in its annual inventory of anthropogenic emissions by sources and removals by sinks of greenhouse gases ... submitted in accordance with relevant decisions of the Conference of the Parties, the necessary supplementary information for the purposes of ensuring compliance with Article 3, to be determined in accordance with paragraph 4 below. 2. Each party included in Annex I shall incorporate in its national communication, submitted under Article 12 of the Convention, the supplementary information necessary to demonstrate compliance with its commitments under this Protocol, to be determined in accordance with paragraph 4 below. 3. Each Party included in Annex I shall submit the information required under paragraph 1 above annually, beginning with the first inventory due under the Convention for the first year of the commitment period after this Protocol has entered into force for that Party. Each such Party shall submit the information required under paragraph 2 above as part of the first national communication due under the Convention after this Protocol has entered into force for it and after the adoption of guidelines as provided for in paragraph 4 below ... ."

"COP/MOP"), and which takes a decision on any matter required for the implementation of the Protocol itself (Article 8.6).

While there is a great variety of approaches towards ensuring compliance with treaties, varying from a soft "managerial" approach to one based on enforcement procedures,[30] the Kyoto Protocol combines both these approaches.

2.2 The Facilitative and Enforcement Branches

The system under the Kyoto Protocol is administered by a Compliance Committee (the "CC"). This body functions as a plenary organ with a bureau consisting of two branches, the facilitative branch and the enforcement branch.[31] They are each required to co-operate with the other,[32] and generally speaking, the system involves highly developed procedures for reporting, expert assessment and the development of appropriate action plans. Emphasis is placed on the input of the non-complying Party itself.

2.2.1 The Facilitative Branch

The facilitative branch is responsible for providing advice and facilitation to the Parties in implementing the Protocol, and for promoting compliance by the Parties with their commitments under the Protocol. It is also responsible for providing early warning of potential non-compliance. Furthermore, the facilitative branch determines whether a Party included in Annex I is not in compliance with the following responsibilities: (a) its quantified emission limitation and reduction commitments ("QELRCs") under Article 3.1 of the Protocol; (b) the methodological and reporting requirements under Articles 4, 5.1-2 and 7.1 of the Protocol; and (c) the eligibility requirements under Articles 6, 12 and 17 of the Protocol (Section V.4 a-c of the procedure). In carrying out its tasks, the facilitative branch (which is required to take into account the principle of common but differentiated responsibilities) may do one or more of the following things: (a) to provide advice and facilitate the provision of assistance to individual Parties regarding the implementation of the Protocol; (b) to facilitate financial and technical assistance, including technology transfer and capacity building, taking into account Article 4.3-5 of the Climate Change Convention; and (c) to assist in the formulation of

---

[30] J. Werksman, "Compliance and the Kyoto Protocol: Building a Backbone into a "Flexible" Regime", 9 *YIEL* (1998), 56.

[31] Article II.1 of the procedure. On the elections to the CC see Article II. 4-6. On the composition of the facilitative branch see Article IV.1-3.

[32] Section II, para. 7 of the procedure.

recommendations to the Party concerned, taking into account Article 4.7 of the Climate Change Convention.[33]

2.2.2 The Enforcement Branch

As well as determining non-compliance by a Party, the enforcement branch also determines whether to apply adjustments or corrections to a Party's emissions obligations in the event of a disagreement between an expert review team under Article 8 of the Protocol and the Party in question (Section V.5 a-b of the procedure). The measures available to the enforcement branch are detailed in Section XV of the procedure. In the event of breach of the obligations under Article 5 (1) or (2) or Article 7 (1) or (4) of the Protocol by either Annex I or Annex II Parties, the enforcement branch may: (a) declare non-compliance; and (b) develop a compliance action plan submitted by the Party itself for review and assessment in accordance with paragraphs 2 and 3 of the compliance procedure. If the enforcement branch determines that an Annex I Party does not meet one or more of the eligibility requirements under Articles 6 (emissions transfer), 12 (clean development mechanism) or 17 (emissions trading), it is required to suspend the eligibility of that Party under those articles. Following such a suspension, the Party's eligibility may be reinstated in accordance with Section X.3 of the compliance procedure.

2.3 Outstanding Issues

2.3.1 The Multilateral Consultative Process

There are, however, unresolved issues concerning the non-compliance procedure under the Kyoto Protocol, such as its relationship with the Multilateral Consultative Process (the "MCP"),[34] and the relationship of the non-compliance procedure with the dispute settlement procedure.[35]

---

[33] Section XIV of the procedure.

[34] Article 16: "The Conference of the Parties serving as the meeting of the Parties to this Protocol shall, as soon as practicable, consider the application to this Protocol of, and modify as appropriate, the multilateral consultative process referred to in Article 13 of the Convention, in the light of any relevant decisions that may be taken by the Conference of the Parties. Any multilateral consultative process that may be applied to this Protocol shall operate without prejudice to the procedures and mechanisms established in accordance with Article 18." Article 13 of the Climate Change Convention reads as follows: "The Conference of the Parties shall, at its first session, consider the establishment of a multilateral consultative process, available to Parties on their request, for the resolution of questions regarding the implementation of the Convention."

[35] Article 19 of the Kyoto Protocol: "The provisions of Article 14 of the Convention on settlement of disputes shall apply *mutatis mutandis* to this Protocol." Article 14 of the Climate

According to the Report of the Climate Change Convention's *Ad Hoc* Group on Article 13, the MCP will in due course implement the Convention on the basis of transparency and co-operation, in a non-judicial, non-confrontational, and timely manner. The Multilateral Consultative Committee (the "MCC") on the other hand, which was established in order to consider the issues of Parties' implementation, will activate the MCP, in the event of non-compliance, at the request of the non-complying Party, another concerned Party (or group of Parties), or the COP. The MCC's task will thus be to advise the Parties, and clarify the issues with a view to resolving the problem. In this regard, the MCC is to make recommendations to the COP on measures to assist the non-complying Party to achieve compliance.[36] Brunnée says:

> The facilitative approach of the MCP reflects the nature of commitments in the [Climate Change Convention]. The MCP is not intended to produce 'findings' of non-compliance but is aimed at bringing about parties' compliance with their convention obligations. By definition, this type of approach cannot adequately address non-compliance with protocol commitments and, in particular, the target-related commitments of Annex I parties. Whether any application of the MCP-type process to the Protocol is appropriate will depend on the non-compliance procedures that the parties end up developing pursuant to Article 18. To the extent that these encompass facilitative approaches, there may be no need for a protocol-specific MCP.[37]

It appears, therefore, that the mandate of the facilitative branch of the Compliance Committee is analogous to the proposed mandate of the MCC. For this reason, in my view, there is really no need to activate the MCP at all.

2.3.2 Relationship between the Non-Compliance Procedure and the Dispute Settlement Procedure

Issues concerning the relationship between the settlement of disputes procedure (the "SDP") and the non-compliance procedure of the Kyoto Protocol form a subset of a broader and still unresolved overall problem in international law of how such procedures should interact with each other.

Exhaustive presentation of that issue, however, exceeds the framework of this study.[38] Suffice it to say that the difficult relationship between these two

---

Change Convention provides for the settlement of disputes by negotiation or non-binding conciliation, or, if the Parties so declare, by the International Court Justice and/or arbitration.

[36] *Ad Hoc* Group on Article 13, UNFCCC UN FCCC/AG13/1998/2 (1998), Decision 10/CP, adopted by the COP 4.

[37] Brunnée, *supra* note 3, at 241-242.

[38] See M. Koskenniemi, "Breach of a Treaty or Non-compliance? Reflections on the Enforcement of the Montreal Protocol", *YIEL*, (1992), at 123; M. Fitzmaurice and C.

regimes was cause for much concern under the Montreal Protocol where no agreement was reached as to the priority between these two systems. As a consequence of the parallel existence of the non-compliance regimes and the SDP, a State in default could find itself subjected to both systems. The position of such a State would be particularly aggravated under the non-compliance system of the Kyoto Protocol if the enforcement branch imposes strong measures against a Party. The possibility of suspension of the rights of a party in default creates a further, grave complication. Suspension arguably places certain parts of the non-compliance procedure within the ambit of the law of state responsibility, including the possibility of countermeasures, and raises serious questions regarding its relationship to the provisions of the VCLT. As a practical matter, there is not only the possibility of unnecessary competition here, but also of actual conflict between different findings resulting from the two regimes.

3. The Kyoto Protocol and the Law of Treaties

3.1 The Kyoto Protocol and Article 30 of the Vienna Convention on the Law of Treaties

3.1.1 The Issue

The manner in which the compliance regime under the Protocol was introduced means that all Parties to the Protocol may be Parties to the amendment containing the compliance regime. In effect, the Protocol with the compliance regime amendment will constitute a later treaty on the same subject matter as the Protocol without the compliance regime. Resolving what the treaty relationship between States that are parties to this later treaty and States that are only parties to the Protocol will, therefore, become an important issue. In the general law of treaties this situation is governed by Article 30 of the VCLT.[39]

Redgwell, "Environmental Non-Compliance Procedures and International Law", *NYIL* (2000), 36, at 43-52.

[39] Vienna Convention Article 30: "1. Subject to Article 103 of the Charter of the United Nations, the rights and obligations of States Parties to successive treaties relating to the same subject-matter shall be determined in accordance with the following paragraphs. 2. When a treaty specifies that it is subject to, or that it is not to be considered as incompatible with, an earlier treaty, the provisions of that other treaty prevail. 3. When all the parties to the earlier treaty are also parties to the later treaty but an earlier treaty is not terminated or suspended in operation under article 59, the earlier treaty applies only to the extent that its provisions are compatible with those of the later treaty. 4. When the parties to the later treaty do not include all the parties to the earlier one: (a) as between States Parties to both treaties the same rule

3.1.2 Article 30 of the VCLT (States Parties to Successive Treaties)

Article 30 of the VCLT represents one of the most complicated and obscure areas in the law of treaties.[40] Sinclair summarises the principles underlying Article 30:

> (a) If a treaty is subject to, or is not to be considered incompatible with, another treaty, that other treaty will prevail;
>
> (b) As between Parties to a treaty who become parties to a later, inconsistent, treaty, the earlier treaty will prevail only where its provisions are not incompatible with the later treaty;
>
> (c) As between a Party to both treaties and a party to only one of them, the treaty to which both are Parties will govern mutual rights and obligations of the States in question.[41]

The most important feature of Article 30 is its residual character. It operates only in the absence of express treaty provisions regulating priority. Although it is not indicated expressly in the text of the Article, its residual character was confirmed by Sir Humphrey Waldock at the Diplomatic Conference in Vienna.[42] One thing that emerged was that not all differences between treaties must entail incompatibility within the meaning of Article 30, paragraph 3.[43] Secondly, the terms "earlier" and "later" treaty are to be interpreted on the basis of the moment of adoption of the text and not of its entry into force. However, the rules laid down in Article 30 bind each Party to a treaty from the date of entry into force of the treaty for that Party.[44] Thirdly, the expression "relating to the same subject matter" must also be understood strictly. Therefore it does not apply to cases where a general treaty has an indirect impact on the content of a particular provision of an earlier treaty, a situation that would be covered by the maxim *generalia*

---

applies as in paragraph 3; (b) as between a State Party to both treaties and a State Party to only one of the treaties, the treaty to which both States are Parties governs their mutual rights and obligations. 5. Paragraph 4 is without prejudice to Article 41, or to any question of the termination or suspension of the operation of the treaty under article 60 or to any question of responsibility which may arise for State from the conclusion of or application of a treaty the provisions of which are incompatible with its obligations towards another State under another treaty." See generally: J.B. Mus, "Conflicts between Treaties in International Law", 45 *NILR* (1998), 208. The Kyoto Protocol does not contain so-called "savings clauses," i.e., clauses indicating that the terms of an earlier agreement prevail over incompatible clauses of a later agreement. Absent a savings clause, the terms of a later agreement prevail over incompatible clauses of an earlier agreement for states parties to both agreements.

[40] Sir Ian Sinclair, *The Vienna Convention on the Law of Treaties* (1984), at 93.

[41] *Id.*, at 94.

[42] *Id.*, at 97.

[43] *Id.*, at 97, citing Yasseen.

[44] *Id.*, at 98.

specialibus non derogant,[45] according to which specific provisions of a treaty retain priority over general ones.

Sinclair considered Article 30 to be "in many respects not entirely satisfactory." He goes on to elaborate that:

> The rules laid down fail to take account of the many complications which arise when there coexist two treaties relating to the same subject-matter, one negotiated at the regional level ... and another negotiated within the framework of a universal organisation. The complications are perhaps such that no attempt to lay down general rules would have disposed of all the difficulties; this is an area where State practice is continually developing, and where it may possibly have been premature to seek to establish fixed guidelines. Perhaps little harm has been done so long as the Convention rules are regarded as residuary in character ...[46]

3.1.3 Article 30 in Relation to the Kyoto Protocol

As discussed in Section 1 above, the Compliance Mechanism of the Kyoto Protocol was adopted by the Conference of the Parties to the Climate Change Convention, in effect in pursuance of Article 18 of the Protocol.[47] The operative words of Article 18, in the present context, are, "Any procedures and mechanisms under this Article entailing binding consequences shall be adopted by means of an amendment to this Protocol." Due to the residual character of Article 30 of the VCLT, when a treaty contains an amendment procedure, that procedure will therefore apply. The Kyoto Protocol contains an amendment procedure in Article 20 which may be summarised as follows:

> (a) Any Party may propose amendments to the Protocol;
>
> (b) The Parties are enjoined to make every effort to reach an agreement on any proposed amendment by consensus. If, however, consensus cannot be reached, as a last resort the amendment will be adopted by a three-fourths majority vote of the Parties present and voting at the meeting.
>
> (c) An amendment adopted in accordance with this procedure will enter into force for those Parties that have accepted it on the ninetieth day after the date of receipt by the Depositary of an instrument of acceptance by at least three-fourths of the Parties.
>
> (d) The amendment will enter into force for any other Party after the date on which that Party deposits with the Depositary its instrument of acceptance.

Under the foregoing procedure, an amendment binds only a Party that accepts it. The principle that a treaty does not create either obligations or

---

[45] *Id.*, at 98.

[46] *Id.*, at 98.

[47] For the text of Article 18, see Section 1.1 above.

rights for a third State without its consent[48] (*pacta tertiis nec nocent nec prosunt*) applies naturally to the amendment of a treaty.[49] Therefore, if the later amendment to the treaty does not include all the Parties to an earlier one, Article 30 paragraph 4 (b) of the VCLT will apply, with the result that the treaty to which both States are party governs their mutual rights and obligations. Therefore, when not all the States Parties to the Kyoto Protocol are also Parties to the amendment introducing the non-compliance procedure, the unamended Protocol would govern the relationship as between States Parties to the Protocol only and States Parties to both the Protocol and the amendment. For States Parties to both, the amended Protocol would apply.

The problem of compatibility between environmental treaties and other treaties with overlapping subject matter is not confined to the Kyoto Protocol and its non-compliance regime.[50] It may be questioned, in fact, whether any regime of detailed formal and inflexible legal rules, such as those in Article 30 of the VCLT, can resolve the complex problem of conflicts between treaties. Safrin describes the problem in the following practical terms:

> ... international lawyers and negotiators may find it more difficult to resolve the substantive issues of whether the parties actually intended to modify their existing international rights and obligations in the event of an unanticipated conflict between successive agreements. Instead, the issue may be reframed into an overarching and perhaps unanswerable question of which set of important international goals reflected in a series of treaties, such as affecting trade, human rights, law enforcement, the environment, and so on, holds greater import.[51]

Some answers may be found to these problems by examining the relationship between environmental treaties and the WTO. There is a cluster of environmental treaties of great importance that preceded the creation of the WTO that potentially clash with the agreements resulting from the 1994 Uruguay Trade Round. Central among them are the 1973 Convention on the International Trade in Endangered Species, the 1987 Montreal Protocol on Substances that Deplete the Ozone Layer and the 1989 Basel Convention on Transboundary Movement of Hazardous Wastes and Their Disposal.

---

[48] VCLT Article 34.

[49] See Sir G. Fitzmaurice, Third Report, YILC (1958), Vol. II, at 43: "Since anything that some of the parties to a treaty do *inter se* under another treaty is clearly *res inter alios acta*, it cannot in law result in any diminution of the obligations of these parties under an earlier treaty, or affect juridically the rights or position of the other parties, which remain legally intact and subsisting."

[50] S. Safrin, "Treaties in Collision? The Biosafety Protocol and the World Trade Organization Agreements", 96 *AJIL* (2002), at 606.

[51] *Id.*, note 51, at 622

The subject of conflict between these treaties and the WTO agreements has been the subject of a voluminous literature.[52] Curiously Safrin observes that: "If anything, the operations of these trade-related multilateral environmental agreements appear remarkably unaffected by the later-time Uruguay Round agreements."[53] With the greatest respect, however, for Safrin's views, her observations do not contain any lasting solution to this problem. The coexistence of conflicting treaties thus far, according to her description of existing practice, has relied entirely on the passive acceptance of the *status quo*. However, this practice may be inadequate to provide a solution in the longer term. In our view, one possible source of such a longer term solution lies in environmental law concepts such as the doctrine of the Common Heritage of Humankind (as contained in the Preamble of the Climate Change Convention)[54] and the concept of Intergenerational Equity, which may be expected to have an important, if indirect, influence on the issue. In our view, the undisputed importance for humankind of environmental issues should prevail over technical legal rules of precedence, a trend that is already evinced in the relationship between the WTO and environmental treaties. We have to look at future practice in relation to these concepts rather than at rules codified in Article 30.

3.2 Article 18 of the Vienna Convention

3.2.1 General Considerations

What obligations, if any, did the signatories to the Kyoto Protocol have prior to the entry into force of the Protocol? Article 18 of the VCLT[55] contains an "interim obligation" not to defeat the object of a treaty prior to its entry into force.[56] That interim obligation becomes operational when the signature of a

---

[52] See e.g. S. Charnovtiz, "Critical Guide to the WTO's Report on Trade and Environment", 14 *Arizona Journal of International and Comparative Law* (1997), 347-348; Safrin, *supra* note 50, at 624.

[53] Safrin, *supra* note 50, at 624.

[54] "Acknowledging that change in the earth's climate and its adverse effects are a common concern of human kind."

[55] Obligation not to defeat the object and purpose prior to its entry into force: "A State is obliged to refrain from acts which would defeat the object and purpose of a treaty when: (a) it has signed the treaty or has exchanged instruments constituting the treaty subject to ratification, acceptance or approval, until it shall have made its intention clear not to become a party to a treaty; or (b) it has expressed its consent to be bound by the treaty, pending the entry into force of the treaty and provided that such entry into force is not unduly delayed."

[56] See generally on this subject: P. McDade, "The Interim Obligation between Signature and Ratification of a Treaty: Issues Raised by the Recent Actions of Signatories to the Law of the Sea Convention with Respect to the Mining of the Deep Seabed", 32 *NILR* (1985), 5; J. Charme, "The Interim Obligation of Article 18 of the Vienna Convention on the Law of

State does not constitute the final stage of its consent to be bound by a treaty, or (even) when a State has expressed its consent to be bound, the treaty has however not yet entered into force. Aust argues that:

> It is sometimes argued that a state which has not yet ratified a treaty must, in accordance with Article 18, nevertheless comply with it, or at least, do nothing inconsistent with its provisions. The argument is clearly wrong, since the act of ratification would then have no purpose because the obligation to perform the treaty would not then be dependent on ratification. The obligation in Article 18 is only to 'refrain' (a relatively weak term) from acts which would 'defeat' (a strong term) the object and purpose of a treaty. The signatory state must therefore not do anything which would affect its *ability* fully to comply with the treaty once it has entered into force. It follows that it does not have to abstain from all acts which will be prohibited after entry into force. But the state may not do an act which would (not merely might) invalidate the basic purpose of the treaty.[57]

3.2.2 The Kyoto Protocol, the 1992 Climate Change Convention and Article 18 of the Vienna Convention

The Kyoto Protocol provides the following procedure for its entry into force:

> This Protocol shall enter into force on the ninetieth day after the date on which not less than 55 Parties to the Convention, incorporating Parties included in Annex I which accounted in total for at least 55 percent of total carbon dioxide emissions for 1990 of the Parties included in Annex I, have deposited their instruments of ratification, acceptance, approval or accession.[58]

Therefore, the Protocol established two triggers for entry into force. The first trigger is the ratification or accession by 55 governments (there are now 124 ratifications or accessions).[59] The second trigger is that ratifying or acceding governments must include developed countries representing at least 55 percent of that group's 1990 carbon dioxide emissions. At this stage the developed countries which have ratified the Protocol account for 43.9 percent of that group's 1990 carbon dioxide emissions. Russia's ratification is also expected soon and since Russia represents 17.4 percent of the group's 1990 emissions, the 55 percent requirement would automatically be met upon Russian ratification.

The Kyoto Protocol was, however, not subject to provisional application either on the basis of the Protocol itself or on the basis of a decision of the

---

Treaties: Making Sense of an Enigma", 25 *George Washington Journal of International Law and Economics* (1991), at 71.

[57] A. Aust, *Modern Treaty Law and Practice* (2000), at 94, footnotes omitted.

[58] Kyoto Protocol, Article 25, paragraph 1.

[59] As of 29 July 2004 (see <http://unfccc.int/resource/convkp.html>).

Parties. Thus far the issues concerning the implementation of the Kyoto Protocol have been addressed at the Conference of the Parties of the Climate Change Convention.[60]

The Conference of the Parties (the "COP") of the Climate Change Convention at its 8th Meeting,[61] serving as a Meeting of the Parties (the "MOP") of the Kyoto Protocol,[62] addressed issues arising from the Kyoto Protocol and took action directed at Parties to the Protocol and to the Climate Change Convention. The COP requested the Parties to the Climate Change Convention included in Annex I that are also Parties to the Kyoto Protocol to submit a report by 1 January 2006 in order to provide the COP with a basis for reviewing progress by 2005 (in accordance with Article 3, paragraph 2 of the Protocol). For example, Switzerland[63], a signatory, submitted in its national report that it agreed to cut its total greenhouse gas emissions by 8 percent of its 1990 emissions levels between 2008 and 2012. National reports on implementation of the Kyoto Protocol were submitted not on the basis of its provisional application, but within the framework of the Climate Change Convention.[64]

By using the Conference of the Parties to implement the Kyoto Protocol, an ingenious procedure therefore appeared to have been created that would allow the adoption of decisions concerning the implementation of a treaty that was not yet in force through the medium of a binding agreement, namely, the Climate Change Convention.[65] The implementation of the

---

[60] According to Article 7 of the Kyoto Protocol, each Party is obliged to incorporate in its annual reporting an inventory of anthropogenic emissions by sources and removal by sinks in accordance with the decision of the Conference of the Parties to the Climate Change Convention, and therefore within the legal framework of the Convention; further, according to Article 7.2, each Party included in Annex I must incorporate in its national communication, submitted under Article 12 of the Convention (communications of information related to implementation), the supplementary information necessary to demonstrate compliance with its commitments under the Protocol. Therefore, the possibility that the Parties to the Kyoto Protocol might, before it was in force, act within the Climate Change Convention, which was already in force, is incorporated in the terms of the Protocol.

[61] 23 October-1 November 2002, New Delhi, <http://unfccc.int/cop8/index/html>.

[62] According to Article 13 of the Kyoto Protocol, the Conference of the Parties of the Climate Change Convention has served as the Meeting of the Parties of the Kyoto Protocol.

[63] Switzerland ratified the Kyoto Protocol on 9 July 2003.

[64] See also, e.g., Report to the UNFCC from the EC on Community Actions Regarding Global Observing Systems, <http://unfcc.int/resources/docs/gcos/engocs.pdf>.

[65] There are several decisions adopted in such manner. See, e.g., FCCC/CP/2001/5/add.2, Decisions in progress on Articles 5, 7 and 8 of the Kyoto Protocol; Fccc/CP/2001/INF.5, Revised decision and guidelines text for Articles 5, 7 and 8 of the Kyoto Protocol; FCCC/CP/2001/MSC.2, Views from Parties on 'demonstrable progress' under Article 3.3 of the Kyoto Protocol; Fccc/SBSTA/2000/7, Draft Guidelines for a review process under article 8 of the Kyoto Protocol; FCCC/SBSTA/2000//INF.5/Add.1, Draft Guidelines for National

Protocol would thus exceed the requirements of Article 18 of the VCLT which only imposes a limited obligation not to frustrate the object and purpose of the treaty. This is so since States are not required at the interim stage to implement the provisions of a treaty. Notably, in this regard, the Parties to the Climate Change Convention have already committed themselves to meeting the emissions targets agreed upon in the Kyoto Protocol and to the introduction of its mechanisms. One reason for this was that the entry into force of the Kyoto Protocol was imminent and its domestic implementation requires the employment of great financial resources and the introduction of structural changes of far reaching nature. Therefore, States would have to start as early as possible to carry out its provisions.[66]

Unlike the Climate Change Convention, which is only a framework convention, the Kyoto Protocol has thereby introduced a strict and structured regime on the reduction of greenhouse gases emissions that States Parties are prepared to follow in order to protect the global climate even before the Protocol entered into force.[67]

3.3 Material Breach of a Treaty and the Kyoto Protocol

An issue concerning the material breach of a treaty in connection with compliance arises, however, in relation to one of the measures that may be adopted under a compliance regime, namely the suspension of a State Party to a treaty. As I pointed out above, the compliance mechanism of the Kyoto Protocol applies only to the Annex I Parties that do not meet one or more of the eligibility requirements under Articles 6, 12 and 17 of Kyoto Protocol.

Systems under article 5.1; FCCC/SBSTAS/2000.MISC.1and Add.1-2; FCCC/SBSTA/2000/MISC.7 and Add..1-2, Submissions from Parties, <http://unfccc.int/issues/art578.html>.

[66] There are many issues relating to the implementation of the Kyoto Protocol which require prompt and global action, such as special situation of developing States; technology transfer and capacity building. It was stated such at the 8th Conference of the Parties of the Climate Change Convention, in Decision CP.8, The Delhi Ministerial Declaration on Climate Change and Sustainable Development in the following terms: "[a]daptation to the adverse effects of climate change is of high priority for all countries. Developing countries are particularly vulnerable, especially the least developed countries and small island developing States. Adaptation requires urgent attention and action on the part of all countries. Effective and result-based measures should be supported for the development of approaches at all levels of vulnerability and adaptation as well as capacity building for the integration of adaptation concerns into sustainable development strategies. The measures should include full implementation of existing commitments under the Convention and the Marrakesh Accords."

[67] See, e.g., L. Thoms, "A Comparative Analysis of International Regimes on Ozone and Climate Change with Implications for Regime Design", 41 *Colum. J. Transnt'l L.* (2003), 795.

Suspension is limited to suspension of the eligibility of the Party concerned under these Articles, and not of the Party's rights under the Kyoto Protocol generally. Articles 6 and 17 relate to emissions trading and Article 12 relates to the CDM.[68] Such compliance regimes may best be viewed as a sort of half-way house between collective suspension of a single obligation under a multilateral treaty and collective suspension of the treaty instrument as a whole.

If a party materially breaches a multilateral treaty, however, Article 60 of the VCLT allows the other parties unanimously, or individual parties under certain circumstances, to suspend the treaty in whole or in part. In order to constitute a material breach under the VCLT, there must be a repudiation of the treaty not sanctioned by the VCLT, or the violation of a provision essential to the accomplishment of the object and purpose of the treaty. Article 60 of the VCLT also provides for termination of a treaty in case of material breach, a means that is, however, not contemplated under non-compliance procedures. On the other hand, the law of state responsibility provides for countermeasures that, in the case of a material breach, could resemble the suspension of treaty obligations under VCLT Article 60.[69] Thus, compliance procedures generally provide for flexible responses outside the realms of both state responsibility/countermeasures and material breach of a treaty, though they may also, at the same time, embody elements of both responses.

Notably, all the current non-compliance procedures, with the exception only of the Kyoto Protocol, refer to suspension "in accordance with the applicable rules of international law concerning suspension of the operation

---

[68] Article 12 defines the purpose of the CDM as being to "assist Parties not included in Annex I in achieving sustainable development and in contributing to the ultimate objective of the Convention, and to assist Parties included in Annex I in achieving compliance with their quantified emission limitation and reduction commitments under Article 3." (Article 12.2). Under Article 12.3 (b), "Parties included in Annex I may use the certified emission reductions accruing from such project activities to contribute to compliance with part of their quantified emission limitation and reduction commitments under Article 3 . . . ."

[69] The difference between countermeasures and VCLT Article 60 has been acknowledged by James Crawford, the Special Rapporteur of the International Law Commission's State Responsibility project. He said: "Countermeasures are to be clearly distinguished from the termination or suspension of treaty relations on account of the material breach of a treaty by another State, as provided for in article 60 of the Vienna Convention on the Law of Treaties. Where a treaty is terminated or suspended in accordance with article 60, the substantive legal obligations of States parties will be affected, but it is quite different from the question of responsibility that may already have arisen from the breach. Countermeasures involve conduct taken in derogation from a subsisting treaty obligation but justified as a necessary measure and proportionate response to an internationally wrongful act of the State against which they are taken. They are essentially temporary measures, taken to achieve a specified end, whose justification terminates once the end is achieved." Report of the 53rd Session of the International Law Commission, 56 UN GAOR, Supp. 10 (A/56/10), at 326 (2001).

of a treaty." It is not entirely clear, however, what is intended by this formulation. It could refer to the provisions of the VCLT concerning suspension (Article 60 and Articles 65-68). However, all the relevant Articles in the VCLT refer to individual or collective responses of the Parties in relation to suspension, while the current non-compliance procedures generally rely on a sort of specialised collective mechanism created by these conventions. Significantly, there is no place under these procedures for individual or collective State responses outside the mechanism specifically provided for. This could mean the exclusion of Article 60 of the VCLT. If so, such references to "international law" would be limited to Articles 65-68 of the VCLT, safeguarding the rights of the Parties.

Under the Montreal Protocol, suspension is, for example, included in an indicative list of measures that might be taken by a meeting of the Parties in respect of non-compliance with the Montreal Protocol. This is couched in the following terms: "Suspension [of a party is permitted], in accordance with the applicable rules of international law concerning the suspension of the operation of a treaty, of specific rights and privileges under the Protocol, whether or not subject to time limits, including those concerned with industrial rationalisation, production, consumption, trade, transfer of technology, financial mechanism and institutional arrangements."[70] Under the Aarhus Convention, the Meeting of the Parties may likewise "suspend, in accordance with the applicable rules of international law concerning the operation of a treaty, the special rights and privileges accorded to the Party concerned under the Convention."[71] The reference to rules of general international law concerning suspension contained in the compliance mechanisms of the Montreal Protocol and the Aarhus Convention could, as I have said, refer to Article 60 of the VCLT, codifying the general rules of international law relating to suspension of rights under a particular treaty as a result of a material breach of that treaty. Even if this is the case, however, Article 60 does not, in any case, expressly apply to non-material breaches. It appears that in the case of non-material breach at least, the law of countermeasures, including the requirement of proportionality, may apply instead.[72]

---

[70] Adopted by Decision IV/5 and Annex IV and V of the Fourth Meeting of the Parties to the Montreal Protocol, UNEP/OzL.Pro.4/15, 25 November 1992.

[71] Economic Commission for Europe, Meeting of the Parties to the Convention on Access to Information, Public Participation in Decision-making and Access to Justice in Environmental Matters, First Meeting, Luca, Italy, 21-23 October 2002, Draft Decision I/7, para. 37(g), UN Doc. MP.PP/2002/9.

[72] See "Naulilaa" (Responsibility of Germany for Damage Caused in the Portuguese Colonies in the South of Africa), *R.I.A.A.* (1928), Vol. II, at 1013; Air Services Agreement of 27 March 1946 (United States v. France); 18 *R.I.A.A.* (1978), 417; see also, Gabčikovo-Nagymaros Project (1997), 1997 ICJ Rep. 55, paragraph 55 . See also D. Bederman, "Counterintuiting

It is worth noting that the Montreal Protocol's non-compliance procedure envisages not only suspension of the operation of a treaty (the Protocol itself), but also of specific rights and privileges under the Protocol, as indicated above. The Aarhus Convention's non-compliance system provides, on the other hand, only for suspension of special rights and privileges, but not for suspension of the operation of the whole treaty. The procedure under the Kyoto Protocol likewise provides that suspension of eligibility regarding Articles 6, 12 and 17 of the Protocol will be effected (only) "in accordance with relevant provisions under those Articles"[73]. While all the other existing non-compliance procedures provide that suspension is implemented by the conference or meeting of the parties as the highest body set up under the treaty, and that, in relation to suspension rules of general international law apply, presumably as codified in the VCLT, the Kyoto Protocol is exceptional in this respect as a decision to suspend a Party would be adopted by the enforcement branch. Yet the provisions of the Kyoto Protocol neither create a detailed procedure nor refer to general rules of international law. The critical question which thus remains to be seen is whether a detailed procedure will be adopted or, if not, whether Article 60 will apply by default.

Article 60 of the VCLT is *lex generalis* regarding material breach of a treaty, and it is subject to the general procedural requirements of Articles 65-68 – relating to notification to other parties of a claimed breach, a three-month waiting period in the absence of special urgency before action is taken, and resort to conciliation if other dispute-settlement methods fail. Nevertheless, parties to a treaty may create their own *lex specialis* which is not subject to the material breach provisions of the VCLT by inserting specific treaty provisions that are applicable in the event of breach.[74] The purpose of such derogation may be either to permit a more severe response on the part of an injured party in an attempt to deter violations. However, it may also be to limit the responses and make them less severe in order to avoid the breakdown of the whole regime.

Countermeasures", 96 *AJIL*, (2002), at 820-822. Article 51 of Articles on Responsibility of States for Internationally Wrongful Acts (2001) sets out a proportionality requirement: "Countermeasures must be commensurate with the injury suffered, taking into account the gravity of the internationally wrongful act and the rights in question." Draft Articles on State Responsibility of States for Wrongful Acts, in *Report of the International Law Commission on the Work of its Fifty-third Session*, UNGAOR, 56th Sess., Supp.No.10, at 43, UN Doc. A/56/10 (2001), available at <http://www.un.org/law/ilc>. The Articles are also annexed to GA Res. 56/83, para.2 (Dec.12, 2001). See also James Crawford, *The International Law Commission's Articles on State Responsibility: Introduction, Text and Commentary* (2002).
[73] XV.4 Compliance Procedure of the Kyoto Protocol.
[74] B. Simma, "Reflections on Article 60 of the Vienna Convention on the Law of Treaties and its Background in General International Law", 20 *ZaöRV* 5 (1970), 82.

It appears that, taken as a whole, the system developed under the Kyoto Protocol is of the latter variety – a *lex specialis* regime with its own elaborate procedures. In this regard, further elaboration of the guidelines for implementation by the COP/MOP, envisaged in the Kyoto Protocol, will apply to the rules relating to suspension of a Party.

In contrast, the procedures in case of suspension are unclear at the level of legal principle in either the Montreal Protocol or the Aarhus Convention. It is difficult to specify in the case of these two regimes whether their compliance procedures are subject to the provisions for suspension under VCLT Article 60 or whether they represent *lex specialis* in relation to Article 60. Under Article 60 (as applicable to multilateral treaties), material breach of a treaty constitutes (for a party specially affected) a ground to be invoked to suspend the operation of the treaty. In other words, its effects are dependent upon the exercise of a right of election by a specially affected State to invoke such breach and its consequences, rather than the material breach itself giving rise *ipso facto* to the termination or suspension of the treaty. Parties not specially affected may seek recourse to the suspension remedy only where the material breach radically changes the position of every party in respect to further performance of its obligations. In addition, whenever a material breach occurs, the other parties may either unanimously suspend the treaty, in whole or in part, or terminate it. In addition, Articles 65-68 of the VCLT impose strict procedural safeguards to forestall a precipitous response to a material breach. These safeguards are rooted in the general principle of reciprocity among parties to the treaty. But environmental treaties, protecting common areas such as the global atmosphere or climate (e.g. the Climate Change Convention and the Kyoto Protocol), are based on non-reciprocal rights and obligations. In this case some complicated questions arise.

In the case of the Kyoto Protocol, it is not clear from the formulation of the relevant provision (Section XV.4) what the applicable law is in case of suspension under its non-compliance procedure. Simma has observed, however, that the *leges generalis* would apply either if the procedural *leges specialis* are affected by a breach from the beginning, or if the State that has breached substantive provisions objects to the application of the special procedural rules in the dispute. In such cases, where the procedure under a special regime (such as the Kyoto Protocol compliance regime) is unclear, the procedural rules in Articles 65-68 of the VCLT would presumably apply nonetheless.[75]

If the "default rules" of the VCLT apply, there remains the important question then of the appropriateness of termination or suspension of an international environmental treaty as a response to breach by one party

---

[75] *Id.*, at 82.

where the treaty in question is normative in character. Wolfrum argues that Article 60 of the VCLT does not adequately address the problem of treaty obligations that are not simply owed reciprocally *but also* serving the interests of the community of States as a whole. He suggests that the normative function of such treaties should

> ... render the validity and the applicability of international agreements immune to actions in reaction to their breach. The object and purpose of agreements for the protection of components of the environment which are of global relevance requires that the standard of protection once achieved should be sustained and even enforced rather than eroded in consequence of the failure to comply therewith.[76]

But Wolfrum's suggestions are aspirational only and do not necessarily reflect international law as it stands. His views appear to call for the development of a rule of general international law that would prohibit the operation of Article 60 in relation to global environmental agreements. In this regard, the compliance mechanisms in environmental treaties, which provide for the withdrawal of the privileges of membership,[77] while leaving intact the obligations entered into by the parties under the treaties concerned (and of which the compliance regime under the Kyoto Protocol is an example), may already be taken as a step in the right direction.

4. Conclusion

This chapter has tried to demonstrate that the Kyoto Protocol and its non-compliance procedure introduce some new and interesting approaches to the problems of compliance with environmental treaty obligations. The implementation of the Kyoto Protocol, even prior to its entry into force, is certainly an original way of implementing treaty provisions that are not yet binding (different from, and indeed far more extensive than, Article 18 of the VCLT).

Difficult interpretative problems will arise in respect of the operation of this non-compliance procedure in connection with the application of the treaties law. One problem, as noted above, is that Article 30 of the VCLT could provide insufficient guidance in relation to the interrelationship and conflict of treaty rules. Article 30 caused much controversy in the ILC and is one of very few Articles of the VCLT that has not well withstood the passage of time. The solution to treaty conflicts may, therefore, have to be found elsewhere when treaty conflicts occur in practice.

---

[76] Wolfrum, *supra* note 8, at 57.
[77] *Id.*, at 57-58.

Other difficult questions would also arise with respect to treaty suspension, or the suspension of particular rights and privileges. Would it be the law of state responsibility (countermeasures) that should be applied, the law of treaties (specifically, Article 60 of the VCLT), or both? Of the treaties discussed, only the Kyoto Protocol specifies the circumstances that would justify suspension.[78] These circumstances (listed under Articles 6, 12 and 17) are material to the accomplishment of the objectives of the Kyoto Protocol. In all other cases, such as the Montreal Protocol, it appears that the materiality of a breach would have to be established separately. Notably however, the Kyoto Protocol's non-compliance procedure does not envisage suspension on the basis of international law at all, and may constitute a species of *lex specialis*. Moreover, the suspension of a Party under a compliance regime is itself an innovative collective institution combining characteristics of both material treaty breach and countermeasures.[79] But suspension has never been implemented in practice. We do not know what it would look like when it does occur. We can only say that, at the present stage of the implementation of these regimes, the facilitative, assistance-based, approach has been the preferred approach and we can at least hope that this will remain the case.

---

[78] See Section 3.3 above.
[79] See M. A. Fitzmaurice and C. Redgwell, "Environmental Non-Compliance Procedures and International Law", 31 *NYIL* (2000), 35-65.

CHAPTER NINE

Conflicts Between Environmental Treaties

1. Introduction

The purpose of this chapter is to examine the position under international law when environmental treaties conflict with each other.[1] The chapter will consider particular provisions in treaties that purport to establish a system of priority between treaties, as well as the position in relation to treaties which do not contain such provisions, or when those provisions themselves conflict or otherwise fail to resolve the conflict. In relation to this latter situation, it will be necessary to examine the rules of general international law, and in particular the role of Article 30 of the 1969 Vienna Convention on the Law of Treaties ("VCLT"), which attempts to deal with incompatibilities between successive agreements relating to the same subject-matter, as well as to a number of other related Articles of the VCLT. This chapter deals only with one formal aspect of the conflict of environmental treaties, primarily based on the analysis of Article 30 of the VCLT and of some clauses included in selected environmental treaties. The possible role of certain "new" concepts emerging in international environmental law (such as Common Heritage of Mankind, the Common Concern of Humankind and Intergenerational Equity) regarding conflicts in international environmental law will also be considered. The chapter also examines the possible pertinence of the concept of the so-called "integral obligation" to the issue of the priority and the legal effects of environmental obligations.

A number of recent works have addressed the question of conflicts between treaties in general.[2] It has been pointed out that the starting-point in

---

[1] See R. Wolfrum and N. Matz, *Conflicts in International Environmental Law* (2003).

[2] For the most thorough analysis of the issue, see S.A. Sadat-Akhavi, *Methods of Resolving Conflicts between Treaties* (2003). The question of conflict of norms, or more precisely competing regimes, of international law will be dealt with as part of the work of the

the resolution of conflicts must be the "holy trinity" of the general principles of the contractual freedom of States, *pacta sunt servanda* and *pacta tertiis*", as follows.[3] The contractual freedom of States permits them to modify their legal relationship with other States, but this contractual freedom may be limited by illegality (e.g. conflict with rules *ius cogens*, integral obligations).[4] Where no question of illegality arises, the legal relationships can be modified as long as the other States involved consent thereto. In the event of the lack of consent, these non-consenting States, on the basis of the *pacta tertiis* rule are not bound and, therefore, following the *pacta sunt servanda* principle, the earlier treaty binds. If this rule is not adhered to, it will result in the international responsibility of the State that does not comply with its obligations:[5] "[c]onflict of norms in international law is governed essentially by priority rules and state responsibility, not by rules invalidating either of the two conflicting norms."[6] What is clear is that Article 30 of the VCLT does not provide all the answers to the issues that may arise for consideration in this regard,[7] and the possibility of a *non-liquet* has been recognized.[8]

With specific reference to environmental treaties, the issue of conflict between successive treaties covering the same subject-matter and involving the same, or some of the same, parties, is an area of particular concern. This is so as successive multilateral conventions – which cover the same, or similar, areas of concern, or cover them with respect to different, though sometimes overlapping geographical areas, or which comprise general framework or umbrella type conventions followed by later particular treaties, amendments or protocols, implementing or developing principles adumbrated in the first convention, or applying them to a particular

---

International Law Commission on Fragmentation of International Law; see the Report of the Study Group on Fragmentation of International Law, UN Doc. A/CN.4/L.628; G. Hafner, feasibility study entitled "Risks Ensuing from Fragmentation of International Law", Official Records of the General Assembly, Fifty-fifth session, Supplement No. 10 (UN Doc. A/58/10), annex; Report of the International Law Commission on "Fragmentation of International Law: Difficulties Arising from the Diversification and Expansion of International Law", in Report of the Work of the International Law Commission at its Fifty-fifth Session (5 May – 6 June and 7 July – 8 August 2003, Official Records of the General Assembly Fifty-fifth session, Supp. 10 (UN Doc. A/58/10)), at 407-435. See also J. Pauwelyn, *Conflict of Norms in Public International Law: How WTO Law Relates to other Rules of International Law* (2003).

[3] *Id.*, Chapters 6 and 7, as summarized at 436-439.

[4] See infra, Section 2.5.

[5] Pauwelyn, note 2, at 436.

[6] Id.

[7] See Sadat-Akhavi, note 2, at 70-84, identifies the following shortcomings of the VCLT: "(a) it does not address the question of conflicting obligations towards different States; (b) problem of determining the "later" treaty; (c) it does not take account of the position of regional treaties; (d) is does not take account of treaties containing obligations erga omnes."

[8] See Pauwelyn, note 2, at 436.

geographical area or reacting to new scientific developments or discoveries –
are the defining feature of the development of modern environmental law. In
general, it may be said that in the case of most bilateral treaties, the situation
is relatively simple and the law relatively clear, and, indeed, satisfactorily
codified in the relevant provisions of the VCLT. Most environmental treaties
are, however, multilateral treaties – in addition, the position is much more
complex, the rules less clear, and the codification in the VCLT widely
considered to be unsatisfactory.

In particular, there are, firstly, a number of possible permutations
involving the extent of overlap between the successive treaties concerned in
terms of their parties – e.g. whether all the parties to the earlier treaty are
also parties to the later one, and if so, whether they are the only parties to the
later treaty, or whether there are additional parties to the later treaty which
were not parties to the earlier[9]. Secondly, there is an issue as to the extent of
overlap of subject-matter that is necessary for a conflict of treaties, which
may affect the continuation or validity of one or the other of them to arise.[10]
A third issue relates to the nature of the obligations contained in the
successive agreements. This issue relates in particular to the distinction, first
fully identified by Fitzmaurice in his Draft Code on Treaty Law which was
contained in his Reports to the ILC, between reciprocal obligations (which
may be contained in both bilateral and multilateral treaties) and non-
reciprocal obligations (which are generally said to arise in relation to
multilateral treaties). This distinction was not followed in terms in the
VCLT, though certain of its provisions do to a limited extent reflect the same
distinction. This will be discussed in greater detail below, but it should be
noted at this stage, firstly, that it is an area in which the law as it stands at
present, and in particular as codified in the VCLT, is not entirely clear or
satisfactory; and, secondly, that it is particularly relevant in the case of
modern environmental treaties, which often embody those types of non-
reciprocal obligations identified by Fitzmaurice. A further problematic issue
relates to so-called "conflict clauses" or other treaty provisions, which
purport to settle the issue of conflict between successive treaties by
establishing a hierarchy between them. General international law as codified

---

[9] A useful analysis of the possible permutations of overlap between parties to successive
treaties is to be found in Article 18 of Fitzmaurice's Draft Code on Treaty Law, in his Third
Report to the ILC. In summary, he identifies the following possibilities, firstly relating to both
bilateral and multilateral treaties: 1. no common parties; 2. common and identical parties; 3.
partly common and partly divergent parties: and, secondly, relating only to situations in which
at least one of the treaties is multilateral: 4. partially common parties, both or all of the parties
to the earlier treaty being also parties (but not the only parties) to the later treaty; and 5.
partially common parties, but were some only of the parties to the earlier one are parties to the
later, which has no other parties. G. Fitzmaurice, Third Report, YILC (1958), Vol. II, at 27.
[10] See Sadat-Akhavi, note 2, at 7-14.

in the VCLT is, as will be seen in the next section of this chapter, largely residual in nature, operating only when parties to successive treaties have failed to establish any hierarchy between them by means of treaty provisions; and the assumption appears generally to have been made that, when the parties to treaties set out to do this, any potential problems would be solved. In fact, as will be seen below, at least in the case of environmental conventions where complex interactions exist between subject-matters, this has not proved necessarily to be the case. There arises, in fact, an issue of conflict between the very conflict clauses that are intended to avoid conflict.

2. The Law Concering Successive Treaties

2.1 Article 30 of the VCLT

Article 30 of the VCLT, dealing with "Application of successive treaties relating to the same subject-matter", provides as follows:[11]

> 1. Subject to Article 103 of the Charter of the United Nations,[12] the rights and obligations of States parties to successive treaties relating to the same subject-matter shall be determined in accordance with the following paragraphs.
>
> 2. When a treaty specifies that it is subject to, or that it is not to be considered as incompatible with, an earlier or later treaty, the provisions of that other treaty prevail.
>
> 3. When all the parties to the earlier treaty are parties also to the later treaty but the earlier treaty is not terminated or suspended in operation under article 59,[13] the earlier treaty applies only to the extent that its provisions are compatible with those of the latter treaty.

---

[11] The footnotes to Article 30 as quoted here are our insertions, and do not form part of the text of Article 30.

[12] Article 103 of the United Nations Charter reads: "In the event of a conflict between the obligations of the Members of the United Nations under the present Charter and their obligations under any other international agreement, their obligations under the present Charter shall prevail".

[13] Article 59 of the VCLT, entitled "Termination or suspension of the operation of a treaty implied by conclusion of a later treaty", provides that

> "1. A treaty shall be considered as terminated if all the parties to it conclude a later treaty relating to the same subject-matter and:
>
> (a) it appears from the later treaty or is otherwise established that the parties intended that the matter should be governed by that treaty; or

4. When the parties to the later treaty do not include all the parties to the earlier one:

(a) as between States parties to both treaties the same rule applies as in paragraph 3;

(b) as between a State party to both treaties and a State party to only one of the treaties, the treaty to which both States are parties governs their mutual rights and obligations.

5. Paragraph 4 is without prejudice to article 41,[14] or to any question of the termination or suspension of the operation of a treaty under article 60[15] or to any question of responsibility which may arise for a State from the conclusion or application of a treaty the provisions of which are incompatible with its obligations towards another State under another treaty. [16]

(b) the provisions of the later treaty are so far incompatible with those of the earlier one that the two treaties are not capable of being applied at the same time.

2. The earlier treaty shall be considered as only suspended in operation if it appears from the later treaty or is otherwise established that such was the intention of the parties.

[14] Article 41 of the VCLT, entitled "Agreements to modify multilateral treaties between certain of the parties only", provides that

"1. Two or more of the parties to a multilateral treaty may conclude an agreement to modify the treaty as between themselves alone if:

(a) the possibility of such a modification is provided for by the treaty; or

(b) the modification in question is not prohibited by the treaty and:

(i) does not affect the enjoyment by the other parties of their rights under the treaty or the performance of their obligations;

(ii) does not relate to a provision, derogation from which is incompatible with the effective execution of the object and purpose of the treaty as a whole.

2. Unless in a case falling under paragraph 1(a) the treaty otherwise provides, the parties in question shall notify the other parties of their intention to conclude the agreement and of the modification to the treaty for which it provides."

[15] Article 60 of the VCLT deals with the termination or suspension of the operation of a treaty as a consequence of its breach.

[16] On Article 30 of the VCLT and conflict of successive treaties generally, in addition to the works cited in notes 1 and 2 above, see K.N Dahl, "The Application of Successive Treaties Dealing with the Same Subject-matter", 17 *Indian Yearbook of International Affairs* (1974), at 279-318; E.W. Vierdag, "The Time of the 'Conclusion' of a Multilateral Treaty: Article 30 of the Vienna Convention on the Law of Treaties and Related Provisions," 59 *BYIL* (1988), at 92-111; W. Czaplinski and G.M. Danilenko, "Conflicts of Norms in International Law", 21 *NYIL* (1990), 3-42, at 12-28; J.B. Mus, "Conflicts between Treaties in International Law",

This text is extremely succinct, notwithstanding that it attempts to cover a variety of very complicated issues, as reflected in the preparatory work.[17] A great deal has been written about Article 30. Sinclair, for instance, summarised the principles underlying the Article as follows:

> (a) If a treaty says that it is subject to, or is not to be considered as incompatible with, another treaty, that other treaty will prevail;
>
> (b) As between parties to a treaty who become parties to a later, inconsistent, treaty, the earlier treaty will apply only where its provisions are not incompatible with the later treaty;
>
> (c) As between a party to both treaties and a party to only one of them, the treaty to which both are parties will govern the mutual rights and obligations of the States concerned.[18]

He nevertheless expressed the opinion that the question of application of successive treaties which relate to the same subject-matter remained a "particularly obscure aspect of the law of treaties",[19] and indeed concluded that Article 30, as drafted in the VCLT, was not entirely satisfactory. He considered that the rules fail to take account of the many complications that arise when two treaties exist relating to the same subject-matter, and one is negotiated at the regional level and another negotiated within the framework of a universal organisation, a situation which is almost commonplace of modern international environmental law.[20] This unsatisfactory situation has led to a number of attempts at analysis and re-categorisation of the situations that may arise in relation to successive conflicting treaties, and the rules applicable to them. However, as Sinclair said:

> The complications are perhaps such that no attempt to lay down general rules would have disposed of all the difficulties; this is an area where State practice is continually developing, and where it may possibly have been premature to

---

NILR (1998), at 208-232. See also the working paper of Professor A. Boyle on Article 30 of the Vienna Convention and the Relationship of Treaties, presented to the International Law Association, Committee on the Law of Treaties.

[17] International Law Commission, YILC (1964), Vol. I, at 127, 131. See also United Nations Conference on the Law of Treaties, Vienna, 9th April 1969, Official Records (UN Doc. A/CONF.39/11/Add.1) (1969), at 253.

[18] Sir Ian Sinclair, *The Vienna Convention on the Law of Treaties* (1984), at 94.

[19] *Id.*, at 93.

[20] One other issue that arises in this context relates to the terms "earlier" and "later" in relation to successive treaties, which are to be interpreted on the basis of the moment of adoption of the text and not of its entry into force. The rules laid down in Article 30 bind each party to a treaty from the date of entry into force of the treaty for that party (see Official Records, Second Session, 91st Meeting, Official Records, First Session, 31st Meeting (Sinclair). However, there are again several issues not resolved by the provisions of Article 30. For an excellent discussion of this issue, see Sadat-Akhavi, note 2, at 75-82.

> seek to establish fixed guidelines. Perhaps little harm has been done so long as the Convention rules are regarded as residuary in character... [21]

This view is important, and it should be recognized that it may have been expecting too much to expect Article 30 to resolve all potential problems that might arise in this regard. The role of cooperation and mutual recognition between treaty regimes with related aims is of great importance. It was clarified at the Diplomatic Conference that not all differences between treaties should be taken as giving rise to incompatibility within the meaning of Article 30, paragraph 3.[22] Also, it was stated that the expression "relating to the same subject matter" should be interpreted restrictively; it does not apply to cases where a general treaty has an indirect impact on the content of particular provisions of an earlier treaty. This instance would be covered by the maxim *generalia specialibus non derogant*,[23] which is not a conflict clause but a rule of general treaty interpretation (Articles 31 and 32 of the VCLT). It was indeed the original intention of the International Law Commission ("ILC") to include a reference to treaty interpretation in paragraph 2 of Article 30 (which underwent numerous changes during its drafting and did not include an explicit reference in the final text). In this respect, Fitzmaurice, in the Commentary to the Article in his Draft Code on Treaty Law entitled "Legality of the object (conflict with previous treaties – normal cases)"[24] also said as follows:

> The whole question of what inconsistency or conflict between two treaties means is a difficult one. Two treaties may be inconsistent in the sense that they set up mutually discordant systems, but so long as these do not have to be applied to or between the same parties, it may be quite possible to apply both. Thus, even though with some difficulty or at some inconvenience, State A may be able to apply one system in regard to State B under treaty X and another in regard to State C under treaty Y. In short, there may be a conflict between the treaties concerned, without this necessarily resulting in any conflict of obligation for any of the parties. Something of this kind is in fact precisely what happens under successive technical conventions concluded under the auspices of various international organisations and agencies. In such a situation, there are many possible permutations and combinations, shades and degrees. It would be very unwise to postulate the invalidity and nullity of a treaty merely because, on the face of it, it contained provisions that were in themselves incompatible with the provisions of an earlier treaty to which the parties to the later treaty were also parties.[25]

---

[21] See note 18, at 98.

[22] Official Records, Second Session, 91st Meeting (Waldock).

[23] Official Records, Second Session, 85th Meeting (Sinclair) and 91st Meeting (Waldock).

[24] Article 18 of the Draft Code, G. Fitzmaurice, Third Report, YILC (1958), Vol. II, at 27.

[25] G. Fitzmaurice, Third Report, YILC (1958), Vol. II, at 44; see also Sadat-Akhavi, note 2, at 7-14.

As will be seen in Section 5 below, the concept of the principle of co-operation between States resolving problems of possible conflicts *stricto sensu* between co-existing regimes which have, nevertheless, common aims, is one of potentially great importance in the field of international environmental protection, so that the above outlined interpretation of rules relating to conflict of successive treaties is extremely relevant.

2.2 Analysis of the Provisions of Article 30

In the introductory section of this chapter, we touched upon a number of the complex variables and issues that arise in the field under consideration. In particular, these included the question of the various permutations of overlap between the parties to successive treaties, the extent of overlap in terms of subject matter, the issue relating to the nature of the obligations contained in the treaties concerned and the distinction between situations in which one or both of the treaties contains some form of express provision purporting to govern the order of priority between the two treaties, and those where there is no such provision.[26] To this may be added the issue of the juridical bases underlying the various rules that exist, such as the question of the nature of the *lex posterior* rule and the rule *legi speciali derogant legi generali*, and the rule *pacta tertiis nec nocent nec prosunt*, and the question of which of these is a rule of interpretation and which is not. These variables and distinctions, so far as they are actually reflected in the Article, are dealt with in the following order.

(a) Subject to the overriding priority, as among UN Member States, of their Charter obligations (paragraph 1, referring to Article 103 of the UN Charter), Article 30 of the VCLT recognises the validity of express provisions contained in one or other of two successive treaties which purport to order their priority. We will consider conflict clauses further below in Section 2.3; but it is necessary at this stage to point out the limited nature of the provisions of Article 30(2) of the VCLT. They apply only to the situation where the parties to a treaty accept the priority of the provisions of another instrument. The provisions of paragraph 2 do not apply in the much more difficult case where the parties to a treaty attempt to accord their own treaty priority over the provisions either of a previous treaty, or even, a situation which is becoming relatively common in the environmental field, over future treaties (considered in section 3.1.2 below). Even this situation, however, gives rise to little difficulty if the parties to the treaties concerned are identical. In this case, the process which has to be undergone is in effect one

---

[26] See Mus, note 16, who adopts this distinction based on the work of the ILC.

of interpretation of the two treaties together. If either contains express provision as to priority, as envisaged in paragraph 2, effect will be given to these provisions. If there is not, then the *lex posterior* rule (really a rule of interpretation) will, as envisaged in paragraph 3 of Article 30, accord priority to the later expressed intention of the parties by giving priority, in case of conflict, to the later treaty. To the extent necessary to do this, there is no problem in treating the earlier treaty as either modified, or even terminated, by agreement of all the parties.

(b) However, the provisions of paragraph 3 of Article 30 of the VCLT actually apply not only to the situation where the parties to the two treaties are identical, but also covers the situation where there are additional parties to the later treaty which were not parties to the earlier one. But this situation also does not, save in one possible respect, give rise to any real problem as all the parties concerned (that is all the parties to the earlier treaty as well as the additional parties to the later one) are parties to the treaty to which precedence is being given. The one possible problem that could, in theory, arise is if there was some reason why the parties to the earlier treaty were, in fact, not free to modify its terms, or to act in contravention of its provisions. In view of the fact that it does appear to be the intention of some environmental treaties now to attempt to do exactly that, by setting up standards or principles from which there would be no possibility of derogation in the future (see further in Section 3 below) it will be necessary to give consideration to this possible problem in relation to the effectiveness of paragraph 3 of Article 30; and we will come back to it in Section 3 below when we consider the impact of the nature of the obligations concerned in relation to conflict of successive treaties.

(c) In paragraph 4 of Article 30, the VCLT attempts to deal with the converse situation to that covered by paragraph 3 (see the previous paragraph) – i.e. the situation in which there remain parties to an earlier treaty, which did not become party to the later treaty. In this case, while there may not be any great difficulty in connection with the interrelationship between those parties which are party to both treaties among themselves (the matter covered by sub-paragraph (a)), there are considerable problems arising concerning the relationship between that group of parties and, firstly, any parties to the later treaty which were not parties to the earlier one, and, secondly, towards the parties to the earlier treaty which have not become parties to the later one (situations covered by sub-paragraph (b)). The core of the problem here is that entry into the later treaty by the group of earlier treaty parties must (where there is conflict between the provisions of the treaties concerning the same or related or overlapping subject-matter) involve, in relation to their performance of the earlier treaty, at least a modification in its terms, and may involve a breach, even a fundamental breach or repudiation of it. The law of treaties does, in fact, envisage the possibility of a group of parties to a multilateral treaty amending its terms as between themselves, but only subject to rather strict limitations. This fact is taken into account in Article 30 in paragraph 5, which makes the provisions of paragraph 4 subject to the provisions of Article 41 (on agreements to modify multilateral treaties between certain of the parties only). If, in fact, entry into the later treaty involves no more than a modification of the earlier treaty without giving rise to any breach of it, there is no problem, and the provisions of paragraph 4 (b) of Article 30 can be applied. If modification of the earlier treaty is not allowed within its terms, then there arises a conflict not only in relation to the interpretation of conflicting clauses, but as between the treaties themselves. These questions require further study of the circumstances in which some parties only to a multilateral treaty are free to modify its terms among themselves, and the effects of such modification on the continued existence of that treaty (both where the modification was allowed within the terms of the earlier treaty and where it constituted a breach). These questions are, in their turn, dependent upon the issue of the categorisation of obligations in multilateral treaties. These issues will be considered more fully in the following subsections.

2.3 The Position and Effect of Express Conflict Clauses

It is now relatively common in multilateral environmental treaties to insert conflict clauses (i.e. clauses which are intended to make express provision to resolve problems arising from a conflict between treaties by according priority to one or other of the treaties, or to certain of the provisions of one of them, also referred to as "savings clauses"). The possibilities relating to these conflict clauses, however, are quite complex, and in certain of the possible situations, their effect is not necessarily entirely clear. In the first place, the conflict clause may be included in either the earlier or the later treaty, or, indeed, in both. And, whichever treaty the clause is included in, it may be aimed either (i) at ensuring the priority of the later treaty (in which case it may in fact do no more than to give expression to the general, *lex posterior*, rule); (ii) at preserving the effect of the earlier treaty, or, (iii) if actually included in the earlier treaty, at preventing States parties from entering into agreements in the future which conflict with the earlier treaty. This latter situation arises not infrequently in the environmental field, either when parties to a treaty want to make its provision subject to, or at least to ensure that they are interpreted so as not to conflict with, the provisions of another treaty which is still in the course of negotiation[27], or when a treaty contains the statement of an important environmental principle which the parties want to ensure is not derogated from in future treaties.[28] It has been written that such a rule has the effect of overcoming the presumption that "as between parties to both agreements, the requirements of the later agreement prevail over incompatible terms of an earlier agreement…".[29]

It should also be noted that Article 30 paragraph 2, which provides that "when a treaty specifies that it is subject to, or it is not considered as incompatible with, an earlier treaty or later treaty, the provision of that other treaty prevail" has the effect of giving priority to conflict clauses over the operation of the general rules (in particular the *lex posterior* rule) which are codified in paragraphs 3 and 4.[30]

The effect of conflict clauses in practice, however, is by no means necessarily as simple and clear-cut as might appear to be the case. In the first place, there are a number of different situations or variables that can exist. These were usefully categorised by Boyle, who suggested the following classification relating to the various situations that may exist when one or

---

[27] For instance, a number of treaties concluded during the course of negotiation of the United Nations Convention on the Law of the Sea ("UNCLOS"), stated that their provisions were to be without prejudice to development of the law of the sea. For instance, Article 18 of the London Convention provides as follows: "Nothing in this Convention shall prejudice the codification and development of the law of the sea by the United Nations Conference on the Law of the Sea convened pursuant to resolution 2750 C (XXV) of the General Assembly of the United Nations nor the present or future claims and legal views of any State concerning the law of the sea and the nature and extent of coastal and flag State jurisdiction".

[28] For instance, Article 11 of the 1989 Basel Convention on Transboundary Trade in Hazardous Waste and their disposal provides that: "… parties may enter into bilateral, multilateral, or regional agreements or arrangements regarding transboundary movement of hazardous wastes or other wastes with Parties or non-Parties provided that such agreements or arrangements do not derogate from the environmentally sound management of hazardous wastes and other wastes as required by this Convention. These agreements or arrangements shall stipulate provisions which are not less environmentally sound than those provided for by this Convention in particular taking into account the interests of developing countries"; see <http://www.basel.int/text/con-e.htm>.

[29] S. Safrin, "Treaties in Collision? The Biosafety Protocol and the World Trade Organisation Agreements", 96 *AJIL* (2002), 606-628, at 613.

[30] This is not expressly stated in Article 30, but is apparent from the position of paragraph 2 within the Article, and it was confirmed as being the case at the Diplomatic Conference, Official Records, Second Session, 91st Meeting. Sir Humphrey Waldock was the Rapporteur at that time, and he explained the need for the provision in the following terms: "These clauses appear in any case of conflict to give priority to the other treaty and therefore be of decisive effect in the application of the two treaties. Accordingly, even if in particular instances the application of these clauses may not differ from the general rules of priority set out in paragraphs 3 and 4, it is thought that they should be made the subject of a special paragraph in the present article", H. Waldock, Third Report, YILC (1964), Vol. II, at 38-40.

other of the treaties does contain some form of express provision governing their relationship:[31]

(a) where a later treaty is expressly subject to or is stated to be not incompatible with an earlier treaty;

(b) where a later treaty replaces or takes priority over an earlier treaty;

(c) where treaties are stated to be without prejudice to later treaties, or where treaties do not preclude subsequent inconsistency;

(d) where treaties do not preclude the later adoption of more stringent rules; and

(e) treaties that preclude the adoption of subsequent inconsistent treaties, or of treaties that are not consistent with their object and purpose.

Furthermore, there may, for instance, be a potential conflict between a conflict clause and the *lex posterior* rule if all the parties to a treaty, which contains a clause claiming priority, decide to conclude a new treaty which does not include a clause regulating the relationship with the existing treaty, and on the basis of the freedom of parties to terminate or amend an existing treaty and to conclude a new one, the new treaty will, in principle, take precedence as expressing the new will of the parties.[32] Nevertheless, it must be emphasised that, in the end, this may well be dependent on careful interpretation of the two treaties. For instance, in order to decide if provisions of the new treaty do, in fact, conflict with the provisions with respect to which the earlier treaty had claimed precedence. This is more so if, as may occur, both treaties claim some kind of general priority regarding the respective principles which they enshrine. In this respect, the potential conflict between the UNCLOS and the 1992 Convention on Biological Diversity ("CBD") (considered in Section 3 below) provides an interesting and pertinent example from the environmental field.

2.4 The Categorisation of the Obligation involved in Relation to Conflict Between Successive Treaties

In Section 2.2(c) above, we concluded that the relationship between two conflicting treaties in cases where there remain parties to the earlier treaty which did not become party to the later treaty, and even possibly the ability of some only of the parties to the earlier treaty to enter into a subsequent conflicting treaty at all, depends on their ability to modify the terms of the

---

[31] A. Boyle, unpublished report for the British Branch of the International Law Association Committee on the Law of Treaties (1995) (on file with the authors).
[32] Mus, note 16, at 216.

earlier treaty, and that that ability, on the basis, *inter alia*, of Article 41 of the VCLT, in turn depends on the nature of the obligations with respect to which the modification is made. The objective of the present section is to consider further the issue of categorisation of obligations, so far as relevant in the present context. In the next section we will consider further the effects that flow from this in relation to conflicts between successive treaties.

As mentioned in Section 1 above, the question of categorisation of obligations was identified by Fitzmaurice in his Draft Code on the Law of Treaties. In particular, the type of obligation involved was relevant to the issues of termination of treaties as a result of fundamental breach,[33] special considerations relating to the termination of multilateral treaties,[34] and the issue of conflict of a treaty with previous treaties.[35] His categorisation is, in fact, though in a less direct and detailed fashion, incorporated in part at least in the provisions of the VCLT.

Fitzmaurice divided treaty obligations into two primary categories, namely, on the one hand, reciprocal obligations, and on the other non-reciprocal obligations. The second, non-reciprocal, category was then further divided into two sub-categories. He referred to the first of these sub-categories as "interdependent" obligations, and to the second sub-category as "integral" or "absolute" obligations.[36]

---

[33] Articles 18 and 19 of the Draft Code, Fitzmaurice, "Second Report", YILC (1957), Vol. II, at 30-31; see also "Third Report", YILC (1958), Vol. II, at 27 (Article 18). See Sadat-Akhavi, note 2, at 67-70.

[34] Article 29 of the Draft Code, Fitzmaurice, "Second Report", YILC (1957), Vol. II, at 35.

[35] Articles 18 and 19 in Fitzmaurice's "Third Report", YILC (1958), Vol. II, at 27. It should be noted that while these articles, which are the main articles in which conflict of treaties is expressly covered, are articles dealing with the legality of object of the later of two conflicting treaties, not much can be deduced from this as to the juridical basis on which Fitzmaurice regarded conflict issues. This is because he did not complete the Draft Code. In particular, in Part III of the First Chapter of the Draft Code, Fitzmaurice had planned a Division C to be entitled "Revision and Modification". In a note, Fitzmaurice said that the essentials of the matter as they affected the specific question of termination had been covered by Article 13 and the commentary on it in paragraphs 74 to 79 in the Second Report. He continued by saying "It may be that the rest would be better placed in a general section on 'Conflicting treaties'", Second Report, p. 70. This chapter is not the place to speculate on what that section might have contained; but one can point out that no particular conclusion can, in the circumstances, be drawn from the fact that conflict of treaties is dealt with in the VCLT in an Article of its own in terms of alternative or rival obligations under the treaties concerned, while, in Fitzmaurice's Draft Code, it appears to be dealt with in terms of the validity of the later treaty.

[36] It may not be necessary to refer to the concept of interdependent obligation as a distinct category. See, e.g., Pauwelyn, note 2, at 59: "Unlike the notions of reciprocal and integral treaties, the concept of interdependent treaties has not been generally used as a distinct category subsequently to Fitzmaurice's reports. For the purposes of conflict of norms

The essential attribute of reciprocal obligations is that they are owed by each party to a multilateral treaty individually to each other party. As Fitzmaurice put it, such obligations are "... based on contractual reciprocity consisting of a reciprocal interchange between the parties, each giving certain treatment to, and receiving it from, each of the others".[37] It is as if there were, within the multilateral treaty, a series of discreet bilateral treaties, one between each pair of parties to the treaty. The essential effect of this in the present context is that a group of parties to a multilateral treaty consisting of such obligations can modify the terms of, or even terminate, their individual mutual obligations without affecting their ability to fully perform their respective mutual obligations with each of the other parties to the treaty, which were not members of the group.

In contrast, "interdependent" obligations (the first of the two kinds of non-reciprocal obligation) are, as Fitzmaurice put it, "... obligations which, by reason of the character of the treaty, are necessarily dependent on a corresponding performance by all the other parties". Viewed from a slightly different angle, one could equally say that such obligations are owed by each party to all the other parties to the treaty jointly, so that, conversely, the *quid pro quo* for the undertaking of each party is the performance of the provision or provisions in question by all the other parties. Typically, such obligations will occur in multilateral treaties in which the parties have a common interest in all of them doing, or refraining from doing, something. Fitzmaurice cites, as an example, disarmament conventions,[38] in which, for example, there is little point in any party reducing its numbers of a particular type of weapon unless all, and not just some, of the others do likewise. But one may equally validly, in the modern world, cite environmental agreements as typically containing provisions of this kind – because to achieve a particular regional or global environmental effect, it is often, if not indeed almost always, necessary for all the States in the region, or for the international community as a whole, to act in accordance with some standard, or to impose upon itself some restraint. The *quid pro quo* for each party acting in accordance with the provisions of most environmental treaties, often not only incurring costs but also other secondary detrimental effects (e.g. in relation to trade) – the benefit which each party seeks from the treaty – is the achievement of that overall object. As soon as that achievement is jeopardised by non-performance of obligations by any party,

---

(essentially the legality of inter se modifications), these interdependent treaties can, indeed, be equated with integral treaties"; See also Chapter 3.

[37] Commentary to Article 18, paragraph 120, Fitzmaurice, "Second Report", YILC (1957), Vol. II, at 53.

[38] Commentary to Article 19, paragraph 91, Fitzmaurice, "Third Report", YILC (1958), Vol. II, at 44.

all the other parties are thereby denied achievement of the benefit they sought.

The second kind of non-reciprocal obligation, the so-called "integral obligation" involves treaties in which, as Fitzmaurice put it, "the obligation of each party [is] altogether independent of performance by any of the others, and would continue for each party even if defaults by others occurred ...".[39] Illustrating the working of such obligations, Fitzmaurice says:

> Thus, a fundamental breach by one party of a treaty on human rights could neither justify termination of the treaty, nor corresponding breaches of the treaty even in respect of nationals of the offending party. The same would apply as regards the obligation of any country to maintain certain standards of working conditions or to prohibit certain practices in consequence of the conventions of the International Labour Organisation; or again under maritime conventions as regards standards of safety at sea. The same principle is now enshrined in express terms in the Geneva Conventions of 12 August 1949 on prisoners of war and other matters. Another type of case is where there exists an international obligation to maintain a certain régime or system in a given area.

The Third Special Rapporteur, Sir H. Waldock, upheld to a certain degree the concept of a reciprocal obligation and its legal consequences, as introduced by Fitzmaurice.[40] The main area of the disagreement concerned the legal nature (in particular its legal consequences) of the integral or interdependent obligation. Briefly speaking, Waldock was of the view that not all subsequent treaties conflicting with a treaty containing an integral type of obligation would be null and void, since this type of obligations was very multifaceted and not all these obligations had a character of the *ius cogens* rules and, further, that many treaties of the same subject-matter including these obligations are often revised *inter se* by another agreement concluded with a view of updating the first agreement, to which only certain States are party. Therefore, this *inter se* agreement would be declared null and void as incompatible with the first agreement, an assertion that, according to Waldock, was not upheld by practice. The ILC further adopted the views of Waldock. However, the groundbreaking division of obligations introduced by Fitzmaurice was reflected to some extent in the VCLT, even if his terms were not used in the VCLT.

In the first place, the VCLT does not contain any provisions that are directly descriptive of the reciprocal type of obligation, but it is apparent that the drafters of the treaty were aware of the distinction between this type of obligation and the interdependent/integral type of obligation from the wording of Article 41 when it limits the right of a group of some (but not all)

---

[39] *Id.*
[40] "The Second Report" on the Law of Treaties, YILC (1964), Vol. II, p. 59, paras. 25-32; see also, YILC (1966), Vol. II, at 217, para.13.

of the parties to a multilateral treaty to modify its terms as between themselves, to a modification which "(i) does not affect the enjoyment by the other parties of their rights under the treaty or the performance of their obligations; and (ii) does not relate to a provision, derogation from which is incompatible with the effective execution of the object and purpose of the treaty as a whole".[41] This is in practical terms virtually indistinguishable from the descriptions quoted above of the interdependent/integral type of obligation.

Again, while the VCLT does not contain any provision in the same terms as the various provisions in Fitzmaurice's Draft Code relating to the "integral" obligation, it does appear to recognise a type of treaty in which the effect of breach is basically the same as that ascribed by Fitzmaurice to the integral type of obligation when it provides that paragraphs 1 to 5 of Article 60, which set out the rights of the other parties in multilateral treaties to breach of obligations by one party, and in particular rights such as to suspend the operation of the treaty in relations between themselves and the defaulting party "... do not apply to provisions relating to the protection of the human person contained in treaties of a humanitarian character, in particular to provisions prohibiting any form of reprisals against persons protected by such treaties".[42]

This provision certainly covers the same ground as the reference to treaties on human rights in the passage from the Fitzmaurice commentary quoted above. Existence of the other forms of treaty he cites is, of course, controversial, and discussion of this is beyond the scope of the present chapter. But it is apparent that, both on the analogy of "conventions as regards standards of safety at sea" and of the concept of an "international obligation to maintain a certain régime or system in a given area" (of which, elsewhere, Fitzmaurice cites the Antarctic treaties as an example), many environmental treaties could fall within the description of "integral obligations".[43]

2.5 Consequences of the Classification of Obligations

It follows from the above analysis that the problems that arise where there are additional parties to an earlier treaty, which did not become party to a later, conflicting treaty, really arise only when the obligations under the earlier treaty (at least those with respect to which the conflict arises) are not of the so-called reciprocal kind. Where they are of the reciprocal kind,

---

[41] Article 41, paragraph 1 (b) (i) and (ii) of the VCLT.

[42] Article 60, paragraph 5, VCLT.

[43] The concept of the "integral obligation" gained currency recently as it formed basis of certain concepts in 2001 Articles on State Responsibility (see below).

Article 41 allows modification of the earlier treaty by "certain of the parties only", so that the provisions of Article 30, paragraph 4 would apply without problem. When, on the other hand, the obligations in question under the earlier treaty are not of the reciprocal kind, their modification by certain of the parties only is not allowed by Article 41. In that case, a series of additional possibilities arise. For instance, the breach may be such as to allow the other parties to the earlier treaty to treat it as at an end (in which case there would no longer be a problem of conflict, though there would be one relating to the liability for breach of obligation by the parties which had entered into the later contract). But if the other parties to the earlier treaty do not, or are not entitled to, treat the earlier treaty as at an end, then other issues arise, such as the extent and manner in which the parties to the later treaty can still hold the remaining parties to the earlier treaty to their obligations. To analyse all these possibilities is beyond the scope of the present chapter, but we may consider briefly what may be the most important issue in practice, namely the question of the conflict for the parties to both the treaties between their obligations to the remaining parties to the earlier treaty under that treaty, and their obligations under the later treaty. This situation would appear to be irresolvable. Mus states, and in the view of the present authors correctly, that where State A is faced with such a conflict of treaty obligations "there is no derogation norm available to limit the scope of obligation of one treaty in favour of the obligation of another treaty. Both conflicting treaty obligations remain valid and applicable. Consequently, this type of treaty conflict is irresolvable."[44]

When placed in a situation like this, a State must decide which treaty to apply and which not to apply, thereby incurring responsibility for breach of one of its international obligations. While this is probably the position in practice, an alternative view, in theory, was expressed by Fitzmaurice. According to him, in effect, the States which were parties to both treaties could be obliged to give priority to their obligations under the earlier treaty over conflicting obligations under the later treaty.[45] Fitzmaurice took the view that this was the position that a tribunal would be obliged to take if the matter came before it, but recognised that in practice this was unlikely; so that, though not sanctioned by international law, in practice the parties which were party to both treaties would have an election. This is not the place to attempt to resolve this issue, which really remains open in view of the fact that it is not resolved by the VCLT. It may, though, be noted that the possibility of the matter coming before a tribunal is not as remote in the case of the kind of obligations involved in modern environmental treaties. For a

---

[44] Mus, note 16, at 231.
[45] See Fitzmaurice Draft Code, Article 18 and commentary thereto in "Third Report", YILC (1958), Vol. II, at 27 and 42.

number of reasons reparation, in accordance with traditional international law, is rarely an adequate response to failure by parties to fulfil their obligations in relation to environmental protection. This is one of the reasons for the development of alternative ways of dispute resolution, such as non-compliance regimes, in environmental treaty systems. It could also be a reason why remaining parties to an earlier treaty in the circumstances we are considering here might indeed call upon a tribunal to make a declaration as to the priority of obligations in the event of such a conflict, rather than merely accepting reparation if the parties to both the treaties elected to honour their obligations under the later rather than under the earlier one.

2.6 Conclusions concerning Article 30 of the VCLT

Article 30, therefore, leaves a number of issues unresolved. For example, the following questions remain: (a) how strictly is "the same subject-matter" requirement to be interpreted; (b) what is the practical application of Article 30 in conjunction with Articles 41 and 59; and (c) what is the practical argument for making a distinction between *lex posterior* (the conflict rule) and *legi speciali derogant legi generali* (the rule of interpretation), especially since the ICJ has often applied them together?[46] There is not even agreement as to the legal character of these two sets of rules. Danilenko and Czaplinski, for example, treat these rules, when applied in relation to conflict of treaties, as "not rules of interpretation but rather as general rules of law accepted by all legal systems."[47] These authors however doubt the usefulness of these rules, for example where parties to the earlier bilateral treaty later became parties to a multilateral treaty dealing with the same issue. Further, we may ask whether certain treaties, due to their particular subject-matter (such as human rights treaties that create the so-called "integral" obligations), are subject to different conflict rules from those specified in Article 30 paragraph 4(b).[48]

---

[46] The Permanent Court of Justice ("PCIJ") applied the combined principles in the Jurisdiction of the European Commission of the Danube Between Gailatz and Braila, Advisory Opinion of 8 December 1927, 1927 PCIJ (Ser.B), No.14, at 23.

[47] Danilenko and Czaplinski, note 16, at 21; the same point is made by Vierdag, note 16, at 96.

[48] See also Pauwelyn, note 2, at 385-415.

3. Practical Application of the Relevant Law in the Environmental Field

3.1 Some Examples of Conventions with Conflict Clauses

Before proceeding, it should be recalled, as discussed in Section 2 above, that the main principle, as enshrined in the VCLT, is that as between parties to both an earlier and a later agreement, the requirements of the later agreement prevail over incompatible terms of an earlier agreement (Article 30(3)). The role of a conflict clause is to reverse such a presumption). This is codified in Article 30(2) of the VCLT. The conflict clause may save the provisions of an earlier agreement that would otherwise be derogated from by incompatible provisions of a later agreement. However, conflict clauses are not operational where a party to one treaty is not a party to the treaty with conflict clause. A treaty to which both States are a party governs relations between these parties. This is provided for in Article 30(4)(b) of the VCLT and it reflects the *pacta tertiis* rule.

3.1.1 CBD and UNCLOS

One relevant conflict clause is that contained in Article 22 of the CBD, which provides as follows:

> 1. The provisions of this Convention shall not affect the rights and obligations of any Contracting Party deriving from any existing international agreement, except where the exercise of those rights and obligations would cause a serious damage or threat to biological diversity.
>
> 2. Contracting Parties shall implement this Convention consistently with the rights and obligations of States under the law of sea.[49]

Under this conflict clause, in the event of conflict between the CBD and an earlier agreement, the earlier agreement would prevail. Article 22 includes an exception, however, that "where the exercise of those rights and obligations would cause a serious damage or threat to biological diversity," the provisions of a later agreement, in this case, the CBD would prevail. The view was expressed that "[t]his exemption to the rule is unusual and can lead to a *de facto* precedence of the Convention on Biological Diversity in respect to other instruments."[50]

---

[49] See extensively on this subject: R. Wolfrum and N. Matz, "The Interplay of the United Nations Convention on the Law of the Sea and the Convention on Biological Diversity", 4 *Max Planck Yearbook of United Nations Law* (2000), at 445-480.

[50] Wolfrum and Matz, note 49, at 475.

The second paragraph of Article 22 represents a different type of conflict clause. It gives priority to the rights and obligations of States under the law of the sea. The problem of the compatibility or in broader terms of the relationship between the CBD and the 1982 Convention on the Law of the Sea ("UNCLOS") is a very difficult one. First of all the regimes differ. As has been observed:

> Fundamental differences relate to the underlying philosophies of the Conventions and their respective focus and structure. This has consequences for the approach to the protection of marine living and genetic resources as well as to marine scientific research and access to generic resources for scientific reasons i.e. for bioprospecting, respectively.[51]

The main purpose of UNCLOS, in relation to environmental protection, is to protect specific marine living resources in order to safeguard human food resources. The CBD is broader and seeks to protect all components of biological diversity – species, genetic diversity and ecosystems, in order to safeguard long-term preservation and sustainable development.[52] The question arises whether Article 30 of the VCLT is of any use in relation to conflicts between these two Conventions. In the first place, the strict definition concerning treaties dealing with the same subject-matter renders them inapplicable in the case of overlapping treaties relating to different aspects of environmental protection. The CBD and UNCLOS cannot properly be considered to be successive treaties on the same subject matter; while they overlap in certain areas of the protection of the marine environment, they have essentially different aims.[53] For example, UNCLOS does not deal with genetic resources directly and its rules on marine resources are not equipped to do so. Therefore, it is a doubtful proposition to suggest that UNCLOS always replaces the CBD in relation to marine resources. It may be surmised that Article 22 paragraph 2 of the CBD instead means, "that the two regimes exist in parallel and supplement and reinforce each other,"[54] and that only if the application of the CBD infringes upon the rights or obligations of States under UNCLOS would the latter prevail.[55]

---

[51] Wolfrum and Matz, note 49, at 464.
[52] See Wolfrum and Matz, note 49, at 477, and 472-477 generally; their discussion is the basis of this discussion on the relationship between the two treaties.
[53] If they are somehow considered to be successive treaties, the conclusion to be reached could be that UNCLOS could preclude the application of large parts of the CBD.
[54] Wolfrum and Matz, note 49, at 476.
[55] Wofrum and Matz, note 49, at 477.

3.1.2. UNCLOS and other MEAs

Also of interest is Article 311 of UNCLOS and its relationship with other environmental treaties.[56] Article 311(1) concerns the relationship between UNCLOS and the 1958 Geneva Conventions on the Law of the Sea, over which, as between States Parties to UNCLOS, the latter prevails in the event of conflict. According to Article 311(2), UNCLOS does not alter the rights and obligations of States Parties that derive from other agreements compatible with it and which do not affect the enjoyment by other States Parties of their rights or the performance of their obligations under it. By implication, UNCLOS, therefore, does alter the rights and obligations of States Parties under other agreements which are not compatible with it or which do affect the enjoyment by other States Parties of their rights, or which do affect the performance of their obligations. It may, thus, be said that UNCLOS claims priority over all other agreements. The same principle operates in relation to subsequent agreements concluded between two or more States Parties to UNCLOS, according to Article 311(3). It follows that all incompatible agreements shall be interpreted, as far as possible, in such a manner as to comply with UNCLOS. Otherwise, the respective provisions cannot be applied at all. This provision affects all other global treaties such as the CBD, insofar as they impose conflicting obligations on Contracting States to UNCLOS. This clearly shows that Article 22(1) of the CBD and Article 311(2) of the UNCLOS are almost mutually exclusive where the exercise of the rights and obligations under UNCLOS would cause serious damage or constitute a threat to biological diversity. Therefore, it appears that even conventions with conflict clauses do conflict, and that the savings clauses may themselves be in conflict. It shows that there is no consistency in the drafting of international (environmental) conventions, proliferation of which makes it difficult to retain coherence.[57]

Additional problems relate to the territorial scope of these conventions, i.e. territorial and archipelagic waters, exclusive economic zone, and the continental shelf. The solution to these problems is not easily found. Wolfrum and Matz conclude that the effectiveness of measures applied under these conventions depends on the degree of cooperation and co-ordination between conventions to promote a more coherent system of protection of marine living resources, at least in the high seas. As to other areas, further cooperation between the institutions of both agreements is necessary in order to address the issues of, e.g., integrated marine and coastal area management, the establishment of protected areas in territorial waters and in the exclusive economic zone, and bioprospecting. Therefore, the success of coexistence between these two conventions does not depend

---

[56] *Id.*
[57] Wolfrum and Matz, note 49, at 477.

on the interpretation of Article 30 of the VCLT, but on the practical issue of the "will of the state community to negotiate for and to comply with duties to conserve and sustainably manage marine areas."[58] It is no doubt correct that

> ... the absence of absolute obligations under the Convention on Biological Diversity (many obligations are qualified by the phrase "as far as possible and as appropriate") reduces the possibility of establishing incompatible conflicts. The implementation of more strict protective criteria for the sustainable management of biological resources and ecosystems especially applies to the territorial sea, for which the Convention on the Law of the Sea does not establish management criteria, but also to the exclusive economic zone as a supplement to the minimum standards established by the Convention on the Law of the Sea.[59]

The relationship between the UNCLOS and conventions relating to the protection and preservation of the marine environment has to be also viewed in the light of Article 237 (Obligations under other conventions on the protection and preservation of the marine environment), which reads as follows:

> 1. ... [t]he provisions of this Part are without prejudice to the specific obligations assumed by States under special conventions and agreements concluded previously which relate to the protection and preservation of the marine environment, and agreements which may be concluded in furtherance of the general principles set forth in this Convention.
>
> 2. Specific obligations assumed by States under special conventions, with respect to the protection and preservation of the marine environment, should be carried out in a manner consistent with the general principles and objectives of the Convention.

First of all, the fundamental difference between Articles 237 and 311 is that Article 311 relates to the general principles governing the relationship between the UNCLOS and other conventions, whilst Article 237 governs the narrower area of the relationship covered by Part XII of UNCLOS on the protection and preservation of the marine environment, which suggests that this Article refers rather to substantive commitments of States than to purely formal conflict of treaty norms as envisaged, i.e. in Article 30 of the VCLT. The main principle employed in paragraph 1 of Article 237 is that all future agreements that are compatible with UNCLOS are allowed and in the case of incompatibility, the obligations stemming from UNCLOS prevail. However, paragraph 2 of Article 237 uses the word "should" in relation to obligations assumed by States under special conventions to be carried out in a manner

---

[58] Wolfrum and Matz, note 49, at 480 and see also at 478-479.
[59] N. Matz, "The Law of the Sea and International Environmental Law", in Wolfrum and Matz, note 1, at 30.

compatible with the UNCLOS, instead of the word "shall".[60] This suggests that it does *not* impose an obligation on State Parties. However, the French text of the Article appears to include an obligation binding on States ("*les Parties s'acquitteront*"). Furthermore,

> ....paragraph 1 preserves future agreements to the extent that they are not inconsistent with the general principles of the Convention. One may wonder why this condition should be applied only to future agreements. It is hardly plausible to say that States must respect the general principles of the Convention in their future agreements but can violate them when carrying out their obligations under prior treaties. If the general principles of the Convention are so important as to justify their priority over inconsistent future agreements, the same will also be valid with respect to prior treaties. In any event, it is clear that under the French text States are obliged to comply with the general principles of the Convention, and whenever the performance of special treaties on the protection of the marine environment conflicts with those principles, priority must be given to the Convention.[61]

This reasoning is, it is submitted, unassailable.[62]

3.1.3 The Biosafety Protocol

Also of interest is the conflict clause in the Biosafety Protocol.[63] The conflict clause in the preamble "emphasises" that "this Protocol shall not be interpreted as implying a change in the rights and obligations of a Party under any existing international agreements" (clause 8 of the preamble). Another clause in the preamble (clause 9) provides that the Protocol "recognises" that "trade and environment agreements should be mutually supportive with a view to achieving sustainable development", while yet

---

[60] Sadat-Akhavi, note 2, at 132-133.

[61] Sadat-Akhavi, note 2, at 132-133.

[62] Also of interest is the relationship between the CBD and the 1997 Kyoto Protocol (see below note 71 for citation). Matz observes that there may be a potential conflict between the fundamental objectives of the CBD as it concerns the protection of forest ecosystems and the indirect incentives stemming from the Kyoto Protocol. The contradiction lies not in incompatible obligations but in "conflicts of implementation, since the Kyoto Protocol does not prescribe the destruction of primary forests to grow wood in plantations.", at 92. The Kyoto Protocol lacks the inclusion of an efficient strategy to incorporate the objectives of the CBD in its programmes in order to achieve its targets without the damage to the environment. In order to remedy such a very unsatisfactory state of affairs, Matz calls for their "respective recognition" and their "harmonisation" as the means to raise their "effectiveness." See N. Matz, "Conflicts between the Convention on Biological Diversity, the Kyoto Protocol and the Convention to Combat Desertification," in Wolfrum and Matz, note 1, at 78-99.

[63] 39 *ILM* 1027 (2000). The solution adopted in this Protocol follows the Convention on the Prior Informed Consent Procedure for Certain Hazardous Chemicals and Pesticides in International Trade ("PIC Convention"), 11 September 1998, 38 *ILM* 1 (1999). See also Safrin, note 29, at 617-628.

another (clause 10) is based on the "understanding" that "the above recital [i.e., conflict clause] is not intended to subordinate this Protocol to other international agreements".

Safrin argues that there are three possible interpretations of these clauses.[64] The first is that these clauses are completely ineffective. The second would allow the assumption that the inclusion of the clauses 9 and 10 essentially undo clause 8, so that, in effect, the Protocol does not include a conflict clause. The third is that the close analysis of the preambular language is that it does preserve parties' rights and obligations under earlier agreements. According to Safrin, the last is the most acceptable. The same author correctly observes that the placement of the conflict clause in the preamble did not diminish its legal value since the preamble, according to Article 31 of the VCLT, constitutes a part of a treaty text; and that the role of the conflict clause, such as it is, is to clarify the relationship between and the agreement and earlier agreements, not to change earlier agreements. The insertion of clause 9, according to her, reveals the "political sentiment" prevailing during negotiations that environmental agreements enjoy no lower status than trade agreements. This results in preservation of the rights of parties acquired under earlier agreements. Safrin explains that clause 9 expresses commonly held "aspirations" "that trade and environmental policies and agreements should support each other" and that this clause "reflected an attempt to protect the environment, on the one hand, "without overburdening trade, on the other"[65]. Clause 10, providing that the conflict clause "is not intended to subordinate the Protocol to other international agreements" is more controversial. Taken at face value, the phrase simply indicates that the inclusion of the conflict clause does not mean that the Protocol is of a lower status than other agreements. In fact, it serves to determine whether a party's rights and obligations under earlier agreements continue or whether such rights and obligations apply only if they are consistent with the provisions of the later agreement. However, it is quite possible to interpret this as meaning that such a clause "undermines or even extinguishes the Protocol".[66] Under this view, the clause would essentially undo the conflict clause that precedes it; therefore, "both clauses, in effect, fall out of the agreement."[67] This would result in the agreement having no conflict clause. The role of Article 30 of the VCLT in this context is limited. Under Article 30 of the VCLT, "the Protocol could be interpreted and understood as being incompatible with or modifying parties' obligations under earlier agreements", so that in the case of a conflict between the Protocol and an earlier agreement, the Protocol will prevail; but this line of

---

[64] Safrin, note 29, at 618-621.
[65] Safrin, note 29, at 620.
[66] *Id.*
[67] *Id.*

reasoning would result in the exact opposite effect of the express language included in the Protocol.[68]

3.1.4 Concluding remarks

It would appear every treaty has to be examined separately, on a case-by-case basis. This would apply to the question, for example, of how the Climate Change Convention relates to other environmental treaties in case of a conflict relating to the overlapping issues without a conflict clause. In a case of a conflict with a later instrument without a conflict clause, according to Article 30 (the general rule), the provisions of a later treaty will prevail, which is not always a desirable solution.

3.2 The Potential Utility of a Hierarchy of Norms in Environmental Treaties

In this section, we will consider the possibility of a role in the resolution of conflicts for certain notions arising from the nature of environmental treaties. Focusing on the Climate Change Convention,[69] we will consider the nature of obligations flowing from environmental treaties, with reference to the concept of integral obligations considered in Section 2 above.

The main object of the Climate Change Convention, as specified in its Article 2, is to stabilise greenhouse gas emissions at a level that would prevent dangerous anthropocentric interference with the climate system. The preamble to the Convention states that the parties acknowledge "that change in the Earth's climate and its adverse effects are a common concern of humankind". In addition, Article 3 of the Climate Change Convention outlines the principles that are to guide the parties to it, one of which is the concept of intergenerational equity.[70] The first Conference of the Parties

---

[68] Safrin, note 29, at 620.

[69] United Nations Framework Convention on Climate Change, opened for signature 4 June, 1992, entered into force 21 March 1994 ("Climate Change Convention"), text in: 31 ILM 849 (1992). See, e.g., R. Churchill and D. Freestone (eds.), *International Law and the Global Climate Change* (1991); D. Bodansky, "Managing Climate Change", *YIEL*, (1992) 60; D. Bodanksy, "The United Nations Framework Convention on Climate Change: A Commentary", 18 Yale JIL (1993), 451-558; S. Nilsson and D.C. Pitt, *Protecting the Atmosphere: The Climate Change Convention and its Context* (1994). On the concepts of the Common Heritage of Mankind and Common Concern of Humankind, see, e.g., K. Baslar, *The Concept of the Common Heritage of Mankind in International Law* (1998).

[70] It has been pointed out that Article 3 takes a novel approach to environmental protection. However, in the context of a dynamic and evolutionary regulatory regime it also has the important merit of providing some predictability regarding the parameters within which the

("COP") to the Climate Change Convention, held in Berlin in 1995, accepted that the commitments of the Convention were inadequate, and gave a mandate for the negotiation of new commitments, that were eventually embodied in the 1997 Kyoto Protocol,[71] which is not yet in force.[72]

For present purposes, two of the principles enumerated in Article 3 of the Climate Change Convention merit some further consideration.

3.2.1 Common Concern of Humankind

The concept of the common concern of humankind ("CCH"), referred to in the preamble to the treaty, was for the first time introduced by the General Assembly Resolution 43/53 in 1988 in relation to climate change.[73] The preamble to the Convention on Biological Diversity[74] ("CBD") also affirms that "the conservation of biological diversity is a common concern of humankind...". The inclusion of the concept of the CCH, as opposed to that of the Common Heritage of Mankind ("CHM"), was a conscious decision of the UNEP Working Group, which was of the view that due to the unclear legal character of biodiversity, it was better to use a concept with less defined legal connotations.[75] Birnie and Boyle are of the view that "'common concern' indicates a legal status both for climate change and biological resources which is distinctively different from the concepts of permanent sovereignty, common property, shared resources or common heritage, which generally determine the international legal status of natural resources".[76] They further explain that the concept of common concern as

---

parties are required to work towards the objective of the convention; see P. Birnie and A. Boyle, *International Law and the Environment* (2002), at 523-533, see also at 524.

[71] Kyoto Protocol to the United Nations Framework Convention on Climate Change, 37 ILM 22 (1998); see also <http://unfccc.int>, UNCCC, Conference of the Parties, 3rd. Sess., UN Doc. FCCC/CP/1997/L.7/Add.1 (1998). On the history of the negotiations of the compliance procedure under the Kyoto Protocol see R. Lefeber, "From The Hague to Bonn to Marrakesh and Beyond: A Negotiating History of the Compliance Regime under the Kyoto Protocol", *The Hague Yearbook of International Law*, (2001), at 25-54. See also, J. Brunnée, "A Fine Balance: Facilitation and Enforcement in the Design of a Compliance Regime for the Kyoto Protocol", 13:2 *Tulane Environmental Law Journal* (2000) at 223-270.

[72] On a further "conflict" issue arising in the context of the Kyoto Protocol, see Chapter 8 above.

[73] "[C]limate change is a common concern of mankind, since climate is an essential condition which sustains life on Earth." See on the subject: A. Boyle, "International Law and the Protection of the Global Atmosphere", in Churchill and Freestone (eds.), note 69, at 7-19; S. Borg, "The Common Concern Concept: A Prerequisite for an International Legal Regime for Protection of Areas beyond National Jurisdiction for Present and Future Generations", 11 *Future Generations Journal* (1993), at 14.

[74] 31 *ILM* 818 (1992).

[75] UNEP/bidiv.SWGB.1/5 Rev.1, 28 November 1990.

[76] Birnie and Boyle, note 70, at 98.

applied to climate change did not make the global atmosphere common property beyond the sovereignty of individual States; rather, and similarly to the ozone layer, it is treated as a "global unity" insofar as injury in the form of global warming or climate change may affect the community of States as a whole. It was not important, according to Birnie and Boyle, whether the global atmosphere comprises airspace under the sovereignty of a subjacent State or not; it is a common resource of vital interest to mankind. Kiss and Shelton, describing the concept of common concern, say the following:

> The concept of the common concern does not connote specific rules and obligations, but establishes the general basis for the international community to act, making clear that the subject matter is one of international concern. The acceptance of both the right and the duty of the international community to protect the global environment implies the need to strike a balance between international action and national sovereignty. In principle, proclaiming that the global environment is a matter of common concern to humanity means that actions affecting it are no longer solely within the domestic jurisdiction of states.[77]

There are, however, some fundamental differences between the concepts of the CCH and the CHM. One of them is the establishment of a special body under UNCLOS (the International Seabed Authority) to deal with the implementation of this concept in relation to 'the Area'. The Area covers the part of the seabed outside the continental shelf, at depths of around 3,500 metres. It was discovered that in this seabed there are manganese nodules that are composed of high-grade metal ore. It may be said that the main features of the CCH as applied to the Area are as follows: no State can claim sovereignty over it, no State can appropriate any part thereof; all resources of the Area are vested in mankind as a whole, on whose behalf the Authority will act; these resources are not subject to alienation. The resources recovered from the Area, however, may only be alienated in accordance with Part XI of the UNCLOS and the rules, regulations and procedures of the Authority (Article 137 of the UNCLOS); the activities in the Area shall be carried out for the benefit of mankind as a whole, taking into particular consideration the interests and needs of developing States (Article 140 of UNCLOS). The use of the Area is exclusively for peaceful purposes (Article 141). The establishment of such a body internationalised the exploitation of natural resources in the Area and turned them into property accessible for sharing by all States, which is not the case under the working of the CCH.

Beyond this, it may justifiably be said that "[i]f 'common concern' is neither common property nor common heritage, and if it entails a reaffirmation of the existing sovereignty of states over their own resources,

---

[77] A. Kiss and D. Shelton, *International Environmental Law* (1999), at 251.

what legal content, if any, does this concept have?"[78] According to these authors there are two basic effects of the application of this doctrine. First, it gives the international community of States both a legitimate interest in resources of global significance and a common responsibility to assist in their sustainable development; and secondly, although the States retain the sovereignty over their natural resources, it must be not unlimited or absolute but must be exercised within the confines of the global responsibilities set out in both in the Climate Change Convention and the CBD and in other important documents, such as the 1992 Rio Declaration on Environment and Development. In conclusion, it may be said that there are many approaches and many views on the matter. Some of the writers approach the concept of CCH in a very broad manner, such as Kiss. He is of the view that this concept should include both international commons and cultural-natural resources such as wildlife, significant wetlands and actions that would affect global climate.[79] Brown-Weiss also advocates such a broad approach. According to this author CCH should extend to all natural and cultural resources.[80]

The varied formulations of concepts of the CCH (as well as the CHM) in conventions, as well as the lack of agreement in doctrine as to their precise scope, make it difficult to ascribe to them precisely defined legal content.[81] It may be presumed, however, that environmental conventions that cover the subject-matter that falls under the CHM of the CCM have a different (higher) status compared to conventions that relate to less important fields. These concepts embody an approach that departs from traditional concepts such as State sovereignty or ownership of natural resources, an approach that is of great importance for strengthening of other human rights.[82]

3.2.2 Intergenerational Equity

The Climate Change Convention also refers to the interests of future generations in Article 3 paragraph 1, which reads as follows:

> The Parties should protect the climate system for the benefit of present and future generations of humankind, on the basis of equity and in accordance with their common but differentiated responsibilities and respective capabilities. Accordingly, the developed country Parties should take the lead in combating climate change and the adverse effect thereof.

---

[78] Birnie and Boyle, note 70, at 98-99.
[79] A.-C. Kiss, "La Notion de Patrimonie Commun de l'Humanité", 175 *RCADI* (1982), at 99-256.
[80] E. Brown-Weiss, *In Fairness to Future Generations: International Law, Common Partimony, Intergenerational Equity* (1989), at 49.
[81] Baslar, note 69, at 109.
[82] *Id.*, at 287-298.

The benefit of present and future generations constitutes one of the elements of so-called theory of intergenerational equity, expounded by Brown-Weiss.[83] The position of future generations and the concept of the wealth of the earth held in trust have been of interest for environmental lawyers for a very long time. As far back as the *Pacific Fur Seals* Arbitration,[84] the concept of trust, which is one of the foundations of the intergenerational equity doctrine, was persuasively expounded. The idea of preservation of the environment for the benefit of present and future generations is not new. For example, the preamble of the 1946 International Convention for the Regulation of Whaling "recognises" the "interest of the nations of the world in safeguarding for future generations the great natural resources represented by the whale stocks...". Furthermore, the Brundtland Commission's definition of sustainable development is phrased as "development that meets the needs of the present without compromising the ability of future generations to meet their own needs."[85] Although this definition is inadequate, it reflects the doctrine of intergenerational equity. There are other numerous examples of the conventions that are based on the interest of present and future generations. For example, the CBD expressly states that its purpose is "to conserve and sustainably use biological diversity for the benefit of present and future generations." Important "soft law" documents such as the 1972 Stockholm Declaration and the 1992 Rio Declaration also rely on this doctrine. Brown-Weiss approaches the position of the future generations on the basis of the concept of trust. She treats the earth and its resources as a trust, enjoyed and passed to us by our ancestors, and to be enjoyed and passed by us to our descendants for their use and enjoyment. Thus, the earth and its resources are held in a kind of "planetary trust" that generates rights and obligations. Intergenerational rights are group rights or "generational rights" that generations may enforce against each other. The fundamental concept is, thus, based on the premise of partnership among all generations. Although the Brown-Weiss' approach has been quite strongly criticised by Birnie and Boyle[86] and Kiss and Shelton,[87] the present authors

---

[83] Note 80; E. Brown-Weiss, "Our Rights and Obligations to Future Generations for the Environment", 84 *AJIL* (1990), at 198; see also C. Redgwell, *Intergenerational Trusts and Environmental Protection* (1999).

[84] Moore, 1 Int.Arb.Awards (1898), 755, rep. in 1 Int. Env.Reps. (1999), 43.

[85] World Commission on Environment and Development, Our Common Future (1987), at 43.

[86] "Despite its conceptual elegance, the apparent simplicity of the theory of intergenerational equity is deceptive. ...viewing inter-generational equity as an element of sustainable development does not resolve the argument for stronger generational rights or international guardianship, nor does it determine the optimal balance between this generation and its successors. Moreover, while accepting the right of present generations to use resources for economic development, it fails to answer the question how we value the environment for the purpose of determining whether future generations will be worse off. Nor does its concentration on relations between one generation and the next convincingly answer the

are of the view that this concept is of considerable significance, and despite its shortcomings, it plays an important part in contemporary international law, and is an element of the concept of sustainable development,[88] one that also expresses the collectivist and cooperational character of environmental protection.

3.2.3 Treaty interpretation, new concepts of environmental law, and creation of 'integral' obligations

The question then is whether it is possible to adopt an approach to the resolution of conflicts in environmental treaties that departs from the traditional and classical system based on the VCLT (including the conflict clauses as inserted in many environmental treaties) and takes account of the concept of "integral obligations", linking it to (emerging) concepts of international law, such as the CCH and intergenerational equity. This approach is of course largely speculative as it has not been tested in practice. The new concepts of environmental law could have an important, if indirect, influence on the "co-existence" of conflicting treaties. The undisputed importance for humankind of environmental issues, as acknowledged in these issues, such as climate change, may play an important role in the resolution of conflicts between treaties.

As noted in Section 3 above, there are some unresolved problems relating to successive treaties that contain integral obligations. While environmental obligations were not envisaged by the ILC during its work on the codification of the law of treaties, these obligations contained in treaties that depend for their implementation on the cooperation of all States, belong to the category of those that create "integral" obligations. "Integral obligations" correspond to what the ILC defined as the type of obligation, the breach of which "necessarily affects the enjoyment of the rights or performance of the obligations" of the other parties. The VCLT deals with such obligations in Articles 41(1)(b)(i), 58(1)(b)(i) and 60(2)(c). The latter concerns the breach of such an obligation and reads as follows: "any party other than a defaulting State [is entitled] to invoke the breach as a ground for suspending the operation of the treaty in whole or in part with respect to itself if the treaty is

---

equally pressing question of how benefits and burdens should be shared within each generation. Thus, although the content of the theory is well defined, it rests on some questionable assumptions concerning the nature of economic equity"; Birnie and Boyle, note 70, at 91.

[87] Kiss and Shelton say as follows: "The very concept of a generation is unclear. ... In fact, there are no distinct generations because every second there are hundreds of human beings who are born and die and at any moment more than five billion people of all ages co-exist." They also point to problems in the concept in relation both to the nature of the possible rights of future generations, and to the possible means of implementing them, note 77, at 255.

[88] See, e.g., Birnie and Boyle, note 70, at 89-91.

of such a character that a material breach of its provisions by one party radically changes the position of every party with respect to the further performance of its obligations under the treaty." In his Report on State Responsibility, the Rapporteur dealt with this aspect of an "integral" obligation,[89] in the context of its breach. He noted that the VCLT is concerned with the treaty instrument as a whole, whilst the Articles on State Responsibility, are concerned with particular obligations, and concludes that there seems to be no difficulty in transposing the notion of integral obligations to the law of state responsibility, and correspondingly, no difficulty in treating each State as individually injured by a breach of an integral obligation."[90]

If we, therefore, treat climate change obligations (contained both in the Climate Change Convention and the Kyoto Protocol) as creating "integral" obligations, which may not be open to any contracting out, the conclusion would be that a later inconsistent treaty constitutes in these circumstances a violation of obligations towards other parties, and as between parties to the earlier treaty the obligations imposed by that treaty would prevail. This view is reflected in Article 30(4)(b) of the VCLT. It may further be argued that obligations falling within the ambit of the concepts of Common Heritage of Humankind and Common Concern of Humankind are also integral obligations. Both concepts presuppose certain common interests and certain common responsibilities and breaches of obligations covered by such concepts radically change the position of other States. Therefore, it would appear that environmental treaties under the regime of either of CHM or CCH which, as just suggested, arguably contain integral obligations, have some priority over the provisions of treaties that can be considered to be of a "lower" order.

What is the importance of conflict clauses for other multilateral agreements such as the Climate Change Convention? It is widely recognised that climate change influences biological diversity, causing, for example, the drying out of wetlands, the habitat loss of estuaries and deltas, major changes in vegetation types and forests, significant losses in some areas such as tundra, losses of land areas etc.[91] Therefore, it may be said that there may be a potential conflict between the CBD and the Climate Change Convention in overlapping areas. It would appear that the conflict clause in the CBD would prevent any significant problems for the States Parties to both Conventions. However, the second part of Article 22 of the CBD ("except where an exercise of those rights and obligations would cause a serious

---

[89] J. Crawford, Third Report on State Responsibility, International Law Commission, Fifty-second session, Geneva, 1 May-9 June, 10 July-18 August 2000, UN Doc. A/CN.4/507 (2000), paragraph 90.
[90] Id., at paragraph 90.
[91] "Biodiversity and Climate Change", at: <http://www.unep-wcmc.org/climate/impacts.htm>

damage or threat to biological diversity") has the potential to cause serious problems. How will the threshold of damage be determined, and what would be the consequences of a decision in favour of the priority of rights and obligations stemming from the CBD? These are questions to which there are at present no easy answers. This underscores the aforementioned limits of the utility of conflict clauses in such situations. The point is that both climate change and the conservation of biological diversity are important goals, and both conventions include reference to, for example, the concept of the CCH, and impose obligations of the integral or interdependent type. Conflicts between treaties at the same point in this suggested hierarchy would still not be easily resolved.

This would mean that the resolution of conflicts between environmental treaties, which would have the same status in this proposed hierarchy, may prove difficult, and the approach suggested here may be of more utility in resolving conflicts between environmental treaties and other treaties. Of course, there is doubt as to the precise legal status of concepts such as intergenerational equity and the CCH. But the role for these concepts as suggested here is a limited one – that they could be useful in resolving conflicts between treaties as aids to interpretation, regardless of their substantive legal status. It has been said that:

> ...rather than formal criteria, an analysis of the actual object and purpose of treaty norms is required to properly answer the question. The evaluation of the States parties purpose, conduct, and objective appears to be an effective instrument for determining to what extent States wish to be bound by an international convention. Therefore, a policy-oriented and teleological interpretation of treaties seems to be a more useful instrument than a purely textual interpretation which is the approach preferred by article 31 para.1 of the Vienna Convention on the Law of Treaties.[92]

---

[92] P. Vigni, "The Interaction between the Antarctic Treaty System and the Other Relevant Conventions Applicable to the Antarctic Area", 4 *Max Planck Yearbook of UN Law* (2000), 481-542, at 539, note 84. Regarding the concept of sustainable development, which suffers from similar difficulties as the CCH and intergenerational equity, a similar approach has been suggested by A.V. Lowe, "Sustainable Development and Unsustainable Arguments", in A.E. Boyle and D.A.C. Freestone (eds.), *International Law and Sustainable Development: Past Achievements and Future Challenges* (1999), at 19, esp. 22-31. Lowe notes that the concept of sustainable development, which, as we argue here, shares the same kinds of limitation regarding their legal status as the CCH and intergenerational equity, cannot "be regarded as having sufficient identifiable normative meaning to be capable of generating a self-contained norm of customary international law, no matter what its utility as a description of policy goals in international treaties might be ... The argument that sustainable development is a norm of customary international law, binding on and directing the conduct of states, and which can be applied by tribunals, is not sustainable" (at 30). He however argues, in favour of the legal relevance of the principle, that the entirety of international law, at least as far as third-party adjudication is concerned, is perhaps not to be sought exclusively within the traditional

4. Concluding Remarks

In conclusion, it may be said that the problem of the hierarchy of treaties and of their conflict remains one of the most complicated and still unresolved issues of international law. The general structure of Article 30 and its link with Articles 40, 41 and 59 of the VCLT, and the problems relating to the scope and content of the "same subject-matter" condition, make it almost impossible to provide a fully coherent analysis of the principles governing the rules of conflict between the treaties and to draw general conclusions about them.[93] It must also be borne in mind that the principle *pacta tertiis nec nocent nec prosunt* plays a fundamental, indeed pivotal, role in the construction of Article 30. As observed above, the emergence of new concepts in international environmental law, such as the CCH and the CHM and intergenerational equity, could add a substantive dimension to the conflict rules enshrined in the VCLT. The question is whether these doctrines (or concepts), due to their importance, are capable of changing the rules codified in Article 30 and to give priority to treaties that otherwise would be subject to other instruments. It has been said that

> The rhetoric in the PIC and biosafety negotiations that demonized savings clauses as setting up a hierarchy of importance in international law could seep

---

sources of international law, for example, as listed in Article 38(1) of the Statute of the International Court of Justice. Taking a lead from dicta in the Separate Opinion of Judge Weeramantry in the Case concerning the Gabčikovo-Nagymaros Project (Hungary/Slovakia), Judgment of 25 September 1997, 1997 ICJ Rep. 7, that all legal systems contain (primary) rules and principles that (potentially) overlap or conflict in relation to a specific set of facts (for example, "the right to development" and "environmental protection"), and there exist "modifying norms", such as sustainable development, that serve to enable a decision-maker to choose which rules or principles are to be given decisive force in a given situation. Sustainable development is of this character, and like other modifying norms (of which canons of interpretation in municipal law and the "Rule of Reason" and the "balancing of interests" test in disputes concerning extraterritorial jurisdiction are also examples) (at p. 33), it does not depend upon state practice and opinio juris; nor does it necessarily carry a prescriptive charge. Lowe states that, "[w]hile the concept is insufficiently precise for it to be possible to say that it requires a state to do this or that, as a goal or policy it is perfectly adequate to offer some guidance to judges in its approach to establishing priorities and accommodations between primary norms", in Boyle and Freestone (at p. 34). As such, sustainable development "can properly claim a normative status as an element of the process of judicial reasoning" (at p. 31), exemplifying "another species of normativity which is of great potential value in the handling of concepts of international environmental law" (at p. 21). The same could apply to the concepts of the CCH and intergenerational equity, as the doubts regarding the legal status and implications of the concept of sustainable development does not prevent it from having a role to play in the manner suggested above.

[93] See also N. Matz, "Approaches to The Coordination of International Environmental Agreements," in Wolfrum and Matz, note 1, 119-213, at 148.

into other negotiations, to the dismay of international lawyers. Unfortunately, international lawyers and negotiators may find it more difficult to resolve the substantive issues of whether the parties actually intended to modify their existing international rights and obligations in the event of an unanticipated conflict between successive agreements. Instead, the issue may be reframed into an overarching and perhaps unanswerable question of which set of important international goals reflected in a series of treaties, such as affecting trade, human rights, law enforcement, the environment, holds greater import.[94]

It also appears that the general, prevailing policy on the coexistence of environmental treaties is that of enhancement of synergies rather than of emphasis on conflict. This is evidenced by the compliance procedure established in the Convention on Access to Information, Public Participation in Decision-making and Access to Justice in Environmental Matters ("Aarhus Convention"),[95] which envisages enhancement of synergies between the Aarhus Convention compliance procedure and compliance procedures under other agreements. To this effect, the Meeting of the Parties of the Aarhus Convention may request the Compliance Committee to communicate as appropriate with the relevant bodies of these agreements and report back to it, and make recommendations, as appropriate. The importance of cooperation between the States as a means of solving conflicts has also been stressed in relation to such areas as Antarctica, covered by the Antarctic Treaty System ("ATS") and indeed, as has been said, in general: "cooperation is probably one of the most effective means for resolving all types of incompatibility between international norms".[96] In the case of the prevention of marine pollution of the Antarctic area, certain aspects of the system under the Madrid Protocol appear to be incompatible with those of the International Convention for the Prevention of Pollution from Ships (1973/1978). In order to avoid a conflict of norms, the suggestion has been made to apply the more effective of the set of norms, rather than to seek a solution in Article 30 of the VCLT.[97]

It is in this context that the approach suggested here might be helpful. Other approaches to the possible solution of conflicts in environmental law (as well sidestepping Article 30 of the VCLT) through some kind of international coordination or harmonisation, such as through the UNEP or "harmonisation conference," or an institution attached to the UNEP endowed with coordination functions, have been proposed.[98] In the absence of such

---

[94] Safrin, note 29, at 622.

[95] Meeting of the Parties to the Convention on Access to Information, Public Participation in Decision-making and Access to justice in Environmental Matters, First Meeting, Lucca, Italy, 21-23 October, 2002), Article XIV.

[96] P. Vigni, note 92, at 508.

[97] Id., at 518.

[98] Wolfrum and Matz, "Conclusions and Outlook," in Wolfrum and Matz, note 1, at 209-213.

approaches, or as a part of such approaches as and when they may materialize, one approach that could reward further consideration, rather than ignoring the problem (which appears to be the favoured policy), is to attempt to coordinate environmental obligations through setting of some kind of hierarchy of norms, perhaps based on the identification of certain concepts of a higher order, such as CCH or intergenerational equity, a hierarchy linked to the concept of integral obligations. As noted above, however, this is not to be expected to resolve all the difficulties arising in this context, but it would be a step towards the solution of conflicts between treaties. Environmental treaties could yet contribute to a deeper understanding of the problems in this field.

CHAPTER TEN

The Gabčikovo-Nagymaros Case and the Law of Treaties[*]

1. Introduction

The main issues in the judgment in the *Gabčikovo-Nagymaros* case[1] focus on the law of treaties, and by rendering its judgment, the ICJ has contributed greatly to the development, or at least clarification, of the law in this field (in addition to other fields such as environmental law and law of international watercourses). The issues covered in this case are numerous, and they include the relationship between the law of treaties and state responsibility; succession of treaties; and territorial régimes. However, this chapter will focus on the following issues: unilateral suspension and abandonment of obligations stemming from a treaty in force; unilateral termination of a treaty; applicability of the 1969 Vienna Convention on the Law of Treaties ("VCLT" or "Vienna Convention");[2] interpretation of Articles 60 and 62 of VCLT (material breach, impossibility of performance, and fundamental change of circumstances); the principle of "approximate application"; and the *pacta sunt servanda* principle, and this chapter will focus on these issues.

---

[*] This chapter is an updated and revised version of M. Fitzmaurice, "The Gabčikovo-Nagymaros case: The Law of Treaties" published in 11:2 *Leiden Journal of International Law* 1998, at 321-344 and reprinted with kind permission of Cambridge University Press.
[1] Gabčikovo-Nagymaros Project (Hungary/Slovakia), Judgment of 25 September 1997, 1997 ICJ Rep. 7 (the "Judgment").
[2] 1969 Vienna Convention on the Law of Treaties, UN Doc. A/CONF.39/27 (1969), reproduced in 8 *ILM* 679 (1969).

2. The Factual Background Relating to the Law of Treaties

2.1 Relevant Terms of the 1977 Treaty

The dispute between Hungary and Czechoslovakia (as it then was) over the Danube River Dam aroused great interest even before it was ruled upon by the ICJ.[3] It is an undisputed fact that the project to build the dam in question arose from the wish to "strengthen the relationships between the two countries and to bring economic development to the region."[4] In order to put the project into effect, the two states concluded the 1977 Treaty Concerning the Construction and Operation of the Gabčikovo-Nagymaros System of Locks (the "1977 Treaty").[5] The 1977 Treaty provided for the construction of a single and indivisible operational system of locks. The head-water installation was to be erected in Hungarian territory at Dunakiliti, which is situated on the border between the two states. The Danube, as a result, would be dammed and an artificial lake would be created of about 60 square kilometres, two thirds of which was to be situated in Czechoslovak territory and one third in Hungarian territory. From there, water would flow for about 17 kilometres through a by-pass canal to the hydro-electric station at Gabčikovo and thence would flow for about 8 kilometres through a canal back to the original bed of the Danube. A second power station was to be built at Nagymaros, about 100 kilometres downstream. As a part of the project, the parties agreed to the modification of the Danube bed between Dunakiliti and Nagymaros (Article 1, paragraphs 1, 2, and 3). The costs of the project were to be borne by the parties jointly in equal measure (Article 1(1)). Each party had specified responsibilities as to the construction and operation of the project (Article 5(1)). All the major constructions were to be

---

[3] See, e.g., E. Hoenderkamp, "The Danube: Damned or Dammed? The Dispute Between Hungary and Slovakia Concerning the Gabčikovo-Nagymaros Project", 8:2 *LJIL* (1995), 287; G.M. Berrisch, "The Danube Dam Dispute Under International Law", 46 *Austrian Journal of International Law* (1994), 231; P.R. Williams, "International Environmental Dispute Resolution: The Dispute Between Slovakia and Hungary Concerning Construction of the Gabčikovo and Nagymaros Dams", 19 *Columbia Journal of Environmental Law* (1994), 1; C. Cepelka, "The Dispute Over the Gabčikovo-Nagymaros Systems of Locks is Drawing to a Close", XX *Polish Yearbook of International Law* (1993), 63; and E. Robert, "L'Affaire relative au project Gabčikovo-Nagymaros (Hongrie/Slovaquie). Un nouveau conflit era matière d'environnement devant la Cour International de Justice?", XLVII, No. 5 *Studia Diplomatica* (1994), 17.

[4] Berrisch, *supra* note 3, at 233.

[5] 1977 Treaty Between the Hungarian People's Republic and the Czechoslovak Socialist Republic Concerning the Construction and Operation of the Gabčikovo-Nagymaros System of Locks, signed in Budapest on 16 September 1977 ("1977 Treaty"), reproduced in 32 *ILM* 1247 (1993).

owned jointly by the parties (Article 8). The parties would jointly use and benefit from the operation of the project (Article 9(1)). An Agreement on Mutual Assistance, concluded by the two parties on 30 June 1978, fixed the schedule of works.[6]

As stated by the Court in its Judgment,

> the Project was to have taken the form of an integrated joint project with two contracting parties on an equal footing in respect to financing, construction and operation of the works. Its single and indivisible nature was to have been realized through the Joint Contractual Plan which complemented the Treaty. In particular, Hungary would have the control of the sluices at Dunakiliti and the works at Nagymaros, whereas Czechoslovakia would have control of the works at Gabčikovo.[7]

There were also a number of provisions in the 1977 Treaty covering additional objectives, such as environmental protection, flood control, and navigation on the relevant stretches of the river Danube. In this respect, the Court found, in a statement to which further reference will be made in Section 5 *infra*,

> that the 1977 Treaty was not only a joint investment project for the production of energy, but it was designed to serve other objectives as well: the improvement of the navigability of the Danube, flood control and regulation of ice-discharge, and the protection of the natural environment. None of these objectives has been given absolute priority over the other, in spite of the emphasis which is given in the Treaty to the construction of a System of Locks for the production of energy.[8]

Finally, on the terms of the 1977 Treaty, it is necessary to note, in view of the considerable importance attached to it by the Court (see Section 5 *infra)* that the Court further found that "[t]he 1977 Treaty never laid down a rigid system, albeit that the construction of a system of locks at Gabčikovo and Nagymaros was prescribed by the Treaty itself.[9] The Court then refers to various manifestations of the parties' desire for, or willingness to contemplate, alterations to aspects of the works as prescribed in the original Treaty, and concludes by stating that "[t]he explicit terms of the Treaty itself were therefore in practice acknowledged by the parties to be negotiable".[10]

---

[6] 1977 Agreement on Mutual Assistance ("Agreement on Mutual Assistance"), reproduced in 32 *ILM* 1263 (1993).

[7] Gabčikovo-Nagymaros Project, *supra,* note 1, para. 20.

[8] *Id.,* para. 135.

[9] *Id.,* para. 138.

[10] *Id.,* para. 139.

2.2 The Course of Work on the Project

The work on the Project started to break down in the early 1980s due to growing scepticism in Hungary as to its ecological viability. This was coupled with economic problems. Hungary subsequently suspended construction of its share of the project.

On 10 October 1983, two Protocols to the 1977 Treaty were signed.[11] One amended Article 4(4) of the 1977 Treaty and the other amended the Agreement on Mutual Assistance,[12] to slow down the works and to postpone putting the power plants into operation. Further, at the request of Hungary, the two states signed a third Protocol on 6 February 1989 ("1989 Protocol").[13] The purpose of this Protocol was to accelerate construction and shorten it to 15 months. On 13 May 1989, the Hungarian government unilaterally announced suspension of the construction works on the Nagymaros Project for two months in order to conduct further studies and to consider the Project alternatives.[14] On 20 July 1989, it extended suspension for a further three months, i.e. until 31 October 1989. This extension related as well to the Dunakiliti and Gabčikovo sites.

In response to these measures, the Czechoslovak government warned of the possibility of the introduction of a unilateral provisional solution. On 31 October 1989, the Hungarian Parliament stopped construction of the entire Project indefinitely and authorized the Hungarian Council of Ministers to conduct negotiations with the other party on the modification of the 1977 Treaty. Negotiations were interrupted by the "velvet revolution" and resumed thereafter, and at the same time domestic experts appointed by both parties were to conduct ecological studies. The new Hungarian government considered construction of the Project a mistake. In 1991, the Hungarian Parliament authorized the termination of the 1977 Treaty, as well as the conclusion of a new agreement, which would provide for the consequences of discontinuation of the Project and the rehabilitation of the Danube area. Czechoslovakia started, on 18 November 1991 to construct within its territory the "provisional solution" (the so-called "Variant C"). The purpose of this was to allow operation of the Gabčikovo Dam without Hungary.

In February 1992, the Hungarian government notified the Czechoslovak Government that it regarded the provisional solution to be incompatible with

---

[11] See 32 *ILM* 1263 (1993).

[12] Agreement on Mutual Assistance, *supra* note 6.

[13] See 32 *ILM* 1263 (1993).

[14] Hungary informed Czechoslovakia on 24 May 1989 of the suspension. See Declaration of the Government of the Republic of Hungary on the Termination of the Treaty Concluded Between the People's Republic of Hungary and the Socialist Republic of Czechoslovakia on the Construction and Joined Operation of the Gabčikovo-Nagymaros Barrage System, reproduced in 32 *ILM* 1260-1290 (1993).

international law and a violation of its territorial integrity. On 16 May 1992, the Hungarian government unilaterally announced termination of the 1977 Treaty. The Czechoslovak government refused to accept this termination on the basis that the declaration of the Hungarian government did not state the grounds for termination, in consequence of which the Czechoslovak government considered the 1977 Treaty to be still in force. On 24 October 1992, the Czechoslovaks began to divert the Danube to the power canal.

An attempt by the European Commission to bring about an interim solution between the parties to the dispute failed. On 1 January 1993, Czechoslovakia dissolved into two separate states: the Czech Republic and the Slovak Republic (also referred to as "Slovakia"). In relation to the Gabčikovo-Nagymaros Project, Slovakia was marked as the sole successor. On 7 April 1993, the Special Agreement between the Republic of Hungary and the Slovak Republic for Submission to the International Court of Justice of the Differences Between Them Concerning the Gabčikovo-Nagymaros Project was concluded.[15]

3. The Terms of the Special Agreement and the Law of Treaties

The Court was asked by the parties to the dispute to decide numerous issues of the law of treaties. Firstly, it was requested to determine the status of the 1977 Treaty. This involved the determination by the Court of "whether the Republic of Hungary was entitled to suspend and subsequently abandon, in 1989, the works on the Nagymaros Project and on the part of the Gabčikovo Project for which the Treaty attributed the responsibility to the Republic of Hungary."[16] and "what are the legal effects of the notification, on 19 May 1992, of the termination of the Treaty by the Republic of Hungary".[17] The Court was also requested to determine the status of the "provisional solution" in that it was asked to answer the question

> whether the Czech and Slovak Federal Republic was entitled to proceed, in November 1992, to the 'provisional solution' and to put into operation from October 1992 this system, described in the Report of the Working Group of Independent Experts of the Commission of the European Communities, the Republic of Hungary and the Czech and Slovak Federal Republic dated 23 November 1992 (damming up of the Danube at the river kilometre 1851.7 on

---

[15] 1993 Special Agreement Between the Republic of Hungary and the Slovak Republic for Submission to the International Court of Justice of the Differences Between Them Concerning the Gabčikovo-Nagymaros Project, reproduced in 32 *ILM* 1293 (1993).

[16] *Id.*, Art. 2(1a). See Gabčikovo-Nagymaros Project, *supra* note 1, para. 2.

[17] *Id.*

the Czechoslovak territory and resulting consequences on water and navigation course).[18]

Finally, the Court was requested "to determine the legal consequences, including the rights and obligations for the Parties, arising from its Judgment on the questions in paragraph 1 of this Article".[19]

4. The Judgment

4.1 The Applicability of the VCLT

The Court remarked, as it has done on many previous occasions, that some rules contained in the VCLT "might be considered as a codification of existing customary law".[20] It may be said that in many respects Articles 60 and 62 of the VCLT,[21] which relate to termination and suspension of treaties, contain such rules. On this point, the parties to the dispute were broadly in agreement. The VCLT is not directly applicable to the 1977 Treaty, since both parties to the dispute ratified the VCLT only after the conclusion of the 1977 Treaty.[22] Nonetheless, the VCLT is applicable to the 1989 Protocol.

4.2 Suspension and Termination of the 1977 Treaty

The starting point of the analysis of this issue is the statement included in the Judgment that "[t]he two parties to this case concur in recognizing that the 1977 Treaty, the above-mentioned Agreement on mutual assistance of 1977 and the Protocol of 1989 were validly concluded and were duly in force when the facts recounted above took place",[23] and that the 1977 Treaty does not contain any provision on its termination. Moreover, the Court could not infer any indication that the parties intended to admit even any possibility of denunciation or withdrawal. The Court was of the view that the contrary conclusion may be drawn, namely, that the 1977 Treaty aimed at the establishment of "a long-standing and durable *régime* of joint investment and joint operation".[24]

---

[18] *Id.*, Art. 2 (1 b) of the Special Agreement, *supra* note 15.
[19] *Id.*, Art 2(2).
[20] See Gabčikovo-Nagymaros Project, *supra* note 1, para. 46.
[21] VCLT, *supra* note 2.
[22] See Gabčikovo-Nagymaros Project, *supra* note 1, para.99.
[23] *Id.*, para. 39.
[24] *Id.*, para. 100.

The Court stated that determination of the issue whether a convention is or is not in force, and whether all conditions to suspend it or denounce it have been fulfilled, is to be made by the Court on the basis of the law of treaties, not on the basis of the law of state responsibility. The Court, however, admitted that

> evaluation of the extent to which the suspensions or denunciation of a convention, seen as incompatible with the law of treaties, involves the responsibility of the State which proceeded to it, is to be made under the law of State responsibility.[25]

The Court interpreted the conduct of Hungary in 1989, i.e. suspending and subsequently abandoning the works, as clearly indicating its unwillingness to comply with at least some provisions of the 1977 Treaty and the 1989 Protocol, as specified in the Joint Contractual Plan.[26] Indeed, the Court put it quite forcefully in saying that "[t]he effect of Hungary's conduct was to render impassible the accomplishment of the system of works the Treaty expressly described as 'single and indivisible'."[27]

The first question that arises is whether a treaty may be suspended or terminated in the absence of a special suspension or termination clause. This topic was considered by the International Law Commission, as well as having been the subject of many publications.[28] The question of unilateral suspension or termination of a treaty in the absence of an explicit provision contained in it, was for the first time taken up at the forum of the ILC by Fitzmaurice and its consideration was subsequently continued by Waldock.[29]

According to Fitzmaurice, in the event of the absence of any provision on termination or suspension of a treaty, there is a presumption that the treaty was intended to be of indefinite duration and could only to be terminated by mutual agreement by all the parties. This presumption may, however, be

---

[25] *Id.*, para. 47.

[26] Joint Contractual Plan, signed on 6 May 1976, reproduced in 32 *ILM* 1248 (1993).

[27] Gabčikovo-Nagymaros case, *supra*, note 1, para. 48.

[28] E.g., K. Widdows, "The Unilateral Denunciation of Treaties Containing No Denunciation Clause", 35 *BYIL* (1982), 83; J. Garner and V. Jobst, "The Unilateral Denunciation of Treaties by One Party Because of Alleged Non-Performance by Another Party or Parties", 24 *AJIL* (1935), 569; S.E. Nahlik, "The Grounds of Invalidity and Termination of Treaties", 65 *AJIL* (1971), 736; B. Simma, "Termination and Suspension of Treaties: Two Recent Austrian Cases", 21 *GYIL* (1979), 74; and H. Briggs, "Unilateral Denunciation of Treaties: The Vienna Convention and the International Court of Justice", 68 *AJIL* (1974), 51.

[29] Second Report of G. Fitzmaurice (Fitzmaurice II), UN Doc. A/CN.4/107, 1957 YILC, Vol. II (Part Two), at 16; Fourth Report of Fitzmaurice (Fitzmaurice IV), UN Doc. A/CN.4/120, 1959 YILC, Vol. II (Part Two), at 37; First Report of Waldock (Waldock I), UN Doc. A/CN.4/144, 1962 YILC, Vol. II (Part Two), at 27; Second Report of Waldock: (Waldock II), UN Doc. A/CN.4/156, 1963 YILC, Vol. II (Part Two), at 36; Fourth Report of Waldock: (Waldock IV), UN Doc. A/CN.4/177, 1965 YILC, Vol. II (Part Two), at 3; and Fifth Report of Waldock (Waldock V), UN Doc. A/CN.4/183, 1966 YILC, Vol. II (Part Two), at 51.

negated a) by necessary inference to be derived from the terms of the treaty in question, which would generally indicate the possibility of its expiry under certain circumstances or an intention to permit unilateral termination or withdrawal; and b) in cases of treaties, which, by their nature, are deemed to belong to a category in which the possibility of withdrawal appears to exist for the parties if the contrary is not indicated. Treaties of alliance or of a commercial character belong to this latter group.[30] In either category of cases, termination or withdrawal may be effected by giving such period of notice as is reasonable, taking into account the nature of the treaty in question and all surrounding circumstances.

Waldock proposed, in his Draft Article 17, a series of rules to deal with the duration of a treaty which contains no provision regarding its duration or termination.[31] In the case of a treaty whose purposes are by their nature limited in duration, the treaty would not be subject to denunciation or withdrawal on notice, but would continue to be in force until devoid of purpose. In cases not falling into this category, a party would have the right to denounce or withdraw from the treaty by giving 12 months' notice to that effect to the depository, or to the other party or parties when the treaty is one of the following: a commercial or trading treaty (other than one establishing an international régime for a particular area, river, or waterway); a treaty of alliance or military co-operation (other than special agreements concluded under Article 43 of the UN Charter); a treaty for technical co-operation in economic, social, cultural, scientific, communications, or any other such matters; or a treaty of arbitration, conciliation, or judicial settlement. He emphasized that a treaty would continue in force indefinitely with respect to each party where the treaty establishes a boundary between two states; or effects a cession of a territory or a grant of rights in or over a territory; establishes a special international régime for a particular area, territory, river, waterway, or air space; is a treaty of peace, a treaty of disarmament or for maintenance of peace; effects a final settlement of an international dispute; or is a general multilateral treaty providing for the codification or progressive development of general international law.[32] In other cases, not enumerated in his Draft Article, a treaty would continue indefinitely, unless it clearly appeared from the nature of the treaty or the circumstances of its conclusion that it was intended to have only temporary application.

Waldock stated in his report that

---

[30] See Fitzmaurice II, *supra* note 29, at 38.
[31] See Waldcock II, *supra* note 29.
[32] *Id.*

> [i]n principle the question is one of the intention of the parties in each case, for the parties are certainly free, as and when they wish, to make their treaty terminable upon notice.[33]

He further stated that the absolute rule of termination only by mutual agreement has become a residuary rule. Since practice appears to be very divergent according to Waldock

> [t]he true position today seems to be that there are certain classes of treaty where by reason of the nature of the treaty the presumption is against a right of denunciation and also certain classes of treaty where by reason of the nature of the treaty it is in favour of such a right.[34]

The residual rule applies perhaps to treaties which fall outside these classes. According to Waldock, the real problem is to define these different categories, i.e. those where the presumption is in favour of a right of denunciation and those where it is against such a presumption. This, and further proposals of Waldock in relation to the codification of unilateral denunciation of treaties without a special provision to this effect, divided the Commission and have proved to be inconclusive. The solution proposed by ILC Draft Article 53 was subject to further criticism in the forum of the Sixth Committee.[35] Draft Article 53 was also not supported by the practice of states. The views expressed by publicists are diverse and do not adhere to one particular view.[36]

The Diplomatic Conference, perhaps predictably, failed to produce any uniform conclusions.[37] Therefore, Article 56 of the VCLT reflects a compromise in relation to the right to denunciation of or withdrawal from a treaty. This Article provides that

> [a] treaty which contains no provision regarding its termination and which does not provide for denunciation or withdrawal is not subject to denunciation or withdrawal unless: a. it is established that the parties intended to admit the

---

[33] *Id.*, at 67.

[34] *Id.*

[35] Official Records of the General Assembly, 22nd Session, 18 October 1967, UN Doc.A/C.6/SR.974, at 94-95.

[36] Lord McNair was of the view that "the normal basis of approach adopted in the United Kingdom and, it is believed, in most States, towards a treaty that it is intended to be of perpetual duration and incapable of unilateral termination, unless, expressly, or by implication, it contains a right of a unilateral termination or some other provision for its coming to an end. There is nothing juridically impossible in the existence of a treaty creating obligations which are incapable of termination except by the agreement of all parties. Some existing British treaties have endured for nearly six centuries, and many for three", see Lord McNair, *The Law of Treaties* (1961), at 493-494.

[37] Official Records of the United Nations Conference on the Law of Treaties, First Session, Vienna, 26 March -25 May 1968, UN Doc. A/CONF.39/11, at 335.

possibility of denunciation or withdrawal; or b. a right of denunciation or withdrawal may be implied from the nature of the treaty.[38]

In this connection, the grounds for termination of a treaty can be grouped into four categories, namely: objective circumstances specified in the treaty itself; objective circumstances for which there is no provision in the treaty; concordant action of the parties; and the actions of one party only.[39]. Suspension of the operation of a treaty, in contrast to termination or denunciation, raises less complicated problems than termination does. It may be said that in many articles of the VCLT, suspension of a treaty has been introduced as an alternative, and by implication, in many circumstances, a preferable solution to its final termination, as it allows for the maintenance of the obligatory force of treaties as far as possible. Termination of a treaty is the last resort.

> [t]he Convention brings to the attention of the parties to any treaty the possibility of suspending its operation instead of acting to bring about its termination whenever either the very occurrence of a ground, or the appraisal of the extent to which it has occurred, may depend upon subjective judgment of a party, or else the occurrence of such a ground does not necessarily mean that it would have become permanent or irrevocable.[40]

In particular, this applies to the following grounds: impossibility of performance, fundamental change of circumstances, and material breach.

The terms of the 1977 Treaty and related documents indicate clearly that recourse to unilateral termination was neither the intention of the parties to it nor to be implied from the nature of the 1977 Treaty. Indeed, the opposite is the case; the parties to the 1977 Treaty intended to create a lasting and durable régime for their mutual benefit. Hungary thus had to rely upon different provisions of the law of treaties to find grounds "in support of the lawfulness, and thus the effectiveness, of its notification of termination".[41] Hungary presented five arguments which are based on the law of treaties, the law of state responsibility, and, finally, environmental considerations, i.e. on the development of new norms of environmental law. In relation to the law of treaties, Hungary in fact invoked three grounds for termination, namely: impossibility of performance; the occurrence of a fundamental change of circumstances; and material breach of the 1977 Treaty by Czechoslovakia.

---

[38] Art. 56 of the VCLT, *supra* note 2.
[39] The VCLT enumerates three possible objective circumstances "which, although not mentioned by the parties in the treaty itself, may be invoked as grounds for its termination"; Nahlik, *supra* note 28, at 747.
[40] *Id.*, at 752.
[41] Gabčikovo-Nagymaros Project, *supra* note 1, para. 92.

4.2.1 Impossibility of performance

According to Nahlik, supervening impossibility of performance is well-established and uncontested as grounds for termination of a treaty. It originates from an ancient concept in civil law and is a principle admitted by international law. The VCLT limits the possibility of invoking this ground to the "permanent disappearance or destruction of an object indispensable for the execution of the treaty";[42] and further that it "cannot be invoked by a party that was itself instrumental in causing it by a breach of its international obligations".[43]

In light of the above, the Court rightly found that "Hungary's interpretation of the wording of Article 61 is, however, not in conformity with the terms of that Article, nor with the intentions of the Diplomatic Conference which adopted the Convention."[44] During the Diplomatic Conference[45] proposals were made to broaden the scope of Article 61. Nonetheless, the parties chose to limit themselves to a narrower concept. The contention of Hungary was that the essential object of the 1977 Treaty, i.e. an economic joint investment which was consistent with environmental considerations, had permanently disappeared and the 1977 Treaty had become impossible to perform. In order to make a decision as to the applicability of Article 61, the Court did not have to determine whether the term "object" in Article 61 could also be understood "to embrace legal régime as in any event, even if that were the case, it would have to conclude that in this instance that régime had not definitively ceased to exist."[46] Further, the Court stated that the 1977 Treaty, in particular its Articles 15, 19, and 20, provided for the parties the necessary means to proceed at any time, through negotiations in order to readjust "between economic imperatives and ecological imperatives"[47] In fact, the Court noticed that if the joint exploitation of the investment was no longer possible, it was due originally to Hungary's failure to perform most of the works for which it was responsible under the 1977 Treaty. As indicated above, according to Article 61(2) of the VCLT, impossibility of performance cannot be invoked by a party as a ground for termination of a treaty when it results from that party's own failure to perform its obligations deriving from that treaty.

---

[42] Nahlik, *supra* note 28, at 747.
[43] *Id.*
[44] Gabčikovo-Nagymaros Project, *supra* note 1, para. 102.
[45] See Diplomatic Conference, *supra* note 37.
[46] Gabčikovo-Nagymaros Project, *supra* note 1, para. 103.
[47] *Id.*

4.2.2 Fundamental change of circumstances

"Fundamental change of circumstances" as a ground to invoke termination of a treaty has been controversial and debatable. The legal nature of this concept was the subject of a heated discussion between its supporters and opponents, both during the Diplomatic Conference[48] and in many publications on the subject.[49] In broad terms, the controversy is based, on one side, upon the principle of primacy of stability of contractual obligations and the conviction that "it is the function of the law to enforce contracts or treaties even if they become burdensome for the party bound by them",[50] and on the other side, upon the view that

> ... one could not insist upon petrifying a state of affairs which had become anachronistic because based on a treaty which either did not contain any specific clause as to its possible termination or which even proclaimed itself to be concluded for all times to come.[51]

The formulation of Article 62 of the VCLT is particularly cautious. The possibility to invoke the principle is admitted, although limited in its scope. It may not be invoked in relation to a treaty which establishes a boundary. Furthermore, no state may invoke it if the change was caused by a breach of its own international obligations, either under tile treaty in question or any other international agreement. In the *Fisheries Jurisdiction* case,[52] the ICJ was equally cautious as to interpretation of this principle. In general, it may be said that the Court, while recognizing the principle as set forth in the 1969 Vienna Convention and in international customary law, "found that the rights were surrounded in each case by substantive conditions limiting their application".[53]

---

[48] See Diplomatic Conference, *supra* note 37.

[49] See references in Chapter 4, note 1, and that chapter generally for further discussion of the subject.

[50] R .Y. Jennings and A.D. Watts (eds.), *Oppenheim's International Law* (1996), Vol. 1, Parts 2 to 4, at 1307. On the subject generally, see also O.J. Lissitzyn, "Treaties and Changed Circumstances (*rebus sic stantibus*)", 61 *AJIL* (1967), 895-922.

[51] Nahlik, *supra* note 28, at 748.

[52] See Fisheries Jurisdiction Case (United Kingdom v. Iceland), Judgment of 2 February 1973, 1973 ICJ Rep. 3, at 18. The Court said as follows: "[i]nternational law admits that a fundamental change in the circumstances which determined the parties to accept the treaty, if it has resulted in radical transformation of the extent of obligations imposed by it, may, under certain conditions, afford the party affected a ground for invoking the termination or suspension of the treaty. This principle, and the conditions and exceptions to which it is subject, have been embodied in Article 62 of the Vienna Convention on the Law of Treaties, which may in many respects be considered as a codification of existing customary law on the subject of termination of a treaty relationship on account of change circumstances".

[53] Briggs, *supra* note 28, at 68.

Hungary identified several "substantive elements" present at the conclusion of the 1977 Treaty which it alleged had changed fundamentally by the date of notification of termination. They were as follows: the notion of "socialist integration" for which the 1977 Treaty originally had been a "vehicle", but which had since disappeared; the "single and indivisible operational system", which was to be replaced by a unilateral scheme; the fact that the basis of the planned joint investment had been frustrated by the sudden emergence of both states into the market economy; the attitude of Czechoslovakia which had turned the "framework treaty" into an "immutable norm"; and, finally, the transformation of a treaty consistent with environmental protection into a "prescription for environmental disaster".[54] Slovakia argued that the changes invoked by Hungary had not altered the nature of the obligations under the 1977 Treaty from those originally undertaken, so no right to terminate it arose from them.[55]

The Court came to the conclusion that the political situation was of relevance to the conclusion of the 1977 Treaty. Nonetheless, the object and purpose of the 1977 Treaty, i.e. a joint investment programme for the production of energy, the control of floods, and the improvement of navigation on the Danube, were not so closely linked to political conditions as to render these an essential basis of the consent of the parties which, in changing, radically altered the extent of the obligations still to be performed.[56] The Court drew the same conclusion as to the economic system in question, and further concluded that even if the estimated profitability of the project had diminished as viewed in 1992 by comparison to 1977, it had not done so to such an extent as to transform parties' obligations in a radical manner as a result. Likewise, new developments in the state of environmental knowledge and of environmental law were not completely unforeseen. Furthermore, Articles 15, 19, and 20 of the 1977 Treaty allowed the parties, as the Court found, to take account of these changes and to accommodate them when implementing the 1977 Treaty provisions. The Court, having analyzed arguments submitted by both parties, was of the view that

> [t]he changed circumstances advanced by Hungary are, in the Court's view, not of such nature, either individually or collectively, that their effect would radically transform the extent of the obligations still to be performed in order to accomplish the Project.[57]

Thus, the Court followed and further developed the cautious approach towards Article 62 of the VCLT adopted by it in the *Fisheries Jurisdiction*

---

[54] See Gabčikovo-Nagymaros Project, *supra* note 1, para. 95.
[55] *Id.*
[56] *Id.*, para. 104.
[57] *Id.*

case[58] and interpreted strictly the manner in which the "fundamental change of circumstances" clause may be invoked. A fundamental change of circumstances must, the Court said,

> have been unforeseen; the existence of the circumstances at the time of the Treaty's conclusion must have constituted an essential basis of the consent of the parties to be bound by the Treaty.[59]

The Court further made an important contribution towards our understanding of Article 62 of the VCLT in having elucidated that the wording of this Article is negative and conditional and that this constitutes a clear indication that "the stability of treaty relations requires that the plea of fundamental change of circumstances be applied only in exceptional cases".[60]

4.2.3 Material breach

The next ground for termination of the 1977 Treaty put forward by Hungary was based on material breach (Article 60 of the VCLT). Hungary claimed that Czechoslovakia violated Articles 15, 19, and 20 of the 1977 Treaty, together with other conventions and rules of international law; and that the planning, construction, and putting into operation of "Variant C" also amounted to a material breach of the 1977 Treaty.

The right of a state based on material breach and involving suspension or termination of a treaty has its roots in the principle of reciprocity and deriving from the *do ut des* aspect of reciprocity which is expressed in the maxim *inadimplenti non est adimplendum*,[61] Article 60 exclusively regulates breaches which have their source in the law of treaties and not those deriving from the law of state responsibility. This limitation of Article 60 has been, widely criticized as one of its shortcomings.[62] The question of material breach was the subject of extensive discussion on the forum of the ILC based on reports by Special Rapporteurs Fitzmaurice and Waldock. The Commission took a cautious approach towards material breach, saying that it

> was agreed that a breach of a treaty, however serious, does not *ipso facto* put an end to the treaty, and also that it is not open to States simply to allege a violation of a treaty and pronounce the treaty at an end. On the other hand, it considered that within certain limits and subject to certain safeguards the right

---

[58] Fisheries Jurisdiction case, *supra* note 52.
[59] Gabčikovo-Nagymaros Project, *supra* note 1, para. 104.
[60] *Id.*
[61] See B. Simma, "Reflections on Article 60 of the Vienna Convention on the Law of Treaties and its Background in General International Law", 20 *ÖZaöRV* (1970), 3-83, at 20. See also chapter Four above for further discussion of the subject.
[62] See, e.g., Simma, *id.*, at 83; and S. Rosenne, *Breach of Treaty* (1985), at 7.

of a party to invoke the breach of a treaty as ground for terminating it or suspending its operation must be recognized.[63]

The intention of the Commission, as it was explained by Waldock at the Diplomatic Conference,[64] was to strike a balance between the need to uphold the stability of treaties and the need to ensure reasonable protection of the innocent victim of the breach of a treaty. In general, however, the ILC approached material breach as a ground for suspension or termination of treaties in a strict manner.[65] The most important aspect of the formulation of the right to suspend or terminate a treaty in relation to material breach in Article 60 of the VCLT is that it does not have an automatic effect on the life of a treaty. It merely provides a faculty of termination or suspension to the innocent party. The allegation of material breach merely to get rid of undesired obligations is extremely harmful for the stability of treaty relationships. "For the sake of legal security and treaty stability [...] termination or suspension have been subjected to many restrictive conditions and limitations to curb any possible abuse".[66] In bilateral relations, suspension or termination of a treaty on the ground of material breach by one of the parties, entitles the other party only to invoke it as a ground for termination (Article 60(1)). The above was the intention of the ILC which said that "[t]he formula "to invoke as a ground" is intended to underline that the right arising under that article is not a right arbitrarily to pronounce the treaty terminated".[67]

The ICJ has made a number of pronouncements concerning material breach. The most well known is that in the South *West Africa* cases where the Court said the following:

> [o]ne of the fundamental principles governing the international relationship thus established is that a party which disowns or does not fulfil its obligations cannot be recognized as retaining the rights which it claims to derive from the relationship.[68]

The judgment in this case was subject to criticism as to the statement of the Court that the general principle of law establishes "a right of termination on account of breach".[69] According to Briggs, such an allegation does not find support in state practice, and moreover finds no recognition in Article 60 of

---

[63] ILC Reports of the Commission to the General Assembly on its 18th Session, 1966 YILC, Vol. II (Part Two), at 255.

[64] See Diplomatic Conference, *supra* note 37.

[65] See Rosenne, *supra* note 62, at 23; *see also* the same view expressed by M.M. Gomaa, *Suspension or Termination of Treaties on Grounds of Breach* (1996), at 183.

[66] Gomaa, *id.,* at 184.

[67] ILC Reports, *supra* note 63, at 254.

[68] South West Africa cases (Ethiopia *v.* South Africa; Liberia *v.* South Africa), Preliminary Objections, Judgment of 21 December 1962, 1962 ICJ Rep. 319, at 331 and 330.

[69] *Id.,* at 320.

the VCLT, which, according to the ICJ, in many respects is a codification of customary law on termination of treaty relations on account of breach. "The only recognition of such an alleged right in the Vienna Convention is found in paragraph 2(a) of Article 60".[70]

Another case which related to material breach was the *ICAO* case.[71] In this case, the Court adopted a limited view as to material breach as a ground for termination. Although the statements of the Court on that matter were in relation to jurisdictional clauses, nonetheless, we may observe that

> much of the rationale advanced by the Court to restrict claims of unilateral right under general international law to terminate or suspend jurisdictional treaties for breach would appear to have cogency in relation to all the treaties, whether or not they contain jurisdictional clauses.[72]

The restrictive approach of the Court in the *ICAO* case was followed by it in the present case. In response to Hungary's reliance on other treaties and general rules of international law in application of material breach, the ICJ was of the view that

> it is only material breach of the treaty itself, by a State party to that treaty, which entitles the other party to rely on it as ground for terminating the treaty.[73]

The Court clarified the position that, while the violation of any other treaty or of rules of general international law may justify the taking of other measures, such as countermeasures, by an injured state, it does not constitute a ground to terminate a treaty under the law of treaties. The Court examined Hungary's contention that Czechoslovakia had violated Articles 15, 19, and 20 of the 1977 Treaty by refusing to enter into negotiations with Hungary to adapt the Joint Contractual Plan to new developments in environmental protection. These Articles were specially designed to oblige the parties to take appropriate measures necessary for the protection of water quality, of nature, and of fishing interests jointly on a continuous basis. The Court stressed that Articles 15 and 19 expressly provide that the obligation contained in them must be implemented by the means specified in the Joint Contractual Plan. The Court found that the failure of the parties to agree on those means was not attributable solely to one party. There was not sufficient evidence to substantiate the claim that Czechoslovakia had consistently refused to consult with Hungary upon the desirability or necessity of measures for the preservation of environment. The Court was of the view that while both parties indicated in principle a willingness to follow further

---

[70] Briggs, *supra* note 28, at 56.
[71] Appeal Relating to the Jurisdiction of the ICAO Council (India *v.* Pakistan), Judgment of 18 August 1972, 48 *ILR* 331 (1975).
[72] Briggs, *supra* note 28, at 60-61.
[73] Gabčikovo-Nagymaros project, *supra* note 1, para. 106.

research, in practice, Czechoslovakia refused to countenance a suspension of the works at Dunakiliti, and at a later stage on "Variant C". Hungary then asked for suspension as a prior condition of environmental research. It claimed that continuation of works would prejudice the outcome of negotiations. The Court observed that suspension of the works by Hungary at Nagymaros and Dunakiliti, was a contributory factor to creation of a situation which was not very favourable for conducting negotiations.[74]

Hungary mainly relied on the construction of "Variant C" by Czechoslovakia as the basis for invoking material breach of the 1977 Treaty (see *infra* Section 2.2.). The Court found that Czechoslovakia only violated the 1977 Treaty when it diverted the waters of the Danube into the bypass canal in October 1992. However, in constructing the works which lead to the operation of "Variant C", Czechoslovakia did not act unlawfully. The Court found that notification of termination by Hungary in 1992 was premature; and that Czechoslovakia had not yet breached the 1977 Treaty. This lead the Court to the conclusion that Hungary was not entitled to invoke any such breach of the 1977 Treaty as a ground for terminating it at the time it did. Moreover, the Court took the view that, Hungary's Declaration terminating the 1977 Treaty issued on 6 May 1992 with effect as from 25 May 1992, was not in accordance with the principle of good faith.[75]

In fact, both parties were in agreement that Articles 65 to 67 of the VCLT, if not codifying customary law, at least generally reflect it, and contain certain procedural principles which are based on good faith. The Court concluded that by its own conduct, Hungary prejudiced its right to terminate the 1977 Treaty. The Court quite forcefully stated that

> this would still have been the case even if Czechoslovakia, by the time of the purported termination, had violated a provision essential to the accomplishment of the object or purpose of the Treaty.[76]

It may be observed that the Court applied the rules and procedures relating to material breach in a very rigorous manner. Not only substantive rules have to be observed, but procedural ones as well. The present Judgment indicates that the Court supports the principle of stability of treaties and that it approaches all rules concerning the possibility of unilateral termination, including those relating to material breach, with due caution.

---

[74] *Id.*, para. 107.
[75] *Id.*, para. 109.
[76] *Id.*, para. 110.

4.3 The Principle of "Approximate Application"

Slovakia invoked the so-called "principle of approximate application" to justify the construction and operation of "Variant C". The application of this principle was, according to Slovakia, the only possibility which remained open to it to fulfil the purposes of the 1977 Treaty and to enable it to continue to implement its obligations deriving from the Treaty in good faith.[77] Another purpose of the employment of this principle was that Czechoslovakia was under a duty to mitigate the damage resulting from Hungary's unlawful actions. Slovakia maintained that "a State which is confronted with a wrongful act of another State is under an obligation to minimize its losses and, thereby, the damages claimable against the wrong-doing State."[78] Slovakia submitted that mitigation of damages constitutes an aspect of performance of obligations in good faith. Slovakia also pleaded, in the alternative, that use of the "principle of approximate application" may be treated as constituting a countermeasure.

Hungary argued that "Variant C" constituted a material breach of the 1977 Treaty.[79] It further pleaded that "Variant C" violated Czechoslovakia's obligations under other treaties, in particular the 1976 Convention on the Regulation of Water Management Issues of Boundary Waters,[80] and its obligations under general international law. Hungary contended that Slovakia's arguments were wrong both in facts and in law. It denied the commission of any violation of its treaty obligations which would justify Slovakia's application of "Variant C". Further, Hungary argued that no "principle of approximate application" exists in international law. As regards the mitigation of damages argument, it claimed that it has to do with quantification of loss, and could not justify action which is unlawful. "Variant C", furthermore, did not satisfy the requirements for lawfulness of countermeasures in international law, i.e. the condition of proportionality.[81]

The "principle of approximate application" was expounded by Sir Hersch Lauterpacht in his Separate Opinion in Admissibility of Hearings of Petitioners by the Committee on South Africa.[82] He said as follows:

> [i]t is a sound principle of law that whenever a legal instrument of continuing validity cannot be applied literally owing to the conduct of one of the parties, it must, without allowing that party to take advantage of its own conduct, be

---

[77] *Id.,* para. 67.

[78] *Id.,* para. 68.

[79] See also *supra* Section 2.2.

[80] Convention on the Regulation of Water Management Issues of Boundary Waters, 31 May 1976.

[81] See Gabčikovo-Nagymaros Project, *supra* note 1, para. 71.

[82] Admissibility of Hearings of Petitioners by the Committee on South Africa, Jurisdiction, Judgment of 1 June 1956, 1956 ICJ Rep. 46 (Judge Lauterpacht, Separate Opinion).

applied in a way approximating most closely to its primary object. To do that is to interpret and to give effect to the instrument–not to change it.[83]

The views of Lauterpacht need to be read in a broader context expressed by him in his Opinion. He was of the view that operation and application of multilateral agreements establishing "an international status, an international régime" exceeds a mere contractual relation.[84] To this effect, their validity continues regardless of changes in states' attitudes or status or existence of individual parties or persons concerned. The unity and operation of any régime created by legal instruments cannot be broken down by an act of one party. Lauterpacht further stated that:

> [t]he treaty as a whole does not terminate as a result of a breach of an individual clause. Neither is it rendered impotent and inoperative as the result of the action or inaction of one of the parties. It continues in being subject to adaptation to circumstances which have arisen.[85]

Lauterpacht, however, made a distinction between treaties creating régimes and as he describes them in his Opinion "ordinary treaties", in that in the latter category "breach creates, as a rule, a right for the injured party to denounce it and claim damages".[86] It appears that he referred the operation of the "principle of approximate application" to multilateral treaties which create an international status.

According to Rosenne, the Opinion of Lauterpacht led to a bifurcation of law. It supplies a philosophical and scientific basis for the view that a breach of treaty provisions must not be assessed in isolation but in the wider context of a treaty regime as a single whole. On the other hand, this principle means that, confronted with a situation of established breach, the parties themselves may in the first instance renegotiate and apply the treaty in good faith or in the event of failure to do that, they may be legally obliged acting through or with assistance of a competent international organ to take steps to redraft or reformulate the sub-system in order to ensure its continued application. In other words, according to Rosenne, this principle

> if skillfully used may serve as a prod to the renegotiation, reinterpretation or readaptation of a treaty which in general lines remains desirable to all parties but which in its details cannot stand up to wear and tear of daily life.[87]

According to the same author, this principle contributes constructively to stability of treaties. The possible juridical bases of this interesting doctrine,

---

[83] *Id.*, at 53-54.
[84] *Id.*, at 48.
[85] *Id.*, at 49. See also Rosenne, *supra* note 61, at 95 – 101.
[86] Admissibility of Hearings of Petitioners by the Committee on South Africa, *supra* note 81, at 48-49.
[87] Rosenne, *supra* note 62, at 100.

which, however, appears to involve some degree of extension of the circumstances in which it may apply even beyond those evidently envisaged by Sir Hersch Lauterpacht.

In the present case, the ICJ made no direct determination on the legal nature of this principle, i.e. whether it is a principle of international law or a general principle of law, or, indeed, even on whether it exists at all. The Court stated that

> even if such a principle existed, it could by definition only be employed within the limits of the treaty in question. In the view of the Court, Variant C does not meet that cardinal condition with regard to the 1977 Treaty.[88]

In support of this, the Court stated that "Variant C" as a unilateral action did not fulfil the conditions which were fundamental for the functioning of the whole system based on the 1977 Treaty. The Court also stated that Czechoslovakia appropriated for its use and benefit between 80 and 90 per cent of the waters of the Danube which is a shared resource and an international boundary river. Even though suspension and withdrawal of consent by Hungary constituted a violation of its treaty obligation, that "cannot mean that Hungary forfeited its basic right to equitable and reasonable sharing of the resources of an international watercourse".[89] In general, the Court reached the conclusion

> that Czechoslovakia, in putting Variant C into operation, was not applying the 1977 Treaty but, on the contrary, violated certain of its express provisions, and, in doing so, committed an internationally wrongful act.[90]

As to the problem of countermeasures, the Court decided

> that Czechoslovakia, by unilaterally assuming control of shared resources, and thereby depriving Hungary of its right to an equitable and reasonable share of the natural resources of the Danube, with the continuing effects of the diversion of these waters on the ecology of the riparian area of the Szigetköz, failed to respect the proportionality which is required in international law.[91]

5. Pacta Sunt Servanda

It may generally be stated that in this case the Court advocated strict observation of the *pacta sunt servarnda* principle. Despite allegations submitted by Hungary that by their conduct both parties had repudiated the 1977 Treaty and that a bilateral treaty repudiated by both parties cannot

---

[88] Gabčikovo-Nagymaros Project, *supra* note 1, para. 76.
[89] *Id.,* para. 78.
[90] *Id.*
[91] *Id.,* para .85.

survive, the Court found that the reciprocal wrongful conduct of both parties "did not bring the Treaty to an end nor justify its termination".[92] The Judgment continued with the following important passage:

> [t]he Court would set a precedent with disturbing implications for treaty relations and the integrity of the rule *pacta sunt servanda* if it were to conclude that a treaty in force between States, which the parties have implemented in considerable measure and at a great cost over a period of years, might be unilaterally set aside on grounds of reciprocal non-compliance.[93]

The Court observed that it would have been a different legal situation if the parties had terminated the 1977 Treaty upon mutual consent.

In taking up this position in the circumstances of the present case, in which both parties were actually in fundamental breach of important obligations with respect to significant parts of the subject matter of the 1977 Treaty, and stating that, notwithstanding these, the 1977 Treaty "cannot be treated as voided by unlawful conduct",[94] the Court indeed adopted a strong, possibly even a fairly extreme, position. Indeed, the Court was faced with something of a dilemma, which it recognized when it said:

> [t]he Court, however, cannot disregard the fact that the Treaty has not been fully implemented by either party for years, and indeed that their acts of commission and omission have contributed to creating the factual situation that now exists. Nor can it overlook that factual situation, or the practical possibilities and impossibilities to which it gives rise, when deciding on the legal requirements for the future conduct of the Parties.[95]

In effect, the Court recognized that, while it had found that the Treaty remained in full force and effect, it could not order the parties to carry out its terms without substantial modification. What the Court did in these circumstances was to apply what appears to be very much like the developed form of the doctrine of "approximate application" outlined by Rosenne.[96] In two important passages of the Judgment, the Court said, firstly, that:

> [w]hat is essential, therefore, is that the factual situation as it has developed since 1989 shall be placed in the context of the preserved and developing treaty relationship, in order to achieve its object and purpose in so far as that is feasible;[97]

and, later

---

[92] *Id.*, para.114.
[93] *Id.*
[94] *Id.*, para. 133.
[95] *Id.*
[96] *Supra,* Section 4.3.
[97] Gabčikovo-Nagymaros project; *supra* note 1, para. 133.

> [w]hat is required in the present case by the rule *pacta sunt servanda,* as reflected in Article 26 of the Vienna Convention of 1969 on the Law of Treaties, is that the Parties find an agreed solution within the co-operative context of the Treaty.[98]

And the Court then continued:

> [a]rticle 26 combines two elements, which are of equal importance. It provides that "Every treaty in force is binding upon the parties to it and must be performed by them in good faith". This latter element, in the Court's view; implies that, in this case, it is the purpose of the Treaty, and the intentions of the parties in concluding it, which should prevail over its literal application. The principle of good faith obliges the Parties to apply it in a reasonable way and in such a manner that its purpose can be realized.[99]

Were this doctrine to be applicable to treaties generally, it would obviously have far-reaching and controversial implications. In fact, however, the Court found itself able to adopt this particular solution in the present case on the basis of particular features of the treaty in question. Three factors may be singled out as having been significant in this respect. Firstly, the Court emphasized the existence of multiple, equal objectives all of which, it appeared to the Court, might still be realized on the basis of an even substantially modified project. Secondly, on its own terms, the 1977 Treaty "never laid down a rigid system", and on the basis of the conduct of the parties in themselves modifying, or expressing willingness to modify the Project "[t]he explicit terms of the Treaty itself were therefore in practice acknowledged by the parties to be negotiable".[100] And, finally, while not expressly referred to again in this operative part of the Judgment, it is not without significance that the Court had found that the 1997 Treaty set up a "territorial régime", at least within the meaning of Article 12 of the 1978 Vienna Convention on state succession.[101]

5. Concluding Remarks

In this important case, which raised a wide range of issues of international law including the law of treaties,[102] the ICJ unconditionally supported the

---

[98] *Id.,* para. 142.

[99] *Id.*

[100] *Id.,* para. 138.

[101] 1978 Vienna Convention on Succession of States With Respect to Treaties, 18 *ILM* 1488 (1978).

[102] From the Key-note address by the President of the ICJ, Judge Stephen M. Schwebel, entitled "The influence of the International Court of Justice on the work of the International Law Commission and the influence of the Commission on the work of the Court", delivered at the United Nations Colloquium on Progressive Development and Codification of

principle of the stability of treaties, and the view that any grounds which may be invoked by states for their termination are treated with great caution. The Court appears to have taken the view that treaties should, at least in general, be terminated upon consent of the parties to them. Thus, the ICJ has, by the Judgment in the present case, and particularly in the declaratory part of its Judgment, strengthened the classical doctrine of the law of treaties, even if the operative part of the Judgment is substantially dependent upon the special features of the 1977 Treaty.[103]

International Law to Commemorate the Fiftieth Anniversary of the International Law Commission, United Nations, New York, 28 October 1997.

[103] This chapter has not dealt with the opinions expressed by individual Judges. These comprised two Declarations appended to the Judgment, namely, by the President Schwebel and Judge Rezek, and Dissenting Opinions of the following Judges: Bedjaoui, Oda, Herczegh, Vereshchetin, Ranjeva, Parra-Aranguren, Vice-President Weeramantry, Fleishhauer, and Judge *ad hoc* Skubiszewski. Of the Dissenting Opinions, those of Judge Fleishhauer and Judge *ad hoc* Skubiszewski contain interesting alternative views relating to a number of the issues of the Law of Treaties.

CHAPTER ELEVEN

The Bakassi Peninsula Case and Article 46 of the Vienna Convention on the Law of Treaties

1. Introduction

A number of questions of general international law were raised and considered by the ICJ in its judgment on the merits of the *Case concerning the Land and Maritime Boundary between Cameroon v. Nigeria (Equatorial Guinea Intervening).*[1] One of these was the question of the validity under international law of a treaty concluded in violation of the internal constitutional law of one of the parties, the applicable rules on which are codified in Article 46 of the VCLT. This chapter will consider the arguments of the Parties to the case on this issue and the treatment of these arguments by the ICJ.[2]

The proceedings in this case were initiated by Cameroon in 1994. The application originally concerned a dispute over the Bakassi Peninsula and the maritime boundary between Cameroon and Nigeria, but in an additional application, Cameroon requested the ICJ to specify definitively the entire frontier between the two States. In its final submissions to the Court, Cameroon requested a ruling that the maritime boundary between the two states follow a particular course. In delimiting the maritime boundary, the Court divided the disputed area into two parts. With respect to one of these two parts, Cameroon argued that the boundary had already been established by an important Anglo-German Agreement of 1913 and by a later treaty, the Maroua Declaration of 1975. It was the validity of this latter treaty that was

---

[1] Case Concerning The Land and Maritime Boundary Between Cameroon and Nigeria (Cameroon *v.* Nigeria: Equatorial Guinnee intervening), Judgment of 10 October 2002, 2002 ICJ Rep. 1.

[2] See the commentary by J. Merrills, 52 *ICLQ* (2003), at 788.

called into question by Nigeria, on the basis that rules of its constitutional law regarding the conclusion of treaties had not been complied with in the conclusion of this treaty.[3]

2. The Rule in Article 46 and General International Law

The effect of non-compliance with the requirements of the constitutional law of a party on the validity of the treaty has been considered widely in the literature and has been the subject of judicial decisions.[4] The doctrinal division is between what has been termed the "internationalist" and the "constitutionalist" schools. The internationalist school, in general, looks to the external manifestations of the expression of a State's consent to be bound, and accordingly holds that non-compliance with the internal constitutional law of States does not affect the validity of a treaty where the agent of the State that concludes the treaty has the apparent authority to bind the State. The constitutionalist school, in contrast, holds that international law leaves it to the internal law of a State to determine the organs and mechanisms through which its consent to be bound by a treaty can be expressed, and that the validity of a treaty in international law depends on compliance of its conclusion with the internal law of that State regarding treaty-making.[5]

In support of the internationalist position,[6] it has been pointed out that state practice does not support the relevance of constitutional requirements,[7] and it has been said that "states do not consider it desirable to tie the validity

---

[3] The question of the validity of the Maroua Declaration was discussed at paragraphs 247-268 of the Judgment.

[4] The most thorough treatment of the subject is perhaps L. Wildhaber, *Treaty-Making Power and Constitution: An International and Comparative Study* (1971), esp. at 146-182. See also, e.g., I. Sinclair, *The Vienna Convention on the Law of Treaties* (1984), at 169-171; R. Jennings and A. Watts (eds.), *Oppenheim's International Law* (1992), at 1284-1288, including a comprehensive bibliography; T.O. Elias, *The Modern Law of Treaties* (1974), at 142-152; H. Blix, *Treaty-Making Power* (1960); S. Riesenfeld and F. Abbott (eds.), *Parliamentary Participation in the Making and Operation of Treaties – A Comparative Study* (1994). For an interesting historical perspective, see P. Haggenmacher, "Some Hints on the European Origins of Legislative Participation in the Treaty-Making Function", 67 *Chicago-Kent Law Review* (1992), at 313; and T. Meron, "The Authority to Make Treaties in the Late Middle Ages", 89 *AJIL* (1995), at 1.

[5] See, e.g., the full discussion of the theories by Wildhaber, *supra* note 4, at 147-153; see also Elias, *supra* note 4, at 144-148, and K. Holloway, *Modern Trends in Treaty Law* (1967), at 123-133.

[6] Wildhaber, *supra* note 4, at 175-178.

[7] *Id.*, at 154-167, for a comprehensive survey of international practice, diplomatic and judicial, on this issue.

of agreements to domestic law procedures".[8] It is also pointed out that the stability of treaties as expressed in the maxim *pacta sunt servanda* would be put at risk if states were allowed to set arbitrary limits on their treaty-making power, and the constitutionalist view could simply provide States with a means of avoiding unwanted treaty obligations. The difficulties in requiring States to inquire into the treaty-making rules and processes of other States are also patent, and it has also been pointed out that even if such inquiries were to be undertaken, states "would ordinarily have to accept the interpretation given to them by the very state officials whose competence they question".[9] It is also sometimes said, in support of the internationalist position, that a State could simply opt for ratification, signature *ad referendum*, acceptance, approval or accession, all of which, *inter alia*, offer a means of protecting its interests against the possibility that its agent might sometimes lack the necessary constitutional authority, by allowing sufficient time to ponder the implications of treaty provisions before they take effect in international law.[10] Where these procedures are not insisted upon, it is argued that the validity of the treaty in international law should be upheld regardless of any internal unconstitutionality.[11] In its Advisory Opinion concerning the *Treatment of Polish Nationals in Danzig*,[12] the PCIJ noted that "while, on the one hand, according to generally accepted principles, a State cannot rely, as against another State, on the provisions of the latter's Constitution, but only on international law and international obligations duly accepted, on the other hand and conversely, a State cannot adduce as against

---

[8] *Id.*, at 167 and 174.

[9] *Id.*, at 176. See also Elias, *supra* note 4, at 147. However, in response to this argument, it should be noted that it is not necessary to require States to undertake their own survey of other States' practice or inquiries into the constitutional requirements of other States. As will be argued in Section IV below, a statement or other representation, which could take a variety of forms, and on which other States could rely, would provide a better basis on which the reliance of other parties to a treaty could rely, and such an explicit rather than implicit representation could strike a better balance between the competing policy considerations reflected in the two schools of thought on the subject.

[10] See Elias, *supra* note 4, at 147. But this argument could apply equally to both the "innocent" state and the state whose constitutional law has been violated. In other words, the "innocent" state could simply stipulate ratification or the other procedures other than entry into force upon signature in order to deal with any constitutional limitation in the law of the other party, just as that other party could insist on those procedures.

[11] See the discussion by Wildhaber (*supra* note 4, at 176) of the distinction between treaties and executive agreements, which he concludes (rightly, in our view) is not of much assistance in the present context. See also Jennings and Watts, *supra* note 4, at 1287.

[12] Treatment of Polish Nationals and Other Persons of Polish Origin or Speech in the Dantzig Territory, 1932 PCIJ Rep. (Series A/B), No. 44, at 24.

another State its Constitution with a view to evading obligations incumbent upon it under international law or treaties in force".[13]

The constitutionalist position,[14] in contrast, attaches greater importance to internal laws, and would appear to regard acts that are not legally valid under domestic law as being equally without legal effect in international law. As to the question of stability of treaties, it has been argued that the implementation or execution of unconstitutional agreements cannot be guaranteed, which makes it important to pay attention to constitutional rules on treaty-making, and it may be added that this could be an important consideration where the actual performance of a treaty obligation is more important than state responsibility and remedies in lieu of the actual implementation or execution of such obligations in cases where the treaty will not be implemented because of the internal unconstitutionality.[15] The constitutionalist approach also appears to favour the requirements of democracy and representative government, and in general appears to shift the burden of the consequences of unconstitutional acts onto the "innocent" treaty party rather than to the State (or, depending on the rules and procedures in that State for control of executive power) whose constitutional law was breached in the conclusion of the treaty. The strength of this approach, it is submitted, depends on the extent to which international law concerns itself with democratic governance, an issue of increasing doctrinal interest in contemporary international law.[16]

On the whole, however, it would appear that the balance of the practice, in modern times, is in favour of the internationalist school, even though there is at least respectable opinion in favour of the constitutionalist school.[17] It is certainly the approach that prevailed, with some modification, at the ILC. Brierly, the first Special Rapporteur on the codification of the law of treaties, favoured the constitutionalist position, and the majority of the members of

---

[13] See also the Case of the Free Zones of Upper Savoy and the District of Gex, (1932 PCIJ Rep. (Series A/B), No. 46, at 170), and the Legal Status of Eastern Greenland case (1933 PCIJ Rep. (Series A/B), No. 53, at 56-71, and 91), for dicta supporting the internationalist position.

[14] For a discussion of the arguments in favour of the constitutionalist position, see Wildhaber, *supra* note 4, at 178-181.

[15] See, in context of the relationship between state responsibility and the validity of the treaty, the interesting formulation of the matter in Article 21 of the Harvard Draft Convention on the Law of Treaties: "A State is not bound by a treaty made on its behalf by an organ or authority not competent under its law to conclude the treaty; however, a State may be responsible for an injury resulting to another State from reasonable reliance by the latter upon a representation that such organ or authority was competent to conclude the treaty"; 29 *AJIL* (Supplement, 1935) at 661.

[16] See, e.g., G.H. Fox and B.R. Roth (eds.), *Democratic Governance and International Law* (2000). We will return to this issue in Sections IV and V below.

[17] See Elias, *supra* note 4, at **???**.

the ILC agreed.[18] The second Special Rapporteur, Lauterpacht, was also in favour of the constitutionalist approach, but his proposed text included greater reference to the importance of the stability of treaty relations.[19] However, his successor, Fitzmaurice,[20] was in favour of the internationalist position, as was the fourth Special Rapporteur, Waldock.[21] The majority opinion that emerged was in favour of the principle that non-observance of constitutional law did not affect the validity of a treaty, but an exception was allowed, at the insistence of some members, where the violation of the provision of internal law regarding competence to conclude treaties was manifest. At the First Session of the Vienna Conference in 1968, two emendations were adopted in order to clarify the scope of this exception.[22] The first, proposed by Peru, required that the rule (whose violation would make it manifest that the State should not be bound by the treaty) be one of "fundamental importance", illustrating the importance attached to the security of treaties. The second, proposed by the United Kingdom, was that the phrase "manifest violation" should mean a violation that would be objectively evident to any State dealing with the matter in accordance with normal practice and in good faith. At the same time, it should be noted that a proposal by Pakistan and Japan to delete the "manifest violation" exception was defeated. The final version of Article 46 of the VCLT provides follows:

> 1. A State may not invoke the fact that its consent to be bound by a treaty has been expressed in violation of a provision of its internal law regarding competence to conclude treaties as invalidating its consent unless that violation was manifest and concerned a rule of its internal law of fundamental importance.
>
> 2. A violation is manifest if it would be objectively evident to any State conducting itself in the matter in accordance with normal practice and in good faith.[23]

In the words of Sinclair, having regard to the conditions set out in Article 46, and to the negative manner in which it is formulated, "it may be conceded that practical cases in which they could be invoked will be rather rare".[24]

---

[18] YILC (1950), Vol. II, at 223, 230-233.

[19] YILC (1953), Vol. II, at 141; "[a] treaty is voidable, at the option of the party concerned, if it has been entered into in disregard of the limitations of its constitutional law and practice" (Article 11(1)).

[20] YILC (1956), Vol. II, at 108-109; YILC (1958), Vol. II, at 25, 33-35; YILC (1959), Vol. II, at 42-43, 48-49, 58-61, 76-78.

[21] YILC (1963), Vol. II, at 41-46.

[22] See Elias, *supra* note 4, at 149-150, and Sinclair, *supra* note 4, at 170-171.

[23] Note also article 47 of the VCLT, which deals with the related matter of a specific restriction on the authority of an agent to bind a state. Such a restriction may be invoked only if it was notified to the other negotiating States prior to his expressing such consent. This confirms the importance attached to the security of treaties.

3. The Arguments of the Parties and the Judgment of the Court

While there had been dicta of greater or lesser relevance to the issue in some cases before the PCIJ,[25] this case afforded the ICJ the opportunity to rule directly on the operation of article 46.[26]

3.1 The Absence of a Requirement of Ratification

Nigeria argued that the Maroua Declaration was not legally valid because it had not been ratified by the Nigerian Supreme Military Council after being signed by the Nigerian Head of State. According to Nigeria, its constitution at the relevant time – June 1975 – required that executive acts were to be carried out by the Supreme Military Council or were at least subject to its approval.[27] Cameroon argued that signing of the Declaration by both Heads of State expressed the consent of the two States to be bound by the treaty; no reservation or condition was expressed in the text and the validity of the instrument was not expressed to be subject to ratification.[28] The Court upheld Cameroon's argument. It stated that, in international practice, a two-step procedure consisting of signature and ratification is frequently provided for in provisions regarding entry into force of a treaty, but that this was not a requirement, and that international law allowed States to choose the particular method by which their treaties entered into force. The Court found that the Maroua Declaration, which provided that "the two Heads of State of Cameroon and Nigeria agreed to extend the delineation of the maritime boundary between the two countries from Point 12 to Point G on the Admiralty Chart No. 3433 annexed to this Declaration", was a treaty that entered into force immediately upon signature.[29]

---

[24] *Supra* note 4, at 172.

[25] *Supra* notes 12 and 13.

[26] The status and effect of the Maroua Declaration were given full and lengthier consideration by Judges *ad hoc* Mbaye (at section 3.1 A-C of his Separate Opinion) and Ajibola (at paragraphs 160-174 of his Dissenting Opinion).

[27] Paragraph 258 of the Judgment.

[28] Paragraphs 253 and 260 of the Judgment.

[29] Paragraph 264 of the judgment, and the Rejoinder of Nigeria, Vol. I, Part I, Chapter 3.

3.2 Non-Compliance with Constitutional Rules and the "Manifest Violation" Exception

Another aspect of Nigeria's argument that the Maroua Declaration was not a valid international treaty was more directly related to the discussion in Section 2 above. In Nigeria's view, Cameroon, according to the objective test contained in the VCLT, either did know or, conducting itself in a normally prudent manner, should have known that the Head of State of Nigeria did not have the authority to make legally binding commitments without referring back to the authority or approval of the Supreme Military Council. In Nigeria's view, it should therefore have been "objectively evident" to Cameroon, within the meaning of Article 46(2) of the VCLT, that the Head of State of Nigeria did not have unrestricted authority.[30] Interestingly, Nigeria argued that "States are normally expected to follow legislative and constitutional developments in neighbouring States which have an impact upon the inter-State relations of those States, and that few limits can be more important than those affecting the treaty-making power".[31] For its part, Cameroon argued that, in the first place, Nigeria had not shown that the Nigerian constitution did in fact require the agreement to be ratified by the Supreme Military Council, and that furthermore, even if there had been a violation of the internal law of Nigeria, the alleged violation was not "manifest", and did not concern a rule of internal law "of fundamental importance" within the meaning of Article 46(1) of the VCLT.[32]

The Court, recalling the wording of Article 46, found that the "rules concerning the authority to sign treaties for a State are constitutional rules of fundamental importance".[33] Accordingly, the requirements of Article 46(1) were satisfied, and to that extent it agreed with Nigeria's characterization of the rules on treaty-making power. However, the Court found that the violation of these rules of fundamental importance was not "manifest" in the sense required by Article 46(2). It stated that according to Article 7(2) of the

---

[30] Nigeria also argued that, nine months before the Maroua Declaration, the Head of State of Nigeria had written to the then Head of State of Cameroon, explaining, with reference to a meeting with the latter in 1972, that "the proposals of the experts based on the documents they prepared on the 4th April 1971 were not acceptable to the Nigerian Government", and that the views and recommendations of the joint commission "must be subject to the agreement of the two Governments", and that this showed that that any arrangements that might be agreed between the two Heads of State were subject to the subsequent and separate approval of the Nigerian Government. See paragraph 258 of the Judgment.

[31] *Id.*

[32] Paragraph 260 of the Judgment.

[33] Paragraph 265 of the Judgment.

VCLT,[34] Heads of State are considered to represent their State "[i]n virtue of their functions and without having to produce full powers", and, unless properly publicized, any restriction in the capacity of a Head of State's capacity was not manifest.[35]

In addition, the Court found that international law does not impose any general legal obligation for States to keep themselves informed of legislative and constitutional developments in other States, which are, or may become, important for the international relations of these States. [36] It found, contrary to Nigeria's argument, that there was nothing in the evidence that could be regarded as a specific warning to Cameroon that the Nigerian Government would not be bound by any commitment entered into by the Head of State.[37]

---

[34] Article 7 of the VCLT, dealing with "Full Powers", provides that

"1. A person is considered as representing a State for the purpose of adopting or authenticating the text of a treaty or for the purpose of expressing the consent of the State to be bound by a treaty if:

(a) he produces appropriate full powers; or

(b) it appears from the practice of the States concerned or from other circumstances that their intention was to consider that person as representing the State for such purposes and to dispense with full powers.

2. In virtue of their functions and without having to produce full powers, the following are considered as representing their State:

(a) Heads of State, Heads of Government and Ministers for Foreign Affairs, for the purpose of performing all acts relating to the conclusion of a treaty;

(b) heads of diplomatic missions, for the purpose of adopting the text of a treaty between the accrediting State and the State to which they are accredited;

(c) representatives accredited by States to an international conference or to an international organization or one of its organs, for the purpose of adopting the text of a treaty in that conference, organization or organ."

[35] Paragraph 265 of the Judgment.

[36] Nigeria had also cited the Fisheries case (United Kingdom v. Norway), 1951 ICJ Reports 126, regarding the argument in that case by the United Kingdom that it was not aware of the Norwegian system of delimitation and that that system lacked the notoriety required to constitute the basis of an historic title enforceable against it. The Court had rejected this argument by the United Kingdom, stating that "[a]s a coastal State on the North Sea, greatly interested in the fisheries in this area, as a maritime Power traditionally concerned particularly to defend the freedom of the seas, the United Kingdom could not have been ignorant" of certain Norwegian legislation that had provoked a request for explanation by other governments . See the Rejoinder of Nigeria, Vol. I, Part I, Chapter 3, paragraph 3.25. The Court did not refer to this argument, which further suggests that, in the Court's view, such notoriety is not to be presumed in the context of Article 46 of the VCLT.

[37] Paragraph 266 of the judgment.

On the contrary, the Court found that the evidence adduced by Nigeria was "part of a pattern which marked the Parties' boundary negotiations between 1970 and 1975, in which the two Heads of State took the initiative of resolving difficulties in those negotiations through person-to-person agreements", including the Maroua Declaration.[38] The Court noted that in July 1975 the two Parties inserted a correction in the Maroua Declaration, that in so acting they treated the Declaration as valid and applicable, and that Nigeria does not claim to have contested its validity or applicability prior to 1977.[39]

3.3 The Scope of Article 7(2) of the VCLT

Cameroon argued that, as a matter of international law, a Head of State is always considered as representing his or her State for the purpose of expressing the consent of the State to be bound by a treaty.[40] Nigeria, however, attempted to circumscribe the effect of Article 7(2) of the VCLT, by arguing that it is "solely concerned with the way in which a person's function as a State's representative is established, but does not deal with the extent of that person's powers when exercising that representative function".[41] The Court rejected Nigeria's argument and upheld Cameroon's, referring to the commentary of the ILC on Article 7(2), which expressly stated that "Heads of State ... are considered as representing their State for the purpose of performing all acts relating to the conclusion of a treaty".[42] The Court thereby rejected Nigeria's distinction between the *representative capacity* of the Head of State, which it argued was established by Article

---

[38] Cameroon had argued that the circumstances confirmed that both itself and Nigeria regarded the Declaration as binding. It argued that "the publication of the Joint Communiqué signed by the Heads of State is also proof of that consent; that the validity of the Maroua Agreement was confirmed by the subsequent exchange of letters between the Heads of State of the two countries correcting a technical error in the calculation of one of the points on the newly agreed line; and that the reference to Yaoundé II in the Maroua Agreement confirms that the legal status of the former is no different from that of the latter ... that these conclusions are confirmed by the publicity given to the partial maritime boundary established by the Maroua Agreement, which was notified to the Secretariat of the United Nations and published in a whole range of publications which have widespread coverage and are well known in the field of maritime boundary delimitation"; see paragraph 253 of the Judgment. See <http://www.icj-cij.org/icjwww/idocket/icn/icncr/icn_icr200206_20020225.PDF> the verbatim record of the public sitting held on Monday 25 February 2002, CR 2002/6, at 2 ff. (Tomuschat). See also paragraph 259 of the Judgment.

[39] Paragraph 267 of the Judgment.

[40] Paragraph 260 of the Judgment.

[41] Paragraph 258 of the Judgment.

[42] Paragraph 265 of the Judgment. See YILC (1966), Vol. II, at 193.

7(2), on the one hand, and the scope of the *powers* that are to be exercised in that capacity, which it argued was not covered by Article 7(2), on the other.[43]

The Court, just as it did in the *Qatar v Bahrain* case, thus confirmed the prevalence of the internationalist position, and confirmed the high threshold set in the VCLT for the operation of the exception in article 46 of the VCLT.[44] Specifically, it is significant that the parties had not specified any special procedure for the entry into force of the treaty, in the light of the dealings between the two Governments and the history of the dealings between the two Governments. The Court confirmed that States are not under an obligation to keep up with internal constitutional developments in neighbouring States even where such developments might be relevant to their relations with those States. Also, the Court confirmed that the rules on treaty-making power are rules of internal law of fundamental importance within the meaning of Article 46(1), but that, particularly where the agent of the State is the Head of State, Article 7(2) of the VCLT makes it difficult for a State to invoke the exception in Article 46, except in the rather unlikely circumstances in which the limits in the power of a Head of State are drawn expressly to the attention of the other party.

Two issues that are significant in that the Court did not refer to them in its Judgment. The first is the argument made (but apparently not dwelled upon) by Nigeria to the effect that, given the circumstances, it voiced its objection to the validity of the Maroua Declaration in a prompt manner.[45] It should be recalled that Article 45 of the VCLT requires prompt and unequivocal action on the part of a State seeking to invoke the invalidity of a treaty after becoming aware of the fact that the treaty is invalid.[46] But the

---

[43] See the Rejoinder of Nigeria, Vol. I, Part I, Chapter 3, paragraphs 3.30-3.31.

[44] See the discussion of the Qatar *v.* Bahrain case (Maritime Delimitation and Territorial Questions between Qatar and Bahrain, Jurisdiction and Admissibility, Judgment of 1 July 1994, 1994 ICJ Rep. 112; Jurisdiction and Admissibility, Judgment of 15 February 1994, 1995 ICJ Rep.6; Merits, Judgement of 16 March 2001, 2001 ICJ Rep. 40) in Chapter 1 above, at note 35 and accompanying text. See, e.g., Merrills, note 2, at 796.

[45] See the Counter-Memorial of Nigeria, at paragraphs 10.12 to 10.14. A few weeks after the Maroua Declaration was adopted, the Head of State that signed it (General Gowon) was deposed by a new Head of State (General Muhammed), who was in office for a matter of months, during which "he was, as would be expected, preoccupied with other affairs of state, and the fact of the non-ratification was not communicated to Cameroon". His successor, according to Nigeria, raised the issue of the non-validity of the Declaration in a meeting between the Heads of State of Nigeria and Cameroon just over a year after coming into office, in 1977.

[46] Article 45 provides that "[a] State may no longer invoke a ground for invalidating, terminating, withdrawing from or suspending the operation of a treaty under articles 46 to 50 or articles 60 and 62 if, after becoming aware of the facts: (a) it shall have expressly agreed that the treaty is valid or remains in force or continues in operation, as the case may be; or (b) it must by reason of its conduct be considered as having acquiesced in the validity of the

Court did not deal with this point. It would, however, appear that the words "after becoming aware of the facts" are important. Presumably, the conduct of Nigeria immediately after the Declaration was signed, to which the Court attached some importance in finding that Nigeria considered the Declaration to be binding, could at least be considered to have taken place in ignorance of the alleged fact of invalidity, and this was the point Nigeria sought to make. Article 45 would seem, from its wording, to allow States in Nigeria's position a period after which the invalidity could be invoked. It is possible that the Court may have considered this possibility in its deliberations, but the absence of reference to it in its Judgment would suggest, again, that the Court set a high threshold for the invocation of exceptions to the principle of the security of treaties. The second issue not addressed by the Court in this Judgment is the subject of the next section.

4. The Declaration of Judge Rezek, Treaties Relating to Territory and "Manifest Violation"

In his Declaration, Judge Rezek raised the question whether, given the circumstances of the bilateral relations between the Parties, the Maroua Declaration could be considered to be a treaty binding on Nigeria. He stated as follows:

> ... je suis d'avis que le Cameroun n'était nullement en droit de croire que la déclaration en cause était vraiment un traité achevé, en vigueur le jour même de sa signature. Je ne connais pas d'ordre juridique qui autoriserait le gouvernant à conclure seul, de manière définitive, et à mettre en vigueur, sur la base de sa seule autorité, un traité concernant une frontière, donc le territoire de l'Etat, qu'il soit terrestre ou maritime. Je me demande s'il y a une partie du monde où ce non-respect des formalités les plus élémentaires serait compatible avec le caractère complexe et éminent d'un traité de frontière international.

Judge Rezek, it appears, cast doubt on the possibility that treaties relating to frontiers between States can fall into the category of "treaties in simplified form". In terms of the wording of Article 46, this argument could be translated as meaning that there could at least be a possibility that a treaty relating to territory, where purportedly in simplified form, should raise the question of compliance with internal constitutional law and procedure, so that the possibility of a "manifest violation" is real in such circumstances. For Judge Rezek, it would appear that was as much the responsibility of Cameroon as it was of Nigeria to have focused on this issue.

treaty or in its maintenance in force or in operation, as the case may be." See Sinclair, discussing the views of Reuter on this point; *supra* note 4, at 171.

This point of view is not completely novel in international law. It has been written, in the slightly different context of cession as a means of acquiring title to territory, that

> The constitutional law of the different states may or may not lay down special rules for the transfer or acquisition of territory. Such rules can have no direct influence upon the rules of international law concerning cession, since municipal law can neither abolish existing nor create new rules of international law. But if such rules contain constitutional restrictions on the government with regard to cession of territory, these restrictions are so far important that such treaties of cession concluded by Heads of State or Government as violate these restrictions are not binding; for if a state's consent to be bound by a treaty of cession was manifestly in violation of a constitutional rule of fundamental importance, the consent may be invalid.[47]

Of course this statement is about cession, and questions may be asked as to whether the circumstances of this case amount to cession in the strict meaning of that term, as distinct from a disposition of territory by treaty other than cession. If it is true that "[i]n the case of a disputed frontier line the boundary treaty which closes the dispute will *create* title, because previously the question of title was unsettled: in contrast a treaty of cession transfers a definitive title",[48] it is submitted that, for present purposes, the difference between cession and other dispositions of the territory of a State by treaty does not affect the point made by Judge Rezek; he did not refer to cession, but only to dispositions of territory by a boundary treaty. The point is that title over the relevant territory is created and is vested in a sovereign where such title did not exist as such prior to the treaty; at best it was disputed.

Nigeria, in its arguments, did refer to this issue. In its Counter-Memorial, Nigeria referred to the first discussion between the Nigerian and Cameroonian Heads of State, in 1977, after the signature of the Maroua Declaration, in which the Nigerian Head of State allegedly stated that "as Nigerian Head of State, he was a trustee of Nigerian property, both land and territorial waters, and he could not give them away unconstitutionally", and that the lack of ratification of the Declaration by the Nigerian Supreme Military Council rendered it a nullity.[49] Similarly, Nigeria argued in its rejoinder that:

> In assessing the significance of the Maroua Declaration, it is necessary to see the episode in the general context of relations between the two States and the impressive evidence of a long existing Nigerian administration in the Bakassi Peninsula. There can be no presumption in favour of relinquishment of title to territory. More particularly, there can be no presumption that, as an incidental

---

[47] See Jennings and Watts, *supra* note 4, at 679-680
[48] See I. Brownlie, *Principles of Public International Law* (6th edn. 2003), at 128-129.
[49] Counter Memorial, paragraph 10.13.

result of the series of meetings concerning the maritime boundary, Nigeria
was surrendering a significant tract of territory in her lawful possession and
populated by 100,000 Nigerians.[50]

And in oral argument, Nigeria argued that there could be "no presumption
that as an incidental result of a series of meetings concerning the maritime
boundary, Nigeria was surrendering a significant tract of territory in its
lawful possession and populated by Nigerians".[51]

It appears that the Court did not consider these statements to be of
significance, as it did not refer to any special considerations arising where
the treaty in question deals with international boundaries. But there is
respectable opinion in doctrine and literature to the effect that special
considerations might apply to treaties in the context of dispositions of State
territory.[52] For his part, Judge Rezek considered, as Nigeria had argued, that
dispositions of territory were not to be presumed lightly.[53] Again, perhaps
the Court, in not addressing the question, was rejecting Nigeria's argument,
and that, in its view, no special considerations apply to boundary treaties,
and that the burden in each case is to fall on the State who alleges non-
compliance with its constitutional law.

Of course, it is an essential attribute of sovereignty that a State can
acquire foreign territory and dispose of its own territory.[54] But it is well-
known that, in addition to the fundamental importance of territory for the
identity of a State in international law, which could put boundary treaties or
treaties of cession in a different category from other treaties for the purposes
of article 46 of the VCLT, the further important dimension that is elided in
upholding the internationalist position in the context of boundary treaties is
the position of the inhabitants of the area that becomes the territory of a new
sovereign. This is a matter that has been the subject of much discussion in

---

[50] Rejoinder, paragraph 3.40.

[51] See   <http://www.icj-cij.org/icjwww/idocket/icn/icncr/icn_icr200220_20020315.pdf>,
verbatim record of the public sitting held on Friday 15 March 2002, CR 2002/20, at 50,
paragraph 7 (Crawford).

[52] See, e.g., Jennings and Watts, *supra* note 4, at 680, footnote 3, also 1285-1288, especially
footnotes 3 and 6. In particular, the decision of the Bangladeshi Supreme Court in Kazi
Mukhlesur Rahman *v.* Bangladesh and Another (1974, 70 ILR at 37, especially at 46-50,
paragraphs 31-38), is instructive. See also A. McNair, *The Law of Treaties* (1961), at 94-110,
regarding the position regarding the conclusion of treaties of cession in the United Kingdom.

[53] Judge Rezek also distinguished the *Eastern Greenland* case (*supra* note 13 above) from the
present case, stating that the unilateral act of the Norwegian Ambassador in that case was not
a treaty, and that the PCIJ did not say that it was a treaty. In his view, "ce qu'il faut se
demander, c'est si un engagement international relatif à la détermination d'une frontière peut
prendre une forme autre que celle du traité au sens étroit, même lorsque les espaces terrestres
ou maritimes concernés sont peu étendus, ou lorsque ladite frontière n'est pas caractérisée par
une longue histoire de contestations et d'incertitudes". His answer was in the negative.

[54] See *Re the Berubari Union* (1960, Indian Supreme Court, 53 ILR at 181, 203).

international law[55] (particularly the question whether the consent of the inhabitants of the territory in question should be required (usually by means of a plebiscite),[56] and this could be a basis for considering it important enough to speak of there being a rule whose violation would be manifest in the sense of Article 46. This should be so even regardless of the representations made to each other by Heads of State attempting to resolve boundary issues *inter se*, representations which might lead them both to believe that each had the authority to dispose of territory. As Jennings and Watts put it, even though it cannot be said that international law requires ratification of every treaty of cession by a plebiscite, "[i] the modern law ... the plebiscite has to be seen rather as a device for securing compliance with the principle of self determination enshrined in the Charter of the United Nations".[57] The point being made here, again, does not depend on the technicalities of cession as a legal category or the distinction between cession and other treaty dispositions of territory, but on the idea that important issues are raised by a change effected by treaty in the sovereignty over populated areas.[58] Such issues, in our view, justify at least a consideration of whether the treaties used to effect such changes comply with internal constitutional rules. The issue of manifest violation in such cases, it is submitted, should arise *ipso facto*.

5. Concluding Remarks

In determining what would amount to a manifest violation, Wildhaber, stating that the answer would depend on the circumstances, expressed the view that "[i]n the treaty relations of pluralistic democracies *inter se*, a violation of a constitutional requirement of legislative approval may perhaps more readily be considered manifest."[59] But it is precisely in cases of non-democratic governments that the need to protect the interests of the State,

---

[55] "The hardship involved for the inhabitants of the territory who remain and lose their old citizenship and are handed over to a new sovereign whether they like it or not, created a movement in favour of the claim that no cession should be valid until the inhabitants had by a plebiscite given their consent to the cession. Several treaties of cession concluded during the nineteenth century stipulated that the cession should only be valid provided the inhabitants consented to it through a plebiscite. But it cannot be said that international law makes it a condition of every cession that it should be ratified by a plebiscite": Jennings and Watts, *supra* note 4, at 683-686.
[56] Plebiscites had indeed taken place in the context of the present dispute; see, e.g., paragraphs 210-214 of the Judgment.
[57] Jennings and Watts, *supra* note 4, at 684.
[58] See also the discussion in Jennings and Watts, *id.*, on the questions of the inhabitants' option of nationality and emigration following the cession of territory they inhabit.
[59] Wildhaber, *supra* note 4, at 181.

specifically its territory and population, would require that care be taken in order to guarantee whatever constitutional safeguards that may exist against arbitrary disposition of territory by treaty. The real issue here, as stated above,[60] is the extent to which international law concerns itself with representative government.[61] It is submitted that it would not require a great deal to consider, like Judge Rezek, treaties disposing of territory as raising, by virtue of their subject-matter, questions of compliance with internal constitutional requirements regarding treaty-making power. It would have been useful for the Court to refer to this issue, regardless of its ultimate finding on the facts of the *Bakassi* case.

It would appear that, ultimately, the question is one of allocation of the burden of establishing the notoriety of the relevant constitutional rule. Judge Rezek's approach would seem to suggest that treaties that dispose of territory should, by their nature, raise the possibility of the existence of manifest violation, so that even an express representation as to the constitutionality of such a treaty being concluded in simplified form by one of the parties may not be sufficient to make the treaty valid. However, such an approach may tilt the balance too strongly against the principle of the security of treaties; as noted above, the difficulties raised in identifying what would be a definitive answer to the question whether one State's constitutional requirements have been met are patent.[62] But while it may be the case that "states do not consider it desirable to tie the validity of agreements to domestic law procedures",[63] what is argued for here is not that States should require research into the complex constitutional rules of other States, but merely that they should obtain a more or less express undertaking as to the constitutionality of a treaty from the other party where there are grounds, as in the case of boundary treaties, for considering that there may be a manifest violation of internal constitutional rules. In other words, the burden in such cases should fall on the "innocent" State as much as the State whose constitutional rules are in question. Seeking such an undertaking – which could be raised when discussing the provisions on entry into force of a treaty – would indicate the good faith of *both* parties, not just one of them, and would serve better the interests of transparency. There is no reason why

---

[60] *Supra* notes 9 and 15 and accompanying text.

[61] See, e.g. Elias, *supra* note 4, at 148-149, who states, in the context of a discussion of the issue at the ILC, as follows: "[t]he view that prevailed, however, is that an exception should be made in a case where there has been a manifest violation of internal law regarding competence to enter into treaties, whether generally or in respect of specified types of which the treaty in question is one. This is because cases have occurred in the past when a Head of State entered into a treaty in sheer disregard or contravention of the State's clear constitutional provisions".

[62] See Section II above.

[63] Wildhaber, *supra* note 4, at 166-167.

there should be such haste in the conclusion and entry into force of treaties disposing of territory. Such an undertaking would also provide a more justifiable basis for holding the entire State bound by the treaty on the basis of the actions of an official, even if it is the Head of State. As it stands, international law appears to attach greater weight to the stability of treaties than to the situation (i.e. the rights, or at least the interests) of the State whose territory is being disposed of, including the inhabitants of that territory, by unconstitutional means. International law, it is submitted, should not properly be seen to be compounding the hardships that may be caused to such populations, while sanctioning the actions of non-representative governments. Requiring compliance with constitutional rules in cases involving disposition of territory, for example by the "innocent" State proposing ratification, would appear to pose few difficulties for States in their practice on the conclusion of treaties, and neither would a radical re-writing of international legal doctrine in this field be called for.

It should be noted that the view proposed in this chapter may not have resulted in a different outcome on the facts of this case. The point being made is a general one regarding what could amount to manifest violations within the meaning of Article 46 of the VCLT. The stability of treaties is a fundamental consideration to be accorded the first importance,[64] but there are other factors to be weighed in the balance, and there are good reasons why treaties involving disposition of territory should be subjected to a stricter procedure in modern international law. Cameroon referred to the fact that "international law comes down unequivocally in favour of the stability and permanence of boundary agreements, whether land or maritime". It is submitted that it is precisely because international law attaches so much importance to such agreements that the procedures for their conclusion and the conditions of their validity should not be taken lightly.

---

[64] Paragraph 253 of the Judgment.

Index